Frommer's®

New Mexico

11th Edition

by Lesley S. King

WILEY
Wiley Publishing, Inc.

ABOUT THE AUTHOR

Lesley S. King grew up on a ranch in northern New Mexico, not far from where she currently lives. She's a freelance writer and photographer, and a columnist for *New Mexico* magazine. Formerly managing editor for *The Santa Fean,* she has written for *The New York Times,* United Airline's *Hemispheres* magazine, and *Audubon,* among other publications. She is the author of *Frommer's Santa Fe, Taos & Albuquerque, Frommer's Great Outdoor Guide to Arizona & New Mexico,* and *New Mexico For Dummies.* She is also the coauthor of *Frommer's American Southwest.* Her newest book, released in 2007, is *King of the Road.*

Published by:
WILEY PUBLISHING, INC.
111 River St.
Hoboken, NJ 07030-5774

ISBN 978-0-470-87617-6 (paper); ISBN 978-1-118-00775-4 (ebk); ISBN 978-1-118-00776-1 (ebk); ISBN 978-1-118-00777-8 (ebk)

Editor: Billy Fox and Cate Latting
Production Editor: Erin Amick
Cartographer: Roberta Stockwell
Photo Editor: Richard Fox
Production by Wiley Indianapolis Composition Services

Front cover photo: Yucca in Sand, White Sand Dunes National Monument, New Mexico ©Susan E. Degginger / Alamy Images.
Back cover photo: Three Rivers Petroglyphs New Mexico ©David Muench / Muench Photography Inc.

For information on our other products and services or to obtain technical support, please contact our Customer Care Department within the U.S. at 877/762-2974, outside the U.S. at 317/572-3993 or fax 317/572-4002.

Wiley also publishes its books in a variety of electronic formats. Some content that appears in print may not be available in electronic formats.

Manufactured in the United States of America
5   4   3   2   1

CONTENTS

12 SOUTHEASTERN NEW MEXICO 349

13 FAST FACTS 386

Index 391

LIST OF MAPS

ACKNOWLEDGMENTS

My sincere thanks goes to Allison Rand, who helped research this book. The assistance of the many tourism agencies, hotel and restaurant owners and managers, and attractions public relations people was invaluable, as was the support of my family, friends, and editor, Billy Fox.

HOW TO CONTACT US

In researching this book, we discovered many wonderful places—hotels, restaurants, shops, and more. We're sure you'll find others. Please tell us about them, so we can share the information with your fellow travelers in upcoming editions. If you were disappointed with a recommendation, we'd love to know that, too. Please write to:

Frommer's New Mexico, 11th Edition
Wiley Publishing, Inc. • 111 River St. • Hoboken, NJ 07030-5774
frommersfeedback@wiley.com

AN ADDITIONAL NOTE

Please be advised that travel information is subject to change at any time—and this is especially true of prices. We therefore suggest that you write or call ahead for confirmation when making your travel plans. The authors, editors, and publisher cannot be held responsible for the experiences of readers while traveling. Your safety is important to us, however, so we encourage you to stay alert and be aware of your surroundings. Keep a close eye on cameras, purses, and wallets, all favorite targets of thieves and pickpockets.

Please be advised that travel information is subject to change at any time—and this is especially true of prices. We therefore suggest that you write or call ahead for confirmation when making your travel plans. The authors, editors, and publisher cannot be held responsible for the experiences of readers while traveling. Your safety is important to us, however, so we encourage you to stay alert and be aware of your surroundings. Keep a close eye on cameras, purses, and wallets, all favorite targets of thieves and pickpockets.

FROMMER'S STAR RATINGS, ICONS & ABBREVIATIONS

Every hotel, restaurant, and attraction listing in this guide has been ranked for quality, value, service, amenities, and special features using a **star-rating system.** In country, state, and regional guides, we also rate towns and regions to help you narrow down your choices and budget your time accordingly. Hotels and restaurants are rated on a scale of zero (recommended) to three stars (exceptional). Attractions, shopping, nightlife, towns, and regions are rated according to the following scale: zero stars (recommended), one star (highly recommended), two stars (very highly recommended), and three stars (must-see).

In addition to the star-rating system, we also use **eight feature icons** that point you to the great deals, in-the-know advice, and unique experiences that separate travelers from tourists. Throughout the book, look for:

special finds—those places only insiders know about

fun facts—details that make travelers more informed and their trips more fun

kids—Best bets for kids and advice for the whole family

special moments—those experiences that memories are made of

overrated—Places or experiences not worth your time or money

insider tips—great ways to save time and money

great values—where to get the best deals

warning—traveler's advisories are usually in effect

The following abbreviations are used for credit cards:

AE	American Express	DISC	Discover	V	Visa
DC	Diners Club	MC	MasterCard		

FROMMERS.COM

Frommer's travel resources don't end with this guide. Frommer's website, **www.frommers. com**, has travel information on more than 4,000 destinations. We update features regularly, giving you access to the most current trip-planning information and the best airfare, lodging, and car-rental bargains. You can also listen to podcasts, connect with other Frommers. com members through our active-reader forums, share your travel photos, read blogs from guidebook editors and fellow travelers, and much more.

THE BEST OF NEW MEXICO

I will never forget when I was in second grade, standing on the dusty playground at Alvarado Elementary School in Albuquerque, pointing west toward the volcanoes. "We went beyond those volcanoes," I bragged to my friend about what my family had done over the weekend. "No way," my friend replied. Actually, a number of times I'd been much farther than the 10 miles between us and the volcanoes, and I now know that the strong impact of the journey's distance had to do with culture rather than miles.

In a half-day drive, we traveled to the Intertribal Indian Ceremonial in Gallup, where I ate blue, crepe-paper-thin *piki* bread and gazed up at people dressed in dreamy rich velvet, their limbs draped in turquoise. I saw painted warriors twirl in the dust and felt drum rhythms pulse in my heart. In short, we had traveled to another world, and that otherworldliness is characteristic of New Mexico.

Never have I taken my strangely exotic home state for granted, nor has more traditional culture let me. When I was a kid, we used to travel to Illinois to visit my grandfather, and when people there heard we were from New Mexico, they would often cock their heads and say things like, "Do you have sidewalks there?" and "This bubble gum must be a real treat for you," as though such inventions hadn't yet arrived in the Southwest.

Our state magazine even dedicates a full page each month to the variety of ways in which New Mexico is forgotten. The most notable was when a New Mexico resident called the Atlanta Olympic committee to reserve tickets and the salesperson insisted that the person contact the international sales office. So, it seems people either don't know the state exists at all, or they believe it's a foreign country south of the border.

Ironically, those naive impressions hold some truth. New Mexico is definitely lost in some kind of time warp. Its history dates from far before Columbus set foot on the continent. The whole attitude here is often slower than that of the rest of the world. Like our neighbors down in Mexico, we use the word *mañana*—which doesn't so much mean "tomorrow" as it does "not today."

When you set foot here, you may find yourself a bit lost within the otherworldliness. You may be shocked at the way people so readily stop

New Mexico

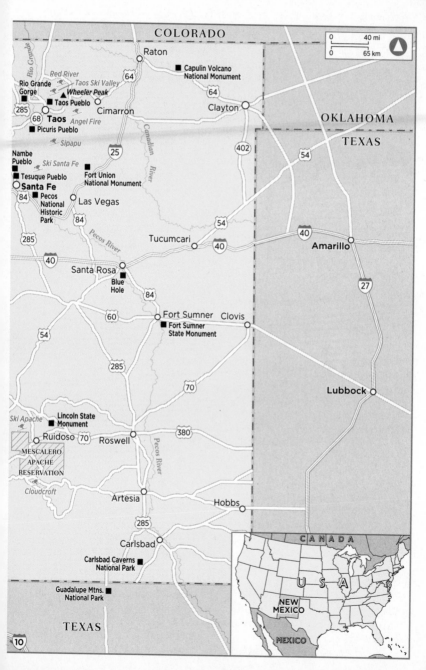

COLORADO

Raton

Capulin Volcano
National Monument

Rio Grande

Red River

Taos Ski Valley

Rio Grande
Gorge

Wheeler Peak

Taos Pueblo   Cimarron

64

64

Clayton

OKLAHOMA

TEXAS

285

68   **Taos**   Angel Fire

Picuris Pueblo

Sipapu

Canadian River

25

402

54

Nambe
Pueblo   Ski Santa Fe

Tesuque Pueblo   Fort Union
National Monument

○**Santa Fe**

84   Pecos
National
Historic
Park   Las Vegas

285   84

Pecos River

54

40

Amarillo

Tucumcari

40

40

27

Santa Rosa

Blue
Hole   84

Fort Sumner   Clovis

60   Fort Sumner
State Monument

54

285

70

Lubbock

Lincoln State
Monument

Ski Apache

Ruidoso   70   Roswell

MESCALERO
APACHE
RESERVATION   380

Pecos River

Cloudcroft

Artesia   Hobbs

285

Carlsbad

Carlsbad Caverns
National Park

Guadalupe Mtns.
National Park

TEXAS

10

0   40 mi
0   65 km

CANADA

U S A

NEW
MEXICO

MEXICO

and converse with you, or you may find yourself in a landscape where there isn't a single landmark from which to negotiate.

In the chapters that follow, I give you some signposts to help you discover for yourself the many treasures of this otherworldly state. But first, here are my most cherished New Mexico experiences.

THE best NEW MEXICO EXPERIENCES

o **New Mexican Enchiladas:** There are few things more New Mexican than the enchilada. You can order red or green chile, or "Christmas"—half and half. Sauces are rich, seasoned with *ajo* (garlic) and oregano. New Mexican cuisine isn't smothered in cheese and sour cream, so the flavors of the chiles, corn, and meats can really be savored. Enchiladas are often served with *frijoles* (beans), *posole* (hominy), and *sopaipillas* (fried bread). See "Eating & Drinking in New Mexico," in chapter 2.

o **High Road to Taos:** This spectacular 80-mile route into the mountains between Santa Fe and Taos takes you through red painted deserts, villages bordered by apple and peach orchards, and the foothills of 13,000-foot peaks. You can stop in Cordova, known for its woodcarvers, or Chimayo, known for its weavers. At the fabled **Santuario de Chimayo,** you can rub healing dust between your fingers. See p. 193.

o **Chaco Culture National Historical Park** (Nageezi; ℂ **505/786-7014;** www. nps.gov/chcu): A combination of a stunning setting and well-preserved ruins makes the long drive to Chaco Canyon an incredible adventure into ancestral Puebloan culture. Many good hikes and bike rides are in the area, and there's also a campground. See p. 267.

o **Santa Fe Opera** (ℂ **800/280-4654** or 505/986-5900; www.santafeopera.org): One of the finest opera companies in the United States has called Santa Fe home for more than 50 years. Performances are held during the summer months in a hilltop, open-air amphitheater. See p. 178.

o **Albuquerque International Balloon Fiesta** (ℂ **505/821-1000;** www.balloon fiesta.com): The world's largest balloon rally assembles some 600 colorful balloons and includes races and contests. Highlights are the mass ascension at sunrise and the special shapes rodeo, in which balloons in all sorts of whimsical forms, from liquor bottles to cows, rise into the sky. See p. 99.

o **María Benitez Teatro Flamenco** (Institute for Spanish Arts, Santa Fe; ℂ **505/470-7828;** www.mariabenitez.com): A native New Mexican, María Benitez was trained in Spain, to which she returns each year to find dancers and prepare her show. Now she brings in professional dance companies and teaches a group of young dancers all performing during the summer at the Lodge at Santa Fe. See p. 179.

o **Taos Pueblo** (Veterans Hwy., Taos Pueblo; ℂ **575/758-1028;** www.taospueblo. com): Possibly the original home of pueblo-style architecture, this bold structure where 200 residents still live much as their ancestors did a thousand years ago is awe-inspiring. Rooms built of mud are poetically stacked to echo the shape of Taos Mountain behind them. As you explore the pueblo, you can visit the residents' studios, munch on bread baked in an *horno* (a beehive-shaped oven), and wander past the fascinating ruins of the old church and cemetery. See p. 223.

THE best OUTDOOR EXPERIENCES

For a list of the best outdoor activities, see chapter 5. Here are a few specific sights:

- **Rio Grande Gorge** (Taos): A hike into this dramatic gorge offers an unforgettable experience. You'll first see it as you come over a rise heading toward Taos. It's a colossal slice in the earth, formed during the late Cretaceous period, 130 million years ago, and the early Tertiary period, about 70 million years ago. Drive about 35 miles north of Taos to the Wild Rivers Recreation Area. From the lip of the canyon, you descend through millions of years of geologic history. If you're visiting during spring and early summer and enjoy an adrenaline rush, be sure to hook up with a professional guide and raft the Taos Box, a 17-mile stretch of class IV white water. See p. 232.
- **Blue Hole** (Santa Rosa): You'll find this odd natural wonder in Santa Rosa, "city of natural lakes." An 81-foot-deep artesian well, its waters are cool and completely clear. Often it resembles a fishbowl, full of scuba divers. See p. 302.
- **Capulin Volcano National Monument** (Capulin; ✆ 575/278-2201; www.nps.gov/cavo): Last active 60,000 years ago, the volcano is located about 27 miles east of Raton. A hike around its rim offers views into neighboring Oklahoma and Colorado, and another walk down into its lush mouth allows you to see the point from which the lava spewed. See p. 298.
- **Carlsbad Caverns National Park** (Carlsbad; ✆ 877/444-6777; www.nps.gov/cave): Truly one of the world's natural wonders, these caverns swallow visitors into what feels like a journey to the center of the earth, where nocturnal creatures thrive and water drips onto your body. Stalactites and stalagmites create another universe of seemingly alien life forms. Kids won't like the fact that they can't go climbing on the formations, but they'll be too fascinated to complain much. See p. 382.
- **White Sands National Monument** (Alamogordo; ✆ 575/679-2599; www.nps.gov/whsa): Like a bizarre, lost land of white, this place is a dream for kids. They can roll around in the fine sand or sled across it, all the while discovering the mysterious creatures that inhabit this truest of deserts. Bring extra clothing, sunglasses, and lots of sunscreen. See p. 358.

THE best NATIVE AMERICAN SIGHTS

- **Indian Pueblo Cultural Center** (2401 12th St. NW, Albuquerque; ✆ 866/855-7902; www.indianpueblo.org): Owned and operated as a nonprofit organization by the 19 pueblos of New Mexico, this is a fine place to begin an exploration of Native American culture. The museum is modeled after Pueblo Bonito, a spectacular 9th-century ruin in Chaco Culture National Historic Park, and it contains a wealth of art and artifacts. See p. 94.

- **Petroglyph National Monument** (6001 Unser Blvd. NW, Albuquerque; ✆ **505/899-0205**; www.nps.gov/petr): This hunting and gathering area for prehistoric Native Americans has 25,000 petroglyphs (prehistoric rock carvings) and provides a variety of hiking trails in differing levels of difficulty, right on the outskirts of Albuquerque. See p. 96.

- **Bandelier National Monument** (Los Alamos; ✆ **505/672-3861**, ext. 517; www.nps.gov/band): These ruins provide a spectacular peek into the lives of the ancestral Puebloan culture, which flourished in the area between A.D. 1100 and 1550, a period later than the time when Chaco Canyon was a cultural center. The most dramatic site is a dwelling and kiva (a room used for religious activities) in a cave 140 feet above the canyon floor—reached by a climb up long pueblo-style ladders. A visitor center and museum offer self-guided and ranger-led tours. See p. 191.

- **Pecos National Historical Park** (Pecos; ✆ **505/757-7200**; www.nps.gov/peco): It's hard to rank New Mexico's many ruins, but this one, sprawled on a plain about 25 miles east of Santa Fe, is one of the most impressive, resonating with the history of the Pueblo Revolt of 1680. You'll see evidence of where the Pecos people burned the mission church before joining in the attack on Santa Fe. You'll also see where the Spanish conquistadors later compromised, allowing sacred kivas to be built next to the reconstructed mission. See p. 188.

- **Acoma Pueblo** (Acoma; ✆ **800/747-0181**; www.skycity.com): This spectacular adobe village sits high atop a sheer rock mesa. Known as "Sky City," it is home to 65 or so inhabitants who still live without electricity and running water. The sculpted mission church and the cemetery seem to be perched on the very edge of the world. Visitors can hike down through a rock cut, once the main entrance to the pueblo. See p. 249.

- **Gila Cliff Dwellings National Monument** (Gila; ✆ **575/536-9461**; www.nps.gov/gicl): Perched in deep caves within a narrow canyon outside Silver City, these ruins tell the mysterious tale of the Mogollon people who lived in the area from the late 1200s through the early 1300s. See p. 345.

THE best MUSEUMS

- **New Mexico History Museum & The Palace of the Governors** (North Plaza, Santa Fe; ✆ **505/476-5100**; www.palaceofthegovernors.org): Take a journey into New Mexico's past in this new 96,000-square-foot museum. A circular exhibit displays Native American, Spanish, and settler history of the state, using voice recording and music to enhance the experience. See p. 156.

- **New Mexico Museum of Art** (107 W. Palace Ave., Santa Fe; ✆ **505/476-5072**; www.museumofnewmexico.org): This museum's permanent collection of more than 8,000 works emphasizes regional art and includes landscapes and portraits by all the Taos masters as well as contemporary artists, including R. C. Gorman, Amado Peña, Jr., and Georgia O'Keeffe. The museum also has a collection of photographic works by such masters as Ansel Adams, Edward Weston, and Elliot Porter. See p. 156.

- **Museum of International Folk Art** (706 Camino Lejo, Santa Fe; ✆ **505/476-1200**; www.moifa.org): Santa Fe's perpetually expanding collection of folk art is the largest in the world, with thousands of objects from more than 100 countries.

You'll find an amazing array of imaginative works, ranging from Hispanic folk art *santos* (carved saints) to Indonesian textiles and African sculptures. See p. 158.

o **Georgia O'Keeffe Museum** (217 Johnson St., Santa Fe; ℂ **505/946-1000;** www.okeeffemuseum.org): This museum contains the largest collection of O'Keeffes in the world: currently 1,149 paintings, drawings, and sculptures, and 1,851 works by other artists of note. It offers visitors poetic views of Southwestern landscapes both vast and minute. See p. 154.

o **Taos Historic Museums** (Taos; ℂ **575/758-0505;** www.taosmuseums.org): What's nice about Taos is that you can see historic homes inside and out. You can wander through Taos Society artist Ernest Blumenschein's home, which is a museum. It was built in 1797 and restored by Blumenschein in 1919. The Martinez Hacienda is an example of a hacienda stronghold. It has been developed into a living museum featuring weavers, blacksmiths, and woodcarvers. See p. 222.

o **El Camino Real International Heritage Center** (30 miles south of Socorro off I-25, exit 115; ℂ **575/854-3600;** www.nmmonuments.org): This museum traces the 1,500-mile historic route between Mexico City and the Española Valley north of Santa Fe. On view are artifacts, art, and devotional items used along the trail, along with state-of-the-art exhibits offering first-person stories of the trail. See p. 310.

o **The Lincoln Historic District** (37 miles northeast of Ruidoso on US 380; ℂ **575/653-4025;** www.nmmonuments.org): One of the last historic yet uncommercialized 19th-century towns remaining in the American West, Lincoln was the focal point of the Lincoln Country War of 1878–79. The town saw some of Billy the Kid's most renowned exploits. See p. 363.

THE best HISTORICAL SIGHTS

o **Old Town** (Albuquerque): Once the center of Albuquerque commerce, Old Town thrived until the early 1880s, when businesses relocated nearer to the railroad tracks. It has been a center of tourism since being rediscovered in the 1930s. Today you can visit shops, galleries, and restaurants in Old Town, as well as the Church of San Felipe de Neri, the first structure built when colonists established Albuquerque in 1706. See p. 95.

o **Georgia O'Keeffe's Home** (Abiquiu; ℂ **505/685-4539;** www.okeeffemuseum. org): Hand-smoothed adobe walls, elk antlers, and a blue door—you'll encounter these images and many more that inspired the famous artist's work. When you view the landscape surrounding her residence in Abiquiu, you'll understand why she was so inspired. Be sure to make a reservation months in advance. See p. 197.

o **Palace of the Governors** (North Plaza, Santa Fe; ℂ **505/476-5100;** www. palaceofthegovernors.org): This is where, in 1680, the only successful Native American uprising took place. Before the uprising, this was the seat of power in the area, and after de Vargas reconquered the American Indians, it resumed that position. Built in 1610 as the original capitol of New Mexico, the palace has been in continuous public use longer than any other structure in the United States. Most notable is the front of the palace, where Native Americans sell jewelry, pottery, and some weavings under the protection of the portal. See p. 156.

o **St. Francis Cathedral** (Cathedral Place at San Francisco St., Santa Fe; ℂ **505/982-5619;** www.cbsfa.org): Santa Fe's grandest religious structure was built between 1869 and 1886 by Archbishop Jean Baptiste Lamy, in the style of the great cathedrals of Europe. Inside the small adobe, Our Lady of the Rosary chapel is full of the romance of Spanish Catholicism. The chapel was built in 1807 and is the only portion that remains from Our Lady of the Assumption Church, founded along with Santa Fe in 1610. See p. 156.

o **San Francisco de Asis church** (Ranchos de Taos Plaza, Taos; © **505/758-2754**): This is one of the world's more beautiful churches. Though some might not see how it could compete with elaborate structures such as Chartres or Notre Dame de Paris, it's like a Picasso sculpture: Simple and direct, it has massive, hand-smoothed adobe walls and a rising sense that nearly lifts the heavy structure off the ground. Maybe that's why such notables as Ansel Adams and Georgia O'Keeffe have recorded its presence in art. See p. 220.

o **El Morro National Monument** (Ramah; © **505/783-4226**; www.nps.gov/elmo): In the Grants area, this sandstone monolith is known as "Inscription Rock," because travelers and explorers documented their journeys for centuries on its smooth face. See p. 254.

o **Cimarron:** Nestled against the eastern slope of the Sangre de Cristo mountain range, this town was a wild and woolly outpost on the Santa Fe Trail between the 1850s and 1880s and a gathering place for area ranchers, traders, gamblers, gunslingers, and other characters. See p. 293.

o **New Mexico Museum of Space History** (NM 2001, Alamogordo; © **877/333-6589** outside New Mexico, or 575/437-2840; www.nmspacemuseum.org): Tracing the story of space travel, this five-story museum recalls the accomplishments of America's Mercury, Gemini, and Apollo programs, including New Mexico's participation in space exploration, from ancient American Indians to rocketry pioneer Robert Goddard to astronauts. See p. 353.

THE best FAMILY EXPERIENCES

o **Albuquerque Aquarium** (2601 Central Ave. NW; © **505/764-6200**; www.cabq.gov/biopark): Exhibits here focus on sea areas fed by the Rio Grande. You'll pass by many large tanks and within an eels' den; the star attraction is a 285,000-gallon shark tank, where many species of fish and 15 to 20 sand tiger, brown, and nurse sharks swim around, looking ominous. See p. 96.

o **Albuquerque Botanic Garden** (2601 Central Ave. NW; © **505/764-6200**; www.cabq.gov/biopark): These gardens provide a perfect place to wander among scented plants, both inside and out. Within a state-of-the-art conservatory, a desert collection features Chihuahuan and Sonoran deserts, and a Mediterranean collection. Outside, kids especially enjoy a model train system and Rio Grande Heritage Farm. See p. 96.

o **Rio Grande Zoo** (903 10th St. SW, Albuquerque; © **505/764-6200**; www.cabq.gov/biopark/zoo): More than 250 species live on 64 acres of riverside bosque among ancient cottonwoods. Open-moat exhibits with animals in naturalized habitats are a treat for zoo-goers. Major exhibits include the polar bears, the giraffes, the sea lions (with underwater viewing), the cat walk, the bird show, and ape country, with its gorillas and orangutans. See p. 98.

- **Sandia Peak Tramway** (10 Tramway Loop NE, Albuquerque; ✆ **505/856-7325;** www.sandiapeak.com): The world's longest "jigback" tramway ferries passengers about 3 miles from Albuquerque's city limits almost to the summit of the 10,678-foot Sandia Peak. On the way, you may see birds of prey and rare Rocky Mountain bighorn sheep. Go in the evening to watch the sun burn its way out of the western sky, then enjoy the glimmering city lights on your way down. See p. 95.
- **El Rancho de las Golondrinas** (334 Los Pinos Rd., Santa Fe; ✆ **505/471-2261;** www.golondrinas.org): This living museum re-creates an 18th- and 19th-century Spanish village. Kids like to visit the working molasses mill, the blacksmith shop, the shearing and weaving rooms, and the water mills, as well as the resident animals. See p. 162.
- **Santa Fe Children's Museum** (1050 Old Pecos Trail; ✆ **505/989-8359;** www.santafechildrensmuseum.org): Designed for the whole family to experience, this museum offers interactive exhibits and hands-on activities in the arts, humanities, science, and technology. Most notable is a 16-foot climbing wall that kids can scale, outfitted with helmets and harnesses. A 1-acre Southwestern horticulture garden features animals, wetlands, and a greenhouse. See p. 164.
- **New Mexico Mining Museum** (100 N. Iron Ave., Grants; ✆ **800/748-2142;** www.grants.org): This museum takes you down into a spooky, low-lit replica mine. You begin in the station where uranium was loaded and unloaded, and travel back into the earth through places defined on wall plaques with such interesting names as "track drift" (where ore comes up in cars from the mine) and "stope" (a room stripped of all ore and off-limits in an actual mine). See p. 251.
- **Living Desert Zoo & Gardens State Park** (1504 Miehls Dr., Carlsbad; ✆ **575/887-5516;** www.emnrd.state.nm.us/prd/livingdesert.htm): Spread across a vast plateau, this park offers visitors an hour-long trek through desert lands full of odd plants that survive on who-knows-what to zoo exhibits of hawks, cats, and bears. What's best about this zoo is that the animals aren't just captive, they're rehabilitating. See p. 378.

THE best SPLURGE HOTELS

- **Hotel Andaluz** (125 Second St. NW, at Copper Ave., Albuquerque; ✆ **877/987-9090** or 505/242-9090; www.hotelandaluz.com): A $30-million makeover to this 1939 classic has brought a cozy Mediterranean ambience. For a real splurge, get a suite here to partake of city views, sumptuous bedding, granite counters, comfy robes, and other luxuries. See p. 82.
- **Hyatt Regency Tamaya Resort and Spa** (1300 Tuyuna Trail, Santa Ana Pueblo; ✆ **800/554-9288** or 505/867-1234; www.tamaya.hyatt.com): Situated on Santa Ana Pueblo land, this grand resort has all a person might need to get away from the world. Three swimming pools, a 16,000-square-foot full-service spa and fitness center, the 18-hole Twin Warriors Championship Golf Course designed by Gary Panks, and views of the Sandia Mountains make for plenty to do. It's only 25 minutes from Albuquerque and 45 minutes from Santa Fe. See p. 85.
- **Sandia Resort & Casino** (30 Rainbow Rd. NE, Albuquerque; ✆ **877/272-9199;** www.sandiaresort.com): One of the state's newer luxury resorts, this

facility offers spacious rooms, an 18-hole golf course, and gambling. With views toward the city and the Sandia Mountains, it's picturesque as well. See p. 82.

o **Bishop's Lodge Ranch Resort & Spa** (Bishop's Lodge Rd., Santa Fe; ℂ 505/983-6377; www.bishopslodge.com): More than a century ago, Bishop Jean Baptiste Lamy often escaped clerical politics by hiking into a valley north of town called Little Tesuque. He built a retreat and chapel that years later have become the Bishop's Lodge. All rooms are spacious and feature handcrafted furniture and local artwork. Activities include horseback riding, hiking, tennis, swimming, and spa treatments. See p. 135.

o **Encantado Resort** (198 State Road 592, Santa Fe; ℂ 877/262-4666; www.encantadoresort.com): An architectural artwork, this Auberge Resort 15 minutes from Santa Fe provides world-class accommodations and views. A spa and fine-dining restaurant add to the all-inclusive nature of the experience. See p. 130.

o **La Posada de Santa Fe Resort and Spa** (330 E. Palace Ave., Santa Fe; ℂ 800/727-5276 or 505/986-0000; www.laposadadesantafe.com): With the feel of a meandering adobe village but the service of a fine hotel, this has become one of New Mexico's premier resorts. It has an elegant spa and pool and spacious spa rooms. Most rooms don't have views but have outdoor patios, and most are tucked back into the quiet compound. See p. 132.

o **Inn of the Five Graces** (150 E. de Vargas St., Santa Fe; ℂ 505/992-0957; www.fivegraces.com): Just a few blocks from the Plaza, this Relais & Châteaux inn spoils guests with floral-decked courtyards and elaborately decorated suites with kilim rugs and ornately carved beds. See p. 131.

o **Ojo Caliente Mineral Springs Resort & Spa** (50 Los Baños Dr., Ojo Caliente; ℂ 800/222-9162; www.ojospa.com): Ojo Caliente's combination of minerals have made it a favorite of spa aficionados for years. Now the resort offers luxury accommodations as well. Reserve a posh cliffside room and you'll soak in a mineral tub on your patio.

o **Rancho de San Juan Country Inn** (US 285 near Española; ℂ 505/753-6818; www.ranchodesanjuan.com): Just 38 miles from Santa Fe, in the enchanting country near Ojo Caliente, this award-winning inn offers complete luxury and the quiet of the country. The rooms in the inn, as well as the casitas set among the hills, are all decorated with impressive art and antiques, and have spectacular views. See p. 199.

o **El Monte Sagrado** (317 Kit Carson Rd., Taos; ℂ 800/828-8267 or 575/758-3502; www.elmontesagrado.com): With guest rooms and casitas set around a grassy "Sacred Circle," this eco-resort is the quintessence of luxury. Every detail, from the waterfalls and chemical-free pool and hot tubs to the authentic theme decor in the rooms, has been created with conscious care. See p. 205.

o **Casa Blanca** (505 E. La Plata St., Farmington; ℂ 800/550-6503; www.casablancanm.com): This inn offers patios, fountains, and lush gardens set on a ridge overlooking Farmington. The rooms have elegant furnishings rich in Native American and world folk art. The full breakfast included with the room is always gourmet. See p. 275.

o **Inn of the Mountain Gods Resort & Casino** (287 Carrizo Canyon Rd., Mescalero; ℂ 800/545-9011; www.innofthemountaingods.com): Although the architecture of this hotel on the Mescalero Apache Indian Reservation is a bit cold, the setting in the pines on the edge of a blue lake compensates, as do the spacious rooms, the lush bedding, and the many activity options, ranging from gambling to fishing to golf to skiing. See p. 365.

- **The Lodge at Cloudcroft** (1 Corona Place, Cloudcroft; ☎ **800/395-6343**; www.thelodgeresort.com): For those who enjoy the Old World style of a Victorian hotel, this lodge nestled on a pine-covered hilltop in southern New Mexico will certainly please. Rooms in the lodge are filled with antiques, from sideboards and lamps to mirrors and steam radiators. A high-elevation golf course and a new spa round out the experience. For a splurge, request a suite. See p. 357.

THE best MODERATELY PRICED HOTELS

- **Hotel Albuquerque at Old Town** (800 Rio Grande Blvd. NW, Albuquerque; ☎ **800/237-2133** for reservations, or 505/843-6300; www.hotelabq.com): This hotel offers lively Spanish Colonial decor and comfortable rooms at a prime location steps from Old Town. See p. 80.
- **El Rey Inn** (1862 Cerrillos Rd., Santa Fe; ☎ **800/521-1349** or 505/982-1931; www.elreyinnsantafe.com): If old-style court motels awaken the road warrior in you, this is your place. Built in the 1930s and added onto over the years, this place provides a variety of types of rooms, all nicely appointed. See p. 137.
- **Santa Fe Motel and Inn** (510 Cerrillos Rd., Santa Fe; ☎ **800/930-5002** or 505/982-1039; www.santafemotel.com): Rooms at this inn are walking distance from the plaza and provide the ambience of the Southwest—bold colors and some handmade furniture—with a standard motel price tag. See p. 135.
- **Old Taos Guesthouse** (1028 Witt Rd., Taos; ☎ **800/758-5448** or 575/758-5448; www.oldtaos.com): Set in a 190-year-old adobe dwelling, this inn offers acres of quiet within minutes of downtown Taos. Rooms range from atmospheric to very practical, all with comfortable beds. It's a family run business, and its owners take good care of their guests. See p. 210.
- **Plaza Hotel** (230 Plaza, Las Vegas; ☎ **800/328-1882** or 505/425-3591; www.plazahotel-nm.com): Set on the plaza, this 1882 gem provides comfortable old-world lodging. Be sure to reserve a room in the recently renovated Ilfeld wing. See p. 292.

THE best DINING EXPERIENCES

- **Jennifer James 101** (4615-A Menaul Blvd. NE, Albuquerque; ☎ **505/884-3860**; www.jenniferjames101.com). In a contemporary setting, one of Albuquerque's best chefs serves imaginative fare using local and seasonal ingredients. The seared duck with a scallion pancake and plum sauce is delicious. See p. 90.
- **The Compound** (653 Canyon Rd., Santa Fe; ☎ **505/982-4353**; www.compoundrestaurant.com): This reincarnation of one of Santa Fe's classic restaurants serves daring contemporary American food in a soulful setting. Such delicacies as grilled beef tenderloin with Italian potatoes and foie gras hollandaise will please sophisticated palates—and probably simpler ones too. See p. 144.

o **Santacafé** (231 Washington Ave., Santa Fe; ☎ **505/984-1788;** www.santacafe. com): This restaurant, my all-time favorite, borrows from an international menu of preparations and offerings. The minimalist decor accentuates the beautiful architecture of the 18th-century Padre Gallegos House. One of their classics is grilled rack of lamb with potato-leek gratin. See p. 147.

o **Geronimo** (724 Canyon Rd., Santa Fe; ☎ **505/982-1500;** www.geronimo restaurant.com): Set in the 1756 Borrego House on Canyon Road, this restaurant offers brilliant flavors in a serene adobe atmosphere. The elk tenderloin here is Santa Fe's most prized entree. See p. 146.

o **The Shed** (113½ E. Palace Ave., Santa Fe; ☎ **505/982-9030;** www.sfshed. com): The Shed, a Santa Fe luncheon institution since 1953, occupies a rambling hacienda that was built in 1692. The sauces here have been refined over the years, creating amazing flavors in basic dishes such as enchiladas, burritos, and stuffed *sopaipillas*. The mocha cake is renowned. See p. 152. Its sister restaurant, **La Choza,** is just as good, with a similar menu. See p. 151.

o **Stakeout Grill & Bar** (101 Stakeout Dr., Taos; ☎ **575/758-2042;** www.stakeout restaurant.com): This elegant restaurant offers delicious New American cuisine and a broad view across sage forest and the Rio Grande Gorge. The filet mignon with béarnaise sauce is excellent. See p. 216.

o **The Bluffs** (3450 E. Main St., Farmington; ☎ **505/325-8155**): Wooden partitions topped with glazed glass shaped like towering bluffs surround diners at this restaurant serving sandwiches and salads at lunch and steaks and seafood at dinner. The turkey bacon club is amazing, as are any of the angus beef steaks. See p. 276.

o **Plaza Hotel's Landmark Grill** (230 Plaza, Las Vegas; ☎ **800/328-1882;** www.plazahotel-nm.com): Set in an 1882 hotel, the Landmark serves three tasty meals daily. Evenings are most notable, with steak and seafood offerings. Best of all is the view of the tree-shaded Las Vegas Plaza. See p. 292.

o **Double Eagle** (2355 Calle de Guadalupe, Las Cruces; ☎ **575/523-6700;** www.double-eagle-mesilla.com): Continental cuisine is alive and well behind the walls of this historic hacienda located in Las Cruces. The decor is lush and dramatic—chandeliers hung with Baccarat crystals—and the food is richly traditional. Steaks are the way to go. See p. 330.

o **Diane's Bakery & Cafe** (510 N. Bullard St., Silver City; ☎ **575/538-8722;** www.dianesrestaurant.com): Diane Barrett, who was once a pastry chef at La Traviata and Eldorado in Santa Fe, has brought refined flavors to the little mining town of Silver City. Come here to feast on sumptuous baked goods and sophisticated meals such as rack of lamb. See p. 343.

o **Trinity Hotel Suites Fine Food & Wine** (201 S. Canal, Carlsbad; ☎ **575/ 234-9891;** www.thetrinityhotel.com): Set in an atmospheric 1882 bank building, this elegant restaurant serves three meals daily. Most notable are the Italian dinners such as lobster ravioli and chicken marsala over pasta. See p. 380.

NEW MEXICO IN DEPTH

When I was a child in New Mexico, we'd sing a song while driving the dusty roads en route to such ruins as Chaco Canyon or Puye Cliff Dwellings. Sung to the tune of "Oh Christmas Tree," it went like this:

> *New Mexico, New Mexico*
> *Don't know why we love you so.*
> *It never rains*
> *It never snows*
> *The winds and sand*
> *They always blow.*
> *And how we live*
> *God only knows*
> *New Mexico, we love you so.*

Although this song exaggerates the conditions here, the truth remains that in many ways New Mexico has an inhospitable environment. So why are so many people drawn here, and why do so many of us stay?

Ironically, the very extremes that this song presents are the reason. In this 121,666-square-mile state, you are met with wildly varied terrain, temperature, and temperament. On a single day you might experience temperatures from 25° to 75°F (–4° to 24°C). From the vast heat and dryness of White Sands in the summer to the 13,161-foot subzero, snow-encrusted Wheeler Peak in the winter, New Mexico's beauty is carved by extremes.

Culturally, this is also the case. Pueblo, Navajo, and Apache tribes occupy much of the state's lands, many of them still speaking their native languages and living within the traditions of their people. Some even live without running water and electricity. Meanwhile, Hispanic culture remains deeply linked to its Spanish roots, practicing a devout Catholicism, and speaking a centuries-old Spanish dialect, some still living by subsistence farming in mountain villages.

New Mexico has its own sense of time and unique social mores. The pace is slower here, the objectives of life less defined. People rarely arrive on time for appointments, and businesses don't always hold to their posted hours. In most cases, people wear whatever they want here. You'll see men dressed for formal occasions wearing a buttoned collar with a bolo tie and women in cowboy boots and broomstick skirts.

All this leads to a certain lost-and-not-caring-to-be-found spell that's akin to some kind of voodoo magic. We find ourselves standing amid the dust or sparkling light, within the extreme heat or cold, not sure whether to speak Spanish or English. That's when we let go completely of society's common goals, its pace, and expectations. We slip into a kayak and let the river take us, or hike a peak and look at the world from a new perspective. Or we climb into a car and drive past ancient ruins being excavated at that instant, past ghost mining towns, and under hot-air balloons, by chile fields and around hand-smoothed *santuarios,* all on the road to nowhere, New Mexico's best destination. At some point in your travels, you'll likely find yourself on this road, and you'll realize that there's no destination so fine.

NEW MEXICO TODAY: FROM FLAMENCO TO CRAPS

Growing Pains

New Mexico is experiencing a reconquest of sorts, as the Anglo population soars and outside money and values again make their way in. The process continues to transform New Mexico's three distinct cultures and their unique ways of life, albeit in a less violent manner than during the Spanish conquest.

Certainly, the Anglos—many of them from large cities—add a cosmopolitan flavor to life here. The variety of restaurants has greatly improved, as have entertainment options. For their small size, towns such as Taos and Santa Fe offer a broad variety of restaurants and cultural events. Santa Fe has developed a strong dance and drama scene, with treats such as flamenco and opera that you'd expect to find in New York or Los Angeles. And Albuquerque has an exciting nightlife scene downtown; you can walk from club to club and hear a wealth of jazz, rock, country, and alternative music.

DATELINE

3000 B.C. First evidence of stable farming settlements in region.

A.D. 700 Earliest evidence of ancestral Puebloan presence.

1540 Francisco Vásquez de Coronado marches to Cíbola in search of a Native American "city of gold."

1542 Coronado returns to New Spain, declaring his mission a failure.

1610 Immigration to New Mexico increases; Don Pedro de Peralta establishes Santa Fe as capital.

1680 Pueblo tribes revolt against Spanish.

1692 Spanish recapture Santa Fe.

1706 Albuquerque established.

1739 First French traders enter Santa Fe.

1779 Tabivo Naritgant, leader of rebellious Comanche tribes, falls to Spanish forces.

1786 Comanches and Utes sign treaty with Spanish.

1821 Mexico gains independence from Spain.

1828 Kit Carson, the legendary frontiersman, arrives in Taos.

Transformation of the local way of life and landscape is also apparent in the stores continually springing up in the area. For some, these are a welcome relief from Western clothing stores and provincial dress shops. The downside is that city plazas, which once contained pharmacies and grocery stores frequented by residents, are now crowded with T-shirt shops and galleries appealing to tourists. Many locals now rarely visit their plazas except during special events.

Environmental threats are another regional reality. Nuclear-waste issues form part of an ongoing conflict affecting the entire Southwest, and a section of southern New Mexico has been designated a nuclear-waste site. Because much of the waste must pass through Santa Fe, the U.S. government, along with the New Mexico state government, constructed a bypass that directs some transit traffic around the west side of the city.

New ways of thinking have also brought positive changes to life here, and many locals have benefited from New Mexico's influx of wealthy newcomers and popularity as a tourist destination. Businesses and industries large and small have come to the area. In Albuquerque, Intel Corporation now employs more than 3,000 workers, and in Santa Fe, the national magazine *Outside* publishes monthly. Local artists and artisans also benefit from growth. Many craftspeople have expanded their businesses. The influx of people has broadened the sensibility of a fairly provincial state. The area has become a refuge for many gay and lesbian people, as well as for political exiles, such as Tibetans. With them has developed a level of creativity and tolerance you would generally find in very large cities but not in smaller communities such as the ones found in New Mexico.

Cultural Questions

Faced with new challenges to their ways of life, both Native Americans and Hispanics are marshaling forces to protect their cultural identities. A prime concern is language. Through the years, many Pueblo people have begun to speak more and more English, with their children getting little exposure to their native tongue. In a number of the pueblos, elders are working with schoolchildren in language classes.

1846	Mexican War breaks out; Gen. Stephen Kearny takes possession of New Mexico for United States.
1847	Revolt in Taos against U.S. control; newly appointed governor Charles Bent killed.
1848	Under provisions of Treaty of Guadalupe Hidalgo, Mexico officially cedes New Mexico to United States.
1861	Victorious Confederate general proclaims all of New Mexico south of the 34th parallel the Confederate territory of Arizona.
1862	Confederates routed from New Mexico.
1864	Navajos relocated to Bosque Redondo Reservation.
1868	Navajos return to their native homeland.
1878–81	Lincoln County War erupts; epitomize the lawlessness and violence of the Wild West.
1879	Atchison, Topeka, and Santa Fe Railroad routes main line through Las Vegas, Albuquerque, El Paso, and Deming, where connection is made with California's South Pacific Line.

continues

Some of the pueblos have even developed written dictionaries, the first time their languages have been systematized in this form.

Many pueblos have introduced programs to conserve the environment, preserve ancient seed strains, and protect religious rites. Because their religion is tied closely to nature, a loss of natural resources would threaten the entire culture. Certain activities have been closed to outsiders, the most notable being some of the rituals of Shalako at Zuni, a popular and elaborate series of year-end ceremonies.

Hispanics, through art and observance of cultural traditions, are also embracing their roots. In northern New Mexico, murals depicting important historic events, such as the Treaty of Guadalupe Hidalgo of 1848, adorn many walls. The **Spanish Market** in Santa Fe has expanded into a grand celebration of traditional arts—from tin working to *santo* carving. Public schools in the area have bilingual education programs, enabling students to embrace their Spanish-speaking roots.

Hispanics are also making their voices heard, insisting on more conscientious development of their neighborhoods and rising to positions of power in government. Congressman Bill Richardson, Hispanic despite his Anglo surname, was appointed U.S. ambassador to the United Nations before becoming energy secretary in President Clinton's cabinet and later running for U.S. president. Currently, he is the governor of New Mexico.

Gambling Wins & Losses

Gambling, a fact of life and source of much-needed revenue for Native American populations across the country, has been a center of controversy in northern New Mexico for a number of years. In 1994, Gov. Gary Johnson signed a compact with tribes in New Mexico, ratified by the U.S. Department of the Interior, to allow full-scale gambling. **Tesuque Pueblo** was one of the first to begin a massive expansion, and many other pueblos followed suit.

Many New Mexicans are concerned about the tone gambling sets in the state. The casinos are for the most part large and unsightly buildings that stand out sorely

1881 Legendary outlaw Billy the Kid killed by Pat Garrett.	1916 Construction of Elephant Butte Dam brings irrigation to southern New Mexican farms.
1886 Apache chief Geronimo captured; signals end of New Mexico's Indian wars.	1924 Native Americans granted full U.S. citizenship.
1898 Painters Ernest Blumenschein and Bert Phillips settle in Taos.	1943 Los Alamos National Laboratory built; "Manhattan Project" scientists spend 2 years in complete seclusion developing nuclear weapons.
1912 New Mexico becomes the 47th state.	1945 First atomic bomb exploded at Trinity Site.
1914 Blumenschein and Phillips form Taos Society of Artists; Taos becomes a major center of influence in midcentury American art and letters.	1947 Reports of a flying saucer crash near Roswell make national headlines, despite U.S. Air Force's denials that it has occurred.

on some of New Mexico's most picturesque land. Though most residents appreciate the boost that gambling can ultimately bring to the Native American economies, many critics wonder where gambling profits actually go—and if the casinos can possibly be a good thing for the pueblos and tribes. Some detractors suspect that profits go directly into the pockets of outside backers.

A LOOK AT THE PAST
In the Beginning

Archaeologists say that humans first migrated to the Southwest, moving southward from the Bering Land Bridge, around 12,000 B.C. Sites such as Sandia Cave and Folsom—where weapon points were discovered that, for the first time, clearly established that our prehistoric ancestors hunted now-extinct mammals such as woolly mammoths—are internationally known. When these large animals died off during the late Ice Age (about 8000 B.C.), people turned to hunting smaller game and gathering wild food.

Stable farming settlements, as evidenced by the remains of domestically grown maize, date from around 3000 B.C. As the nomadic peoples became more sedentary, they built permanent residences and pit houses and made pottery. Cultural differences began to emerge in their choice of architecture and decoration: The **Mogollon people,** in the southwestern part of modern New Mexico, created brown and red pottery and built large community lodges; the **ancestral Puebloans,** or **Anasazi,** in the north, made gray pottery and smaller lodges for extended families.

The Mogollon, whose pottery dates from around 100 B.C., were the first of the sophisticated village cultures. They lived primarily in modern-day Catron and Grant counties. The most important Mogollon ruins are in the Gila River Valley, including Gila Cliff Dwellings National Monument, north of Silver City.

By about A.D. 700, and perhaps a couple centuries earlier, the ancestral Puebloans of the northwest had absorbed village life and expanded through what is now known

1972 Pioneer balloonist Sid Cutter establishes Albuquerque International Balloon Fiesta.

1981 The Very Large Array, the world's most powerful radio telescope, begins observations of distant galaxies from the desert west of Socorro.

1982 U.S. space shuttle *Columbia* lands at Holloman Air Force Base, near White Sands National Monument.

1984 New Mexico's last remaining section of famed Route 66, near San Jon, is abandoned.

1990 New Mexico's last uranium mine, near Grants, closes.

1994 Under pressure from Congress, U.S. Air Force reopens investigation of the 1947 flying saucer crash reports, concluding that the debris found was likely from tests of a secret Cold War spy balloon; UFO believers allege a cover-up.

1998 The Waste Isolation Pilot Project, the nation's first deep-geologic repository for permanent disposal of radioactive waste, receives

continues

as the Four Corners region (where New Mexico, Arizona, Utah, and Colorado come together). Around A.D. 1000, their culture eclipsed that of the Mogollon. Chaco Culture National Historic Park, Aztec Ruins National Monument, and Salmon Ruins all exhibit architectural excellence and skill, as well as a scientific sensitivity to nature, that mark this as one of America's classic pre-Columbian civilizations.

Condominium-style communities of stone and mud adobe bricks, three and four stories high, were focused around central plazas. The villages incorporated circular spiritual chambers called kivas. The ancestral Puebloans also developed means to irrigate their fields of corn, beans, and squash by controlling the flow of water from the San Juan River and its tributaries. From Chaco Canyon, they built a complex system of well-engineered roads leading in four directions to other towns or ceremonial centers. Artifacts found during excavation, such as seashells and macaw feathers, indicate that they had a far-reaching trade network. The incorporation of solar alignments into some of their architecture has caused some to speculate on the importance of the equinoxes to their religion.

The diminishing of the Anasazi culture, and the emergence of the **Pueblo culture** in its place, is something of a mystery today. Historians disagree as to why the ancestral Puebloans left their villages around the 13th century. Some suggest drought or soil exhaustion; others posit invasion, epidemic, or social unrest. But by the time the first Spanish arrived in the 1500s, the ancestral Puebloans were long gone and the Pueblo culture was well established throughout northern and western New Mexico, from Taos to Zuni, near Gallup. Most of the people lived on the east side of the Continental Divide, in the Rio Grande Valley.

The Pueblos absorbed certain elements of the ancestral Puebloan civilization, including the apartment-like adobe architecture, the creation of rather elaborate pottery, and the use of irrigation or flood farming in their fields. Agriculture, especially corn, was the economic mainstay.

Each village fiercely guarded its independence. When the Spanish arrived, no alliances existed between them. No more than a few hundred people lived in any

go-ahead to begin storage operations.

2002 80th anniversary of the Inter-Tribal Indian Ceremonial is held at Gallup.

2006 Spaceport America, the world's first purpose-built commercial spaceport, initiated in the desert 45 miles north of Las Cruces, with plans to one day launch commercial flights into outer space.

2010 Santa Fe celebrates 400-year anniversary.

one, an indication that the natives had learned to keep their population (which totaled 40,000–50,000) down in order to preserve their soil and other natural resources. But not all was peaceful: They alternately fought and traded with each other, as well as with nomadic Apaches. Even before the Spanish arrived, a pattern had been established.

The Arrival of the Spanish

The Spanish controlled New Mexico for 300 years, from the mid-16th to the mid-19th century—twice as long as the United States has. The Hispanic legacy in language and culture is stronger today in New Mexico than anywhere else in the Southwest, no doubt a result of the prominence of the Rio Grande Valley as the oldest and most populous fringe province of the viceroyalty of New Spain.

The spark that sent the first European explorers into what is now New Mexico was a fabulous medieval myth that seven Spanish bishops had fled the Moorish invasion of the 8th century, sailed westward to the legendary isle of Antilia, and built themselves seven cities of gold. Hernán Cortés's 1519 discovery and conquest of the Aztecs' treasure-laden capital of Tenochtitlán, now Mexico City, fueled belief in the myth. When a Franciscan friar 20 years later claimed to have sighted, from a distance, "a very beautiful city" in a region known as Cíbola while on a reconnaissance mission for the viceroyalty, the gates were opened.

Francisco Vásquez de Coronado, the ambitious young governor of New Spain's western province of Nueva Galicia, was commissioned to lead an expedition to the "seven cities." Several hundred soldiers, accompanied by servants and missionaries, marched overland to Cíbola with him in 1540, along with a support fleet of three ships in the Gulf of California. What they discovered, after 6 hard months on the trail, was a bitter disappointment: Instead of a city of gold, they found a rock-and-mud pueblo at Hawikuh, the westernmost of the Zuni towns. The expedition wintered at Tiguex, on the Rio Grande near modern Santa Fe, before proceeding to the Great Plains, seeking more treasure at Quivira, in what is now Kansas. The grass houses of the Wichita Indians were all they found.

Coronado returned to New Spain in 1542, admitting failure. Historically, though, his expedition was a great success, contributing the first widespread knowledge of the Southwest and Great Plains, and encountering the Grand Canyon en route.

By the 1580s, after important silver discoveries in the mountains of Mexico, the Spanish began to wonder if the wealth of the Pueblo country might lie in its land rather than its cities. They were convinced that they had been divinely appointed to convert the natives of the New World to Christianity. And so a northward migration began, orchestrated and directed by the royal government. It was a mere trickle in the late 16th century. Juan de Oñate established a capital in 1598 at San Gabriel, near San Juan Pueblo, but a variety of factors led to its failure. In 1610, under **Don Pedro de Peralta,** the migration began in earnest.

It was not dissimilar to America's schoolbook stereotype. Bands of armored conquistadors did troop through the desert with humble robed friars striding by their sides. But most of the pioneers came up the Rio Grande Valley, with oxcarts and mule trains rather than armor, intent on transplanting their Hispanic traditions of government, religion, and material culture to this new world.

Peralta built his new capital at Santa Fe and named it La Villa Real de la Santa Fe de San Francisco de Asis, the Royal City of the Holy Faith of St. Francis of Assisi.

His capitol building, the Palace of the Governors, has been continuously occupied as a public building ever since by Spanish, Mexicans, Americans, and, for 12 years (1680–92), the Pueblo Indians. Today, it's a museum.

Religion & Revolt

The 17th century in New Mexico was essentially a missionary era, as Franciscan priests attempted to turn the Indians into model Hispanic peasants. Their churches became the focal point of every pueblo, with Catholic schools a mandatory adjunct. By 1625, the Rio Grande Valley was home to an estimated 50 churches.

But the Native Americans weren't enthused about doing "God's work"—building new adobe missions, tilling fields for the Spanish, and weaving garments for export to Mexico—so soldiers backed the padres in extracting labor, a system known as *repartimiento*. Simultaneously, the *encomienda* system provided that a yearly tribute in corn and blankets be levied upon each Indian. The Pueblos were amenable to taking part in Catholic religious ceremonies and proclaiming themselves converts.

To them, spiritual forces were actively involved in the material world. If establishing harmony with the cosmos meant absorbing Jesus Christ and various saints into their hierarchy of *katsinas* and other spiritual beings, so much the better. But the Spanish friars demanded that they do away with their traditional singing, masked dancing, and other "pagan practices." When the Pueblo religion was violently crushed and driven literally underground, resentment toward the Spanish grew and festered. Rebellions at Taos and Jemez in the 1630s left village priests dead, but the Pueblos were savagely repressed.

> ### Impressions
>
> *"In New Mexico he always awoke a young man; not until he rose and began to shave did he realize that he was growing older."*
> —Archbishop Latour in Willa Cather's *Death Comes for the Archbishop*, 1927

A power struggle between church and state in New Mexico weakened the hand of the Spanish colonists, and a long drought in the 1660s and 1670s gave the Apaches reason to scourge the Spanish and Pueblo settlements for food. The Pueblos blamed the friars, and their ban on traditional rain dances, for the drought. The hanging of four medicine men as "sorcerers" and the imprisonment of 43 others was the last straw for the Rio Grande natives. In 1680, the Pueblo Revolt erupted.

Popé (Poh-*pay*), a San Juan shaman, catalyzed the revolt. Assisted by other Pueblo leaders, he unified the far-flung Native Americans, who had never before confederated. They pillaged and burned the province's outlying settlements, and then turned their attention on Santa Fe, besieging the citizens who had fled to the Palace of the Governors. After 9 days, having reconquered Spain's northernmost American province, they let the refugees retreat south to Mexico.

Popé ordered that the Pueblos should return to the lifestyle they had before the arrival of the Spanish. All Hispanic items, from tools to fruit trees, were to be destroyed, and the blemish of baptism was to be washed away in the river. But the shaman misjudged the influence of the Spanish on the Pueblo people. They were not the people they had been a century earlier, and they *liked* much of the material culture they had absorbed from the Europeans. What's more, they had no intention of remaining confederated; their independent streaks were too strong.

In 1692, led by newly appointed **Gov. Don Diego de Vargas,** the Spanish recaptured Santa Fe without bloodshed. Popé had died, and without a leader to reunify them, the Pueblos were no match for the Spanish. Vargas pledged not to punish them but to pardon and convert. Still, when he returned the following year with 70 families to recolonize the city, he did use force. And for the next several years, bloody battles persisted throughout the Pueblo country.

By the turn of the 18th century, Nuevo Mexico was firmly in Spanish hands. This time, however, the colonists seemed to have learned from some of their past errors. They were more tolerant in their religion and less ruthless in their demands and punishments.

The Arrival of the Anglos

By the 1700s, there were signals that new interlopers were about to arrive in New Mexico. The French had laid plans to begin colonizing the Mississippi River, and hostile Native American tribes were on the warpath. The Spanish viceroyalty fortified its position in Santa Fe as a defensive bastion and established a new villa at Albuquerque in 1706.

In 1739, the first French trade mission entered Santa Fe and was welcomed by the citizenry but not by the government. For 24 years, until 1763, a black-market trade thrived between Louisiana and New Mexico. It ended only when France lost its toehold on its North American claims during the French and Indian War.

Other Native Americans were more fearsome foes. Apaches, Comanches, Utes, and Navajos launched raids against each other and the Rio Grande settlements for most of the 18th century, which led the Spanish and Pueblos to pull closer together for mutual protection. Pueblo and Hispanic militias fought side by side in campaigns against the invaders. But by the 1770s, the attacks had become so savage and destructive that the viceroy in Mexico City created a military jurisdiction in the province, and **Gov. Juan Bautista de Anza** led a force north to Colorado to defeat Tabivo Naritgant, the most feared of the Comanche chiefs, in 1779. Seven years later, the Comanches and Utes signed a lasting treaty with the Spanish and thereafter helped keep the Apaches in check.

France sold the Louisiana Territory to the young United States in 1803, and the Spanish suddenly had a new intruder to fear. The Lewis and Clark expedition of 1803 went unchallenged, much as the Spanish would have liked to challenge it; but in 1807, when **Lt. Zebulon Pike** built a stockade on a Rio Grande tributary in Colorado, he and his troops were taken prisoner by troops from Santa Fe. Pike was taken to the New Mexican capital, where he was interrogated extensively, and then to Chihuahua, Mexico. The report he wrote upon his return was the United States' first inside look at Spain's frontier province.

At first, pioneering American merchants—excited by Pike's observations of New Mexico's economy—were summarily expelled from Santa Fe or jailed, and their goods were confiscated. But after Mexico gained independence from Spain in 1821, traders were welcomed. The wagon ruts of the Santa Fe Trail soon extended from Missouri to New Mexico, and from there to Chihuahua. (Later, it became the primary southern highway to California.)

As merchants hastened to Santa Fe, Anglo-American and French-Canadian fur trappers headed into the wilderness. Their commercial hub became Taos, a tiny village near a large pueblo a few days' ride north of Santa Fe. Many married into native or Hispanic families. Perhaps the best known was **Kit Carson,** a sometime federal agent, sometime scout, whose legend is inextricably interwoven with that of early Taos. He spent 40 years in Taos, until his death in 1868.

In 1846, the **Mexican-American War** broke out, and New Mexico became a territory of the United States. There were several causes of the war, including the U.S. annexation of Texas in 1845, disagreement over the international boundary, and unpaid claims owed to American citizens by the Mexican government. But foremost was the prevailing U.S. sentiment of "manifest destiny," the belief that the Union should extend "from sea to shining sea." **Gen. Stephen Kearny** marched south from Colorado; on the Las Vegas plaza, he announced that he had come to take possession of New Mexico for the United States. His arrival in Santa Fe on August 18, 1846, went unopposed.

An 1847 revolt in Taos resulted in the slaying of the new governor of New Mexico, Charles Bent, but U.S. troops defeated the rebels and executed their leaders. That was the last threat to American sovereignty in the territory. In 1848, the **Treaty of Guadalupe Hidalgo** officially transferred the title of New Mexico, along with Texas, Arizona, and California, to the United States.

Kearney promised New Mexicans that the United States would respect their religion and property rights and would safeguard their homes and possessions from hostile Indians. His troops behaved with a rigid decorum. The United States upheld Spanish policy toward the Pueblos, assuring the survival of their ancestral lands, their traditional culture, and their old religion—which even 3 centuries of Hispanic Catholicism could not do away with.

The Civil War

As conflict between the North and South flared east of the Mississippi, New Mexico found itself caught in the debate over **slavery.** Southerners wanted to expand slavery to the Western territories, but abolitionists bitterly opposed them. New Mexicans themselves voted against slavery twice, while their delegate to Congress engineered the adoption of a slavery code. In 1861, the Confederacy laid plans to make New Mexico theirs as a first step toward capturing the West.

In fact, southern New Mexicans, including those in Tucson (Arizona was then a part of the New Mexico Territory), were disenchanted with the attention paid them by Santa Fe and were already threatening to form their own state. So when Confederate Lt. Col. John Baylor captured Fort Fillmore, near Mesilla, and on August 1, 1861, proclaimed all of New Mexico south of the 34th parallel to be the new territory of Arizona, few complained.

The following year, Confederate Gen. Henry Sibley assembled three regiments of 2,600 Texans and moved up the Rio Grande. They defeated Union loyalists in a bloody battle at Valverde, near Socorro; easily took Albuquerque and Santa Fe; and proceeded toward the federal arsenal at Fort Union, 90 miles east of Santa Fe. Sibley planned to replenish his supplies there before continuing north to Colorado, and then west to California.

On March 27 and 28, 1862, the Confederates were met head-on in **Glorieta Pass,** about 16 miles outside Santa Fe, by regular troops from Fort Union, supported by a regiment of Colorado volunteers. By the second day, the rebels were in control, until a detachment of Coloradans circled behind the Confederate troops and destroyed their poorly defended supply train. Sibley was forced into a retreat down the Rio Grande. A few months later, Mesilla was reclaimed for the Union, ending the Confederate presence in New Mexico.

The Land Wars

The various tribes had not missed the fact that whites were fighting among themselves, and they took advantage of this weakness to step up their raids on border settlements. The U.S. government retaliated. In 1864, the government rounded up 10,000 Navajos and forced them to walk some 450 miles, on what is now called the Long Walk, to Bosque Redondo on the Pecos River at Fort Sumner, in east-central New Mexico. Col. Kit Carson led New Mexico troops in this venture, a position to which he acceded as a moderating influence between the Navajos and those who called for their unconditional surrender or extermination.

Moving the Navajos was an ill-advised decision: The land could not support 9,000 people, the government failed to supply adequate provisions, and the Navajos were unable to live peacefully with the **Mescaleros.** By late 1868, the tribes retraced their routes to their homelands, where the Navajos gave up their warlike past. The Mescaleros' raids were squashed in the 1870s, and they were confined to a reservation in southern New Mexico.

Corralling the rogue **Apaches** of southwestern New Mexico presented the territory with its biggest challenge. Led by chiefs Victorio, Nana, and Geronimo, these bands wreaked havoc on the mining region around Silver City. Eventually, however, they succumbed, and the capture of Geronimo in 1886 was the final chapter in New Mexico's long history of Indian wars.

As the Native American threat decreased, more and more livestock and sheep **ranchers** established themselves on the vast plains east of the Rio Grande, in the San Juan basin of the northwest, and in other equally inviting parts of the territory. Cattle drives up the Pecos Valley, on the Goodnight-Loving Trail, are the stuff of legend; so, too, was Roswell cattle baron John Chisum, whose 80,000 head of beef probably represented the largest herd in America in the late 1870s.

Mining grew as well. Albuquerque blossomed in the wake of a series of major gold strikes in the Madrid Valley, close to ancient turquoise mines; other gold and silver discoveries through the 1870s gave birth to boomtowns—now mostly ghost towns—such as Hillsboro, Mogollon, Pinos Altos, and White Oaks. The copper mines of Santa Rita del Cobre, near Silver City, are still thriving.

In 1879, the Atchison, Topeka, and Santa Fe Railway sent its main line through Las Vegas, Albuquerque, El Paso, and Deming, where it joined with the Southern Pacific line coming from California. (The Santa Fe station was, and is, at Lamy, 17 miles southeast of the capital.) Now linked by **railroad** to the great markets of America, New Mexico's economic boom period was assured.

But ranching invites cattle rustling and range wars, mining beckons feuds and land fraud, and the construction of railroads often brings political corruption and swindles. New Mexico had all of them, especially during the latter part of the 19th century. Best known of a great many conflicts was the **Lincoln County War** (1878–81), which began as a feud between rival factions of ranchers and merchants. It led to such utter lawlessness that President Rutherford B. Hayes ordered a federal investigation of the territorial government and the installation of Gen. Lew Wallace as governor (whose novel *Ben-Hur* was published in 1880).

One of the central figures of the Lincoln County War was **William "Billy the Kid" Bonney** (1858–81), a headstrong youth who became probably the best-known outlaw of the American West. Legend says he blazed a trail of bloodshed from Silver City to Mesilla, Santa Fe to Lincoln, and Artesia to Fort Sumner, where he was finally killed by Sheriff Pat Garrett in July 1881. Really, though, in his short life, he killed four people.

By the turn of the 20th century, most of the violence had been checked. The mineral lodes were drying up, and ranching was taking on increased importance. Economic and social stability were coming to New Mexico.

> ### Reflections
>
> *"I wasn't the leader of any gang. I was for Billy all the time."*
> —Billy the Kid
> To a Las Vegas, New Mexico reporter, after his capture at Stinking Springs

Statehood, Art & Atoms

Early in the 20th century, its Hispanic citizens having proved their loyalty to the U.S. by serving gallantly with Theodore Roosevelt's Rough Riders during the Spanish-American War, New Mexico's long-awaited dream of becoming an integral part of the Union was finally recognized. On January 6, 1912, President William Howard Taft signed a bill making New Mexico the **47th state.**

Within a few years, Taos began gaining fame as an artists' community. Two painters from the East Coast, **Ernest Blumenschein** and **Bert Phillips,** settled in Taos in 1898, lured others to join them, and in 1914 formed the **Taos Society of Artists,** one of the most influential schools of art in America. Writers and other intellectuals soon followed, including patron **Mabel Dodge Luhan,** novelists **D. H. Lawrence** and **Willa Cather,** and poet-activist **John Collier.** Other artists settled in Santa Fe and elsewhere in New Mexico; the best known was **Georgia O'Keeffe,** who lived miles from anywhere in tiny Abiquiu. Today, Santa Fe and Taos are world renowned for their contributions to art and culture.

The construction in 1916 of the Elephant Butte Dam near Hot Springs (now Truth or Consequences) brought irrigated farming back to a drought-ravaged southern New Mexico. Potash mining boomed in the southeast in the 1930s. Native Americans gained full citizenship in 1924, 2 years after the **All Pueblo Council** was formed to fight passage in Congress of a bill that would have given white squatters rights to Indian lands. And in 1934, tribes were accorded partial self-government. Hispanics, meanwhile, became the most powerful force in state politics and remain so today.

The most dramatic development in 20th-century New Mexico was induced by World War II. In 1943, the U.S. government sealed off a tract of land on the Pajarito Plateau, west of Santa Fe, that previously had been an exclusive boys' school. On this site, it built the Los Alamos National Laboratory, otherwise known as Project Y of the Manhattan Engineer District—the **"Manhattan Project."** Its goal: to split the atom and develop the first nuclear weapons.

Under the direction of **J. Robert Oppenheimer,** later succeeded by **Norris E. Bradbury,** a team of 30 to 100 scientists and hundreds of support staff lived and worked in almost complete seclusion for 2 years. Their work resulted in the atomic bomb, tested for the first time at the Trinity Site, north of White Sands, on July 16, 1945. The bombings of Hiroshima and Nagasaki, Japan, 3 weeks later, signaled to the world that the nuclear age had arrived.

Even before that time, New Mexico was gaining stature in America's scientific community. **Robert H. Goddard,** considered the founder of modern rocketry, conducted many of his experiments near Roswell in the 1930s, during which time he became the first person to shoot a liquid-fuel rocket faster than the speed of sound. **Clyde Tombaugh,** who discovered Pluto in 1930, helped establish the department of astronomy at New Mexico State University in Las Cruces. And former **Sen. Harrison (Jack) Schmitt,** an exogeologist and the first civilian to walk on the moon in 1972, is a native of the Silver City area.

Today, the **White Sands Missile Range** is one of America's most important astrophysics sites, and the **International Space Hall of Fame** in nearby Alamogordo honors men and women from around the world who have devoted their lives to space exploration. Aerospace research and defense contracts are economic mainstays in Albuquerque, and **Kirtland Air Force Base** is the home of the Air Force Special Weapons Center. **Los Alamos,** of course, continues to be a national leader in nuclear technology. Now under construction, **Spaceport America** near Las Cruces may launch privately funded space flights as early as 2012.

> ### Reflections
>
> *"I am become death, the shatterer of worlds."*
> —J. Robert Oppenheimer, quoting from ancient Hindu texts

Despite the arrival of the 21st century in many parts of the state, other areas are still struggling to be a part of the 20th. Many Native Americans, be they Pueblo, Navajo, or Apache, and Hispanic farmers, who till small plots in isolated rural regions, hearken to a time when life was slower paced.

ART & ARCHITECTURE
A Land of Art

It's all in the light—or at least that's what many artists claim drew them to New Mexico. In truth, the light is only part of the attraction: Nature in this part of the country, with its awe-inspiring thunderheads, endless expanse of blue skies, and rugged desert, is itself a canvas. To record the wonders of earth and sky, the early natives of the area, the ancestral Puebloans, imprinted images (in the form of petroglyphs and pictographs) on the sides of caves and on stones, as well as on the sides of pots they shaped from clay dug in the hills.

Today's Native American tribes carry on that legacy, as do the other cultures that have settled here. Life in New Mexico is shaped by the arts. Everywhere you turn, you see pottery, paintings, jewelry, and weavings.

The area is full of little villages that maintain their own artistic specialties. Each Indian pueblo has a trademark design, such as **Santa Clara**'s and **San Ildefonso**'s black pottery and **Zuni's** needlepoint silverwork. Bear in mind that the images used often have symbolic meaning. When purchasing art or an artifact, you may want to talk to its maker about what the symbols mean.

Hispanic villages are also distinguished by their artistic identities. **Chimayo** has become a center for Hispanic weaving, and the village of **Cordova** is known for its *santo* (icon) carving. *Santos, retablos* (paintings), and *bultos* (sculptures), as well as works in tin, are traditional devotional arts tied to the Roman Catholic faith. Often, these works are sold out of artists' homes in villages, allowing you to glimpse the lives of the artists and the surroundings that inspire them.

Hispanic and Native American villagers take their goods to the cities, where for centuries people have bought and traded. Under the portals along the plazas of Santa Fe, Taos, and Albuquerque, you'll find a variety of works in silver, stone, and pottery for sale. In the cities, you'll find streets lined with galleries. At major markets, such as the **Spanish Market** and **Indian Market** in Santa Fe, some of the top artists from the area sell their works. Smaller shows at the pueblos also attract artists and artisans. The **Northern Pueblo Artists and Craftsman Show,** revolving each July to a different pueblo, continues to grow.

Drawn by the beauty of the local landscape and respect for indigenous art, artists from all over have flocked here, particularly during the 20th century. They have established locally important art societies; one of the most notable is the **Taos Society of Artists.** In 1898, artists Bert Phillips and Ernest L. Blumenschein were traveling through the area from Colorado on a mission to sketch the Southwest when their wagon broke down north of Taos. The scenery so overwhelmed them that they abandoned their journey and stayed. Joseph Sharp joined them, and still later came Oscar Berninghaus, Walter Ufner, Herbert Dunton, and others. You can see a brilliant collection of some of their romantically lit portraits and landscapes at the Taos Art Museum.

A major player in the development of Taos as an artists' community was the arts patron **Mabel Dodge Luhan.** A writer who financed the work of many an artist, in the 1920s Luhan held court for many notables, including Georgia O'Keeffe, Willa Cather, and D. H. Lawrence. This illustrious history goes a long way to explaining how it is that Taos—a town of about 5,000 inhabitants—has more than 100 arts-and-crafts galleries and many resident painters.

> ## Impressions
>
> *[Sun-bleached bones] were most won-derful against the blue/that blue that will always be there as it is now after all man's destruction is finished.*
> —Georgia O'Keeffe, on the desert skies of New Mexico

Santa Fe has its own art society, begun in the 1920s by a nucleus of five painters who became known as **Los Cinco Pintores.** Jozef Bakos, Fremont Ellis, Walter Mruk, Willard Nash, and Will Shuster lived in the area of Canyon Road (now the arts center of Santa Fe). Despite its small size, Santa Fe is considered one of the top three art markets in the U.S.

Perhaps the most celebrated artist associated with New Mexico was **Georgia O'Keeffe** (1887–1986), a painter who worked and lived most of her later years in the region. O'Keeffe's first sojourn to New Mexico in 1917 inspired her sensuous paintings of the area's desert landscape and bleached animal skulls. The house where she lived in Abiquiu (42 miles northwest of Santa Fe on US 84) is now open for limited public tours (see chapter 7 for details). The **Georgia O'Keeffe Museum** in Santa Fe is the only museum in the United States entirely dedicated to an internationally known woman artist.

Santa Fe is also home to the **Institute of American Indian Arts,** where many of today's leading Native American artists have studied, including the Apache sculptor Allan Houser (whose works you can see near the state capitol building and in other public areas in Santa Fe). The best-known Native American painter is the late R. C. Gorman, an Arizona Navajo who made his home in Taos for more than 3 decades. Gorman is internationally acclaimed for his bright, somewhat surrealistic depictions of Navajo women. Another artist who has achieved national fame is Dan Namingha, a Hopi painter and sculptor who weaves native symbology together with contemporary concerns.

If you look closely, you'll find notable works from a number of local artists. Tammy Garcia is a young Taos potter who year after year continues to sweep the awards at Indian Market with her intricately shaped and carved pots. Cippy Crazyhorse, a Cochiti, has acquired a steady following of patrons for his silver jewelry. All around the area you'll see the frescoes of Frederico Vigil, a noted muralist and Santa Fe native.

For the visitor interested in art, however, some caution should be exercised; a lot of schlock out there targets the tourist trade. But if you persist, you're likely to find some very inspiring work as well.

A Rich Architectural Melting Pot

Nowhere else in the United States are you likely to see such extremes of architectural style as in New Mexico. The state's distinctive architecture reflects the diversity of cultures that have left their imprint on the region. The first people in the area were the ancestral Puebloans, the Anasazi, who built stone and mud homes at the bottom of canyons and inside caves. **Pueblo-style adobe architecture** evolved and became the basis for traditional New Mexican homes: sun-dried clay bricks mixed with grass for strength, mud-mortared, and covered with additional protective layers of mud. Roofs are supported by a network of vigas—long beams whose ends protrude through the outer facades—and *latillas,* smaller stripped branches layered between the vigas. Other adapted Pueblo architectural elements include plastered adobe-brick kiva fireplaces, *bancos* (adobe benches that protrude from walls), and *nichos* (small indentations within a wall in which religious icons are placed). These adobe homes are characterized by flat roofs and soft, rounded contours.

Spaniards wedded many elements to Pueblo style, such as portals (porches held up with posts, often running the length of a home) and enclosed patios, as well as the simple, dramatic sculptural shapes of Spanish mission arches and bell towers. They also brought elements from the Moorish architecture found in southern Spain: heavy wooden doors and elaborate *corbels*—carved wooden supports for the vertical posts.

With the opening of the Santa Fe Trail in 1821 and later the 1860s gold boom, both of which brought more Anglo settlers, came the next wave of building. New arrivals contributed architectural elements such as neo-Grecian and Victorian influences popular in the middle part of the U.S. at the time. Distinguishing features of what came to be known as **Territorial-style** architecture can be seen today; they include brick facades and cornices as well as porches, often placed on the second story. You'll also note millwork on doors and wood trim around windows and doorways, double-hung windows, and Victorian bric-a-brac.

Santa Fe Plaza is an excellent example of the convergence of these early architectural styles. On the west side is a Territorial-style balcony, while the Palace of Governors is marked by Pueblo-style vigas and oversized Spanish/Moorish doors. Nearby, you'll see the Romanesque architecture of the **St. Francis Cathedral** and **Loretto chapel,** initiated by Archbishop Lamy from France, as well as the railroad station built in the **Spanish Mission style**—popular in the early part of the 20th century.

Most notable architecturally in Taos is **Taos Pueblo,** the site of two structures emulated in homes and business buildings throughout the Southwest. Built to resemble Taos Mountain, which stands behind it, the two structures are pyramidal in form, with the different levels reached by ladders. Also quite prevalent is architecture echoing colonial hacienda style. What's nice about Taos is that you can see historic homes inside and out. You can wander through artist **Ernest Blumenschein's home.** Built in 1797 and restored by Blumenschein in 1919, it represents another New Mexico architectural phenomenon: homes that were added onto year after year. Doorways are typically low, and floors rise and fall at the whim of the earth beneath them. The **Martinez Hacienda** is an example of a hacienda stronghold. Built without windows facing outward, it originally had 20 small rooms, many with doors opening out to the courtyard. It is one of the few refurbished examples of colonial New Mexico architecture.

As you head into villages in the north, you'll see steep pitched roofs on most homes. This is because the common flat-roof style doesn't shed snow; the water builds up and causes roof problems. In just about any town in northern New Mexico, you may detect the strong smell of tar, a sure sign that another resident is laying out thousands to fix his enchanting but frustratingly flat roof.

Today, very few new homes are built of adobe. Instead, most are constructed with wood frames and plasterboard, and then stuccoed over. Several local architects are currently employing innovative architecture to create a Pueblo-style feel. They incorporate straw bales, pumice-crete, rammed earth, old tires, even aluminum cans in the construction of homes. Most of these elements are used in the same way bricks are used, stacked and layered, and then covered over with plaster and made to look like adobe. Often it's difficult to distinguish homes built with these materials from those built with wood-frame construction. West of Taos, a number of "earth ships" have been built. Many of these homes are constructed with alternative materials, most bermed into the sides of hills, utilizing the earth as insulation and the sun as an energy source.

A visitor could spend an entire trip to New Mexico focusing on the architecture. As well as relishing the wealth of architectural styles, you'll find more subtle elements everywhere. You may encounter an ox-blood floor, for example. An old Spanish tradition, ox blood is spread in layers and left to dry, hardening into a glossy finish that's known to last centuries. You're also likely to see coyote fences—narrow cedar posts lined up side by side—a system early settlers devised to ensure safety of their animals. Winding around homes and buildings you'll see *acequias,* ancient irrigation canals still maintained by locals for watering crops and trees.

THE LAY OF THE LAND

It would be easy, and accurate, to call New Mexico "high and dry" and leave it at that. The lowest point in the state, in the southeastern corner, is still over 2,800 feet in elevation, higher than the highest point in at least a dozen other states. The southern **Rocky Mountains** extend well into New Mexico, rising above 13,000 feet in the **Sangre de Cristo range** and sending a final afterthought above 10,000 feet, just east of Alamogordo. Volcanic activity created the mountain range—and its aftereffects can be seen throughout the state, from Shiprock (the remaining core of a long-eroded volcano) to Capulin Volcano National Monument. Two fault lines, which created the Rio Grande Rift Valley, home to the **Rio Grande,** run through the center of the state, and seismic activity continues to change the face of New Mexico even today.

Although archaeologists have discovered fossils indicating that most of New Mexico was once covered by ancient seas, the surface area of the state is now quite dry. The greater portion of New Mexico receives fewer than 20 inches of precipitation annually, the bulk of that coming either as summer afternoon thunderstorms or winter snowfall. In an area of 121,666 square miles—the fifth-largest U.S. state—there are only 221 square miles of water. Rivers and lakes occupy less than 0.2% of the landscape. The most important source of water is the Rio Grande. It nourishes hundreds of small farms from the **Pueblo country** of the north to the bone-dry **Chihuahuan Desert** of the far south.

However, there's more water than meets the eye in New Mexico. Systems circulating beneath the earth's surface have created all sorts of beautiful and fascinating geologic formations, including the natural wonder known as **Carlsbad Caverns,** one of the greatest cave systems in the world. Other caves have formed throughout the state, many of which have collapsed over the centuries, creating large sinkholes. These sinkholes have since filled with water and formed beautiful lakes. **Bottomless Lakes State Park,** near the town of Roswell, is a good example of this type of geological activity.

> **Impressions**
>
> *"New Mexico is old, stupendously old and dry and brown, and wind-worn by the ages. I went to New Mexico . . . to be overcome again by oldness."*
> —Charles Kuralt, *Charles Kuralt's America,* 1995

Other natural wonders you'll encounter during a visit to New Mexico include red-, yellow-, and orange-hued high, flat **mesas,** and the 275-square-mile **White Sands National Monument** that contains more than 8 billion tons of pure white gypsum and is the largest field of sand dunes of this kind in the entire world. Here, mountains meet desert, and the sky is arguably bigger, bluer, and more fascinating than any other place in the country. Words can't do justice to the spectacular colors of the landscape, and the blues, browns, greens, reds, oranges, and yellows in every imaginable variation make this land a living canvas. This is truly big sky country, where it seems you can see forever.

BOOKS, FILMS & MUSIC
Books

Many well-known writers made their homes in New Mexico in the 20th century. In the 1920s, the most celebrated were **D. H. Lawrence** and **Willa Cather,** both short-term Taos residents. Lawrence, the romantic and controversial English novelist, spent time here between 1922 and 1925; he reflected on his sojourn in *Mornings in Mexico* and *Etruscan Places.* Lawrence's Taos period is described in *Lorenzo in Taos,* which his patron, Mabel Dodge Luhan, wrote. Cather, a Pulitzer-prize winner famous for her depictions of the pioneer spirit, penned *Death Comes for the*

Archbishop, among other works. This fictionalized account of the 19th-century Santa Fe bishop, Jean-Baptiste Lamy, grew out of her stay in the region. Frank Waters gives a strong sense of Native American tradition in the region in his classics *People of the Valley* and *The Man Who Killed the Deer.*

Many contemporary authors also live in and write about New Mexico. John Nichols, of Taos, whose *Milagro Beanfield War* was made into a Robert Redford movie in 1987, writes insightfully about the problems of poor Hispanic farming communities. Albuquerque's Tony Hillerman has for decades woven mysteries around Navajo tribal police in books such as *Listening Woman* and *A Thief of Time.* In more recent years, Sarah Lovett has joined Hillerman's ranks with a series of gripping mysteries, most notably *Dangerous Attachments.* The Hispanic novelist Rudolfo Anaya's *Bless Me, Ultima,* and Pueblo writer Leslie Marmon Silko's *Ceremony* capture the lifestyles of their respective peoples. A coming-of-age story, Richard Bradford's *Red Sky at Morning* juxtaposes the various cultures of New Mexico. Edward Abbey wrote of the desert environment and politics; his *Fire on the Mountain,* set in New Mexico, was one of his most powerful works.

Excellent works about Native Americans of New Mexico include *The Pueblo Indians of North America* (Holt, Rinehart & Winston, 1970) by Edward P. Dozier and *Living the Sky: The Cosmos of the American Indian* (University of Oklahoma Press, 1987) by Ray A. Williamson. Also look for *American Indian Literature 1979–1994* (Ballantine, 1996), an anthology edited by Paula Gunn Allen.

For general histories of the state, try Myra Ellen Jenkins and Albert H. Schroeder's *A Brief History of New Mexico* (University of New Mexico Press, 1974) and Marc Simmons's *New Mexico: An Interpretive History* (University of New Mexico Press, 1988). In addition, Claire Morrill's *A Taos Mosaic: Portrait of a New Mexico Village* (University of New Mexico Press, 1973) does an excellent job of portraying the history of that small New Mexican town. I have also enjoyed Tony Hillerman's (editor) *The Spell of New Mexico* (University of New Mexico Press, 1976) and John Nichols and William Davis's *If Mountains Die: A New Mexico Memoir* (Alfred A. Knopf, 1979). *Talking Ground* (University of New Mexico Press, 1996), by Santa Fe author Douglas Preston, tells of a contemporary horseback trip through Navajoland, exploring the native mythology. One of my favorite texts is *Enchantment and Exploitation* (University of New Mexico Press, 1985) by William deBuys. An extensive book that attempts to capture the multiplicity of the region is *Legends of the American Southwest* (Alfred A. Knopf, 1997) by Alex Shoumatoff.

Enduring Visions: 1,000 Years of Southwestern Indian Art by the Aspen Center for the Visual Arts (Publishing Center for Cultural Resources, 1969) and Roland F. Dickey's *New Mexico Village Arts* (University of New Mexico Press, 1990) are both excellent resources for those interested in Native American art. If you become intrigued with Spanish art during your visit to New Mexico, you'll find E. Boyd's *Popular Arts of Spanish New Mexico* (Museum of New Mexico Press, 1974) to be quite informative.

If you like to combine walking with literary history, pick up Barbara Harrelson's *Walks in Literary Santa Fe: A Guide to Landmarks, Legends, and Lore* (Gibbs-Smith, 2008).

Films

If you like to start traveling before you climb onto the plane or into the car, you can do so easily by watching any number of movies filmed in the state. Over the years

King of the Road

If you like road trip stories to small New Mexico towns, check out my book *King of the Road* (New Mexico Magazine Press, 2007). It's a compilation of articles from my monthly column in *New Mexico Magazine,* in which locals tell the stories of their hometowns. It's illustrated with my photos too. You can order the book online at www.nm magazine.com and www.amazon.com.

so many have been filmed that I won't list them all. Instead, I'll give the ones that provide a glimpse into the true nature of New Mexico. *Silverado* (1985), a light-hearted Western, and the heartfelt miniseries *Lonesome Dove* (1989), based on a Larry McMurtry novel, start my list. Billy Bob Thorton's film adaptation (2000) of the novel *All the Pretty Horses*, Ron Howard's film version of *The Missing* (2003), and Billy Crystal in *City Slickers,* are also some of my favorite Westerns.

Favorite classics include *Butch Cassidy and the Sundance Kid* (1969), filmed in Taos and Chama; *The Cowboys* (1972), with John Wayne; Clint Eastwood's *Every Which Way But Loose* (1978); and Dennis Hopper in the 1960s classic *Easy Rider* (1969).

More contemporary themes are explored in *Contact* (1997), which features the National Radio Astronomy Very Large Array in western New Mexico, as did *Independence Day* (1996). Also exploring alien themes, *The Man Who Fell to Earth* (1976), with David Bowie, was filmed in southern New Mexico.

In recent years, thanks to state tax credits given to film companies, many films have been shot in New Mexico. Among these recent additions is the 2009 double-Oscar winner *Crazy Heart.*

Music

Such musical legends as Bo Diddley, Buddy Holly, Roy Orbison, and the Fireballs basked in New Mexico's light for parts of their careers. More recent musicians whose music really reflects the state include Mansanares, two brothers who grew up in Abiquiu, known for their Spanish guitar and soulful vocals. Look for their album *Nuevo Latino.* Master flute player Robert Mirabal's music is informed by the ceremonial music he grew up with at Taos Pueblo. Check out his 2006 Grammy Award–winning album *Sacred Ground.* Using New Mexico as his creative retreat since the 1980s, Michael Martin Murphey often plays live here, where fans always cheer for his most notable song, "Wildfire." *The Best of Michael Martin Murphey* gives a good taste of his music. Country music superstar Randy Travis calls Santa Fe home. His newest release, *Around the Bend,* is a treasure, as are his classics. My favorite musician who resides in Santa Fe is Ottmar Liebert and his band, the Luna Negra. All of their flamenco-inspired music is rich with New Mexico tones. Check out their CD *Leaning into the Night.*

EATING & DRINKING IN NEW MEXICO

You know you're in a food-conscious place when the local newspaper uses chiles (and onions) to rate movies, as does Santa Fe's *New Mexican.* A large part of that city's cachet as a chic destination derives from its famous cuisine, while Taos and Albuquerque, are developing notable reputations themselves. The competition among restaurants is fierce, which means that visitors have plenty of options from which to choose. Aside from establishments serving New Mexican cuisine that the region is famed for, you can also find French, Italian, Asian, Indian, and interesting hybrids of those. Luckily, not all the top restaurants are high-end; several hidden gems satisfy your taste buds without emptying your wallet.

Reservations are always recommended at the higher-end restaurants and are essential during peak seasons. Only a few restaurants serve late, so be sure to plan dinner before 8pm. Most restaurants are casual, so almost any attire is fine, though for the more expensive ones, dressing up is a good idea.

At the beginning of each city's dining section I give more details about the dining scene there.

Food here isn't the same as Mexican cuisine or even those American variations of Tex-Mex and Cal-Mex. New Mexican cooking is a product of Southwestern history: Native Americans taught the Spanish conquerors about corn—how to roast it and how to make corn pudding, stewed corn, cornbread, cornmeal, and *posole* (hominy)—and they also taught the Spanish how to use chile peppers, a crop indigenous to the New World, having been first harvested in the Andean highlands as early as 4000 B.C. The Spaniards brought the practice of eating beef to the area.

Newcomers have introduced other elements to the food here. From Mexico came the interest in seafood. Regional New American cuisine combines elements from various parts of Mexico, such as sauces from the Yucatán Peninsula, and fried bananas served with bean dishes, typical of Central American locales. You'll also find Asian elements mixed in.

The basic ingredients of New Mexico cooking are three indispensable, locally grown foods: **chile, beans,** and **corn.** Of these, perhaps the most crucial is the **chile,** whether brilliant red or green and with various levels of spicy bite. Chile forms the base for the red and green sauces that top most New Mexico dishes such as enchiladas and burritos. One is not necessarily hotter than the other; spiciness depends on the type, and where and during what kind of season (dry or wet) the chiles were grown.

Spotted or painted **pinto beans** with a nutty taste are simmered with garlic, onion, cumin, and red chile powder and served as a side dish. When mashed and refried in oil, they become *frijoles refritos.* **Corn** supplies the vital dough for tortillas and tamales called *masa.* New Mexican corn comes in six colors, of which yellow, white, and blue are the most common.

Even if you're familiar with Mexican cooking, the dishes you know and love are likely to be prepared differently here. The following is a rundown of some regional dishes, a number of which aren't widely known outside the Southwest:

BISCOCHITO A cookie made with anise.

CARNE ADOVADA Tender pork marinated in red chile sauce, herbs, and spices, and then baked.

CHILE RELLENOS Peppers stuffed with cheese, deep-fried, and then covered with green chile sauce.

CHORIZO BURRITO Mexican sausage, scrambled eggs, potatoes, and scallions wrapped in a flour tortilla with red or green chile sauce and melted Jack cheese. Also called a "breakfast burrito."

YOU SAY chili, WE SAY chile

You'll never see "chili" on a menu in New Mexico. New Mexicans are adamant that *chile,* the Spanish spelling of the word, is the only way to spell it—no matter what your dictionary may say.

Virtually anything you order in a restaurant is likely to be topped with a chile sauce. If you're not accustomed to spicy foods, certain varieties will make your eyes water, your sinuses drain, and your palate feel as if it's on fire. ***Warning:*** No amount of water or beer will alleviate the sting. (Drink milk. A *sopaipilla* drizzled with honey is also helpful.)

But don't let these words of caution scare you away from genuine New Mexico chiles. The pleasure of eating them far outweighs the pain. Start slowly, with salsas and chile sauces first, perhaps *rellenos* (stuffed peppers) next. Before long, you'll be buying chile *ristras* (chiles strung on rope).

EMPANADA   A fried pie with nuts and currants.

ENCHILADAS   Tortillas either rolled or layered with chicken, beef, or cheese, topped with chile sauce.

FRY BREAD   A crispy Native American bread fried in oil, served with honey or smothered with meat and chile.

GREEN CHILE STEW   Locally grown chiles cooked in a stew with chunks of meat, beans, and potatoes.

HUEVOS RANCHEROS   Fried eggs on corn tortillas, topped with cheese and red or green chile, served with pinto beans.

POSOLE   A corn soup or stew (called hominy in other parts of the south), sometimes prepared with pork and chile.

SOPAIPILLA   A lightly fried puff pastry served with honey as a dessert or stuffed with meat and vegetables as a main dish. *Sopaipillas* with honey have a cooling effect on your palate after you've eaten a spicy dish.

TACOS   Spiced chicken or beef served either in soft tortillas or crispy shells.

TAMALES   A dish made from cornmeal mush, wrapped in husks and steamed.

PLANNING YOUR TRIP TO NEW MEXICO

3

A trip to New Mexico may affect your attitude. You may return home and find that your response to the world is completely different from the way it used to be. (That is, if you return at all.) The Land of Enchantment has few customary points of reference. Rather than sharp-cornered buildings, you find adobe ones made of mud bricks. Rather than hearing a single language on the street, you hear many, from Navajo and the Pueblo Tiwa and Tewa to Spanish and English. The pace here is slow and the objectives are less obvious than in most places.

And New Mexico has its own unique terrain and climate as well. Travelers often think that because this is the desert, it should have saguaro cactus and always be warm. Think again. Much of the area lies upwards of 5,000 feet in elevation, which means that four full seasons act upon the land. So, when you're planning, be sure to take a look at the "When to Go" section so you can be prepared.

That said, preparation to come here is simple. Even though many people mistake New Mexico for our lovely neighbor to the south, really, traveling here is much like anywhere in the U.S. You can drink the water and eat all the food you care to eat, except you'll want to take care, as some of the chiles can be very hot. The sun at these elevations can also be scorching, so come readied with a hat and plenty of sunscreen. In fact, the elements here may present the greatest challenge, so be sure to review the section "Staying Healthy," later in this chapter.

Another point to be aware of is the distance between cities. Your best bet is to travel by car here, as many of the "must see" attractions are located off the main thoroughfares traversed by the few public transportation options available here. Besides, there are few enjoyments so great as driving in the sparkling light through crooked farming villages, past ancient ruins, around plazas, and over mountain passes.

As with any trip, a little preparation is essential before you start your journey to New Mexico. This chapter provides a variety of planning tools, including information on when to go and how to get there. For additional help in planning your trip and for more on-the-ground resources in New Mexico, please turn to "Fast Facts," on p. 386.

WHEN TO GO

Forget any preconceptions you may have about the New Mexico "desert." The high desert climate of this part of the world is generally dry but not always warm. Summers are hot throughout most of the state, though distinctly cooler at higher elevations. Winters are relatively mild in the south, harsher in the north and in the mountains. Spring and fall have pleasant temperatures, though in spring the wind blows throughout the state. Rainfall is sparse except in the higher mountains; summer afternoon thunderstorms and winter snows account for most precipitation.

Santa Fe and Taos, at 7,000 feet, have midsummer highs in the low 90s (about 32°C), overnight midwinter lows in the teens (btw. −12° and −7°C). Temperatures in Albuquerque, at 5,300 feet, often run about 10°F warmer than elsewhere in the northern region. Snowfall is common November through March, and sometimes as late as May, though it seldom lasts long. Santa Fe averages 32 inches total annual snowfall. At the high-mountain ski resorts, as much as 300 inches may fall—and stay—in a season. The plains and deserts of the southeast and south commonly have summer temperatures in excess of 100°F (38°C).

New Mexico Temperatures (High/Low) & Precipitation

		JAN	APR	JULY	OCT	ANNUAL PRECIPITATION (INCHES)
Alamogordo	(°F)	57/28	78/40	95/65	79/42	7.5
	(°C)	14/-2	26/4	35/18	26/6	
Albuquerque	(°F)	47/28	70/41	92/66	74/45	8.5
	(°C)	8/-2	21/5	33/19	22/7	
Carlsbad	(°F)	60/28	81/46	96/67	80/49	12.6
	(°C)	16/-2	27/7	36/19	27/9	
Chama	(°F)	33/3	54/22	73/37	52/18	20.9
	(°C)	-1/-16	12/-6	23/3	11/-8	
Cloudcroft	(°F)	41/19	56/33	73/48	59/36	26.5
	(°C)	5/-7	13/-1	23/9	15/2	
Farmington	(°F)	44/16	70/36	92/58	70/37	8.2
	(°C)	7/-9	21/2	33/14	21/3	
Las Cruces	(°F)	56/29	79/48	96/68	78/50	8.6
	(°C)	13/-2	26/9	36/20	26/10	
Roswell	(°F)	56/24	78/42	91/65	79/46	12.7
	(°C)	13/-4	26/6	33/18	26/7	
Ruidoso	(°F)	50/17	65/28	82/48	68/31	21.4
	(°C)	10/-8	18/-2	28/9	20/-1	
Santa Fe	(°F)	47/18	64/33	85/56	67/38	11.4
	(°C)	8/-8	18/1	29/13	19/3	
Taos	(°F)	40/10	64/29	87/50	75/32	12.0
	(°C)	4/-12	18/-2	31/10	24/0	
Truth or Consequences	(°F)	54/27	75/449	2/66	75/47	9.9
	(°C)	12/-3	24/7	33/19	24/8	

New Mexico Calendar of Events

A good resource for events is **www.newmexico.org/calendar**. Here are some of my favorites. For an exhaustive list of events beyond those listed here, check **http://events.frommers.com**, where you'll find a searchable, up-to-the-minute roster of what's happening in cities all over the world.

JANUARY

New Year's Day. Transfer of canes to new officials and various dances at most pueblos. Turtle Dance at Taos Pueblo (no photography allowed). Call © **575/758-1028** or go to www.taospueblo.com for more information. January 1.

Winter Wine Festival. A variety of wine offerings and food tastings prepared by local chefs take place in the Taos Ski Valley. Call © **505/438-8060** for details or go to www.taoswinterwinefest.com. Mid-January.

FEBRUARY

Mt. Taylor Winter Quadrathlon. Hundreds of athletes come from all over the West to bicycle, run, cross-country ski, and snowshoe up and down this mountain. For information, call © **800/748-2142**. Early February.

Just Desserts Eat, Ski or Snowshoe. Cross-country skiers and snow-shoers travel from point to point on the Enchanted Forest course near Red River, tasting decadent desserts supplied by area restaurants. Call © **575/754-2374** or go to www.enchantedforestxc.com. Late February.

MARCH

National Fiery Foods/Barbecue Show. Here's your chance to taste the hottest of the hot and plenty of milder flavors, too. Some 13,000 general-public attendees show up to taste sauces, salsas, candies, and more at the Sandia Resort & Casino. For information, call © **505/873-8680** or go to www.fiery-foods.com. Early March.

Rio Grande Arts and Crafts Festival. A juried show featuring 200 artists and craftspeople from around the country takes place at Expo New Mexico in Albuquerque. Call © **505/292-7457** for more information, or visit www.riograndefestivals.com. (Also check out their Oct balloon Fiesta show and Nov holiday show.) Second week of March.

Chimayo Pilgrimage. On Good Friday, thousands of pilgrims trek on foot to the Santuario de Chimayo, a small church north of Santa Fe that's believed to aid in miracles. For information, call © **505/351-9961;** www.elsantuariodechimayo.org.

Rockhound Roundup. Gems, jewelry, tools, and crafted items are displayed and sold at the Southwest New Mexico State Fairgrounds in Deming. Contact (© **575/543-8915** or 575/267-4399; www.dgms.bravehost.com. Second weekend in March.

APRIL

Easter Weekend Celebration. Celebrations include Masses, parades, corn dances, and other dances, such as the bow and arrow dance at Nambe. Call © **505/843-7270** for information.

American Indian Week. A celebration of Native American traditions and culture at the Indian Pueblo Cultural Center, Albuquerque. Call © **505/843-7270** or go to www.indianpueblo.org. Late April.

Gathering of Nations Powwow. Dance competitions, arts-and-crafts exhibitions, and Miss Indian World contest. At the University Football Stadium, Albuquerque. Call © **505/836-2810** or visit www.gatheringofnations.com. Late April.

MAY

Cinco de Mayo Fiestas. The restoration of the Mexican republic (from French occupation during 1863–67) is celebrated in, among other places, Las Cruces at Old Mesilla Plaza (other celebrations are held statewide). For information go to www.oldmesilla.org. First weekend in May.

Taos Spring Arts Festival. Contemporary visual, performing, and literary arts are highlighted during 2 weeks of gallery openings, studio tours, performances by visiting theatrical and dance troupes, live musical events, traditional ethnic entertainment, literary readings, and more.

Events are held at venues throughout Taos and Taos County. For dates and ticket info call ✆ **575/751-8800** or visit www.taoschamber.com. All month.

JUNE

Aztec Fiesta Days. Celebrate the arrival of summer with three parades, games, food, arts and crafts, and a carnival in Aztec. Contact ✆ **505/334-9551** or visit www.aztecchamber.com. First full weekend in June.

Rodeo de Santa Fe. This 4-day event features a Western parade, free concert, and five rodeo performances with more than 600 contestants from all over the world, who compete for sizable purses in such events as Brahma bull and bronco riding, roping, steer wrestling, barrel racing, and clown antics.

The rodeo grounds are at 3237 Rodeo Rd., at Richards Avenue, 5½ miles south of the plaza. Performances are in the evening Wednesday to Saturday, and on Saturday afternoon. For tickets and information, call ✆ **505/471-4300** or visit www.rodeodesantafe.org. It takes place sometime around the fourth weekend in June.

Rodeo de Taos. A fun event at the County Fairgrounds in Taos, featuring local and regional participants. For information, call ✆ **575/758-5700,** or in mid- to late June call ✆ 575/758-3974. Third or fourth weekend in June.

Taos Solar Music Festival. Sit out on the grass, under the sun, and listen to major players at this event celebrating the summer solstice. A tribute to solar energy, the event has a stage powered by a solar generator and educational displays within a "Solar Village." Held at the Kit Carson Municipal Park, Taos. For information, contact ✆ **575/758-9191** or www.solarmusicfest.com. Late June.

New Mexico Arts and Crafts Fair. A tradition for 43 years, this juried show offers work from more than 200 New Mexico artisans, accompanied by nonstop entertainment for the whole family. This can be a good place to find Hispanic arts and crafts.

The fair is held at Expo New Mexico in Albuquerque. Admission cost varies. For information, call ✆ **505/884-9043** or check online at www.nmartsandcraftsfair.org. Last full weekend in June.

JULY

Apache Maidens' Puberty Rites. This 4-day ceremony in Mescalero concludes with a rodeo and the dance of the mountain spirits. Call ✆ **575/464-4494** for more information. July 1 to 4.

Fourth of July celebrations. Held all over New Mexico, celebrations include fireworks displays. Call the chambers of commerce in specific towns and cities for information. One of the best is the **Fiestas de Las Vegas,** at the plaza, which includes a parade, concerts, and food booths. Contact ✆ **800/832-5947** or 505/425-8631; www.lvsmchamber.org.

Pancake Breakfast on the Plaza. Rub elbows with Santa Fe residents at this locals' event on the plaza that raises funds for charities and draws some 10,000 hungry folks. For information call ✆ **505/982-2002;** www.uwsfc.org. July 4th.

UFO Festival. This festival celebrates all manner of extraterrestrial oddity that has sprung to life since the alleged 1947 alien crash in Roswell. More than 7,000 visitors fill the town of Roswell to attend lectures and participate in a costume contest and parade. Contact ✆ **888/767-3378;** www.roswellufofestival.com. Early July.

Santa Fe International Folk Art Market. This has fast become one of the city's most popular summer events. Artisans from all over the world come to display and sell works ranging from basketry to textiles outside the International Museum of Folk Art. Concerts, dance performances, and children's programs charge the air, while the scent of delectable food wafts about. Contact ✆ **505-476-1197** or go to www. folkartmarket.org. Early July.

Taos Pueblo Powwow. Intertribal competition in traditional and contemporary dances. Call ✆ **575/758-1028** for more information, or visit www.taospueblopow wow.com. Second weekend in July.

Taste of Santa Fe. Sample some 50 of Santa Fe's best chefs' food, including appetizers, entrees, and desserts at the Santa Fe Railyard. For information, call ✆ **505/982-6366,** ext. 107, or go to www.tasteof santafe.com. Held in mid-July.

Eight Northern Pueblos Artist and Craftsman Show. More than 600 Native American artists exhibit their work at the eight northern pueblos. Traditional dances and food booths; location varies. Contact ✆ **505/747-1593** or www.enipc.org for location and exact dates. Third weekend in July.

Fiestas de Santiago y Santa Ana. The celebration begins with a Friday-night Mass at one of the three Taos-area parishes, where the fiesta queen is crowned. During the weekend there are candlelight processions, special Masses, music, dancing, parades, crafts, and food booths.

Taos Plaza hosts many events and most are free. For information, contact ✆ **800/732-8267** or www.fiestasdetaos.com. Third weekend in July.

Spanish Market. More than 500 traditional and contemporary Hispanic artists from New Mexico and southern Colorado exhibit and sell their work in this lively community event. Artists are featured in special demonstrations, while an entertaining mix of traditional Hispanic music, dance, foods, and pageantry creates the ambience of a village celebration. Artwork for sale includes *santos* (painted and carved saints), textiles, tinwork, furniture, straw appliqué, and metalwork.

The markets are found at the Santa Fe plaza. For information, contact the Spanish Colonial Arts Society (✆ **505/982-2226;** www.spanishmarket.org). Last full weekend in July.

Bat Flight Breakfast. An early morning buffet breakfast is served at Carlsbad Caverns National Park while visitors watch the bats return to the cave. Contact ✆ **575/785-3012** or www.nps.gov/cave for details and exact date. Mid- to late July or early August.

Old Lincoln Days and Billy the Kid Pageant. The main attraction is a reenactment of Billy the Kid's escape from the Lincoln jail. There are also a fiddling contest and living-history demonstrations (such as weaving and blacksmithing). Contact ✆ **575/653-4372** or www.nmmonuments. org for more information. Last weekend in July or first weekend in August.

AUGUST

Inter-tribal Indian Ceremonial. Thirty tribes from the United States and Mexico participate in rodeos, parades, dances, athletic competitions, and an arts and crafts show at Red Rock Park, east of Gallup. Contact ✆ **505/863-3896** or visit www. theceremonial.com. Late July or early to mid-August.

Pueblo Independence Day. Participants from many of the Pueblos convene at Jemez State Monument to celebrate the Pueblo Revolt of 1680. Food, art booths, dances, and live music fill the sunny plaza. Contact ✆ **575/829-3530** or go to www. nmmonuments.org. Mid-August.

Zuni Arts & Cultural Expo. This 3-day event features arts-and-crafts sales and traditional food and dances. Contact ✆ **575/782-7238** or www.zunitourism.com for more information. Second week in August.

Chama Days. A rodeo, parade, and arts-and-crafts fair highlight this mountain-town event. Contact the Chama Valley Chamber of Commerce (✆ **800/477-0149** or 575/756-2306; www.chamavalley.com). Second weekend of August.

The Indian Market. This is the largest all-Native American market in the country.

About 1,000 artisans display their baskets and blankets, jewelry, pottery, woodcarvings, rugs, sand paintings, and sculptures at rows of booths around Santa Fe Plaza, surrounding streets, and de Vargas Mall. Sales are brisk. Costumed tribal dancing and crafts demonstrations are scheduled in the afternoon.

The market is free, but hotels are booked months in advance. For information, contact the Southwestern Association for Indian Arts (📞 **505/983-5220;** www. swaia.org). Third weekend in August.

Music from Angel Fire. World-class musicians gather in Angel Fire to perform classical and chamber music. For information and schedules, call 📞 **575/377-3233** or go to www.musicfromangelfire.org. Mid-August to the first week in September.

Great American Duck Race. Devised in a bar in 1979, this event has grown to include a parade, a tortilla toss, an outhouse race, ballooning, dances, and, of course, the duck race. It takes place on the Deming courthouse lawn ("Duck Downs"). Call 📞 **888/345-1125** or visit www.demingduckrace.com. Fourth weekend in August.

SEPTEMBER

Artist Studio Tours take place all over New Mexico in the fall. For specific detail see "High on Art" in chapter 7.

The All American Futurity. With a purse of $2 million, this is the world's richest quarter-horse race. At Ruidoso Downs, Ruidoso. Contact 📞 **575/378-4431** or www.ruidownsracing.com. Labor Day.

Chile Festival. New Mexicans celebrate their favorite fiery food item with a festival in Hatch, the "Chile Capital of the World." Contact 📞 **575/267-5483** or www.hatchchilefest.com. Labor Day weekend.

New Mexico Wine Festival. New Mexico wines are showcased at this annual event in Bernalillo, near Albuquerque, which features wine tastings, an art show, and live entertainment. For a schedule of events, call 📞 **505/867-3311** or go to www.newmexicowinefestival.com. Labor Day weekend.

Las Fiestas de Santa Fe. An exuberant combination of spirit, history, and general merrymaking, Las Fiestas is the oldest community celebration in the United States. The first fiesta was celebrated in 1712, 20 years after the peaceful resettlement of New Mexico by Spanish conquistadors in 1692. The celebration includes Masses, a parade for children and their pets, a historical/hysterical parade, mariachi concerts, dances, food, and arts, as well as local entertainment on the plaza. Zozobra, "Old Man Gloom," a 40-foot-tall effigy made of wood, canvas, and paper, is burned at dusk on Thursday to revitalize the community. For information, contact 📞 **505/204-1598;** www.santafefiesta.org. Weekend following Labor Day.

Enchanted Circle Century Bike Tour. About 600 cyclists turn out to ride 100 miles of scenic mountain roads, starting and ending in Red River. All levels of riders are welcome, though not everyone completes this test of endurance. Call 📞 **575/754-2366** or go to www.redrivernewmex.com. Weekend following Labor Day.

New Mexico State Fair and Rodeo. This is one of America's top state fairs; it features parimutuel horse racing, a nationally acclaimed rodeo, entertainment by top country artists, Native American and Spanish villages, the requisite midway, livestock shows, and arts and crafts.

The fair and rodeo, which last 17 days, are held at Expo New Mexico in Albuquerque. Advance tickets can be ordered by calling 📞 **505/265-3976** or visiting www.exponm.com. Early September.

Taos Trade Fair. La Hacienda de los Martinez, Lower Ranchitos Road, Taos. This 1-day affair reenacts Spanish colonial life of the mid-1820s and features Hispanic and Native American music, weaving and crafts demonstrations, traditional foods, dancing, and visits by mountain men. Call 📞 **575/758-0505.** Last full weekend in September.

San Geronimo Vespers Sundown Dance and Trade Fair. This event, at Taos Pueblo, features a Mass and procession; traditional corn, buffalo, and Comanche dances; an arts-and-crafts fair; foot races; and pole climbs by clowns. Call ✆ **575/758-1028** for details or go to www.taospueblo.com. Last weekend in September.

Santa Fe Wine & Chile Fiesta. This lively celebration boasts 5 days of wine and food events, including seminars, guest chef demonstrations and luncheons, tours, a grand tasting and reserve tasting, an auction, and a golf tournament. It takes place at many venues in downtown Santa Fe with the big event on the last Saturday. Tickets go on sale in early July and sell out quickly. For information, call ✆ **505/438-8060** or visit www.santafewineandchile.org. Last Wednesday through Sunday in September.

Stone Lake Fiesta. Jicarilla Reservation, 19 miles south of Dulce. This Apache festival features a rodeo, ceremonial dances, and a foot race. For more information call ✆ **575/759-3242**, ext. 275 or 277, or go to www.jicarillaonline.com. September 15.

Mexican Independence Day. A parade and dances take place in Las Cruces at Old Mesilla Plaza (✆ **505/524-3262,** ext. 117; www.vivamesilla.org) and Carlsbad at San Jose Plaza (✆ **575/887-6516;** www.carlsbadchamber.com). Weekend closest to September 16.

Taos Fall Arts Festival. Highlights include arts-and-crafts exhibitions and competitions, studio tours, gallery openings, lectures, concerts, dances, and stage plays. Simultaneous events include the **Trade Fair, Wool Festival,** and **San Geronimo Day** at Taos Pueblo.

The festival is held throughout Taos and Taos County. Events, schedules, and tickets (where required) can be obtained from the Taos County Chamber of Commerce (✆ **800/732-8267** or 575/751-8800; www.taosfallarts.com). Mid-September (or the third weekend) to the first week in October.

The Whole Enchilada Fiesta. The world's biggest enchilada (sometimes over 7 ft. wide) is created and eaten in Las Cruces.

Contact ✆ **575/562-1938** or visit www.enchiladafiesta.com. Late September or early October.

OCTOBER

Shiprock Navajo Fair. The oldest and most traditional Navajo fair, it features a rodeo, dancing and singing, a parade, and arts-and-crafts exhibits. Contact ✆ **505/368-3727** or www.shiprocknavajofair.org. Early October.

Albuquerque International Balloon Fiesta. The world's largest balloon rally, this 9-day festival brings together more than 600 colorful balloons and includes races and contests. There are mass ascensions at sunrise, "balloon glows" in the evening, and balloon rides for those desiring a little lift. Various special events are staged all week.

Balloons lift off at Balloon Fiesta Park (at I-25 and Alameda NE) on Albuquerque's northern city limits. For information, call ✆ **505/821-1000** or visit www.balloonfiesta.com. First full week in October.

NOVEMBER

Weems Artfest. Approximately 260 artisans, who work in a variety of media, come from throughout the world to attend this 3-day fair, held at Expo New Mexico in Albuquerque. It's one of the top-100 arts-and-crafts fairs in the country. For details, call ✆ **505/293-6133** or go to www.weemsgallery.com. Early November.

Festival of the Cranes. People come from all over the world to attend this bird-watching event just 1½ hours south of Albuquerque at Bosque del Apache National Wildlife Refuge, near Socorro. Call ✆ **575/835-1828** or go to www.friendsofthebosque.org. Weekend before Thanksgiving.

Yuletide in Taos. This holiday event emphasizes northern New Mexican traditions, culture, and arts, with carols, festive classical music, Hispanic and Native American songs and dances, historic walking tours, art exhibitions, dance performances, candlelight dinners, and more.

Events are staged by the Taos County Chamber of Commerce (✆ **575/751-8800;**

www.taoschamber.com). From Thanksgiving through New Year's Day.

DECEMBER

Christmas on the Pecos. In Carlsbad, pontoon-boat rides take place each evening, past a brilliant display of Christmas lights on riverside homes and businesses. Contact ✆ **800/221-1224** or 575/877-6516; www.christmasonthepecos.com. Thanksgiving to New Year's Eve (except Christmas Eve).

Santa Fe Film Festival. At venues throughout the city, presenting engaging local New Mexican films and international films in a variety of genres. Post-screening parties often feature film stars. Call ✆ **505/988-7414** or go to www.santafefilmfestival.com. Early December.

Winter Spanish Market. At the Santa Fe Community Convention Center. Approximately 150 artists show their wares at this little sister to July's major event. See the Spanish Market in July (above) for more information. Call ✆ **505/982-2226;** www.spanishmarket.org. First full weekend in December.

Christmas in Madrid Open House. Even if you never get out of your car, it's worth going to see the spectacular lights display in this village between Albuquerque and Santa Fe on the Turquoise Trail. You'll also find entertainment, refreshments in shops, and Santa Claus. For additional information, call ✆ **505/471-1054.** First two weekends in December.

Canyon Road Farolito Walk. Locals and visitors to Santa Fe bundle up and stroll Canyon Road, where streets and rooftops are lined with *farolitos* (candle lamps). Musicians play and carolers sing around *luminarias* (little fires). Though it's not responsible for the event, the **Santa Fe Convention and Visitors Bureau** (✆ **505/955-6200**) can help direct you there; or ask your hotel concierge. Christmas Eve at dusk.

Christmas Native American Celebrations. Many pueblos celebrate the Christmas holiday with dances. The Dance of the Matachines takes place at Picuris and San Juan pueblos on Christmas Day. Call ✆ **505/843-7270** or go to www.indianpueblo.org. Christmas Eve and Christmas Day.

Our Lady of Guadalupe Fiesta. This pilgrimage to Tortugas Mountain (near Las Cruces) and torchlight descent is followed by a Mass and traditional Native American and Hispanic dances. Call ✆ **575/526-8171** for more information. December 10 to 12.

Torchlight Procession. Brave skiers in the Taos Ski Valley carve down a steep run named Snakedance in the dark while carrying golden fire. For information call ✆ **866/968-7386** or visit www.skitaos.org. December 31.

ENTRY REQUIREMENTS

Passports

Virtually every air traveler entering the U.S. is required to show a passport. All persons, including U.S. citizens, traveling by air between the United States and Canada, Mexico, Central and South America, the Caribbean, and Bermuda are required to present a valid passport. *Note:* U.S. and Canadian citizens entering the U. S. at land and sea ports of entry from within the western hemisphere must now also present a passport or other documents compliant with the Western Hemisphere Travel Initiative (WHTI; see www.getyouhome.gov for details). Children 15 and under may continue entering with only a U.S. birth certificate, or other proof of U.S. citizenship.

It is advised to always have at least one or two consecutive blank pages in your passport to allow space for visas and stamps that need to appear together. It is also important to note when your passport expires. Many countries require your passport to have at least 6 months left before its expiration in order to allow you into the destination.

Visas

For information on obtaining a Visa, please visit "Fast Facts," on p. 389.

The U.S. State Department has a **Visa Waiver Program (VWP)** allowing citizens of the following countries to enter the United States without a visa for stays of up to 90 days: Andorra, Australia, Austria, Belgium, Brunei, Czech Republic, Denmark, Estonia, Finland, France, Germany, Greece, Hungary, Iceland, Ireland, Italy, Japan, Latvia, Liechtenstein, Lithuania, Luxembourg, Malta, Monaco, the Netherlands, New Zealand, Norway, Portugal, San Marino, Singapore, Slovakia, Slovenia, South Korea, Spain, Sweden, Switzerland, and the United Kingdom. (**Note:** This list was accurate at press time; for the most up-to-date list of countries in the VWP, consult www.travel.state.gov/visa.) Even though a visa isn't necessary, in an effort to help U.S. officials check travelers against terror watch lists before they arrive at U.S. borders, visitors from VWP countries must register online through the Electronic System for Travel Authorization (ESTA) before boarding a plane or a boat to the U.S. Travelers must complete an electronic application providing basic personal and travel eligibility information. The Department of Homeland Security recommends filling out the form at least 3 days before traveling. Authorizations will be valid for up to 2 years or until the traveler's passport expires, whichever comes first. Currently, there is no fee for the online application. **Note:** Any passport issued on or after October 26, 2006, by a VWP country must be an **e-Passport** for VWP travelers to be eligible to enter the U.S. without a visa. Citizens of these nations also need to present a round-trip air or cruise ticket upon arrival. E-Passports contain computer chips capable of storing biometric information, such as the required digital photograph of the holder. If your passport doesn't have this feature, you can still travel without a visa if the valid passport was issued before October 26, 2005, and includes a machine-readable zone; or if the valid passport was issued between October 26, 2005, and October 25, 2006, and includes a digital photograph. For more information, go to **www.travel.state.gov/visa**. Canadian citizens may enter the United States without visas, but will need to show passports and proof of residence.

Citizens of all other countries must have (1) a valid passport that expires at least 6 months later than the scheduled end of their visit to the U.S.; and (2) a tourist visa.

Customs

WHAT YOU CAN BRING INTO THE U.S.

Every visitor 21 years of age or older may bring in, free of duty, the following: (1) 1 U.S. quart of alcohol; (2) 200 cigarettes, 50 cigars (but not from Cuba), or 3 pounds of smoking tobacco; and (3) $100 worth of gifts. These exemptions are offered to travelers who spend at least 72 hours in the United States and who have not claimed them within the preceding 6 months. It is forbidden to bring into the country almost any meat products (including canned, fresh, and dried meat products such as bouillon, soup mixes, and so on). Generally, condiments including vinegars, oils, pickled goods, spices, coffee, tea, and some cheeses and baked goods are permitted. Avoid rice products, as rice can often harbor insects. Bringing fruits and vegetables is prohibited since they may harbor pests or disease. International visitors may carry in or out up to $10,000 in U.S. or foreign currency with no formalities; larger sums must be declared to U.S. Customs on entering or leaving, which includes filing form CM 4790. For details regarding U.S. Customs and Border Protection, consult your nearest U.S. embassy or consulate, or **U.S. Customs** (www.customs.gov).

WHAT YOU CAN TAKE HOME

For information on what you're allowed to bring home, contact one of the following agencies:

U.S. Citizens: U.S. Customs & Border Protection (CBP), 1300 Pennsylvania Ave., NW, Washington, DC 20229 (✆ **877/287-8667;** www.cbp.gov).

Canadian Citizens: Canada Border Services Agency, Ottawa, Ontario, K1A 0L8 (✆ **800/461-9999** in Canada, or 204/983-3500; www.cbsa-asfc.gc.ca).

U.K. Citizens: HM Customs & Excise, Crownhill Court, Tailyour Road, Plymouth, PL6 5BZ (✆ **0845/010-9000,** or 020/8929-0152 from outside the U.K.; www.hmce.gov.uk).

Australian Citizens: Australian Customs Service, Customs House, 5 Constitution Avenue, Canberra City, ACT 2601 (✆ **1300/363-263,** or 612/6275-6666 from outside Australia; www.customs.gov.au).

New Zealand Citizens: New Zealand Customs, The Customhouse, 17–21 Whitmore St., Box 2218, Wellington, 6140 (✆ **04/473-6099** or 0800/428-786; www.customs.govt.nz).

Medical Requirements

Unless you're arriving from an area known to be suffering from an epidemic (particularly cholera or yellow fever), inoculations or vaccinations are not required for entry into the United States.

GETTING THERE & AROUND

Getting to New Mexico

BY PLANE

The gateway to Santa Fe, Taos, Albuquerque, and other New Mexico communities is the **Albuquerque International Sunport** (ABQ; ✆ **505/244-7700** for the administrative offices; www.cabq.gov/airport).

A secondary hub for southern New Mexico is **El Paso International Airport** (ELP; ✆ **915/780-4749;** www.elpasointernationalairport.com) in western Texas.

To find out which airlines travel to New Mexico, see "Airline Websites," p. 390. A little more costly, visitors can now fly into the **Santa Fe Municipal Airport** (SAF; ✆ **505/955-2900;** www.santafenm.gov. In conjunction with American Airlines, flights are offered by **American Eagle** (✆ **800/433-7300;** www.aa.com).

Getting into Town from the Airport

Most hotels have courtesy vans to meet their guests and take them to their respective destinations. In addition, **Sunport Shuttle** (✆ **505/883-4966;** www.sunport shuttle.com) in Albuquerque runs vans to and from city hotels. In Santa Fe, **Roadrunner Shuttle** (✆ **505/424-3367**) meets flights and takes visitors anywhere in Santa Fe. See "By Bus" and "By Train," below, to find out how to get from the Albuquerque Sunport to Santa Fe. **Las Cruces Shuttle Service** (✆ **800/288-1784;**

www.lascrucesshuttle.com) travels between the El Paso International Airport and Las Cruces.

BY CAR

Driving is the best way to see New Mexico, so you'll want to either drive here or rent a car. All major rental car companies are represented here.

Three interstate highways cross New Mexico. The north-south I-25 bisects the state, passing through Albuquerque and Las Cruces. The east-west I-40 follows the path of the old Route 66 through Gallup, Albuquerque, and Tucumcari in the north; I-10 from San Diego crosses southwestern New Mexico until intersecting I-25 at Las Cruces.

Parking is readily available and reasonably priced throughout the state both at meters and in city parking garages.

International visitors should note that insurance and taxes are almost never included in quoted rental car rates in the U.S. Be sure to ask your rental agency about additional fees for these. They can add a significant cost to your car rental.

The following table shows the approximate mileage to Santa Fe from various cities around the United States.

Distances to Santa Fe (in Miles)

FROM	DISTANCE	FROM	DISTANCE
Atlanta	1,417	Minneapolis	1,199
Boston	2,190	New Orleans	1,181
Chicago	1,293	New York	1,971
Cleveland	1,558	Oklahoma City	533
Dallas	663	Phoenix	595
Denver	391	St. Louis	993
Detroit	1,514	Salt Lake City	634
Houston	900	San Francisco	1,149
Los Angeles	860	Seattle	1,477
Miami	2,011	Washington, D.C.	1,825

BY TRAIN

Northern New Mexico recently gained rail transport with **New Mexico Rail Runner Express** (© **866/795-7245**; www.nmrailrunner.com). Trains run daily from various points in Albuquerque to various ones in Santa Fe, with connecting buses to the Albuquerque International Sunport and to Taos.

Amtrak (© **866/795-7245** or 505/842-9650; www.amtrak.com) has two routes through the state. Greyhound bus lines provide through-ticketing for Amtrak between Albuquerque and El Paso.

You can get a copy of Amtrak's National Timetable at **www.amtrak.com**. A photo ID is required for check-in.

BY BUS

Because Santa Fe is only about 58 miles northeast of Albuquerque via I-40, most visitors to Santa Fe take the bus directly from the Albuquerque airport, at a cost of $20 to $25 one-way. **Sandia Shuttle Express** buses (© **888/775-5696** or 505/474-5696; www.sandiashuttle.com) make the 70-minute run between the airport and Santa Fe hotels 10 times daily each way (from Albuquerque to Santa Fe, 6:30am–6pm; from Santa Fe to Albuquerque, 8:45am–8:20pm). Reservations are required, ideally 48 hours in advance. Two other bus services shuttle between Albuquerque and Taos (via Santa Fe) for $25 to $35 one-way: **Faust's Transportation** (📞 **888/830-3410** or 505/758-3410) and **Twin Heart Express & Transportation** (📞 **800/654-9456** or 575/751-1201).

The **public bus depot** in Albuquerque is located at 100 1st St. SW. Contact **Greyhound** 📞 **800/231-2222;** www.greyhound.com) for information and schedules. Buses no longer run to Santa Fe and Taos.

Getting Around
BY PLANE
New Mexico doesn't have many carriers flying between its cities, which is just as well. The best parts of the region happen *between* the major destinations.

If you don't have a car and don't want to rent one, there are a few flights. The principal carrier is **Great Lakes Airlines** (📞 **800/554-5111;** www.flygreatlakes.com), which flies from Albuquerque to Farmington and Grant County Airport near Silver City. As well, the **Roswell Airport,** at Roswell Industrial Air Center, is served commercially by **American Eagle Airlines** (📞 **800/433-7300;** www.aa.com), directly from Dallas, Texas, twice daily. And **New Mexico Airlines** (📞 **888/564-6119;** www.pacificwings.com/nma) provides daily flights between Albuquerque and **Cavern City Air Terminal** near Carlsbad.

Some large airlines offer transatlantic or transpacific passengers special discount tickets under the name **Visit USA,** which allows mostly one-way travel from one U.S. destination to another at very low prices. Unavailable in the U.S., these discount tickets must be purchased abroad in conjunction with your international fare. This system is the easiest, fastest, cheapest way to see the country.

BY CAR
The most convenient, and scenic, way to get around New Mexico is by private car. Auto and RV rentals are widely available for those who arrive without their own transportation, either at the Albuquerque airport or at locations around each city.

If you plan to drive your own vehicle to and around New Mexico, give it a thorough road check before starting out. The state offers plenty of wide-open desert and wilderness spaces, and it's not fun to be stranded in the heat or cold with a vehicle that doesn't run. Check with your auto-insurance company to make sure you're covered when out of state or when driving a rental car.

Gasoline is readily available at service stations throughout the state. Prices are cheapest in Albuquerque and 10% to 15% more expensive in more isolated communities. All prices are subject to the same fluctuations as elsewhere in the United States.

Indian reservations are considered sovereign nations, and they enforce their own laws. For instance, on the Navajo reservation (New Mexico's largest), it's pro-

> ### Drive Carefully
>
> US 491, formerly US 666, between Gallup and Shiprock, was at one time labeled America's "most dangerous highway" by *USA Today*. Though in recent years it has become safer, it still merits cautious driving. In addition, New Mexico has a high per-capita rate of traffic deaths. Drive carefully!

hibited to transport alcoholic beverages, to leave established roadways, or to travel without a seat belt. While there, abide by speed limits and follow traffic signs.

Drivers who need wheelchair-accessible transportation should call **Wheelchair Getaways of New Mexico,** 1015 Tramway Lane NE, Albuquerque (© **800/408-2626** or 505/247-2626; www.wheelchairgetaways.com); the company rents vans by the day, week, or month.

If you're visiting from abroad and plan to rent a car in the United States, keep in mind that foreign driver's licenses are usually recognized in the U.S., but you may want to consider obtaining an international driver's license.

BY TRAIN

New Mexico Rail Runner Express (© **866/795-7245;** www.nmrailrunner.com) runs daily from various points in Albuquerque to various ones in Santa Fe, with connecting buses to the Albuquerque International Sunport and to Taos.

Amtrak's northern New Mexico line, the *Southwest Chief,* runs west-east and east-west once daily, with stops in Gallup, Grants, Albuquerque, Lamy (for Santa Fe), Las Vegas, and Raton. The *Sunset Unlimited* connects Lordsburg and Deming with El Paso, Texas, three times weekly each direction. Greyhound provides through-ticketing for Amtrak passengers between Albuquerque and El Paso. Contact **Amtrak** (© **800/872-7245** or 505/842-9650; www.amtrak.com) for more information.

International visitors can buy a **USA Rail Pass,** good for 15, 30, or 45 days of unlimited travel on **Amtrak.** The pass is available online or through many overseas travel agents. See Amtrak's website for the cost of travel within the western, eastern, or northwestern United States. Reservations are generally required and should be made as early as possible. Regional rail passes are also available.

BY BUS

Greyhound (© **800/231-2222;** www.greyhound.com) is the sole nationwide bus line. It no longer runs between New Mexico cities; however I list shuttle buses that do in the "Getting There" section above. International visitors can obtain information about the **Greyhound North American Discovery Pass.** The pass, which offers unlimited travel and stopovers in the U.S. and Canada, can be obtained from foreign travel agents or through **www.discoverypass.com.**

MONEY & COSTS

THE VALUE OF U.S. DOLLARS VS. OTHER POPULAR CURRENCIES

US$	C$	£	€	A$	NZ$
1	1.03	.70	.80	1.14	1.43

Frommer's lists exact prices in the local currency. The currency conversions quoted above were correct at press time. However, rates fluctuate, so before departing consult a currency exchange website such as **www.xe.com** to check up-to-the-minute rates.

If you come from a major city such as New York or London, you may find New Mexico overall fairly inexpensive. In Taos and Albuquerque, you can still get good accommodations and meals without wincing. Santa Fe, however, may hurt a bit, especially if you hit the hottest spots in town, which cater to sophisticated tastes.

WHAT THINGS COST IN SANTA FE	US$
Double room in high season at La Posada de Santa Fe Resort and Spa	361.00
Double room in high season at Santa Fe Sage Inn	140.00
Dinner for two at Geronimo, without drinks, tax, or tip	115.00
Dinner for two at La Choza, without drinks, tax, or tip	25.00
Imported Mexican beer at the Dragon Room	4.00
Hour massage at Ten Thousand Waves Japanese Health Spa	99.00
Adult admission to the Museum of International Folk Art	9.00

The easiest and best way to get cash away from home is from an ATM (automated teller machine), sometimes referred to as a "cash machine," or "cashpoint." **Note:** They are widely available in the main towns, but can be scarce in small villages. The **Cirrus** (✆ **800/424-7787;** www.mastercard.com) and **PLUS** (www.visa.com) networks span the globe; look at the back of your bank card to see which network you're on, then call or check online for ATM locations at your destination. Be sure you know your personal identification number (PIN) and daily withdrawal limit before you depart. **Note:** Remember that many banks impose a fee every time you use a card at another bank's ATM, and that fee can be higher for international transactions (up to $5 or more) than for domestic ones (where they're rarely more than $2). In addition, the bank from which you withdraw cash may charge its own fee. For international withdrawal fees, ask your bank.

Beware of hidden credit-card fees while traveling. Check with your credit or debit card issuer to see what fees, if any, will be charged for overseas transactions. Recent reform legislation in the U.S., for example, has curbed some exploitative lending practices. But many banks have responded by increasing fees in other areas, including fees for customers who use credit and debit cards while out of the country—even if those charges were made in U.S. dollars. Fees can amount to 3% or more of the purchase price. Check with your bank before departing to avoid any surprise charges on your statement.

STAYING HEALTHY

One thing that sets New Mexico apart from most other states is its elevation. Santa Fe and Taos are about 7,000 feet above sea level; Albuquerque is more than 5,000 feet above sea level. The reduced oxygen and humidity can yield some unique problems, as noted below. The desert environment can also present some challenges.

Regional Health Concerns

HIGH DESERT CHALLENGES One of the most common ailments in New Mexico is acute mountain sickness. In its early stages, you might experience headaches, shortness of breath, loss of appetite and/or nausea, tingling in the fingers or toes, lethargy, and insomnia. The condition can usually be treated by taking aspirin as well as getting plenty of rest, avoiding large meals, and drinking lots of

WHAT THINGS COST IN LAS CRUCES	US$
Double room in high season at the Hotel Encanto	159.00
Double room in high season at La Quinta	97.00
Dinner for two at the Double Eagle, without drinks, tax, or tip	80.00
Dinner for two at Chope's Bar & Cafe, without drinks, tax, or tip	20.00
An imported Mexican beer at La Posta de Mesilla	3.75
Hiking in the Organ Mountains	Free
Adult admission to the New Mexico Farm and Ranch Heritage Museum	5.00

nonalcoholic fluids (especially water). If the condition persists or worsens, you must return to a lower altitude. Other dangers of higher elevations include hypothermia and sun exposure, and these should be taken seriously. To avoid dehydration, drink water as often as possible.

Limit your exposure to the sun, especially during the first few days of your trip and, thereafter, between 11am and 2pm. Liberally apply sunscreen with a high protection factor. Remember that children need more protection than adults do. It's important to monitor your children's health while in New Mexico. They are just as susceptible to mountain sickness, hypothermia, sunburn, and dehydration as you are.

DIETARY RED FLAGS   Though some places in New Mexico can have the feel of towns in our neighboring Mexico, the food and water here are safe. As well, a broad range of food is available, so that even vegetarians can usually find something to eat; small cafes often offer beans and rice. One of the few dietary concerns is the spicy chile, so be sure to ask how hot it is before ordering.

BUGS, BITES & OTHER WILDLIFE CONCERNS   If you're an outdoorsperson, be on the lookout for snakes—particularly rattlers. Avoid them. Don't even get close enough to take a picture (unless you have a very good zoom lens). As well, watch for black widows, which have a bulbous body and an hourglass image on their belly; a bite from this spider can make you very sick. The same goes for scorpions, which are crablike spiders with a curled stinging tail. If you get bitten by a snake or spider, or stung by a scorpion, seek professional medical help immediately.

Visitors to the state should also be careful of contracting the plague and hantavirus, a few cases of each reported annually in the state. Both diseases can be fatal, and both are transmitted through exposure to infected rodent droppings. Though it's unlikely that you'll be exposed to such things while traveling, be careful anytime you note the presence of mice or other rodents.

WEATHER CONCERNS   You'll also want to be wary of arroyos, or creek beds in the desert where flash floods can occur without warning. If water is flowing across a road, *do not* try to drive through it because chances are the water is deeper and flowing faster than you think. Just wait it out. Arroyo floods don't last long.

If You Get Sick

The most reliable hospitals are **Christus St. Vincent Regional Medical Center,** 455 St. Michaels Dr. in Santa Fe (© **505/983-5250;** www.stvn.org); **Presbyterian Hospital,** 1100 Central Ave. SE in Albuquerque (© **505/841-1819,** or 505/841-1111 for emergency service; www.phs.org); and **Memorial Medical Center,** 2450 S. Telshor Blvd. in Las Cruces (© **575/521-2286;** www.mmclc.org).

CRIME & SAFETY

Tourist areas as a rule are safe, but, despite recent reports of decreases in violent crime in Santa Fe, it would be wise to check with the tourist offices in Santa Fe, Taos, and Albuquerque if you are in doubt about which neighborhoods are safe. (See the "Orientation" sections in chapters 6, 7, and 8 for the names and addresses of the specific tourist bureaus.)

Remember that hotels are open to the public, and in a large hotel, security may not be able to screen everyone who enters. Always lock your room door; don't assume that once inside your hotel you are automatically safe and no longer need to be aware of your surroundings.

Be aware that New Mexico has a higher-than-average reported incidence of rape. Women should not walk alone in isolated places, particularly at night.

SPECIALIZED TRAVEL RESOURCES

In addition to the destination-specific resources listed below, please visit **Frommers.com** for other specialized travel resources.

LGBT Travelers

New Mexico is a pretty gay-friendly place in general, especially in Santa Fe, with its cosmopolitan attitude. Only in the smaller villages will locals look askance.

Common Bond (© **505/891-3647;** www.commonbond.org) provides information and outreach services for Albuquerque's gay and lesbian community as well as referrals for other New Mexico cities. A recorded message on this phone line gives lists of bars and clubs, businesses, and publications, as well as health and crisis information and a calendar of events. Volunteers are on hand (generally in the evenings) to answer questions. Another good resource is **www.gaynm.org**, a website that provides news, resources, and lists of events.

For more gay and lesbian travel resources, visit **www.frommers.com**.

Travelers with Disabilities

Throughout New Mexico, measures have been taken to provide access for travelers with disabilities. Several bed-and-breakfasts have made one or more of their rooms completely wheelchair accessible. The **Center for Development & Disability Info in NM** (© **800/552-8195** or 505/272-8549) accesses a database with lists of services ranging from restaurants and hotels to wheelchair rentals. The *Access New Mexico* guide lists accessible hotels, attractions, and restaurants throughout the state. For more information, contact the **Governor's Commission on Disabilities,** 491 Old Santa Fe Trail, Lamy Building Room 117, Santa Fe, NM 87503 (© **505/827-6465;** www.gcd.state.nm.us).

The chambers of commerce in Santa Fe, Taos, and Albuquerque will answer questions regarding accessibility in their areas. It is advisable to call hotels, restaurants, and attractions in advance to be sure that they are fully accessible.

Family Travel

If you have enough trouble getting your kids out of the house in the morning, dragging them thousands of miles away may seem like an insurmountable challenge. But family travel can be immensely rewarding, giving you new ways of seeing the world through smaller pairs of eyes.

Be aware that family travel in New Mexico may be a little different from what you're accustomed to. You'll find few huge Disney-like attractions here. Instead, the draws are culture and the outdoors. Rather than spending time in theme parks, you may go white-water rafting down the Rio Grande, skiing at one of the many family-friendly areas, climbing a wooden ladder up to a cliff dwelling, or trekking through the wilderness with a llama.

If your brood is not very adventurous, don't worry. Some of the hotels and resorts listed in this book have inviting pools to laze around or on-site activities planned especially for kids. Whatever your choice, New Mexico will definitely offer your children a new perspective on the United States by exposing them to ancient ruins, Southwestern cuisine, and Hispanic and Native American cultures that they may not experience elsewhere.

The Santa Fe quarterly *Tumbleweeds* (© **505/984-3171;** www.sftumbleweeds. com) offers useful articles on family-oriented subjects in the Santa Fe area, a quarterly day-by-day calendar of family events, and a seasonal directory of children's classes, camps, and programs. Free in locations all over Santa Fe or by mail for $15.

To locate accommodations, restaurants, and attractions that are particularly kid-friendly, look for the "Kids" icon throughout this guide.

Senior Travel

Recommended publications offering travel resources and discounts for seniors include the Albuquerque-based monthly tabloid *Prime Time* (© **505/880-0470;** www.primetimemonthly.com), which publishes a variety of articles aimed at those 50 years and older.

Members of **AARP,** 601 E St. NW, Washington, DC 20049 (© **888/687-2277;** www.aarp.org), get discounts on hotels, airfares, and car rentals. AARP offers members a wide range of benefits, including *AARP The Magazine* and a monthly newsletter. Anyone over 50 can join.

Recommended publications offering travel resources and discounts for seniors include the quarterly magazine *Travel 50 & Beyond* (www.travel50andbeyond. com) and the bestselling paperback *Unbelievably Good Deals and Great Adventures That You Absolutely Can't Get Unless You're Over 50* (McGraw-Hill), by Joann Rattner Heilman.

Frommers.com offers more information and resources on travel for seniors.

RESPONSIBLE TOURISM

New Mexico is the first state in the U.S. to launch an ecotourism initiative. It has three focuses: Cultural Heritage, Nature and Conservancy, and Outdoor Adventure. What this means to travelers is yet to be seen, but it is important that the state is looking to help expand this part of its travel offering.

Most of New Mexico's 19 Native American communities still preserve their traditional ways. In order for them to continue to do so, we all must respect their requests. When visiting these cultures, be sure to honor their posted boundaries and their rules. In chapter 6, I list some important tips on Pueblo Etiquette; see p. 110.

The main environmental challenge in New Mexico's high desert is **water.** For many years, the region has been experiencing a drought to the degree that citizens in Albuquerque and Santa Fe monitor their landscape irrigation. This has led businesses to become more accountable for their water use as well. Some recycle their water, using it to irrigate landscaping. Others plant xeric (natural) gardens. Many have extended their green practices to include recycling paper, glass, and other materials, and, when possible, eliminating paper filing systems in favor of electronic ones. New Mexico has also become conscious of its **CO_2 footprint** in relation to food. More and more residents and restaurants now buy produce from local farmers, rather than large suppliers who ship long distances. Such practices support small, often organic, agriculture, which helps protect the region's clean water from pesticides and rural land from development. Yet, there is still massive waste of water and other resources here. Golf courses, including those on Native American–owned lands, have become more and more common, with only a few that are desert oriented.

Public transportation is relatively scarce, though the recent introduction of the New Mexico Rail Runner Express train has helped reduce some of the automobile travel between Albuquerque and Santa Fe and outlying communities. Visitors to the region will likely still want to have a car handy because many of the sights and activities are in outlying areas. But you can help in other ways. Look for hotels that are taking steps toward the green measures mentioned above and eat in restaurants that use local, seasonal ingredients when possible. Play golf at the few desert courses, even if they may be more challenging than standard ones.

A few ecotourism lodgings in the region have initiated green measures. These include in Santa Fe **Bishop's Lodge Ranch Resort & Spa** (© 505/983-6377; www.bishopslodge.com) and **La Posada Resort & Spa** (© 800/727-5276; www.rockresorts.com); in Taos, **El Monte Sagrado** (© 800/828-8267; www.elmontesagrado.com) and the **Old Taos Guesthouse** (© 800/758-5448; www.oldtaos.com); and in Albuquerque, the new **Andaluz** (© 505/242-9090; www.hotelandaluz.com).

In the "Where to Dine" sections in this book, I mention a number of restaurants that use local, seasonal ingredients, which will help you support the region's environmental efforts.

If you're a duffer and want to play on an ecofriendly course, check out **Marty Sanchez Links de Santa Fe** (© 505/955-4400; www.linksdesantafe.com), **Paa-Ko Ridge** (© 866/361-7443; www.resortlifestylecommunities.com/paakoridge) east of Albuquerque, and the **Twin Warriors Golf Club** at the Hyatt Regency Tamaya Resort & Spa (© 505/867-1234; www.tamaya.hyatt.com).

GENERAL RESOURCES FOR responsible travel

In addition to the resources for New Mexico listed above, the following websites provide valuable wide-ranging information on sustainable travel.

○ **Responsible Travel** (www.responsibletravel.com) is a great source of sustainable travel ideas; the site is run by a spokesperson for ethical tourism in the travel industry. **Sustainable Travel International** (www.sustainabletravelinternational.org) promotes ethical tourism practices, and manages an extensive directory of sustainable properties and tour operators around the world.

○ **Carbonfund** (www.carbonfund.org), **TerraPass** (www.terrapass.org), and **Cool Climate** (http://coolclimate.berkeley.edu) provide info on "carbon offsetting," or offsetting the greenhouse gas emitted during flights.

○ **Greenhotels** (www.greenhotels.com) recommends green-rated member hotels around the world that fulfill the company's stringent environmental requirements. **Environmentally Friendly Hotels** (www.environmentallyfriendlyhotels.com) offers more green accommodation ratings.

○ **Volunteer International** (www.volunteerinternational.org) has a list of questions to help you determine the intentions and the nature of a volunteer program. For general info on volunteer travel, visit **www.volunteerabroad.org** and **www.idealist.org**.

For more all-inclusive travel in Santa Fe, **Santa Fe Mountain Adventures** (© **800/965-4010** or 505/988-4000; www.santafemountainadventures.com) leads programs that combine outdoor adventures with arts and cultural experiences, and spa treatments. This ecoconscious business is a collaborative effort in conjunction with *Outside* magazine.

SPECIAL-INTEREST & ESCORTED TRIPS

Academic & Cultural Trips

Those who like a scholarly bent to their vacations can hook up with **Southwest Seminars** (© 505/466-2775; www.southwestseminars.org) and its "Travels with a Scholar" program. This organization arranges tours throughout the Southwest, led by museum directors, historians, geologists, archaeologists, anthropologists, and authors. Southwest Seminars is able to arrange visits to sites that are not open to the general public such as archaeological sites, petroglyph panels, volcanic calderas, contemporary Indian pueblos, and native artists' homes and studios. **Note:** Each Monday at 6pm, talks are given by regional scholars that are well worth checking out.

Photography & Art Trips

Some of the world's most outstanding photographers convene in Santa Fe at various times during the year for the **Santa Fe Workshops,** P.O. Box 9916, Santa Fe, NM

87504, at a delightful campus in the hills on the east side of town (© **505/983-1400;** www.santafeworkshops.com). Most courses are full time, lasting a week. Food and lodging packages are available.

If you'd like to pursue an artistic adventure, check out the weeklong classes in such media as painting, Native American pottery making, and weaving offered by **Taos Art School** (© **505/758-0350;** www.taosartschool.org). This organization is especially known for its weaving and horseback-riding creative "odyssey." Open since 1989, the school is a virtual campus in which classes go where they need to be. For instance, a painting class on Georgia O'Keeffe is held in Abiquiu and a Pueblo pottery class at Taos Pueblo. The fees vary from class to class and include lodging and meals.

Great Expeditions (© **800/663-3364;** www.greatexpeditions.com) offers an "Opera in Santa Fe" trip, which focuses on more than the opera, but also partakes of this world-class entertainment.

Adventure & Wellness Trips

If you're looking for an active adventure and some relaxation too there are a few options. One excellent operator is **Santa Fe Mountain Adventures** (© **800/965-4010** or 505/988-4000; www.santafemountainadventures.com), which combines outdoor adventures such as hiking and river running with cultural activities such as visits to pueblos or museums, with more relaxing ones such as spa treatments and meditation practices. A collaborative effort in conjunction with *Outside* magazine, the business is ecoconscious.

Bicycle Adventures, P.O. Box 11219, Olympia, WA 98508 (© **800/443-6060** or 425/250-5540; www.bicycleadventures.com), offers tours to New Mexico. Riders get to experience some of the region's most lovely routes such as the High Road to Taos and the Enchanted Circle. Participants visit major sights such as Santa Fe's Canyon Road and Taos Pueblo and can even opt for a river trip. In business for more than 2 decades, this company knows how to put together a good tour.

Food & Wine Trips

Jane Butel Cooking School, 2655 Pan American NE, Suite F (© **800/473-8226** or 505/243-2622; www.janebutelcooking.com), offers weeklong and weekend packages with a hotel stay and full-participation classes. The weekend classes are held in noted chef and television personality Jane Butel's home kitchen in Corrales, a village along the Rio Grande on the edge of Albuquerque. The weeklong classes are in Santa Fe.

Volunteer & Working Trips

Sierra Club Outings (© **415/977-5522;** www.sierraclub.org/outings/national/service.asp) organizes working vacations all over the world, with some work to be done in New Mexico. **Global Citizens Network** offers volunteer vacations to worldwide destinations as well, including, at times, New Mexico. To check its schedule, contact © **800/644-9292;** www.globalcitizens.org.

Escorted General Interest Tours

Escorted tours are structured group tours, with a group leader. The price usually includes everything from airfare to hotels, meals, tours, admission costs, and local transportation.

Not many escorted tours are offered in New Mexico. Most visitors have such disparate interests it's difficult to create packages to please everyone. Still, a few tour companies can help you arrange a variety of day trips during your visit and can also secure lodging. **Tauck World Discovery,** 10 Norden Place, Norwalk, CT 06855 (✆ **800/788-7885;** www.tauck.com), offers weeklong cultural trips to New Mexico. **Destination Southwest, Inc.,** 20 First Plaza Galeria, Suite 212, Albuquerque, NM 87102 (✆ **800/999-3109** or 505/766-9068; www.destinationsouthwest.com), offers an escorted tour to the Albuquerque International Balloon Fiesta. **Rojotours & Services,** P.O. Box 15744, Santa Fe, NM 87506-5744 (✆ **505/474-8333;** www.rojotours.com), can help with a variety of day trips during your visit.

For more information on escorted tours, including questions to ask before booking your trip, visit **www.frommers.com**.

STAYING CONNECTED

Mobile Phones

Since this region is a GSM network, your cellphone will likely work in the major cities. Be aware, though, that in rural areas, reception will be spotty.

Internet & E-mail

Wi-Fi and traditional Internet access are widely available in the cities in the region. Most hotels now offer free Wi-Fi, and all cities in the region have cafes with wireless access. In order to find one near you, log onto **www.jiwire.com**; its Hotspot Finder holds the world's largest directory of public wireless hotspots. To find wireless cafes, check out **www.cybercafe.com**.

Newspapers & Magazines

National newspapers include the *New York Times, USA Today,* and the *Wall Street Journal.* National news weeklies include *Newsweek, Time,* and *U.S. News & World Report.* In large cities, most newsstands offer a small selection of the most popular foreign periodicals and newspapers, such as *The Economist* and *Le Monde.*

Telephones

Many convenience groceries and packaging services sell **prepaid calling cards** in denominations up to $50. Many public pay phones at airports now accept American Express, MasterCard, and Visa. **Local calls** made from most pay phones cost either 25¢ or 35¢. Most long-distance and international calls can be dialed directly from any phone. **To make calls within the United States and to Canada,** dial 1 followed by the area code and the seven-digit number. **For other international calls,** dial 011 followed by the country code, city code, and the number you are calling.

Calls to area codes **800, 888, 877,** and **866** are toll-free. However, calls to area codes **700** and **900** (chat lines, bulletin boards, "dating" services, and so on) can be expensive—charges of 95¢ to $3 or more per minute. Some numbers have minimum charges that can run $15 or more.

For **reversed-charge or collect calls,** and for person-to-person calls, dial the number 0 then the area code and number; an operator will come on the line, and you should specify whether you are calling collect, person-to-person, or both. If your operator-assisted call is international, ask for the overseas operator.

For **directory assistance** ("Information"), dial 411 for local and national numbers in the U.S. and Canada. For dedicated long-distance information, dial 1, then the appropriate area code plus 555-1212.

TIPS ON ACCOMMODATIONS

No two travelers are alike; fortunately, New Mexico has a broad-enough range of accommodations to satisfy even the most eccentric adventurer. If you long to be pampered, you'll find a few swanky resorts within the region, with a variety of luxury options such as pool and exercise facilities, golf, tennis, horseback riding, and spa treatments. Of course, none of it comes cheap.

If you're looking to really savor the flavor of New Mexico, you may want to opt for one of its historic hotels. This may include a hacienda-style inn—an adobe one- or two-story structure often built around a courtyard. You'll also find some Victorian inns that have a frontier flavor. Within this variety of architecture, the amenities vary, from places with antique but workable plumbing and no television, to those with hot tubs and Wi-Fi in rooms.

In recent years, bed-and-breakfast inns (B&Bs) have proliferated in New Mexico. Though you can find traditional Victorian-style B&Bs here (and some lovely ones at that), complete with lacy bedding and elaborately carved accents, you can also choose from old hacienda-style homes or tiered adobe structures. All are comfortable and a few luxurious, with prices in the moderate to expensive range.

We all have those nights when only predictability will do. That's when a chain hotel comes in handy. You'll find all the major ones in New Mexico, though not quite everywhere. The small villages still shun such cookie-cutter establishments, but most everywhere else you can find them along the highways or in the town centers.

For tips on surfing for hotel deals online, visit **www.frommers.com**.

SUGGESTED NEW MEXICO ITINERARIES

4

You may already have an idea of how you want to spend your time in New Mexico—power shopping, perhaps, or time-traveling through ancient cultures. But if you're not sure what to do, here are four suggested itineraries, outlined in 1-week and 2-week segments. For each one, I assume that you're starting in Albuquerque, either by driving in your own car or flying into the Albuquerque International Sunport, the air transportation hub of the state, and then renting a car.

New Mexico has a mix of museums and indoor activities, but the real attractions here are the living culture and spectacular scenery en route. With this in mind, I've combined scenic drives with city stays in these tours. In order to get a true sense of this place, take your time—linger at a cafe or wander a plaza for an hour. You might be surprised at how easily you get enveloped into the experience of being a New Mexican.

The Regions in Brief

North-Central New Mexico The most highly populated and well-traveled area of the state, north-central New Mexico roughly includes the cities of Albuquerque, Santa Fe, and Taos. It's also the economic center of New Mexico. In this portion of the state, lush mountains seem to rise directly out of the parched plateaus that have made New Mexico's landscape famous. Temperatures are generally lower in this area than they are in the rest of the state, and skiing is one of the most popular winter activities in both Santa Fe and Taos.

Northwestern New Mexico Head to this region if you're interested in Native American culture. Sandstone bluffs here mark the homes of Pueblo, Navajo, and Apache Indians, in an area once inhabited by the ancestral Puebloans (also known as Anasazi) of the past. My favorite places to visit in this section of the state are Acoma Pueblo, Chaco Culture National Historical Park, and Aztec Ruins National Monument. A major portion of the northwestern region is part of a Navajo reservation, the largest in the country. This is also the gateway to the famous Four Corners region. The town of Grants, near Acoma, offers a glimpse into uranium mining. Railroad fanatics, hikers, hunters, and fishers should make a trip to Chama, home of the Cumbres & Toltec Railroad and a popular starting point for outdoor adventures.

Northeastern New Mexico Covering the area north of I-40 and east of the Sangre de Cristo Mountains, northeastern New Mexico is prairie land once inhabited or visited by some of the West's most legendary gunslingers. Towns to visit for a bit of Wild West history are Cimarron and Las Vegas. The northeastern portion of the state also includes attractions such as Fort Union National Monument, a portion of the Santa Fe Trail, Kiowa and Rita Blanca National Grasslands, and Capulin Volcano National Monument. Due to its abundance of state parks and wildlife reserves, as well as the fact that it borders the ski resort towns of Angel Fire, Taos, Red River, and Santa Fe, this region is an excellent area for sports enthusiasts.

Southwestern New Mexico This region, like northeastern New Mexico, is another great place to visit if you're interested in the history of the Wild West and Native American culture, as it was once home to Billy the Kid and Geronimo. The Rio Grande, lifeline to this part of the state, acts as a border between the southwestern and southeastern portions of the state.

Attractions west of the river include Gila National Forest, once home to the Mogollon Indians, whose past is preserved in the Gila Cliff Dwellings National Monument. The Chiricahua Apaches, a tribe once led by Geronimo, also lived in this area. The town of Silver City, which survives as an economic center of this area, was once a booming mining town. Surrounding ghost towns weren't as lucky. Las Cruces, at the foot of the Organ Mountains, is the state's second largest city, and Truth or Consequences, named for a television and radio game show, offers abundant hot springs.

Southeastern New Mexico Bounded on the west by the Rio Grande, to the north by I-40, and to the east by Texas, southeastern New Mexico is home to two of the most interesting natural wonders in this part of the country: Carlsbad Caverns and White Sands National Monument. The underground caverns, filled with stalactites and stalagmites, are infinitely interesting and hauntingly beautiful. Snow-white dunes at White Sands National Monument, which rise out of the desert landscape, are an extraordinary sight as you make the drive to Alamogordo. White Sands is a great place to camp out and watch the sunrise. This portion of the state is yet another former home of Billy the Kid. It's also where he died. Southeastern New Mexico has something of a controversial past as well: The world's first atomic bomb was detonated here.

CULTURE CRUISING: NORTHERN NEW MEXICO IN A WEEK

New Mexico is a big state. Covering it all in 1 week would only wear a traveler out. That's why I've relegated this tour to the northern part, which has the highest concentration of sights. You can gaze at ancient petroglyphs etched on stone at the Petroglyph National Monument, shop one of the world's top art markets on Canyon Road in Santa Fe, marvel at the play of light on the Rio Grande Gorge in Taos—and even take a white-water rafting trip if you choose. You can do this trip during any season, though the warmer months offer the mildest climate and the most options.

Days 1–2: Albuquerque

If you have some energy left after traveling, head to **Old Town** (p. 95), where you can wander through the **plaza** and peruse some shops. Be sure to tuck into

Suggested New Mexico Itineraries

Northern New Mexico in a Week

1-2 Albuquerque
3 The Turquoise Trail & Santa Fe
4 Santa Fe Arts
5 Bandelier National Moument & North to Taos
6 Taos Pueblo
7 The High Road

New Mexico in 2 Weeks

WEEK 1

1-4 Albuquerque & Santa Fe
5 The High Road
6 Taos
7 Cumbres & Toltec Scenic Railroad

WEEK 2

8 Chaco Culture National Historic Park
9 Acoma Pueblo
10 Birds & Lava
11 Ruidoso
12 White Sands National Monument
13 Carlsbad Caverns National Park
14 Alien Sightings

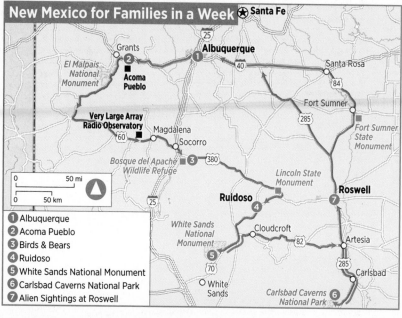

New Mexico for Families in a Week

★ Santa Fe

1. Albuquerque
2. Acoma Pueblo
3. Birds & Bears
4. Ruidoso
5. White Sands National Monument
6. Carlsbad Caverns National Park
7. Alien Sightings at Roswell

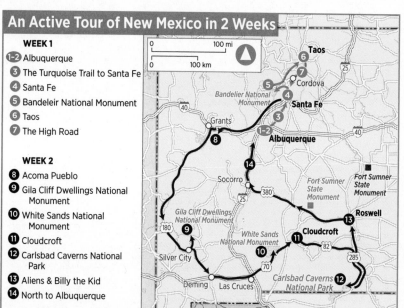

An Active Tour of New Mexico in 2 Weeks

WEEK 1

1-2 Albuquerque
3. The Turquoise Trail to Santa Fe
4. Santa Fe
5. Bandeleir National Monument
6. Taos
7. The High Road

WEEK 2

8. Acoma Pueblo
9. Gila Cliff Dwellings National Monument
10. White Sands National Monument
11. Cloudcroft
12. Carlsbad Caverns National Park
13. Aliens & Billy the Kid
14. North to Albuquerque

some of the back alleyways and little nooks—you'll uncover some of the city's most inventive shops in these areas. Next, head over to the **Albuquerque Museum of Art and History** (p. 92) to get a good sense of this land's story. Finish the day with one of New Mexico's premier treats—an enchilada at **Mary & Tito's** (p. 89).

Start out your second day in Albuquerque at the **Indian Pueblo Cultural Center** (p. 94), where you'll get a sense of the cultures you'll encounter up north, and then head to the **Albuquerque Biological Park** (p. 96), both in the vicinity of **Old Town Plaza.** From here, go west of town to visit the **Petroglyph National Monument** (p. 96). If it's summer, you may want to go during the cooler early morning. In the late afternoon, find your way to Central Avenue, just south of Old Town, and drive east on **Route 66.** This takes you right through downtown, to the Nob Hill district and the Sandia Mountains foothills, respectively. Finish your day with a ride up the **Sandia Peak Tramway** (p. 95). Ideally, you should ride up during daylight and back down at night for a view of the city lights. You may even want to dine at the top.

Day 3: The Turquoise Trail ★★ & Santa Fe

Today, strike out for the ghost towns and other sights along the **Turquoise Trail** (p. 118) to Santa Fe, stopping to peruse some of the galleries in **Madrid** (p. 120). This will put you in Santa Fe in time to do some sightseeing. Head straight to the **plaza** (p. 157), the **New Mexico History Museum & the Palace of the Governors** (p. 156), and **St. Francis Cathedral** (p. 156). If you shop from the Native Americans selling under the portal, be sure to ask about the art you buy; the symbols on it may have interesting significance. Next, make your way over to the **Georgia O'Keeffe Museum** (p. 154). Finish your day with an enchilada at the **Shed** (p. 152). In the evening, depending on the season, you may want to check out Santa Fe's excellent arts scene; try the **Santa Fe Opera** (p. 178) or the **Santa Fe Chamber Music Festival** (p. 178).

Day 4: Santa Fe Arts

In the morning, head up to Museum Hill, where you can take your pick from four unique museums: the **Museum of International Folk Art** (p. 158), the **Museum of Indian Arts & Culture** (p. 158), the **Wheelwright Museum of the American Indian** (p. 160), and the **Museum of Spanish Colonial Art** (p. 159). You can have lunch at the **Museum Hill Café** (p. 158). On your way back to the plaza, take a stroll and do some shopping on **Canyon Road** (p. 170). At sunset during the warmer months, you can enjoy a cocktail at the bell tower of the historic **La Fonda Hotel** (p. 132). Eat dinner at **Santacafé** (p. 147)—or if you lingered over your shopping, stop in at **Geronimo** (p. 146) or the **Compound** (p. 144) on Canyon Road.

Day 5: Bandelier National Monument ★★★ & North to Taos

Head out of town today to **Bandelier National Monument** (p. 191). Explore the ruins and be sure to climb the ladders to see the kiva set high above the canyon floor. Then continue north to Taos. On your way into the city, stop at the **San Francisco de Asis church** (p. 220). And if you like music, head out to the **Sagebrush Inn** (p. 239) for some country-and-western or rock dancing.

Day 6: Taos Pueblo ★★★

Spend your morning exploring **Taos Pueblo** (p. 223), the **Millicent Rogers Museum** (p. 220), and the **Rio Grande Gorge Bridge** (p. 226). You can then ditch your car for the afternoon and step out on foot. Do some shopping around **Taos Plaza.** At cocktail hour, head to the **Adobe Bar** (p. 239) at the Historic Taos Inn or the **Anaconda Bar** (p. 239) at the new El Monte Sagrado.

Day 7: The High Road ★★

On your last day, enjoy a leisurely morning and then head south on the **High Road to Taos** (p. 192). Be sure to spend some time at the **Santuario de Chimayo** (p. 193), where you can rub healing dust between your fingers. You may want to spend the night at a bed-and-breakfast in **Chimayo** (p. 192) or have lunch at **Rancho de Chimayo** (p. 193) along the way. Depending on your flight time the next morning, stay the night in Santa Fe or Albuquerque.

NEW MEXICO IN 2 WEEKS

If you have 2 weeks to spend exploring the region, consider yourself fortunate. You'll not only be able to hit the highlights in the north, but you'll also be able to spend time getting to know such places as Chaco National Cultural Park, White Sands National Monument, and Carlsbad Caverns National Park. This trip is fun any time of year. In winter, the north will be cold and the south will be cool. In the warmer months, the north will be warm and the south very hot.

Days 1–4: Albuquerque & Santa Fe

For days 1 through 4, follow those days as outlined in the previous itinerary, "Culture Cruising: Northern New Mexico in a Week."

Day 5: The High Road ★★

Today, travel the **High Road to Taos** (p. 192), stopping at the little galleries and art studios along the way. Be sure to rub healing dust between your fingers at **Santuario de Chimayo** (p. 193). On the way into Taos, visit the **San Francisco de Asis Church** (p. 220). If you like nightlife, head out to the **Sagebrush Inn** (p. 239) to dance to country-and-western or rock music or to the **Anaconda Bar** (p. 239) to hear some jazz or other music.

Day 6: Taos

Spend the morning at **Taos Pueblo** (p. 223). Next head over to the **Millicent Rogers Museum** (p. 220) and the **Rio Grande Gorge Bridge** (p. 226). During the afternoon, do some shopping around the **Taos Plaza** (p. 235) and then visit the **Taos Art Museum** (p. 222). At cocktail hour, head to the **Adobe Bar** (p. 239) at the Historic Taos Inn.

Day 7: Cumbres & Toltec Scenic Railroad ★★

This morning, get up early and head west on a scenic drive to Chama, where you can spend the day riding the **Cumbres & Toltec Scenic Railroad** (p. 279). Be sure to check departure times for the train and make reservations in advance. Spend the night in Chama.

Day 8: Chaco Culture National Historic Park ★★★

From Chama, drive across the Jicarilla Apache Indian Reservation on NM 537 to **Chaco Culture National Historical Park** (p. 267). Though it's a long and dusty drive, Chaco's combination of stunning setting and expansive ruins makes the day worthwhile. In fact, Chaco is the Holy Grail for Southwest history buffs. If you have camping equipment, spend the night at Chaco. If not, stay the night in Grants.

Day 9: Acoma Pueblo ★★★

Head east on I-40 to **Acoma Pueblo** (p. 249). Upon arrival, spend some time in the pueblo's 40,000-square-foot museum to get a sense of the culture before taking the bus to the top of Sky City. Next, head south on NM 117, one of the state's prettiest drives, to **El Malpais** (p. 253), where you can stretch your legs on a short or long hike. Continue south through Quemado, then turn east, and drive to Magdalena, where you can stop for a meal at **Magdalena Café & Steakhouse** (p. 310). This is a long drive, so you'll need a refresher. Spend the night in **Socorro** (p. 309), or continue south to San Antonio, where you can stay at the **Casa Blanca** B&B (p. 275).

Day 10: Birds & Lava

If it's wintertime, wake up before dawn today and head out to **Bosque del Apache National Wildlife Refuge** (p. 313), where you can watch thousands of cranes and snow geese take flight. (Even if it's not winter—when thousands of cranes and geese fill the sky—you can still tour the refuge to see birds and wildlife.) From the refuge, head east on US 380 to the **Valley of Fires Recreation Area** (p. 371), an amazing lava field, where you can stretch your legs before lunch. Your next stop is Carrizozo to feast on a green-chile cheeseburger at the **Outpost** (p. 370). Next, you'll want to make your way east along the **Lincoln Loop** (p. 369) to Lincoln, where you can visit the **Lincoln Historic District** (p. 363) and walk in the footsteps of Billy the Kid. Spend the night in Lincoln or Ruidoso.

Day 11: Ruidoso

If you like to hike, stop at the Lincoln National Forest Ranger Station for directions to the many trails in the area. Otherwise, you may want to shop a little. If it's winter, you can ski at **Ski Apache** (p. 352). Or, if you have an interest in horses, head over to the **Hubbard Museum of the American West** (p. 361) and then take in some horse racing at **Ruidoso Downs** (p. 361). Spend the night in Ruidoso, and if you feel like splurging, stay at the **Inn of the Mountain Gods** (p. 365). Even if you don't stay there, you may want to drive to the inn for an evening stroll around the lake and a little throw of the dice in its casino.

Day 12: White Sands National Monument ★★★

This day takes you southwest out of Ruidoso through the **Mescalero Apache Indian Reservation** on US 70 to **Alamogordo.** Here, you'll visit the **New Mexico Museum of Space History** (p. 353) and one of the stars of this trip: **White Sands National Monument** (p. 358). Spend the night in Alamogordo.

Day 13: Carlsbad Caverns National Park ★★★

Strike out early for **Cloudcroft** (p. 354), a darling mountain town where you can stretch your legs and have breakfast at **The Lodge at Cloudcroft** (p. 357). Spend the rest of the morning driving to **Carlsbad** (p. 377) and have lunch in the town itself. If you like zoos, you may want to visit the **Living Desert Zoo & Gardens State Park** (p. 378), but be sure to save energy for your afternoon. Head south to the most spectacular sight in New Mexico, **Carlsbad Caverns National Park** (p. 382), where you want to walk down into the cave, rather than ride the elevator (trust me). End your day by strolling along the water at the **river walk** (p. 377), or if it's summertime, by relaxing at your hotel pool.

Day 14: Alien Sightings

Spend your last day on a long cruise north to Albuquerque. Take US 285 to Roswell, where you can feed your *X-Files* fantasies at the **International UFO Museum and Research Center** (p. 372). History buffs may want to detour to Fort Sumner to see **Billy the Kid's grave** (p. 376), but more importantly to see the tragedy presented at **Fort Sumner State Monument** (p. 375). If you choose this option, stop for a bite afterward at **Joe's** (p. 304) in Santa Rosa. In Albuquerque, you can finish the trip with a delicious meal at **Jennifer James 101** (p. 90).

NEW MEXICO FOR FAMILIES IN A WEEK

Although it's wonderful, northern New Mexico is not the most suitable vacationland for kids—unless they have a precocious interest in history and architecture. Some hearts are better suited to Wild West action and natural wonders than gourmet food and history, and those kinds of attractions mainly reside in the state's southern half. If you prefer a more active vacation, this 1-week trip is for you, whatever your age. The climate in this region is fairly mild, but summers in the south can be quite hot. *Tip:* Parents who are first-time visitors to New Mexico may want to trade the day 1 and day 2 schedules for a trip north to **Santa Fe** (see chapter 7) to take in the cultural sights there. You can then shoot down I-25 and resume the itinerary in Socorro on the evening of day 2.

Day 1: Albuquerque

On your first day, head to **Old Town** (p. 95), where you can wander the **plaza**, peruse some shops, and head over to the **Explora** (p. 97). Next, visit the **Albuquerque Biological Park** (p. 96). Be sure to check out the Biological Park's butterfly exhibit. Or, you may want to visit the **Rio Grande Zoo** (p. 98). Don't miss the polar bears there. Finish the day with one of New Mexico's premier treats—an enchilada at **Mary & Tito's** (p. 89). If you have any energy left, ride the **Sandia Peak Tramway** (p. 95) in time to watch the sunset.

Day 2: Acoma Pueblo ★★★

You'll cover a lot of ground this day, so head out early. Drive west about 70 miles to **Acoma Pueblo** (p. 249), taking time to see the museum there before you ride the bus up to Sky City. Next, head south on NM 117 to **El Malpais** (p. 253), where you can stretch your legs on a short hike. Continue south through Quemado, then turn east, and drive to Magdalena, where you can stop for a snack or meal at **Magdalena Café & Steak House** (p. 310). Spend the night in Socorro or continue south to San Antonio, where you can stay at **Casa Blanca** B&B (p. 275).

Day 3: Birds & Bears

On day 3, if it's wintertime, wake before dawn and head out to **Bosque del Apache National Wildlife Refuge** (p. 313). Even though it's early for kids, they're usually amazed to see thousands of cranes and snow geese take flight, and hear the air fill with their calls. (Even if it's not winter—when thousands of cranes and geese fill the sky—you can still tour the refuge to see birds and wildlife, and take a hike to a high point to view the scene from above.) From the refuge, head east on US 380 to the **Valley of Fires Recreation Area** (p. 371), an amazing lava field. Your next stop is Carrizozo to feast on a green-chile cheeseburger at the **Outpost** (p. 370). Continue east to **Capitan** and **Smokey Bear Historical State Park** (p. 370). Farther east along the Lincoln Loop, stop at the **Lincoln Historic District** (p. 363). Spend the night in Lincoln or Ruidoso.

Day 4: Ruidoso

This morning, if you like to hike, head to the Lincoln National Forest Ranger Station for directions to the many trails in the area. Otherwise, you may want to shop a little. If it's winter, you can ski at **Ski Apache** (p. 352). Or, if your kids have any interest in horses, head over to the **Hubbard Museum of the American West** (p. 361). In the evening, check out the **Flying J Ranch** (p. 362) for a chuck-wagon dinner and an Old West show. Spend the night in Ruidoso.

Day 5: White Sands National Monument ★★★

This day takes you southwest out of Ruidoso through the **Mescalero Apache Indian Reservation** on US 70 to **Alamogordo.** Here, you'll visit the **New Mexico Museum of Space History** (p. 353) and one of the stars of this trip: **White Sands National Monument** (p. 358). Spend the night in Alamogordo.

Day 6: Carlsbad Caverns National Park ★★★

Strike out early for **Cloudcroft** (p. 354), a darling mountain town where you can stretch your legs and have breakfast at **The Lodge at Cloudcroft** (p. 357). Spend the rest of the morning driving to **Carlsbad** (p. 377) and have lunch in the town itself. If you like zoos, you may want to visit the **Living Desert Zoo & Gardens State Park** (p. 378), but be sure to save energy for your afternoon. Head south to the most spectacular sight in New Mexico, **Carlsbad Caverns National Park** (p. 382), where you want to walk down into the cave, rather than ride the elevator (trust me). End your day by strolling along the water at the **river walk** (p. 377), or if it's summertime, by relaxing at your hotel pool.

Day 7: Alien Sightings at Roswell

Spend your last day on a long cruise north to Albuquerque. Take US 285 to Roswell, where your kids can stock up on little-green-men stickers and see the

International UFO Museum and Research Center (p. 372). History buffs may want to detour to Fort Sumner to see **Billy the Kid's grave** (p. 376) and the tragedy presented at **Fort Sumner State Monument** (p. 375). If you take this option, stop for a bite afterward at **Joe's** (p. 304) in Santa Rosa.

AN ACTIVE TOUR OF NEW MEXICO IN 2 WEEKS

Anyone who skis, hikes, mountain bikes, or rafts knows that the Southwest is unsurpassed in its offerings for outdoor enthusiasts. New Mexico is no exception. This trip is for the road-warrior type of sportsperson. It takes in New Mexico's full sphere of terrain, from the Rocky Mountains in the north to the desert of White Sands in the South and the caves at Carlsbad. Be aware that the region is known for its mercurial weather conditions—always be prepared for extremes. Also, northern New Mexico is over 6,000 feet in elevation, so it may take you time to catch your breath. Be patient on those long upward hills. The sports you do will, of course, depend a lot on the season. For the full benefit of this trip, take it in late March or early April. With a little advance preparation, you might be able to ski and river raft on the same trip!

Days 1–2: Albuquerque

When you arrive in Albuquerque, you may want to get acclimated to the city by strolling through **Old Town** (p. 95). Next, visit the **Albuquerque Biological Park** (p. 96) to get a sense of the nature in the area and the **Pueblo Cultural Center** (p. 94) to get acquainted with the culture you'll encounter as you head north.

On day 2, for a truly unique experience, you may want to schedule a **balloon ride** (p. 99). *Tip:* Make reservations for this activity in advance, especially because you fly first thing in the morning. If you're a bike rider or hiker, head to **Petroglyph National Monument** (p. 96) for a ride or hike to see thousands of symbols etched on stone. In the evening, ride the **Sandia Peak Tramway** (p. 95) and do a little hiking along the crest. If you'd like, you can have dinner at the top and view the city lights as you come down.

Day 3: The Turquoise Trail ★★ to Santa Fe

On day 3, head for the ghost towns and other sights along the **Turquoise Trail** (p. 118) to Santa Fe. If you like to ride horses, schedule a ride in Cerrillos with **Broken Saddle Riding Company** (p. 120). This will put you in Santa Fe in time to do some late-afternoon sightseeing. Head straight to the **plaza** (p. 157), the **New Mexico History Museum & the Palace of the Governors** (p. 156), and **St. Francis Cathedral** (p. 156). Have an enchilada at **The Shed** (p. 152).

Day 4: Santa Fe

Either use your own bike or rent a cruiser in town to ride around the plaza and up **Canyon Road** (p. 124). Stop at the top of Canyon at the **Randall Davey Audubon Center** (p. 161) to do some bird-watching. Or, you may want to head to the mountains to do some hiking on the **Aspen Vista Trail** (p. 168) or, if it's winter, some skiing at **Ski Santa Fe** (p. 169). Finish your day at one of the fun restaurants or cafes on **Canyon Road** (p. 170). In the evening, depending on the season, you may want to take in some of Santa Fe's excellent arts, such as the **Santa Fe Opera** (p. 178) or the **Santa Fe Chamber Music Festival** (p. 178).

Day 5: Bandelier National Monument ★★★

Head out from Santa Fe to **Bandelier National Monument** (p. 191) and hike among ancient ruins. Follow the Frijoles Trail as far up as you'd like, making sure you stop to climb the ladders to the kiva perched high on the canyon wall. Trail runners like to jog the Frijoles Trail, with its easy descent back to the start. Next, follow the Rio Grande River north and you'll come to Taos. On the way into town, stop at the **San Francisco de Asis church** (p. 220). Spend the evening strolling around the Taos **plaza** to get a feel of the city.

Day 6: Taos

Sports lovers have many options in this town. If you like to ride horses, take a **ride on Taos Pueblo** (p. 232) land. Or, you may want to take a **llama trek** (p. 233) into the Rio Grande Gorge, or hike up to the top of **Wheeler Peak** (p. 232), New Mexico's highest, a full-day trek. If it's ski season, you'll definitely want to spend the day at **Taos Ski Valley** (p. 227). If it's spring and the rivers are running, take either the full-day, heart-throbbing romp through the **Taos Box** (p. 233), or a half-day trip at **Pilar** (p. 233).

Day 7: The High Road ★★★

Take a leisurely drive south toward Santa Fe. You'll want to take the **High Road** (p. 192) through the art villages of Cordova and Chimayo. Stop at the **Santuario de Chimayo** (p. 193) and have lunch on the patio at **Rancho de Chimayo** (p. 193). Spend the night in Albuquerque.

Day 8: Acoma Pueblo ★★★

Head east on Interstate 40 to **Acoma Pueblo** (p. 249) and spend some time in its 40,000-square-foot museum to get a sense of the area's culture before taking the bus to the top of Sky City. You may want to eat at Acoma or in Grants because dining options are few for the rest of the day. Next, head south on NM 117, one of the state's prettiest drives, to **El Malpais** (p. 253), where you'll see great views and some wonderful history. Continue south through Quemado and Reserve to the **Catwalk National Recreation Trail** (p. 347), where you'll stretch your legs on an easy hike. Then make your way to Silver City to spend the night. Have dinner at **Diane's Bakery & Cafe** (p. 343).

Day 9: Gila Cliff Dwellings National Monument ★★★

Before you head out of town this morning, pick up supplies for a picnic. This day takes you deep into the Gila Wilderness to see the ruins at **Gila Cliff Dwellings National Monument** (p. 345). After you've toured the ruins, head up the Middle Fork Trail; the trail head is near the cliff dwellings. The trail follows the Gila River through the wilderness and offers some lovely picnic spots along the way. As you return to town, take a detour through Pinos Altos and stop for dinner at the **Buckhorn Saloon & Opera House** (p. 343). Return to Silver City, where you'll spend the night.

Day 10: White Sands National Monument ★★★

This day takes you southeast, with a quick stop at **City of Rocks State Park** (p. 336) to see lovely rock formations. Have lunch in Las Cruces at one of the restaurants in the vicinity of **Old Mesilla** (p. 330), a lovely plaza where you can shop and stroll. In the afternoon, drive northeast on US 70 to **White Sands National Monument** (p. 358), where you'll want to spend the late afternoon and early evening. For the night, head to the **Lodge at Cloudcroft** (p. 357).

Day 11: Cloudcroft

Today, get ready to burn some calories as you hike or bike the Sacramento Mountains around **Cloudcroft** (p. 354). The **Rim Trail** (p. 351), which offers views out across White Sands, is considered one of the top bike trails in the United States. Or choose one of the excellent hiking trails in the area. Spend the night in Cloudcroft.

Day 12: Carlsbad Caverns National Park ★★★

Head east to **Carlsbad** to visit the **Living Desert Zoo & Gardens State Park** (p. 378). Have lunch in Carlsbad and then drive out to the most spectacular sight in New Mexico, **Carlsbad Caverns National Park** (p. 382), where you want to walk down into the cave, rather than ride the elevator. If you're a serious spelunker, arrange in advance for one of the special tours. End your day at the **river walk** (p. 377), where you can swim and pedal paddleboats, or at your hotel pool.

Day 13: Aliens & Billy the Kid

Take US 285 to Roswell, where you can decide for yourself whether or not aliens landed there in the 1940s. Visit the **International UFO Museum and Research Center** (p. 372). From there, head west to **Lincoln Historic District** (p. 363). Spend the night there at **Ellis Store and Co. Country Inn** (p. 366) or the **Wortley Hotel** (p. 366).

Day 14: North to Albuquerque

Spend a leisurely morning enjoying the quiet village of Lincoln. Then go west to Capitan, where you can learn about the history of forest fire prevention at **Smokey Bear Historical State Park** (p. 370). Have lunch in Carrizozo, where you can feast on a green-chile cheeseburger at the **Outpost** (p. 370). Continue west to see the **Valley of Fires Recreation Area** (p. 371), an amazing lava field. Then drive to San Antonio to the **Bosque del Apache National Wildlife Refuge** (p. 313), arriving in time to see the birds fly in to the lakes after a day in the fields. This takes place in winter at dusk, but there are still plenty of birds to see at other times of year. Finally, head north to Albuquerque, where you can cool down in the pool for the evening and have an enchilada before you catch your plane home.

THE ACTIVE VACATION PLANNER

Y ou may be pleasantly surprised at the range of outdoor fun available in this state. From the dry flatlands of the southern regions to the mountains and forests of the north-central part of the state, diversity reigns here. Whether you're interested in a short day hike or an overnight horse trip, groomed ski trails or backcountry adventures, you won't be disappointed.

For more in-depth coverage of the activities that follow, contact some of the local outfitters or organizations that are listed in the "Outdoor Activities" and "Getting Outside" sections in the later chapters in this book.

For tips on staying healthy outdoors, see "Staying Healthy," in chapter 3.

BALLOONING

New Mexico could just be *the* place to go **hot-air ballooning.** Its open spaces and relatively mild climate are ideal for the sport. In fact, one of the state's greatest attractions is the annual Albuquerque International Balloon Fiesta in early October (see "New Mexico Calendar of Events," in chapter 3), which draws thousands of people from all over the world. It is possible to charter hot-air balloon rides in most regions of the state. The outfitters offer a variety of packages, from a standard flight to a more elaborate all-day affair that includes meals. For more information, see the "Outdoor Activities" sections in chapters 6 and 7, and "More Outdoor Activities," in chapter 8; for other cities, contact individual chambers of commerce.

BIRD-WATCHING

New Mexico is directly on the Central Flyway, which makes it a great spot for bird-watching all year long. Each region of the state offers refuge to a wide variety of birds, including doves, finches, bluebirds, and roadrunners (the state bird). The bald eagle is also frequently spotted during winter and spring migrations. A good place to pull out your binoculars is the **Gila National Forest** (© 575/388-8201; www.fs.fed.us/r3/gila) near Silver

City. The area around Lake Roberts is especially known for its high concentration and variety of hummingbirds. Also check out the wildlife refuge centers in New Mexico, most notably the **Bosque del Apache National Wildlife Refuge,** 93 miles south of Albuquerque (© **575/835-1828;** www.fws.gov/southwest/refuges/newmex/ bosque). Others include the **Rio Grande Nature Center State Park,** Albuquerque (© **505/344-7240;** www.nmparks.com), the **Las Vegas National Wildlife Refuge,** 5 miles southeast of Las Vegas (© **505/425-3581;** www.fws.gov/refuges), and **Bitter Lake National Wildlife Refuge,** 13 miles northeast of Roswell (© **575/622-6755;** www.fws.gov/refuges). Some common sightings at these areas include sandhill cranes, snow geese, a wide variety of ducks, and falcons. New Mexico is also home to an amazing variety of hummingbirds. The number of verified species in New Mexico is now 478. New Mexico ranks fourth (behind Texas, California, and Arizona) in the number of birds that live in or have passed through the state.

To find out about bird-watching activities in New Mexico, contact the state office of the **National Audubon Society,** 1800 Upper Canyon Rd., Santa Fe, NM 87504 (© **505/983-4609;** www.audubon.org).

FISHING

You'll find scores of **fishing** opportunities in New Mexico. Warm-water lakes and streams are home to large- and small-mouth bass, walleye, stripers, catfish, crappie, and bluegill. In cold-water lakes and streams, look for the state fish, the Rio Grande cutthroat, as well as kokanee salmon and rainbow, brown, lake, and brook trout.

Two of the best places for fishing are the **San Juan River** near Farmington (see chapter 9) and **Elephant Butte Lake** (see chapter 11), not far from Truth or Consequences. The San Juan River offers excellent trout fishing and is extremely popular with fly fishers. Elephant Butte Lake is great for bass fishing; in fact, it's considered one of the top 10 bass-fishing locations in the United States.

All sorts of other possibilities are available, such as the Rio Grande, the Chama, Jemez, and Gila watershed areas, and the Pecos River. I recommend Taylor Streit's *Fly Fishing in New Mexico* (David Communications). This excellent and wonderfully comprehensive book provides options for beginner and advanced fishers. Also of note is *49 Trout Streams of New Mexico,* by Raymond C. Shewnack and William J. Fangos (University of New Mexico Press), which offers a comprehensive view of fishing in the state.

For information on obtaining a fishing license, call the **New Mexico Game and Fish Department,** 1 Wildlife Way, Santa Fe, NM 87507 (© **505/476-8000;** www.wildlife.state.nm.us).

Although it is not necessary to have a fishing license in order to fish on Native American reservation land, you must still receive written permission and an official tribal document before setting out on any fishing trips there. Phone numbers for tribes and pueblos are listed separately in the regional and city chapters in this book.

GOLF

New Mexico provides the clear air and oft-cool climates that draw many golfers. In northern New Mexico, golfers can find great packages for eight respected courses

The drought that has spread across the Southwest in recent years has caused the U.S. Forest Service to close trails in many New Mexico mountains during the summer in order to reduce fire hazard. Before you head out in this area, contact the ranger district nearest your destination. The contact information is in the "Great Outdoors" sections in chapters 9 through 12 of this book.

from **Golf on the Santa Fe Trail** (© 866/465-3660; www.santafetrailgolf.com). The most challenging course in the state is the **University of New Mexico Championship Golf Course,** 3601 University Blvd. SE, Albuquerque (© 505/277-4546; www.unmgolf.com), and one of the most scenic is the **Cochiti Lake Golf Course,** 5200 Cochiti Hwy., Cochiti Lake, NM (© 505/465-2239; www.pueblode cochiti.org). If you're in the Farmington area, check out **Piñon Hills Golf Course,** 2101 Sunrise Pkwy. (© 505/326-6066; www.fmtn.org), rated a few years ago by *Golf Digest* as the "best public golf course" in New Mexico. In the south, you can enjoy views, a challenging course, and cool climes even in summer at the **Links at Sierra Blanca,** in Ruidoso, 105 Sierra Blanca Dr. (© 800/854-6571 or 575/258-5330; www.thelinksatsierrablanca.com). See individual chapters for more suggestions.

HIKING

Everywhere you go in New Mexico you'll find opportunities for hiking adventures. The terrain and climate vary from the heat and flatness of the desert plains to the cold, forested alpine areas of the northern region of the state. You can visit both (going from 3,000–13,000 ft. in elevation) and anything in between in the same day without much trouble. You can go hiking virtually anywhere you please (except on private land or Native American land without permission); however, it's wise to stick to designated trails.

I mention some of the best hiking trails in each region of the state below. See later chapters for details about outfitters, guides, llama trekking services, and who to contact for maps and other information.

Best Hikes

If you're around **Santa Fe,** I recommend hiking Santa Fe Baldy. Once you get to the top, you'll have panoramic views of the Sangre de Cristo and Jemez mountains, as well as the Rio Grande Valley. It's a hike you can do in a day if you start out early, or you might want to camp and take 2 days. Be aware that it is a strenuous hike. A more leisurely option is Aspen Vista, which offers spectacular views, especially in the autumn.

If you're looking for something more challenging in the **north-central region** of the state, head to Taos and give Wheeler Peak your best shot. The hike up New Mexico's highest peak is about 15 miles round-trip. If you're incredibly well conditioned, you may be able to do the hike in a day. Otherwise, plan to hike and camp for several days. The pain of getting to the top is worth it—at the top you'll find some of New Mexico's most spectacular views. See chapter 8 for details.

For a much easier hike in the Taos area, try hiking down into Rio Grande Gorge. It's beautiful and can be hiked year-round. See chapter 8 for details.

In the **northeastern region** of New Mexico, I recommend taking the 1-mile loop around Capulin Volcano. The crater rim offers stunning views in all directions. The trail has a few steep sections, so you'll want to pace yourself. If you don't care to exert yourself that much take the short hike into the crater, which is easier. Any time except winter is good for this hike. See chapter 10 for details.

If you're heading to the **northwestern region** of the state, try hiking the Bisti/De-Na-Zin Wilderness, 37 miles south of Farmington. Though there are no marked trails, the hiking is easy in this area of low, eroded hills and fanciful rock formations. You may see petrified wood or fossils from the dinosaurs that lived here millions of years ago. A walk to one of the more interesting areas is about 4 miles round-trip and is best taken in spring or fall. See chapter 9 for details.

The northwestern region is also home to El Malpais National Monument, where you can hike into great lava tubes. The hiking is easy, but it's also easy to get lost in this area, so be sure to carry a compass and a topographical map. Also in the area is El Morro National Monument, known as Inscription Rock. This is a 200-foot-tall bluff which holds inscriptions dating from as far back as 1605. As well as history, it offers one of my favorite hikes in the state, a moderate ascent to a summit, which has stunning views and an ancestral Puebloan ruin. The hike is especially good in spring and fall. See chapter 9 for details.

In the **southwestern region** is the Gila National Forest, which has approximately 1,500 miles of trails, with varying ranges of length and difficulty. Your best bet is to purchase a guidebook devoted entirely to hiking the Gila Forest, but popular areas include the Crest Trail, the West Fork Trail, and the Aldo Leopold Wilderness. One favorite day hike in the forest is the Catwalk, a moderately strenuous hike along a series of steel bridges and walkways suspended over Whitewater Canyon. See chapter 11 for details.

In the **southeastern region,** you'll find one of my favorite places in all of New Mexico: White Sands National Monument. Hiking the white-sand dunes is easy, if sometimes awkward, and the magnificence of the views is unsurpassed. Be sure to take sunscreen and sunglasses, plenty of water, and a compass on this hike; there's no shade, and it's difficult to tell one dune from another here. See chapter 12 for more information.

Of course, you can choose from hundreds of other hikes. You can purchase a hiking book or contact the National Park Service, National Forest Service, Bureau of Land Management, or other appropriate agency directly. The best guides for the region are 50 *Hikes in Northern New Mexico: From Chaco Canyon to the High Peaks of the Sangre de Cristos* (Countryman), by Kai Huschke, and *100 Hikes in New Mexico,* 3rd edition, by Craig Martin (the Mountaineers). A popular guide with Santa Feans is *Day Hikes in the Santa Fe Area,* published by the local branch of the Sierra Club and available in most local bookstores.

HORSEBACK RIDING

What's unique about much of New Mexico's horseback riding is its variety. You'll find a broad range of riding terrain, from open plains to high mountain wilderness. In the Santa Fe area, you can ride across the plains of the spectacular Galisteo basin with **Santa Fe Detours,** 54½ E. San Francisco St. (© **800/338-6877** or 505/983-6565; www.sfdetours.com) or **Broken Saddle Riding Company** (© **505/424-7774**; www.brokensaddle.com). In Taos, you can explore secluded Taos Pueblo land with the **Taos Indian Horse Ranch,** on Pueblo land off Ski Valley Road, just before Arroyo Seco (© **800/659-3210** or 505/758-3212; www. taosindianhorseranch.com). In the southeast, try **Inn of the Mountain Gods Resort & Casino,** Carrizo Canyon Road (© **800/545-9011** or 575/464-4100; www.innofthemountaingods.com). If you're looking for a resort horseback riding experience, contact **Bishop's Lodge Ranch Resort & Spa,** Bishop's Lodge Road, Santa Fe (© **800/732-2240** or 505/983-6377; www.bishopslodge.com). If you want an authentic cowpoke experience, I recommend the **Double E Guest Ranch,** 67 Double E Ranch Rd., Gila (© **866/242-3500** or 575/535-2048; www. doubleeranch.com), in the Silver City area.

MOUNTAIN BIKING

New Mexico offers not only fun and exciting biking terrain but also ancient history. Just about the entire state is conducive to the sport, making it one of the most popular places in the United States for avid mountain bikers.

Albuquerque has some excellent and very challenging trails in the Sandia Mountains, as well as less strenuous routes west of town, through Petroglyph National Monument (see chapter 6). In **Santa Fe,** you'll find some very rugged and steep mountain trails, most accessed off the road to Ski Santa Fe (see chapter 7). **Taos** is a rider's paradise, with lots of extreme mountain trails, as well as some that are purely scenic, such as the west rim of the Rio Grande Gorge (see chapter 8).

In northwestern New Mexico, you can ride around El Malpais National Monument in the **Grants** area. You can also take your bike with you to Chaco Culture National Historical Park and ride from ancestral Puebloan ruin to ruin. The **Farmington** area has its renowned Road Apple Trail within Lions Wilderness Park, which you can ride even through the winter. See chapter 9.

In the southwestern region, bikes are not allowed in the Gila Wilderness, but they are permitted in other parts of Gila National Forest; you'll find terrific trails that originate in **Silver City** (see chapter 11). In the southeastern region, the **Cloudcroft** area has some excellent trails; there are a few that explore history as well as natural terrain, most notably the 17-mile Rim Trail (see chapter 12).

Some books to check out are *Mountain Biking Northern New Mexico: A Guide to Taos, Santa Fe, and Albuquerque Areas' Greatest Off-Road Bicycle Rides* (Falcon) by Bob D'Antonio, which details 40 rides, and *Mountain Biking New Mexico* (Falcon) by Sarah Bennett, which covers the whole state.

Known World Guides, in Velarde (© **800/983-7756** or 505/983-7756; www. knownworldguides.com), offers single-day and multiday trips all over New Mexico, with options such as 3 days in the Jemez Mountains west of Santa Fe or 5 days in the Gila National Forest in Silver City. **Mellow Velo,** 636 Old Santa Fe Trail, Santa Fe (© **505/982-8986**; www.mellowvelo.com), runs bike tours to some of the most spectacular spots in northern New Mexico. Trips range from the easy Train Tour south of Santa Fe, to a challenging Borrego Bust ride in the Santa Fe National Forest.

SKIING & SNOWBOARDING

New Mexico has some of the best **downhill skiing** in the United States. With most alpine areas above 10,000 feet and many above 12,000 feet, several ski areas offer vertical drops of over 2,000 feet. Average annual snowfall at the nine major areas ranges from 100 to 300 inches. Many areas, aided by vigorous snow-making efforts, are able to open around Thanksgiving, and most open by mid-December, making New Mexico a popular vacation spot around the holidays. As a result, you'll see a definite rise in hotel room rates in or around ski areas during the holiday season. The ski season runs through March and often into the first week in April.

Some of the best skiing and snowboarding in the state is at Taos and the nearby resort towns of Angel Fire and Red River (see chapter 8). In addition, Taos Ski Valley is home to one of the best ski schools in the country. Ski areas in New Mexico offer runs for a variety of skill levels, and all-day adult lift tickets range from about $39 to $69. Also, some of the best **cross-country skiing** in the region can be found at the Enchanted Forest near Red River and in Chama.

Equipment for alpine, telemark, and cross-country skiing, as well as for snowboarding, can be rented at ski areas and nearby towns. Lessons are widely available.

For more information about individual ski areas, see regional and city chapters later in this book.

WATERSPORTS

Watersports in New Mexico? Absolutely! Here you'll find a variety of watersports activities, ranging from pleasure boating to white-water rafting and windsurfing.

New Mexico offers fantastic opportunities for **white-water rafting** and **kayaking.** The waters in the Chama River and the Rio Grande are generally at their best during the spring and summer (May–July). I've listed my favorite outfitters in chapters 8 and 9. If you're an experienced rafter or kayaker and intend to head out on your own, you still may want to contact one of the outfitters listed in order to get tips on how to negotiate New Mexico's waters. In addition to calling outfitters, you can also contact the **Bureau of Land Management,** 226 Cruz Alta Rd., Taos, NM 87571 (© **575/758-8851;** www.nm.blm.gov), for information.

Opportunities for **pleasure boating** are available on many of New Mexico's lakes and reservoirs, with boat ramps at more than 45 state parks, dams, and lakes. Elephant Butte Lake is one of the best and most beautiful spots for boating (see chapter 11). Unfortunately, the rules and regulations vary greatly from one body of water to another, so you'll have to contact the governing agencies for each place in which you intend to go boating.

The **U.S. Army Corps of Engineers,** 4101 Jefferson Plaza NE, Albuquerque (© **505/342-3100;** www.usace.army.mil), oversees the following lakes: Abiquiu, Cochiti, Conchas, Galisteo, Jemez, Santa Rosa, and Two Rivers. Most other boating areas are regulated by the **State Parks Division,** 1220 S. St. Francis, Santa Fe (© **888/667-2757** or 505/476-3355; www.nmparks.com), or by the **New Mexico Game and Fish Department,** 1 Wildlife Way, Santa Fe (© **505/476-8000;** www. wildlife.state.nm.us). Some are overseen by tribes and pueblos, and in those cases, you'll have to contact them directly.

Another popular pastime, particularly at Cochiti and Storrie lakes in summer, is **windsurfing.** Elephant Butte is also good for windsurfing all year.

OTHER OUTDOOR ACTIVITIES

In addition to the activities listed so far in this chapter, many other recreational opportunities are available in New Mexico. **Hot springs,** for example, are quite popular with locals and visitors. They take many different forms and offer a wide variety of facilities and amenities; some, which aren't owned and operated by anyone but Mother Nature, offer no amenities. You'll find hot springs in the Jemez, Taos, and Las Vegas areas as well as in the southwestern region of New Mexico. Many of them are listed later in this book.

Rockhounding

New Mexico abounds in rockhounding opportunities. Of course, you can't just go around picking up and taking rocks whenever it strikes your fancy—in many places it's illegal to take rocks—but a few places not only allow rockhounding, but also encourage it. **Rockhound State Park** (✆ **575/546-6182;** www.nmparks.com), about 14 miles from Deming, is one such place (see chapter 11 for information). Rockhounds from all over the country descend on this part of the state to find great rocks, such as agate, jasper, and opal. At Rockhound State Park, you're allowed to camp and take a handful or two of rocks home with you. For information on other popular rockhounding sites, contact the **New Mexico Bureau of Geology & Mineral Resources** (✆ **575/835-5420;** www.geoinfo.nmt.edu).

Tennis

Although New Mexico's high and dry climate is ideal for tennis much of the year, the sport is somewhat underdeveloped in the state. Certainly each of the major cities has municipal courts, information about which you'll find in the city and regional chapters of this book. If you're looking for a tennis resort experience, try **Bishop's Lodge Ranch Resort & Spa,** Bishop's Lodge Road, Santa Fe (✆ **800/732-2240** or 505/983-6377; www.bishopslodge.com).

ALBUQUERQUE | 6

Albuquerque is the gateway to New Mexico, the portal through which most domestic and international visitors pass before traveling on to Santa Fe and Taos. But it's worth stopping here for a day or two in order to get a feel for the history of this area.

From the rocky crest of Sandia Peak at sunset, one can see the lights of this city of more than a half million people spread out across 16 miles of high desert grassland. As the sun drops beyond the western horizon, it reflects off the Rio Grande River, flowing through Albuquerque more than a mile below.

This waterway is the bloodline for the area, what allowed a city to spring up in this vast desert, and it continues to be at the center of the area's growth. Farming villages that line its banks are being stampeded by expansion. As the west side of the city sprawls, more means for transporting traffic across the river have been built.

The railroad, which set up a major stop here in 1880, prompted much of Albuquerque's initial growth, but that economic explosion was nothing compared with what happened since World War II. Designated a major national center for military research and production, Albuquerque became a trading center for New Mexico, whose populace is spread widely across the land. Look closely, and you'll see ranchers, Native Americans, and Hispanic villagers stocking up on goods to take back to the New Mexico boot heel or the Texas panhandle.

Climbing out of the valley is **Route 66,** well worth a drive, if only to see the rust that time has left. Old court motels still line the street, many with their funky '50s signage. One enclave on this route is the **University of New Mexico and Nob Hill district,** with a number of fun cafes and shops.

Farther downhill, you come to **downtown Albuquerque.** During the day, this area is all suits and heels, but at night it boasts a hip nightlife scene. People from all over the state come to Albuquerque to check out the live music and dance clubs, most within walking distance from each other.

The section called **Old Town** is worth a visit. Though it's the most touristy part of town, it's also a unique Southwestern village with a beautiful and intact plaza. Also in this area are Albuquerque's aquarium and botanical gardens, as well as its zoo.

ORIENTATION

Arriving

Albuquerque is the transportation hub for New Mexico, so getting in and out of town is easy. For more detailed information, see "Getting There & Around," in chapter 3.

BY PLANE   The **Albuquerque International Sunport** (© **505/842-4366**; www.cabq.gov/airport) is in the south-central part of the city, between I-25 on the west and Kirtland Air Force Base on the east, just south of Gibson Boulevard. Sleek and efficient, the airport is served by most national airlines and two local ones.

Most hotels have courtesy vans to meet their guests and take them to their respective destinations. In addition, **Sunport Shuttle** (© **866/505-4966**; www.sunport-shuttle.com) runs services to and from city hotels. **ABQ Ride** (© **505/243-7433**; www.cabq.gov/transit), Albuquerque's public bus system, also makes airport stops. There is efficient taxi service to and from the airport, and there are numerous car-rental agencies.

BY TRAIN   Amtrak's *Southwest Chief* arrives and departs daily to and from Los Angeles and Chicago. The station is at the Alvarado Transportation Center, 300 2nd St. SW (at the corner of Lead and Second; © **800/872-7245** or 505/842-9650; www.amtrak.com). The **New Mexico Rail Runner Express** (© **866/795-7245**; www.nmrailrunner.com) runs trains daily from various points in Albuquerque to various ones in Santa Fe, with connecting busses to the Albuquerque International Sunport and to Taos.

BY BUS   Greyhound/Trailways (© **800/231-2222**; www.greyhound.com) arrives and departs from the Alvarado Transportation Center, 300 2nd St. SW (at the corner of Lead and Second).

BY CAR   If you're driving, you'll probably arrive via either the east-west I-40 or the north-south I-25. Exits are well marked. For information and advice on driving in New Mexico, see "Getting There & Around," in chapter 3.

Visitor Information

The main office of the **Albuquerque Convention and Visitors Bureau** is at 20 First Plaza NW (© **800/284-2282** or 505/842-9918; www.itsatrip.org). It's open Monday to Friday 8am to 5pm. There are information centers at the airport, on the lower level at the bottom of the escalator, open daily 9:30am to 8pm; and in Old Town at 303 Romero St. NW, Ste. 107, open daily 10am to 5pm. Recorded information about current local events is available from the bureau after 5pm weekdays and all day Saturday and Sunday. Call © **800/284-2282.**

City Layout

The city's sprawl takes a while to get used to. A visitor's first impression is of a grid of arteries lined with shopping malls and fast-food eateries, with residences tucked behind on side streets.

If you look at a map of Albuquerque, you'll notice that it lies at the crossroads of I-25 north-south and I-40 east-west. Focus your attention on the southwest quadrant: Here, you'll find both downtown Albuquerque and Old Town, site of many tourist attractions. Lomas Boulevard and Central Avenue, the old Route 66 (US 66),

Greater Albuquerque

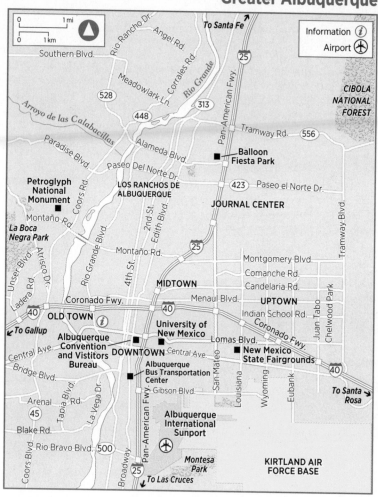

0   1 mi
0   1 km

Rio Rancho Dr.
Angel Rd.
To Santa Fe
25

Southern Blvd.

Information ⓘ
Airport ✈

Meadowlark Ln.
Corrales Rd.
Rio Grande
Pan-American Fwy.

CIBOLA NATIONAL FOREST

528
448
313

Arroyo de las Calabacillas

Tramway Rd.   556

Paradise Blvd.
Alameda Blvd.

■ **Balloon Fiesta Park**

Paseo Del Norte Dr.

Petroglyph National Monument ■

Coors Rd.
LOS RANCHOS DE ALBUQUERQUE

423   Paseo el Norte Dr.

Montaño Rd.

JOURNAL CENTER

Tramway Blvd.

La Boca Negra Park

Rio Grande Blvd.
2nd St.
Edith Blvd.

Unser Blvd.
Atrisco Dr.

Montaño Rd.
25

Montgomery Blvd.
Comanche Rd.
Candelaria Rd.

Ladera Rd.

MIDTOWN

Coronado Fwy.
Menaul Blvd.
UPTOWN

Juan Tabo
Chelwood Park

40

OLD TOWN ⓘ

Indian School Rd.
Coronado Fwy.

◀ **To Gallup**

University of New Mexico

40

Albuquerque Convention and Vistitors Bureau

4th St.

Central Ave.   **DOWNTOWN**   Central Ave.

Lomas Blvd.

■ **New Mexico State Fairgrounds**

San Mateo
Louisiana
Wyoming
Eubank

To Santa Rosa ▶

Central Ave.
Bridge Blvd.

■ **Albuquerque Bus Transportation Center**

Gibson Blvd.

Arenal Rd.
Tapia Blvd.
La Vega Dr.

45

Blake Rd.

Rio Bravo Blvd.   500

Coors Blvd.

Pan-American Fwy.

Albuquerque International Sunport
✈

Montesa Park

KIRTLAND AIR FORCE BASE

Broadway
25
↓ **To Las Cruces**

flank downtown on the north and south. They come together 2 miles west of downtown near Old Town Plaza, the historical and spiritual heart of the city. Lomas and Central continue east across I-25, staying about half a mile apart as they pass by the University of New Mexico (UNM) and the Expo New Mexico fairgrounds. The airport is directly south of the UNM campus, about 3 miles via Yale Boulevard. Kirtland Air Force Base—site of Sandia National Laboratories—is an equal distance south of the fairgrounds, on Louisiana Boulevard.

Roughly paralleling I-40 to the north is Menaul Boulevard, the focus of midtown and uptown shopping, as well as the hotel districts. As Albuquerque expands northward, the Journal Center business park area, about 4½ miles north of the freeway interchange, is expanding. Near there is home to the Albuquerque International Balloon Fiesta and the new Balloon Museum. East of Eubank Boulevard lie the Sandia Foothills, where the alluvial plain slants a bit more steeply toward the mountains.

When looking for an address, it is helpful to know that Central Avenue divides the city into north and south, and the railroad tracks—which run just east of First Street downtown—comprise the dividing line between east and west. Street names are followed by a directional: NE, NW, SE, or SW.

MAPS The most comprehensive Albuquerque street map is distributed by the Convention and Visitors Bureau, 20 First Plaza NW (© **800/284-2282** or 505/842-9918).

GETTING AROUND

Albuquerque is easy to get around, thanks to its wide thoroughfares and grid layout, combined with its efficient transportation systems.

BY PUBLIC TRANSPORTATION ABQ Ride (© **505/243-7433**) cloaks the arterials with its city bus network. Call for information on routes and fares.

BY TAXI Yellow Cab (© **505/247-8888**) serves the city and surrounding area 24 hours a day.

BY CAR The Yellow Pages list more than 30 car-rental agencies in Albuquerque. Among them are the following well-known national firms: **Alamo,** 3400 University Blvd. SE (© **505/842-4057;** www.alamo.com); **Avis,** at the airport (© **505/842-4080;** www.avis.com); **Budget,** at the airport (© **505/247-3443;** www.budget.com); **Hertz,** at the airport (© **505/842-4235;** www.hertz.com); **Rent-A-Wreck,** 2001 Ridegcrest Dr. SE (© **505/232-7552;** www.rentawreck.com/nm.htm); and **Thrifty,** 2039 Yale Blvd. SE (© **505/842-8733;** www.thrifty.com). Those not located at the airport itself are close by and can provide rapid airport pickup and delivery service.

Parking is generally not difficult in Albuquerque. Meters operate weekdays 8am to 6pm and are not monitored at other times. Only the large downtown hotels charge for parking. Traffic is a problem only at certain hours. Avoid I-25 and I-40 at the center of town around 8am and 5pm.

[FastFACTS] ALBUQUERQUE

Airport See "Orientation," above.

Area Code For the northwestern section of New Mexico, including Santa Fe and Albuquerque, the area code is **505,** while the rest of the state is **575.**

ATMs You can find ATMs all over town, at supermarkets, banks, and drive-throughs.

Business Hours

Offices and **stores** are generally open Monday to Friday, 9am to 5pm, with many stores also open Friday night, Saturday, and Sunday in the summer season. Most **banks** are also open Monday to Friday, 9am to 5pm. Some may be open Saturday morning. Most branches have ATMs available 24 hours. Call establishments for specific hours.

Car Rentals See "Getting There & Around," in chapter 3, or "Getting Around," above.

Climate See "When to Go," in chapter 3.

Currency Exchange Foreign currency can be exchanged at any of the branches of **Bank of America** (its main office is at 303 Roma NW; ✆ **505/282-2450**).

Dentists Contact **Emergency Dental USA of Albuquerque** at ✆ **505/296-9911** (www.albuquerqueemergencydental.com).

Doctors Call the **Greater Albuquerque Medical Association,** at ✆ **505/821-4583,** for information.

Emergencies For police, fire, or ambulance, dial ✆ **911.**

Hospitals The major hospital facilities are **Presbyterian Hospital,** 1100 Central Ave. SE (✆ **505/841-1234,** or 505/841-1111 for emergency services), and **University of New Mexico Hospital,** 2211 Lomas Blvd. NE (✆ **505/272-2111,** or 505/272-2411 for emergency services).

Hot Lines The following hot lines are available in Albuquerque: rape crisis (✆ **505/266-7711**), poison control (✆ **800/432-6866**), suicide (✆ **505/247-1121**), and Psychiatric Emergency Services (✆ **505/272-2920**).

Information See "Visitor Information," under "Orientation," above.

Internet Access **Fedex Kinko's** provides high-speed Internet access at five locations throughout the city. Two convenient ones are 6220 San Mateo Blvd. NE at Academy Boulevard (✆ **505/821-2222**) and 2706 Central Ave. SE at Princeton Boulevard (✆ **505/255-9673**).

Library The Albuquerque/Bernalillo County Public Library's **main branch** is at 501 Copper Ave. NW, between Fifth and Sixth streets (✆ **505/768-5140**). You can find the locations of the 17 other library facilities in the area by checking online at **www.cabq.gov/library**.

Liquor Laws The legal drinking age is 21 throughout New Mexico. Bars may remain open until 2am Monday to Saturday and until midnight on Sunday. Wine, beer, and spirits are sold at licensed supermarkets and liquor stores. It is illegal to transport liquor through most Native American reservations.

Lost Property Contact the city police at ✆ **505/768-2229.**

Newspapers & Magazines The daily newspaper is the **Albuquerque Journal** (✆ **505/823-7777;** www.abqjournal.com). You can pick up the **Alibi** (✆ **505/346-0660;** www.alibi.com), Albuquerque's alternative weekly, for free at newsstands all over town, especially around the University of New Mexico. It offers entertainment listings and alternative views on a variety of subjects.

Pharmacies **Walgreens** (www.walgreens.com) has many locations throughout Albuquerque. To find one near you, call ✆ **800/925-4733.** Two centrally located ones that are open 24 hours are 8011 Harper Dr. NE at Wyoming Boulevard (✆ **505/858-3134**) and 5001 Montgomery Blvd. NE at San Mateo (✆ **505/881-5210**).

Police For emergencies, call ✆ **911.** For other business, contact the **Albuquerque City Police** (✆ **505/242-COPS** [2677]) or the **New Mexico State Police** (✆ **505/841-9256**).

Post Offices To find the nearest U.S. Post Office, dial ✆ **800/275-8777.** The service will ask for your zip code and give you the closest post office address and hours.

Radio The local AM station **KKOB** (770) broadcasts news and events. FM band stations include **KUNM** (89.9), the University of New Mexico station, which broadcasts Public Radio programming and a variety of music; **KPEK** (100.3), which plays adult contemporary music; and **KHFM** (95.5), which broadcasts classical music.

Taxes In Albuquerque, the sales tax is 6.25%. An additional hotel tax of 6% will be added to your bill.

Taxis See "Getting Around," above.

Television There are five Albuquerque network affiliates: **KOB-TV** (Channel 4, NBC), **KOAT-TV** (Channel 7, ABC), **KQRE-TV** (Channel 13, CBS), **KASA-TV** (Channel 2, FOX), and **KNME-TV** (Channel 5, PBS).

Time As is true throughout New Mexico, Albuquerque is on **Mountain Standard Time**. It's 2 hours earlier than New York, 1 hour earlier than Chicago, and 1 hour later than Los Angeles. Daylight saving time is in effect from mid-March to early November.

Transit Information **ABQ Ride** is the public bus system. Call ✆ **505/243-7433** for schedules and information.

Useful Telephone Numbers For **road information,** call ✆ **800/432-4269;** for **emergency road service** (AAA), call ✆ **505/291-6600.**

Weather For **time** and **temperature,** call ✆ **505/821-1111.** To get **weather forecasts** on the Internet, check **www.accu weather.com** and use the Albuquerque zip code, 87104.

WHERE TO STAY

Albuquerque's hotel glut is good news for travelers looking for quality rooms at a reasonable cost. Except during peak periods—specifically, the New Mexico Arts and Crafts Fair (late June), the New Mexico State Fair (Sept), and the Albuquerque International Balloon Fiesta (early Oct)—most of the city's hotels have vacant rooms, so guests can frequently request and get lower room rates than the ones posted.

A tax of approximately 12.25% is added to every hotel bill. All hotels and bed-and-breakfasts listed offer rooms for nonsmokers and travelers with disabilities.

Hotels/Motels
EXPENSIVE

Albuquerque Marriott Pyramid North ★★ About a 15-minute drive from Old Town and downtown, this Aztec pyramid–shaped structure provides well-appointed rooms in an interesting environment. The 10 guest floors are grouped around a skylit atrium. Vines drape from planter boxes on the balconies, and water falls five stories to a pool between the two glass elevators. The rooms are spacious, all with picture windows and ample views. The third stage of a $10-million renovation was completed in 2008. With lots of convention space at the hotel, you're likely to encounter name-tagged conventioneers here. Overall, the service seems to be good enough to handle the crowds, but there are only two elevators, so guests often must wait.

5151 San Francisco Rd. NE, Albuquerque, NM 87109. ✆ **800/262-2043** or 505/821-3333. Fax 505/822-8115. www.marriott.com/abqmc. 310 units. $109–$185 double; $185 and up suite. Ask about special weekend and package rates. AE, DC, DISC, MC, V. Free parking. **Amenities:** Restaurant; lounge; concierge; exercise room; Jacuzzi; indoor/outdoor pool; room service. *In room:* A/C, TV, hair dryer, Wi-Fi.

Hotel Albuquerque at Old Town ★★ 🍴 This hotel, just a 5-minute walk from Old Town, offers artfully decorated rooms with views and excellent service. No Albuquerque hotel is closer to top tourist attractions than the Hotel Albuquerque. The cathedral-style lobby has Spanish colonial furnishings and art, a theme that carries into the guest rooms. They're medium size, with handcrafted furniture, comfortable beds, and medium-size bathrooms with outer vanities. Request a south-side room,

Where to Stay in Central Albuquerque

Albuquerque Central KOA **12**
Albuquerque Marriott Pyramid North **8**
Albuquerque North Bernalillo KOA **9**
Best Western Rio Grande Inn **2**
Böttger Mansion of Old Town **4**
Hacienda Antigua **7**
Hotel Albuquerque at Old Town **3**
Hotel Andaluz **5**
Hyatt Regency Tamaya Resort and Spa **9**
La Quinta Inn **10**
Los Poblanos Inn **1**
Nativo Lodge **11**
Sandia Resort & Casino **9**
Sheraton Albuquerque Airport Hotel **6**

and you'll get a balcony with a view over Old Town. A north-side room yields mountain views but no balconies (this is the side to request during the Balloon Fiesta). The lovely grounds have a long trellis portal and a quaint chapel. One of the prettiest pools in town offers a great place to cool off after touring the city. The Q Bar is one of Albuquerque's chicest night spots, with a good tapas menu and a dance floor.

800 Rio Grande Blvd. NW, Albuquerque, NM 87104. © **800/237-2133** (reservations only), or 505/843-6300. Fax 505/842-8426. www.hotelabq.com. 188 units. $119–$219 double; $149–$350 junior suite. Children stay free in parent's room. AE, DC, DISC, MC, V. Free parking. **Amenities:** 2 restaurants; lounge; concierge; exercise room; Jacuzzi; outdoor pool (summer only); room service. *In room:* A/C, TV, hair dryer, Wi-Fi.

Hotel Andaluz ★★★ 🛏 Built in 1939 by Conrad Hilton as the La Posada de Albuquerque, this hotel recently received a $30-million makeover and the new name Andaluz. The hotel at the center of downtown is listed on the National Register of Historic Places and is ecofriendly, with solar hot water and use of earth-friendly paint, varnishes, and carpeting. The lobby, a center of activities many nights when live music plays, offers a sophisticated ambience utilizing Moroccan and Spanish architectural elements around a central fountain. The elegance carries into the guest rooms decorated in warm earth tones. They have fine linens, granite counter tops, and views of the city and mountains. The hotel caters to business and leisure travelers with kiosks on the mezzanine that offer descriptions to and ticket sales for cultural events in the area. Andaluz also has an excellent restaurant and nightclub.

125 2nd St. NW, at Copper Ave., Albuquerque, NM 87102. © **877/987-9090** or 505/242-9090. Fax 505/923-9015. www.hotelandaluz.com. 107 units. $119–$229 double; $450 suite. AE, DISC, MC, V. Self-parking $10 per day, valet parking $16 per day. **Amenities:** Restaurant; lounge; nightclub; concierge; exercise room; room service. *In room:* A/C, TV, hair dryer, MP3 docking station, Wi-Fi.

Nativo Lodge ★ This full-service hotel provides comfortable rooms with a Native American theme, utilizing high-tech elements as well. It's part of the Heritage Hotels & Resorts group, which, in recent years, has renovated a number of New Mexico hotels such as the Hotel Encanto in Las Cruces and Hotel Albuquerque at Old Town. The five-story building, renovated in 2004, has tan walls throughout the two-tiered lobby and standard-size guest rooms. The rooms are tastefully decorated with Native American geometric patterns, creating a cozy feel, with comfortable beds and good linens, a desk, and small balcony. The bathrooms are small but functional. Be sure to request a room well away from the lounge area, which can be noisy on weekend nights. The service is thoughtful and efficient. This is a good home base for the Balloon Fiesta, as well as to explore the city. The property even has a tepee used for special events.

6000 Pan American Fwy. NE, Albuquerque, NM 87109. © **888/628-4861** or 505/798-4300. Fax 505/798-4305. www.nativolodge.com. $119–$129 double. AE, DC, DISC, MC, V. Free parking. **Amenities:** Restaurant; lounge; exercise room; Jacuzzi; indoor/outdoor pool; room service; sauna. *In room:* A/C, TV, fridge (in suites), hair dryer, Wi-Fi.

Sandia Resort & Casino ★★★ On the Sandia Reservation at the north end of town in a grand nine-story pueblo-style structure, this resort offers plenty of fun activities in a scenic setting. The hotel has spectacular views of the Sandia Mountains and the Albuquerque skyline. The lobby, constructed in a majestic mission church style, offers space for lounging, and just off it, a casino with 1,800 slots, Vegas-style gambling, and all the blinking lights that a gambler could want. The spacious rooms, decorated in an elegant Native American motif, have very comfortable beds, a lounge chair, desk, and louvered blackout blinds, as well as many amenities. The bathrooms are large, with Italian tile throughout, and robes. The suites are even more spacious. Be aware that this resort best serves active people who like to play into the night. If you're looking for a more relaxing stay, you might choose the Hyatt Tamaya.

30 Rainbow Rd. NE, Albuquerque, NM 87113. ℭ **877/272-9199** reservations, 800/526-9366 or 505/798-3930. Fax 505/796-7606. 228 units. www.sandiaresort.com. $139–$299 double; $319–$389 1-bedroom suite; $699 2-bedroom suite. AE, DC, DISC, MC, V. Free valet parking. **Amenities:** 3 restaurants; lounge; free airport transfers; concierge; exercise room; golf course; Jacuzzi; large outdoor pool (weather permitting); room service; spa. *In room:* A/C, TV, hair dryer, Wi-Fi.

MODERATE

Best Western Rio Grande Inn ★ ☺ A 10-minute walk from Old Town, this well-cared for hotel offers comfortable accommodations at a reasonable price. It sits close to I-40, so be sure to request a south-facing room, which will be quieter. The medium-size rooms are accessed off of interior corridors and have earth-tone upholstery and walls, a desk, and comfortable chair. With a restaurant on-site and a fenced pool, this is a good option for families.

1015 Rio Grande Blvd. NW, Albuquerque, NM, 87104. ℭ **800/959-4726** or 505/843-9500. Fax 505/843-9238. www.riograndeinn.com. $89–$129 double. AE, DISC, MC, V. Free parking. Pets welcome ($25 one-time fee). **Amenities:** Restaurant; free airport transfer; exercise room, Jacuzzi, outdoor pool (heated year-round). *In room:* A/C, TV, hair dryer, Wi-Fi.

Sheraton Albuquerque Airport Hotel ★★ This 15-story hotel right at the airport provides spacious rooms with a touch of elegance. The lobby, grill, and lounge areas employ a lot of sandstone, wood, copper, and tile to lend an Anasazi feel, which carries into the rooms, each with a broad view from a balcony. A recent remodel brought new, comfortable mattresses and bright contemporary furnishings. Air travelers enjoy this hotel's location, but because it has good access to freeways and excellent views, it could also be a wise choice for a few days of browsing around Albuquerque. Of course, you will hear some jet noise. The Rojo Grill serves a variety of American and uniquely Southwestern dishes.

2910 Yale Blvd. SE, Albuquerque, NM 87106. ℭ **505/843-7000.** Fax 505/246-8188. www.albuquerquegrandairporthotel.com. 276 units. $79–$176 double. AE, DC, DISC, MC, V. Free parking. Pets welcome. **Amenities:** Restaurant; lounge; concierge; outdoor pool (summer only). *In room:* A/C, TV, fridge, hair dryer, Wi-Fi.

INEXPENSIVE

La Quinta Inn La Quinta offers reliable, clean rooms at a decent price. Rooms are tastefully decorated, fairly spacious, and comfortable, each with a table and chairs and a shower-only bathroom big enough to move around in. Each king room has a recliner, and two-room suites are available. If you're headed to the Balloon Fiesta, this is a good choice because it's not far from the launch site, though you'll have to reserve as much as a year in advance.

There's another La Quinta near the airport (2116 Yale Blvd. SE); you can make reservations for either branch at the toll-free number.

5241 San Antonio Dr. NE, Albuquerque, NM 87109. ℭ **800/753-3757** or 505/821-9000. Fax 505/821-2399. www.lq.com. 130 units. $72–$79 double (higher during Balloon Fiesta). Children stay free in parent's room. AE, DC, DISC, MC, V. Free parking. Pets welcome. **Amenities:** Outdoor pool (heated May–Oct). *In room:* A/C, TV, hair dryer, Wi-Fi.

Bed & Breakfasts

Böttger Mansion of Old Town ★ Decorated with a mixture of antiques and contemporary furnishings, this 1910 historic inn situated right in Old Town offers a sweet taste of a past era. Currently the innkeepers are in the process of retheming the rooms to bring more Albuquerque history into the guests' stay. This includes one room with railroad and another with Route 66 memorabilia. All rooms are medium size and have excellent beds; most have small bathrooms. The rooms facing south let in the most sun but pick up a bit of street noise from nearby Central Avenue and a nearby elementary school. The school quiets down at night, but light sleepers might want a room at the back of the inn to avoid street noise. A guest computer and printer are available in the main living room. Breakfast, such as green-chile polenta quiche with a blueberry muffin, is served in the sunroom. All day, treats are available from the guest snack bar (try the chocolate cookies with a little chile in them). During warm months, the patio is lovely.

110 San Felipe NW, Albuquerque, NM 87104. © **800/758-3639** or 505/243-3639. www.bottger.com. 7 units. $115–$179 double. Rates include full breakfast and snack bar. AE, DISC, MC, V. *In room:* A/C, TV, hair dryer, Wi-Fi.

Hacienda Antigua ★★ 🛍 This adobe home built in 1790 was once the first stagecoach stop out of Old Town in Albuquerque. Now, it's one of Albuquerque's more elegant inns. The artistically landscaped courtyard, with its large cottonwood tree and abundance of greenery, offers a welcome respite for tired travelers. The rooms are gracefully and comfortably furnished with antiques. My favorites all open onto the Great Room. La Capilla, the home's former chapel, has a serene and holy feel, and is furnished with a queen-size bed, a fireplace, and a carving of St. Francis (the patron saint of the garden). All the rooms are equipped with fireplaces. Two more modern rooms built in 2000 aren't quite as atmospheric as those in the main house. A gourmet breakfast, such as pecan waffles, is served in the garden during warm weather and by the fire in winter. The inn is a 15-minute drive from Old Town.

6708 Tierra Dr. NW, Albuquerque, NM 87107. © **800/201-2986** or 505/345-5399. Fax 505/345-3855. www.haciendantigua.com. 8 units. $129–$209 double. Additional person $25. Rates include gourmet breakfast. AE, MC, V. Free parking. Pets welcome ($30 fee). **Amenities:** Concierge; Jacuzzi; outdoor pool. *In room:* A/C, fridge, hair dryer, Wi-Fi.

Los Poblanos Inn ★★ Nestled among century-old cottonwoods, this bed-and-breakfast sits on 25 acres of European-style gardens and peasantlike vegetable and lavender fields, providing one of the state's richest country living experiences. Notable architect John Gaw Meem built the structure, a 7-minute drive from Old Town, in the 1930s. Each of the six guest rooms, most arranged around a poetically planted courtyard with a fountain, has unique touches such as hand-carved doors, traditional tin fixtures, fireplaces, and views across the lushly landscaped grounds. The rooms vary in size. All are comfortable, tastefully decorated with good linens, and offer organic shampoo and soap scented with lavender from the inn's garden. At breakfast, you might feast on eggs Florentine made with eggs from the inn's chickens, spinach from the garden, and artisanal bread made locally, while watching peacocks preen outside the windows of the very Mexican-feeling, boldly decorated cantina. Light sleepers should be aware that the peacocks may caw at night. Fortunately, the inn provides earplugs.

4803 Rio Grande Blvd. NW, Albuquerque, NM 87107. ☏ **866/344-9297** or 505/344-9297. Fax 505/342-1302. www.lospoblanos.com. 7 units. $130–$280 double. $25 additional person. Rates include full breakfast. AE, MC, V. Free parking. **Amenities:** Bike rentals; concierge; outdoor pool (summer only). *In room:* A/C, TV/DVD (some rooms), hair dryer, Wi-Fi.

Near Albuquerque

Hyatt Regency Tamaya Resort and Spa ★★★ This is the spot for a get-away-from-it-all luxury vacation. Set in the hills above the lush Rio Grande Valley on the Santa Ana Pueblo, this pueblo-style resort offers a 16,000-square-foot full-service spa and fitness center, an 18-hole Twin Warriors Championship Golf Course designed by Gary Panks, and views of the Sandia Mountains. Rooms are spacious, with large tile bathrooms. Request one that faces the mountains for one of the state's more spectacular vistas. Other rooms look out across a large courtyard, where the pools and hot tub are. Though the resort is surrounded by acres of quiet countryside, it's only 20 minutes from Albuquerque and 50 minutes from Santa Fe. The concierge offers trips to attractions daily, as well as on-site activities such as hot-air balloon rides, horseback rides, and nature/cultural walks or carriage rides by the river.

1300 Tuyuna Trail, Santa Ana Pueblo, NM 87004. ☏ **800/554-9288** or 505/867-1234. www.tamaya.hyatt.com. 350 units. May–Oct $249–$459 double; Nov–Apr $153–$239 double. Suite rates available upon request. Inquire about spa, horseback riding, golf, and family packages. AE, DC, DISC, MC, V. Free parking. From I-25 take exit 242, following US 550 west to Tamaya Blvd.; drive 1½ miles to the resort. **Amenities:** 2 restaurants; 2 snack bars; lounge; children's programs; concierge; golf course; health club; Jacuzzi; 3 pools (heated year-round); room service; his/hers spa with steam room and sauna. *In room:* A/C, TV, fridge, hair dryer, Wi-Fi.

RV Parks

Albuquerque Central KOA This RV park in the foothills east of Albuquerque is a good choice for those who want to be close to town. It offers some shade trees, lots of amenities, and convenient freeway access. Cabins are available.

 ## CRUISING corrales

If you'd like to travel along meadows and apple orchards into a place where life is a little slower and sweeter, head 20 minutes north of Albuquerque to the village of Corrales. Home to farmers, artists, and affluent landowners, this is a fun place to roam through shops and galleries, and, in the fall, sample vegetables from roadside vendors. Two excellent restaurants, both serving imaginative new American cuisine, sit on the main street. **Indigo Crow ★**, 4515 Corrales Rd. (☏ **505/898-7000;** www.indogocrowcafe.com), serves lunch and dinner Tuesday to Saturday 11:30am to 9pm, and brunch and dinner on Sunday 10am to 9pm. If you'd like to stay in the village, contact the **Sandhill Crane Bed-and-Breakfast ★**, 389 Camino Hermosa (☏ **800/375-2445** or 505/898-2445; www.sandhillcranebandb.com).

The town also has a nature preserve and a historic church. In September, the Harvest Festival is well worth the trip. For more information about Corrales, contact Corrales Village (☏ **505/897-0502;** www.corrales-nm.org).

To get to the village, head north on either I-25 or Rio Grande Boulevard, turn west on Alameda Boulevard, cross the Rio Grande, and turn north on Corrales Road (NM 448). The village is just a few minutes up the road.

12400 Skyline Rd. NE, Albuquerque, NM 87123. ✆ **800/562-7781** or 505/296-2729. www.koa.com. $25–$30 tent site; $35–$65 RV site, depending on hookup; $45–$85 1-room cabin; $48–$95 2-room cabin. All prices valid for up to 2 people. Additional adult $5, child $3. AE, DISC, MC, V. Free parking. Pets welcome. **Amenities:** Bathhouse; bike rentals; fenced dog park; Jacuzzi; miniature golf; playground; outdoor pool; wheelchair-accessible restroom; Wi-Fi access throughout the park.

Albuquerque North Bernalillo KOA ★   More than 1,000 cottonwood and pine trees shade this park, and you'll see many flowers in the warm months. At the foot of the mountains, 14 miles from Albuquerque, this campground has plenty of amenities. Guests enjoy a free pancake breakfast daily and free outdoor movies. Reservations are recommended. Six camping cabins are also available.

555 Hill Rd., Bernalillo, NM 87004. ✆ **800/562-3616** or 505/867-5227. www.koa.com. $21–$23 tent site; $30–$39 RV site, depending on hookup; $38 1-bedroom cabin; $48 2-bedroom cabin. Rates include pancake breakfast and are valid for up to 2 people. Additional person $3. Children 6 and under free with parent. AE, DISC, MC, V. Free parking. Pets welcome. **Amenities:** Restaurant; playground; outdoor pool (summer only); store; Wi-Fi access throughout the park.

WHERE TO DINE
In or Near Old Town
EXPENSIVE

Seasons Rotisserie & Grill ★★ NEW AMERICAN/STEAK/SEAFOOD   Between sunshine-colored walls and under an arched ceiling, this restaurant serves sophisticated flavors just steps from Old Town. It's a sweet oasis at midday and a romantic spot in the evening. The upstairs cantina bustles at sundown, with folks drinking margaritas. Service is excellent. At lunch you can't go wrong with the Angus burger with lemon aioli and roasted poblano chiles, served with herb fries. For the lighter eater, a number of salads head the menu. Dinner brings more sophisticated offerings. The grilled pork chop with goat cheese and roasted potatoes is tasty, as is the hoisin-glazed Atlantic salmon with jasmine rice. A full bar and an imaginative wine and beer list accompany the menu. On Saturday and Sunday evenings in summer, live jazz is played.

2031 Mountain Rd. NW. ✆ **505/766-5100.** Reservations recommended at dinner. Main courses $7–$14 lunch, $16–$40 dinner. AE, DC, DISC, MC, V. Mon–Fri 11:30am–2:30pm; daily 5–10:30pm. Cantina daily 4pm–midnight (Mon–Thurs until 11pm).

MODERATE

La Crêpe Michel ★★ FRENCH   Locals love this small cafe tucked away in a secluded walkway not far from the plaza, where the food is fun and imaginatively prepared. Run by chef Claudie Zamet-Wilcox from France, it has a cozy, informal European feel, with white table coverings and simple furnishings. Service is friendly and calm, which makes this a good place for a romantic meal. The *crêpe aux fruits de mer* (blend of sea scallops, bay scallops, and shrimp in a *velouté* sauce with mushrooms) is especially nice, as is the *crêpe à la volaille* (chunks of chicken in a cream sauce with mushrooms and Madeira wine). For a heartier meal, try one of the specials listed on the board on the wall, such as the beef filet or the *saumon au champagne* (filet of salmon with a white wine–and-cream sauce). For dessert, don't leave without having a *crêpe aux chocolat* (chocolate crepe).

400 San Felipe C2. ✆ **505/242-1251.** www.lacrepemichel.com. Main courses $7–$14 lunch, $10–$27 dinner. AE, DISC, MC, V. Tues–Sun 11:30am–2pm; Tues–Sat 6–9pm.

Where to Dine in Central Albuquerque

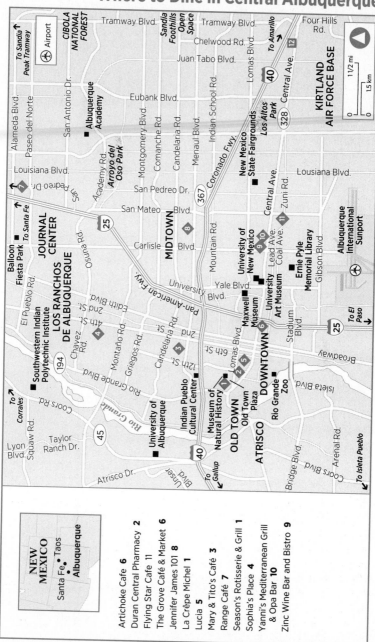

Artichoke Café **6**
Duran Central Pharmacy **2**
Flying Star Cafe **11**
The Grove Café & Market **6**
Jennifer James 101 **8**
La Crêpe Michel **5**
Lucia **5**
Mary & Tito's Café **3**
Range Café **7**
Season's Rotisserie & Grill **1**
Sophia's Place **4**
Yanni's Mediterranean Grill & Opa Bar **10**
Zinc Wine Bar and Bistro **9**

GASTROblog

If you're looking for an in-depth look at Albuquerque's restaurants, check out **Gil's Thrilling (and filling) Blog ★★** at www.nmgastronome.com/blog. Food critic and New Mexico native Gil Garduño has dined at more than 1,000 restaurants in northern New Mexico. In his blog he provides in-depth accounts and ratings, of the food and the experience of dining at most of them. You may spend hours reading up on his favorites, or just take a quick peek to get a recommendation.

INEXPENSIVE

Duran Central Pharmacy ★ 📷 NEW MEXICAN   Sounds like an odd place to eat, I know. You could go to one of the touristy New Mexican restaurants in the middle of Old Town and have lots of atmosphere and mediocre food—or you could come here, where locals eat, and feast on better, more authentic fare. It's a few blocks up Central, east of Old Town. On your way through the pharmacy, you may want to stock up on specialty soaps; there's a pretty good variety here. The restaurant itself is plain, with a red-tile floor and small tables, as well as a counter, where you can eavesdrop on the chefs as they speak Spanish. For years, I used to come here for a bowl of green-chile stew and a homemade tortilla, which is still an excellent choice. Now I go for the full meals, such as the blue-corn enchilada plate or the huevos rancheros (eggs over corn tortillas, smothered with chile). The menu is short, but you can count on authentic northern New Mexican food.

1815 Central Ave. NW. 🕿 **505/247-4141.** Menu items $6–$10. No credit cards. Mon–Fri 9am–6:20pm; Sat 9am–2pm.

Sophia's Place ★★ 📷 NEW MEXICAN   Don't be daunted by the modest exterior of this bustling little cafe—it has very sophisticated and delectable flavors. Between sun-colored walls and vigas shining with multicolored Christmas lights, diners order at a counter and the food is brought to the table. It's tough to make suggestions because everything is delicious. Breakfast is served all day and includes stellar blue-corn pancakes and excellent huevos rancheros—two eggs on corn tortillas topped with meat or veggie chile and cheese and served with beans and potatoes. At lunch, the tacos with cod are some of the best I've had anywhere: soft corn tortillas with salsa crema, a side salad, beans, and rice. You can also order them with salmon or scallops. For dessert, try the pumpkin brownies. During warm months, diners enjoy sitting at picnic tables on the patio.

6313 4th St. NW 🕿 **505/345-3935.** Main courses $5–$12. AE, DISC, MC, V. Mon–Fri 7am–3pm; Sat–Sun 9am–2pm.

Downtown

EXPENSIVE

Artichoke Cafe ★★ NEW AMERICAN   An art gallery as well as a restaurant, this popular spot has modern paintings and sculptures, offering bursts of color set against calm earth tones, a hint at the innovative dining experience offered here. Set in three rooms, this is a nice romantic place. The service is friendly and efficient. At lunch, a number of gourmet sandwiches top the menu along with salads. One of my favorites is the grilled Greek lamb salad, with tomatoes, capers, feta, and grilled eggplant. At dinner, you might start with roasted garlic with Montrachet goat cheese, and then move on to the house-made asparagus and mushroom ravioli in a fresh basil beurre blanc sauce or sea scallops wrapped in prosciutto served with green beans and small potatoes. A carefully selected beer and wine (*Wine Spectator* award-winning) list accompanies the menu. Recently the Artichoke has opened a wine bar on the premises, a fun, cozy spot to sample their wine list.

424 Central Ave. SE. © **505/243-0200.** www.artichokecafe.com. Reservations recommended. Main courses $9–$15 lunch, $18–$31 dinner. AE, DC, DISC, MC, V. Mon–Fri 11am–2pm; Sun–Mon 5:30–9pm; Tues–Sat 5:30–10pm.

Lucia ★★ NEW AMERICAN At the new Hotel Andaluz, this restaurant serves delectable meals in a warm, contemporary ambience. The place has high ceilings with hanging halogen lamps, lots of good wood, and an exhibition kitchen. Like the hotel, the menu here is inspired by Mediterranean flavors, using local and seasonal ingredients, when possible. At breakfast, you might try the lemon ricotta pancakes with maple syrup and at lunch a club with applewood-smoked bacon, egg, lettuce, tomato, and baby Gouda on sourdough bread. A vegetarian special tops the menu each day. Dinner might start with a beet and heirloom tomato salad with sherry-walnut dressing and herbed goat cheese and move on to—my favorite here—roasted butternut-squash ravioli with baby artichokes and a brown-butter sauce. Finish with mango-honey-lavender flan. A thoughtful international wine list accompanies the menu.

At Hotel Andaluz, 125 2nd St. NW, at Copper Ave. © **505/923-9080.** www.hotelandaluz.com. Reservations recommended. Main courses $7–$15 breakfast, $9–$13 lunch, $10–$35 dinner. AE, DISC, MC, V. Mon–Sat 7–10:30am, 11am–2:30pm, and 5:30–10pm; Sun 9am–noon and 5:30–10pm. Free valet parking.

MODERATE

The Grove Café & Market ★★ 🍴 DELI/CAFE Albuquerque's hippest new dining spot in the EDo district offers fresh breakfasts and lunches utilizing organic and locally grown produce in a fun and open space. Colorful nature paintings hang on sky blue walls, and a patio opens during warm months. Breakfast, served all day, offers creative twists on standards, such as French-style pancakes with fruit and crème fraîche, but the real winner here is the *croque madame*—Black Forest ham, tomato, and Gruyère cheese on rustic farm loaf, topped with a sunny-side-up egg. Lunch offers an array of salads and sandwiches. My favorites are the pressed ones such as the BLT, with applewood smoked bacon and guacamole on whole wheat. With cupcakes "in" these days, this place makes six flavors. My favorite is the strawberry cheesecake with mascarpone frosting. Wash it all down with latte or chai tea. This is also an excellent place to stock a picnic basket and purchase specialty teas and local truffles in the market portion of the restaurant.

600 Central Ave. SE (just west of I-25). © **505/248-9800.** www.thegrovecafemarket.com. All main courses under $11. AE, MC, V. Tues–Sat 7am–4pm; Sun 8am–3pm.

INEXPENSIVE

Mary & Tito's Café ★★ 🍴 NEW MEXICAN In a modest setting with arched windows, a tile floor, and turquoise booths, this cafe has been serving some of the region's best New Mexican food for 48 years. It's so good that it received the James Beard Foundation's American Classic Restaurant award in 2010, a real surprise for the humble owner, Mary Gonzales, who, along with many family members, runs the

family-friendly RESTAURANTS

Flying Star Cafe (p. 91)   With a huge selection, a relaxed atmosphere, and a number of locations, the whole family can enjoy this place.

Range Café (p. 91)   The fun and funky decor and Taos Cow Ice Cream makes this a good spot for kids.

cafe. The focus here is on the chile, made fresh and extremely flavorful. Their signature dish, *carne adovada* (pork simmered in red chile) is cooked for 5 hours and served with beans, rice, and a tortilla. On a recent visit, I enjoyed the blue-corn chicken enchiladas with red and green chile, served with beans, rice, and tortillas. Stuffed *sopaipillas* are also a big hit here, as is the combination plate, with beef tacos, a *relleno,* and cheese enchiladas. What's most unique about any of these dishes is that they are absolutely smothered with the best chile you've ever eaten, with only a minimum of extras such as cheese and sour cream to dilute the flavor. For dessert, the Mexican wedding cake is moist and delectable.

2711 4th St. NW. ⓒ **505/344-6266.** Main courses $5.50–$8.50. MC, V. Mon–Thurs 9am–6pm; Fri–Sat 9am–8pm.

The Northeast Heights

EXPENSIVE

Jennifer James 101 ★★★ 🎁 NEW AMERICAN   This restaurant's namesake may be Albuquerque's most notable chef. Unfortunately, she doesn't seem to have much longevity with her eateries. I hope this one will last. It's a comfortable place to spend an evening relishing delightful flavors. The setting is contemporary, with hardwood floors, drum-shaped light fixtures, and an exhibition kitchen in back. The food, too, hearkens back to elemental flavors, which is why she named the restaurant "101." But, really, nothing about this place is simple. James uses local, seasonal ingredients in completely imaginative ways, and the service is knowledgeable and efficient. The short menu features appetizers such as an arugula salad with dried apricots and hazelnut vinaigrette. For an entree, I've enjoyed almond-crusted halibut over basmati rice with a light curry sauce and French-style carrots. A dessert of hot milk cake with strawberries and cream is the best version of the traditional strawberry shortcake I've had. A select wine and beer list accompanies the menu.

4615-A Menaul Blvd. NE. ⓒ **505/884-3860.** www.jenniferjames101.com. Reservations highly recommended. Main courses $16–$25. AE, DISC, MC, V. Tues–Sat 5–10pm.

University & Nob Hill

EXPENSIVE

Zinc Wine Bar and Bistro ★★ NEW AMERICAN   In a moody, urban atmosphere with wood floors and a high ceiling, this Nob Hill in-place serves imaginative food, using meticulously prepared seasonal ingredients. The bi-level dining room with well-spaced tables can get crowded and noisy at peak hours (especially under the balcony, so avoid sitting there then). Service is congenial but inconsistent. The lunch menu offers a variety of salads and sandwiches, as well as inventive dishes. One of my favorites is the mango-glazed chicken breast stir-fry. At dinner, the wild Alaskan halibut is tasty, as is the vegetarian crostada (also served at lunch), which is a baked pastry filled with vegetables and cheese. Sunday brunch is also offered, with items such as green-chile eggs Benedict. An extensive wine list accompanies the menu, or you may simply opt for a martini from the full bar. In the lower level, a lounge serves less formally in a wine cellar atmosphere with live music playing 2 to 3 nights a week.

3009 Central Ave. NE. ⓒ **505/254-9462.** www.zincabq.com. Reservations recommended. Main courses $8–$14 lunch, $17–$27 dinner. AE, DC, DISC, MC, V. Tues–Fri and Sun 11am–2:30pm; Mon–Thurs 5–10pm; Fri–Sun 5–11pm. Wine bar Mon–Sat 5pm–1am, with food served till midnight.

MODERATE

Yanni's Mediterranean Grill and Opa Bar ★★ GREEK   With bright blue and white decor, Athenian-style pillars, and Mediterranean paintings on the walls, this is a great place for a festive meal. Locals crowd the cafe and patio with big windows looking out on Central Avenue. Service is friendly, though overworked during peak hours. All food is made fresh, with specials daily. You might start with jumbo sea scallops seared and served with grilled tomato, and then move on to one of the excellent specials such as wild opah (a white fish) roasted with oranges, or, my favorite, oven-roasted lamb. The menu hosts a variety of pasta dishes and, of course, moussaka. Entrees come with a salad, bread, vegetable, and a potato or rice side. The Greek potatoes seasoned with olive oil, garlic, and oregano are yummy. For dessert, try the tiramisu or baklava sundae. An international wine list featuring Greek offerings and a full bar accompany the menu. And the attached Opa! Bar provides live entertainment on weekends.

3109 Central Ave. NE. ⓒ **505/268-9250.** www.yannisandopabar.com. Reservations recommended. Main courses $7–$14 lunch, $13–$27 dinner. AE, DISC, MC, V. Mon–Thurs 11am–10pm; Fri–Sat 11am–11pm; Sun noon–9pm.

INEXPENSIVE

Flying Star Cafe ★ ☺ AMERICAN/CAFE/BAKERY   The Flying Star Cafe makes good on its promise of uptown food with down-home ingredients. It's a fun and friendly place with excellent contemporary international food. But beware: During mealtime, the university location on Central Avenue gets packed and rowdy. The selections range broadly, all made with local and organic produce, when possible. You can choose from 16 different breakfast options to homemade soups and salads to sandwiches and pasta (and pizza at the Juan Tabo and Rio Grande locations). Try the Rancher's Melt (New Zealand sirloin sautéed with green chile, provolone, and horseradish on sourdough) or the Buddha's Bowl (sautéed vegetables in ginger sauce with tofu over jasmine rice). Flying Star also has locations at 4501 Juan Tabo Blvd. NE (ⓒ **505/275-8311**), 8001 Menaul Blvd. NE (ⓒ **505/293-6911**), and 4026 Rio Grande Blvd. NW (ⓒ **505/344-6714**). They don't serve alcohol, but they do brew up plenty of espresso and cappuccino. Kids enjoy the relaxed atmosphere and their own selections from the menu. Though hours vary for each location, they are all open daily for breakfast, lunch, and dinner.

3416 Central Ave. SE. ⓒ **505/255-6633.** www.flyingstarcafe.com. All menu items under $15. AE, DISC, MC, V. Daily 6am–11:30pm.

Outside Albuquerque

Range Café ★ ☺ NEW MEXICAN/AMERICAN   This cafe on the main drag of Bernalillo, about 20 minutes north of Albuquerque, is a perfect place to stop on your way to or from town. Housed in what was once an old drugstore, the restaurant has a pressed-tin ceiling and is decorated with western touches, such as cowboy boots and whimsical art. The food ranges from enchiladas and burritos to chicken-fried steak to more elegantly prepared meals. For breakfast, try the pancakes or the breakfast burrito. For lunch or dinner, I recommend Tom's meatloaf, served with roasted-garlic mashed potatoes, mushroom gravy, and sautéed vegetables. For dinner, you might try pan-seared scallops with roasted poblano corn salsa, green beans and *arroz verde*. Taos Cow ice cream is the order for dessert, or try the baked goods and specialty drinks from the full bar. In the same locale, the Range has opened the Lizard Rodeo Lounge, a hoppin' place with Wild West decor that offers live music many nights a week. There's also a retail space that sells local art and New Mexico wines. Two other branches of the restaurant in Albuquerque have similar food offerings (4200 Wyoming Blvd. NE, ✆ **505/293-2633;** and 2200 Menaul Blvd. NE, ✆ **505/888-1660**).

925 Camino del Pueblo (P.O. Box 1780), Bernalillo. ✆ **505/867-1700.** www.rangecafe.com. Breakfast and lunch $7–$18; dinner $10–$19. AE, DISC, MC, V. Summer daily 7:30am–9:30pm (Fri–Sat till 10pm); winter daily 7:30am–9pm (Fri–Sat till 9:30pm). Closed Thanksgiving, Christmas.

WHAT TO SEE & DO

Albuquerque's original town site, known today as Old Town, is the central point of interest for visitors. Here, grouped around the plaza, are the venerable Church of San Felipe de Neri and numerous restaurants, art galleries, and crafts shops. Several important museums are close by. Within a few blocks are the 25,000-square-foot Albuquerque Aquarium and the 50-acre Rio Grande Botanic Garden (near Central Ave. and Tingley Dr. NW), both well worth a visit.

But don't get stuck in Old Town. Elsewhere, you'll find the Sandia Peak Tramway, the new Balloon Museum, and a number of natural attractions. Within day-trip range are several pueblos and significant monuments (see "Touring the Pueblos Around Albequerque," later in this chapter).

The Top Attractions

Albuquerque Museum of Art and History ★ ☺   Take an interesting journey into New Mexico's present and past in this museum on the outskirts of Old Town. Most notable for me here are works from the museum's art collection, which includes large canvases by Fritz Scholder, Peter Hurd, Ernest Blumenshein, and Georgia O'Keeffe, as well as contemporary woodwork by Luis Tapia. Downstairs you'll take a trip through history, represented by an impressive collection of Spanish colonial artifacts. Displays here include Don Quixote–style helmets, swords, and horse armor, a 19th-century house compound and chapel, and gear used by *vaqueros,* the original cowboys who came to the area in the 16th century. In an old-style theater, two films on Albuquerque history are shown. An Old Town walking tour originates here at 11am Tuesday to Sunday during spring, summer, and fall. A gift shop sells books and jewelry, and a cafe serves upscale sandwiches and soups. Plan to spend 1 to 2 hours here.

2000 Mountain Rd. NW. ✆ **505/243-7255.** www.cabq.gov/museum. Admission $4 adults, $2 seniors 65 and older, $1 children 4-12. Tues–Sun 9am–5pm. Closed major holidays.

Albuquerque Biological Park:
Aquarium & Botanic Garden **3**
Albuquerque Museum of Art
and History **6**
American International Rattlesnake
Museum **4**
Balloon Museum **10**
Explora **6**
Indian Pueblo Cultural Center **5**
National Hispanic Cultural Center **9**
National Museum of Nuclear
Science & History **12**
New Mexico Museum of Natural
History & Science **6**
Petroglyph National Monument **1**
Rio Grande Nature Center State
Park **2**
Rio Grande Zoo **8**
The Rio Line **7**
Sandia Peak Tramway **11**

Balloon Museum ★★ ☺ The Anderson-Abruzzo Albuquerque International Balloon Museum holds special significance for me, as my parents owned part of the first hot-air balloon in Albuquerque over 30 years ago. Today, with the Albuquerque International Balloon Fiesta drawing hundreds of brilliantly colored and imaginatively shaped balloons to the city each October (p. 40), this museum's time has come. It tells the history of ballooning, from the first flight in France in 1783, with a rooster, sheep, and duck as passengers, to the use of balloons in military, science, and aerospace research. Most poignant are displays of Albuquerque balloonists Maxie Anderson and Ben Abruzzo, who, with Larry Newman, completed the first manned crossing of the Atlantic Ocean in 1978. Originals and replicas of various historic crafts dot the three-story-tall space, and windows look out at the Sandia Mountains and Rio Grande Valley. Kids will enjoy the flight simulator, which tests their ability to fly and land a balloon on target. Plan on spending at least an hour here.

9201 Balloon Museum Dr. NE. ☏ **505/768-6020.** www.cabq.gov/balloon.com. Admission $4 adults, $2 seniors 65 and older, $1 children 4-12, free for children 3 and under. Tues–Sun 9am-5pm. Closed New Year's Day, Thanksgiving, Christmas, city holidays.

Indian Pueblo Cultural Center ★ ☺ Owned and operated as a nonprofit organization by the 19 pueblos of New Mexico, this is a fine place to begin an exploration of Native American culture. About a mile northeast of Old Town, this museum—modeled after Pueblo Bonito, a spectacular 9th-century ruin in Chaco Culture National Historic Park—consists of several parts.

You'll want to spend 1 to 2 hours here. Begin above ground, where you'll find changing shows of contemporary Puebloan arts and crafts. Next, head to the basement, where a permanent exhibit depicts the evolution of the various pueblos from prehistory to present, including displays of the distinctive handicrafts of each community. Note especially how pottery differs in concept and design from pueblo to pueblo. In the main building is an enormous (10,000-sq.-ft.) **gift shop** featuring fine pottery, rugs, sand paintings, *katsinas*, drums, and jewelry, among other things. Southwestern clothing and souvenirs are also available. Prices here are quite reasonable.

Throughout the year, Native American dancers perform in an outdoor arena surrounded by original murals. Dances are performed Saturday and Sunday at noon in winter, and Saturday and Sunday at 11am and 2pm in spring. In summer, dances are scheduled at 2pm on Thursday and Friday, and 11am and 2pm Saturday. Often, artisans demonstrate their crafts as well. During certain weeks of the year, such as the Balloon Fiesta, dances are performed daily.

The restaurant serves traditional Native American foods. It's a good place for some Indian fry bread and a bowl of *posole*.

2401 12th St. NW. ☏ **866/855-7902** or 505/843-7270. www.indianpueblo.org. Admission $6 adults, $5.50 seniors, $3 students, free for children 4 and under. AE, DISC, MC, V. Daily 9am-5pm; restaurant Mon–Thurs 8am-8:30pm, Fri-Sat 8am-9pm, Sun 8am-4pm. Closed New Year's Day, July 4, Labor Day, Thanksgiving, Christmas.

National Hispanic Cultural Center ★ In the historic Barelas neighborhood on the Camino Real, this gem of Albuquerque museums offers a rich cultural journey through hundreds of years of history and across the globe. It explores Hispanic arts and lifestyles with visual arts, drama, music, dance, and other programs. I most enjoy the 11,000-square-foot gallery space, which exhibits exciting contemporary and traditional works, as well as changing exhibits. A restaurant offers New Mexican and American food for breakfast and lunch. It's a good spot to sample authentic regional dishes such as tacos, enchiladas, and the rich custard dessert called flan. The shop offers a broad range of fun gifts from Latin America and New Mexico. Plan to spend 1 to 2 hours here, or watch for events and come in conjunction with them.

1701 4th St. SW (corner of 4th St. and Av. Cesar Chavez). © **505/246-2261.** Fax 505/246-2613. www. nhccnm.org. Admission Tues–Sat $3 adults, $2 seniors 60 and over, free for children 16 and under; Sun free for all ages. AE, DISC, MC, V. Tues–Sun 10am–5pm. Restaurant Tues–Fri 9am–3pm; Sat 8am–3pm; Sun 9am–3pm. Closed New Year's Day, Memorial Day, Labor Day, Christmas.

Old Town ★★　A maze of cobbled courtyard walkways leads to hidden patios and gardens, where many of Old Town's 150 galleries and shops are located. Adobe buildings, many refurbished in the pueblo revival style of the 1950s, are grouped around the tree-shaded plaza, created in 1780. Pueblo and Navajo artisans often display their pottery, blankets, and silver jewelry on the sidewalks lining the plaza.

The buildings of Old Town once served as mercantile shops, grocery stores, and government offices, but the importance of Old Town as Albuquerque's commercial center declined after 1880, when the railroad came through 1¼ miles east of the plaza and businesses relocated to be closer to the trains. Old Town clung to its historical and sentimental roots, but the quarter fell into disrepair until the 1930s and 1940s, when artisans and other shop owners rediscovered it and the tourism industry burgeoned.

When Albuquerque was established in 1706, the first building erected by the settlers was the **Church of San Felipe de Neri,** which faces the plaza on its north side. It's a cozy church with wonderful stained-glass windows and vivid *retablos* (religious paintings). This house of worship has been in almost continuous use for nearly 300 years.

Though you'll wade through a few trinket and T-shirt shops on the plaza, don't be fooled: Old Town is an excellent place to shop. Look for good buys from the Native Americans selling jewelry on the plaza, especially silver bracelets and strung turquoise. If you want to take something fun home and spend very little, buy a dyed corn necklace. Your best bet when wandering around Old Town is to peek into shops, but there are a few places in which you'll definitely want to spend time. See "Shopping," later in this chapter, for a list of recommendations. An excellent Old Town historic walking tour originates at the Albuquerque Museum of Art and History (see above) at 11am Tuesday to Sunday during spring, summer, and fall.

Plan to spend 2 to 3 hours strolling around.

Northeast of Central Ave. and Rio Grande Blvd. NW. Old Town Visitor Center: 303 Romero St. NW, Albuquerque, NM 87104 (across the street from the Church of San Felipe de Neri). © **505/243-3215.** Visitor Center daily 10am–6pm summer; daily 10am–4:30pm rest of the year.

Sandia Peak Tramway ★★ ☺　This fun and exciting half-day or evening outing allows incredible views of the Albuquerque landscape and wildlife. The Sandia Peak Tram is a "jigback"; in other words, as one car approaches the top, the other nears the bottom. The two pass halfway through the trip, in the midst of a 1½-mile "clear span" of unsupported cable between the second tower and the upper terminal.

Several hiking trails are available on Sandia Peak, and one of them—La Luz Trail— takes you on a steep and rigorous trek from the base to the summit. The views in all directions are extraordinary. *Note:* The trails on Sandia may not be suitable for children. If you'd like to enjoy a meal during your trip, you can eat lunch (salads, burgers, and pasta dishes) or dinner (steaks, seafood, and pasta) at the **High Finance Restaurant and Tavern** at the top of the tram. Special tram rates apply with dinner reservations. Be aware that the tram does not operate on very windy days.

10 Tramway Loop NE. ℂ **505/856-7325.** Fax 505/856-6335. www.sandiapeak.com. Admission $18 adults, $15 seniors and ages 13–20, $10 children 5–12, free for children 5 and under. Memorial Day to Labor Day daily 9am–9pm; ski season, spring, and fall Wed–Mon 9am–8pm, Tues 5–8pm. Closed 2 weeks each spring and fall for maintenance; check the website for details. Parking $1 daily. AE, DISC, MC, V. To reach the base of the tram, take I-25 north to Tramway Rd. (exit 234), then proceed east about 5 miles on Tramway Rd. (NM 556); or take I-40 to Tramway Blvd., exit 167 (NM 556), and head north 8½ miles.

Other Attractions

National Museum of Nuclear Science & History ★ ☺ Set in a new 30,000-square-foot building with 12 acres of exterior space, this museum offers the next-best introduction to the nuclear age after the Bradbury Science Museum in Los Alamos, making for an interesting 1- to 2-hour perusal. It traces the history of nuclear-weapons development, beginning with the top-secret Manhattan Project of the 1940s, and continues with explanations of nuclear use in power, medicine, and energy. The displays utilize interactive and touch-screen devices—one even calculates your exposure to radiation. There's also a kid's area that explores the science of Albert Einstein. You'll find full-scale casings of the "Fat Man" and "Little Boy" bombs, as well as a running roster of films exploring the atomic age.

601 Eubank SE (at Southern). ℂ **505/245-2137.** Fax 505/242-4537. www.atomicmuseum.com. Admission $8 adults, $7 seniors, $7 children 6–17, free for children 5 and under. Children 11 and under not admitted without adult. Group rates available. Daily 9am–5pm. Closed New Year's Day, Easter, Thanksgiving, Christmas.

Petroglyph National Monument ★★ ☺ These lava flows were once a hunting and gathering area for prehistoric Native Americans, who left a chronicle of their beliefs etched on the dark basalt boulders. Some 25,000 petroglyphs provide a nice outdoor adventure after a morning in a museum. You'll want to stop at the visitor center to get a map and check out the interactive computer. From there, you can drive north to the Boca Negra area, where you'll have a choice of three trails. Take the Mesa Point Trail (30 min.) that climbs quickly up the side of a hill, offering many petroglyph sightings as well as an outstanding view of the Sandia Mountains. If you're traveling with your dog, you can bring her along on the Rinconada Trail. Hikers can have fun searching the rocks for more petroglyphs; there are many yet to be found. This trail (a few miles south of the visitor center) runs for miles around a huge *rincon* (corner) at the base of the lava flow. Camping is not permitted in the park; it's strictly for day use, with picnic areas, drinking water, and restrooms provided.

6001 Unser Blvd. NW (3 miles north of I-40 at Unser and Western Trail). ℂ **505/899-0205.** Fax 505/899-0207. www.nps.gov/petr. Admission $1 per vehicle on weekdays, $2 weekends. DISC, MC, V. Visitor Center and Boca Negra area daily 8am–5pm. Closed New Year's Day, Thanksgiving, Christmas.

ESPECIALLY FOR KIDS

Albuquerque Biological Park: Aquarium and Botanic Garden ★★ ☺ For those of us born and raised in the desert, this attraction quenches years of soul thirst. The self-guided aquarium tour begins with a number of films, including a 9-minute one that describes the course of the Rio Grande from its origin to the Gulf

Coast. Then, you'll move on to the ray pool, and next the eel tank—an arched aquarium you get to walk under. A colorful coral-reef exhibit comes next. Finally, culminating the show, is a 285,000-gallon shark tank.

The Botanic Garden offers an excellent place to stroll through fragrant flowers with a few treats for kids as well. You'll pass through a number of gardens en route to a 10,000-square-foot conservatory, housing a desert collection and a Mediterranean collection. Beyond that, you can see a *curandera* (herb doctor) garden, with medicinal plants, and the Rio Grande Heritage Farm, with corrals, a vineyard, and orchard. Allow at least 2 hours to see both parks. There is a cafe on the premises. May to September, the PNM Butterfly Pavilion fills with the colors of several hundred North American butterflies.

2601 Central Ave. NW. ⓒ **505/764-6200.** www.cabq.gov/biopark. Admission $7 adults ($12 with Rio Grande Zoo admission), $3 seniors 65 and over and children 3–12 ($5 with Rio Grande Zoo admission). Ticket sales stop a half-hour before closing. MC, V. Daily 9am–5pm; (June–Aug Sat–Sun until 6pm). Closed New Year's Day, Thanksgiving, Christmas.

American International Rattlesnake Museum ★ 👜 ☺

This unique museum, just off Old Town Plaza, has living specimens of common, uncommon, and very rare rattlesnakes of North, Central, and South America in naturally landscaped habitats. Oddities such as albino and patternless rattlesnakes are included, as is a display popular with youngsters: baby rattlesnakes. More than 30 species can be seen, followed by a 7-minute film on this contributor to the ecological balance of our hemisphere. Throughout the museum are rattlesnake artifacts from early American history, Native American culture, medicine, the arts, and advertising. You'll also find a gift shop that specializes in Native American jewelry, T-shirts, and other memorabilia related to the natural world and the Southwest, all with an emphasis on rattlesnakes.

202 San Felipe St. NW. ⓒ **505/242-6569.** www.rattlesnakes.com. Admission $5 adults, $4 seniors, $3 children. AE, DISC, MC, V. June–Aug Mon–Sat 10am–6pm, Sun 1–5pm; Sept–May Mon–Fri 11:30am–5:30pm, Sat 10am–6pm, Sun 1–5pm.

Explora ★ ☺

As a center for lifelong learning, Explora houses more than 250 hands-on exhibits in science, technology, and art. Visitors of all ages make their way through the mazelike museum exploring topics as diverse as water, the Rio Grande, light and optics, biological perception, and energy. The exhibits utilize technology that is creatively accessible to the public. My favorite is the Laminar Flow Fountain in which water leaps across spaces, seeming to come alive. Little kids especially enjoy the arts-and-crafts workshop where they can make art to take home. You could spend 1½ hours to a full day here.

1701 Mountain Rd. NW. ⓒ **505/224-8300.** Fax 505/224-8325. www.explora.us. Admission $7 ages 12–64, $5 seniors 65 and over, $3 children 1–11. Mon–Sat 10am–6pm; Sun noon–6pm.

New Mexico Museum of Natural History and Science ★★ ☺

A trip through this museum will take you through 12 billion years of natural history, from the formation of the universe to the present day. You'll stroll through the "Age Jurassic Super Giants" display, where you'll find dinosaur skeletons cast from the real bones and see the latest display "Triassic: Dawn of the Dinosaur." You can ride the Evolator (kids love this!), a simulated time-travel experience that moves and rumbles, taking you 1¼ miles down through 38 million years of history. Soon, you'll find yourself in the age of the mammoths and moving through the Ice Age. Be sure to check out the museum's planetarium. Those exhibits, as well as the DynaTheater, which surrounds you with images and sound, cost an additional fee. A gift shop on the ground floor sells imaginative nature games and other curios. This museum has good access for people with disabilities. Plan to spend 1 to 2 hours here, more if you take in extra attractions.

1801 Mountain Rd. NW. © **505/841-2800.** www.nmnaturalhistory.org. Admission $7 adults, $6 seniors, $4 children 3–12, free for children 2 and under. DynaTheater, planetarium, and Virtual Voyages cost extra, with prices in the $7 range for adults and $4 range for children. Discount ticket combinations are available. Daily 9am–5pm. Closed on nonholiday Mon in Jan and Sept, New Year's Day, Thanksgiving, Christmas.

Rio Grande Nature Center State Park ★ ☺   This center, just a few miles north of Old Town, spans 270 acres of riverside forest and meadows that include stands of 100-year-old cottonwoods and a 3-acre pond. On the Rio Grande Flyway, an important migratory route for many birds, it's an excellent place to see sandhill cranes, Canadian geese, and quail—more than 260 bird species have made this their temporary or permanent home. In a protected area where dogs aren't allowed (you can bring dogs on most of the 2 miles of trails), you'll find exhibits of native grasses, wildflowers, and herbs. Inside a building built half above and half below ground, you can sit next to the pond in a glassed-in viewing area and comfortably watch ducks and other birds in their avian antics. There are 21 self-guided interpretive exhibits as well as photo exhibits, a library, a small nature store, and a children's resource room.

2901 Candelaria Rd. NW. © **505/344-7240.** Fax 505/344-4505. www.nmparks.com. Admission $3 per vehicle. No credit cards (cash and checks only). Daily 10am–5pm; store Mon–Fri 11am–3pm, Sat–Sun 10am–4pm. Closed New Year's Day, Thanksgiving, Christmas.

Rio Grande Zoo ★ ☺   Some 250 species live on 64 acres of riverside bosque here among ancient cottonwoods. Open-moat exhibits with animals in naturalized habitats are a treat for zoogoers. Major exhibits include polar bears, giraffes, sea lions (with underwater viewing), the cat walk, the bird show, and ape country, with gorillas and orangutans. The zoo has an especially fine collection of elephants, koalas, polar bears, reptiles, and native Southwestern species. The Thunderbird Express Train operates in a nonstop loop around the zoo, except on Mondays. As well, the Rio Line operates between the zoo and the Albuquerque Biological Park (p. 96). There are numerous snack bars on the zoo grounds, and La Ventana Gift Shop carries film and souvenirs. Check out the seal and sea lion feeding daily at 10:30am and 3:30pm, the polar bear feeding at 2:30 daily, and the summer Zoo Music Concert Series.

903 10th St. SW. © **505/764-6200.** www.cabq.gov/biopark/zoo. Admission $7 adults ($12 with Aquarium and Botanic Garden admission), $3 seniors and children 3–12 ($5 with Aquarium and Botanic Garden admission), free for children 2 and under. MC, V. Daily 9am–5pm (summer weekends till 6pm). Closed New Year's Day, Thanksgiving, Christmas.

The Rio Line ★ ☺   This miniature train travels between the Tingley Train Station, the Albuquerque Biological Park, and the Rio Grande Zoo, stopping at each facility, with tickets available at each as well. Conductors give an interpretive tour and answer your questions as you ride. A round-trip journey lasts approximately 1 hour. This is a fun trip for families. **Note:** If you purchase a "combo ticket" for the Biological Park and Rio Grande Zoo, you get free between all stations. Also, during summer weekends, because of the high volume of visitors, only those with combo tickets can ride the Rio Line.

903 10th St. SW (station at Tingley Beach on Tingley Dr.) ℭ **505/768-2000.** www.cabq.gov/biopark/ trains.html. Train ride $2 adult, $1 children 3-12. MC, V. The train operates Tues–Sun approximately 10am–3:45pm. The last trains leave the Aquarium/Garden Station and the Asia Station at the zoo at 3:45pm, and the Tingley Station at 3pm.

ORGANIZED TOURS

Bus, Car & Trolley Tours

ABQ Trolly Company ★   A great way to get acquainted with the city, this open-air trolley tour takes visitors to 11 sights in 66 minutes. It starts in Old Town, heads up Route 66 to the Nob Hill shopping district, past the University of New Mexico, to the historic Barelas neighborhood, and to Tingley Beach.

Departs from 303 Romero St. NW in Old Town. ℭ **505/240-8000.** www.abqtrolley.com. $25 adults, $20 seniors 65 and older and students, $13 children 12 and under. AE, DISC, MC, V. Operates 2-4 times daily Tues–Sun Apr–Oct.

OUTDOOR ACTIVITIES

Ballooning

Visitors have a choice of several hot-air balloon operators; rates start at about $160 per person per hour. Call **Rainbow Ryders,** 5601 Eagle Rock Ave. NE (ℭ **505/823-1111;** www.rainbowryders.com), or **World Balloon Corporation,** 1103 La Poblana NW (ℭ **505/293-6800;** www.worldballoon.com).

If you'd rather just watch, go to the annual **Albuquerque International Balloon Fiesta** ★★★, which is held the first through second weekends of October (see "The Most Unforgettable New Mexico Experiences," in chapter 1, and "New Mexico Calendar of Events," in chapter 3, for details).

Biking

Albuquerque is a major bicycling hub in the summer, for both road racers and mountain bikers. For an excellent map of Albuquerque bicycle routes, call the **Albuquerque Parks & Recreation Department** at ℭ **505/768-5300.** You can also find links to many recreation opportunities for adults and kids at **www.cabq.gov/visiting. html**. A great place to bike is **Sandia Peak** (ℭ **505/242-9133;** www.sandiapeak. com) in Cíbola National Forest. You can't take your bike on the tram, but chairlift no. 1 is available for up- or downhill transportation with a bike. Bike rentals are available at the top and bottom of the chairlift. They cost $40 for adult bikes and $30 for junior ones. The lift costs $16 and runs on Saturday and Sunday, with Friday added in July and August, though you'll want to call to be sure. Helmets are mandatory. Bike maps are available; the clearly marked trails range from easy to very difficult.

Down in the valley, there's a **bosque trail** that runs along the Rio Grande, accessed through the Rio Grande Nature Center (see "Especially for Kids," above). To the east, the **Foothills Trail** runs along the base of the mountains. It's a fun, 7-mile-long trail that offers excellent views. Access it by driving east from downtown on Montgomery Boulevard, past the intersection with Tramway Boulevard. Go left on Glenwood Hills Drive and head north about ½ mile before turning right onto a short road that leads to the Embudito trail head.

Northeast Cyclery, 8305 Menaul Blvd. NE (© **505/299-1210**), rents bikes at the rate of $25 per day for front-suspension mountain bikes and $35 per day for road bikes. Multiday discounts are available. Unfortunately, the shop doesn't rent children's bikes. Rentals come with helmets.

Bird-Watching

Bosque del Apache National Wildlife Refuge ★★ (© **505/835-1828;** www.fws.gov/southwest/refuges/newmex/bosque/index.html) is a haven for migratory waterfowl such as snow geese and cranes. It's 90 miles south of Albuquerque on I-25, and it's well worth the drive. See chapter 11 for more details. Closer to town, check out the **Rio Grande Nature Center State Park** (see "Especially for Kids," above).

Fishing

Albuquerque's most notable fishing spot is **Tingley Beach** (© **505/764-6281;** www.cabq.gov/biopark/tingley), stocked weekly with trout, bass, and catfish. It's open daily and is free. To access Tingley from Rio Grande Boulevard, head west to Tingley Drive (Pkwy.) and turn south. Another option is **Shady Lakes** (© **505/898-2568**). Nestled among cottonwood trees, it's near I-25 on Albuquerque's north side. The most common catches are rainbow trout, black bass, bluegill, and channel catfish. To reach Shady Lakes, take I-25 north to the Tramway exit. Follow Tramway Road west for a mile and then go right on NM 313 for ½ mile. **Sandia Lakes Recreational Area** (© **505/771-5190;** www.sandiapueblo.nsn.us), also on NM 313, is another popular fishing spot. There is a bait and tackle shop there.

Golf

There are quite a few public courses in the Albuquerque area. The **Championship Golf Course at the University of New Mexico,** 3601 University Blvd. SE (© **505/277-4546;** www.unmgolf.com), is one of the best in the Southwest and was rated one of the country's top-25 public links by *Golf Digest.* **Desert Greens Golf Course,** 10035 Country Club Lane NW (© **505/898-7001;** www.desertgreensgolf.com), is a popular 18-hole golf course on the west side of town.

golf ON THE SANTA FE TRAIL

Those golfers traveling through Albuquerque and northward will appreciate the nine respected courses that have teamed together to offer customized golf packages, including accommodations. **Golf on the Santa Fe Trail** (© **866/465-3660;** www.santafetrailgolf.com) includes such prestigious courses as the **Black Mesa Golf Club,** just north of Albuquerque at Santa Ana Pueblo (© **505/747-8946;** www.blackmesagolfclub.com), one of the state's premier golf settings since opening in 2003; and **Towa Golf Resort,** north of Santa Fe at Pojoaque Pueblo (© **877/465-3489;** www.golfnewmexico.com), where 9 of the 18 holes were designed by Hale Irwin. To explore the other courses involved, check out their website.

Other Albuquerque courses to check with for tee times are **Ladera**, 3401 Ladera Dr. NW (☎ **505/836-4449**); **Los Altos,** 9717 Copper Ave. NE (☎ **505/298-1897;** www.cabq.gov/golf/los-altos); **Puerto del Sol,** 1800 Girard Blvd. SE (☎ **505/265-5636;** www.cabq.gov/golf/puerto-del-sol); **Arroyo del Oso,** 7001 Osuna Rd. NE (☎ **505/884-7505;** www.cabq.gov/golf/arroyo-del-oso); and **Sandia Golf Club** (☎ **505/798-3990;** www.sandiagolf.com), located at Sandia Resort and Casino on the north end of town.

If you're willing to drive a short distance just outside Albuquerque, you can play at the **Santa Ana Golf Club at Santa Ana Pueblo,** 288 Prairie Star Rd., Bernalillo, NM 87004 (☎ **505/867-9464;** www.santaanagolf.com), which was rated by the *New York Times* as one of the best public golf courses in the country. Club rentals are available (call for information). In addition, **Isleta Pueblo,** 4001 NM 47 (☎ **866/475-3822;** www.isletapueblo.com), south of Albuquerque, has an 18-hole course.

Hiking

The 1½-million-acre **Cíbola National Forest** offers ample hiking opportunities. Within town, the best hike is the **Embudito Trail,** which heads up into the foothills, with spectacular views down across Albuquerque. The 5.5-mile one-way hike is moderate to difficult. Allow 1 to 8 hours, depending on how far you want to go. Access it by driving east from downtown on Montgomery Boulevard past the intersection with Tramway Boulevard. Go left on Glenwood Hills Drive and head north about a half mile before turning right onto a short road that leads to the trail head. The premier Sandia Mountain hike is **La Luz Trail,** a very strenuous journey from the Sandia foothills to the top of the Crest. It's a 15-mile round-trip jaunt, and it's half that if you take the Sandia Peak Tramway (see "The Top Attractions," earlier in this chapter) either up or down. Allow a full day for this hike. Access is off Tramway Boulevard and Forest Service Road 333. For more details contact **Sandia Ranger Station,** NM 337 south toward Tijeras (☎ **505/346-3900;** www.fs.fed.us/r3/cibola).

Horseback Riding

Sometimes I just have to get in a saddle and eat some trail dust. If you get similar hankerings, call the **Hyatt Regency Tamaya Resort and Spa,** 1300 Tuyuna Trail, Santa Ana Pueblo (☎ **505/771-6060;** www.tamaya.hyatt.com). The resort offers 2½-hour-long rides near the Rio Grande for $75 per person. Children must be over 7 years of age and over 4 feet tall. The resort is about 15 miles north of Albuquerque. From I-25 take exit 242, following US 550 west to Tamaya Boulevard, and drive 1½ miles to the resort.

Skiing

The **Sandia Peak Ski Area** is a good place for family skiing. There are plenty of beginner and intermediate runs. (If you're looking for more challenge or more variety, you'd better head north to Santa Fe or Taos.) The ski area has twin base-to-summit chairlifts to its upper slopes at 10,360 feet and a 1,700-foot vertical drop. There are 30 runs (35% beginner, 55% intermediate, 10% advanced) above the day lodge and ski-rental shop. Four chairs and two Pomas accommodate 3,400 skiers an hour. All-day lift tickets are $50 for adults, $40 for ages 6 to 20 and seniors 62 to 71; free for children 46 inches tall or less in ski boots and seniors ages 72 and over.

GETTING PAMPERED: the spa scene

If you're looking to get pampered, you have a few options. **Mark Prado Salon & Spa** (© 505/298-2983 all locations) offers treatments at four locations: 1100 Juan Tabo Blvd. NE; 8001 Wyoming Blvd. NE; 3500 Central Ave. SE 7-B; and Cottonwood Mall, 10,000 Coors Blvd. NE.

Albuquerque's top-two luxurious spa experiences are at the **Hyatt Regency Tamaya Resort & Spa,** 1300 Tuyuna Trail, Santa Ana Pueblo (© 505/867-1234; www.tamaya.hyatt. com), and the **Sandia Resort & Casino,** 30 Rainbow Rd. NE (© 800/526-9366 or 505/796-7500; www.sandiacasino. com). Each offers a broad array of treatments, as well as a sauna and a steam room, in refined atmospheres. The Tamaya is 15 minutes north of Albuquerque, near the village of Bernalillo, while the Sandia is on the north end of town, off Tramway Boulevard.

Rental packages are available. The season runs mid-December to mid-March. Contact the ski area, 10 Tramway Loop NE (© **505/242-9052;** www.sandiapeak.com), for more information, or call the hot line for ski conditions (© **505/857-8977**).

Cross-country skiers can enjoy the trails of the Sandia Wilderness from the ski area, or they can go an hour north to the remote Jemez Wilderness and its hot springs.

Tennis

Albuquerque has 29 public parks with tennis courts. Because of the city's size, your best bet is to call the **Albuquerque Convention and Visitors Bureau** (© **800/284-2282;** www.itsatrip.org) to find out which park is closest to your hotel.

SPECTATOR SPORTS

Baseball

The **Albuquerque Isotopes** play 72 home games as part of the Pacific Coast League in Isotopes Park. Tickets range in price from $6 to $24. For information, contact © **505/924-2255** (www.albuquerquebaseball.com). Isotopes Park is at 1601 Avenida Cesar Chavez SE. Take I-25 south of town to Avenida Cesar Chavez and go east; the stadium is at the intersection of Avenida Cesar Chavez and University Boulevard.

Basketball

The University of New Mexico team, **the Lobos,** plays an average of 16 home games from late November to early March. Capacity crowds cheer the team at the 17,121-seat University Arena (fondly called "the Pit") at University and Stadium boulevards. For tickets and information, call © **505/925-5626** (www.golobos.com).

Football

The **UNM Lobos** football team plays a September-to-November season, usually with five home games, at the 30,000-seat University of New Mexico Stadium, opposite both Albuquerque Sports Stadium and University Arena at University and Stadium boulevards. For tickets and information call © **505/925-5626** (www.golobos.com).

Horse Racing

The **Downs at Albuquerque Racetrack and Casino,** Expo New Mexico fairgrounds (© **505/266-5555** for post times; www.abqdowns.com) is near Lomas and Louisiana boulevards NE. Racing and betting—on thoroughbreds and quarter horses—take place mid-August through mid-November (including the New Mexico State Fair in Sept). The Downs has a glass-enclosed grandstand and exclusive club seating. General admission is free. Simulcast racing happens year-round daily, except Christmas. The 340-slot casino is open daily 10am to 2am, with drinks and dining in the Jockey Club.

SHOPPING A TO Z

Visitors seeking regional specialties will find many **local artists** and **galleries** of interest in Albuquerque, although not as many as in Santa Fe and Taos. The galleries and regional fashion designers around the plaza in Old Town comprise a kind of shopping center for travelers, with more than 40 merchants represented. The Sandia Pueblo runs its own **crafts market** at the reservation, off I-25 at Tramway Road, just beyond Albuquerque's northern city limits.

Albuquerque has three of the largest **shopping malls** in New Mexico, two within 2 blocks of each other on Louisiana Boulevard just north of I-40—Coronado Center and Winrock Center. The other is the Cottonwood Mall on the west mesa, at 10,000 Coors Blvd. NW (© **505/899-7467**). But the city's best mall is the **ABQ Uptown ★★** at Louisiana Boulevard NE and Indian School Road NE (© **505/883-7676;** www. abquptown.com), an outdoor mall with such anchors as Williams Sonoma, Pottery Barn, Sharper Image, Chicos, and Ann Taylor.

Business hours vary, but shops are generally open Monday to Saturday 10am to 6pm; many have extended hours; some have reduced hours; and a few, especially in shopping malls or during the high tourist season, are open on Sunday.

Best Buys

The best buys in Albuquerque are Southwestern regional items, including **arts and crafts** of all kinds—traditional Native American and Hispanic as well as contemporary works. In local Native American art, look for silver and turquoise jewelry, pottery, weavings, baskets, sand paintings, and Hopi *katsina* dolls. Hispanic folk art—handcrafted furniture, tinwork and *retablos,* and religious paintings—is worth seeking out. The best contemporary art is in paintings, sculpture, jewelry, ceramics, and fiber art, including weaving.

Other items of potential interest are Southwestern fashions, gourmet foods, and unique local Native American and Hispanic creations.

By far, the most **galleries** are in Old Town; others are spread around the city, with smaller groupings in the university district and the northeast heights. Consult the brochure published by the **Albuquerque Gallery Association,** *A Select Guide to Albuquerque Galleries,* or Wingspread Communications's annual *The Collector's Guide to Albuquerque,* widely distributed at shops. Once a month, usually from 5 to 9pm on the third Friday, the **Albuquerque Art Business Association** (© **505/244-0362;** www.artscrawlabq.org for information) sponsors an ArtsCrawl to dozens of galleries and studios. It's a great way to meet the artists.

You'll find some interesting shops in the Nob Hill area, which is just west of the University of New Mexico and has an Art Deco feel.

Following are some shopping recommendations for the greater Albuquerque area.

Arts & Crafts

Amapola Gallery ★ Fifty artists and craftspeople show their talents at this lovely cooperative gallery upstairs in the historic 1849 Romero House. You'll find pottery, paintings, textiles, carvings, baskets, jewelry, and other items. 205 Romero St. ⓒ **505/242-4311.** www.amapolagallery.com.

Andrews Pueblo Pottery ★ Carrying Pueblo pottery ranging from the black firings of San Ildefonso to the sand-colored Acoma, this gallery is a place for rich perusing as well as serious buying. Also of note here are Zuni stone fetishes and Hopi *katsinas*. 303 N. Romero NW, Old Town. ⓒ **877/606-0543.** www.andrewspp.com.

Bien Mur Indian Market Center ★ Sandia Pueblo's crafts market, on the reservation, sells turquoise and silver jewelry, pottery, baskets, *katsina* dolls, hand-woven rugs, sand paintings, and other arts and crafts. The market is open Monday through Saturday from 9:30am to 5:30pm and Sunday from 11am to 5:30pm. I-25 at Tramway Rd. NE. ⓒ **800/365-5400** or 505/821-5400. www.sandiapueblo.nsn.us/bienmur.html.

Gallery One This gallery features folk art, jewelry, contemporary crafts, cards and paper, and natural-fiber clothing. In the Nob Hill Shopping Center, 3500 Central Ave. SE. ⓒ **505/268-7449.**

Hispaniae in Old Town ★ 📖 Day of the Dead people and Frida Kahlo faces greet you at this wild shop with everything from kitschy Mexican tableware to fine Oaxacan woodcarvings. 410 Romero St. NW, Old Town. ⓒ **505/244-1533.** www.hispaniae.com.

La Casita de Kaleidoscopes ★ This shop carries kaleidoscopes in a dizzying array (some 500) of styles, from egg- and tepee-shaped to fountains to little paper ones, with over 60 artists represented. 326-D San Felipe NW, in the Poco a Poco Patio in Old Town. ⓒ **505/247-4242.** www.casitascopes.com.

Mariposa Gallery ★★ 🖌 Eclectic contemporary art, jewelry, blown glass, and sculpture fill this Nob Hill shop, with prices that even a travel writer can afford. In the Nob Hill Shopping Center, 3500 Central Ave. SE. ⓒ **505/268-6828.** www.mariposa-gallery.com.

Ortega's Indian Arts and Crafts An institution in Gallup, adjacent to the Navajo Reservation, Ortega's now has this Albuquerque store. It sells, repairs, and appraises silver and turquoise jewelry. 6600 Menaul Blvd. NE, no. 359. ⓒ **505/-881-1231.**

Skip Maisel's 🖌 If you want a real bargain in Native American arts and crafts, this is the place to shop. You'll find a broad range of quality and price here in goods such as pottery, weavings, and *katsinas*. Be sure to check out the 1933 murals by notable Navajo painter Harrison Begay and Pueblo painter Pablita Velarde, which adorn the outside of the store. 510 Central Ave. SW. ⓒ **505/242-6526.**

Tanner Chaney Galleries ★ In business since 1875, this gallery has fine Native American jewelry, pottery, rugs, and more. Most of these items are purchased directly from the artists who make them by hand. 323 Romero NW St., no. 4, Old Town. ⓒ **800/444-2242** or 505/247-2242. www.tannerchaney.com.

Wright's Collection of Indian Art This gallery, first opened in 1907, features a free private museum and carries fine handmade Native American arts and crafts, both contemporary and traditional. 1100 San Mateo Blvd. NE. ☏ **505/266-0120.** www.wrights gallery.com.

Books

Barnes & Noble   On the west side, just north of Cottonwood Mall, this huge bookstore offers plenty of browsing room and a Starbucks Cafe for lounging. The store is known for its large children's section and weekly story-time readings. 3701 Ellison Dr. NW, no. A. ☏ **505/792-4234.** Or at the Coronado Center, 6600 Menaul Blvd. NE. ☏ **505/883-8200.** www.barnesandnoble.com.

Bookworks ★   Selling both new and used books, Bookworks has one of the most complete Southwestern nonfiction and fiction sections in the region. A good place to linger, the store has a coffee bar and an area for readings. It also carries CDs, cassettes, and books on tape. 4022 Rio Grande Blvd. NW. ☏ **505/344-8139.** www.bkwrks.com.

Borders   This branch of the popular chain provides a broad range of books, music, and videos, and hosts in-store appearances by authors, musicians, and artists. Uptown Center, 2240 Q St. NE. ☏ **505/884-7711.** www.borders.com.

Page One ★   This popular local bookstore offers a broad range of new and used books, DVDs, and CDs and often hosts readings by authors. Check out their website to find out the schedule. 11018 Montgomery NE. ☏ **800/521-4122** or 505/294-2026. www.page1 book.com.

Food

The Candy Lady   Having made chocolate for more than 30 years, the Candy Lady is especially known for 21 varieties of fudge, including jalapeño flavor. The chile-*piñon* brittle has a nice zing. 524 Romero St. NW, Old Town. ☏ **800/214-7731** or 505/243-6239. www.thecandylady.com.

Fashion

Albuquerque Pendleton ★   Cuddle up in a large selection of blankets and shawls, and haul them away in a handbag. 1100 San Mateo NE Blvd., Stes. 2 and 4. ☏ **505/255-6444.**

A TASTE OF THE grape

In addition to New Mexico's many enchanting sights, wineries drape the state, providing an excellent way to taste some of the 400-year-old growing tradition. Call to find out about their wine-tasting hours. Two Albuquerque wineries just a short, scenic drive from Old Town include **Anderson Valley Vineyards,** 4920 Rio Grande Blvd. NW, Albuquerque, NM 87107 (☏ **505/344-7266**); and **Casa Rondeña Winery,** 733 Chavez Rd., Los Ranchos de Albuquerque, NM 87107 (☏ **800/706-1699**; www.casa rondena.com). **Sandia Shadows Vineyard and Winery,** 11704 Coronado NE, Albuquerque, NM 87122 (☏ **505/856-1006;** www.vivanewmexico.com/nm/wines.central.sandia.html) and **Gruet Winery,** 8400 Pan-American Hwy. NE, Albuquerque, NM 87113 (☏ **505/821-0055;** www.gruetwinery.com), are in the northeast heights.

All That Glitters Is on Gold

For years, downtown Albuquerque has been reinventing itself and nowhere is the luster more brilliant than on Gold Avenue. A funky boutique street, it's the home of many unique shops and restaurants, well worth a morning or afternoon perusal. Look for "fine, fun, and funky" functional art at **Patrician Design**, 216 Gold Ave. SW (© 505/242-7646; www.patriciandesign.com). Down the street, step into **Ooh! Aah! Jewelry**, 110 Amherst SE (© 505/242-7101; www.oohaahjewelry.com), to find a wide selection of contemporary jewelry and handbags. If you work up an appetite, head to **Gold Street Caffè**.

Gertrude Zachary ★★ This large well of imagination has beaded velvet scarves and elaborate antique furniture, but the real buy here is jewelry, ranging from traditional Native American bracelets and necklaces to wildly kitschy butterfly concho belts. Purses, beaded lamps—this place has anything that a contemporary gal could want. 3300 Central Ave. SE (in the Nob Hill area at Wellsley). © **505/766-4700.** www.gertrudezachary.com.

Gifts/Souvenirs

Jackalope International ★★ Wandering through this vast shopping area is like an adventure to another land—to many lands, really. You'll find Mexican *trasteros* (armoires) next to Balinese puppets. The store sells sculpture, pottery, and Christmas ornaments as well. 6400 San Mateo Blvd. © **505/349-0955.** Also at 834 US 550 in Bernalillo. © **505/867-9813.** www.jackalope.com.

Home Furnishings

Ernest Thompson Furniture ★ Original-design, handcrafted furniture is exhibited in the factory showroom. Thompson is a fifth-generation furniture maker who still uses traditional production techniques. 4531 Osuna Rd. NE (¼ block west of I-25 and ½ block north on Osuna Rd.). © **800/568-2344** or 505/344-1994. www.ernestthompson.com.

El Paso Import Company ★ Advertising "unique furnishings from around the world," this place in the Nob Hill Shopping Center is packed with all manner of tables, *trasteros,* and chairs, most with aged and chipped paint for those who love the worn look. It's a fun place to browse even if you don't buy. 3500 Central SE, Nob Hill. © **888/999-3773.** www.elpasoimportco.com.

Strictly Southwestern You'll find nice, solid pine and oak Southwestern-style furniture here. Lighting, art, pottery, and other interior items are also available. 1321 Eubank Blvd. NE. © **800/336-7838.** www.strictlysouthwestern.com.

Markets

Flea Market Every Saturday and Sunday, year-round, the fairgrounds host this market from 7am to 6pm. It's a great place to browse for turquoise and silver jewelry and locally made crafts, as well as newly manufactured inexpensive goods such as socks and T-shirts. The place takes on a fair atmosphere, with the smell of cotton candy filling the air. There's no admission charge. Expo New Mexico fairgrounds. For information, call the Albuquerque Convention and Visitors Bureau, © **800/284-2282.** www.exponm.com/en/fleamarket.com.

ALBUQUERQUE AFTER DARK

Albuquerque has an active performing-arts and nightlife scene, as befits a city of half a million people. As also befits this area, the performing arts are multicultural, with Hispanic and (to a lesser extent) Native American productions sharing stage space with Anglo works, including theater, opera, symphony, and dance. Albuquerque also attracts many national touring companies. Nightclubs cover the gamut, with rock, jazz, and country predominant.

Complete information on all major cultural events can be obtained from the **Albuquerque Convention and Visitors Bureau** (✆ **800/284-2282;** staffed Mon–Fri 9am–5pm, with recorded information after hours). Current listings appear in the two daily newspapers; detailed weekend arts calendars can be found in Friday's *Journal.* The monthly *On the Scene* also carries entertainment listings.

Tickets for nearly all major entertainment and sporting events can be obtained from **Ticketmaster,** 4004 Carlisle Blvd. NE (✆ **800/745-3000**). Discount tickets are often available for midweek and matinee performances; check with individual theater or concert hall box offices.

The Performing Arts
CLASSICAL MUSIC

New Mexico Ballet Company   Founded in 1972, the state's oldest ballet company holds most of its performances at Popejoy Hall. Typically there's a fall production such as *Dracula,* a holiday one such as *The Nutcracker* or *A Christmas Carol,* and a contemporary spring production. 4200 Wyoming Blvd. NE, Ste. B2, Albuquerque, NM 87154-1518. ✆ **505/292-4245.** www.newmexicoballet.org. Tickets $15–$40, depending on the performance and venue.

New Mexico Symphony Orchestra ★   My first introduction to symphony was with the NMSO. Although I was so young that I didn't quite understand the novelty of hearing live symphony, I loved picking out the distinct sounds and following as they melded together. The NMSO first played in 1932 (long before I attended, thank you) and has continued as a strong cultural force throughout the state. The

THE MAJOR concert & performance HALLS

- **Journal Pavilion,** 5601 University Blvd. NE (✆ **505/452-5100**).
- **Keller Hall,** University of New Mexico, Cornell Street at Redondo Drive South NE (✆ **505/277-4569**).
- **KiMo Theatre ★★**, 423 Central Ave. NW (✆ **505/768-3544**). Take a self-guided tour of this historic 1927 theater to see elaborate corbels and mosaic tile

work in Pueblo Deco style. It's open Tuesday to Friday 8:30am to 4:30pm and Saturday 11am to 5pm.
- **Popejoy Hall,** University of New Mexico, Cornell Street at Redondo Drive South NE (✆ **505/277-3824**).
- **South Broadway Cultural Center,** 1025 Broadway Blvd. SE (✆ **505/848-1320**).

symphony performs classics and pops, as well as family and neighborhood concerts. It plays for more than 20,000 grade-school students and visits communities throughout the state in its annual tour program. Concert venues are generally Popejoy Hall on the University of New Mexico campus, the National Hispanic Cultural Center, and the Rio Grande Zoo, all of which are accessible to people with disabilities. Guillermo Figueroa is the music director and conductor. I recommend going to one of the outdoor concerts at the band shell at the Rio Grande Zoo. 4407 Menaul Blvd. NE. © **800/251-6676** for tickets and information, or 505/881-9590. www.nmso.org. Ticket prices vary with concert; call for details.

Theater

Albuquerque Little Theatre   The Albuquerque Little Theatre has been offering a variety of productions ranging from comedies to dramas to musicals since 1930. Eight plays are presented here annually during a July-to-June season. Located across from Old Town, the theater offers plenty of free parking. 224 San Pasquale Ave. SW. © **505/242-4750.** www.albuquerquelittletheatre.org. Tickets $22; $10 for student rush tickets purchased 30 min. before showtime; $20 seniors. Box office Mon–Fri 11am–5:30pm.

Vortex Theatre ★   A 35-year-old community theater known for its innovative productions, the Vortex is Albuquerque's "Off-Broadway" theater, presenting a range of plays from classic to original. You'll see such plays as *I Hate Hamlet* by Paul Rudnik and *Death & the Maiden* by Ariel Dorfman. Performances take place on Friday and Saturday at 8pm and on Sunday at 6pm. The black-box theater seats 90. 2004½ Central Ave. SE. © **505/247-8600.** www.vortexabq.org. All tickets $15; student rush 5 min. prior $10.

The Club & Music Scene

ROCK/JAZZ

Burt's Tiki Lounge   This club won the weekly paper *Alibi's* award for the best variety of drinks. The club offers live music Monday to Saturday 8pm to 2am and charges no cover. 313 Gold Ave. © **505/247-2878.** www.burtstikilounge.com.

Ibiza ★★   At Hotel Andaluz, this glossy rooftop hotspot with a Mediterranean ambience features city views, a broad patio, and DJ or live music. It's a great place to dance. Happy hour is Wednesday to Friday 5 to 8pm; the club is open Wednesday to Saturday 9pm to 1:30am with a $10 cover. 125 2nd St. NW. © **505/243-9090.** www. hotelandaluz.com.

Kelly's BYOB ★   Near the university, Kelly's is a local brewpub, set in a renovated auto-body shop. The place has tasty pub fare, excellent brew specials, and live music for special events. 3222 Central SE. © **505/262-2739.** www.kellysbrewpub.com.

Nob Hill Bar & Grill   The college and post-college crowd flocks this restaurant to savor a broad selection of beers, tequilas, and whiskeys and nosh on Kobe beef burgers and fish tacos. 3128 Central Ave. SE. © **505/266-4455.** www.upscalejoint.com.

One Up Elevated Lounge ★   In a contemporary setting with city views and cushy couches, this spot offers something new nightly. Dance music ranges from salsa to R&B to rock, with food and drink specials to complement the mood. Check out their website to see what's happening that week. 301 Central NW, 2nd floor. © **505/242-1966.** www.oneupabq.com.

O'Niell's Pub   A favorite club in the University of New Mexico area, this Irish bar serves up good pub fare as well as live local music on Saturday nights and Celtic and bluegrass on Sunday evenings. 4310 Central SE. ✆ **505/255-6782.** www.oniells.com.

Q Bar ★   With sophisticated decor—lots of plush couches and comfy chairs in bright tones—this lounge in the Hotel Albuquerque at Old Town offers innovative cuisine, often live entertainment, and a dance floor. On weekend nights it's packed with 20- and 30-somethings. It's open Tuesday to Saturday 4pm to 1am. 800 Rio Grande Blvd. NW. ✆ **505/843-6300.**

More Entertainment

Albuquerque's best nighttime attraction is the **Sandia Peak Tramway,** from which you can enjoy a view nonpareil of the Rio Grande Valley and the city lights.

The best place to catch foreign films, art films, and limited-release productions is the **Guild Cinema,** 3405 Central Ave. NE (✆ **505/255-1848**). For film classics, check out the **Southwest Film Center,** on the UNM campus (✆ **505/277-5608**), which has double features, changing nightly (when classes are in session). In addition, Albuquerque has a number of first-run movie theaters whose numbers you can find in the local telephone directory.

Many travelers like to include a little dice-throw and slot-machine play in their trip to New Mexico. Those who do are in luck, with the expansive **Sandia Resort & Casino,** north of I-25 and ¼ mile east on Tramway Boulevard (✆ **800/526-9366;** www.sandiacasino.com). The $80-million structure sits on Sandia Pueblo land and has outstanding views of the Sandia Mountains. Built in pueblo architectural style, the graceful casino has a 3,650-seat outdoor amphitheater, three restaurants, a lounge, more than 1,800 slot and video poker machines, the largest poker room in the state, and blackjack, roulette, and craps tables. It's open from 8am to 4am Sunday to Wednesday and 24 hours Thursday to Saturday. Fifteen minutes south of town, the **Hard Rock Hotel & Casino Albuquerque,** 11000 Broadway SE (✆ **877/747-5382** or 505/724-3800; www.hardrockcasinoabq.com), is a luxurious, air-conditioned casino (featuring blackjack, poker, slots, bingo, and keno) with a full-service restaurant, nonsmoking section, and free bus transportation on request. It's open Thursday to Saturday 24 hours, Sunday to Wednesday 9am to 5pm.

TOURING THE PUEBLOS AROUND ALBUQUERQUE

Ten Native American pueblos are located within an hour's drive of central Albuquerque. Two of them, Acoma and Laguna, are discussed in chapter 9, "Northwestern New Mexico." The others, from south to north, are discussed here, followed by Coronado and Jemez state monuments, which preserve ancient pueblo ruins. If you'd like to combine a tour of the archaeological sites and inhabited pueblos, consider driving the **Jemez Mountain Trail ★**. Head north on I-25 to Bernalillo, where you can visit the Coronado State Monument. Continue west on US 550 to Zia Pueblo. Six miles farther on US 550 takes you to NM 4, where you'll turn north and drive through orchards and along narrow cornfields of Jemez Pueblo. Farther north on NM 4, you'll find another archaeological site, the Jemez State Monument.

PUEBLO ETIQUETTE: do's & don'ts

Those who are not Native American are welcome to visit Indian pueblos and reservations; however, there are some guidelines you should follow as a guest on tribal land.

Native American reservations and pueblos have their own systems of government and, therefore, their own laws and regulations. If you don't follow their laws, you will be subject to punishment as outlined by the American Indian government. The best thing that could happen is that you'd simply be asked to leave.

Stay out of cemeteries and ceremonial rooms, such as kivas, as these are sacred grounds. Remember, these are not museums or tourist attractions in their own right; they are people's homes. Don't peek into doors and windows, and don't climb on top of buildings.

Most pueblos require a permit to carry a camera or to sketch or paint on location, and many prohibit photography at any time. If you want to take pictures, make a video, or sketch anything on pueblo or reservation land, find out about permits and fees in advance.

Do not wander around on your own if the residents have asked that you visit the pueblo only by guided tour. If, on a guided tour, you are asked not to take pictures of something, or are asked to stay out of a certain area, please follow the guidelines. If you don't have to visit by guided tour, don't go into private buildings without being escorted by someone who lives there or who has the authority to take you inside.

Be respectful of ceremonial dances. Do not speak during dances or ceremonies and don't applaud at the end of the dance—they aren't dancing for your amusement; they are dancing as part of their ceremony.

In short, be courteous and don't do anything you wouldn't do in your own mother's house.

You'll also find Jemez Springs, where you can stop for a hot soak. The road continues to the Los Alamos area, where you can see the spectacular ruins at Bandelier National Monument. From there you have the option of returning the way you came or via Santa Fe.

Area Pueblos

ISLETA PUEBLO

Located just 14 miles south of Albuquerque, off I-25 or US 85, **Isleta Pueblo,** P.O. Box 1270, Isleta, NM 87022 (© **505/869-3111;** www.isletapueblo.com), is the largest of the Tiwa-speaking pueblos, comprising several settlements on the west side of the Rio Grande. The largest village, Shiaw-iba, contains the Mission of San Agustin de Isleta, built in 1613, partially destroyed during the Pueblo Revolt, and then rebuilt in 1716. On the quiet plaza is Isleta's church, St. Augustine, built in 1629, with thick adobe walls and vigas adorning the ceiling. It is one of the oldest churches in New Mexico.

Isleta women potters make red wares distinctive for their red-and-black designs on white backgrounds. The tribe operates the **Hard Rock Casino and Resort** (© **877/747-5382** or 505/724-3800; www.hardrockcasinoabq.com) and fishing and camping areas at Isleta Lakes. An RV site costs $30. No tent sites are available. A fishing permit is $15 and can be purchased at the recreation area.

Excursions from Albuquerque

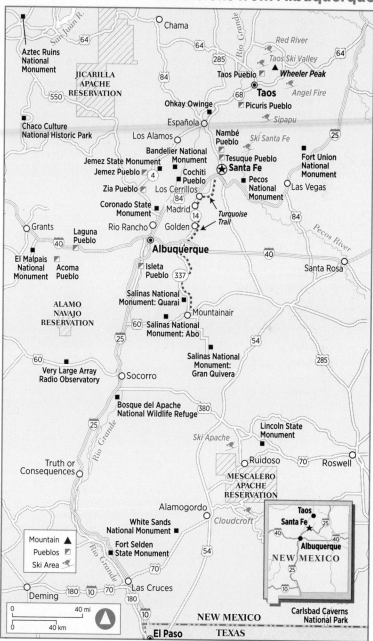

Aztec Ruins National Monument

JICARILLA APACHE RESERVATION

Chaco Culture National Historic Park

San Juan R.

Chama

Rio Grande

Red River

Taos Ski Valley

Wheeler Peak

Taos Pueblo

Taos

Angel Fire

Ohkay Owinge

Picuris Pueblo

Española

Sipapu

Los Alamos

Ohkay Owinge

Nambé Pueblo

Ski Santa Fe

Bandelier National Monument

Fort Union National Monument

Jemez State Monument

Tesuque Pueblo

Santa Fe

Jemez Pueblo

Cochiti Pueblo

Zia Pueblo

Los Cerrillos

Pecos National Monument

Las Vegas

Coronado State Monument

Madrid

Turquoise Trail

Pecos River

Grants

Laguna Pueblo

Rio Rancho

Golden

El Malpais National Monument

Acoma Pueblo

Albuquerque

Santa Rosa

Isleta Pueblo

ALAMO NAVAJO RESERVATION

Salinas National Monument: Quarai

Mountainair

Salinas National Monument: Abo

Very Large Array Radio Observatory

Socorro

Salinas National Monument: Gran Quivera

Bosque del Apache National Wildlife Refuge

Lincoln State Monument

Ski Apache

Truth or Consequences

Ruidoso

Roswell

MESCALERO APACHE RESERVATION

Alamogordo

Cloudcroft

White Sands National Monument

Mountain

Pueblos

Ski Area

Fort Selden State Monument

Taos

Santa Fe

Albuquerque

NEW MEXICO

Rio Grande

Deming

Las Cruces

0   40 mi

0   40 km

NEW MEXICO

TEXAS

El Paso

Carlsbad Caverns National Park

The Isleta hold an evergreen dance sometime in late February. The big day of the year is the feast day honoring St. Augustine, August 28, when a morning Mass and procession are followed by an afternoon harvest dance.

The pueblo is open to visitors daily during daylight hours. Admission is free. Photography is limited to the church.

SANDIA PUEBLO

Established about 1300, **Sandia Pueblo,** 481 Sandia Loop, Bernalillo, NM 87004 (© **505/867-3317;** www.sandiapueblo.nsn.us), is one of the few pueblos visited by Coronado's contingent in 1540. Remains of that village, known as Nafiat, or "sandy," are still visible near the present church. The Sandia people temporarily fled to Hopi country after the Pueblo rebellion of 1680, but they returned to the Rio Grande in 1742. Many of today's 4,000 Tiwa-speaking (Tanoan) inhabitants work in Albuquerque or at Pueblo Enterprises. They also run the **Bien Mur Indian Market Center** on Tramway Road (© **800/365-5400** or 505/821-5400) and **Sandia Casino** (© **800/526-9366;** www.sandiacasino.com). It's about 5 miles north of Albuquerque off I-25.

The pueblo celebrates its St. Anthony feast day on June 13, with a midmorning Mass, procession, and afternoon corn dance. Another dance honors newly elected governors in January.

The pueblo is open to visitors weekdays during daylight hours, and admission is free. No photographing, video recording, or sketching is allowed.

SANTA ANA PUEBLO

Though partially abandoned, **Santa Ana Pueblo,** 2 Dove Rd., Santa Ana Pueblo, NM 87004 (© **505/771-6700;** www.santaana.org), on the lower Jemez River, claims a population of about 500. Many "residents" who maintain family homes at the pueblo actually live nearer the stream's confluence with the Rio Grande, in Ranchos de Santa Ana, near Bernalillo, where farming is more productive. A handful of craftspeople in the old village produce pottery, woodcarvings, ceremonial bands, red-cloth belts, and unique wooden crosses with straw inlay.

Guests are normally welcomed only on ceremonial days. Pueblo members perform the turtle and corn dances on New Year's Day; the eagle, elk, buffalo, and deer dances on January 6; and several days of dances at Christmastime. Feast Day celebrations honoring Saint Ann take place on July 26.

The pueblo is about 15 to 20 miles north of Albuquerque, reached via I-25 to Bernalillo, and then 8 miles northwest on US 550. Admission is free and allowed only on dance days; photography is prohibited. Visitors can stay on Santa Ana Pueblo land at the **Hyatt Regency Tamaya Resort** (p. 85). The **Santa Ana Star Casino** (© **505/867-0000;** www.santaanastar.com) offers all manner of gambling.

ZIA PUEBLO

Zia Pueblo, 135 Capitol Square Dr., Zia Pueblo, NM, 87053 (© **505/867-3304**), which has 720 inhabitants, blends in so perfectly with the soft tans of the stone and sand of the desertlike land around it that it's very hard to see—it's like a chameleon on a tree trunk. The pueblo is best known for its famous sun symbol—now the official symbol of the state of New Mexico—adapted from a pottery design showing three rays going in each of the four directions from a sun, or circle. It is hailed in the pledge to the state flag as "a symbol of perfect friendship among united cultures."

Zia has a reputation for excellence in pottery making. Its pottery is identified by its unglazed terra-cotta coloring, traditional geometric designs, and plant and animal motifs painted on a white slip. Paintings, weaving, and sculptures are also prized products of the artists of the Zia community. Their work can be viewed at the **Zia Cultural Center** located at the pueblo. Our Lady of the Assumption, the patron saint, is given a celebratory corn dance on her day, August 15.

The pueblo is about 17 miles northwest of Bernalillo, just off of US 550. It's open to visitors daily during daylight hours, and admission is free. Photography is not permitted.

JEMEZ PUEBLO

The more than 2,500 **Jemez Pueblo** natives—including descendants of the Pecos Pueblo, east of Santa Fe, abandoned in 1838—are the only remaining people to speak the Towa dialect of the Tanoan group. The Jemez are famous for their excellent dancing and feast-making; their feast days attract residents from other pueblos, turning the celebrations into multitribal fairs. Two rectangular kivas are central points for groups of dancers. However, in recent years the pueblo has been closed to visitors. Though they are allowed to visit on dance days, the pueblo has become close-mouthed about when dances occur. However, visitors can partake of the crafts at local shops along NM 4 and at the Walatowa Visitor Center (see "Historic Culture with a Hint of Honey," below). The primary craft is Jemez pottery.

On weekends April through mid-October, weather permitting, arts and crafts and traditional foods are sold across the street from the visitor center at the **Jemez Red Rocks Open-Air Market.**

You can enjoy fishing and picnicking along the Jemez River on government forestlands and camping at the Dragonfly Recreation Area. Call about getting permits. The pueblo, P.O. Box 100, Jemez Pueblo, NM 87024 (© **575/834-7539;** www.jemezpueblo.org), is 55 miles northwest of Albuquerque via I-25 to Bernalillo, US 550 to San Ysidro, and NM 4 for 6 final miles.

SAN FELIPE PUEBLO

San Felipe Pueblo, a conservative pueblo of 3,500 people, located on a mesa on the west bank of the Rio Grande, is known for its beautiful ritual ceremonies. The plaza has been worn into the shape of a bowl by the feet of San Felipe's dancers over the centuries. In the grandest of these dances, hundreds of men, women, and children move through their rhythmic steps all day long in the spring corn dance on May 1, performed in honor of the pueblo's patron, St. Philip (San Felipe). The dancing is done to a great chorus of male singers intoning music that reaches back into prehistory and evokes strong emotions in participants and in visitors, too. Another notable event here is a corn dance on January 6.

San Felipe Pueblo, P.O. Box 4339, San Felipe, NM 87001 (© **505/867-3381**), is 30 miles northeast of Albuquerque via I-25 and an access road. Admission is free. Photography and sketching are not permitted. The pueblo is open to visitors during daylight hours. **Casino Hollywood,** exit 252 off I-25 north of Albuquerque (© **505/867-6700;** www.sanfelipecasino.com), offers most types of gambling.

A visit to the **Kasha-Katuwe Tent Rocks National Monument** ★★, north of Albuquerque (© 505/761-8700; www.blm.gov/nm/st/en.html; see "Visit Us," then "Special Areas"), offers a lunar landscape pocked by white cone-shaped rocks. Hikers follow a wash through the formations, ending above them. It's a good hike for kids, since the round-trip distance is only 2 miles—about 1½ hours—and it's the kind of place to wander. No supplies are available, so it's best to get them in Albuquerque or Santa Fe. To reach the monument from Albuquerque, take I-25 north to the exit for Santo Domingo/Cochiti Lake Recreation Area (exit 259) onto NM 22. Follow the signs. Admission is $5 per vehicle. The monument is open daily April to October 7am to 7pm, and November to March 8am to 5pm.

SANTO DOMINGO PUEBLO

One of New Mexico's largest pueblos, with 3,500 residents, this farming community on the east bank of the Rio Grande is also one of the state's most traditional. Craftspeople are known for their beautiful silver jewelry, unique necklaces of *heishi* (shell fragments), innovative pottery, and fine weaving.

At the dramatic **Santo Domingo Pueblo** feast day, August 4, the corn dance is performed as it is done nowhere else. It is a lavish production involving clowns, scores of singers and drummers, and 500 tireless and skilled dancers in imaginative traditional costumes. Other festive occasions during the year include the Easter spring corn dance and basket dance and an arts-and-crafts festival on Labor Day weekend, with more than 300 artisans in attendance.

Santo Domingo Pueblo, P.O. Box 99, Santo Domingo, NM 87052 (© **505/465-2214**), is 40 miles northeast of Albuquerque via I-25 north to NM 22. The pueblo is open daily to visitors during daylight hours. Admission is free, but no photography or sketching is permitted.

COCHITI PUEBLO

Occupied continuously since about the 13th century, **Cochiti Pueblo,** P.O. Box 70, Cochiti Pueblo, NM 87072 (© **505/465-2244;** www.pueblodecochiti.org), the northernmost of the Keresan-speaking pueblos, stretches along the Rio Grande. Its Church of San Buenaventura, though rebuilt and remodeled since, still contains sections of its original 1628 structure.

Cochiti (pop. 1,500) is well known for its pottery, especially the famous "storyteller" figures created by Helen Cordero. Beadwork and soft leather moccasins are other craft specialties. The pueblo's double-headed dance drums, made from hollowed-out cottonwood logs and covered with leather, are used in ceremonies throughout the Rio Grande area.

San Buenaventura Feast Day, when the corn and rain dances are performed, is July 14. Other events include a buffalo dance December 25, and other dances December 26 to 29.

The pueblo is about 40 miles north of Albuquerque, via I-25, and then north on NM 22. It is open to visitors daily during daylight hours; admission is free. Photography, sketching, and tape recording are not permitted. Cochiti Lake, though fairly silty, is popular for watersports, especially windsurfing. Tent Rocks National Monument, on Cochiti Pueblo land, is a fun place to hike.

A State Monument in the Area

Coronado State Monument ★   When Spanish explorer Francisco Vásquez de Coronado traveled through this region in 1540–41 while searching for the Seven Cities of Cíbola, he wintered at a village on the west bank of the Rio Grande—probably one of the ruins of the ancient Anasazi Pueblo known as Kuaua. Those excavated ruins have been preserved in this state monument.

Hundreds of rooms can be seen, and a kiva has been restored so that visitors can descend a ladder into the enclosed space, once the site of sacred rites. Unique multicolored murals, depicting human and animal forms, were found on successive layers of wall plaster in this and other kivas here; some examples are displayed in the monument's small archaeological museum.

485 Kuaua Rd., Bernalillo. ✆ **505/867-5351.** www.nmmonuments.org. Admission $3 adults, free for children 16 and under. Wed–Mon 8:30am–5pm. Closed New Year's Day, Easter, Thanksgiving, Christmas. Located 20 miles north of Albuquerque; take I-25 to Bernalillo and US 550 west for 1¾ miles.

Jemez Springs

Getting to this village along the Jemez River is half the fun. You'll drive the **Jemez Mountain Trail** ★ into the Jemez Mountains, a trip that can provide a relaxing retreat and/or an exhilarating adventure. In the area are historic sites and relaxing hot springs, as well as excellent stream fishing, hiking, and cross-country skiing. You may want to combine a drive through this area with a visit to Los Alamos and Bandelier National Monument (see chapter 7).

Historic Culture with a Hint of Honey

Jemez Pueblo, home to more than 3,000, no longer welcomes visitors except on selected days. However, visitors can get a taste of the Jemez culture at the **Walatowa Visitor Center,** on NM 4, 8 miles north of the junction with US 550 (✆ **575/834-7235;** www.jemez-pueblo.org). A museum presents the history of the Jemez people and displays pottery and drums. A gift shop sells mostly fake Native American art, but also a few real pieces from the pueblo. The shop also offers information about hiking and scenic tour routes. While in the area, you may encounter Jemez people sitting under *ramadas* (thatch-roofed lean-tos) selling home-baked bread, cookies, and pies. If you're lucky, they may also be making fry bread, which you can smother with honey for one of New Mexico's more delectable treats. The center is open Tuesday to Saturday 10am to 5pm, Sunday noon to 5pm.

SAMPLING NATURE'S nectars

The waters running through the Jemez area are high in mineral content. In fact, the manager of **Jemez Springs Bath House,** 62 NM 4, on the Jemez Springs Plaza (☏ **575/829-3303;** www.jemezspringsbathhouse.com), says they are so healing, more than once she's had to run after visitors who walked off without their canes. This bathhouse was one of the first structures to be built in what is now Jemez Springs. Built in the 1870s of river rock and mud, it has thick walls and a richly herbal scent. You soak in individual tubs in either the men's side or the women's side. In back are a series of massage rooms, where the spa offers a full range of treatments. In front is a gift shop packed with interesting soaps and soulful gifts. Jemez Springs Bath House is open daily 10am to 8pm.

Another option in town is the **Giggling Springs** ★ (☏ **575/829-9175;** www.gigglingsprings.com), across the street from the Laughing Lizard. A small

outdoor pool, surrounded by sandstone and funky art, highlights this place. The Jemez River acts as a cold plunge. It's open Wednesday to Sunday 11am to 8pm, with an abbreviated schedule in winter. Reservations recommended.

At **Ponderosa Valley Vineyard & Winery,** 3171 NM 290, Ponderosa, NM 87044 (☏ **800/946-3657** or 575/834-7487; www.ponderosawinery.com), 3 miles off NM 4 south of Jemez Springs, you'll find a quaint country store with some of New Mexico's best wines. The vintners preside over a small curved bar and will pour you delectable tastes while telling stories of the history of wine in New Mexico and of the Jemez area, where they have lived and grown grapes for more than 3 decades. A 10- to 15-minute tour will take you through the cellar and production buildings. You'll likely want to take a bottle with you. They range in price from $12 to $30.

North of town you'll come to the **Soda Dam,** a strange and beautiful mineral mass formed by travertine deposits—minerals that precipitate out of geothermal springs. Considered a sacred site by Native Americans, it has a gushing waterfall and caves. During the warm months, it's a popular swimming hole.

Jemez State Monument ★ A stop at this small monument takes you on a journey through the history of the Jemez people. The journey begins in the museum, which tells the tale of Giusewa, "place of boiling waters," the original Tewa name of the area. Then it moves out into the mission ruins, whose story is told on small plaques that juxtapose the first impressions of the missionaries against the reality of the Jemez life. The missionaries saw the Jemez people as barbaric and set out to settle them. Part of the process involved hauling up river stones and erecting 6-foot-thick walls of the Mission of San José de los Jemez (founded in 1621) in the early 17th century. Excavations in 1921–22 and 1935–37 unearthed this massive complex through which you may wander. You enter through a broad doorway to a room that once held elaborate fresco paintings, the room tapering back to the nave, with a giant bell tower above.

18160 NM 4 (P.O. Box 143), Jemez Springs. ☏ **505/829-3530.** www.nmmonuments.org. Admission $3 adults, free for children 17 and under. Wed–Mon 8:30am–5pm. Closed New Year's Day, Easter, Thanksgiving, Christmas. From Albuquerque, take NM 550 (NM 44) to NM 4 and then continue on NM 4 for about 18 miles.

WHERE TO STAY & DINE

Cañon del Rio Retreat & Spa ★   Set above a cottonwood-shaded arch of the Jemez River, the adobe-style Cañon del Rio offers comfortable rooms around a courtyard, each named after a Native American tribe. Each has a sliding glass door that opens out to a patio where there's a (not very clean) fountain. Located a short walk from the river, guests can fish if they'd like. The lap pool, heated in summer, offers sunbathing and swimming. The beds are comfortable, and the bathrooms are very functional. The Great Room has a cozy, welcoming feel, with a big-screen TV, as well as a large table where breakfast (such as blue-corn blueberry pancakes) is served family style. An elegant new spa offers a variety of treatments.

16445 NM 4, Jemez Springs, NM 87025. © **505/829-4377.** www.canondelrio.com. 6 units. $119–$200 double, depending on the season. Rates include full gourmet breakfast. AE, DISC, MC, V. **Amenities:** Jacuzzi; outdoor pool; spa. *In room:* A/C, hair dryer, Wi-Fi.

The Laughing Lizard Inn & Cafe ★ AMERICAN   This is the kind of small-town cafe that doesn't have to try to have a personality. It already has thick adobe walls, wood floors, and a wood-burning stove for its innate charm. Added touches are the brightly painted walls and funky old tables. The menu is eclectic—most dishes have a bit of an imaginative flair. The burritos come in a variety of types, such as fresh spinach with black beans, mushrooms, jack cheese, salsa, and guacamole. The homemade pizzas, made with blue-corn crusts, feature ingredients such as pesto, sun-dried tomatoes, and feta, or more basic ones with red sauce as well. Beer and wine are served, and there are daily dessert treats such as *piñon* pie, chocolate mousse, and berry cobbler. The staff is friendly and accommodating. A small inn attached to the cafe provides inexpensive rooms that are clean but a bit timeworn.

17526 NM 4, Jemez Springs, NM 87025. © **575/829-3108.** www.thelaughinglizard.com. Main courses $5–$10 lunch, and $6–$18 dinner. DISC, MC, V. Wed–Sat 8am–7:45pm; Sun 8am–4:45pm.

THREE HISTORIC MISSIONS

Salinas Pueblo Missions National Monument ★ 🎁   These rarely visited ruins provide a unique glimpse into history. The Spanish conquistadors' Salinas Jurisdiction, on the east side of the Manzano Mountains (southeast of Albuquerque), was an important 17th-century trade center because of the salt extracted by the Native Americans from the salt lakes. Franciscan priests, utilizing native labor, constructed missions of Abo red sandstone and blue-gray limestone for the native converts. The ruins of some of the most durable missions—along with evidence of preexisting Anasazi and Mogollon cultures—are the highlights of a visit here. The monument consists of three separate units: the ruins of Abo, Quarai, and Gran Quivira. They are situated around the quiet town of Mountainair, 75 miles southeast of Albuquerque at the junction of US 60 and NM 55.

Abo (© **505/847-2400**) boasts the 40-foot-high ruins of the **Mission of San Gregorio de Abo,** a rare example of medieval architecture in the United States.

A RENOVATED relic

In Mountainair, the **Shaffer Hotel and Restaurant ★**, 103 W. Main St. (*©* **888/595-2888** or 505/847-2888; www.shafferhotel.com), offers a fun glimpse into the past. Renovated by Joel Marks, who stumbled on the place while riding his Harley through the Manzano Mountains, it has a stone fireplace and molded tin ceiling, as well as original Tiffany stained-glass windows. The attached restaurant is even more remarkable, with bright Southwest Art Deco murals on the ceiling, and

chandeliers sporting Native American symbols. Diners enjoy huevos rancheros and breakfast burritos. Built in the 1920s by blacksmith Clem "Pop" Shaffer, it also has a curios shop named after the founder, selling turquoise jewelry, dreamcatchers, and *katsinas*. The hotel includes 19 rooms, some with shared bathroom. The rooms are fairly basic, but will serve those who like frontier-style antique hotels. Prices range from $28 to $89.

Quarai (*©* **505/847-2290**) preserves the largely intact remains of the **Mission of La Purísima Concepción de Cuarac** (1630). Its vast size, 100 feet long and 40 feet high, contrasts with the modest size of the pueblo mounds. A small museum in the visitor center has a scale model of the original church, along with a selection of artifacts found at the site. **Gran Quivira** (*©* **505/847-2770**) once had a population of 1,500. The pueblo has 300 rooms and 7 kivas. Rooms dating from 1300 can be seen. There are indications that an older village, dating from 800, may have previously stood here. Ruins of two churches (one almost 140 ft. long) and a convent have been preserved. The visitor center includes a museum with many artifacts from the site and shows a 40-minute movie about the excavation of some 200 rooms, plus a short video of the pueblo's history. All three pueblos and the churches that were constructed above them are believed to have been abandoned in the 1670s.

Self-guided tour pamphlets can be obtained at the units' respective visitor centers and at the **Salinas Pueblo Missions National Monument Visitor Center** in Mountainair, on US 60, 1 block west of the intersection of US 60 and NM 55. The visitor center offers an audiovisual presentation on the region's history, a bookstore, and an art exhibit.

P.O. Box 517, Mountainair. *©* **505/847-2585.** www.nps.gov/sapu. Free admission. Sites summer daily 9am–6pm (till 5pm rest of year). Visitor center in Mountainair daily 8am–5pm. Closed New Year's Day, Thanksgiving, Christmas. Abo is 9 miles west of Mountainair on US 60. Quarai is 8 miles north of Mountainair on NM 55. Gran Quivira is 25 miles south of Mountainair on NM 55. All roads are paved.

EN ROUTE TO SANTA FE: THE TURQUOISE TRAIL ★★

NM 14, known as "the Turquoise Trail," begins about 16 miles east of downtown Albuquerque, at I-40's Cedar Crest exit, and winds some 46 miles to Santa Fe along the east side of the Sandia Mountains. This state-designated scenic and historic route traverses the revived ghost towns of Golden, Madrid, and Cerrillos, where gold, silver, coal, and turquoise were once mined in great quantities. Modern-day settlers, mostly artists and craftspeople, have brought a renewed frontier spirit to the old mining towns.

SANDIA CREST   As you start along the Turquoise Trail, you may want to turn left onto Sandia Crest Road and drive about 5 minutes to the **Tinkertown Museum ★**, 121 Sandia Crest Rd. (© **505/281-5233;** www.tinkertown.com). The creation of Ross Ward, who took 40 years to carve, collect, and construct the place, it is mostly a miniatures museum, featuring dollhouse-type exhibits of a mining town, a circus, and other venues, with push buttons to make the little characters move. The building itself is constructed of glass bottles, wagon wheels, and horseshoes, among other ingredients. Great fun for the kids here. It's open daily from April to October from 9am to 6pm. Adults $3, children 4 to 16 $1.

GOLDEN   Golden is approximately 10 miles north of the Sandia Park junction on NM 14. Its sagging houses, with their missing boards and the wind whistling through the broken eaves, make it a purist's ghost town. There's a general store widely known for its large selection of well-priced jewelry, and across the street, a bottle seller's "glass garden." Be sure to slow down and look for the village church, a great photo opportunity, on the east side of the road. Nearby are the ruins of a pueblo called **Paako,** abandoned around 1670.

Mining Town Art Walk

Once a fabled mining town, Madrid has become a notable arts village, a great place to wander on a sunny day. Start on the south end of town at **Al Leedom Studio,** 2485 NM 14 (© 505/473-2054; www.alleedom.com), where the studio's namesake sells inventive glassware, made in New Mexico from recycled glass. Around the corner, step into the **Painted Horse Gallery,** 2850 NM 14 (© 505/473-5900; www.loonesome-dovey.com), an intimate place showing modern landscape paintings by Dean Dovey, as well as jewelry and gifts. Just down the street, **Jezebel,** 2860 NM 14 (© 505/471-3795; www.jezebelgallery.com), has lamps with dazzling slumped-glass shades. The shop also has a soda fountain selling Starbucks Coffee, breakfast items, and burgers.

Next door, **Indigo Gallery ★**, 2584 NM 14 (© 505/438-6202; www.indigogallery.com), represents 20 artists who live in New Mexico, their colorful work ranging from realism to abstract. Stop for coffee and pastries at **Java Junction,** 2855 NM 14 (© 505/438-2772; www.java-junction.com), where you'll want to gawk over their vast hot sauce collection, including brands named "Scorned Woman," "Cowboy Cayenne," and "Original Death Sauce." If you'd like to stay the night, inquire about their Victorian suite upstairs. On the north end of town, check out **Seppanen & Daughters Fine Textiles ★**, 2879 NM 14 (© 505/424-7470; www.finetextiles.com), a quaint house draped floor to ceiling with weavings from lands as near as Navajo and as distant as Tibet.

MADRID Madrid (pronounced *Mah*-drid) is about 12 miles north of Golden. This town and neighboring Cerrillos were in a fabled turquoise-mining area dating back to prehistory. Gold and silver mines followed, and when they faltered, there was coal. The Turquoise Trail towns supplied fuel for the locomotives of the Santa Fe Railroad until the 1950s, when the railroad converted to diesel fuel. Madrid used to produce 100,000 tons of coal a year and was a true "company town," but the mine closed in 1956. Today, this is a village of artists and craftspeople seemingly stuck in the 1960s: Its funky, ramshackle houses have many counterculture residents who operate several crafts stores and galleries.

The **Old Coal Mine Museum and Old West Saloon** (© **505/438-3780**) invites visitors to peek into a mine that was saved when the town was abandoned. You can see the old mine's offices, steam engines, machines, and tools. It's open daily; admission is $5 for adults, $3 for seniors, and free for children 5 and under.

Next door, the **Mine Shaft Tavern** (© **505/473-0743**) continues its colorful career by offering a variety of burgers (try the green-chile cheeseburger) and presenting live music Saturday nights and Sunday afternoons; it's open for meals in summer Monday to Thursday 11am to 6pm and Friday to Sunday 11:30am to 7:30pm. In winter, meals are served Monday to Thursday from noon to 4pm and Friday to Sunday noon to 8pm. The bar is open in summer Sunday to Thursday 11am to 11pm and Friday to Saturday 11am to 1am. In winter the bar is open from Sunday to Thursday noon to 10pm and Friday to Saturday noon to 1am. Next door is the **Madrid Engine House Theater** (© **505/438-3780**), offering melodrama during the summer. Its back doors open out so a steam locomotive can take center stage.

A healthier dining option than the Mine Shaft is **Mama Lisa's Ghost Town Kitchen ★**, 2859 NM 14 (© **505/471-5769**). You'll find salads, sandwiches, and New Mexican specialties, all prepared with fresh ingredients. During the summer, it's open Friday to Sunday from 11am to 4:30pm. In winter, it's open intermittently, so call ahead.

CERRILLOS & GALISTEO Cerrillos, about 3 miles north of Madrid, is a village of dirt roads that sprawls along Galisteo Creek. It appears to have changed very little since it was founded during a lead strike in 1879; the old hotel, the saloon, and even the sheriff's office look very much like parts of an Old West movie set. You may want to stop in at **Casa Grande Trading Post,** 17 Waldo St. (© **505/438-3008;** www. casagrandetradingpost.com), a shop that was featured on PBS's *Antiques Roadshow.* You'll find lots of jewelry and rocks, as well as the **Cerrillos Turquoise Mining Museum,** full of artifacts from this region's mining era.

A good horseback-riding outfitter in the Galisteo Basin is **Broken Saddle Riding Company.** A 1¼-hour ride is $55 a person, a 2-hour ride is $80, a 3-hour ride is $100, and the 1½-hour sunset ride is $75. Riders are grouped according to skill level. For more information, call © **505/424-7774** and listen to the recorded message, or go to www.brokensaddle.com.

If you're getting hungry on the outskirts of Santa Fe, stop by the **San Marcos Café ★**, 3877 NM 14, near Lone Butte (© **505/471-9298**). Set next to a feed store in a curvaceous old adobe with wood-plank floors and lots of Southwest ambience, this cafe serves creative fare such as cinnamon rolls and their special Eggs San Marcos—tortillas stuffed with scrambled eggs and topped with guacamole, pinto beans, jack cheese, and red chile. The cafe is open daily 8am to 2pm (stops serving at 1:50pm).

SANTA FE

A city of 72,000 people living 7,000 feet above sea level, Santa Fe, nicknamed "The City Different," is an exotic and sophisticated place. The Native Americans enlighten the area with viewpoints and lifestyles deeply tied to nature and completely contrary to the American norm. Many of the Hispanics here still live within extended families and practice a devout Catholicism; they bring a slower pace to the city and an appreciation for deep-rooted ties. Meanwhile, a strong cosmopolitan element contributes cutting-edge cuisine, world-class opera, first-run art films, and some of the finest artwork in the world, seen easily while wandering on foot from gallery to gallery, museum to museum.

The city's history is told through its architecture. For its first 2 centuries, it was constructed mainly of adobe bricks. When the U.S. took over the territory from Mexico in 1846 and trade began flowing from the eastern states, new tools and materials began to change the face of the city. The old adobe took on brick facades and roof decoration in what became known as the Territorial style. But the flat roofs were retained so that the city never lost its unique, low profile, creating a sense of serenity found in no other U.S. city.

Bishop Jean Baptiste Lamy—the inspiration for the character of Bishop Latour in Willa Cather's *Death Comes for the Archbishop*—built the French Romanesque St. Francis Cathedral shortly after he was appointed to head the diocese in 1851. Other structures still standing include what is claimed to be the oldest house in the United States. The San Miguel Mission is the oldest mission church in the country, while the state capitol, built in the circular form of a ceremonial Indian kiva, is among the newest in the U.S.

The city was originally named La Villa Real de la Santa Fe de San Francisco de Asis (the Royal City of the Holy Faith of St. Francis of Assisi) by its founder, Spanish governor Don Pedro de Peralta. He built the Palace of the Governors as his capitol on the central plaza; today it (and the attached New Mexico History Museum) tells the story of the region. It is one of the major attractions in the Southwest, and under its portico, Native Americans sell their crafts to eager travelers, as they have done for decades.

The plaza is the focus of numerous bustling art markets and Santa Fe's early September fiesta, celebrated annually since 1770. The fiesta commemorates the time following the years of the Pueblo revolt, when Spanish governor Don Diego de Vargas reconquered the city in 1692. The plaza was also the terminus of the Santa Fe Trail from Missouri, and of the earlier Camino Real (Royal Rd.) from Mexico, when the city thrived on the wool and fur of the Chihuahua trade. Today, a central **gazebo** makes a fun venue for summer concerts.

What captures the eye most, though, is the city's setting, backed by the rolling hills and the blue peaks of the Sangre de Cristo Mountains. In the summer, thunderheads build into giant swirling structures above those peaks and move over the city, dropping cool rain. In the winter, snow often covers the many flat-roofed adobe homes, creating a poetic abstraction that at every glance convinces you that the place itself is exotic art.

ORIENTATION

Part of the charm of Santa Fe is that it's so easy to get around. Like most cities of Hispanic origin, it was built around a parklike central plaza. Centuries-old adobe buildings and churches still line the narrow streets; many of them house shops, restaurants, art galleries, and museums.

Santa Fe sits high and dry at the foot of the Sangre de Cristo range. Santa Fe Baldy rises to more than 12,600 feet, a mere 12 miles northeast of the plaza. The city's downtown straddles the Santa Fe River, a tiny tributary of the Rio Grande that is little more than a trickle for much of the year. North is the Española Valley and, about 70 miles beyond that, the village of Taos (see chapter 8). South are ancient Indian turquoise mines in the Cerrillos Hills; southwest is metropolitan Albuquerque, 58 miles away (see chapter 6). To the west, across the Caja del Rio Plateau, is the Rio Grande, and beyond that, the 11,000-foot Jemez Mountains and Valle Grande, an ancient and massive volcanic caldera. Native American pueblos dot the entire Rio Grande valley; they're an hour's drive in any direction.

Arriving

BY PLANE   Many people choose to fly into the Albuquerque International Sunport. However, if you want to save time and don't mind paying a bit more, you may be able to fly into the **Santa Fe Municipal Airport** (**SAF**; © **505/955-2900;** www.santafenm.gov), just outside the southwestern city limits on Airport Road. In conjunction with American Airlines, commuter flights are offered by **American Eagle** (© **800/433-7300;** www.aa.com).

If you do fly into Albuquerque, you can rent a car or take one of the bus services. See "Getting There & Around," in chapter 3, for details.

From the Santa Fe Municipal Airport, **Roadrunner Shuttle** (© **505/424-3367**) meets every commercial flight and takes visitors anywhere in Santa Fe. From the Albuquerque Sunport to Santa Fe, **Sandia Shuttle Express** (© **888/775-5696** or 505/474-5696; www.sandiashuttle.com) runs shuttles daily from 8:45am to 10:45pm. **New Mexico Rail Runner Express** (see below) also runs to Santa Fe, with a shuttle bus taking travelers from the airport to the train.

BY TRAIN & BUS   Daily train service from Albuquerque to Santa Fe is now provided by **New Mexico Rail Runner Express** (© **866/795-7245;** www.

nmrailrunner.com). For more information about train and bus service to Santa Fe, see "Getting There & Getting Around," in chapter 3.

BY CAR   I-25 skims past Santa Fe's southern city limits, connecting it along one continuous highway from Billings, Montana, to El Paso, Texas. I-40, the state's major east-west thoroughfare, which bisects Albuquerque, affords coast-to-coast access to Santa Fe. From the west, motorists leave I-40 in Albuquerque and take I-25 north; from the east, travelers exit I-40 at Clines Corners and continue 52 miles to Santa Fe on US 285. For those coming from the northwest, the most direct route is via Durango, Colorado, on US 160, entering Santa Fe on US 84.

For information on car rentals in Albuquerque, see "Getting Around" in chapter 3; for agencies in Santa Fe, see "Getting Around," below.

Visitor Information

The **Santa Fe Convention and Visitors Bureau** is located downtown at 201 W. Marcy St. (P.O. Box 909), Santa Fe, NM 87504-0909 (© **800/777-2489** or 505/955-6200). You can also log on to the bureau's website, at www.santafe.org.

City Layout

MAIN ARTERIES & STREETS   The limits of downtown Santa Fe are demarcated on three sides by the horseshoe-shaped Paseo de Peralta and on the west by St. Francis Drive, otherwise known as US 84/285. Alameda Street follows the north side of the Santa Fe River through downtown, with the State Capitol and other government buildings on the south side of the river, and most buildings of historic and tourist interest on the north, east of Guadalupe Street.

The plaza is Santa Fe's universally accepted point of orientation. Its four diagonal walkways meet at a central fountain, around which a strange and wonderful assortment of people of all ages, nationalities, and lifestyles can be found at nearly any hour of the day or night.

If you stand in the center of the plaza looking north, you'll be gazing directly at the Palace of the Governors. In front of you is Palace Avenue; behind you, San Francisco Street. To your left is Lincoln Avenue, and to your right is Washington Avenue, which divides the downtown avenues into east and west. St. Francis Cathedral is the massive Romanesque structure a block east, down San Francisco Street. Alameda Street is 2 full blocks behind you.

Near the intersection of Alameda Street and Paseo de Peralta, you'll find Canyon Road running east toward the mountains. Much of this street is one-way. The best way to see it is to walk up or down, taking time to explore shops and galleries and even have lunch or dinner.

Running to the southwest from the downtown area, beginning opposite the state office buildings on Galisteo Avenue, is Cerrillos Road. Once the main north-south highway connecting New Mexico's state capital with its largest city, Albuquerque, it is now a 6-mile-long motel and fast-food strip. St. Francis Drive, which crosses Cerrillos Road 3 blocks south of Guadalupe Street, is a far less tawdry byway, linking Santa Fe with I-25, 4 miles southwest of downtown. The Old Pecos Trail, on the east side of the city, also joins downtown and the freeway. St. Michael's Drive connects the three arteries.

FINDING AN ADDRESS The city's layout makes it difficult to know exactly where to look for a particular address. It's best to call ahead for directions.

MAPS Free city and state maps can be obtained at tourist information offices. An excellent state highway map is published by the **New Mexico Department of Tourism,** 491 Old Santa Fe Trail, Lamy Building, Santa Fe, NM 87501 (© **800/733-6396** or 505/827-7400, www.newmexico.org; to receive a tourism guide call © 800/777-2489). There's also a Santa Fe visitor center in the same building. More specific county and city maps are available from the **State Highway and Transportation Department,** 1120 Cerrillos Rd., Santa Fe, NM 87504 (© **505/827-5100**). Members of the **American Automobile Association (AAA),** 1644 St. Michael's Dr. (© **505/471-6620;** www.aaa.com), can obtain free maps from the AAA office. Other good regional maps can be purchased at area bookstores.

GETTING AROUND

The best way to see downtown Santa Fe is on foot. Free **walking-tour maps** are available at the **Santa Fe Convention and Visitors Bureau,** 201 W. Marcy St. (© **800/777-2489** or 505/955-6200), and several guided walking tours are listed later in this chapter.

By Bus

In 1993, Santa Fe opened **Santa Fe Trails** (© **505/955-2001;** www.santafenm. gov), its first public bus system. There are seven routes, and visitors can pick up a map from the Convention and Visitors Bureau. Most buses operate Monday to Friday 6:30am to 9:30pm and Saturday 8am to 8pm. There is limited service on Sunday and holidays. Call for a current schedule and fare information. Be aware that the buses don't always run on time.

> **Driving Warning**
>
> New Mexico has one of the highest per-capita rates of traffic deaths in the nation (mostly due to drunk driving). Although the number has been dropping in recent years, it's still a good idea to drive carefully!

By Car

Cars can be rented from any of the following firms in Santa Fe: **Avis,** Santa Fe Airport (© **505/471-5892**); **Budget,** 1946 Cerrillos Rd. (© **505/984-1596**); **Enterprise,** 4462 Cerrillos Rd. and 1611 St. Michael's; (© **505/473-3600**); and **Hertz,** Santa Fe Airport (© **505/471-7189**).

If Santa Fe is merely your base for an extended driving exploration of New Mexico, be sure to give the vehicle you rent a thorough road check before starting out. There are a lot of wide-open desert and wilderness spaces here, so if you break down, you could be stranded for hours before someone passes by, and cellphones don't tend to work in these remote areas.

Make sure your driver's license and auto club membership (if you have one) are valid before you leave home. Check with your auto-insurance company to make sure you're covered when out of state and/or when driving a rental car.

Note: In 2002, the Santa Fe City Council imposed a law prohibiting use of cell-phones while driving within the city limits, with strict fines imposed. If you need to make a call, be sure to pull off the road or use a hands-free device.

Street parking is difficult to find during summer months. There's a metered parking lot near the federal courthouse, 2 blocks north of the plaza; a city lot behind Santa Fe Village, a block south of the plaza; another city lot at Water and Sandoval streets, and one underneath the Santa Fe Community Convention Center. If you stop by the Santa Fe Convention and Visitors Bureau (see above), you can pick up a wallet-size guide to Santa Fe parking areas. The map shows both street and lot parking.

Unless otherwise posted, the speed limit on freeways is 75 mph; on most other two-lane open roads it's 60 to 65 mph. The minimum age for drivers is 16. Seat belts are required for drivers and all passengers ages 5 and over; children 4 and under must use approved child seats.

Since Native American reservations enjoy a measure of self-rule, they can legally enforce certain designated laws. For instance, on the Navajo reservation, it is forbidden to transport alcoholic beverages, leave established roadways, or go without a seat belt. Motorcyclists must wear helmets. If you are caught breaking reservation laws, you are subject to reservation punishment—often stiff fines and, in some instances, detainment.

The **State Highway and Transportation Department** has a toll-free hot line (© 800/432-4269) that provides up-to-the-hour information on road closures and conditions.

By Taxi

Cabs are difficult to flag from the street, but you can call for one. Expect to pay a standard fee of $3 for the service and an average of about $3 per mile. **Capital City Cab** (© 505/438-0000) is the main company in Santa Fe. On Friday and Saturday nights from 5:30pm to 2:30am, service is $5 for two people ($10 for three or more) anywhere within the city limits. This reduced cost service is provided between a bar, club, or restaurant and a person's home, not from bar to bar.

By Bicycle

Riding a bicycle is a good way to get around town, though you'll have to ride cautiously because there are few designated bike paths. Check with **Mellow Velo,** 638 Old Santa Fe Trail (© 505/982-8986; www.mellowvelo.com); **Bike-N-Sport,** 524 Cordova Rd. (© 505/820-0809; www.nmbikensport.com); or **Santa Fe Mountain Sports,** 1221 Flag Man Way (© 505/988-3337; www.santafemountainsports.com), for rentals.

[Fast FACTS] SANTA FE

Airport See "Orientation," p. 123.

Area Code In 2007 New Mexico added a new area code. The northwestern section, including Santa Fe and Albuquerque, retained the **505** code, while the rest of the state changed to 575.

ATM Networks As in most U.S. destinations, ATMs are ubiquitous in the cities of New Mexico. However, in the small mountain towns, they're scarce. ATMs are linked to a network that most likely includes your bank at home. **Cirrus** (© 800/424-7787; www.mastercard.

com) and **PLUS**
(☎ **800/843-7587;** www.
visa.com) are the two
most popular networks in
the United States and in
this region.

Babysitters Most hotels
can arrange for sitters on
request. Alternatively, call
the professional, licensed
sitter **Linda Iverson**
(☎ **505/982-9327**).

Business Hours
Offices and **stores** are
generally open Monday to
Friday, 9am to 5pm, with
many stores also open Friday night, Saturday, and
Sunday in the summer
season. Most **banks** are
open Monday to Thursday,
9am to 5pm, and Friday,
9am to 6pm. Some may
also be open Saturday
morning. Most branches
have ATMs available 24
hours. Call establishments
for specific hours.

Car Rentals See "Get-
ting Around," in chapter 3,
and "Getting Around,"
above.

Climate See "When to
Go," in chapter 3.

Currency Exchange
You can exchange foreign
currency at **Wells Fargo**
for $5 at 241 Washington
St. (☎ **505/984-0500**).

Dentists **Dr. Gilman
Stenzhorn** (☎ **505/982-
4317** or 505/983-4491)
offers emergency service.
He's located at 1496 St.
Francis Dr., in the St. Francis Professional Center.

Doctors **ABQ Health
Partners,** 465 St. Michaels
Dr., Suite 101

(☎ **505/995-2400**), is
open Monday to Friday
8am to 5pm. For physician
and surgeon referral and
information services, call
the **American Board of
Medical Specialties**
(☎ **866/275-2267**).

Emergencies For
police, fire, or ambulance
emergencies, dial ☎ **911.**

Etiquette & Customs
Certain rules of etiquette
should be observed when
visiting the pueblos. See
chapter 6 for details.

Hospitals **Christus St.
Vincent Regional Medical
Center,** 455 St. Michaels
Dr. (☎ **505/983-3361,** or
505/995-3934 for emer-
gency services; www.stvin.
org), is a 248-bed regional
health center. Patient services include urgent and
emergency-room care and
ambulatory surgery. Health
services are also available
at the **Women's Health
Services Family Care and
Counseling Center**
(☎ **505/988-8869;** www.
whssf.org). **Ultimed,** 707
Paseo de Peralta
(☎ **505/989-8707;** www.
ultimed.com), an urgent-
care facility near the plaza,
offers comprehensive
health care.

Hot Lines The following
hot lines are available in
Santa Fe: **battered families**
(☎ **505/473-5200;** www.
esperanzashelter.org), **poison control** (☎ **800/432-
6866**), **psychiatric
emergencies** (☎ **888/920-
6333** or 505/820-6333),

and **sexual assault**
(☎ **505/986-9111**).

Internet Access Head
to the **Santa Fe Public
Library** at 145 Washington
Ave. (☎ **505/955-6780**),
or **FedEx,** 301 N. Guadalupe (☎ **505/982-6311**).

Libraries The **Santa Fe
Public Library** is half a
block from the plaza, at
145 Washington Ave.
(☎ **505/955-6780**). The
Oliver La Farge Branch
library is at 1730 Llano St.,
just off St. Michael's Drive,
and the Southside Library
is at 6599 Jaguar Dr., at
the intersection with Country Club Road. **The New
Mexico State Library** is at
1209 Camino Carlos Rey
(☎ **505/476-9700**).

Liquor Laws The legal
drinking age is 21 throughout New Mexico. Bars may
remain open until 2am
Monday to Saturday and
until midnight on Sunday.
Wine, beer, and spirits are
sold at licensed supermarkets and liquor stores, but
there are no package sales
on election days until after
7pm, and on Sundays
before noon. It is illegal to
transport liquor through
most Native American
reservations.

Lost Property Contact
the city police at
☎ **505/955-5030.**

**Newspapers & Maga-
zines** The *New Mexi-
can*—Santa Fe's daily
paper—is the oldest news-
paper in the West. Its main
office is at 202 E. Marcy
St. (☎ **505/983-3303;**

www.santafenewmexican. com). The weekly **Santa Fe Reporter,** 132 E. Marcy St. (✆ **505/988-5541;** www. sfreporter.com), published on Wednesdays and available free at stands all over town, is often more controversial, and its entertainment listings are excellent. Regional magazines published locally are **New Mexico** magazine (monthly, statewide interest; www.nmmagazine. com) and the **Santa Fean** magazine (six times a year, Southwestern lifestyles; www.santafean.com).

Pharmacies **Del Norte Pharmacy,** at 1691 Galisteo St. (✆ **505/988-9797**), is open Monday to Friday 8am to 6pm, and Saturday 8am to noon. Delivery service is available.

Police In case of emergency, dial ✆ **911.** For all other inquiries, call the **Santa Fe Police Department,** 2515 Camino Entrada (✆ **505/428-3710**). The **Santa Fe County Sheriff,** with jurisdiction outside the city limits, is at 35 Camino Justicia (✆ **505/986-2400**).

Post Offices The **main post office** is at 120 S. Federal Place (✆ **505/988-2239**), 2

blocks north and 1 block west of the plaza. It's open Monday to Friday 7:30am to 5:30pm and Saturday 9am to 4pm. The **Coronado Station branch** is at 2071 S. Pacheco St. (✆ **800/275-8777**), and is open Monday to Friday 8am to 6pm, and Saturday 9am to 4pm. Some of the major hotels have stamp machines and mailboxes with twice-daily pickup.

Radio Local radio stations are **KLBU** (102.9), which plays contemporary jazz, and **KBAC** (98.1), which plays alternative rock and folk music.

Safety Although the tourist district appears very safe, Santa Fe is not on the whole a safe city; theft and the number of reported rapes have risen. The good news is that Santa Fe's overall crime statistics do appear to be falling. Still, when walking the city streets, guard your purse carefully because there are many bag-grab thefts, particularly during the summer tourist months. Also, be as aware of your surroundings as you would in any other major city.

Taxes A tax of about 8% is added to

all purchases, with an additional 7% added to lodging bills.

Taxis See "Getting Around," above.

Television There are five Albuquerque network affiliates: **KOB-TV** (Channel 4, NBC), **KOAT-TV** (Channel 7, ABC), **KQRE-TV** (Channel 13, CBS), **KASA-TV** (Channel 2, FOX), and **KNME-TV** (Channel 5, PBS).

Time Zone New Mexico is on **Mountain Standard Time,** 1 hour ahead of the West Coast and 2 hours behind the East Coast. When it's 10am in Santa Fe, it's noon in New York, 11am in Chicago, and 9am in San Francisco. Daylight saving time is in effect from early March to early November.

Useful Telephone Numbers Information on **road conditions** in the Santa Fe area can be obtained by calling the State Highway and Transportation Department (✆ **800/432-4269**). For **time and temperature,** call ✆ **505/473-2211.**

Weather For weather forecasts call ✆ **505/988-5151.**

WHERE TO STAY

The City Different offers a broad range of accommodations. From downtown hotels to Cerrillos Road motels, ranch-style resorts to quaint bed-and-breakfasts, the standard is almost universally high.

You should be aware of the seasonal nature of the tourist industry in Santa Fe. Accommodations are often booked through the summer months, the Christmas

Where to Stay in Downtown Santa Fe

Adobe Abode **5**

Don Gaspar Inn **9**

Eldorado Hotel & Spa **6**

El Farolito **8**

Four Kachinas Inn **10**

Garrett's Desert Inn **17**

Hacienda Nicholas **19**

Hotel Plaza Real **12**

Hotel St. Francis **11**

Hotel Santa Fe **4**

Inn & Spa at Loretto **15**

Inn of the Anasazi **13**

Inn of the Five Graces **16**

Inn on the Alameda **18**

La Fonda **14**

La Posada de Santa Fe Resort and Spa **20**

The Lodge at Santa Fe **1**

Old Santa Fe Inn **7**

Santa Fe Motel and Inn **3**

Water Street Inn **2**

holiday, and Easter, and most places raise their prices accordingly. Rates increase even more during Indian Market, the third weekend of August. During these periods, it's essential to make reservations well in advance.

No matter the season, discounts are often available to seniors, affiliated groups, corporate employees, and others. If you have any questions about your eligibility for these lower rates, be sure to ask.

A combined city-state tax of about 15% is added to every hotel bill in Santa Fe. And unless otherwise indicated, all recommended accommodations come with a private bathroom.

RESERVATIONS SERVICES Year-round reservation assistance is available from **Santafehotels.com** (☎ 800/745-9910), the **Accommodation Hot Line** (☎ 800/338-6877), **All Santa Fe Reservations** (☎ 877/737-7366), and **Santa Fe Stay,** which specializes in casitas (☎ 800/995-2272). **Emergency Lodging Assistance** is available free daily after 4pm (☎ 505/986-0038). All of the above are private companies and may have biases toward certain properties. Do your own research before calling.

Hotels/Motels

DOWNTOWN

Everything within the horseshoe-shaped Paseo de Peralta and east a few blocks along either side of the Santa Fe River is considered downtown Santa Fe. All these accommodations are within walking distance of the plaza.

Very Expensive

Eldorado Hotel & Spa ★★ Since its opening in 1986, the Eldorado has been a model hotel for the city. In a large structure, the architects managed to meld pueblo revival style with an interesting cathedral feel, inside and out. The lobby has a high ceiling that continues into the court area and the cafe, all adorned with well over a million dollars' worth of Southwestern art. The spacious, quiet rooms received a makeover in 2006, maintaining an artistic motif, with a warm feel created by custom-made furniture in all and kiva fireplaces in many. You'll find families, businesspeople, and conference-goers staying here. Most of the rooms have views of downtown Santa Fe, many from balconies. The Nidah Spa offers a full range of treatments, including turquoise gemstone therapy. The Eldorado also manages the nearby Zona Rosa condominiums, which are two-, three-, and four-bedroom suites with full kitchens. The hotel's innovative and elegant restaurant, the Old House serves creative American cuisine.

309 W. San Francisco St., Santa Fe, NM 87501. ☎ **800/955-4455** or 505/988-4455. Fax 505/995-4544. www.eldoradohotel.com. 219 units. $139–$389 double. Seasonal package rates available. AE, DC, DISC, MC, V. Valet parking $18 per night. Pets accepted, $50 fee. **Amenities:** 2 restaurants; lounge; concierge; executive-level rooms; medium-size health club; Jacuzzi; heated rooftop pool; room service; his-and-hers saunas and steam baths; spa. *In room:* A/C, TV, CD player, hair dryer, MP3 docking station, Wi-Fi.

Encantado Resort ★★★ This Auberge Resort, set in pink foothills of the Sangre de Cristo Mountains about 15 minutes from Santa Fe, offers 65 elegant casitas, an artfully kiva-shaped spa, and gourmet dining. The resort melds contemporary architecture with traditional Pueblo style, using textured art and earth tones to add warmth to the design. Broad windows blur the boundary between indoor and out, with views from nearly every vantage point. In the casitas, polished concrete floors, kiva fireplaces, vaulted ceilings, and patios with stunning vistas west toward the Jemez Mountains add to the "mystical" quality the resort touts. In addition, the spa features a full range of treatments, including Ayurvedic techniques and regionally inspired massages. Steam rooms, soaking pools, and a fitness facility add to the experience. The resort's restaurant, Terra, opened to national rave reviews.

198 NM 592, Santa Fe, NM 87506. ✆ **877/262-4666.** Fax 505/946-5888. www.encantadoresort.com. 65 casitas. $305–$695 casita double; $650–$1,100 suite. AE, DISC, MC, V. **Amenities:** Restaurant; lounge; concierge; exercise room; Jacuzzi; outdoor pool; room service; sauna; spa. *In room:* A/C, TV/DVD, hair dryer, minibar, MP3 docking station, Wi-Fi.

Inn of the Anasazi ★★★   The designers of this fine luxury hotel have crafted a feeling of grandness in a very limited space. The rooms have bold splashes of color, and flagstone floors create a warm and welcoming ambience that evokes the feeling of an Anasazi cliff dwelling. Oversize cacti complete the look. A half-block off the plaza, this hotel was built in 1991 to cater to travelers who know their hotels. On the ground floor are a living room and library with oversize furniture and replicas of Anasazi pottery and Navajo rugs. The rooms range from medium-size to spacious, with pearl-finished walls, comfortable four-poster beds, and novelties such as iron candle sconces, gas-lit kiva fireplaces (in some), and humidifiers. All the rooms are quiet and comfortable, though none have dramatic views. The Anasazi Restaurant serves creative Southwestern cuisine.

113 Washington Ave., Santa Fe, NM 87501. ✆ **800/688-8100** or 505/988-3030. Fax 505/988-3277. www.innoftheanasazi.com. 57 units. Jan–Feb $217–$269 double; Mar–Apr $217–$362 double; May–Dec $325–$525 double. AE, DC, DISC, MC, V. Valet parking $15 per day. **Amenities:** Restaurant; concierge; library/boardroom; room service. *In room:* A/C, TV/DVD, hair dryer, minibar, Wi-Fi.

Inn of the Five Graces ★★★ 🏨   In the historic Barrio de Analco, just a few blocks from the plaza, this Relais & Châteaux inn holds true to its stated theme: "Here the Orient and the Old West meet, surprisingly at home in each other's arms." With floral-decked courtyards, elaborately decorated suites with *kilim* rugs, embroidered bedspreads, and ornately carved beds, this is a chic place. All rooms are suites, with sitting areas and fireplaces. Most have large bathrooms with elaborate broken-tile mosaics and soaking or jetted tubs. It's of the same caliber as Inn of the Anasazi, but with more flair. In recent years, the inn acquired the atmospheric Pink Adobe restaurant next door; every other evening the inn holds a wine-and-cheese reception in the Pink's lounge. All rooms have robes, stocked fridges, patios, and CD players; some have kitchenettes. This is a nontipping property, and all amenities are included with the room rate.

150 E. de Vargas St., Santa Fe, NM 87501. ✆ **505/992-0957.** www.fivegraces.com. 24 units. $360–$900 double, depending on the season and type of room. Price includes full breakfast with specialty items and afternoon treats. AE, MC, V. Free parking. Pets welcome ($75 per night). **Amenities:** Restaurant; lounge; concierge. *In room:* A/C, TV, CD player, fridge, hair dryer, kitchen (in some), MP3 docking station, Wi-Fi.

Inn & Spa at Loretto ★★   This much-photographed hotel, just 2 blocks from the plaza, was built in 1975 to resemble Taos Pueblo. Light and shadow dance upon the five-level structure as the sun crosses the sky. With a multimillion-dollar renovation in 2008, this has become a comfortable and elegant place to stay. The medium-size rooms employ a Navajo motif, with comfortable beds and fine linens, while the medium-size bathrooms have fine tiling and robes. Be aware that the Loretto likes convention traffic, so sometimes service lags for travelers. Overall, it is fairly quiet and has nice views—especially on the northeast side, where you'll see both the historic St. Francis Cathedral and the Loretto Chapel (with its "miraculous" spiral staircase; p. 160). The Spa Terre offers a range of treatments, from facials to massages, in intimate, Southwest-meets-Asia rooms. Their restaurant, Luminaria, and lobby lounge are excellent places to relax and sate your hunger.

211 Old Santa Fe Trail (P.O. Box 1417), Santa Fe, NM 87501. ☎ **800/727-5531** or 505/988-5531. Fax 505/984-7968. www.innatloretto.com. 134 units. Jan–Mar $189–$279 double; Apr–June $219–$349 double; July–Oct $329–$499 double; Nov–Dec $209–$299 double. Additional person $30. Children 17 and under stay free in parent's room. Resort fee of $12 per night. AE, DC, DISC, MC, V. Valet parking $18 per night. AE, DC, DISC, MC, V. **Amenities:** Restaurant; lounge; concierge; exercise room; outdoor pool (heated year-round); room service; spa. *In room:* A/C, TV, hair dryer, stocked minibar, MP3 docking station (some rooms), Wi-Fi.

La Fonda ★★   This historic hotel right on the plaza offers a glimpse into Santa Fe's past. It was once the inn at the end of the Santa Fe Trail, hosting trappers and traders, as well as notables such as President Rutherford B. Hayes and General Ulysses S. Grant. The original inn was razed in 1920 and replaced by the current La Fonda, built in pueblo revival style. Inside, the lobby is richly textured and slightly dark, with people bustling about, sitting in the cafe, and buying jewelry from Native Americans.

No two rooms are the same, but all have fine bedding and graceful touches such as hand-painted furnishings and some have fireplaces and private balconies. The elegant Terrace suites have handcrafted furniture, balconies, and city views. La Fiesta Lounge draws many locals, and the newly renovated La Plazuela offers excellent Southwestern cuisine in a skylit garden patio. The Bell Tower Bar, the highest point downtown, is a great place for a cocktail and a view of the city.

100 E. San Francisco St. (P.O. Box 1209), Santa Fe, NM 87501. ☎ **800/523-5002** or 505/982-5511. Fax 505/988-2952. www.lafondasantafe.com. 168 units. $229–$319 double; $249–$359 deluxe double; $309–$469 suite. Additional person $15. Children 12 and under stay free in parent's room. AE, DC, DISC, MC, V. Parking $12 per day in a covered garage. **Amenities:** Restaurant; 2 lounges; babysitting; concierge; exercise room; Jacuzzi; outdoor pool (heated in summer); room service; sauna; spa. *In room:* A/C, TV, hair dryer, Wi-Fi.

La Posada de Santa Fe Resort and Spa ★★   Three blocks from the plaza, this century-old New Mexico adobe hotel was once an art colony, and the original part was a Victorian mansion built in 1882. It is said that the first owner's widow, who died in 1896, continues to haunt the place. If you like tasteful Victorian interiors more than Santa Fe style, these rooms are a good bet.

The rest of the hotel offers pueblo-style architecture. Here, you get to experience squeaky maple floors, vigas and *latillas,* and kiva fireplaces. Be aware that unless you've secured a deluxe room or suite, the rooms tend to be fairly small. Fortunately, the hotel benefited from major remodels in recent years, including a $6-million one in 2008, so all the bathrooms are modern with artful granite throughout. Most notable are the Zen-Southwestern–style spa rooms, as well as a few "gallery suites," appointed with original artwork. Most rooms don't have views but have outdoor patios, and most are tucked back into the quiet compound. This hotel has taken many actions toward being "green."

330 E. Palace Ave., Santa Fe, NM 87501. ☎ **800/727-5276** or 505/986-0000. Fax 505/982-6850. www.laposada.rockresorts.com. 157 units. $169–$361 double; $239–$401 deluxe double; $419–$1,131

suite. Various vacation packages available. AE, DC, DISC, MC, V. $30 resort fee per day includes parking. **Amenities:** Restaurant; lounge; babysitting; concierge; exercise room; Jacuzzi; outdoor pool (heated year-round); room service; spa w/full treatments. *In room:* A/C, TV, hair dryer, minibar, Wi-Fi.

Expensive

Don Gaspar Inn ★★ 🎁   In a historic neighborhood only a 10-minute walk from the plaza, the Don Gaspar occupies three homes, connected by brilliant gardens and brick walkways. Rooms vary in size, though all are plenty spacious, most with patios, some with kitchenettes, and there's even a full house for rent. Travelers looking for an adventure beyond a hotel stay, but without the close interaction of a B&B, enjoy this place. Though the rooms don't have views, all are quiet. The Courtyard Casita, with a kitchenette and a sleeper couch in its own room, is nice for a small family. The Territorial Suite, with carpet throughout and Italian marble in the bathroom, is perfect for a romantic getaway. All rooms have bathrobes and fireplaces. The friendly staff serves a full breakfast such as green-chile stew with fresh baked items on the patio under a peach tree (the fruit from which they make cobbler) in the warm months and in the atrium in winter.

623 Don Gaspar Ave., Santa Fe, NM 87505. ✆ **888/986-8664** or 505/986-8664. Fax 505/986-0696. www.dongaspar.com. 10 units. $165–$185 double; $165–$225 suite; $205–$255 casita; $345–$385 house. Rates include full breakfast. AE, DISC, MC, V. Free parking. *In room:* A/C, TV/DVD, hair dryer, Wi-Fi.

Hotel Plaza Real ★ 🥄   This Territorial-style hotel provides comfortable, creatively appointed rooms near the plaza. The lobby is rustically elegant, built around a fireplace with balconies perched above. Clean and attractively decorated rooms have Southwestern-style furniture, many with French doors opening onto balconies or terraces that surround a quiet courtyard decorated with *ristras* (strung chiles). Beds are comfortably soft and bathrooms are small but with an outer sink vanity. The junior suites have an especially nice layout, with a sitting area near a fireplace and good light from the north and south.

125 Washington Ave., Santa Fe, NM 87501. ✆ **877/901-7666** or 505/988-4900. Fax 505/983-9322. www.hhandr.com. 56 units. $109–$149 double; $149–$289 suite, depending on time of year and type of room. Additional person $20. Children 11 and under stay free in parent's room. AE, DC, DISC, MC, V. Parking $14 per day. Pets $50 per stay. **Amenities:** Lounge; concierge. *In room:* A/C, TV, fridge (in some), Wi-Fi.

Hotel St. Francis ★★   Two blocks from the plaza, this 1880 building was renovated in 2009 with an artful Spanish monastery atmosphere. The lobby is crowned by a stone fireplace and has marble arches and travertine tile floors. Devotional art decorates all public spaces and rooms. The standard rooms here are small, but sparsely enough decorated so they feel more cozy than cramped. If possible, opt for a deluxe room and you'll have more space. Each room in the hotel has a unique footprint, some with hardwood floors, some with carpets. All have a carved *trastero* housing the television, a sink in the room, and fairly small but nicely tiled bathroom. Request a room facing east, and you'll wake each day to a view of the mountains. Enjoy high tea in the lobby Thursday to Saturday from 3 to 5pm. Their restaurant, called Table, serves quality New Mexican/American food.

210 Don Gaspar Ave., Santa Fe, NM 87501. ✆ **800/529-5700** or 505/983-5700. Fax 505/989-7690. www.hotelstfrancis.com. 81 units. $109–$349 double, depending on the season. Children 11 and under stay free in parent's room. AE, DC, DISC, MC, V. Parking $9 per day. **Amenities:** Restaurant; lounge; babysitting; concierge; exercise room; room service; access to nearby spa. *In room:* A/C, TV, fridge (in deluxe rooms), MP3 docking station, Wi-Fi.

Hotel Santa Fe ★★ 🛍 A 10-minute walk south of the plaza, this is the only Native American–owned hotel in Santa Fe. Picuris Pueblo is the majority stockholder, and part of the pleasure of staying here is the culture the Picuris bring to your visit. This is not to say that you'll experience the rusticity of a pueblo—this is a sophisticated hotel decorated in Southwestern style. The rooms are medium size, with clean lines and comfortable beds, the decor accented with pine Taos-style furniture. Rooms on the north side get less street noise and have better views of the mountains, but they don't have the sun shining onto their balconies. In the summer, Picuris dancers come to perform and bread bakers uncover the *horno* (oven) and prepare loaves for sale.

The **Hacienda at Hotel Santa Fe** ★★ is a unique addition and features 35 luxurious rooms and suites, all with cozy fireplaces, 10-foot ceilings, handcrafted Southwestern furnishings, and plush duvets to snuggle under on chilly nights. The Amaya restaurant serves a standard breakfast, but for lunch and dinner you can dine on what they call "native" cuisine from all over the Americas.

1501 Paseo de Peralta, Santa Fe, NM 87501. ⓒ **800/825-9876** or 505/982-1200. Fax 505/984-2211. www.hotelsantafe.com. 163 units. $129–$199 double; $239–$459 suite, depending on the season. Hacienda rooms and suites $199–$459. Additional person $20. Children 17 and under stay free in parent's room. AE, DC, DISC, MC, V. Free parking. Pets accepted with $20 fee. **Amenities:** Restaurant; babysitting; concierge; executive-level rooms; exercise room; Jacuzzi; outdoor pool; room service. *In room:* A/C, TV, minibar (in suites), Wi-Fi.

Inn on the Alameda ★★ Just across the street from the bosque-shaded Santa Fe River sits the Inn on the Alameda, a cozy stop for those who like the services of a hotel with the intimacy of an inn. It's a little like a village, with a number of pueblo-style adobe buildings and casitas. The owner has used red brick in the dining area and Mexican *equipae* (wicker) furniture in the lobby, as well as thick vigas and shiny *latillas* in a sitting area set around a grand fireplace. Some rooms have kiva fireplaces, and all have comfortable beds, good linens, robes, and well-planned bathrooms with tile. A full-service bar is open nightly. Breakfast is delicious, with bakery and organic items, as well as dairy-free and gluten-free options.

303 E. Alameda, Santa Fe, NM 87501. ⓒ **800/289-2122** or 505/984-2121. Fax 505/986-8325. www.innonthealameda.com. 71 units. $125–$230 queen; $180–$305 king; $240–$390 suite. Additional adult $25. Reduced off-season rates are available. Rates include breakfast and afternoon wine-and-cheese reception. AE, DC, DISC, MC, V. Free parking. Small pets under 30 lb. welcome with $30 fee. **Amenities:** Lounge; babysitting; concierge; exercise room; 2 open-air Jacuzzis; pet amenities and a pet-walking map. *In room:* A/C, TV, CD player, fridge (in some), hair dryer, Wi-Fi.

Moderate

Garrett's Desert Inn 🦎 The closest budget hotel to the plaza (just 3 blocks), Garrett's offers decent and comfortable accommodations. It's a clean, two-story, concrete-block building around a broad parking lot. Renovation on the hotel is ongoing but don't expect the consistency of a chain hotel here. Instead you'll find some '50s elements, such as Art Deco tile in the bathrooms and plenty of space in the rooms. If you're traveling in winter, ask for a south-facing room and you might be able to sunbathe under the portal. Minisuites have refrigerators and microwaves. The outdoor pool here is one of the nicest in town.

311 Old Santa Fe Trail, Santa Fe, NM 87501. ⓒ **800/888-2145** or 505/982-1851. Fax 505/989-1647. www.garrettsdesertinn.com. 83 units. $89–$169 double, depending on season and type of room. AE, DISC, MC, V. **Amenities:** Restaurant; exercise room; heated outdoor pool (open in summer). *In room:* A/C, TV, hair dryer, Wi-Fi.

Old Santa Fe Inn ★ 👜 Want to stay downtown and savor Santa Fe–style ambience without wearing out your plastic? This is your hotel. A multi-million-dollar renovation to this 1930s court motel has created a comfortable, quiet inn just a few blocks from the plaza. Rooms verge on small but are decorated with such lovely handcrafted colonial-style furniture that you probably won't mind. All have small Mexican-tiled bathrooms, and some have gas fireplaces and DVD players. You have a choice of king, queen, or twin bedrooms as well as suites. Breakfast is served in an atmospheric dining room next to a comfortable library. This inn jacks prices *way* up during special event times such as the Indian Market.

320 Galisteo St., Santa Fe, NM 87501. ℂ **800/745-9910** or 505/995-0800. Fax 505/995-0400. www.oldsantafeinn.com. 43 units. $90–$129 double; $179–$500 suite depending on season. Rates include full hot breakfast. AE, DC, DISC, MC, V. *In room:* A/C, TV, Wi-Fi.

Santa Fe Motel and Inn ★ If you like walking to the plaza and restaurants but don't want to pay big bucks, this little compound is a good choice. Rooms here are larger than at the Old Santa Fe Inn and have more personality than those at Garrett's Desert Inn. Ask for one of the casitas in back—you'll pay more but get a little turn-of-the-20th-century charm, plus more quiet and privacy. Some have vigas; others have skylights, fireplaces, and patios. The main part of the motel, built in 1955, is two-story Territorial style, with upstairs rooms that open onto a portal with a bit of a view. All guest rooms are decorated with a Southwest motif and some have antique furnishings. All have medium-size bathrooms and comfortable beds. A full breakfast, including Sage Bakehouse bread, is served each morning in the Southwest-style dining room or on a quaint patio.

510 Cerrillos Rd., Santa Fe, NM 87501. ℂ **800/930-5002** or 505/982-1039. Fax 505/986-1275. www.santafemotel.com. 23 units. $79–$139 double; $99–$159 deluxe double depending on season. Additional person $10. Rates include full breakfast. AE, DC, MC, V. Free parking. *In room:* A/C, TV, hair dryer, kitchenette (in some), Wi-Fi.

Inexpensive

Santa Fe Sage Inn 🏷️ ☺ If you're looking for a convenient, almost-downtown location at a reasonable price, this is one of your best bets. This two-story stucco adobe motel with portals is spread through five buildings and is about a 10-minute walk from the plaza. The hotel also provides shuttle service to local businesses. Built in 1985, it was remodeled in 2005. The smallish rooms have Southwestern furnishings, with comfortable beds and small bathrooms. There's a park in the back and an outdoor pool set in a secluded fenced area, a good place for kids. To avoid street noise, ask for a room at the back of the property.

725 Cerrillos Rd., Santa Fe, NM 87501. ℂ **866/433-0335** or 505/982-5952. Fax 505/984-8879. www.santafesageinn.com. 156 units. $50–$140 double. Rates include continental breakfast. Additional person $10. Pets welcome. AE, DC, DISC, MC, V. Free parking. **Amenities:** Exercise room; heated outdoor pool. *In room:* A/C, TV, hair dryer, Wi-Fi.

THE NORTH SIDE

Within easy reach of the plaza, the north side encompasses the area that lies north of the loop of Paseo de Peralta.

Very Expensive

Bishop's Lodge Ranch Resort & Spa ★★★ ☺ 📷 This resort holds special significance for me because my parents met in the lodge and were later married in

family-friendly HOTELS

Bishop's Lodge Ranch Resort & Spa (p. 135) Riding lessons, tennis courts with instruction, a pool with a lifeguard, a stocked trout pond just for kids, a summer daytime program, horseback trail trips, and more make this a veritable day camp for all ages.

El Rey Inn (p. 137) A picnic area and playground in a courtyard set back away from the street make this a nice place for families to commune in summer.

The Lodge at Santa Fe (p. 136) Built above the city, with a bit of a country-club feel, this place offers a nice outdoor pool and condo units that serve family needs well.

Residence Inn (p. 137) Spacious suites house families comfortably. An outdoor pool, fully equipped kitchens, and patio grills add to the appeal.

Santa Fe Sage Inn (p. 135) With its fenced-in pool and reasonable prices, this is a good spot for families.

the chapel. More than a century ago, when Bishop Jean-Baptiste Lamy was the spiritual leader of northern New Mexico's Roman Catholic population, he often escaped clerical politics by hiking into this valley called Little Tesuque. He built a retreat and a humble chapel (now on the National Register of Historic Places) with high-vaulted ceilings and a hand-built altar. Today, Lamy's 450-acre getaway has become Bishop's Lodge.

In recent years, a $17-million renovation spruced up the place and added a spa. The guest rooms, spread through many buildings, feature handcrafted furniture and regional artwork, and many have balconies or patios. The newer Ridge Rooms are spacious, with high ceilings, vigas, gas fireplaces, patios or balconies, and most with views. The newest addition are villas: spectacular two- and three-bedroom town houses, filled with amenities, including full kitchens, fireplaces, patios, and views, a great option for families or couples who travel together. The Bishop's Lodge is an active resort three seasons of the year, with activities such as horseback riding, nature walks, and cookouts; in the winter, it takes on the character of a romantic country retreat. A children's program keeps kids busy for much of the day.

Bishop's Lodge Rd. (P.O. Box 2367), Santa Fe, NM 87504. © **505/983-6377.** Fax 505/989-8939. www. bishopslodge.com. 111 units. Summer $299–$489 double; fall and spring $259–$399 double; midwinter $189–$309 double; $599–$1,800 villa. Resort fee $15 per person per day. Additional person $15. Children 3 and under stay free in parent's room. Ask about packages that include meals. AE, DC, DISC, MC, V. Free parking. **Amenities:** Restaurant; lounge; babysitting; children's center; concierge; Jacuzzi; outdoor pool; room service; spa; tennis courts. *In room:* A/C, TV, fridge, hair dryer, Wi-Fi.

Expensive

The Lodge at Santa Fe ★ ☺ Set on a hill as you head north toward the Santa Fe Opera, this three-story hotel is a convenient and relaxing place to stay. The theme is Native American, with Anasazi-style stacked sandstone throughout the lobby and dining room, a theme that carries into the guest rooms. They are medium size, decorated in earth tones with bold prints, some with views of the mountains, others overlooking the pool. Premium rooms are more spacious, some with large living rooms and private balconies. Each parlor suite has a Murphy bed and kiva fireplace in the living room, a big dining area, a wet bar and refrigerator, and a jetted bathtub. The suites nearby come with fully equipped kitchens, fireplaces, and private decks. Be aware that this hotel is ready for a remodel; the rooms can be a little worn around the edges. The lodge offers free shuttle service to downtown.

750 N. St. Francis Dr., Santa Fe, NM 87501. ℭ **800/563-4373** or 505/992-5800. Fax 505/992-5856. www.lodgeatsantafe.com. 128 units. $89–$179 double; $129–$199 suite; $200–$300 condo. AE, DC, DISC, MC, V. Free parking. **Amenities:** Restaurant; bar; babysitting; exercise room; Jacuzzi; heated outdoor pool. *In room:* A/C, TV, fridge, hair dryer, kitchen (in suites), Wi-Fi.

THE SOUTH SIDE

Santa Fe's major strip, Cerrillos Road, is US 85, the main route to and from Albuquerque and the I-25 freeway. It's about 5¼ miles from the plaza to the Santa Fe mall, which marks the southern boundary of the city. Most motels are on this strip, although several of them are to the east, closer to St. Francis Drive (US 84) or the Las Vegas Highway.

Expensive

Residence Inn by Marriott ★ ☺ Designed to look like a neighborhood, this inn provides the efficient stay you'd expect from a Marriott. It's a 10-minute drive from the plaza, through a few quiet neighborhoods. The lobby and breakfast area are warmly decorated in tile, with a fireplace and Southwestern accents. There are three sizes of suites, each roomy, each with a fully equipped kitchen. All rooms have fireplaces and are decorated with Southwestern furnishings. Many have balconies. Outside, plenty of amenities keep family members happy, including barbecue grills on the patio. Most who stay here are leisure travelers, but you'll also encounter some government workers and business travelers. Guests gather for complimentary hors d'oeuvres Monday through Wednesday from 5 to 6:30pm.

1698 Galisteo St., Santa Fe, NM 87505. ℭ **800/331-3131** or 505/988-7300. Fax 505/988-3243. www. marriot.com. 120 suites. $139–$249 studio suite and double suite; $179–$289 penthouse suite. Rates vary according to season. Rates include hot breakfast buffet and Mon–Wed evening hors d'oeuvres. AE, DC, DISC, MC, V. Free parking. **Amenities:** Exercise room; 3 Jacuzzis; jogging trail; outdoor pool; sports court. *In room:* A/C, TV, kitchen, Wi-Fi.

Moderate

El Rey Inn ★ 🛍☺ Staying at "the King" makes you feel as if you're traveling the old Route 66 through the Southwest. Opened in the 1930s, it received additions in the 1950s, and remodeling is ongoing. No two rooms are alike. The oldest section, nearest the lobby, feels a bit cramped, though the rooms have Art Deco tile in the bathrooms and vigas on the ceilings. Some have little patios. Be sure to request a room as far back as possible from Cerrillos Road. The two stories of suites around the Spanish colonial courtyard have the ambience of a Spanish inn, with carved furniture and cozy couches. Some rooms have kitchenettes. To the north sit 10 deluxe units around the courtyard. These rooms offer more upscale amenities and gas log fireplaces, as well as distinctive furnishings and artwork. There's also a sitting room with a library and games tables, as well as a picnic area, a playground, and an exercise room.

1862 Cerrillos Rd. (P.O. Box 4759), Santa Fe, NM 87502. ℭ **800/521-1349** or 505/982-1931. Fax 505/989-9249. www.elreyinnsantafe.com. 86 units. $99–$165 double; $125–$225 suite. Rates include continental breakfast. AE, DC, DISC, MC, V. Free parking. **Amenities:** Exercise room; 2 Jacuzzis; outdoor pool (summer only); sauna. *In room:* A/C, TV, fridge, hair dryer, kitchenette (in some), Wi-Fi.

Greater Santa Fe

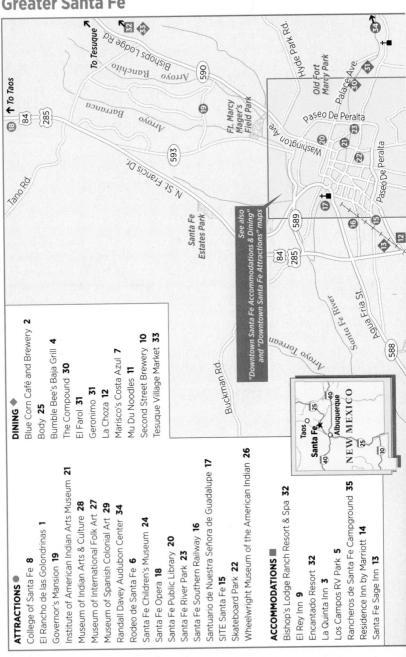

ATTRACTIONS ●

College of Santa Fe **8**
El Rancho de las Golondrinas **1**
Governor's Mansion **19**
Institute of American Indian Arts Museum **21**
Museum of Indian Arts & Culture **28**
Museum of International Folk Art **27**
Museum of Spanish Colonial Art **29**
Randall Davey Audubon Center **34**
Rodeo de Santa Fe **6**
Santa Fe Children's Museum **24**
Santa Fe Opera **18**
Santa Fe Public Library **20**
Santa Fe River Park **23**
Santa Fe Southern Railway **16**
Santuario de Nuestra Señora de Guadalupe **17**
SITE Santa Fe **15**
Skateboard Park **22**
Wheelwright Museum of the American Indian **26**

ACCOMMODATIONS ■

Bishop's Lodge Ranch Resort & Spa **32**
El Rey Inn **9**
Encantado Resort **32**
La Quinta Inn **3**
Los Campos RV Park **5**
Rancheros de Santa Fe Campground **35**
Residence Inn by Marriott **14**
Santa Fe Sage Inn **13**

DINING ◆

Blue Corn Café and Brewery **2**
Body **25**
Bumble Bee's Baja Grill **4**
The Compound **30**
El Farol **31**
Geronimo **31**
La Choza **12**
Marisco's Costa Azul **7**
Mu Du Noodles **11**
Second Street Brewery **10**
Tesuque Village Market **33**

Talaya
Hill
Resevoir

Camino del
Monte Sol

Old Santa Fe Trail

To Roswell
& Las Vegas

Garcia St.

Old Santa Fe Trail

Las Vegas Hwy.

Cordova St.

Don Gaspar Ave.

Old Pecos Trail

Lupita Rd.

Botulph Rd.

E. San Mateo Rd.

Salvador
Perez Park

Fairview
Cemetery

S. St. Francis Dr.

St. Michael's Dr.

Mateo Rd.

W. San

Ashbaugh
Park

Zia Rd.

Ragle
Park

Arroyo de los Chamisos

Siringo Rd.

Gen. Franklin
E. Miles Park

Agua Fria St.

Santa Fe River

Cerrillos Rd.

Rodeo Rd.

Richards Ave.

Rodeo Rd.

Villa Linda
Mall

Church

Railway

To Albuquerque

1/2 mi

0.5 km

139

Inexpensive

La Quinta Inn Though it's a good 15-minute drive from the plaza, this is a good choice among the economical Cerrillos Road chain hotels. Built in 1986, it has had ongoing remodeling to keep the rooms comfortable and tasteful. The rooms within the three-story building have an unexpectedly elegant feel, with lots of deep colors and Art Deco tile in the bathrooms. There's plenty of space in these rooms, and they're lit for mood as well as for reading. The heated outdoor kidney-shaped pool has a nice lounging area. The hotel is just across a parking lot from the Santa Fe Place mall, which shoppers and moviegoers will appreciate. The Flying Tortilla coffee shop is adjacent.

4298 Cerrillos Rd., Santa Fe, NM 87507. © **800/753-3757** or 505/471-1142. Fax 505/438-7219. www. lq.com. 130 units. June to mid-Oct $92–$119 double; late Oct to May $79–$89 double. Children 18 and under stay free in parent's room. Rates include continental breakfast. AE, DC, DISC, MC, V. Free parking. Maximum 2 pets stay free. **Amenities:** Executive-level rooms; outdoor heated pool (open May–Oct). *In room:* A/C, TV, fridge, hair dryer, microwave (in some), Wi-Fi.

Bed & Breakfasts

If you prefer a homey, intimate setting to the sometimes impersonal ambience of a large hotel, one of Santa Fe's bed-and-breakfast inns may be right for you. All those listed here are in or close to the downtown area and offer comfortable accommodations at expensive to moderate prices.

Adobe Abode ★ A short walk from the plaza, in the same quiet residential neighborhood as the Georgia O'Keeffe Museum, Adobe Abode is one of Santa Fe's most imaginative B&Bs. The living room is cozy, decorated with folk art. The creativity shines in each of the guest rooms as well, some in the main house, which was built in 1907. Others, in back, are newer. The Galisteo Suite is decorated with Spanish colonial furniture and artwork, while the Bronco Room is filled with cowboy paraphernalia: hats, Pendleton blankets, pioneer chests, and an entire shelf lined with children's cowboy boots. Two rooms have fireplaces, and several have private patios. Complimentary sherry, fruit, and cookies are served daily in the living room. Every morning, a full breakfast of fresh fruit and a hot dish such as green-chile corn soufflé is served in the country-style kitchen.

202 Chapelle St., Santa Fe, NM 87501. © **505/983-3133.** Fax 505/983-3132. www.adobeabode.com. 6 units. $155–$225 double. Rates include full gourmet breakfast and afternoon snacks. DISC, MC, V. Limited free parking. *In room:* A/C, TV, hair dryer, Wi-Fi.

El Farolito ★★ Within walking distance of the plaza, themes here include the Native American Room, decorated with rugs and pottery; the South-of-the-Border Room, with Mexican folk art; and the elegant Santa Fe–style Opera Room, with hand-carved, lavishly upholstered furniture. A two-room suite has been added in the main building, with a queen-size iron bed and Southwestern decor. The walls of most of the rooms were rubbed with beeswax during plastering to give them a golden finish. All rooms have kiva fireplaces and private patios. Part of the inn was built before 1912, and the rest is new, but the old-world elegance carries through. For breakfast, the focus is on healthy food with a little decadence thrown in. You'll enjoy fresh fruit and home-baked breads and pastries. Under the same stellar ownership (but a little less expensive) is the nearby **Four Kachinas Inn** ★ (© **888/634-8782;** www. fourkachinas.com), where Southwestern-style rooms sit around a sunny courtyard.

514 Galisteo St., Santa Fe, NM 87501. ℂ **888/634-8782** or 505/988-1631. Fax 505/988-4589. www. farolito.com. 8 units. $150–$280 casita. Rates include hot entree breakfast buffet. AE, DISC, MC, V. Free parking. **Amenities:** Babysitting by appointment. *In room:* A/C, TV, fridge, hair dryer, Wi-Fi.

Hacienda Nicholas ★★   A few blocks from the plaza, this inn has a delightful Southwest hacienda feel. Rooms surround a sunny patio; my favorite is the bright Cottonwood, with a serene feel created by the sunshine-colored walls, wood floors, and a kiva fireplace. The luxurious Sunflower has French doors, plenty of space, and also a fireplace. The rooms off the sitting room are more modest but have a warm "Southwest meets Provence" feel. All beds are comfortable and bathrooms range from small (with showers only) to larger (with tub/showers). A full breakfast—including such delicacies as homemade granola and red-and-green chile breakfast burritos—and afternoon wine and cheese are served in the lovely Great Room or on the patio, both with fireplaces. Under the same ownership, **Alexander's Inn** (ℂ **888/321-5123** or 505/986-1431; www.alexanders-inn.com) has long been one of the city's finest B&Bs. The inn itself has closed, but the same managers rent four charming casitas in the older district of Santa Fe.

320 E. Marcy St., Santa Fe, NM 87501. ℂ **888/284-3170** or 505/992-0888. Fax 505/982-8572. www. haciendanicholas.com. 7 units. $100–$240 double. Additional person $25. Rates include breakfast and afternoon wine and cheese. AE, DISC, MC, V. Free parking. Pets accepted with $20 fee. **Amenities:** Concierge. *In room:* A/C, TV, hair dryer, Wi-Fi.

Water Street Inn ★★   An award-winning adobe restoration 4 blocks from the plaza, this friendly inn features elegant Southwestern-style rooms, with antique furnishings, and several with kiva fireplaces. Rooms are medium size to large, some with four-poster beds, all comfortable with fine linens and well-planned Mexican-tiled bathrooms. Four suites have elegant contemporary Southwestern furnishings and outdoor private patios with fountains. Most rooms have balconies or patios. The hot breakfast here is always gourmet.

427 W. Water St., Santa Fe, NM 87501. ℂ **800/646-6752** or 505/984-1193. Fax 505/984-6235. www. waterstreetinn.com. 11 units. $195–$275 double. Rates include hot gourmet breakfast. AE, DISC, MC, V. Free parking. Children and pets welcome with prior approval. **Amenities:** Jacuzzi; concierge; room service. *In room:* A/C, TV/VCR/DVD, hair dryer, Wi-Fi.

RV Parks & Campgrounds
RV PARKS
tAt least four private camping areas, mainly for recreational vehicles, are located within a few minutes' drive of downtown Santa Fe. Typical rates are $30 for full RV hookups, $20 for tents. Be sure to book ahead at busy times.

Los Campos RV Resort   The resort has 95 spaces with full hookups, picnic tables, and covered pavilion for use with reservation at no charge. It's just 5 miles south of the plaza, so it's plenty convenient, but keep in mind that it is surrounded by the city. The campground honors a variety of discounts. Wireless Internet access is available in half the park.

3574 Cerrillos Rd., Santa Fe, NM 87507. ℂ **800/852-8160.** Fax 505/471-9220. $36–$45 daily; $220–$258 weekly; $500 monthly in winter, $550 monthly in summer. AE, DISC, MC, V. Pets welcome. **Amenities:** Grills; outdoor pool; restrooms; showers; vending machines; free cable TV.

Rancheros de Santa Fe Campground ★   Tents, motor homes, and trailers requiring full hookups are welcome here. The park's 127 sites are situated on 22 acres of *piñon* and juniper forest. Cabins are also available. It's about 6 miles south-east of Santa Fe and is open March 15 to October 31. Wireless Internet access is available throughout the park and high-speed Internet access is available in the lobby. Free nightly movies are shown May through September.

736 Old Las Vegas Hwy. (exit 290 off I-25), Santa Fe, NM 87505. ✆ **800/426-9259** or 505/466-3482. www.rancheros.com. Tent site $20–$22; RV hookup $24–$38. AE, DISC, MC, V. **Amenities:** Cable TV hookup; grills; grocery store; nature trails; picnic tables; playground; outdoor pool; propane; recreation room; restrooms; showers.

Santa Fe KOA   This campground, about 11 miles northeast of Santa Fe, sits among the foothills of the Sangre de Cristo Mountains, an excellent place to enjoy northern New Mexico's pine-filled high desert. It offers full hookups, pull-through sites, and tent sites. Ten cabins are available. Wireless Internet access is available throughout the park.

934 Old Las Vegas Hwy. (exit 290 or 294 off I-25), Santa Fe, NM 87505. ✆ **800/KOA-1514** (562-1514), or 505/466-1419 for reservations. www.santafekoa.com. Tent site $14; cabins $55; RV hookup $29–$40. AE, MC, V. **Amenities:** Cable TV hookup; dumping station; gift shop; picnic tables; playground; propane; recreation room; restrooms; showers.

Campgrounds

There are three forested sites along NM 475 on the way to Ski Santa Fe. All are open from May to October. Overnight rates start at about $12.

Hyde Memorial State Park ★   About 8 miles from the city, this pine-surrounded park offers a quiet retreat. Seven RV pads with electrical pedestals and an RV dumping station are available. There are nature and hiking trails and a playground.

740 Hyde Park Rd., Santa Fe, NM 87501. ✆ **505/983-7175.** www.nmparks.com. **Amenities:** Picnic tables; group shelters (for social events in inclement weather); vault toilets; water.

Santa Fe National Forest ★★   You'll reach **Black Canyon campground,** with 44 sites, before you arrive at Hyde State Park. It's one of the only campgrounds in the state for which you can make a reservation (✆ **877/444-6777;** www.recreation.gov). The sites sit within thick forest, with hiking trails nearby. **Big Tesuque,** a first-come, first-served campground with 10 newly rehabilitated sites, is about 12 miles from town. The sites here are closer to the road and sit at the edge of aspen forests. Both Black Canyon and Big Tesuque campgrounds, along the Santa Fe Scenic Byway, NM 475, are equipped with vault toilets.

1474 Rodeo Rd., Santa Fe, NM 87505. ✆ **505/438-5300** or 505/753-7331 (Espanola District). www.fs.fed.us/r3/sfe. **Amenities:** Vault toilets; drinking and all-purpose water.

WHERE TO DINE

Santa Fe abounds in dining options, with hundreds of restaurants in all categories. Competition among them is steep, and spots are continually opening and closing. Locals watch closely to see which ones will survive. Some chefs create dishes that incorporate traditional Southwestern foods with ingredients not indigenous to the region; their restaurants are referred to in the listings as New American. There is also standard regional New Mexican cuisine, and beyond that, diners can opt for excellent steak and seafood, as well as Continental, European, Asian, and, of course, Mexican menus. On the south end of town, Santa Fe has the requisite

Where to Dine in Downtown Santa Fe

Adobe Abode **5**

Don Gaspar Inn **9**

Eldorado Hotel & Spa **6**

El Farolito **8**

Four Kachinas Inn **10**

Garrett's Desert Inn **17**

Hacienda Nicholas **19**

Hotel Plaza Real **12**

Hotel St. Francis **11**

Hotel Santa Fe **4**

Inn & Spa at Loretto **15**

Inn of the Anasazi **13**

Inn of the Five Graces **16**

Inn on the Alameda **18**

La Fonda **14**

La Posada de Santa Fe Resort and Spa **20**

The Lodge at Santa Fe **1**

Old Santa Fe Inn **7**

Santa Fe Motel and Inn **3**

Water Street Inn **2**

chain establishments such as **Outback Steakhouse,** 2574 Camino Entrada (© **505/424-6800**), **Olive Garden,** 3781 Cerrillos Rd. (© **505/438-7109**), and **Red Lobster,** 4450 Rodeo Rd. (© **505/473-1610**).

Especially during peak tourist seasons, dinner reservations may be essential. Reservations are always recommended at better restaurants.

Downtown

This area includes the circle defined by the Paseo de Peralta and St. Francis Drive, as well as Canyon Road.

EXPENSIVE

¡A La Mesa! Bistro & Wine Bar ★★ NEW AMERICAN   Since its opening in late 2008, this cozy restaurant has drawn crowds. Serving what it calls "classy comfort food from all over the world," it lives up to its goal. The atmosphere melds the curves of a century-old adobe with modern touches such as a beaded shimmer screen covering one wall. The service is refined. Your meal might start with a frisée salad with mushroom confit, bacon, and a basil vinaigrette. For a main course, the steak frites with green peppercorn and cognac sauce and, of course, french fries, offers brilliant flavor, as does the honey-lacquered duck with sour cherry sauce and mascarpone polenta. A diverse and reasonable international wine list accompanies the menu. For dessert, try the *pithivier,* a puff pastry with almond marzipan cream on a bed crème anglaise.

428 Agua Fria St. © **505/988-2836.** Reservations recommended. Main courses $18–$25; brunch $8–$20. AE, DISC, MC, V. June–Aug Wed–Sun 11:30am–2pm (with a brunch menu Sun) and daily 5:30–9:30pm; Sept–May Mon–Sat 5:30–9:30pm. The schedule may change, so call to confirm.

Cafe Pasqual's ★★ NEW AMERICAN/MEXICAN   Pasqual's owner uses mostly organic ingredients in her dishes, and the walls are lined with murals depicting villagers playing guitars and drinking. It's a festive place, though it's also excellent for a romantic dinner. My favorite dish for breakfast or lunch is the *huevos motuleños* (two eggs over easy on blue-corn tortillas and black beans topped with sautéed bananas, feta cheese, salsa, and green chile). Soups and salads are also served for lunch, and there's a delectable grilled-salmon burrito with herbed goat cheese and cucumber salsa. The frequently changing dinner menu offers grilled meats and seafood, plus vegetarian specials. Start with the Mexican prawn cocktail with lime, tomato, and avocado, and move on to the chicken mole enchiladas with cilantro rice and orange-jicama salad. There's a communal table for those who would like to meet new people over a meal. Pasqual's offers imported beers and wine by the bottle or glass. Try to go at an odd hour—late morning or afternoon—or make a reservation for dinner; otherwise, you'll have to wait.

121 Don Gaspar Ave. © **505/983-9340.** www.pasquals.com. Reservations recommended for dinner. Main courses $8–$15 breakfast, $9–$17 lunch, $19–$39 dinner. AE, MC, V. Daily 8am–3pm and 5:30–9:30pm.

The Compound ★★★ NEW AMERICAN/CONTINENTAL   This reincarnation of one of Santa Fe's classic restaurants serves some of the most flavorful and daring food in the Southwest. Inside, it's an elegant old adobe with white walls often offset by bold splashes of flowers. Outside, during warm months, a broad patio shelters diners from the city bustle. With friendly, efficient service, this is an excellent place for a romantic dinner or a relaxing lunch. Chef and owner Mark Kiffin (a James

Beard award winner and the former chef at Coyote Café) lets his creativity soar. For lunch, monkfish chorizo with watercress is outrageously tasty. At dinner, you might start off with tuna tartare topped with Osetra caviar. For an entree, a signature dish is the grilled beef tenderloin with Italian potatoes and foie gras hollandaise, the beef so tender you won't quite believe it. Finish with a warm bittersweet liquid-chocolate cake. A carefully selected beer and wine list accompanies the menu.

653 Canyon Rd. ✆ **505/982-4353.** www.compoundrestaurant.com. Reservations recommended. Main courses $12–$20 lunch, $25–$40 dinner. AE, DC, DISC, MC, V. Mon–Sat noon–2pm; daily 6–9pm. Bar opens nightly at 5pm.

Coyote Café ★★ NEW AMERICAN World-renowned chef and cookbook author Mark Miller put this place on the map decades ago. Now under new ownership, it has gained new popularity as a place for innovative food in a festive environment. The atmosphere blends warm colors, sculpted adobe, and creative lighting to make for a memorable meal. The waitstaff is efficient and friendly. The menu changes seasonally. Past favorites have included sautéed Italian porcinis or prawns over corn cakes with chipotle butter and guacamole. For a main course, look for delights such as pan-seared white miso halibut with roasted lobster jus, wasabi mashed potatoes, and braised baby bok choy; or the Cowboy Cut, a rib-eye with "borracho" beans, red-chile onion rings, and roasted fingerling potatoes. You can order drinks from the full bar or wine by the glass.

Coyote Café has an adjunct establishment. In summer, the place to be seen is the **Rooftop Cantina,** where light Mexican fare and cocktails are served on a festively painted terrace. Try the guacamole and chips, tacos, and burgers.

132 Water St. ✆ **505/983-1615.** www.coyotecafe.com. Reservations recommended. Main courses $19–$36 (Coyote Café), $6–$16 (Rooftop Cantina). AE, DC, DISC, MC, V. Dining room daily 5:30–10pm; Rooftop Cantina daily 11:30am–9:30pm.

El Farol ★★ SPANISH This is the place to head for local ambience and flavors of Spain, Santa Fe, and Mexico. El Farol (the Lantern), set in an 1835 adobe building, is the Canyon Road artists' quarter's original neighborhood bar. The restaurant has cozy low ceilings and hand-smoothed adobe walls. Thirty-five varieties of tapas are offered, including such delicacies as *gambas al ajillo* (shrimp with chile, garlic, Madeira, and lime) and *puerco asado* (pork tenderloin with figs). You can make a meal out of two or three tapas shared with your friends, or order a full dinner such as the paella or the mixed grill, with lamb, chorizo, and shrimp over potatoes. There is live entertainment 7 nights a week—including jazz/swing, folk, and Latin guitar music—starting at 9:30pm. In summer, two outdoor patios are open to diners. Check the web to find out about their flamenco dinner shows. The restaurant offers some of the finest wines and sherries in the world.

808 Canyon Rd. ✆ **505/983-9912.** www.elfarolsf.com. Reservations recommended. Tapas $5–$10; main courses $8.75–$18 lunch, $26–$33 dinner. AE, DC, DISC, MC, V. Daily 11:30am–3pm and 5:30–10pm. Bar until 2am Mon–Sat; until midnight Sun.

Galisteo Bistro & Wine Bar ★★★ 🍴 NEW AMERICAN In a cozy setting that sparkles with conviviality, chefs Robert and Marge Chickering serve innovative cuisine that spans the globe. The bistro features an exhibition kitchen that puts on an active show during the busy dining hours here. Chef Robert greets diners at the door and follows up throughout the meal. Each night features a short list of specials, as well as a carefully planned menu with seasonal offerings. You might start with a buffalo bratwurst with mushrooms and sauerkraut. A popular entree is the chicken saltimbocca—pan-roasted chicken layered with sage, prosciutto, and fontina in a Madeira sauce with vegetables and orzo. As a recent special I had a delectable duck Marsala—served over gnocchi and finished with mushrooms, tomatoes, and cream. For dessert, definitely choose the Mud Puddle—layers of coffee ice cream, chocolate mousse and whipped cream, large enough to share. The wine list here features local and international selections that compliment the menu.

227 Galisteo St. ℰ **505/982-3700.** www.galisteobistro.com. Reservations highly recommended. Tapas $9–$12; main courses $23–$29. AE, DISC, MC, V. Wed–Sun 5–9pm.

Geronimo ★★★ NEW AMERICAN/CONTINENTAL This elegant restaurant offers one of Santa's Fe's most delectable and atmospheric dining experiences. Occupying an adobe structure known as the Borrego House—which was built by Geronimo Lopez in 1756—it retains the feel of an old Santa Fe home. The food is simply fantastic, always using seasonal produce. If you enjoy dining outside, reserve a spot under the portal and watch the action on Canyon Road. You might order the pan-roasted caramel quail with brie and Reggiano polenta, or a *Kurobuta* pork tenderloin with a soy peach glaze and scallion risotto. If you want to try one of Santa Fe's most renowned entrees, order the peppery elk tenderloin with applewood-smoked bacon served with mashed Yukon gold potatoes. For dessert try the white-chocolate mascarpone cheesecake. The menu changes seasonally, and there's a thoughtful wine list, with a primary focus on boutique American vineyards.

724 Canyon Rd. ℰ **505/982-1500.** www.geronimorestaurant.com. Reservations recommended. Main courses $28–$43 dinner. AE, MC, V. Daily 5:45–9:30pm.

La Casa Sena ★★ NEW AMERICAN/NEW MEXICAN This is one of Santa Fe's favorite restaurants, though the food here isn't as precise and flavorful as at Santacafé or Geronimo. It sits in a Territorial-style adobe house built in 1867 by Civil War hero Major José Sena. The house, which surrounds a garden courtyard, is today a veritable art gallery, with museum-quality landscapes on the walls and Taos-style handcrafted furniture. During the warm months, this restaurant has the best patio in town. One of my favorite lunches is the fish tacos with Cuban-*mojo napa* slaw. In the evening, diners might start with a salad of garden greens and New Mexico feta cheese, then move onto a red-chile-crusted pork loin with roasted sweet potatoes.

In the adjacent **La Cantina,** waitstaff sings Broadway show tunes as they carry platters. The Cantina offers the likes of enchiladas with black beans and Mexican rice. Both restaurants have exquisite desserts; try the black-and-white bittersweet chocolate terrine with raspberry sauce. The award-winning wine list features more than 850 selections.

125 E. Palace Ave. ℰ **505/988-9232.** www.lacasasena.com. Reservations recommended. La Casa Sena main courses $8–$19 lunch, $21–$39 dinner; 5-course chef's tasting menu $63, varies with wine price. La Cantina main courses $13–$28. AE, DC, DISC, MC, V. Mon–Sat 11:30am–3pm; Sun brunch 11am–3pm; daily 5:30–10pm.

Restaurant Martín ★★★ NEW AMERICAN Santa Fe's stand-out newcomer offers casual elegance in the historic 1944 Ortiz home, with hardwood floors and bold paintings, as well as sprawling patios perfect for a summer lunch. Opened in 2009, the restaurant is the creation of Chef Martín Rios. A native of Guadalajara,

Mexico, he grew up in Santa Fe, where he started his career as a dishwasher. After formal training, he became executive chef at some of the city's finest restaurants. Finally at his own eatery, he serves innovative flavors often utilizing chile peppers and local, seasonal ingredients. At lunch the delicious grilled-vegetable panini has eggplant, camembert, and golden tomatoes. The restaurant's signature appetizer is an ahi tuna tartare with avocado and jalapeño parfait and toasted nori pancakes. For a dinner entree, the Maine Diver sea scallops with potato-shallot puree and chorizo offers a tasty mix of flavors. For dessert try the bittersweet chocolate truffle cake. The well-conceived wine and beer list is accessible to many wallets.

526 Galisteo St. ✆ **505/820-0919.** www.restaurantmartinsantafe.com. Reservations recommended. Main courses $9–$14 lunch, $19–$30 dinner. AE, DISC, MC, V. Tues–Sun 11:30am–2pm and 5:30–9pm.

Rio Chama Steakhouse ★★ STEAK/SEAFOOD Serving tasty steaks in a refined ranch atmosphere, this is one of Santa Fe's most popular restaurants, with a bright patio during warm months. I suggest sticking to the meat dishes here, though the fish and pasta dishes can be quite good, too. At lunch or dinner you might start with the Capitol Salad, with lots of fresh greens, piñon nuts, and blue cheese crumbles. My favorite for lunch is the green-chile cheeseburger made with New Mexico grass-fed beef. Lunch also brings more formal dishes such as a grilled Atlantic salmon with grilled vegetables and mango salsa. At dinner, the prime rib is a big hit, as is the filet mignon, both served with a potato and vegetable. For dessert, try the chocolate pot. The bar here romps during happy hour, when the booths fill up, martinis nearly overflow, and reasonably priced menu items sate postwork appetites.

414 Old Santa Fe Trail. ✆ **505/955-0765.** www.riochamasteakhouse.com. Reservations recommended on weekend nights. Main courses $8.50–$17 lunch, $18–$39 dinner. AE, DC, DISC, MC, V. Daily 11am–3pm and 5–10pm. Patio bar 5pm–closing.

Santacafé ★★★ 📷 NEW AMERICAN This is where I go to celebrate special occasions. The food combines the best of many cuisines, from Asian to Southwestern, served in an elegant setting with minimalist decor. The white walls are decorated only with deer antlers, and each room contains a fireplace. In warm months you can sit under elm trees in the charming courtyard. Beware that on busy nights the rooms are noisy. Their Sunday brunch menu offers such delights as a mascarpone-stuffed French toast and poached eggs with corned beef. For a lunch or dinner starter, try the shiitake and cactus spring rolls with Southwestern *ponzu*. One of my favorite lunches is the baby spinach niçoise salad with tuna seared to perfection. At dinner I've enjoyed the grilled rack of lamb with rosemary risotto. There's an extensive whole- and half-bottle wine list, with wine by the glass as well. Desserts, as elegant as the rest of the food, are made in-house; try the warm chocolate upside-down cake with vanilla ice cream.

231 Washington Ave. ✆ **505/984-1788.** www.santacafe.com. Reservations recommended. Main courses $6.50–$11 lunch, $19–$33 dinner. AE, DISC, MC, V. Daily 11:30am–2pm and 5:30–9pm.

315 Restaurant & Wine Bar ★★ BISTRO/FRENCH This classy French bistro enjoyed instant success when it opened in 1995 because the food is simply excellent. The cozy atmosphere provides a perfect setting for a romantic meal, and during warm months the patio is a popular place to people-watch, with little white lights setting the whole place aglow. Service is excellent. The menu changes seasonally and more recently offers a number of Italian dishes. The daily prix-fixe menu offers some great

family-friendly RESTAURANTS

Blue Corn Cafe (p. 150)   A relaxed atmosphere and their own menu pleases kids, while excellent brewpub beer pleases parents.

Bumble Bee's Baja Grill (p. 150)   A casual atmosphere allows parents to relax while their kids chow down on quesadillas and burritos.

deals. You might start with the grilled prawn skewer with tomato chutney and move on to the roasted halibut served with baby carrots and asparagus. Save room for dessert, such as the flourless chocolate cake with pistachio ice cream and Grand Marnier sauce. The wine list includes more than 250 offerings from France to California to Australia, with many by-the-glass selections served at table or at the new wine bar.

315 Old Santa Fe Trail. ✆ **505/986-9190.** www.315santafe.com. Reservations recommended. Main courses $9–$17 lunch, $18–$33 dinner. AE, DISC, MC, V. Sun–Thurs 5:30–9pm; Fri–Sat 5:30–9:30pm; summer only Fri 11:30am–2pm.

MODERATE

Cowgirl Hall of Fame ★ REGIONAL AMERICAN/BARBECUE/CAJUN   This raucous bar/restaurant serves decent food in a festive atmosphere. The main room is a bar—a hip hangout spot, and a good place to eat as well. The back room is quieter, with wood floors and tables and plenty of cowgirl memorabilia. Best of all is sitting out on a brick patio lit with strings of white lights during the warm season. The service is at times brusque, and the food varies. In winter, my favorite is a big bowl of gumbo or crawfish étouffée, and the rest of the time, I order Jamaican jerk chicken or pork tenderloin when it's a special. Careful, both can be hot. The daily blue-plate special is a real buy, especially on Tuesday nights, when it's *chile rellenos*. There's even a special "kid's corral" that has horseshoes, a rocking horse, a horse-shaped rubber tire swing, hay bales, and a beanbag toss. Happy hour is daily from 3 to 6pm. There is also live music almost every night, a pool hall, and a deli.

319 S. Guadalupe St. ✆ **505/982-2565.** www.cowgirlsantafe.com. Reservations recommended. Main courses $7–$13 lunch, $8–$23 dinner. AE, DISC, MC, V. Mon–Fri 11am–midnight; Sat 10am–midnight; Sun 10am–11pm. Bar Mon–Sat until 2am; Sun until midnight.

Il Piatto Cucina Italiano ★★ 🍴 NORTHERN ITALIAN   This simple Italian cafe brings innovative flavors to thinner wallets. It's simple and elegant, with contemporary art on the walls—nice for a romantic evening. Service is efficient, though on a busy night, overworked. The menu changes seasonally, complemented by a few perennial standards. For a starter, try the grilled calamari with shaved fennel and aioli. Among entrees, my favorite is the pancetta-wrapped trout with grilled polenta and wild mushrooms. The Gorgonzola-walnut ravioli is a favorite of many, though not quite enough food to fill me up, so I order an appetizer. A full wine and beer menu is available.

95 W. Marcy St. ✆ **505/984-1091.** www.ilpiattosantafe.com. Reservations recommended. Main courses $15–$22. AE, DISC, MC, V. Mon–Fri 11:30am–2pm; daily 5:30–9pm. Closed July 4.

India Palace ★★ INDIAN   Once every few weeks, I get a craving for the lamb vindaloo served at this restaurant in the center of downtown. A festive ambience, with pink walls painted with mosque rooflines, makes this a nice place for a relaxed meal. The service is efficient, and most of the waiters are from India, as is the chef. The tandoori chicken, fish, lamb, and shrimp are rich and flavorful, and the *baingan bhartha* (eggplant) makes a nice accompaniment. A lunch buffet provides an excellent selection of both vegetarian and nonvegetarian dishes at a reasonable price. Beer and wine are available, or you might want some chai tea.

227 Don Gaspar Ave. (inside the Water St. parking compound). © **505/986-5859.** www.indiapalace. com. Reservations recommended. Main courses $11–$26; luncheon buffet $9.50. AE, DC, DISC, MC, V. Daily 11:30am–2:30pm and 5–10pm. Closed Super Bowl Sunday.

La Boca ★★ 🎁 SPANISH/MEDITERRANEAN   Amid cream-colored walls and sparse decor, with simple white-clothed tables set close together, Chef James Campbell Caruso brings the sensations of southern Spain to your palate. Utilizing traditional Spanish foods with mixtures of Arabic and Moroccan flavors, the menu always has welcome surprises. Such artistry has garnered the restaurant acclaim in *Travel + Leisure, Esquire,* and the *New York Times.* Only tapas are served at dinner, emphasizing a social way of dining, since dishes circulate—along with conversation—around the table. You may sample Velarde peaches wrapped in *jamón serrano* or a grilled hanger steak draped with smoked sea-salt-caramel sauce. Full entrees such as paella are available as well. Accenting the experience are selections from a handpicked wine list focusing on Spanish, Italian, and South American vineyards—all served by a knowledgeable and conscientious waitstaff.

72 W. Marcy St. © **505/982-3433.** www.labocasf.com. Reservations recommended. Main courses $8–$24 lunch; dinner tapas $6–$14; 3-, 4-, and 5-course tasting menus $45–$65. AE, DISC, MC, V. Mon–Sat 11:30am–10pm; Sun 5–10pm.

Shohko Cafe ★★ ASIAN   Santa Fe's favorite sushi restaurant serves fresh fish in a 150-year-old adobe building that was once a bordello. The atmosphere is sparse and comfortable, a blending of New Mexican decor (such as ceiling vigas and Mexican tile floors) with traditional Japanese decorative touches (rice-paper screens, for instance). Up to 30 fresh varieties of raw seafood, including sushi and sashimi, are served at plain pine tables in various rooms or at the sushi bar. Request the sushi bar, where the atmosphere is coziest, and you can watch the chefs at work. My mother likes the tempura combination with veggies, shrimp, and scallops. On an odd night, I'll order the salmon teriyaki, but most nights I have sushi, particularly the *anago* and spicy tuna roll—though if you're daring, you might try the Santa Fe Roll (with green chile, shrimp tempura, and *masago*). Wine, imported beers, and hot sake are available.

321 Johnson St. © **505/982-9708.** Reservations recommended. Main courses $5–$19 lunch, $8.50–$25 dinner. AE, DISC, MC, V. Mon–Fri 11:30am–2pm; Mon–Thurs 5:30–9pm; Fri–Sat 5:30–9:30pm.

Vinaigrette ★★ BISTRO   This new restaurant serves inventive salads, soups, and sandwiches on one of the city's best patios. It's a delightful place to sit and sip herbal iced tea under shade trees, but allow plenty of time because the patio fills quickly. Inside, vermillion-colored chairs and butcher-block tables create a contemporary ambience that appeals to some more than others and tends to be noisy. Still, the food uses seasonal ingredients, much of them sourced from the chef's own farm in Nambé, north of Santa Fe. The salad selections include classics such as a Greek and Cobb, but also signature ones such as an Asian beef—marinated steak over arugula, roasted cherry tomatoes, and rice noodles with a Thai peanut vinaigrette. Daily soup and sandwich specials also accompany the regular menu, as does an inventive wine and beer list.

709 Don Cubero Alley. ✆ **505/820-9205.** Reservations accepted for dinner only. Main courses $8–$16. AE, DISC, MC, V. Mon–Sat 11am–9pm.

INEXPENSIVE

Blue Corn Cafe ★ ☺ NEW MEXICAN/MICROBREWERY   Within a breezy decor—wooden tables and abstract art—you'll find a raucous and buoyant atmosphere. The overworked waitstaff may be slow, but they're friendly. I recommend sampling dishes from the combination menu, which includes such favorites as enchiladas and tamales. You can get two to five items served with your choice of rice, beans, or one of the best *posoles* (hominy and chile) that I've tasted. Kids have their own menu and crayons to keep them occupied. Nightly specials include the tasty shrimp fajitas, served with guacamole and the usual toppings. Because this is also a brewery, you might want to sample the High Altitude Pale Ale or Sleeping Dog Stout. My beverage choice is the prickly-pear iced tea (black tea with enough cactus juice to give it a zing). The Spanish flan is tasty and large enough to share. **The Blue Corn Cafe & Brewery,** 4056 Cerrillos Rd., Suite G (✆ **505/438-1800**), on the south side at the corner of Cerrillos and Rodeo roads, has similar fare and atmosphere.

133 W. Water St. ✆ **505/984-1800.** www.bluecorncafe.com. Reservations accepted for parties of 6 or more. Main courses $10–$12. AE, DC, DISC, MC, V. Daily 11am–10pm.

Body ★★ ASIAN/HEALTH FOOD   My best friend and I eat lunch here every week in order to partake of the calming atmosphere. The cafe atmosphere is quiet, with wood floors and dark wood tables. The service, though good-natured, seems to be perpetually in training. The main draws for us are the mostly organic offerings that always leave us feeling healthy. Breakfast, served all day, includes an excellent granola and a number of egg dishes such as an omelet with goat cheese, basil pesto, tomatoes, and spinach, served with potatoes and toast. Lunch and dinner (same menu) offer such simply delicious food as grilled vegetables with tofu (or chicken or salmon, if you'd prefer), and a very light lemon grass, coconut, and ginger curry, with lots of vegetables. Salads, sandwiches, and a selection of raw entrees round out the menu, as well as smoothies, chai tea, and desserts such as a yummy mixed berry pie. Organic beers and wines are offered as well.

333 Cordova Rd. ✆ **505/986-0362.** www.bodyofsantafe.com. Main courses $6–$11. AE, DISC, MC, V. Daily 7am–9pm.

Bumble Bee's Baja Grill ★ 🎁 ☺ MEXICAN   This new "beestro" offers a refreshing twist on fast food: It's actually healthy! The secret? Tacos are made Mexican style, with a tortilla folded around quality meat, fish, and poultry grilled with veggies. You pick from an array of salsas. Waist watchers can sample from a selection of salads, including one with grilled chicken and avocado. Rotisserie chicken and various burritos round out the main menu, while kids have their own options, such as the quesadillas. Diners order at a counter, and a waiter brings the food. The decor is a bit Formica-esque for my tastes, though the primary colors are fun. During warm months, I try to nab a patio table. Evenings often offer live jazz music, when folks sit back and sip beer and wine. There's also a drive-through window. There's another **Bumble Bee's Baja Grill** at 3777 Cerrillos Rd (🕿 **505/988-3278**), with similar decor and offerings, on the south side of town.

301 Jefferson St. (from W. San Francisco St., take Guadalupe 2 blocks north). 🕿 **505/820-2862.** www.bumblebeesbajagrill.com. Main courses $7–$12. AE, MC, V. Daily 11am–9pm.

Guadalupe Cafe ★★ NEW MEXICAN A real locals' choice for New Mexican food, this casually elegant cafe occupies a white stucco building that's warm and friendly and has a nice-size patio for dining in warmer months. Service is conscientious. For breakfast, try the spinach-mushroom burritos or huevos rancheros, and for lunch, the chalupas or stuffed *sopaipillas*. Any other time, I'd start with fresh roasted *ancho* chiles (filled with a combination of Montrachet and Monterey Jack cheeses and piñon nuts, and topped with your choice of chile) and move on to the sour-cream chicken enchilada or any of the other New Mexican dishes. Order both red and green chile ("Christmas") so that you can sample some of the best sauces in town. Beware, though: The chile here can be hot, and the chef won't put it on the side. Diners can order from a choice of delicious salads, such as a Caesar with chicken. Daily specials are available, and don't miss the famous chocolate-amaretto adobe pie for dessert. Beer and wine are served.

422 Old Santa Fe Trail. 🕿 **505/982-9762.** Main courses $5.50–$10 breakfast, $6–$12 lunch, $8–$17 dinner. DISC, MC, V. Tues–Fri 7am–2pm; Sat–Sun 8am–2pm; Tues–Sat 5–9pm.

La Choza ★★ NEW MEXICAN This sister restaurant of the Shed (see below) offers some of the best New Mexican food in town at a convenient location near the intersection of Cerrillos Road and St. Francis Drive. When other restaurants are packed, you'll only wait a little while here. It's a warm, casual eatery with vividly painted walls; it's especially popular on cold days, when diners gather around the wood-burning stove and fireplace. The patio is delightful in summer. Service is friendly and efficient. The menu offers enchiladas, tacos, and burritos, as well as green-chile stew, chile con carne, and *carne adovada*. The portions are medium size, so if you're hungry, start with guacamole or nachos. For dessert, you can't leave without trying the mocha cake (chocolate cake with a mocha pudding filling, served with whipped cream). Vegetarians and children have their own menus. Beer and wine are available. La Choza now boasts a full bar.

905 Alarid St. 🕿 **505/982-0909.** Main courses $9–$12. AE, DISC, MC, V. Summer Mon–Sat 11am–2:30pm and 5–9pm; winter Mon–Thurs 11am–2:30pm and 5–8pm, Fri–Sat 11am–2:30pm and 5–9pm.

Plaza Cafe ★ AMERICAN/DELI/NEW MEXICAN/GREEK Santa Fe's best example of diner-style eating, this cafe has excellent food in a bright and friendly atmosphere right on the plaza. A restaurant since the turn of the 20th century, the decor has changed only enough to stay comfortable and clean, with red upholstered banquettes, Art Deco tile, and a soda fountain–style service counter. Service is always quick and conscientious, and only during the heavy tourist seasons will you have to wait long for a table. Breakfasts are excellent and large, and the hamburgers and sandwiches at lunch and dinner are good. I also like the soups and New Mexican dishes, such as the bowl of green-chile stew, or, if you're more adventurous, the pumpkin *posole*. Check out the Greek dishes, such as vegetable moussaka or beef and lamb gyros. Beer and wine are available.

54 Lincoln Ave. (on the plaza). 🕿 **505/982-1664.** www.thefamousplazacafe.com. Reservations not accepted. Main courses $8–$17. AE, DISC, MC, V. Daily 7am–9pm.

DINING ON THE outskirts

If you're on the south or east side of Santa Fe, you might want to try some of the excellent restaurants on the city's outskirts. Toward the east is the famed **Harry's Roadhouse ★★**, Old Las Vegas Highway (℃ **505/989-4629**), always packed with locals, but worth a wait to sample from their menu of inventive diner-style food. Try the burgers or the salmon with a mustard glaze. It's open daily 7am to 9:30pm. Also in that vicinity, try **Real Food Nation ★★**, 624 Old Las Vegas Hwy. (℃ **505/466-3886;** www.realfoodnation.biz). Greenhouses, orchards, and gardens are on-site, so nearly every item is locally grown. Their veggie burger is homemade and hearty, and the cookies are big enough to share.

The Shed ★★ NEW MEXICAN   This longtime locals' favorite is so popular that during lunch lines often form outside. Half a block east of the plaza and a luncheon institution since 1953, it occupies several rooms and the patio of a rambling hacienda that was built in 1692. Festive folk art adorns the doorways and walls. The food is delicious, some of the best in the state, and a fine example of traditional Hispanic and Pueblo cooking. The red-chile cheese enchilada is renowned in Santa Fe. Tacos and burritos are good, too. The green-chile stew is a local favorite. The Shed has added vegetarian and low-fat Mexican foods to the menu, as well as a variety of soups and salads and grilled chicken and steak. Don't leave without trying the mocha cake, possibly the best dessert you'll ever eat. In addition to wine and a number of beers, there's full bar service. The cantina-style bar is a fun place to schmooze, and the brick patio is well shaded.

113½ E. Palace Ave. ℃ **505/982-9030.** www.sfshed.com. Reservations accepted at dinner. Main courses $6.75–$11 lunch, $8–$19 dinner. AE, DC, DISC, MC, V. Mon–Sat 11am–2:30pm and 5:30–9pm. Bar opens at 4pm.

Tomasita's Cafe ★ NEW MEXICAN   When I was in high school, I used to eat at Tomasita's, a little dive on a back street. I always ordered a burrito, and I think people used to bring liquor in bags. It's now in a modern building near the train station, and its food has become renowned. The atmosphere is simple—hanging plants and wood accents—with lots of families sitting at booths or tables and a festive spillover from the bar, where many come to drink margaritas. Service is quick, even a little rushed, which is my biggest gripe about Tomasita's. Sure, the food is still tasty, but unless you go at some totally odd hour, you'll wait for a table, and once you're seated, you may eat and be out again in less than an hour. The burritos are still excellent, though you may want to try the *chile rellenos*, a house specialty. Vegetarian dishes, burgers, steaks, and daily specials are also offered. There's full bar service.

500 S. Guadalupe St. ℃ **505/983-5721.** Main courses $6–$15 lunch, $6.25–$16 dinner. AE, DISC, MC, V. Mon–Sat 11am–10pm.

The North Side

MODERATE

Tesuque Village Market ★ AMERICAN/NEW MEXICAN   Located under a canopy of cottonwoods at the center of this quaint village, the restaurant doesn't have the greatest food but makes for a nice adventure 10 minutes north of town. During warmer months, you can sit on the porch; in other seasons, the interior is comfortable, with plain wooden tables next to a deli counter and upscale market. For me, this is a breakfast place, where blue-corn pancakes rule. Friends of mine like the breakfast burritos and huevos rancheros. Lunch and dinner are also popular, and there's always a crowd (though, if you have to wait for a table, the wait is usually brief). For lunch, I recommend the burgers, and for dinner, one of the hearty specials, such as lasagna. A kids' menu is available.

At the junction of Bishop's Lodge Rd. and NM 591, in Tesuque Village. © **505/988-8848.** www.tesuquevillagemarket.com. Reservations recommended for holidays. Main courses $4–$15 breakfast, $7–$14 lunch and dinner. MC, V. Daily 7am–9pm.

South Side

Santa Fe's motel strip and other streets south of Paseo de Peralta have their share of good, reasonably priced restaurants. Take note that the highly recommended **Bumble Bee's Baja Grill** and the **Blue Corn Cafe** have a south-side location (see above for both). Also, Marisco's La Playa has a second location on Cerrillos Road, called **Marisco's Costa Azul.**

MODERATE

Mu Du Noodles ★★ ASIAN   If you're ready for a light, healthy meal with lots of flavor, head to this small restaurant about an 8-minute drive from downtown. The two main rooms, with coral- and butter-colored walls, plain pine tables and chairs, and Asian prints on the walls provide a cozy ambience. The woodsy-feeling patio is definitely worth requesting during the warmer months. Chef Mu uses organic produce and meats and wild seafood whenever she can. My favorite appetizer is the lamb *martabak,* Indonesian dumplings served with a cilantro-mint dipping sauce. For an entree I often order the Malaysian *laksa,* thick rice noodles in a blend of

DINING ON THE outskirts—north

If you'd like to take a little drive en route to dinner, or are cruising into Santa Fe from the north, you'll find a number of excellent dining options. You can have a little history with your crab cakes or filet mignon at **Las Fuentes Restaurant & Bar** ★★ at Bishop's Lodge Ranch Resort & Spa, 1297 Bishop's Lodge Rd. (© **505/819-4035;** www.bishopslodge.com). When you finish feasting, ask for a key at the front desk and then take a short walk up some steps to the 1853 chapel, which once served as Bishop Jean-Baptiste Lamy's retreat. Las Fuentes is open daily for breakfast, lunch, and dinner. Among the pink hills north of Santa Fe at Encantado Resort, **Terra** ★★, 198 NM 592 (© **877/262-4666;** www.encantadoresort.com) serves New American cuisine with one of the city's finest sunset views. You might try lobster spaghettini. Terra is open daily for breakfast, lunch, and dinner. Feast on the region's best guacamole, mixed tableside at **Gabriel's** ★★ on US 84/285 (© **505/455-7000;** www.restauranteur.com/gabriels), 15 minutes north of Santa Fe. The steak tacos are excellent. The restaurant is open Sunday to Thursday 11:30am to 9pm and Friday and Saturday 11:30am to 10pm.

coconut milk, hazelnuts, onions, and red curry, stir-fried with chicken or tofu and julienned vegetables and sprouts. If you're eating with others, you may each want to order a different dish and share. Definitely check out the daily specials, which usually include a fish dish. An interesting selection of beers, wines, and boutique sakes is available, tailored to the menu.

1494 Cerrillos Rd. ✆ **505/983-1411.** www.mudunoodles.com. Reservations for parties of 3 or larger only. Main courses $9–$18. AE, DC, DISC, MC, V. Tues–Sat 5:30–9pm (sometimes 10pm in summer).

Second Street Brewery ★ MICROBREWERY/AMERICAN   In both its 2nd Street location and its Santa Fe Railyard one, this brewery creates a lively pub scene and fairly warm atmosphere. The decor includes contemporary art and wooden tables. It's a party type of place, especially during the warm months, when diners and beer drinkers sit out on the patio. The beers are quite tasty, and you can get a 4-ounce sampler size for $1.25 and try a few different brews. The food isn't extremely memorable, but in winter, it can warm a hearty appetite with such home-style dishes as chicken potpie (as a special) and shepherd's pie. The fish and chips is a big seller, as are the burgers topped with green chile and cheese. The menu also offers lighter fare, such as quiches, soups, and salads. There's a kids' menu, and wines are available. Look for their "Hoppy" Hour, when beer prices are reduced. There are also darts all the time and live entertainment several nights a week.

1814 2nd St. (at the railroad tracks). ✆ **505/982-3030.** Downtown Railyard location: 1607 Paseo del Peralta. ✆ **505/989-3278.** www.secondstreetbrewery.com. Main courses $5–$13. AE, DISC, MC, V. Mon–Thurs 11am–10pm; Fri–Sat 11am–11pm (bar until later); Sun noon–9pm.

WHAT TO SEE & DO

One of the oldest cities in the United States, Santa Fe has long been a center for the creative and performing arts, so it's not surprising that most of the city's major sights are related to local history and the arts. The city's Museum of New Mexico, art galleries and studios, historic churches, and cultural sights associated with local Native American and Hispanic communities all merit a visit. It would be easy to spend a full week sightseeing in the city, without ever heading out to any nearby attractions.

The Top Attractions

Georgia O'Keeffe Museum ★★   The Georgia O'Keeffe Museum, inaugurated in July 1997, contains the largest collection of O'Keeffes in the world: currently 1,149 paintings, drawings, and sculptures, and 1,851 works by other artists of note. It's the largest museum in the United States dedicated solely to an internationally known woman artist. You can see such remarkable O'Keeffes as *Jimson Weed,* painted in 1932, and *Evening Star No. VI,* from 1917. The museum presents special exhibitions that are either devoted entirely to O'Keeffe's work or combine examples of her art with works by her American modernist contemporaries. My favorite in recent years brought together works of O'Keeffe and photographer Ansel Adams. The rich and varied collection adorns the walls of a cathedral-like, 13,000-square-foot space—a former Baptist church with adobe walls. O'Keeffe's images are tied inextricably to local desert landscapes. She first visited New Mexico in 1929 and returned for extended periods from the '20s through the '40s. In 1949 she moved here permanently. An excellent film at the museum depicts her life.

Downtown Santa Fe Attractions

Church ✚
Information ⓘ
Post Office ✉

Georgia O'Keefe Museum **2**

Institute of American Indian Arts Museum **5**

Loretto Chapel Museum **7**

Mission of San Miguel **9**

New Mexico Museum of Art **3**

New Mexico State Capitol (Roundhouse) **8**

New Mexico History Museum
  & the Palace of the Governors **4**

Santuario de Nuestra Señora de Guadalupe **1**

St. Francis Cathedral **6**

217 Johnson St. © **505/946-1000.** www.okeeffemuseum.org. Admission $9, free for students and children 18 and under, free for all first Fri of each month 5-8pm. Daily 10am-5pm (Fri until 8pm). Closed Tues Nov-May.

New Mexico History Museum and the Palace of the Governors ★★   Open in 2009, the New Mexico History Museum presents the state's unique role in world history. Set in 96,000 square feet of exhibit space, the museum offers visitors an interactive experience utilizing voice recordings, music and electronic media to explore the region occupied by Pueblo, Navajo, and Apache people, followed by the arrival of the Spanish in the 1500s, and, finally, the present day.

You'll enter through the Palace of the Governors. Built in 1610 as the original capital of New Mexico, the palace has been in continuous public use longer than any other structure in the United States. Its defining moment was when the Pueblo people took it over during the Pueblo Revolt of 1680. Begin out front, where Native Americans sell jewelry, pottery, and some weavings under the protection of the portal. This is a good place to buy, and it's a fun place to shop, especially if you take the time to visit with the artisans about their work. When you buy a piece, you may learn its history, a treasure as valuable as the piece itself. Plan to spend 2 or more hours exploring the museum and shopping here.

Two shops are of particular interest. One is the bookstore/gift shop, which has an excellent selection of art, history, and anthropology books. The other is the print shop and bindery, where limited-edition works are produced on hand-operated presses. Free docent tours are offered daily, as are downtown walking tours April through October. Call for the schedule.

North plaza. © **505/476-5100.** www.palaceofthegovernors.org. Admission $8 adults, free for children 16 and under, free for all Fri 5-8pm. 4-day passes (good at all branches of the Museum of New Mexico and the Museum of Spanish Colonial Art) $20 for adults. Tues-Sun in winter and daily in summer 10am-5pm (Fri until 8pm).

New Mexico Museum of Art ★   Opposite the Palace of the Governors, this was one of the first Pueblo revival–style buildings constructed in Santa Fe (in 1917). The museum's permanent collection of more than 20,000 works emphasizes regional art and includes landscapes and portraits by all the Taos masters, *los Cincos Pintores* (a 1920s organization of Santa Fe artists), and contemporary artists. The museum also has a collection of photographic works by such masters as Ansel Adams and Eliot Porter. Modern artists are featured in temporary exhibits throughout the year. Two sculpture gardens present a range of three-dimensional art, from the traditional to the abstract.

Graceful **St. Francis Auditorium,** patterned after the interiors of traditional Hispanic mission churches, adjoins the art museum. A museum shop sells gifts, art books, prints, and postcards of the collection.

107 W. Palace (at Lincoln Ave.). © **505/476-5072.** www.nmartmuseum.org. Admission $9 adults, free for seniors Wed, free for children 16 and under, free for all Fri 5-8pm. 4-day passes (good at all branches of the Museum of New Mexico and the Museum of Spanish Colonial Art) $20 for adults. Tues-Sun 10am-5pm (Fri until 8pm). Closed New Year's Day, Easter, Thanksgiving, Christmas.

St. Francis Cathedral ★   Santa Fe's grandest religious structure is an architectural anomaly in Santa Fe because its design is French. Just a block east of the plaza, it was built between 1869 and 1886 by Archbishop Jean-Baptiste Lamy in the style of the great cathedrals of Europe. French architects designed the Romanesque

museum BINGEING

If you're a museum buff, pick up a **Museum of New Mexico's 4-day pass.** It's good at all branches of the Museum of New Mexico: the Palace of the Governors, the Museum of Art, the Museum of International Folk Art, and the Museum of Indian Arts & Culture, with the Museum of Spanish Colonial Art thrown in for good measure. The cost is $20 for adults. Also ask about the new **Culture Pass,** which provides full one-time admission to each of the state's 14 museums during a 12-month period for $25.

building—named after Santa Fe's patron saint—and Italian masons assisted with its construction. The small adobe Our Lady of the Rosary chapel on the northeast side of the cathedral has a Spanish look. Built in 1807, it's the only portion that remains from Our Lady of the Assumption Church, founded along with Santa Fe in 1610. The new cathedral was built over and around the old church.

A wooden icon set in a niche in the wall of the north chapel, Our Lady of Peace, is the oldest representation of the Madonna in the United States. Rescued from the old church during the 1680 Pueblo Rebellion, it was brought back by Don Diego de Vargas on his (mostly peaceful) reconquest 12 years later—thus, the name. Today, Our Lady of Peace plays an important part in the annual Feast of Corpus Christi in June and July.

The cathedral's front doors feature 16 carved panels of historic note and a plaque memorializing the 38 Franciscan friars who were martyred during New Mexico's early years. There's also a large bronze statue of Archbishop Lamy himself; his grave is under the main altar of the cathedral.

Cathedral Place at San Francisco St. ✆ **505/982-5619.** Donations appreciated. Daily 8am–5pm. Mass Mon-Sat 7am and 5:15pm; Sun 8, 10am, noon, and 5:15pm. Free parking in city lot next to the cathedral.

Santa Fe Plaza ★★ ▣ This square has been the heart and soul of Santa Fe, as well as its literal center, since the city was established in 1610. Originally designed as a meeting place, it has been the site of innumerable festivals and other historical, cultural, and social events. Long ago the plaza was a dusty hive of activity as the staging ground and terminus of the Santa Fe Trail. Today, those who congregate around the central monument enjoy the best people-watching in New Mexico. Live music and dancing are often staged on the gazebo/bandstand in summer. At Christmastime the plaza is decked out with lights. Santa Feans understandably feel nostalgic for the days when the plaza, now the hub of the tourist trade, still belonged to locals rather than outside commercial interests.

At the corner of San Francisco St. and Lincoln Ave. Daily 24 hr.

More Attractions

Institute of American Indian Arts Museum ★ A visit to this museum (with more than 7,000 works, often called the "national collection of contemporary Native American art") offers a profound look into the lives of a people negotiating two worlds: traditional and contemporary. Here, you'll see cutting-edge art that pushes the limits of many media, from creative writing to textile manufacturing to painting.

Much of the work originates from artists from the Institute of American Indian Arts (IAIA), the nation's only congressionally chartered institute of higher education devoted solely to the study and practice of the artistic and cultural traditions of all American Indian and Alaska Native peoples.

Exhibits change periodically, while a more permanent collection of Allan Houser's monumental sculpture is on display in the museum's Art Park. The museum store offers a broad collection of contemporary jewelry, pottery, and other crafts, as well as books and music.

108 Cathedral Place. *©* **505/983-1777.** www.iaia.edu. Admission $5 adults, $2.50 seniors and students, free for children 16 and under. Mon–Sat 10am–5pm; Sun noon–5pm.

Museum of Indian Arts & Culture ★★   An interactive permanent exhibit here has made this one of the most exciting Native American museum experiences in the Southwest. "Here, Now and Always" takes visitors through thousands of years of Native American history. More than 70,000 pieces of basketry, pottery, clothing, carpets, and jewelry—much of it quite old—are on continual rotating display. You begin by entering through a tunnel that symbolizes the *sipapu*, the ancestral Puebloan entrance into the upper worlds; you're greeted by the sounds of trickling water, drums, and Native American music. Videos show Native Americans telling creation stories. Visitors can reflect on the lives of modern-day Native Americans by seeing a traditional Pueblo kitchen juxtaposed with a modern kitchen. You can step into a Navajo hogan (log and mud hut) and stroll through a trading post. The rest of the museum houses an expansive pottery collection as well as changing exhibits. There's always a contemporary show.

Look for demonstrations of traditional skills by tribal artisans and regular programs in a 70-seat multimedia theater. Call for information on year-round lectures and classes on native traditions and arts, as well as performances of Native American music and dancing by tribal groups. The Roland Discovery Corner offers space for kids to build puzzles and stack fake sandstone into a house. The museum shop offers a broad range of jewelry, pottery, books, and music.

710 Camino Lejo. *©* **505/476-1250.** www.miaclab.org. Admission $9 adults, free for children 16 and under. 4-day passes (good at all branches of the Museum of New Mexico and the Museum of Spanish Colonial Art) $20 for adults. Tues–Sun 10am–5pm (also Mon in summer). Drive southeast on Old Santa Fe Trail (beware: Old Santa Fe Trail takes a left turn; if you find yourself on Old Pecos Trail, you missed the turn). Look for signs pointing right onto Camino Lejo.

Museum of International Folk Art ★★★ ☺   This branch of the Museum of New Mexico may not seem quite as typically Southwestern as other Santa Fe museums, but it's the largest of its kind in the world. With a collection of some 130,000 objects from more than 100 countries, it's my favorite city museum, well worth an hour or two of perusing. It was founded in 1953 by the Chicago collector Florence Dibell Bartlett, who said, "If peoples of different countries could have the opportunity to study each other's cultures, it would be one avenue for a closer understanding between men." That's the basis on which the museum operates today.

The special collections include Spanish colonial silver, traditional and contemporary New Mexican religious art, Mexican tribal costumes and majolica ceramics, Brazilian folk art, European glass, African sculptures, and East Indian textiles. Particularly delightful are numerous dioramas of people around the world at work and play in typical town, village, and home settings, which children enjoy.

The Hispanic Heritage Wing houses a fine collection of Spanish colonial and contemporary Hispanic folk art. Folk-art demonstrations, performances, and workshops are often presented here. The 80,000-square-foot museum also has a lecture room, a research library, and two gift shops, where a variety of folk art is available for purchase.

706 Camino Lejo. ℂ **505/476-1200.** www.moifa.org. Admission $9 adults, free for children 16 and under. 4-day passes (good at all branches of the Museum of New Mexico and at the Museum of Spanish Colonial Art) $20 for adults. Daily 10am–5pm (closed Mon Labor Day to Memorial Day). The museum is about 2 miles southeast of the plaza. Drive southeast on Old Santa Fe Trail (beware: Old Santa Fe Trail takes a left turn; if you find yourself on Old Pecos Trail, you missed the turn). Look for signs pointing right onto Camino Lejo.

Museum of Spanish Colonial Art ★   Ironically, beauty sometimes follows in the wake of imperialism. A good example of this is Spanish colonial art, which has flourished from Europe across the Americas and even in the Philippines. This newer museum, located in the same compound as the Museum of International Folk Art, the Museum of Indian Arts & Culture, and the Wheelwright Museum of the American Indian, celebrates this art with a collection of 3,000 devotional and decorative works and utilitarian artifacts. Housed in a home built by noted architect John Gaw Meem, the museum displays *retablos* (religious paintings on wood), *bultos* (free-standing religious sculptures), furniture, metalwork, and textiles and, outside, an 18th-century wooden colonial house from Mexico.

750 Camino Lejo. ℂ **505/982-2226.** www.spanishcolonial.org. Admission $9 adults, free for children 16 and under. 4-day passes (good at all branches of the Museum of New Mexico and this one) $20 for adults. Tues–Sun 10am–5pm. The museum is located about 2 miles southeast of the plaza. Drive southeast on Old Santa Fe Trail (beware: Old Santa Fe Trail takes a left turn; if you find yourself on Old Pecos Trail, you missed the turn). Look for signs pointing right onto Camino Lejo.

SITE Santa Fe ★   This not-for-profit, 18,000-square-foot contemporary art space without a permanent collection has made a place for itself in the City Different, as well as in the international art scene. It's no wonder, with shows by some of the world's most noted contemporary artists. As well as bringing cutting-edge visual art to Santa Fe, SITE sponsors an art and culture series of lectures, multidisciplinary programs, and artist dialogues.

1606 Paseo de Peralta. ℂ **505/989-1199.** www.sitesantafe.org. $10 adults, $5 students and seniors, free for SITE Santa Fe members, free for all Fri–Sat 10–noon during the Farmer's Market. Wed–Sat 10am–5pm (Fri until 7pm); Sun noon–5pm. Closed Thanksgiving, Christmas Eve, Christmas, New Year's Eve, New Year's Day. Call for information about docent tours and tours in Spanish.

Wheelwright Museum of the American Indian ★ ☺ Next door to the folk art museum, this museum resembles a Navajo hogan, with its doorway facing east (toward the rising sun) and its ceiling formed in the interlocking "whirling log" style. It was founded in 1937 by Boston scholar Mary Cabot Wheelwright, in collaboration with a Navajo medicine man, Hastiin Klah, to preserve and document Navajo ritual beliefs and practices. Klah took the designs of sand paintings used in healing ceremonies and adapted them into the woven pictographs that are a major part of the museum's treasure. In 1976, the museum's focus was altered to include the living arts of all Native American cultures. The museum offers three or four exhibits per year. You may see a basketry exhibit, mixed-media Navajo toys, or contemporary Navajo rugs. An added treat here is the Case Trading Post, an arts-and-crafts shop built to resemble the typical turn-of-the-20th-century trading post found on the Navajo reservation. Docent tours of the exhibition are Monday through Friday at 2pm and Saturday at 1pm. Year-round each Saturday and Tuesday morning at 10:15am and Sunday at 2pm, the Trading Post presents a lively and informative introduction to Southwestern Indian art. The museum has excellent access for travelers with disabilities. Best of all here are the **storytelling sessions** ★★ given by Joe Hayes, scheduled in July and August on Saturday and Sunday evenings at 7pm. Check the Web schedule for more details.

704 Camino Lejo. ⓒ **800/607-4636** or 505/982-4636. Fax 505/989-7386. www.wheelwright.org. Donations appreciated. Mon–Sat 10am–5pm; Sun 1–5pm. Closed New Year's Day, Thanksgiving, Christmas. Drive southeast on Old Santa Fe Trail (beware: Old Santa Fe Trail takes a left turn; if you find yourself on Old Pecos Trail, you missed the turn). Look for signs pointing right onto Camino Lejo.

Churches

Loretto Chapel Museum ★★ Though no longer consecrated for worship, the Loretto Chapel is an important site in Santa Fe. Patterned after the famous Sainte-Chapelle in Paris, it was constructed in 1873—by the same French architects and Italian masons who were building Archbishop Lamy's cathedral—as a chapel for the Sisters of Loretto, who had established a school for young women in Santa Fe in 1852.

The chapel is especially notable for its remarkable spiral staircase: It makes two complete 360-degree turns, with no central or other visible support. The structure is steeped in legend. The building was nearly finished in 1878, when workers realized the stairs to the choir loft wouldn't fit. Hoping for a solution more attractive than a ladder, the sisters made a novena (9-day prayer) to St. Joseph—and were rewarded when a mysterious carpenter appeared astride a donkey and offered to build a staircase. Armed with only a saw, a hammer, and a T-square, the master constructed this work of genius by soaking slats of wood in tubs of water to curve them and holding them together with wooden pegs. Then he disappeared without bothering to collect his fee.

207 Old Santa Fe Trail (btw. Alameda and Water sts.). ⓒ **505/982-0092.** www.lorettochapel.com. Admission $2.50 adults, $2 children 7–12 and seniors 65 and over, free for children 6 and under. Mon–Sat 9am–5pm; Sun 10:30am–5pm.

Mission of San Miguel If you really want to get the feel of colonial Catholicism, visit this church. Better yet, attend Mass here. You won't be disappointed. Built in 1610, the church has massive adobe walls, high windows, an elegant altar screen (erected in 1798), and a 780-pound San José bell (now found inside), which was cast in Spain in 1356. It also houses buffalo-hide and deerskin Bible paintings used in 1630 by Franciscan missionaries to teach the Native Americans. Anthropologists have excavated near the altar, down to the original floor that some claim to be part of a 12th-century pueblo. A small store just off the sanctuary sells religious articles.

401 Old Santa Fe Trail (at E. de Vargas St.). ℂ **505/983-3974.** Admission $1 adults, free for children 6 and under. Mon–Sat 9am–5pm; Sun 9am–4pm. Summer hours start earlier. Mass Sun 5pm.

Santuario de Nuestra Señora de Guadalupe ★   This church, built between 1776 and 1796 at the end of El Camino Real by Franciscan missionaries, is believed to be the oldest shrine in the United States honoring the Virgin of Guadalupe, the patron saint of Mexico. Better known as Santuario de Guadalupe, the shrine's adobe walls are almost 3 feet thick, and the deep-red plaster wall behind the altar was dyed with oxblood in traditional fashion when the church was restored early in the 20th century.

It is well worth a visit to see photographs of the transformation of the building over time; its styles have ranged from flat-topped pueblo to New England town meeting and today's northern New Mexico style. On one wall is a famous oil painting, *Our Lady of Guadalupe,* created in 1783 by the renowned Mexican artist José de Alzibar. Painted expressly for this church, it was brought from Mexico City by mule caravan. One of Santa Fe's newest landmarks, the graceful 12-foot, 4,000-pound statue of Our Lady of Guadalupe by Mexican sculptor Georgina "Gogy" Farias, was erected in 2008.

100 S. Guadalupe St. ℂ **505/983-8868.** Donations appreciated. Mon–Fri 9am–4pm. Labor Day to Memorial Day Sun–Fri 9am–6pm. Mass Mon–Fri 6:30am, Sun noon.

Parks & Refuges

Old Fort Marcy Park   Marking the 1846 site of the first U.S. military reservation in the Southwest, this park overlooks the northeast corner of downtown. Only a few mounds remain from the fort, but the Cross of the Martyrs, at the top of a winding brick walkway from Paseo de Peralta near Otero Street, is a popular spot for bird's-eye photographs. The cross was erected in 1920 by the Knights of Columbus and the Historical Society of New Mexico to commemorate the Franciscans killed during the Pueblo Rebellion of 1680. It has since played a role in numerous religious processions. The park is open daily 24 hours, though it's dark and not safe at night.

617 Paseo de Peralta (or travel 3 blocks up Artist Rd. and turn right).

Randall Davey Audubon Center ★   Named for the late Santa Fe artist who willed his home to the National Audubon Society, this wildlife refuge occupies 135 acres at the mouth of Santa Fe Canyon. Just a few minutes' drive from the plaza, it's an excellent escape. More than 100 species of birds and 120 types of plants live here, and varied mammals have been spotted—including black bears, mule deer, mountain lions, bobcats, raccoons, and coyotes. Trails winding through more than 100 acres of the nature sanctuary are open to day hikers, but not to dogs. There's also a natural history bookstore on site.

1800 Upper Canyon Rd. ℂ **505/983-4609.** http://nm.audubon.org. Trail admission $2 adults, $1 children. Daily 9am–5pm. House tours conducted Mon and Fri at 2pm, $5 per person. Free 1-hr. guided bird walk Sat at 8:30am. Gift shop daily 10am–4pm (call for winter hours).

Santa Fe River Park   This is a lovely spot for an early morning jog, a midday walk beneath the trees, or perhaps a sack lunch at a picnic table. The green strip follows the midtown stream for about 4 miles as it meanders along Alameda from St. Francis Drive upstream beyond Camino Cabra, near its source. It's open daily 24 hours, but it's not safe at night.

Alameda St. ✆ **505/955-6977.**

Other Attractions

El Rancho de las Golondrinas ★★ ☺   This 200-acre ranch, about 15 minutes south of the plaza via I-25, was once the last stopping place on the 1,000-mile El Camino Real from Mexico City to Santa Fe. Today, it's a living 18th- and 19th-century Spanish village, comprising a hacienda, a village store, a schoolhouse, and several chapels and kitchens. There's also a working molasses mill, wheelwright and blacksmith shops, shearing and weaving rooms, a threshing ground, a winery and vineyard, and four water mills, as well as dozens of farm animals. A walk around the entire property is 1¼ miles in length, with amazing scenery and plenty of room for the kids to romp.

The Spring Festival (the first full weekend of June) and the Harvest Festival (the first full weekend of Oct) are the year's highlights at Las Golondrinas (the Swallows). On these festival Sundays, the museum opens with a procession and Mass dedicated to San Ysidro, patron saint of farmers. Volunteers in authentic costumes demonstrate shearing, spinning, weaving, embroidery, woodcarving, grain milling, blacksmithing, tinsmithing, soap making, and other activities. There's an exciting atmosphere of Spanish folk dancing, music, theater, and food.

334 Los Pinos Rd. ✆ **505/471-2261.** www.golondrinas.org. Admission $6 adults, $4 seniors and teens, $2 children 5–12, free for children 4 and under. Festival weekends $8 adults, $5 seniors and teens, $3 children 5–12. June–Sept Wed–Sun 10am–4pm; Apr–May and Oct by advance arrangement. From Santa Fe, drive south on I-25, taking exit 276; this will lead to NM 599 going north; turn left on W. Frontage Rd.; drive ½ mile; turn right on Los Pinos Rd.; travel 3 miles to the museum.

New Mexico State Capitol (Roundhouse)   This is the only round capitol building in the U.S. Built in 1966, it's designed in the shape of a Zia Pueblo emblem (or sun sign, which is also the state symbol). It symbolizes the Circle of Life: four winds, four seasons, four directions, and four sacred obligations. Surrounding the capitol is a lush 6½-acre garden boasting more than 100 varieties of plants, including roses, plums, almonds, nectarines, Russian olive trees, and sequoias. Inside you'll find standard functional offices, with New Mexican art hanging on the walls. Check out the Governor's Gallery and the Capitol Art Collection. Self-guided tours are available year-round Monday through Friday 7am to 6pm; Memorial Day to Labor Day guided tours are available Monday through Saturday at 10am and 2pm. All tours and self-guided brochures are free to the public.

Paseo de Peralta and Old Santa Fe Trail. ✆ **505/986-4589.** www.legis.state.nm.us. Free admission. Memorial Day to last Sat in Aug Mon–Sat 7am–7pm, tours Sat 10am and 2pm; rest of year Mon–Fri 7am–6pm, tours by appointment. Free parking.

Santa Fe Southern Railway ★   ["]Riding the old Santa Fe" always referred to riding the Atchison, Topeka & Santa Fe railroad. Ironically, the main route of the AT&SF bypassed Santa Fe, which probably forestalled some development for the capital city. A spur was run off the main line to Santa Fe in 1880, and today, an 18-mile ride along that spur offers views of some of New Mexico's most spectacular scenery.

The Santa Fe Depot is a well-preserved tribute to the Mission architecture that the railroad brought to the West in the early 1900s. Characterized by light-colored stuccoed walls, arched openings, and tiled roofs, this style was part of an architectural revolution in Santa Fe at a time when builders snubbed the traditional pueblo style.

Inside the restored coach, passengers are surrounded by aged mahogany and faded velvet seats. The train snakes through Santa Fe and into the Galisteo Basin, broad landscapes spotted with *piñon* and chamisa, with views of the Sandia and Ortiz mountains. Arriving in the small track town of Lamy, you get another glimpse of a Mission-style station, this one surrounded by spacious lawns where passengers picnic. Check out the sunset rides on weekends and specialty trains throughout the year.

410 S. Guadalupe St. (🕻 **888/989-8600** or 505/989-8600. Fax 505/983-7620. www.thetraininsantafe. com. Tickets $32 adults, $18 children 3–13; evening High Ball Train $28–$35 adults, children not encouraged; evening Barbecue Train $58–$70 adults, $35–$55 children. Discounts available. Depending on the season, trains depart the Santa Fe Depot (call to check schedule) 9:30am–1pm Mon–Sat. Rides also available Fri–Sat evening and Sun afternoon.

Cooking, Art & Photography Classes

If you're looking for something to do that's a little off the beaten tourist path, you might consider taking a class.

You can master the flavors of Santa Fe with an entertaining 3-hour demonstration cooking class at the **Santa Fe School of Cooking and Market ★**, on the upper level of the Plaza Mercado, 116 W. San Francisco St. (🕻 **800/982-4688** or 505/983-4511; www.santafeschoolofcooking.com). The class teaches about the flavors and history of traditional New Mexican and contemporary Southwestern cuisines. "Cooking Light" classes are available as well. Prices range from $40 to $150 and include a meal; call for a class schedule. The adjoining market offers a variety of regional foods and cookbooks, with gift baskets available.

If Southwestern art has you hooked, you can take a drawing and painting class led by Santa Fe artist Jane Shoenfeld. Students sketch such outdoor subjects as the Santa Fe landscape and adobe architecture. In case of inclement weather, classes are held in the studio. Each class lasts for 3 hours, and art materials are included in the fee, which is $125. Private lessons can also be arranged. All levels of experience are welcome. Children's classes can be arranged, and discounts are available for families. You can create your own personal art adventure with one of Shoenfeld's 1-day classes at Ghost Ranch in Abiquiu. Contact Jane at **Sketching Santa Fe ★**, P.O. Box 5912, Santa Fe, NM 87502 (🕻 **505/986-1108;** www.skyfields.net).

Some of the world's most outstanding photographers convene in Santa Fe at various times during the year for the **Santa Fe Workshops ★★**, P.O. Box 9916, Santa Fe, NM 87504, at a delightful campus in the hills on the east side of town (🕻 **505/983-1400;** www.santafeworkshops.com). Most courses are full time, lasting a week. Food and lodging packages are available.

Wine Tastings

If you enjoy sampling regional wines, consider visiting the wineries within easy driving distance of Santa Fe: **Santa Fe Vineyards,** with a retail outlet at 235 Don Gaspar Ave., in Santa Fe (🕻 **505/982-3474;** www.nmwine.com), or the vineyard itself about

20 miles north of Santa Fe to the Nambe Road on 106 W. Shining Sun (© **505/455-2826**); and the **Black Mesa Winery,** 1502 Hwy. 68, in Velarde (© **800/852-6372**), north on US 84/285 to NM 68 (about 1-hr. drive). Be sure to call in advance to find out when the wineries are open for tastings and to get specific directions.

7 Especially for Kids

Don't miss taking the kids to the **Museum of International Folk Art** (p. 158), where they'll love the international dioramas and the toys. Also visit the tepee at the **Wheelwright Museum of the American Indian** (p. 160), where storyteller Joe Hayes spins traditional Spanish *cuentos*, Native American folk tales, and Wild West tall tales on weekend evenings. **The Bishop's Lodge Ranch Resort and Spa** (p. 160) has extensive children's programs during the summer. These include horseback riding, swimming, arts-and-crafts programs, and special activities such as archery and tennis. Kids are sure to enjoy **El Rancho de las Golondrinas** (p. 162), a living 18th- and 19th-century Spanish village comprising a hacienda, a village store, a schoolhouse, and several chapels and kitchens.

The **Genoveva Chavez Community Center,** 3221 Rodeo Rd., is a full-service family recreation center on the south side of Santa Fe. The complex includes a 50m pool, a leisure pool, a therapy pool, an ice-skating rink, three gyms, a workout room, racquetball courts, and an indoor running track, as well as a spa and sauna. For hours and more information, call © **505/955-4001** (www.chavezcenter.com).

Santa Fe Children's Museum ★   This museum offers interactive exhibits and hands-on activities in the arts, humanities, and science. The most notable features include a 16-foot climbing wall that kids—outfitted with helmets and harnesses—can scale, and a 1-acre Southwestern horticulture garden, complete with animals, wetlands, and a greenhouse. This fascinating area serves as an outdoor classroom for ongoing environmental educational programs. Special performances and hands-on sessions with artists and scientists are regularly scheduled. *Family Life* magazine named this as one of the 10 hottest children's museums in the nation.

1050 Old Pecos Trail. © **505/989-8359.** www.santafechildrensmuseum.org. Admission $8 for non-residents; $4 New Mexico residents; $4 children 12 and under. Wed–Sat 10am–5pm; Sun noon–5pm.

Santa Fe Public Library   Special programs, such as storytelling and magic shows, can be found here weekly throughout the summer. The library is in the center of town, 1 block from the plaza.

145 Washington Ave. © **505/955-6780.** www.santafelibrary.org. Mon–Thurs 10am–9pm; Fri–Sat 10am–6pm; Sun 1–5pm. Call for information on current events.

Skateboard Park   Split-level ramps for daredevils, park benches for onlookers, and climbing structures for youngsters are located at this park near downtown.

At the intersection of de Vargas and Sandoval sts. © **505/955-2100.** Free admission. Daily 24 hr.

ORGANIZED TOURS

Bus, Car & Tram Tours

Loretto Line ★   For an open-air tour of the city covering history and sights, contact this company that has been running tours for some 20 years. Tours last 1¼ hours and are offered daily from April to October. They depart at 10am, noon, and 2pm—and sometimes more frequently in high summer.

At the Hotel Loretto, 211 Old Santa Fe Trail. Tours depart from the Loretto Chapel. ℂ **505/983-3701.** www.toursofsantafe.com. Tours $14 adults, $10 children 12 and under.

Walking Tours

As with the independent strolls described above, the following are the best way to get an appreciable feel for Santa Fe's history and culture.

Storytellers and the Southwest: A Literary Walking Tour ★   Barbara Harrelson, a former Smithsonian museum docent and local writer, takes you on a 2-hour literary walking tour of downtown, exploring the history, legends, characters, and authors of the region through its landmarks and historic sites. It's a great way to absorb the unique character of Santa Fe. Tours take place by appointment. Harrelson's book, *Walks in Literary Santa Fe: A Guide to Landmarks, Legends, and Lore* (Gibbs Smith) allows for self-guided tours and is available in local bookstores and online.

924 Old Taos Hwy. ℂ **505/989-4561.** barbarah@newmexico.com. Apr–Oct. Tours $20 per person, with a $40 minimum.

Walking Tour of Santa Fe ★   One of Santa Fe's best walking tours begins under the T-shirt tree at Tees & Skis, 107 Washington Ave., near the northeast corner of the plaza (daily at 9:30am and afternoons by reservation). It lasts about 2½ hours. From November through March, the tour runs by reservation only.

54½ E. San Francisco St. ℂ **800/338-6877** or 505/983-6565. Tours $10 adults, free for children 12 and under.

Miscellaneous Tours

Pathways Customized Tours ★   Don Dietz offers several planned tours, including a downtown Santa Fe walking tour, a full city tour, a trip to the cliff dwellings and native pueblos, a "Taos adventure," and a trip to Georgia O'Keeffe country (with a focus on the landscape that inspired the art now viewable in the O'Keeffe Museum). He will try to accommodate any special requests you might have. These tours last anywhere from 2 to 9 hours, depending on the one you choose. Don has extensive knowledge of the area's culture, history, geology, and flora and fauna, and will help you make the most of your precious vacation time.

161-F Calle Ojo Feliz. ℂ **505/982-5382.** www.santafepathways.com. Tours for 2 or more people $60 (and up) per day. No credit cards.

Rain Parrish ★   A Navajo anthropologist, artist, and curator, Rain Parrish offers custom guide services focusing on cultural anthropology, Native American arts, and the history of the Native Americans of the Southwest. Some of these are true adventures to insider locations. Ms. Parrish includes visits to local Pueblo villages.

704 Kathryn St. ℂ **505/984-8236.** 4-hr. tours for 2 people $135. Additional person $30 per hour, and discounted group rates available.

Santa Fe Detours ★   Santa Fe's most extensive tour-booking agency accommodates almost all travelers' tastes, from bus and rail tours to river rafting, backpacking, and cross-country skiing. The agency can also facilitate hotel reservations, from budget to high end.

54½ E. San Francisco St. (summer tour desk, 107 Washington Ave.). © **800/338-6877** or 505/983-6565. www.sfdetours.com.

Southwest Safaris ★★   This tour is one of the most interesting Southwestern experiences available. You'll fly in a small plane 1,000 feet off the ground to various destinations while pilot Bruce Adams explains millions of years of geologic history. En route to the Grand Canyon, for instance, you may pass by the ancient ruins of Chaco Canyon and over the vivid colors of the Painted Desert, and then, of course, over the spectacular Grand Canyon itself. Trips to many Southwestern destinations are available.

Departs from Santa Fe Airport. © **800/842-4246** or 505/988-4246. www.southwestsafaris.com. Tours $89–$799 per person.

OUTDOOR ACTIVITIES

Set between the granite peaks of the Sangre de Cristo Mountains and the subtler volcanic Jemez Mountains, and with the Rio Grande flowing through, the Santa Fe area offers outdoor enthusiasts many opportunities to play. This is the land of high desert, where temperatures vary with the elevation, allowing for a full range of activities throughout the year.

Ballooning

New Mexico is renowned for its spectacular Balloon Fiesta, which takes place annually in Albuquerque (p. 40). If you want to take a ride, you'll probably have to go to Albuquerque or Taos, but you can book your trip in Santa Fe through **Santa Fe Detours,** 54½ E. San Francisco St. (tour desk for summer, 107 Washington Ave.; © **800/338-6877** or 505/983-6565; www.sfdetours.com). Flights take place early in the day. Rates begin at around $175 a flight. If you have your heart set on a balloon flight, I suggest that you reserve a time early in your trip because flights are sometimes canceled due to bad weather. That way, if you have to reschedule, you'll have enough time to do so.

Biking

You can cycle along main roadways and paved country roads year-round in Santa Fe, but be aware that traffic is particularly heavy around the plaza—and all over town, motorists are not particularly attentive to bicyclists, so you need to be especially alert. Mountain-biking interest has blossomed here and is especially popular in the spring, summer, and fall; the high-desert terrain is rugged and challenging, but mountain bikers of all levels can find exhilarating rides. The Santa Fe Convention and Visitors Bureau can supply you with bike maps.

I recommend the following trails: West of Santa Fe, the **Caja del Rio** area has nice dirt roads and some light-to-moderate technical biking; the **railroad tracks south of Santa Fe** provide wide-open biking on beginner-to-intermediate technical trails; and the **Borrego Trail** up toward the Santa Fe Ski Area is a challenging technical ride that links in with the **Windsor Trail,** a nationally renowned technical romp with plenty of verticality.

In Santa Fe bookstores, or online at sites like Amazon.com, look for *Mountain Biking Northern New Mexico: A Guide to Taos, Santa Fe, and Albuquerque Areas'*

Greatest Off-Road Bicycle Rides, by Bob D'Antonio (Falcon). The book details 40 rides ranging in difficulty from beginning to advanced. **Santa Fe Mountain Sports,** 1221 Flagman Way (© **505/988-3337;** www.santafemountainsports. com), rents hard-tail mountain bikes for $20 per half-day and $25 per full day, or full-suspension bikes for $35 per full day. **Mellow Velo Bikes,** 638 Old Santa Fe Trail (© **505/982-8986;** www.mellowvelo.com), rents front-suspension mountain bikes for $23 per half-day and $30 per full day. Town cruisers run $23 per half-day and $30 per full day. Full-suspension bikes run $55 per day. Add $7, and Mellow Velo will deliver to and pick up from your hotel (in the Santa Fe area). Price per day decreases with multiday rentals. Both shops supply accessories such as helmets, locks, maps, and trail information, usually at an additional cost.

Bird-Watching

Bird-watchers flock to the **Randall Davey Audubon Center** ★ (see "Parks & Refuges," earlier in this chapter), 1800 Upper Canyon Rd. (© **505/983-4609**), to see more than 100 species of birds and many other animals. For guided bird-watching tours all over the region, contact **Wings West** (© **800/583-6928;** wingswestnm.com). Bill West guides half-day tours to local spots such as the Santa Fe Mountains and Cochiti Lake ($105 for one to two people) and full-day ones farther afield ($195 for one to two people).

Fishing

In the lakes and waterways around Santa Fe, anglers typically catch trout (there are five varieties in the area). Other local fish include bass, perch, and kokanee salmon. The most popular fishing holes are Cochiti and Abiquiu lakes, as well as the Rio Chama, Pecos River, and the Rio Grande. A world-renowned fly-fishing destination, the **San Juan River,** near Farmington, is worth a visit and can make for an exciting 2-day trip in combination with a tour around **Chaco Culture National Historic Park** (see chapter 9). Check with the **New Mexico Game and Fish Department** (© **505/476-8000;** www.wildlife.state.nm.us) for information (including maps of area waters), licenses, and fishing proclamations. **High Desert Angler,** 460 Cerrillos Rd. (© **505/988-7688;** www.highdesertangler.com), specializes in fly-fishing gear and guide services.

Golf

There are three courses in the Santa Fe area: the 18-hole **Santa Fe Country Club,** on Airport Road (© **505/471-2626;** www.santafecountryclub.com); the often-praised 18-hole **Cochiti Lake Golf Course,** 5200 Cochiti Hwy., Cochiti Lake, about 35 miles southwest of Santa Fe via I-25 and NM 16 and 22 (© **505/465-2239;** www.pueblodecochiti.org); and Santa Fe's newest 18-hole course, **Marty Sanchez Links de Santa Fe,** 205 Caja del Rio (© **505/955-4400;** www.linksdesantafe.com). Both the Santa Fe Country Club and the Marty Sanchez Links offer driving ranges as well. North of Santa Fe on Pojoaque Pueblo land, the **Towa Golf Resort,** Buffalo Thunder Resort, 12 miles north of Santa Fe on US 285/84 (© **877/465-3489** or 505/455-9000; www.buffalothunderresort.com), offers 36 holes, 27 of them designed by Hale Irwin and William Phillips, set with views of the Jemez and Sangre de Cristo Mountains.

Hiking

It's hard to decide which of the 1,000 miles of nearby national forest trails to tackle. Four wilderness areas are nearby, most notably **Pecos Wilderness,** with 223,000 acres east of Santa Fe. Also visit the 58,000-acre **Jemez Mountain National Recreation Area.** Information on these and other wilderness areas is available from the **Santa Fe National Forest,** P.O. Box 1689 (1474 Rodeo Rd.), Santa Fe, NM 87504 (✆ **505/438-7840;** www.fs.fed.us). If you're looking for company on your trek, contact the Santa Fe branch of the **Sierra Club,** 1807 Second St. (✆ **505/983-2703;** www.riogrande.sierraclub.org). A hiking schedule can be found in the local newsletter; you can pick one up outside the office. Some people enjoy taking a chairlift ride to the summit of the **Santa Fe Ski Area** (✆ **505/982-4429;** www.skisantafe.com) and hiking around up there during the summer. A popular guide with Santa Feans is *Day Hikes in the Santa Fe Area,* published by the local branch of the Sierra Club.

The most popular hiking trails are the **Borrego Trail,** a moderate 4-mile jaunt through aspens and ponderosa pines, ending at a creek, and **Aspen Vista,** an easy 1- to 5-mile hike through aspen forest with views to the east. Both are easy to find; simply head up Hyde Park Road toward Ski Santa Fe. The Borrego Trail is 8¼ miles up, while Aspen Vista is 10 miles. In recent years an energetic crew has cut the **Dale Ball Trails** (✆ **505/955-6977;** www.santafenm.gov), miles of hiking/biking trails throughout the Santa Fe foothills. The easiest access is off Hyde Park Road toward Ski Santa Fe. Drive 2 miles from Bishop's Lodge Road and watch for the trail head on the left. If you're looking for "outspiration" (versus inspiration) on a guided day-hiking experience, call **Outspire** (✆ **505/660-0394;** www.outspire.com). They'll set you up with a guide and design just the hike for your ability level and interest. A 3- to 4-hour hike begins at $150. Outspire also guides snowshoeing trips.

Horseback Riding

Trips ranging in length from a few hours to overnight can be arranged by **Santa Fe Detours,** 54½ E. San Francisco St. (summer tour desk, 107 Washington Ave.; ✆ **800/338-6877** or 505/983-6565; www.sfdetours.com). You'll ride with "experienced wranglers" and they can even arrange a trip that includes a cookout or brunch. Rides are also major activities at the **Bishop's Lodge** (p. 135). The **Broken Saddle Riding Company** (✆ **505/424-7774**) offers rides through the stunning Galisteo Basin south of Santa Fe.

Hunting

Elk and mule deer are taken by hunters in the Pecos Wilderness and Jemez Mountains, as are occasional black bears and bighorn sheep. Wild turkeys and grouse are frequently bagged in the uplands, geese and ducks at lower elevations. Check with the **New Mexico Game and Fish Department** (✆ **505/476-8000;** www.wildlife.state.nm.us) for information and licenses.

River Rafting & Kayaking

Although Taos is the real rafting center of New Mexico, several companies serve Santa Fe during the April-to-August white-water season. They include **New Wave Rafting,** 2110 Hwy. 68, Embudo, NM 87531 (✆ **800/984-1444** or 505/579-0075;

GETTING PAMPERED: the spa scene

If traveling, skiing, or other activities have left you weary, Santa Fe has a number of relaxation options. **Absolute Nirvana Spa & Gardens ★★** (✆ 866/585-7942; www.absolute nirvana.com) offers imaginative Indo-Asian spa "experiences" as well as massages and facials. Their signature treatment, the Javanese Lulur, includes a full-body massage with jasmine oil, a sandalwood/rice powder exfoliation and yogurt/honey wrap, followed by a steam shower and decadent rose petal bath, all accompanied by tea, fruit, and a house-made truffle. The spa is open Sunday to Thursday 10am to 6pm and Friday and Saturday 10am to 8pm. Prices range from $105 to $240. Another option with a more Japanese bent is **Ten Thousand Waves ★★**, a spa about 3 miles north-east of Santa Fe on Hyde Park Road (✆ 505/982-9304; www.tenthousand waves.com). This serene retreat, nestled in a grove of *piñons,* offers hot tubs, saunas, and cold plunges, plus a variety of massage and other bodywork techniques. Bathing suits are optional in both the communal hot tub (during the day) and the women's communal tub, where you can stay as long as you want for $19. Nine private hot tubs cost $30 to $40 an hour, with discounts for seniors and children. A premium bath is offered at $49 for 90 minutes. You can also arrange therapeutic massage, hot-oil massage, in-water *Watsu* massage, herbal wraps, salt glows, facials, dry brush aromatherapy treatments, Ayurvedic treatments, and the much-praised Japanese Hot Stone Massage. If you call far enough in advance, you may be able to find lodging at Ten Thousand Waves as well. The spa is open Monday, Wednesday, and Thursday from 10:30am to 10:30pm; Tuesday from noon to 10:30pm; and Friday through Sunday from 9am to 10:30pm (winter hours are shorter, so be sure to call). Reservations are recommended, especially on weekends.

www.newwaverafting.com), and **Santa Fe Rafting Co.,** 1000 Cerrillos Rd., Santa Fe, NM 87505 (✆ **888/988-4914** or 505/988-4914; www.santaferafting.com). You can expect the cost of a full-day trip to range from about $110 to $125 per person before tax and the 3% federal land-use fee. The day of the week (weekdays are less expensive) and group size may also affect the price.

Running

Despite its elevation, Santa Fe is popular with runners and hosts numerous competitions, including the annual **Old Santa Fe Trail Run** on Labor Day. The **Santa Fe Striders** website (www.santafestriders.org) lists various runs during the year, as well as weekly runs. This is a great opportunity for travelers to find their way and to meet some locals.

Skiing

There's something available for every ability level at **Ski Santa Fe,** about 16 miles northeast of Santa Fe via Hyde Park (Ski Basin) Road. Lots of locals ski here, particularly on weekends; if you can, go on weekdays. It's a good family area and fairly small, so it's easy to split off from and later reconnect with your party. Built on the upper reaches of 12,000-foot Tesuque Peak, the area has an average annual snowfall of 225 inches and a vertical drop of 1,725 feet. Seven lifts, including a 5,000-foot triple chair and a quad chair, serve 69 runs and 660 acres of terrain, with a total capacity of 7,800 riders an hour. Base facilities, at 10,350 feet, center around **La Casa Mall,** with a cafeteria, lounge, ski shop, and boutique. A restaurant, **Totem-off's,** has a midmountain patio.

The ski area is open daily from 9am to 4pm; the season often runs from Thanksgiving to early April, depending on snow conditions. Rates for all lifts are $58 for adults, $46 for those ages 13 to 20, $40 for children 12 and under and seniors; half-day (morning or afternoon) tickets run $42. Tickets are free for kids less than 46 inches tall (in their ski boots), and for seniors 72 and older. For more information, contact **Ski Santa Fe,** 2209 Brothers Rd., Suite 220 (② **505/982-4429;** www.skisantafe.com). For 24-hour reports on snow conditions, call ② **505/983-9155.** Ski packages are available through **SantaFeHotels.com** (② **800/745-9910**).

Cross-country skiers find seemingly endless miles of snow to track in the **Santa Fe National Forest** (② **505/438-5300;** www.fs.fed.us). A favorite place to start is at the Black Canyon campground, about 9 miles from downtown en route to Ski Santa Fe. In the same area are the **Borrego Trail** (high intermediate), **Aspen Vista Trail,** and the **Norski Trail,** all en route to Ski Santa Fe as well. Other popular activities at the ski area in winter include snowshoeing, snowboarding, sledding, and inner tubing. Ski, snowboard, and snowshoe rentals are available at a number of downtown shops and the ski area.

Swimming

There's a public pool at the **Fort Marcy Complex** (② **505/955-2500;** www.santafenm.gov) on Camino Santiago, off Bishop's Lodge Road. In summer, the public **Bicentennial Pool,** 1121 Alto St. (② **505/955-4778**), offers outdoor swimming. Admission to both is less than $2 for all ages.

Tennis

Santa Fe has 44 public tennis courts and four major private facilities. The **City Recreation Department** (② **505/955-2602;** www.santafenm.gov) can help you locate indoor, outdoor, and lighted public courts.

SHOPPING

Santa Fe offers a broad range of art, from very traditional Native American crafts and Hispanic folk art to extremely innovative contemporary work. Some call Santa Fe one of the top art markets in the world. Galleries speckle the downtown area, and as an artists' thoroughfare, Canyon Road is preeminent. The greatest concentration of Native American crafts is displayed beneath the portal of the Palace of the Governors.

Any serious arts aficionado should try to attend one or more of the city's great arts festivals—the Spring Festival of the Arts in May, the Spanish Market in July, the Indian Market in August, and the Fall Festival of the Arts in October.

Few visitors to Santa Fe leave the city without acquiring at least one item from the Native American artisans at the Palace of the Governors. You can also peruse the outstanding **gallery catalogs** for an introduction to local dealers. They're available for free in many galleries and hotels. They include *The Collector's Guide to Art in*

Santa Fe and Taos by Wingspread Incorporated (www.collectorsguide.com), *The Essential Guide to Santa Fe & Taos* by Essential Guides (www.essentialguide.com), and others. For a current listing of gallery openings, with recommendations on which ones to attend, purchase a copy of the monthly magazine the *Santa Fean* by Santa Fean, 466 W. San Francisco St., Santa Fe, NM 87501 (www.santafean.com). Also check in the "Pasatiempo" section of the local newspaper, the *New Mexican* (www.santafenewmexican.com), every Friday.

Business hours vary quite a bit among establishments, but most are open at least Monday through Friday from 10am to 5pm, with mall stores open until 8 or 9pm. Most shops are open similar hours on Saturday, and many also open on Sunday afternoon during the summer. Winter hours tend to be more limited.

After the high-rolling 1980s, during which art markets around the country prospered, came the penny-pinching 1990s and the fearful 2000s. Many galleries in Santa Fe have been forced to shut their doors. Those that remain tend to specialize in particular types of art, a refinement process that has improved the gallery scene here. Some locals worry that the lack of serious art buyers in the area leads to fewer good galleries and more T-shirt and trinket stores. The plaza has its share of those, but still has a good number of serious galleries appealing to those buyers whose interests run to accessible art—Southwestern landscapes and the like. On Canyon Road, the art is often more experimental and diverse.

The Top Galleries

CONTEMPORARY ART

Canyon Road Contemporary Art   This gallery represents some of the finest emerging U.S. contemporary artists, as well as internationally known artists. You'll find figurative, landscape, and abstract paintings, as well as raku pottery. 403 Canyon Rd. ✆ **505/983-0433.** www.crcainc.com.

Hahn Ross Gallery   Owners Tom Ross and Elizabeth Hahn, a children's book illustrator and surrealist painter, respectively, specialize in representing artists who create colorful, fantasy-oriented works. Check out the sculpture garden here. 409 Canyon Rd. ✆ **505/984-8434.** www.hahnross.com.

LewAllen Galleries ★★ 🎁   This is one of Santa Fe's most prized galleries. You'll find bizarre and beautiful contemporary works in a range of media, from granite to clay to twigs. There are always exciting works on canvas. They have a second location at the railyard on 1613 Paseo del Peralta. 129 W. Palace Ave. ✆ **505/988-8997.** www. lewallencontemporary.com.

Linda Durham Contemporary Art ★   Linda Durham has devoted more than 30 years to representing New Mexico–based artists in a range of mediums including painting, sculpture, photography, and others. These are often daring and always soulful works from a strong roster of talent, including Greg Erf. 1807 2nd St., no. 107. ✆ **505/466-6600.** www.lindadurham.com.

Manitou Galleries ★   This expansive space just off the plaza presents bold contemporary images of the Southwest and beyond through a variety of mediums, including paintings, prints, sculpture, glass, and jewelry. Look for the work of Miguel Martinez and Roger Hayden Johnson. 123 W. Palace Ave. ✆ **800/283-0440** or 505/986-0440. www.manitougalleries.com.

Peyton Wright Gallery ★   Housed within the Historic Spiegelberg House (a refurbished Victorian adobe), this excellent gallery offers contemporary, American Modernism, Spanish Colonial, Russian, and 18th-century New Mexico *bultos* and *santos*. In addition to representing such artists as Orlando Leyba, Roni Stretch, and Tim Murphy, the gallery features monthly exhibitions—including contemporary paintings, sculptures, and works on paper. 237 E. Palace Ave. ✆ **800/879-8898** or 505/989-9888. www.peytonwright.com.

Shidoni Foundry, Gallery, and Sculpture Gardens ★★ 📷   Shidoni Foundry is one of the area's most exciting spots for sculptors and sculpture enthusiasts. At the foundry, visitors may take a tour through the facilities to view casting processes. In addition, Shidoni Foundry includes a 5,000-square-foot contemporary gallery, a bronze gallery, and a wonderful sculpture garden—a great place for a picnic. Bishop's Lodge Rd., Tesuque. ✆ **505/988-8001.** www.shidoni.com.

NATIVE AMERICAN & OTHER INDIGENOUS ART

Andrea Fisher Fine Pottery ★   This expansive gallery is a wonderland of authentic Southwestern Indian pottery. You'll find real showpieces here, including the work of renowned San Ildefonso Pueblo potter Maria Martinez. 100 W. San Francisco St. ✆ **505/986-1234.** www.andreafisherpottery.com.

Frank Howell Gallery   If you've never seen the wonderful illustrative hand of the late Frank Howell, you'll want to visit this gallery. You'll find a variety of works by contemporary American Indian artists. The gallery also features sculpture, jewelry, and graphics. 103 Washington Ave. ✆ **505/984-1074.** www.frankhowellgallery.com.

Morning Star Gallery ★★ 🎁   This is one of my favorite places to browse. Throughout the rambling gallery are American Indian art masterpieces, all elegantly displayed. You'll see a broad range of works, from late-19th-century Navajo blankets to 1920s Zuni needlepoint jewelry. 513 Canyon Rd. ✆ **505/982-8187.** www.morningstargallery.com.

Ortega's on the Plaza   A hearty shopper could spend hours here, perusing inventive turquoise and silver jewelry and especially fine-strung beadwork, as well as rugs and pottery. An adjacent room showcases a wide array of clothing, all with a hip Southwestern flair. 101 W. San Francisco St. ✆ **505/988-1866.** www.ortegasontheplaza.net.

Sherwoods ★   Set in the historic Bandelier House, this gallery features museum-quality Plains Indians antiquities such as an 1870 Nez Perce beaded dress and a Crow war shirt. Some paintings hang here as well, including works by Santa Fe masters such as J. H. Sharp and Gene Kloss. Firearm buffs will go ballistic over the gun room here. 1005 Paseo de Peralta. ✆ **505/988-1776.** www.sherwoodsspirit.com.

PHOTOGRAPHY

Andrew Smith Gallery ★   I'm always amazed when I enter this gallery and notice works I've seen reprinted in major magazines for years. There they are, photographic prints, large and beautiful, hanging on the wall. Here, you'll see famous works by Edward Curtis, Henri Cartier-Bresson, Ansel Adams, Annie Leibovitz, and others. A new gallery at the corner of Grant and Johnson streets extends this collection. 122 Grant Ave. ✆ **505/984-1234.** www.andrewsmithgallery.com.

Photo-Eye Gallery   You're bound to be surprised each time you step into this gallery a few blocks off Canyon Road. Dealing in contemporary photography, the

gallery represents both internationally renowned and emerging artists. 370 Garcia St.
📞 **505/988-5152.** www.photoeye.com.

TRADITIONAL ART

Altermann Galleries   This is a well of interesting traditional art, mostly 19th-, 20th-, and 21st-century American paintings and sculpture. The gallery represents Remington and Russell, in addition to Taos founders, Santa Fe artists, and members of the Cowboy Artists of America and the National Academy of Western Art. Stroll through the sculpture garden among whimsical bronzes of children and dogs. 225 Canyon Rd. 📞 **505/983-1590.** www.altermann.com.

Gerald Peters Gallery ★★   Displayed throughout a graceful Pueblo-style building, the works here are so fine you'll feel as though you're in a museum. You'll find 19th-, 20th-, and 21st-century American painting and sculpture, featuring the art of Georgia O'Keeffe, William Wegman, and the founders of the Santa Fe and Taos artist colonies, as well as more contemporary works. 1011 Paseo de Peralta. 📞 **505/954-5700.** www.gpgallery.com.

The Mayans Gallery Ltd.   Established in 1977, this is one of the oldest galleries in Santa Fe. You'll find 20th-century American and Latin American paintings, photography, prints, and sculpture. 601 Canyon Rd. 📞 **505/983-8068.**

Nedra Matteucci Galleries ★★   As you approach this gallery, note the elaborately crafted stone and adobe wall that surrounds it, merely a taste of what's to come. The gallery specializes in 19th-, 20th-, and 21st-century American art. Inside, you'll find a lot of high-ticket works such as those of early Taos and Santa Fe painters, as well as classic American Impressionism, historical Western modernism, and contemporary Southwestern landscapes and sculpture. Another excellent gallery, Nedra Matteucci Fine Art, is located at 555 Canyon Rd. There look for the fabulous impressionist works by Evelyne Boren. 1075 Paseo de Peralta. 📞 **505/982-4631.** www.matteucci.com.

Owings-Dewey Fine Art ★   These are treasure-filled rooms. You'll find 19th-, 20th-, and 21st-century American painting and sculpture, including works by Georgia O'Keeffe, Robert Henri, Maynard Dixon, Fremont Ellis, and Andrew Dasburg, as well as antique works such as Spanish colonial *retablos, bultos,* and tin works. Look for the exciting bird sculptures by Peter Woytuk. There's a second shop at 120 E. Marcy St. 76 E. San Francisco St., upstairs. 📞 **505/982-6244.** www.owingsgallery.com.

Zaplin Lampert Gallery ★★   Art aficionados as well as those who just like a nice landscape will enjoy this gallery, one of Santa Fe's classics. Hanging on old adobe walls are works by some of the region's early masters, including Bert Phillips, Gene Kloss, and Gustauve Baumann. 651 Canyon Rd. 📞 **505/982-6100.** www.zaplinlampert.com.

More Shopping A to Z

ANTIQUES

El Paso Import Company ★   Whenever I'm in the vicinity of this shop, I always stop in. It's packed—and I mean packed—with colorful, weathered colonial and ranchero furniture. The affordable home furnishings and folk art here are imported from Mexico, India, and Romania. 418 Sandoval St. 📞 **505/982-5698.** www.elpasoimportco.com.

Jackalope ★ ☺ 🔥   Spread over 7 acres of land, this is a wild place to spend a morning or an afternoon browsing through exotic furnishings from India and Mexico,

ARCADE SHOPPING ON THE plaza

Opened in 2004, the **Santa Fe Arcade,** 60 E. San Francisco St. (✆ **505/988-5792**), on the south side of the plaza, offers three stories of shops in a sleek, glassy European-style space. It's a far cry from the Woolworth's that once lived there. Showy Western wear, fine Indian jewelry, and hip clothing fill the display windows of some 60 spaces in the mall. To pamper yourself with natural products, many made in northern New Mexico, step into **Sombria,** Ste. 222 (✆ **888/480-5554** or 505/982-7383). Look for their margarita salt glow, made with salt from Utah's Great Salt Lake. Prima Fine Jewelry's **Oro Fino,** Ste. 218

(✆ **505/983-9699**), sells contemporary and Southwestern inlaid jewelry in silver, gold, and platinum. After all the shopping, if you find yourself hungry, head to the **Rooftop Pizzeria ★**, top floor (✆ **505/984-0008;** www.rooftoppizzeria.com), for some of the city's best pizza. Two types of crust, an "artisan" or a blue corn, are topped with imaginative concoctions such as smoked duck and roasted garlic or wild mushroom and Alfredo sauce. Salads, pasta dishes, and beer and wine are also available. It's open Sunday through Thursday 11am to 10pm and Friday and Saturday 11am to 11pm.

as well as imported textiles, pottery, jewelry, and clothing. It's a great place to find gifts. Kids will love the prairie-dog village. 2820 Cerrillos Rd. ✆ **505/471-8539.** www.jackalope.com.

BOOKS

Borders   With close to 200 stores nationwide, this chain provides a broad range of books, music, and videos, and it hosts in-store appearances by authors, musicians, and artists. 500 Montezuma Ave. ✆ **505/954-4707.** www.borders.com.

Collected Works Bookstore ★★   This is an excellent downtown book source, with carefully recommended books up front, in case you're not sure what you want, and shelves of Southwest, travel, nature, and other books. The shop includes a coffeehouse and hosts weekly readings and talks by notable authors. 202 Galisteo St. ✆ **505/988-4226.** www.cwbookstore.com.

Garcia Street Books ★   One of Santa Fe's best shops for perusing, this gem stocks a broad range of titles on the Southwest and collectibles. Not sure what to read? The knowledgeable staff here will help you decide. 376 Garcia St. ✆ **866/986-0151** or 505/986-0151. www.garciastreetbooks.com.

CHILDREN

Gypsy Baby   This shop sells bright clothes, beaded slippers, and mustang rocking horses, all mindful of the slogan "Born to be spoiled." 318 S. Guadalupe St. ✆ **505/820-1898.** www.gypsybabies.com.

CRAFTS

Davis Mather Folk Art Gallery   This small shop is a wild-animal adventure. You'll find New Mexican animal woodcarvings in shapes of lions, tigers, and bears— even chickens—as well as other folk and Hispanic arts. 141 Lincoln Ave. ✆ **505/983-1660.** www.santafefolkartgallery.com.

Nambe ★ 🎁   The cooking, serving, and decorating pieces here are fashioned from an exquisite sand-cast and handcrafted alloy. These items are also available at the Nambe stores at 104 W. San Francisco St. (📞 **505/988-3574**) and in Taos at 109 North Plaza (📞 **575/758-8221**). 924 Paseo de Peralta.📞 **505/988-5528.** www.nambe.com.

FASHIONS
Back at the Ranch ★   This shop has chic Western wear and what it calls the "largest selection of handmade cowboy boots in the country." 209 E. Marcy St. 📞 **888/962-6687** or 505/989-8110. www.backattheranch.com.

Origins ★ 📷   A little like a Guatemalan or Turkish marketplace, this store is packed with wearable art, folk art, and the work of local designers. Look for good buys on ethnic jewelry. Throughout the summer there are trunk shows, which offer opportunities to meet the artists. 135 W. San Francisco St. 📞 **505/988-2323.** www.origins santafe.com.

Overland Sheepskin Company   The rich smell of leather will draw you in the door, and possibly hold onto you until you purchase a coat, blazer, hat, or other finely made leather item. 74 E. San Francisco St.📞 **505/983-4727.** www.overland.com.

FOOD
The Chile Shop   This store has too many cheap trinketlike items for me, but many people find some novelty items to take back home. You'll find everything from salsas to cornmeal and tortilla chips. The shop also stocks cookbooks and pottery items. 109 E. Water St.📞 **505/983-6080.** www.thechileshop.com.

Señor Murphy Candy Maker   Unlike any candy store you'll find in other parts of the country—everything here is made with local ingredients. The chile–piñon nut brittle is a taste sensation! Señor Murphy has another shop in the Santa Fe Place mall (📞 **505/471-8899**). 100 E. San Francisco St. (La Fonda hotel).📞 **505/982-0461.** www. senormurphy.com.

FURNITURE
Southwest Spanish Craftsmen   The Spanish colonial and Spanish provincial furniture, doors, and home accessories in this store are a bit too elaborate for my tastes, but if you find yourself dreaming of carved wood, this is your place. 314 S. Guadalupe St.📞 **505/982-1767.** www.nussbaumerfineart.com.

GIFTS & SOUVENIRS
El Nicho ✎   If you want to take a little piece of Santa Fe home with you, you'll likely find it at this shop. You'll find handcrafted Navajo folk art as well as jewelry and other items by local artisans, including woodcarvings (watch for the *santos!*) by the renowned Ortega family. 227 Don Gaspar Ave.📞 **505/984-2830.**

HATS
Montecristi Custom Hat Works ★   This fun shop hand-makes fine Panama and felt hats in a range of styles, from Australian outback to Mexican bolero. 322 McKenzie St.📞 **505/983-9598.** www.montecristihats.com.

JEWELRY
Packards ★   Opened by a notable trader, Al Packard, and later sold to new owners, this store on the plaza is worth checking out to see some of the best jewelry

available. You'll also find exquisite rugs and pottery. 61 Old Santa Fe Trail. ℂ **505/983-9241.** www.packards-santafe.com.

Tresa Vorenberg Goldsmiths You'll find some wildly imaginative designs in this jewelry store, where more than 40 artisans are represented. All items are hand-crafted, and custom commissions are welcomed. 656 Canyon Rd. ℂ **505/988-7215.** www. tvgoldsmiths.com.

MALLS & SHOPPING CENTERS

De Vargas Center There are approximately 50 merchants and restaurants in this mall just northwest of downtown. This is Santa Fe's small, more intimate mall, with anchors Ross and Office Depot; it's open Monday to Friday 10am to 7pm, Saturday 10am to 6pm, and Sunday noon to 5pm. N. Guadalupe St. and Paseo de Peralta. ℂ **505/982-2655.** www.devargascenter.com.

Fashion Outlets of Santa Fe Outlet shopping fans will enjoy this open-air mall on the south end of town. Anchors include Brooks Brothers, Jones New York, and Coach. 8380 Cerrillos Rd. ℂ **505/474-4000.** www.fashionoutletssantafe.com.

Sanbusco Market Center ★ Unique shops and restaurants occupy this remodeled warehouse near the old Santa Fe Railyard. Many of the shops are overpriced, but it's a fun place to window-shop. Borders (see above) is here as well. It's open Monday to Saturday 10am to 6pm, Sunday noon to 5pm. 500 Montezuma St. ℂ **505/989-9390.** www.sanbusco.com.

Santa Fe Place Santa Fe's largest mall is near the southwestern city limits, not far from the I-25 on-ramp. If you're from a major city, you'll probably find shopping here very provincial. Anchors include JCPenney, Sears, Dillard's, and Mervyn's. Hours are Monday to Saturday 10am to 9pm, Sunday noon to 6pm. 4250 Cerrillos Rd. (at Rodeo Rd.). ℂ **505/473-4253.** www.shopsantafeplace.com.

MARKETS

Santa Fe Farmers' Market ★★ 🎁 This farmers' market has everything from fruits, vegetables, and flowers to cheeses, cider, and salsas. Great local treats! If you're an early riser, stroll through and enjoy good coffee, excellent breakfast burritos, and music ranging from flute to fiddle. In 2008, the market moved into a beautiful new building in the railyard district. It's open April to mid-November Tuesday and Saturday 7am to noon. In winter, an abbreviated version takes place indoors. In the Santa Fe Railyard, off Paseo de Peralta. ℂ **505/983-4098.** www.santafefarmersmarket.com.

Tesuque Flea Market ★ 📷 If you're a flea-market hound, you'll be happy to discover this one. More than 500 vendors sell everything from used cowboy boots (you might find some real beauties) to clothing, jewelry, books, and furniture, all against a big northern New Mexico view. The flea market runs March to late November Friday to Sunday. Vendors start selling at about 7:30am and stay open until about 6:30pm, weather permitting. US 84/285 (about 8 miles north of Santa Fe). No phone. www.pueblooftesuquefleamarket.com.

NATURAL ART

Mineral & Fossil Gallery of Santa Fe ★ You'll find ancient artwork here, from fossils to geodes in all sizes and shapes. Natural mineral jewelry and decorative items for the home, including lamps, wall clocks, furniture, art glass, and carvings are also on hand. Mineral & Fossil also has galleries in Taos, and in Scottsdale and Sedona, Arizona. 127 W. San Francisco St.✆ **800/762-9777** or 505/984-1682. www.mineralgallery.net.

Stone Forest ★★ 🎒 Proprietor Michael Zimber travels to China and other Asian countries every year to collaborate with the stone carvers who create the fountains, sculptures, and bath fixtures that fill this inventive shop and garden not far from the plaza. 213 St. Francis Dr.✆ **505/986-8883.** www.stoneforest.com.

POTTERY & TILES

Artesanos Imports Company ★ 📷 Coming here is like taking a trip south of the border, with all the scents and colors you'd expect on such a journey. You'll find a wide selection of Talavera tile and pottery, as well as light fixtures and many other accessories for the home. 1414 Maclovia St.✆ **505/471-8020.** www.artesanos.com.

Santa Fe Pottery at Double Take The work of more than 120 master potters from New Mexico and the Southwest is on display here; you'll find everything from mugs and lamps to home furnishings. 323 S. Guadalupe St.✆ **505/989-3363.**

RUGS

Seret & Sons Rugs, Furnishings, and Architectural Pieces ★ If you're like me and find Middle Eastern decor irresistible, you'll want to wander through this shop. You'll find *kilims* and Persian and Turkish rugs, as well as some of the Moorish-style ancient doors and furnishings that you see around Santa Fe. 224 Galisteo St. ✆ **505/988-9151** or 505/983-5008. www.seretandsons.com.

SANTA FE AFTER DARK

Santa Fe is a city committed to the arts, so it's no surprise that the Santa Fe night scene is dominated by highbrow cultural events, beginning with the world-famous Santa Fe Opera. The club and popular music scene runs a distant second.

Information on all major cultural events can be obtained from the **Santa Fe Convention and Visitors Bureau** (✆ **800/777-2489** or 505/955-6200) or from the **City of Santa Fe Arts Commission** (✆ **505/955-6707**). Current listings are published each Friday in the "Pasatiempo" section of *The New Mexican* (www.santafenewmexican.com), the city's daily newspaper, and in the *Santa Fe Reporter* (www.sfreporter.com), published every Wednesday.

You can also order tickets to events by phone from **Ticketmaster** (✆ **800/745-3000**). Discount tickets may be available on the night of a performance; for example, the opera offers standing-room tickets on the day of the performance. Sales start at 10am.

A variety of free concerts, lectures, and other events are presented in the summer, cosponsored by the City of Santa Fe and the Chamber of Commerce. Many of these musical and cultural events take place on the plaza; check in the "Pasatiempo" section for current listings and information.

Many performing-arts groups flourish in this city of 72,000. Some of them perform year-round, while others are seasonal. The acclaimed Santa Fe Opera, for instance, has a 2-month summer season: late June to August.

Note: Many companies noted here perform at locations other than their listed addresses, so check the site of the performance you plan to attend.

Major Performing Arts Companies
OPERA & CLASSICAL MUSIC

Santa Fe Opera ★★★   Many rank the Santa Fe Opera second only to the Metropolitan Opera of New York in the United States. Established in 1957, it consistently attracts famed conductors, directors, and singers. At the height of the season, the company is 500 strong. It's noted for its performances of the classics, little-known works by classical European composers, and American premieres of 21st-century works. The theater, completed for the 1998 season, sits on a wooded hilltop 7 miles north of the city, off US 84/285. It's partially open air, with open sides. A controversial structure, this new theater replaced the original, built in 1968, but preserved the sweeping curves attuned to the contour of the surrounding terrain. At night, the lights of Los Alamos can still be seen in the distance under clear skies.

The 8-week, 40-performance opera season runs from late June through late August. Highlights for 2011 include the first major U.S. production of Vivaldi's *Griselda,* Gian Carlo Menotti's *The Last Savage,* Gounod's *Faust,* and Puccini's *La Bohême.* All performances begin at 9pm, until the end of July when performances start at 8:30pm, and the last week of the season when performances begin at 8pm. A small screen in front of each seat shows the libretto during the performance. A gift shop has been added, as has additional parking. The entire theater is wheelchair accessible. P.O. Box 2408. ✆ **800/280-4654** or 505/986-5900. www.santafeopera.org. Tickets $28–$180; standing room $10; Opening Night Gala $1,750–$3,000. Backstage tours June–Aug Mon–Sat at 9am; $5 adults, free for children 5–17.

ORCHESTRAL & CHAMBER MUSIC

Santa Fe Pro Musica Chamber Orchestra & Ensemble ★   Nominated in 2008 for a Grammy Award, this chamber ensemble performs everything from Bach to Vivaldi to contemporary masters. During Holy Week, the Santa Fe Pro Musica presents its annual Mozart and Hayden Concert at the St. Francis Cathedral. Christmas brings candlelight chamber ensemble concerts. Pro Musica's season runs September to May. Students and teachers get half off ticket prices. 1405 Luisa St., Ste. 10. ✆ **505/988-4640.** www.santafepromusica.com. Tickets $15–$70.

Santa Fe Symphony Orchestra and Chorus ★   This 60-piece professional symphony orchestra has grown rapidly in stature since its founding in 1984. Matinee and evening performances of classical and popular works are presented in a subscription series at the Lensic Performing Arts Center from August to May. There's a preconcert lecture before each performance. During the spring, the orchestra presents music festivals (call for details). P.O. Box 9692. ✆ **800/480-1319** or 505/983-1414. www. santafesymphony.org. Tickets $20–$75.

Music Festivals & Concert Series

Santa Fe Chamber Music Festival ★★   An extraordinary group of international artists comes to Santa Fe every summer for this festival. Its 6-week season runs mid-July to mid-August and is held in the St. Francis Auditorium and the Lensic Performing Arts Center. Each festival features chamber-music masterpieces, new music by a composer in residence, jazz, free youth concerts, preconcert lectures, and open rehearsals. Performances are Monday, Tuesday, Thursday, and Friday at 8pm; Saturday at various evening times; and Sunday at 6pm. Open rehearsals, youth concerts, and preconcert lectures are free to the public. 239 Johnson St., Ste. B (P.O. Box 2227).℃ **505/983-2075** or 505/982-1890 for box office (after the third week of June). www.sfcmf.org. Tickets $10–$62.

Santa Fe Concert Association ★   Founded in 1937, this oldest musical organization in northern New Mexico has a September-to-May season that includes a six-performance series. Among them are a "Great Performances" series and an "Adventures" series, which feature renowned instrumental and vocal soloists and chamber ensembles. The association also hosts special holiday concerts around Christmas and New Year's. Performances are held at the Lensic Performing Arts Center; tickets are available at the Lensic box office. 210 E. Marcy St., Ste. 15.℃ **505/988-1234,** 800/905-3315 (www.tickets.com), or 505/984-8759. www.santaconcerts.org. Tickets $20–$175.

Theater Companies

Santa Fe Playhouse ★   Founded in the 1920s, this is the oldest extant theater group in New Mexico. Still performing in a historic adobe theater in the Barrio de Analco, it attracts thousands for its dramas, avant-garde theater, and musical comedy. Its popular one-act melodramas call on the public to boo the sneering villain and swoon for the damsel in distress. 142 E. de Vargas St. ℃ **505/988-4262.** www.santafe playhouse.org. Tickets "pay what you wish" to $20, depending on the show.

Theater Grottesco ★★ 📖   This troupe combines the best of comedy, drama, and dance in its original productions performed each spring, summer, or fall, at whatever venue suits the performance. Expect to be romanced, shocked, intellectually stimulated, and, above all, struck silly with laughter. Look for upcoming winter shows as well. 551 W. Cordova Rd., no. 8400.℃ **505/474-8400.** www.theatergrottesco.org. Tickets $10–$25.

Theaterwork Studio ★   This community theater goes out of its way to present refreshing, at times risky, plays. In an intimate space on the south end of town, Theaterwork offers seven main-stage productions a year, a broad variety including new plays and classics by regional and national playwrights. Expect to see works by such names as Brecht, Shakespeare, and Victor Hugo. 1336 Rufina Circle. ℃ **505/471-1799.** www.theaterwork.org. Tickets $10–$18.

Dance Companies

Aspen Santa Fe Ballet ★   In its second decade, the Aspen Santa Fe Ballet brings classically trained dancers to Santa Fe and Aspen. Performances are an eclectic repertoire by some of the world's foremost choreographers. The season is year-round, with performances at the Lensic Performing Arts Center. 550-B St. Michael's Dr. ℃ **505/983-5591.** www.aspensantafeballet.com. Purchase tickets at the Lensic ℃ 505/988-1234). Tickets $20–$72.

María Benitez Teatro Flamenco ★ 📖   True flamenco is one of the most thrilling of dance forms, displaying the inner spirit and verve of the gypsies of Spanish Andalusia. María Benitez, trained in Spain, choreographs a troupe of vibrant young dancers called Flamenco's Next Generation. Their summer series holds matinee performances from mid-July to mid-August on Sundays at 2pm. The María Benitez Theater at the Lodge at Santa Fe is modern and showy, and yet it's intimate enough so you're immersed in the art. Institute for Spanish Arts, P.O. Box 8418.℃ **505/470-7828.** www. mariabenitez.com. Tickets $5–$15.

Major Concert Halls & All-Purpose Auditoriums

Center for Contemporary Arts and Cinematheque ★   CCA presents the work of internationally, nationally, and regionally known contemporary artists in art exhibitions, dance, music concerts, poetry readings, performance-art events, theater, and video screenings. The Cinematheque screens films from around the world nightly, with special series presented regularly. CCA's galleries are open daily noon to 7:30pm. 1050 Old Pecos Trail. ℂ **505/982-1338.** www.ccasantafe.org. Film tickets $8. Art exhibitions are free; performances range broadly in price.

Lensic Performing Arts Center ★★   The Santa Fe arts scene's best venue, the Lensic hosts many of the city's major performances, including the Santa Fe Chamber Music Festival and the Santa Fe Symphony Orchestra and Chorus, among others. The setting is wonderfully atmospheric; a multimillion-dollar face-lift brought out the 1931 movie palace's Arabian Nights charm. 211 W. San Francisco St. ℂ **505/988-7050.** www.lensic.com.

St. Francis Auditorium   This atmospheric music hall, patterned after the interiors of traditional Hispanic mission churches, is noted for its excellent acoustics. The hall hosts a wide variety of musical events, including the Santa Fe Chamber Music Festival in July and August. Museum of Fine Arts, Lincoln and Palace aves. ℂ **505/476-5072.** Ticket prices vary; see above for specific performing-arts companies.

The Club & Music Scene

In addition to the clubs and bars listed below, there are a number of hotels whose bars and lounges feature some type of entertainment (see "Where to Stay," earlier in this chapter).

COUNTRY, JAZZ & LATIN

Chispa! ★   A tapas bar with the *chispa* or "spark" of fun entertainment and dancing, this hot spot next to the dining room at El Meson draws locals of all types. Music ranges from guitar duos to jazz combos and Brazilian music, with flamenco dancers performing on some Saturday nights. On Tango Tuesdays, locals turn out in their tightest dance clothes to party. The tapas are excellent. It's open Tuesday to Saturday. 213 Washington Ave. ℂ **505/983-6756.** www.elmeson-santafe.com. Cover charge for select performances.

Cowgirl Hall of Fame ★   It's difficult to categorize what goes on in this bar and restaurant, but there's live entertainment nightly. Some nights there's blues guitar, others folk music; you might also find progressive rock, comedy, reggae, karaoke, or cowboy poetry. In the summer, this is a great place to sit under the stars and listen to music. 319 S. Guadalupe St. ℂ **505/982-2565.** No cover for music Sun–Mon and Wed; Tues and Thurs–Sat $3–$5 cover. Special performances $10.

Eldorado Hotel ★   In a grand lobby-lounge full of fine art, classical guitarists and pianists perform nightly. 309 W. San Francisco St. ℂ **505/988-4455.** www.eldoradohotel.com.

El Farol ★   This original neighborhood bar of the Canyon Road artists' quarter (its name means "the lantern") is the place to head for local ambience. Its cozy interior is home to Santa Fe's largest and most unusual selection of tapas. Jazz, swing, folk, and most notably, salsa and flamenco musicians (and dancers)—some of national note—perform most nights. On Friday nights the Flamenco Dinner Show starts at 7pm for $25. 808 Canyon Rd.© **505/983-9912.** www.elfarolsf.com. Cover $5.

La Fiesta Lounge ★   Set in the notable La Fonda hotel on the plaza, this night-club offers excellent country bands on weekends, with old- and new-timers two-stepping across the floor. This lively lobby bar offers cocktails, an appetizer menu, and live entertainment nightly. It's a great authentic Santa Fe spot. La Fonda hotel, 110 E. San Francisco St.© **505/982-5511.** www.lafondasantafe.com.

ROCK & DISCO

Catamount Bar and Grille   The postcollege crowd hangs out at this bar, where live rock and blues music play on weekends. Food is served until 11pm, and there is also a billiards room. 125 E. Water St. © **505/988-7222.**

THE BAR SCENE

The Dragon Room ★   A number of years ago, *International Newsweek* named the Dragon Room at the Pink Adobe one of the top 20 bars in the world. The reason is its spirited but comfortable ambience, which draws students, artists, politicians, and even an occasional celebrity. The decor theme is dragons, which you'll find carved on the front doors as well as depicted on the walls, all within low-lit, aged elegance akin to the Pink Adobe's interior. Live trees also grow through the roof. In addition to the tempting lunch and bar menu, there's always a complimentary bowl of popcorn close at hand. 406 Old Santa Fe Trail.© **505/983-7712.**

El Paseo Bar and Grill   You can almost always catch live music at this casual, unpretentious place. The crowd here is somewhat younger than at most other down-town establishments, and on certain nights, the bar is completely packed. In addi-tion to the open mic night on Tuesdays, a variety of local bands play here regularly—cranking out many types of music, from blues to rock to jazz to bluegrass. Friday happy hour is from 4 to 6pm. 208 Galisteo St.© **505/992-2848.** www.elpaseobar.com. Cover $3-$5 weekends.

Evangelo's   A popular downtown hangout, with tropical decor and a mahogany bar, this place can get raucous at times. It's a bit seedy, but more than 200 varieties of imported beer are available, and pool tables are an added attraction. On Friday and Saturday nights starting at 9pm and Wednesdays at 7:30pm, live bands play (jazz, rock, or reggae). Evangelo's has reached new fame as one of the bars where Jeff Bridges sang in the 2009 movie *Crazy Heart*. You'll find your share of businesspeople, artists, and even bikers here. The bar downstairs attracts a younger crowd and music. It's open Monday to Saturday noon to 1:30am and Sunday until midnight. 200 W. San Francisco St.© **505/982-9014.** Cover for special performances only.

Milagro 139   This restaurant and lounge that opened in 2010 transports the flavor and feel of New Orleans to the desert. After dinner hours the lounge becomes a dance spot in a courtyard with climbing bougainvilleas and a live tree growing in the middle. A broad range of ages shows up to sip martinis and margaritas and to enjoy live music on Thursday through Saturday nights. Hours are daily 4pm to midnight, later on weekends. 139 W. San Francisco St. ℰ **505/995-0139.** www.milagro139.com.

Vanessie of Santa Fe ★   This is unquestionably Santa Fe's most popular piano bar. The talented Doug Montgomery and Charles Tichenor have a loyal local following. Their repertoire ranges from Bach to Billy Joel, Gershwin to Barry Manilow. They play nightly from 8pm until closing, which could be anywhere from midnight to 2am. There's an extra microphone, so if you're daring (or drunk), you can stand up and accompany the piano and vocals (though this is *not* a karaoke scene). National celebrities have even joined in—including Harry Connick, Jr. Vanessie's offers a great bar menu. 434 W. San Francisco St. ℰ **505/982-9966.** www.vanessiesantafe.com.

TOURING THE PUEBLOS AROUND SANTA FE

Of the eight northern pueblos, Tesuque, Pojoaque, Nambe, San Ildefonso, San Juan, and Santa Clara are within about 30 miles of Santa Fe. Picuris (San Lorenzo) is on the High Road to Taos (see "Taking the High Road to Taos," later in this chapter), and Taos Pueblo is just outside the town of Taos (p. 192).

The six pueblos described in this section can easily be visited in a single day's round-trip from Santa Fe, though I suggest visiting just the two that really give a feel of the ancient lifestyle: San Ildefonso, with its broad plaza, and Ohkay Owinge, with its pastoral setting along the Rio Grande. In an easy day trip from Santa Fe you can take in both, with some delicious New Mexican food in Española en route. If you're in the area at a time when you can catch certain rituals, that's when you should see some of the other pueblos.

Tesuque Pueblo

Tesuque (Te-*soo*-keh) Pueblo is about 9 miles north of Santa Fe on US 84/285. You'll know that you're approaching the pueblo when you see a large store near the highway. If you're driving north and you get to the unusual Camel Rock and a large roadside casino, you've missed the pueblo entrance.

The 800 pueblo dwellers at Tesuque are faithful to their traditional religion, rituals, and ceremonies. Excavations confirm that a pueblo has existed here at least since A.D. 1200; accordingly, this pueblo is now on the National Register of Historic Places. When you come to the welcome sign at the pueblo, turn right, go a block, and park on the right. You'll see the plaza off to the left. There's not a lot to see; in recent years renovation has brought a new look to some of the homes around it. There's a big open area where dances are held and the **San Diego Church,** completed in 2004 on the site of an 1888 structure that burned down. It's the fifth church on the pueblo's plaza since 1641. Visitors are asked to remain in this area.

Some Tesuque women are skilled potters; Ignacia Duran's black-and-white and red micaceous pottery and Teresa Tapia's miniatures and pots with animal figures are especially noteworthy. You'll find many crafts at a gallery on the plaza's southeast corner. The **San Diego Feast Day,** which may feature harvest, buffalo, deer, flag, or Comanche dances, is November 12.

Pueblo Etiquette

When you visit pueblos, it is important to observe certain rules of etiquette. These are personal dwellings and/or important historic sites and must be respected as such. Don't climb on the buildings or peek into doors or windows. Don't enter sacred grounds, such as cemeteries and kivas. If you attend a dance or ceremony, remain silent while it is taking place and refrain from applause when it's over. Many pueblos prohibit photography or sketches; others require you to pay a fee for a permit. If you don't respect the privacy of the Native Americans who live at the pueblo, you'll be asked to leave.

The Tesuque Pueblo's address is Route 42, Box 360-T, Santa Fe, NM 87501 (© 505/983-2667). Admission to the pueblo is free; however, there is a $20 charge for use of still cameras; special permission is required for filming, sketching, and painting. The pueblo is open daily from 8am to 5pm. **Camel Rock Casino** (© 505/984-8414; www.camelrockcasino.com) is open Sunday to Wednesday from 8am to 4am, and Thursday to Saturday for 24 hours; it has a snack bar on the premises.

Pojoaque Pueblo

About 6 miles farther north of Tesuque Pueblo on US 84/285, at the junction of NM 502, Pojoaque (Po-*hwa*-keh) Pueblo provides a roadside peek into Pueblo arts. Though small (pop. 2,712) and without a definable village (more modern dwellings exist now), Pojoaque is important as a center for traveler services; in fact, Pojoaque, in its Tewa form, means "water-drinking place." The historical accounts of the Pojoaque people are sketchy, but we do know that in 1890 smallpox took its toll on the Pojoaque population, forcing most of the pueblo residents to abandon their village. Since the 1930s, the population has gradually increased, and in 1990, a war chief and two war captains were appointed. Today, visitors won't find a historic village, but the **Poeh Cultural Center and Museum,** on US 84/285, operated by the pueblo, features a museum, a cultural center, and artists' studios. It's situated within a complex of adobe buildings, including the three-story Sun Tower. There are frequent artist demonstrations, exhibitions, and, in the warmer months, traditional ceremonial dances. Indigenous pottery, embroidery, silverwork, and beadwork are available for sale at the Pojoaque Pueblo Visitor Center nearby.

If you leave US 84/285 and travel on the frontage road back to where the pueblo actually was, you'll encounter lovely orchards and alfalfa fields backed by desert and mountains. There's a modern community center near the site of the old pueblo and church. On December 12, the annual feast day of **Our Lady of Guadalupe** features a buffalo dance.

The pueblo's address is Rte. 11, Box 71, Santa Fe, NM 87506 (© 505/455-2278). The pueblo is open every day during daylight hours. The Poeh Center is at 78 Cities of Gold Rd. (© 505/455-3334; www.poehcenter.com). Admission is free, and it's open daily 8am to 5pm. Sketching, photography, and filming are prohibited.

WHERE TO STAY & DINE

Hilton Santa Fe Golf Resort & Spa at Buffalo Thunder ★★★ Twenty minutes north of Santa Fe, this lively resort offers luxury accommodations and plenty to do for those seeking fun. The structure itself is gigantic, though designers have managed to impart an intimate feel. The rooms pay special attention to details and texture, with carved headboards, Native American art, and granite counter tops. The suites are spacious and have sleeper sofas—a good option for small families. Most rooms have balconies.

Owned by the Pueblo of Pojoaque, the resort features a number of restaurants and lounges, and a contemporary nightclub. The resort offers duffers 36 holes at the Towa Golf Course, Gamblers test their luck with 1,200 slots, a variety of table games, poker and simulcast horse and dog racing. Spa fans enjoy 16,000 square feet of relaxation. In artful treatment rooms, staff members provide a full range of massages and salt glows.

20 Buffalo Thunder Trail, Pojoaque, NM, 87506 *C* **505/455-5555.** Fax 505/455-0200. www.buffalo thunderresort.com. 395 units. $149–$189 double; $209–$389 suite. AE, DISC, MC, V. Free parking. **Amenities:** 6 restaurants; lounge; casino; children's center; concierge; executive-level rooms; exercise room; golf course; Jacuzzi; 2 pools; room service; sauna; spa; tennis courts. *In room:* A/C, TV, CD player, hair dryer, minibar, Wi-Fi.

Nambe Pueblo

If you're still on US 84/285, continue north from Pojoaque about 3 miles until you come to NM 503; turn right, and travel until you see the Bureau of Reclamation sign for Nambe Falls; turn right on NP 101. Approximately 2 miles farther is Nambe ("mound of earth in the corner"), a 700-year-old Tewa-speaking pueblo (pop. 500), with a solar-powered tribal headquarters, at the foot of the Sangre de Cristo range. Only a few original pueblo buildings remain, including a large round kiva, used today in ceremonies. Pueblo artisans make woven belts, beadwork, and brown micaceous pottery. One of my favorite reasons for visiting this pueblo is to see the small herd of bison that roams on 179 acres set aside for them.

Nambe Falls make a stunning three-tier drop through a cleft in a rock face about 4 miles beyond the pueblo. You can reach the falls via a 15-minute hike on a rocky, clearly marked path that leaves from the picnic area. A recreational site at the reservoir offers fishing, boating (nonmotor boats only), hiking, camping, and picnicking. The **Waterfall Dances** on July 4 and the **Saint Francis of Assisi Feast Day** on October 4, which has buffalo and deer dances, are observed at the pueblo. Recent dry weather has caused cancellations; before setting out, call the pueblo.

The address is Rte. 1, Box 117-BB, Santa Fe, NM 87506 (*C* **505/455-2036,** or 505/455-2304 for the Ranger Station). Admission to the pueblo is free, and no photography is allowed. Filming and sketching are prohibited. The pueblo is open daily 8am to 5pm. The recreational site is open 8am to noon and 1 to 5pm April to October.

San Ildefonso Pueblo ★★

Pox Oge, as San Ildefonso Pueblo is called in its own Tewa language, means "place where the water cuts down through," possibly named such because of the way the Rio Grande cuts through the mountains nearby. At Pojoaque, head west on NM 502 and drive about 6 miles to the turnoff. This pueblo has a broad, dusty plaza, with a kiva on one side, ancient dwellings on the other, and a church at the far end. It's nationally famous for its matte-finish, black-on-black pottery, developed by tribeswoman María Martinez in the 1920s. One of the most visited pueblos in northern New Mexico (pop. 1,524), San Ildefonso attracts more than 20,000 visitors a year.

The San Ildefonsos could best be described as rebellious because this was one of the last pueblos to succumb to the reconquest spearheaded by Don Diego de Vargas in 1692. Within view of the pueblo is the volcanic Black Mesa, a symbol of the San Ildefonso people's strength. Through the years, each time San Ildefonso felt itself threatened by enemy forces, the residents, along with members of other pueblos, would hide out up on the butte, returning to the valley only when starvation set in. Today, a visit to the pueblo is valuable mainly in order to see or buy rich black pottery. A few shops surround the plaza, and there's the **San Ildefonso Pueblo Museum** tucked away in the governor's office beyond the plaza. I especially recommend visiting during ceremonial days. **San Ildefonso Feast Day,** on January 23, features the buffalo and Comanche dances in alternate years. **Corn dances,** held in late August or early September, commemorate a basic element in pueblo life, the importance of fertility in all creatures—humans as well as animals—and plants.

The pueblo has a 4½-acre fishing lake that is surrounded by *bosque* (Spanish for "forest"), open April to October. Picnicking is encouraged, though you may want to look at the sites before you decide to stay; some are nicer than others. Camping is not allowed.

The pueblo's address is Rte. 5, Box 315A, Santa Fe, NM 87506 (© **505/455-3549**). The admission charge is $7 per car. The charge for taking photographs is $10; you'll pay $20 to film and $25 to sketch. If you plan to fish, the charge is $10 for adults and $5 for seniors and children 11 and under, but you'll want to call to be sure the lake is open. The pueblo is open in the summer daily 8am to 5pm; call for weekend hours. In the winter, it's open Monday to Friday 8am to 4:30pm. It's closed for major holidays and tribal events.

Ohkay Owinge (San Juan Pueblo) ★

If you continue north on US 84/285, you will reach Ohkay Owinge, via NM 74, a mile off NM 68, about 4 miles north of Española.

The largest (pop. 6,748) and northernmost of the Tewa-speaking pueblos and headquarters of the Eight Northern Indian Pueblos Council, San Juan is on the east side of the Rio Grande—opposite the 1598 site of San Gabriel, the first Spanish settlement west of the Mississippi River and the first capital of New Spain. In 1598, the Spanish, impressed with the openness and helpfulness of the people of San Juan, decided to establish a capital there (it was moved to Santa Fe 10 years later), making San Juan Pueblo the first to be subjected to Spanish colonization. The Indians were generous, providing food, clothing, shelter, and fuel—they even helped sustain the settlement when its leader, Conquistador Juan de Oñate, became preoccupied with his search for gold and neglected the needs of his people.

The past and present cohabit here. Though many of the tribe members are Catholics, most of the San Juan tribe still practice traditional religious rituals. Thus, two rectangular kivas flank the church in the main plaza, and *caciques* (pueblo priests) share power with civil authorities. The annual **San Juan Fiesta** is held June 23 and 24; it features buffalo and Comanche dances. Another annual ceremony is the **turtle dance** on December 26. The **Matachine dance,** performed here Christmas Day, vividly depicts the subjugation of the Native Americans by the Catholic Spaniards (p. 323).

The address of the pueblo is P.O. Box 1099, San Juan Pueblo, NM 87566 (© **505/852-4400** or 505/852-4210). Admission is free. Photography or sketching may be allowed for a fee with prior permission from the governor's office. For information, call the number above. The charge for fishing is $8 for adults and $5 for children and seniors. The pueblo is open every day during daylight hours.

The **Eight Northern Indian Pueblos Council** (© **505/747-1593**) is a sort of chamber of commerce and social-service agency.

Fishing and picnicking are encouraged at the **San Juan Tribal Lakes,** open year-round. **Ohkay Casino** (© **505/747-1668;** www.ohkay.com) offers table games and slot machines, as well as live music nightly Tuesday through Saturday. It's open 24 hours on weekends.

Santa Clara Pueblo

Close to Española (on NM 5), Santa Clara, with a population of 1,944, is one of the largest pueblos. You'll see the village sprawling across the river basin near the beautiful Black Mesa, rows of tract homes surrounding an adobe central area. Although it's in an incredible setting, the pueblo itself is not much to see; however, a trip through it will give a real feel for the contemporary lives of these people. Though stories vary, the Santa Clarans teach their children that their ancestors once lived in cliffside dwellings named Puye and migrated down to the river bottom in the 13th century. This pueblo is noted for its language program. Artisan elders work with children to teach them their native Tewa language, on the brink of extinction because so many now speak English. This pueblo is also the home of noted potter Nancy Youngblood, who comes from a long line of famous potters and now does alluring contemporary work.

Follow the main route to the old village, where you come to the visitor center, also known as the neighborhood center. There you can get directions to small shops that sell distinctive black incised Santa Clara pottery, red burnished pottery, baskets, and other crafts. One stunning sight here is the cemetery. Stop on the west side of the church and look over the 4-foot wall. It's a primitive site, with plain wooden crosses and some graves adorned with plastic flowers.

There are corn and harvest dances on **Santa Clara Feast Day** (Aug 12); information on other special days (including the corn or harvest dances, as well as children's dances) can be obtained from the pueblo office.

The famed **Puye Cliff Dwellings** (see below) are on the Santa Clara reservation. The pueblo's address is P.O. Box 580, Española, NM 87532 (© **505/753-7326**). A permit is required from the governor's office to enter the pueblo. The fee is $5 and includes permission for photography; filming and sketching are not allowed. The pueblo is open every day from 8am to 4:30pm.

PUYE CLIFFS ★★

The Puye Cliff Dwellings offer a view of centuries of culture so well preserved you can almost hear ancient life clamoring around you. You'll first visit the Harvey House and exhibit hall, which tells some of the history of the site. Next, with a guide, you'll take a fairly steep hike up to a 200-foot cliff face where you'll see caves that were once part of dwellings believed to have been built around 1450. Next, either by bus or ladder, you will travel to the mesa top to see stone dwellings dating from 1200. By 1540, this community's population was at its height, and Puye was the center for a number of villages of the Pajarito Plateau. The guides, ancestors of this culture, help interpret the site.

Unfortunately, Santa Clara Pueblo, which owns Puye, is currently charging a steep price for a visit, as you'll see below. For this reason, I would recommend a visit to Bandelier National Monument (see below) instead. But if you have money and plenty of time (the guided tours—the only way to see the ruins—take upwards of 2 hours), then by all means go. Your best bet is to check the website or call to make sure tours are available.

From the Monday after Easter to Labor Day, the site is open daily 8:30am to 6pm, with tours on the hour from 9am to 5pm. After Labor Day to the week before Easter, daily hours are 9:30am to 3pm, with tours on the hour from 10am to 2pm. The site is closed the week before Easter, June 13, August 12, Christmas Day, and during inclement weather.

Admission is $35 per person for adults, $33 for children ages 5 to 14, free for ages 4 and under. To reach Puye from Santa Fe, on US 285, drive 28 miles to Española. Turn left onto US 84 and travel just under a mile. You will cross the Rio Grande. Turn left onto NM 30 and travel south 2 miles to the Puye Cliffs Welcome Center. From there you will travel on Indian Rte. 601 for 7 miles to Puye. Call © 888/320-5008 (www.puyecliffs.com) for information.

PECOS NATIONAL HISTORICAL PARK ★★

About 15 miles east of Santa Fe, I-25 meanders through **Glorieta Pass,** site of an important Civil War skirmish. In March 1862, volunteers from Colorado and New Mexico, along with Fort Union regulars, defeated a Confederate force marching on Santa Fe, thereby turning the tide of Southern encroachment in the West.

Follow NM 50 east to **Pecos** for about 7 miles. This quaint town, well off the beaten track since the interstate was constructed, is the site of a noted **Benedictine monastery.** About 26 miles north of here on NM 63 is the village of **Cowles,** gateway to the natural wonderland of the **Pecos Wilderness.** There are many camping, picnicking, and fishing locales en route.

Pecos National Historical Park ★★ (© 505/757-7200; www.nps.gov/peco), about 2 miles south of the town of Pecos off NM 63, contains the ruins of a 15th-century pueblo and 17th- and 18th-century missions that jut up spectacularly from a high meadow. Coronado mentioned Pecos Pueblo in 1540: "It is feared through the land," he wrote. The approximately 2,000 Native Americans here farmed in irrigated fields and hunted wild game. Their pueblo had 660 rooms and many kivas. By 1620, Franciscan monks had established a church and convent. Military and natural disasters took their toll on the pueblo, and in 1838, the 20 surviving Pecos went to live with relatives at the Jemez Pueblo.

The **E. E. Fogelson Visitor Center** tells the history of the Pecos people in a well-done, chronologically organized exhibit, complete with dioramas. A 1.5-mile loop trail begins at the center and continues through Pecos Pueblo and the **Misión de Nuestra Señora de Los Angeles de Porciuncula** (as the church was formerly called). This excavated structure—170 feet long and 90 feet wide at the transept—was once the most magnificent church north of Mexico City.

Pecos National Historical Park is open daily 8am to 6pm (until 5pm Labor Day to Memorial Day). It's closed January 1 and December 25. Admission is $3 per person age 17 and over.

LOS ALAMOS & BANDELIER NATIONAL MONUMENT

Pueblo tribes lived in the rugged Los Alamos area for well over 1,000 years, and an exclusive boys' school operated atop the 7,300-foot plateau from 1918 to 1943. Then, the **Los Alamos National Laboratory** was established here in secrecy, code-named Site Y of the Manhattan Project, the hush-hush wartime program that developed the world's first atomic bombs.

Project director J. Robert Oppenheimer, later succeeded by Norris E. Bradbury, worked along with thousands of scientists, engineers, and technicians in research, development, and production of those early weapons. Today, with an annual budget of $2 billion, the lab operates more than 2,100 facilities and employs about 11,000 people, making it the largest employer in northern New Mexico. The lab is operated by Los Alamos National Security, currently under a contract through the U.S. Department of Energy.

The laboratory is one of the world's foremost scientific institutions. It primarily focuses on nuclear weapons research—the Trident and Minuteman strategic warheads were designed here, for example—and has many other interdisciplinary research programs, including international nuclear safeguards and nonproliferation, space, and atmospheric studies; supercomputing; theoretical physics; biomedical and materials science; and environmental restoration.

Currently Los Alamos National Laboratory is building a limited number of replacement plutonium pits for use in the enduring U.S. nuclear weapons stockpile. The lab has the only plutonium-processing facility in the United States that is capable of producing those components.

An unusual town, Los Alamos has the highest per capita Ph.D. population in the nation—22 percent. If you listen closely you may hear people talk of such complexities as quantum cryptography, trapdoor functions of polynomial integers, reciprocal space and heterogeneous multicores. With researchers convening here from all over the world, the accents range from Russian to French to Japanese and even a Texas twang or two.

Orientation/Useful Information

Los Alamos is about 35 miles west of Santa Fe and about 65 miles southwest of Taos. From Santa Fe, take US 84/285 north approximately 16 miles to the Pojoaque junction, then turn west on NM 502. Driving time is only about 50 minutes.

Los Alamos is a town of 18,000, spread over the colorful, fingerlike mesas of the Pajarito Plateau, between the Jemez Mountains and the Rio Grande Valley. As NM 502 enters Los Alamos from Santa Fe, it follows Trinity Drive, where accommodations, restaurants, and other services are located. Central Avenue parallels Trinity Drive and has restaurants, galleries, and shops.

The **Los Alamos Chamber of Commerce,** P.O. Box 460, Los Alamos, NM 87544 (✆ **505/662-8105;** fax 505/662-8399; www.losalamoschamber.com), runs a visitor center that is open Monday to Saturday 9am to 5pm and Sunday 10am to 3pm. It's at 109 Central Park Sq. (across from the Bradbury Science Museum).

What to See & Do

Aside from the sights described below, Los Alamos offers the **Pajarito Mountain ski area,** Camp May Road (P.O. Box 155), Los Alamos, NM 87544 (© 505/662-5725; www.skipajarito.com), with five chairlifts—it's only open on Friday through Sunday and federal holidays. It's an outstanding ski area that rarely gets crowded; many trails are steep and have moguls. Los Alamos also offers the **Los Alamos Golf Course,** 4250 Diamond Dr. (© 505/662-8139; www.losalamosgolf.org), where greens fees are around $28 for 18 holes and $17 for 9 holes; and the **Larry R. Walkup Aquatic Center,** 2760 Canyon Rd. (© 505/662-8170; www.los alamosnm.us), the highest-altitude indoor Olympic-size swimming pool in the United States. Not far from downtown is the outdoor **Los Alamos County Ice Rink,** with a snack bar and skate rentals, open Thanksgiving to late February (© 505/662-4500; www.losalamosnm.us). It's at 4475 West Rd. (take Trinity Dr. to Diamond St., turn left, and watch for the sign on your right). There are no outstanding restaurants in Los Alamos, but if you get hungry, you can stop at the **Central Avenue Grill & Quark Bar ★,** 1789 Central Ave., Ste. 8 (© 505/662-2005), a festive gathering place at the center of town that serves salads, sandwiches, pasta dishes and sushi. Science-minded folks gather here in the evenings over drinks. The chamber of commerce has maps for self-guided historical walking tours, and you can find self-guided driving-tour tapes at stores and hotels around town.

The Art Center at Fuller Lodge This is a public showcase for work by visual artists from northern New Mexico and the surrounding region. Two annual arts-and-crafts fairs are also held here in August and October. The gallery shop sells local crafts at good prices.

In the same building is the **Los Alamos Arts Council** (© 505/663-0477), a multidisciplinary organization that sponsors an art fair in May, as well as evening and noontime cultural programs.

2132 Central Ave., Los Alamos. © **505/662-9331.** www.artfulnm.org. Free admission. Mon–Sat 10am–4pm.

Bradbury Science Museum ★ This is a great place to get acquainted with what goes on at a weapons production facility after nuclear proliferation. Although the museum is run by Los Alamos National Laboratory, which definitely puts a positive spin on the business of producing weapons, it's a fascinating place to learn about—through dozens of interactive exhibits—the lab's many contributions to science.

Begin in the History Gallery, where you'll learn about the evolution of the site from the Los Alamos Ranch School days through the Manhattan Project to the present, including a 1939 letter from Albert Einstein to President Franklin D. Roosevelt, suggesting research into uranium as a new and important source of energy. Next, move into the Research and Technology Gallery, where you can see work that's been done on the Human Genome Project, including a computer map of human DNA. You can try out a laser and learn about the workings of a particle accelerator. Meanwhile, listen for announcement of the film *The Town That Never Was,* a 16-minute presentation on this community that grew up shrouded in secrecy (shown in the auditorium). Further exploration will take you to the Defense Gallery, where you can test the heaviness of plutonium against that of other substances, see an actual 5-ton Little Boy nuclear bomb (like the one dropped on Hiroshima), and see firsthand how Los Alamos conducts worldwide surveillance of nuclear explosions.

15th St. and Central Ave., Los Alamos. © **505/667-4444.** www.lanl.gov/museum. Free admission. Tues–Sat 10am–5pm; Sun–Mon 1–5pm. Closed New Year's Day, Thanksgiving, Christmas.

Los Alamos Historical Museum ★ Start your visit to this museum next door at Fuller Lodge, a massive vertical-log building built by John Gaw Meem in 1928. The log work is intricate and artistic, and the feel of the old place is warm and majestic. It once housed the dining and recreation hall for the Los Alamos Ranch School for boys and is now a National Historic Landmark. Its current occupants include the museum office and research archives and the Art Center at Fuller Lodge (see above). The museum, located in the small log-and-stone building to the north of Fuller Lodge, depicts area history from prehistoric cliff dwellers to the present. Exhibits range from Native American artifacts to school memorabilia and an excellent Manhattan Project exhibit that offers a more realistic view of the devastation resulting from use of atomic bombs than is offered at the Bradbury Science Museum.

1921 Juniper St., Los Alamos. © **505/662-4493.** www.losalamoshistory.org. Free admission. Summer Mon–Sat 9:30am–4:30pm, Sun 1–4pm; winter Mon–Sat 10am–4pm, Sun 1–4pm. Closed New Year's Day, Easter, Thanksgiving, Christmas.

NEARBY

Bandelier National Monument ★★★ Less than 15 miles south of Los Alamos along NM 4, this site contains stunningly preserved ruins of the ancient cliff-dwelling ancestral Puebloan (Anasazi) culture within 46 square miles of canyon-and-mesa wilderness. The national monument is named after the Swiss-American archaeologist Adolph Bandelier, who explored here in the 1880s. During busy summer months, head out early—there can be a waiting line for cars to park.

After an orientation stop at the visitor center and museum to learn about the culture that flourished here between 1100 and 1550, most visitors follow a trail along Frijoles Creek to the principal ruins. The pueblo site, including an underground kiva, has been stabilized. The biggest thrill for most folks is climbing hardy ponderosa pine ladders to visit an alcove—140 feet above the canyon floor—that was once home to prehistoric people. Tours are self-guided or led by a National Park Service ranger. Be aware that dogs are not allowed on trails.

On summer nights, rangers offer campfire talks about the history, culture, and geology of the area. During the day, nature programs are sometimes offered for adults and children. The small museum at the visitor center displays artifacts found in the area.

Elsewhere in the monument area, 70 miles of maintained trails lead to more ruins, waterfalls, and wildlife habitats. However, a number of years ago a fire decimated parts of this area, so periodic closings take place in order to allow the land to reforest.

The separate **Tsankawi** section, reached by an ancient 2-mile trail close to **White Rock,** has a large unexcavated ruin on a high mesa overlooking the Rio Grande Valley. The town of White Rock, about 10 miles southeast of Los Alamos on NM 4, offers spectacular panoramas of the river valley in the direction of Santa Fe; the **White Rock Overlook** is a great picnic spot. Within Bandelier, areas have been set aside for picnicking and camping.

INSIDE A volcano

While you're in the area, check out the **Valles Caldera National Preserve,** past Bandelier National Monument on NM 4, beginning about 15 miles from Los Alamos. The reserve is all that remains of a volcanic caldera created by a collapse after eruptions nearly a million years ago. When the mountain spewed ashes and dust as far away as Kansas and Nebraska, its underground magma chambers collapsed, forming this great valley—one of the largest volcanic calderas in the world. Lava domes that pushed up after the collapse obstruct a full view across the expanse, but the beauty of the place is still within grasp. Visitors have many guided options for exploring the preserve, from sleigh rides and snowshoeing in winter to fly-fishing and horseback riding in summer. For more information, contact ℂ **866/382-5537** (www.vallescaldera.gov).

NM 4 (HCR 1, Box 1, Ste. 15, Los Alamos). ℂ **505/672-3861,** ext 517. www.nps.gov/band. Admission $12 per vehicle. Daily during daylight hours. No pets allowed on trails. Closed New Year's Day, Christmas. From Santa Fe take US 84/285 north to Pojoaque. Exit west onto NM 502 toward Los Alamos. Bear right onto NM 4 toward White Rock and continue for 12 miles. Bandelier is on the left. Travel time is approximately 1 hr.

TAKING THE HIGH ROAD TO TAOS ★★

Unless you're in a hurry to get from Santa Fe to Taos, the High Road—also called the Mountain Road or the King's Road—is by far the most fascinating route between the two cities. It begins in lowlands of mystically formed pink and yellow stone, passing by apple and peach orchards and chile farms in the weaving village of **Chimayo.** Then it climbs toward the highlands to the village of **Cordova,** known for its woodcarvers, and higher still to **Truchas,** a renegade arts town where Hispanic traditions and ways of life continue much as they did a century ago. Though I've described this tour from south to north, the most scenic way to see it is from north to south, when you travel down off the mountains rather than up into them. This way, you see more expansive views.

Chimayo

About 28 miles north of Santa Fe on NM 76/285 is the historic weaving center of Chimayo. It's approximately 16 miles past the Pojoaque junction, at the junction of NM 520 and NM 76 via NM 503. In this small village, families still maintain the tradition of crafting hand-woven textiles initiated by their ancestors seven generations ago, in the early 1800s. One such family is the Ortegas, and **Ortega's Weaving Shop** (ℂ **505/351-4215;** www.ortegasweaving.com) and **Galeria Ortega ★** (ℂ **505/351-2288;** www.galeriaortegainc.com), both at the corner of NM 520 and NM 76, are fine places to take a close look at this ancient craft. A more humble spot is **Trujillo Weaving Shop** (ℂ **505/351-4457**) on NM 76. If you're lucky enough to find the proprietors in, you might get a weaving history lesson. You can see a 100-year-old loom and an even older shuttle carved from apricot wood. The weavings you'll find are some of the best of the Rio Grande style, with rich patterns, many made from naturally dyed wool. Also on display are some fine Cordova woodcarvings. Also check out **Centinela Traditional Arts,** 946 NM 76 (© **505/351-2180;** www.chimayoweavers.com), for a good selection of rugs made by weavers from up and down the Rio Grande Valley. Watch for the chenille shawls by Lore Wills.

One of the best places to shop in Chimayo, **Chimayo Trading and Mercantile ★** (© **505/351-4566**), on NM 76, is a richly cluttered store carrying Pueblo pottery, Navajo weavings, and local arts and crafts as well as select imports. It has a good selection of *katsinas* and Hopi corn maidens. Look for George Zarolinski's fused glass.

Many people come to Chimayo to visit **El Santuario de Nuestro Señor de Esquipulas (The Shrine of Our Lord of Esquipulas) ★★** (© 505/351-4360; holyfamily@cybermesa.com), better known simply as El Santuario de Chimayo. Ascribed with miraculous powers of healing, this church has attracted thousands of pilgrims since its construction in 1816. Up to 30,000 people participate in the annual Good Friday pilgrimage, many of them walking from as far away as Albuquerque. Although only the earth in the anteroom beside the altar is presumed to have the gift of healing powers, the entire shrine radiates true serenity. A National Historic Landmark, the church has five beautiful *reredos* (panels of sacred paintings)— one behind the main altar and two on each side of the nave. Each year during the fourth weekend in July, the military exploits of the 9th-century Spanish saint Santiago are celebrated in a weekend fiesta, including games and music. The Santuario is open daily March to September 9am to 6pm and October to February 9am to 5pm. Please remember that this is a place of worship, so quiet is always appreciated.

WHERE TO STAY

Casa Escondida ★   On the outskirts of Chimayo, this inn is a good home base for exploring the Sangre de Cristo Mountains and their many soulful farming villages. Decor is simple and classic, with Mission-style furniture lending a colonial feel. The breakfast room is a sunny atrium with French doors that open out in summer to a grassy yard spotted with apricot trees. The rooms are varied; all of my favorites are within the main house. The Sun Room catches all that passionate northern New Mexico sun upon its red brick floors and on its private flagstone patio as well. It has an elegant feel and connects with a smaller room, so it's a good choice for families. The Vista is on the second story. It has a wrought-iron queen-size bed as well a twin, and it opens out onto a large deck offering spectacular sunset views. The casita adjacent to the main house has a kiva fireplace, a stove, and a minifridge, as well as nice meadow views.

P.O. Box 142, Chimayo, NM 87522. © **800/643-7201** or 505/351-4805. Fax 505/351-2575. www. casaescondida.com. 8 units. $99–$159 double. Rates include full breakfast. MC, V. Pets welcome in four rooms for a small fee; prearrangement required. **Amenities:** Jacuzzi. *In room:* Kitchenette (in 1 room), no phone.

WHERE TO DINE

Restaurante Rancho de Chimayo ★★ NEW MEXICAN   For as long as I can remember, my family and many of my friends' families have scheduled trips into northern New Mexico to coincide with lunch or dinner at this atmospheric restaurant. In an adobe home built by Hermenegildo Jaramillo in the 1880s, it's now run as a restaurant by his descendants. Over the years the restaurant has become so famous that tour buses now stop here. However, the food is still delicious. In the

HIGH ON art

If you really like art and want to meet artists, check out one of the **Art Studio Tours** held in the fall in the region. Artists spend months preparing their best work, then open their doors to visitors. Wares range from pottery and paintings to furniture and woodcarvings to *ristras* and dried-flower arrangements. The most notable tour is the **High Road Studio Art Tour** (www.highroadnewmexico. com) in mid- to late September. If you're not in the region during that time, watch the newspapers (such as the *Santa Fe New Mexican*'s Friday edition, "Pasatiempo") for notices of other art-studio tours. Good ones are held in **Galisteo** (in mid-Oct; www.galisteostudiotour. com); **Abiquiu** (early Sept; www.abiquiustudiotour.org); **El Rito** (mid-Oct; www. elritostudiotour.org); and **Dixon** (early Nov; www.dixonarts.org). If you're not here during those times, you can still visit many of the galleries listed on the websites.

warmer months, request to dine on the terraced patio. During winter, you'll be seated in the atrium or one of a number of cozy rooms with thick viga ceilings. The food is native New Mexican, prepared from generations-old Jaramillo family recipes. You can't go wrong with the chicken enchiladas with green chile. For variety you might want to try the *combinación picante* (*carne adovada,* tamale, enchilada, beans, and *posole*). Each plate comes with a fluffy *sopaipilla.* With a little honey, who needs dessert? The full bar serves tasty margaritas.

300 CR 98 (¼ mile west of the Santuario), Chimayo, NM 87522. ⓒ **505/984-2100.** www.ranchodechimayo.com. Reservations recommended. Main courses $7–$10 lunch, $9–$21 dinner. AE, DC, DISC, MC, V. May–Oct daily 11:30am–9pm, Sat–Sun breakfast 8:30–10:30am; Nov–Apr Tues–Sun 11:30am–8:30pm.

Cordova

Just as Chimayo is famous for its weaving, the village of Cordova, about 7 miles east on NM 76, is noted for its woodcarving. It's easy to whiz by this village, nestled below the High Road, but don't. Just a short way through this truly traditional northern New Mexico town is a gem: **The Castillo Gallery** ★ (ⓒ **505/351-4067**), a mile into the village of Cordova, carries moody and colorful acrylic paintings by Paula Castillo, as well as her metal welded sculptures. It also carries the work of Terry Enseñat Mulert, whose contemporary woodcarvings are treasures of the high country. En route to the Castillo, you may want to stop in at two other local carvers' galleries. The first you'll come to is that of **Sabinita Lopez Ortiz;** the second belongs to her cousin, **Gloria Ortiz.** Both are descendants of the noted José Dolores Lopez. Carved from cedar wood and aspen, their works range from simple *santos* (statues of saints) to elaborate scenes of birds.

Truchas

Robert Redford's 1988 movie *The Milagro Beanfield War* featured the town of Truchas (which means "trout"). A former Spanish colonial outpost built on top of an 8,000-foot mesa, 4 miles east of Cordova, it was chosen as the site for the film in part because traditional Hispanic culture is still very much in evidence. Subsistence farming is prevalent here. The scenery is spectacular: 13,101-foot Truchas Peak dominates one side of the mesa, and the broad Rio Grande Valley dominates the other.

Look for the **High Road Marketplace** ★ (© 866/343-5381 or 505/689-2689), an artists' co-op gallery with a variety of offerings ranging from jewelry to landscape paintings to a broad range of crosses made from tin, rusted metal, and nails. Be sure to find your way into the **Cordovas' Handweaving Workshop** (© 505/689-1124). In the center of town, this tiny shop is run by Harry Cordova, a fourth-generation weaver with a unique style. His works tend to be simpler than many Rio Grande weavings, using mainly stripes in the designs.

Just down the road from Cordovas' is **Hand Artes Gallery** (© 800/689-2441 or 505/689-2443), a definite surprise in this remote region. Here you'll find an array of contemporary as well as representational art from noted regional artists. Look for Sheila Keeffe's worldly painted panels, and Norbert Voelkel's colorful paintings and monoprints.

About 6 miles east of Truchas on NM 76 is the small town of **Las Trampas,** noted for its 1780 **San José de Gracia Church,** which, with its thick walls and elegant lines, might possibly be the most beautiful of all New Mexico churches built during the Spanish colonial period.

Picuris (San Lorenzo) Pueblo & Peñasco

Not far from the regional education center of Peñasco, about 24 miles from Chimayo, near the intersection of NM 75 and NM 76, is the Picuris (San Lorenzo) Pueblo (© 575/587-2519; www.indianpueblo.org/19pueblos/picuris.html). The 375 citizens of this 15,000-acre mountain pueblo, native Tewa speakers, consider themselves a sovereign nation: Their forebears never made a treaty with any foreign country, including the United States. Thus, they observe a traditional form of tribal council government. A few of the original mud-and-stone houses still stand, as does a lovely church. A striking aboveground ceremonial kiva called "the Roundhouse," built at least 700 years ago, and some historic excavated kivas and storerooms are on a hill above the pueblo and are open to visitors. The **annual feast days** at San Lorenzo Church are August 9 and 10.

The people here are modern enough to have fully computerized their public showcase operations as Picuris Tribal Enterprises. Besides running the Hotel Santa Fe in the state capital, they own the **Picuris Pueblo Museum and Visitor's Center,** where weaving, beadwork, and distinctive reddish-brown clay cooking pottery are exhibited daily 8am to 5pm. Self-guided tours through the old village ruins begin at the museum and cost $5; the camera fee is $6; sketching and video camera fees are $25. There's also an information center, crafts shop, and restaurant. Fishing permits ($11 for all ages) are available, as are permits to camp ($8) at Tu-Tah Lake, which is regularly stocked with trout.

You might want to plan your High Road trip to include a visit to **Sugar Nymphs Bistro** ★★, 15046 NM 75 (© 575/587-0311), for some inventive food. Inside a vintage theater in the little farming village of Peñasco, Kai Harper, former executive chef at Greens in San Francisco, prepares contemporary bistro cuisine, using local and seasonal ingredients. Lunch brings imaginative pizza, salads, and burgers, while dinner includes a full range of entrees. Some of my favorites include a goat-cheese salad and a chicken breast with green-chile cream. All breads and desserts are baked in-house by Kai's partner, Ki Holste, including a delectable chocolate-pecan pie. It goes great with a range of coffee drinks, including a perfect latte. The Bistro also sponsors family-oriented events in the theater. In summer, the cafe is open Tuesday to Saturday 11:30am to 3pm and Thursday to Saturday 5:30 to 7:30 or 8pm, with Sunday brunch 10am to 2pm. In winter, spring, and fall, the schedule is abbreviated. Call ahead to be sure it's open.

Dixon & Embudo

Taos is about 24 miles north of Peñasco via NM 518, but day-trippers from Santa Fe can loop back to the capital by taking NM 75 west from Picuris Pueblo. Dixon, approximately 12 miles west of Picuris, and its twin village Embudo, a mile farther on NM 68 at the Rio Grande, are home to many artists and craftspeople who exhibit their works during the annual **autumn show** sponsored by the Dixon Arts Association. If you get to Embudo at mealtime, stop in at **Embudo Station** (© 505/852-4707; www.embudostation.com), a restaurant right on the banks of the Rio Grande. From mid-April to October—the only time it's open—you can sit on the patio under giant cottonwoods and sip the restaurant's own microbrewed beer (try the green-chile ale, its most celebrated) and signature wines while watching the peaceful Rio flow by. The specialty here is Southwestern food, but you'll find other tantalizing tastes as well. Try the rainbow trout roasted on a cedar plank. The restaurant is generally open Tuesday to Sunday noon to 9pm, but call before making plans. It's especially known for its jazz on Sunday, an affair that PBS once featured.

To taste more of the local grape, follow signs to **La Chiripada Winery** (© 505/579-4437; www.lachiripada.com), whose product is quite good, especially to those who don't know that New Mexico has a long winemaking history. Local pottery is also sold in the tasting room. The winery is open Monday to Saturday 10am to 5pm, Sunday noon to 5pm.

Two more small villages lie in the Rio Grande Valley at 6-mile intervals south of Embudo on NM 68. **Velarde** is a fruit-growing center; in fall, the road here is lined with stands selling fresh fruit or crimson chile *ristras* and wreaths of native plants. **Alcalde** is the site of Los Luceros, a restored early-17th-century home that will soon house a school for Native American and Hispanic filmmakers. The school is a collaboration between the state of New Mexico and actor Robert Redford. The unique

 lowriders: CAR ART

While cruising Española's main drag, don't drop your jaw if you see the front of a car rise up off the ground and then sink down again, or if you witness another that appears to be scraping its underbelly on the pavement. These novelties are part of a car culture that thrives in northern New Mexico. Traditionally, the owners use late-model cars, which they soup up with such novelties as elaborate chrome, metal chain steering wheels, even portraits of Our Lady of Guadalupe painted on the hood. If you're interested in seeing the Custom Car and Truck Show put on by local car clubs (and often cosponsored by local casinos), call the Española Valley Chamber of Commerce for information (© 505/753-2831; www.espanolanm chamber.com).

Dance of the Matachines, a Moorish-style ritual brought from Spain, is performed here on holidays and feast days.

Española

The commercial center of Española (pop. 9,688) no longer has the railroad that led to its establishment in the 1880s, but it may have New Mexico's greatest concentration of **lowriders.** These are late-model customized cars, so called because their suspension leaves them sitting quite close to the ground. For details, see the box below.

Sights of interest in Española include the **Bond House Museum** (© **505/747-8535**), a Victorian-era adobe home that exhibits local history and art, and the **Santa Cruz Church,** built in 1733 and renovated in 1979, which houses many fine examples of Spanish colonial religious art. The **Convento,** built to resemble a colonial cathedral, on the Española Plaza (at the junction of NM 30 and US 84), houses a variety of shops, including a trading post and an antiques gallery, as well as a display room for the Historical Society. Major events include the July **Fiesta de Oñate,** commemorating the valley's founding in 1596; the October **Tri-Cultural Art Festival** on the Northern New Mexico Community College campus; the week-long **Summer Solstice** celebration staged in June by the nearby Hacienda de Guru Ram Das (© **888/346-2420**); and **Peace Prayer Day,** an outdoor festival in mid-June—featuring art, music, food, guest speakers, and more—in the Jemez Mountains (© **877/707-3221;** www.peaceprayerday.org).

Complete information on Española and the vicinity can be obtained from the **Española Valley Chamber of Commerce,** no. 1 Calle de Las Espanolas, NM 87532 (© **505/753-2831;** www.espanolanmchamber.com).

If you admire the work of Georgia O'Keeffe, try to plan a short trip to **Abiquiu,** a tiny town at a bend of the Rio Chama, 14 miles south of Ghost Ranch and 22 miles north of Española on US 84. When you see the surrounding terrain, it will be clear that this was the inspiration for many of her startling landscapes. **O'Keeffe's adobe home ★** (where she lived and painted) is open for public tours. However, a reservation must be made in advance; the fee for adults is $30 (some discounts apply) for a 1-hour tour. A number of tours are given each week—on Tuesday, Thursday, and Friday (mid-Mar to late Nov only)—and a limited number of people are accepted per tour. Visitors are not permitted to take pictures. Fortunately, O'Keeffe's home remains as it was when she lived there (until 1986). Call several months in advance for reservations (© **505/685-4539;** www.okeeffemuseum.org).

If you're in the area and need gas for your car or a snack for yourself (or goodies for a picnic), stop in at **Bode's** on US 84 in Abiquiu (© **505/685-4422**). The general store for the area, this place has shovels and irrigation boots, and better yet, cold drinks, gourmet sandwiches, and other deli items—even a hearty green-chile stew.

WHERE TO STAY & DINE

A fun side trip while in the area is the village of **El Rito.** One of the state's best chile spots is there, at the family-owned restaurant **El Farolito ★★** at 1212 Main St. (© **575/581-9509**). The remote place has been written about in *Gourmet* and *Travel + Leisure,* and it's no wonder—their enchiladas are some of the best in the state. The hours vary, so call ahead.

GEORGIA O'KEEFFE & NEW MEXICO:
a desert romance

In June 1917, during a short visit to the Southwest, the painter Georgia O'Keeffe (b. 1887) visited New Mexico for the first time. She was immediately enchanted by the stark scenery; even after her return to the energy and chaos of New York City, her mind wandered frequently to New Mexico's arid land and undulating mesas. However, not until coaxed by the arts patron and "collector of people" Mabel Dodge Luhan 12 years later did O'Keeffe return to the multihued desert of her daydreams.

O'Keeffe was reportedly ill, both physically and emotionally, when she arrived in Santa Fe in April 1929. New Mexico seemed to soothe her spirit and heal her physical ailments almost magically. Two days after her arrival, Luhan persuaded O'Keeffe to move into her home in Taos. There, she would be free to paint and socialize as she liked.

In Taos, O'Keeffe began painting what would become some of her best-known canvases—close-ups of desert flowers and objects such as cow and horse skulls. "The color up there is different . . . the blue-green of the sage and the mountains, the wildflowers in bloom," O'Keeffe once said of Taos. "It's a different kind of color from any I've ever seen—there's nothing like that in north Texas or even in Colorado." Taos transformed not only her art, but her personality as well. She bought a car and learned to drive. Sometimes, on warm days, she ran naked through the sage fields. That August, a new, rejuvenated O'Keeffe rejoined her husband, photographer Alfred Stieglitz, in New York.

The artist returned to New Mexico year after year, spending time with Luhan as well as staying at the isolated Ghost Ranch. She drove through the countryside in her snappy Ford, stopping to paint in her favorite spots along the way. Until 1949, O'Keeffe always returned to New York in the fall. Three years after Stieglitz's death, though, O'Keeffe relocated permanently to New Mexico, spending each winter and spring in Abiquiu and each summer and fall at Ghost Ranch. Georgia O'Keeffe died in Santa Fe in 1986.

A great way to see Ghost Ranch is on a hike that climbs above the mystical area. Take US 84 north from Española about 36 miles to Ghost Ranch and follow the road to the Ghost Ranch office. The ranch is owned by the Presbyterian Church, and the staff will supply you with a primitive map for the **Kitchen Mesa** and **Chimney Rock** hikes. If you hike there, be sure to check in at the front desk, which is open Monday to Saturday from 8am to 5pm. For more information, contact **Ghost Ranch,** 401 Old Taos Hwy., Santa Fe (☎ **505/685-4333;** www. ghostranch.org).

El Paragua ★ NORTHERN NEW MEXICAN   Every time I enter El Paragua (which means "the umbrella"), with its red-tile floors and colorful Saltillo-tile trimmings, I feel as though I've stepped into Mexico. The restaurant opened in 1958 as a small taco stand owned by two brothers, and through the years it has received praise from many sources, including *Gourmet* magazine and N. Scott Momaday, writing for the *New York Times.* You can't go wrong ordering the enchilada suprema, a chicken-and-cheese enchilada with onion and sour cream. Also on the menu are fajitas and a variety of seafood dishes and steaks, including the *churrasco Argentino.*

Served at your table in a hot brazier, it's cooked in a green-herb salsa chimichurri. There's a full bar from which you may want to try Don Luis's Italian coffee, made with a coffee-flavored liquor called Tuaca. For equally excellent but faster food, skip next door to the kin restaurant **El Parasol ★** and order a guacamole chicken taco—the best in the region.

603 Santa Cruz Rd., Española (off the main drag; turn east at Long John Silver's). ℂ **505/753-3211.** www.elparagua.com. Reservations recommended. Main courses $11–$22. AE, DISC, MC, V. Mon-Fri 11am–9pm; Sat 9am–9pm; Sun 9am–8pm.

Ojo Caliente Mineral Springs Resort & Spa ★★ 📷

This newly renovated retreat offers fine lodging and quality soaks and spa treatments. A National Historic Site, no other hot spring in the world has Ojo Caliente's combination of minerals, and these are split into separate pools so visitors can partake of the healing qualities of each. If the weather is warm enough, the outdoor mud bath is a treat.

The lodging options range from posh cliffside rooms with fireplaces and their own mineral soaking tubs on a patio to very basic ones with a shared shower. Lodging rates include access to all mineral pools for both the day of arrival and the day of departure.

The pools are open daily 8am to 10pm. Children 12 and under are welcome in the springs from 10am to 6pm in the large pool only and with adult supervision. Mineral springs entry Monday to Thursday costs $16 adult and $12 for children 12 and under; Friday to Sunday and holidays, it's $24 adult and $18 children, with reduced rates after 6pm. Private pools are available.

50 Los Baños Dr., Ojo Caliente, NM 87549. ℂ **800/222-9162.** Fax 505/583-9198. www.ojospa.com. 48 units. $119–$329 double; $399–$449 house for 4 guests. Additional person $50. AE, DISC, MC, V. **Amenities:** Restaurant; lounge; bikes; concierge; pool; sauna; spa; steam room. *In room:* A/C, TV, fridge, hair dryer, Wi-Fi. On US 285, 45 miles northwest of Santa Fe and 50 miles southwest of Taos.

Rancho de San Juan Country Inn & Three Forks Restaurant ★★★

Thirty-eight miles from Santa Fe, between Española and Ojo Caliente, this inn set on 225 acres provides an authentic northern New Mexico desert experience with the comforts of a luxury hotel. The original part of the inn comprises four recently renovated and enlarged rooms around a central courtyard, all with fireplaces. Additional casitas with kitchens are in the outlying hills. Rooms here are open, bright, and decorated with a creative mix from the owners' personal art collections. From private patios, you'll enjoy spectacular views of desert landscapes and distant, snow-capped peaks. The Kiva Suite is the most innovative, with a round bedroom and a skylight just above the bed, perfect for stargazing. Meals at the **Three Forks Restaurant** are delicious, served in a room with contemporary decor that looks out on the desert.

US 285 (en route to Ojo Caliente), P.O. Box 4140, Fairview Station, Española, NM 87533. ℂ **505/753-6818.** www.ranchodesanjuan.com. 13 units. $285–$485 double. AE, MC, V. **Amenities:** Restaurant; concierge; massage and other spa treatments. *In room:* A/C (in most), CD player, fridge, hair dryer.

TAOS

New Mexico's favorite arts town sits in a masterpiece setting. It's wedged between the towering peaks of the Rocky Mountains and the plunging chasm of the Rio Grande Gorge.

Located about 70 miles north of Santa Fe, this town of 5,000 residents combines 1960s hippiedom (thanks to communes set up in the hills back then) with the ancient culture of Taos Pueblo (some people still live without electricity and running water, as their ancestors did 1,000 years ago). It can be an odd place, where some completely eschew materialism and live "off the grid" in half-underground houses called earth ships. But there are plenty of more mainstream attractions as well—Taos boasts some of the best restaurants in the state, a hot and funky arts scene, and incredible outdoors action, including world-class skiing.

Its history is rich. Throughout the Taos valley, ruins and artifacts attest to a Native American presence dating back 5,000 years. The Spanish first visited this area in 1540, colonizing it in 1598. In the last 2 decades of the 17th century, they put down three rebellions at Taos Pueblo. During the 18th and 19th centuries, Taos was an important trade center: New Mexico's annual caravan to Chihuahua, Mexico, couldn't leave until after the annual midsummer **Taos Fair.** French trappers began attending the fair in 1739. Even though the Plains tribes often attacked the pueblos at other times, they would attend the market festival under a temporary annual truce. By the early 1800s, Taos had become a meeting place for American mountain men, the most famous of whom, Kit Carson, made his home in Taos from 1826 to 1868.

Taos remained loyal to Mexico during the U.S.-Mexican War of 1846. The town rebelled against its new U.S. landlord in 1847, even killing newly appointed Governor Charles Bent in his Taos home. Nevertheless, the town was eventually incorporated into the Territory of New Mexico in 1850. During the Civil War, Taos fell into Confederate hands for 6 weeks; afterward, Carson and two other men raised the Union flag over Taos Plaza and guarded it day and night. Since then, Taos has had the honor of flying the flag 24 hours a day.

Taos's population declined when the railroad bypassed it in favor of Santa Fe. In 1898, two East Coast artists—Ernest Blumenschein and Bert Phillips—discovered the dramatic, varied effects of sunlight on the natural environment of the Taos valley and depicted them on canvas. By 1912, thanks to the growing influence of the **Taos Society of Artists,** the town had gained a worldwide reputation as a cultural center. Today, it is estimated that more than 15% of the population are painters, sculptors, writers, or musicians, or in some other way earn their income from artistic pursuits.

The town of Taos is merely the focal point of rugged 2,200-square-mile Taos County. Two features dominate this sparsely populated region: the high desert mesa, split in two by the 650-foot-deep chasm of the **Rio Grande;** and the **Sangre de Cristo** range, which tops out at 13,161-foot Wheeler Peak, New Mexico's highest mountain. From the forested uplands to the sage-carpeted mesa, the county is home to a large variety of wildlife. The human element includes Native Americans who are still living in ancient pueblos and Hispanic farmers who continue to irrigate their farmlands using centuries-old methods.

Taos is also inhabited by many people who have chosen to retreat from, or altogether drop out of, mainstream society. There's a laid-back attitude here, even more pronounced than the general *mañana* attitude for which New Mexico is known. Most Taoseños live here to play here—and that means outdoors. Many work at the ski area all winter (skiing whenever they can) and work for raft companies in the summer (to get on the river as much as they can). Others are into rock climbing, mountain biking, and backpacking. That's not to say that Taos is just a resort town. With the Hispanic and Native American populations' histories in the area, there's a richness and depth here that most resort towns lack.

Taos's biggest task these days is to try to stem the tide of overdevelopment that is flooding northern New Mexico. In "New Mexico Today" (p. 14), I address the city's success in battling back airport expansion and some housing developments. A grassroots community program has been implemented that gives neighborhoods a say in how their area is developed.

ORIENTATION

Arriving

BY PLANE The **Taos Regional Airport** (© 575/758-4995) is about 8 miles northwest of town on US 64. Most people opt to fly into Albuquerque International Sunport, rent a car, and drive up to Taos from there. The drive takes approximately 2½ hours. If you'd rather be picked up at Albuquerque International Sunport, call **Faust's Transportation, Inc.** (© 575/758-3410), which offers daily service, as well as taxi service between Taos and Taos Ski Valley.

BY BUS/TRAIN Besides Faust's Transportation (above) the only way to arrive in Taos by bus is via Rail Runner. The **New Mexico Rail Runner Express** train service connects Santa Fe to Taos via the Taos Express Shuttle Service on Fridays through Sundays. Contact © 866/799-7245 or www.nmrailrunner.com/bus_san-tafe_depot.asp. For more information on this and other bus services to and from Albuquerque and Santa Fe, see "Getting There & Around," in chapter 3.

BY CAR Most visitors arrive in Taos via either NM 68 or US 64. Northbound travelers should exit I-25 at Santa Fe, follow US 285 as far as Española, and then continue on the divided highway when it becomes NM 68. Taos is about 79 miles from the I-25 junction. Southbound travelers from Denver on I-25 should exit about 6 miles south of Raton at US 64 and then follow it about 95 miles to Taos. Another major route is US 64 from the west (214 miles from Farmington).

Warning for Drivers

En route to many recreation sites, reliable paved roads often give way to poorer forest roads, where gas stations and cafes are scarce. Four-wheel-drive vehicles are recommended on snow and much of the unpaved terrain of the region. If you're doing some off-road adventuring, it's wise to go with a full gas tank, extra food and water, and warm clothing—just in case. At the higher-than-10,000-foot elevations of northern New Mexico, sudden summer snowstorms can occur.

Visitor Information

The **Taos County Chamber of Commerce,** at 108 Kit Carson Rd., Taos, NM 87571 (𝓒 **575/751-8800;** www.taoschamber.com), is open Monday to Friday 9am to 5pm in summer and 1 to 5pm in winter. It's closed on major holidays.

City Layout

The **plaza** is a short block west of Taos's major intersection—where US 64 (Kit Carson Rd.) from the east joins NM 68, **Paseo del Pueblo Sur.** US 64 proceeds north from the intersection as **Paseo del Pueblo Norte. Camino de la Placita (Placita Rd.)** circles the west side of downtown, passing within a block of the other side of the plaza. Many of the streets that join these thoroughfares are winding lanes lined by traditional adobe homes, many of them over 100 years old.

Most of the art galleries are located on or near the plaza, which was paved over with bricks several years ago, and along neighboring streets. Others are in the **Ranchos de Taos** area, a few miles south of the plaza.

MAPS To find your way around town, pick up a free Taos map from the **Town of Taos Visitor Center,** 1139 Paseo del Pueblo Sur (𝓒 **800/732-8267** or 575/758-3873). Good, detailed city maps can be found at area bookstores as well. **Carson National Forest** information and maps are available in the same building.

GETTING AROUND

By Car

With offices at the Taos airport, **Enterprise** (𝓒 **575/751-7490**) is reliable and efficient. Other car-rental agencies are available out of Albuquerque. See "Getting Around," in chapter 6, for details.

PARKING Parking can be difficult during the summer rush, when the stream of tourists' cars moving north and south through town never ceases. If you can't find parking on the street or in the plaza, check out some of the nearby roads (Kit Carson Rd., for instance); there are plenty of metered and unmetered lots in Taos.

ROAD CONDITIONS Information on highway conditions throughout the state can be obtained from the **State Highway Department** (𝓒 **800/432-4269**).

By Bus & Taxi

If you're in Taos without a car, you're in luck because there's local bus service, provided by **Chile Line Town of Taos Transit** (© **575/751-4459;** www.taosgov. com). It operates on the half-hour Monday to Saturday 7am to 7pm in summer, 7am to 6pm in winter, and on the hour Sunday 8am to 5pm. Two simultaneous routes run southbound from Taos Pueblo and northbound from the Ranchos de Taos Post Office. Each route makes stops at the casino and various hotels in town, as well as at Taos RV Park. Bus fares are 50¢ one-way, $1 round-trip, $5 for a 7-day pass, and $20 for a 31-day pass.

In addition, **Faust's Transportation** (© **575/758-3410**) has a taxi service linking town hotels and Taos Ski Valley. Faust's Transportation also offers shuttle service and on-call taxi service daily from 8am to 5pm (special arrangements made for after hours; Sun by appointment only), with fares of about $10 anywhere within the city limits for up to two people. Bus service to and from the mountain is 50¢ one-way, exact change only.

By Bicycle

Bicycle rentals are available from **Gearing Up Bicycle Shop,** 129 Paseo del Pueblo Sur (© **575/751-0365;** www.gearingupbikes.com); daily rentals run $35 for a full day and $25 for a half-day for a mountain bike with front suspension. From April to October, **Native Sons Adventures,** 1334 Paseo del Pueblo Sur (© **800/753-7559** or 575/758-9342; www.nativesonsadventures.com), also rents front-suspension bikes for $35 for a full day and $25 for a half-day. It also rents car racks for $5. Each shop supplies helmets and water bottles with rentals.

[FastFACTS] TAOS

Airport See "Orientation," above.

Area Code The telephone area code for Taos is **575.**

ATMs You can find ATMs all over town, at supermarkets, banks, and drive-throughs.

Business Hours Most **businesses** are open at least Monday to Friday 10am to 5pm, though some may open an hour earlier and close an hour later. Many **tourist-oriented shops** are also open on Saturday morning, and some **art galleries** are open all day Saturday and

Sunday, especially during peak tourist seasons.

Banks are generally open Monday to Thursday 9am to 5pm and often for longer hours on Friday. Some may be open Saturday morning. Most branches have cash machines available 24 hours. Call establishments for specific hours.

Car Rentals See "Getting Around," in chapter 3, or "Getting Around," above.

Climate Taos's climate is similar to that of Santa Fe. Summer days are dry and sunny, except for frequent

afternoon thunderstorms. Winter days are often bracing, with snowfalls common but rarely lasting too long. Average **summer temperatures** range from 50° to 87°F (10°–31°C). **Winter temperatures** vary between 9° and 40°F (−13° to 4°C). **Annual rainfall** is 12 inches; annual snowfall is 35 inches in town and as much as 300 inches at Taos Ski Valley, where the elevation is 9,207 feet. (A foot of snow is equal to an inch of rain.)

Currency Exchange Foreign currency can be exchanged at the **Centinel**

Bank of Taos, 512 Paseo del Pueblo Sur (☏ **575/758-6700**), for a $35 fee.

Dentists If you need dental work, try **Dr. Walter Jakiela,** 1392 Weimer Rd. (☏ **575/758-8654**); **Dr. Michael Rivera,** 107 Plaza Garcia, Suite E (☏ **575/758-0531**); or **Dr. Tom Simms,** 1392 Weimer Rd. (☏ **575/758-8303**).

Doctors Members of the **Taos Medical Group,** on Weimer Road (☏ **575/758-2224**), are highly respected. Also recommended are **Family Practice Associates of Taos,** 630 Paseo del Pueblo Sur, Ste. 150 (☏ **575/758-3005**).

Emergencies Dial ☏ **911** for police, fire, and ambulance.

Hospital Holy Cross Hospital, 1397 Weimer Rd., off Paseo del Canyon (☏ **575/758-8883**), has a 24-hour emergency service. Serious cases are transferred to Santa Fe or Albuquerque.

Hot Lines The **crisis hot line** (☏ **575/758-9888**) is available for emergency counseling.

Information See "Visitor Information," above.

Internet Access You can retrieve your e-mail via Wi-Fi or the cafe's computers at **Sustaining Cultures,** 114 Doña Luz (☏ **575/613-3490;** www.sustainingcultures.org). It's located 1 block west of the plaza. And the Taos

County Chamber of Commerce, 108 Kit Carson Rd., Ste. F (☏ **575/751-8800;** www.taoschamber.com), just off the plaza, offers free access. As well, the **Taos Public Library** offers free access.

Library The **Taos Public Library,** 402 Camino de la Placita (☏ **575/758-3063** or 575/737-2590; www.taoslibrary.org), has a general collection for Taos residents, a children's library, and special collections on the Southwest and Taos art.

Lost Property Check with the **Taos police** at ☏ **575/758-2216.**

Newspapers & Magazines *The Taos News* (☏ **575/758-2241;** www.taosnews.com) and the *Sangre de Cristo Chronicle* (☏ **575/377-2358;** www.sangrechronicle.com) are published every Thursday. *Taos Magazine* is also a good source of local information. The *Albuquerque Journal* (www.abqjournal.com) and Santa Fe's *New Mexican* (www.santafenewmexican.com) are easily obtained at book and convenience stores.

Pharmacies There are several full-service pharmacies in Taos. **Sav-on Drug** (☏ **575/758-1203**), **Smith's Pharmacy** (☏ **575/758-4824**), and **Wal-Mart Pharmacy** (☏ **575/758-2743**) are all on Pueblo Sur and are easily seen from the road.

Police In case of emergency, dial ☏ **911.** All other inquiries should be directed to the **Taos police,** Civic Plaza Drive (☏ **575/758-2216**). The **Taos County Sheriff,** with jurisdiction outside the city limits, is in the county courthouse on Paseo del Pueblo Sur (☏ **575/758-3361**).

Post Offices The main **Taos post office** is at 318 Paseo del Pueblo Norte (☏ **575/758-2081**), a few blocks north of the plaza traffic light; it's open Monday to Friday 8:30am to 5pm. There are smaller offices in **Ranchos de Taos** (☏ **575/758-3944;** Mon–Fri 8:30am–5pm, Sat 9am–noon) and at **El Prado** (☏ **575/758-4810;** Mon–Fri 8am–4:30pm, Sat 8:30–11:30am). The zip code for Taos is 87571.

Radio A local station is **KTAOS-FM** (101.9), which broadcasts an entertainment calendar daily (☏ **575/758-5826**); National Public Radio can be found on **KUNM-FM** (98.5) from Albuquerque.

Road Conditions For **emergency road service** in the Taos area, call the state police at ☏ **575/758-8878;** for **road conditions** dial ☏ **800/432-4269** (within New Mexico) for the state highway department.

Taxes Gross receipts tax for the city of Taos is 8.06%, and for Taos County it's 7%. There is an additional lodgers' tax of 5% in both the city of Taos and in Taos County.

Taxis See "Getting Around," above.

Television Channel 2, the local access station, is available in most hotels. For a few hours a day it shows local programming.

Cable networks carry Santa Fe and Albuquerque stations.

Time As is true throughout New Mexico, Taos is on **Mountain Standard Time.** It's 2 hours earlier than New York, 1 hour earlier than Chicago, and 1 hour later than Los Angeles. Clocks change the second Sunday in March and the first Sunday in November.

Weather Taos has no number to call for weather forecasts, but you can log on to **www.taosnews.com/ weather**.

WHERE TO STAY

A tiny town with a big tourist market, Taos has thousands of rooms in hotels, motels, condominiums, and bed-and-breakfasts. In the slower seasons—January through early February and April through early May—when competition for travelers is steep, you may even want to try bargaining your room rate down. Most of the hotels and motels are on Paseo del Pueblo Sur and Norte, with a few located just east of the town center, along Kit Carson Road. The condos and bed-and-breakfasts are generally scattered throughout Taos's back streets.

During peak seasons, visitors without reservations may have difficulty finding vacant rooms. **Taos Chamber of Commerce,** 108 S. Kit Carson Rd. (© **575/751-8800**), might be able to help.

Rocky Mountain Tours (© **800/233-2300,** ext. 3442; www.rockymountain-tours.com) will help you find accommodations ranging from bed-and-breakfasts to home rentals, hotels, and cabins throughout Taos, Taos Ski Valley, and the rest of northern New Mexico. It'll also help you arrange package trips for outdoor activities such as skiing, horseback riding, hot-air ballooning, and snowmobiling.

There are two high seasons in Taos: winter (the Christmas-to-Easter ski season, except for Jan, which is notoriously slow) and June through September. Spring and fall are shoulder seasons, often with lower rates. The period between Easter and Memorial Day is also slow in the tourist industry here, and many proprietors of restaurants and other businesses take their annual vacations at this time. Book well ahead for ski holiday periods (especially Christmas) and for the annual arts festivals (late May to mid-June and late Sept to early Oct).

Taos
HOTELS/MOTELS
Expensive

El Monte Sagrado ★★★ 🖻 New to Taos in 2003, this resort near the center of town offers a feast for the senses. Water running over falls, lush landscaping, and delicious food and drink lull guests into a state of relaxation. Rooms range in theme from the Caribbean casita, a medium-size room that evokes the feel of an African jungle, to the Argentina global suite, a huge two-bedroom decorated in cowboy-contemporary style with wood floors, leather furniture, and two large bathrooms featuring mosaic-decorated shower and tub. In 2007, the inn nearly doubled in size with a series of more reasonably priced rooms. All rooms are serene, with patios or balconies and views. In line with the resort's commitment to responsible development, the resort recycles its water, using it to irrigate the cottonwood-shaded Sacred Circle, at the resort's center. The intimate spa offers a full range of treatments and free classes such as yoga and tai chi. The **Anaconda Bar** (p. 239) and **De La Tierra** restaurant (p. 213) combine a contemporary feel with elegant Asian touches.

317 Kit Carson Rd., Taos, NM 87571. © **800/828-8267** or 575/758-3502. www.elmontesagrado.com. 84 units. $169–$229 1-bedroom casita; $199–$519 suite. AE, DC, DISC, MC, V. Valet parking $12. **Amenities:** Restaurant; bar; concierge; health club; Jacuzzi; indoor pool; spa. *In room:* A/C, TV, CD player, hair dryer, minibar (stocked on request), Wi-Fi.

The Historic Taos Inn ★ Here, you'll be surrounded by 21st-century luxury without ever forgetting that you're within the thick walls of 19th-century homes. It's listed on the State and National Registers of Historic Places. The lobby doubles as the popular **Adobe Bar,** which surrounds a wishing well that was once the old town well. A number of rooms open onto a balcony that overlooks this area. I don't recommend these rooms, as they can be noisy. All the other rooms sit among a number of "houses" separated by walkways and grass. Some have modest style, with lower ceilings and Spanish Colonial furnishings, while others are more chic. My favorites are no. 204 in the Sandoval House, decorated with antiques, and any room in the recently built **Helen House ★★**. These rooms, with Saltillo tile floors and kiva fireplaces, will appeal to travelers who don't appreciate the whims of an older building, but still enjoy character. **Doc Martin's** (p. 214) is a good bet for any meal.

125 Paseo del Pueblo Norte, Taos, NM 87571. © **800/826-7466** or 575/758-2233. Fax 575/758-5776. www.taosinn.com. 44 units. $75–$120 double; $195–$275 suite. AE, DISC, MC, V. **Amenities:** Restaurant; lounge; Jacuzzi; room service; Wi-Fi in lobby. *In room:* A/C, TV, hair dryer.

Hotel La Fonda de Taos ★ Taos now has a recommendable hotel on the plaza. A $3-million renovation to this historic property built in 1880 has turned it into a comfortable, fun spot with a stellar location. The charismatic Taos figure Saki Kavaras put this hotel on the society map in the 1930s when, most notably, British author D. H. Lawrence frequented it. His legacy is preserved in a unique museum, where some of his risqué paintings hang—a must-see even if you don't stay here (free for guests; $3 for nonguests). Rooms are set off broad hallways, each styled in earth tones, Southwestern furnishings, and tile bathrooms. Standards are small, each with a queen-size bed. Your better bet is to reserve a plaza or deluxe plaza room, or a suite. These are larger, with king beds. My favorite rooms are nos. 201 and 301, which overlook the plaza. Groups can rent the whole top floor (or the whole hotel), which includes a full kitchen suite.

108 South Plaza, Taos, NM 87571. © **800/833-2211** or 575/758-2211. Fax 575/758-8508. www.lafonda taos.com. 25 units. $119–$179 standard double; $129–$249 plaza and deluxe plaza double; $179–$229 suite. AE, DISC, MC, V. Free parking. **Amenities:** Restaurant; coffee shop; lounge. *In room:* A/C, TV, hair dryer, high-speed Internet.

Inger Jirby's Guest Houses ★★ Two blocks from the plaza, between the R. C. Gorman Gallery and the Ernest L. Blumenschein Museum, this inn provides a stay in an artistic ancient adobe. Painter Inger Jirby has chosen this for her gallery space as well as a home for travelers. From the remains of a 400-year-old adobe, she's carved and added these lively dwellings and adorned them with her unique style. Full of rich Mexican and Balinese art, and then accented by her own vivid land-

Where to Stay in the Taos Area

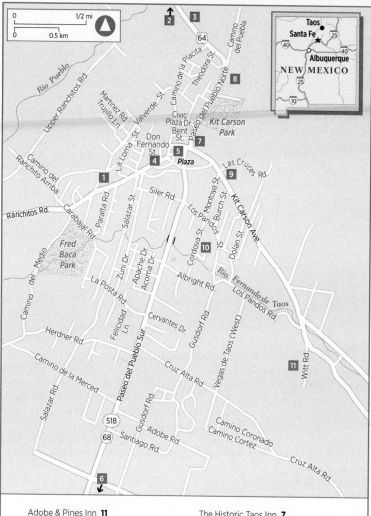

Adobe & Pines Inn **11**

Adobe and Stars
  Bed and Breakfast Inn **2**

Best Western Kachina Lodge **8**

Carson National Forest **2**

Casa del las Chimeneas **10**

El Monte Sagrado **9**

Hacienda del Sol **3**

The Historic Taos Inn **7**

Hotel La Fonda de Taos **5**

Inger Jirby's Guest Houses **4**

Inn on La Loma Plaza **1**

Little Tree Bed & Breakfast **2**

Old Taos Guesthouse **11**

Taos Hampton Inn **6**

Taos Valley RV Park and Campground **6**

scapes of the Southwest and beyond, the casitas are artsy as well as comfortable. Both have a full kitchen, flagstone floors, large windows, and sleeping lofts. (Very large or elderly people might have trouble maneuvering the spiral staircases in these.) They also have fold-out couches, so they're a great option for families. Both are equipped with stereos and robes. More than anywhere else in town, these casitas provide a real home away from home. The attached Inger Jirby Gallery provides Internet access for guests.

207 Ledoux St., Taos, NM 87571. © **575/758-7333.** www.jirby.com. 2 units. $175–$225 double (up to $275 during holidays). Additional person $25–$35. *In room:* TV/DVD, hair dryer, kitchen.

Moderate

Taos Hampton Inn ★ ☺   The most reliable moderately priced hotel in town, the Hampton is about 5 minutes (by car) from the plaza. Rooms are medium size with either two queens or one king bed, a few with Jacuzzis and mountain views. All have nice pine furnishings, quality bedding, and a hint of Southwestern decor, some with desks, others with a table and chair. The beds are comfortable and the medium-size bathrooms very clean and functional. The medium-size indoor pool keeps kids entertained year-round.

1515 Paseo del Pueblo Sur, Taos, NM 87571. **800/426-7866** or 575/737-5700. Fax 575/737-5701. www.hampton.com. 71 units. $109–$149 double. Rates include full hot breakfast and afternoon snack. AE, DC, DISC, MC, V. **Amenities:** Exercise room; Jacuzzi; indoor pool. *In room:* A/C, TV, hair dryer, Wi-Fi.

Inexpensive

Best Western Kachina Lodge & Meeting Center ☺   Built in the early 1960s, this lodge on the north end of town, within walking distance of the plaza, has a lot of charm despite the fact that it's a motor hotel. Unfortunately, it needs a major remodel. It does receive periodic minor ones, such as new linens and painted trim. If you don't mind crumbling sidewalks and frayed carpeting, the place will suit you fine. Some of the Southwestern-style rooms have couches and most have Taos-style *trasteros* (armoires) that hold the TVs. Rooms sit around a grassy courtyard studded with huge blue spruce trees, allowing kids room to run. In the center is a stage where a family from Taos Pueblo builds a bonfire and dances nightly in the summer and explains the significance of the dances—a real treat for anyone intrigued by the Pueblo rituals.

413 Paseo del Pueblo Norte (P.O. Box NM), Taos, NM 87571. © **800/522-4462** or 575/758-2275. Fax 575/758-9207. www.kachinalodge.com. 118 units. $69–$149 double. Rates includes half-price breakfast and half-price cocktail. Additional person $15. Children 11 and under stay free in parent's room. AE, DISC, MC, V. **Amenities:** 2 restaurants; lounge; outdoor pool (summer only). *In room:* A/C, TV, hair dryer, Wi-Fi.

BED & BREAKFASTS
Expensive

Adobe & Pines Inn ★★   This inn occupies a 180-year-old adobe directly off NM 68, less than half a mile south of St. Francis Plaza (about a 10-min. drive from Taos Plaza). The inn is set around a courtyard marked by an 80-foot-long grand portal and surrounded by pine and fruit trees. Each room has a private entrance and fireplace (three rooms have a fireplace in their bathroom!), and each is uniquely decorated. Colors are richly displayed on the walls and in the furnishings. Puerta Azul, a good value, is cozy with blue accents and thick adobe walls, and Puerto Roja has bold maroon walls, a comfortable couch, and kitchenette. Many rooms have Jacuzzi tubs, including three with private outdoor hot tubs. Because this inn is near the highway, at times cars can be heard on the grounds, but the rooms themselves are quiet. Morning brings a delicious full gourmet breakfast in the atrium. Guests also enjoy a labyrinth and Zen garden.

NM 68, Ranchos de Taos, NM 87557. © **800/723-8267** or 575/751-0947. Fax 575/758-8423. www. adobepines.com. 8 units. $98–$225 double; $215–$225 suite. Additional person $25. Rates include full gourmet breakfast. MC, V. Pets accepted with prior arrangement, one-time $25 fee. *In room:* A/C, TV, kitchenette (in some), no phone, Wi-Fi (in some).

Adobe and Stars Bed and Breakfast Inn ★★ This inn sitting on the mesa between Taos town and Taos Ski Valley offers chic Southwestern-style rooms with a focus on fine detail in a quiet country setting. The breakfast area and common room are sunny, with large windows facing the mountains. A few rooms are upstairs, such as La Luna, my favorite, with views in every direction and a heart-shaped Jacuzzi tub for two. All rooms have kiva fireplaces and private decks or patios. Most of the downstairs rooms open onto a portal. All are decorated with hand-crafted Southwestern-style furniture, and many have Jacuzzi tubs. As well, guests enjoy an outdoor hot tub under the stars, reserved by the half-hour. The full breakfast may vary from New Mexican dishes such as breakfast burritos with green chile to gingerbread waffles with whipped cream. In the afternoons, a glass of New Mexico wine is served with a snack. A courtesy computer with Internet is available for guest use.

At the corner of State Hwy. 150 and Valdez Rim Rd. (P.O. Box 2285), Taos, NM 87571. © **800/211-7076** or 575/776-2776. Fax 575/776-2872. www.taosadobe.com. 8 units. $95–$180 double. Rates include full breakfast and refreshments. AE, MC, V. Pets accepted with $15 per-pet fee and $50 damage deposit. **Amenities:** Jacuzzi. *In room:* A/C, TV, CD player, hair dryer, Wi-Fi.

Casa de las Chimeneas ★★★ This 82-year-old adobe home set on spacious grounds has, since its opening as a luxury inn in 1988, been a model of Southwestern elegance. Adding to its appeal is a spa with a small fitness room and sauna, as well as complete massage and facial treatments for an additional charge. I recommend the Sombraje Room; with old-world elegance, it has high ceilings, a gas fireplace, and two queen beds. The Rio Grande has tile floors, handcrafted furniture, and a large jetted tub. Each room in the inn is decorated with original works of art and has elegant bedding, a private entrance, and robes. All rooms have kiva fireplaces, and most look out on flower and herb gardens. Breakfasts are delicious. Specialties include an artichoke-heart and mushroom omelet or ricotta cream-cheese blintz. In the evenings the inn offers a full dinner, which may include corn-crusted tilapia or roasted chicken served with vegetables from a local organic farm. End the day at the large hot tub in the courtyard.

405 Cordoba Rd., at Los Pandos Rd. (5303 NDCBU), Taos, NM 87571. © **877/758-4777** or 575/758-4777. Fax 575/758-3976. www.visittaos.com. 8 units. $195–$290 double; $325 suite. Rates include breakfast and light evening supper. AE, DC, DISC, MC, V. **Amenities:** Concierge; small exercise room; Jacuzzi; sauna; spa. *In room:* TV/VCR/DVD, hair dryer, free stocked nonalcoholic minibar, MP3 docking station, Wi-Fi.

Hacienda del Sol ★★ ☺ This inn offers spectacular views of Taos Mountain and elegant comfort in both modern and historic rooms. The 1¼-acre property borders Taos Pueblo, providing a rural feel. The inn was once owned by arts patron Mabel Dodge Luhan, and Frank Waters wrote *The People of the Valley* here. You'll find bold splashes of color from the gardens—where in summer tulips, pansies, and flax bloom—to the rooms themselves—where woven bedspreads and original art lend a

Mexican feel. The main house is 204 years old, so it has the wonderful curves of adobe as well as thick vigas. My favorite is the Mabel's Salon, with wood floors and a kiva fireplace. Other guestrooms are newer and yet also atmospheric. The Cowgirl and Cowboy suites have adjoining rooms, perfect for children. Most rooms have fireplaces, three have private Jacuzzis, and four have private steam showers. A delicious breakfast, with favorites such as a mushroom frittata with bacon and toast, is served in the Spanish-hacienda-style dining area. The outdoor hot tub has a mountain view.

109 Mabel Dodge Lane (P.O. Box 177), Taos, NM 87571. © **866/333-4459** or 575/758-0287. Fax 575/758-5895. www.taoshaciendadelsol.com. 11 units. $135–$325 double; $190–$305 suite. Additional person $25. Rates include full breakfast and evening sweets. AE, DISC, MC, V. **Amenities:** Concierge; privileges at nearby health club; Jacuzzi. *In room:* CD player, fridge (in some), hair dryer, Wi-Fi.

Inn on La Loma Plaza ★★ Named by *American Historic Inns* as one of the 10 most romantic inns in America, this inn is on a historic neighborhood plaza, complete with dirt streets and a tiny central park. A 10-minute walk from Taos Plaza, the inn is in a 200-year-old home, complete with aged vigas and maple floors, decorated tastefully with comfortable furniture and Middle Eastern rugs. Three new rooms offer Southwest style and modern convenience. These are spacious, with viga ceilings and elaborate bathrooms. Each room is unique, most with sponge-painted walls and Talavera tile in the bathrooms to provide an eclectic ambience. All have robes, slippers, lighted makeup mirrors, bottled water, and fireplaces, and most have balconies or terraces and views. The Happy Trails Room features knotty pine paneling, a brass bed, old chaps, and decorative hanging spurs. Guests dine on such delights as breakfast burritos or green-chile casserole in a plant-filled sunroom or on the patio.

315 Ranchitos Rd., Taos, NM 87571. © **800/530-3040** or 575/758-1717. Fax 575/751-0155. www.vacationtaos.com. 10 units. $155–$240 double; $275–$325 artist's studio; $425–$590 suite. Additional person $25. Children 12 and under stay free in parent's room. Discounts available. Rates include full breakfast. AE, DISC, MC, V. **Amenities:** Concierge; Internet; Jacuzzi; pool and spa privileges at nearby Taos Spa. *In room:* TV/VCR/DVD, hair dryer, kitchenette (in some), Wi-Fi.

Little Tree Bed & Breakfast ★★ 📖 Little Tree is one of my favorite Taos bed-and-breakfasts. It's in a beautiful, secluded setting, and constructed with real adobe that's been left in its raw state, lending the place an authentic hacienda feel. Two miles down a country road, about midway between Taos and the ski area, it's surrounded by sage and *piñon*. The charming rooms have radiant heat under the floors, queen-size beds (one with a king-size), and access to the portal and courtyard garden, at the center of which is the little tree for which the inn is named. The Piñon (my favorite) and Juniper rooms are equipped with fireplaces and private entrances. The Piñon and Aspen rooms offer sunset views. The Spruce Room has a private patio and outdoor hot tub. In the main building, the living room has *tierra blanca* adobe (adobe that's naturally white; if you look closely at it, you can see little pieces of mica and straw). Visiting hummingbirds enchant guests as they enjoy a scrumptious breakfast on the portal during warmer months.

County Rd. B-143 (P.O. Box 509), Arroyo Hondo, NM 87513. © **800/334-8467** or 575/776-8467. www.littletreebandb.com. 4 units. $135–$175 double. Rates include breakfast and afternoon snack. MC, V. *In room:* TV/VCR, Wi-Fi.

Moderate

Old Taos Guesthouse ★ ☺ This 190-year-old adobe hacienda has been extensively restored but maintains its country charm: Mexican tile in the bathrooms, vigas on the ceilings, and kiva-style fireplaces in most of the rooms. Each room has an entrance from the outside, some off the broad portal that shades the front of the hacienda, some from a grassy lawn in the back, with a view toward the mountains. Some rooms are more utilitarian, some quainter, so make a request depending on your needs. One of my favorites is the Taos Suite, with a king-size bed, a big picture window, and a full kitchen. Less than 2 miles from the plaza, this inn sits on 7½ acres and provides a cozy northern New Mexico rural experience, complete with birds galore and a healthy breakfast. Kids enjoy the inn's dogs and plenty of space to run free.

1028 Witt Rd., Taos, NM 87571. ℂ **800/758-5448** or 575/758-5448. www.oldtaos.com. 10 units. $90–$185 double. Rates include a full breakfast. Ask about seasonal rates. DISC, MC, V. Pets accepted in some rooms with one-time $25 fee. **Amenities:** Babysitting; concierge; Jacuzzi; Wi-Fi (in some). *In room:* TV (in some rooms), hair dryer, kitchen (in some).

RV PARKS & CAMPGROUNDS

Carson National Forest   There are nine national forest camping areas within 20 miles of Taos; these developed areas are open from Memorial Day to Labor Day. They range from woodsy, streamside sites on the road to Taos Ski Valley to open lowlands with lots of sage. Call the Forest Service to discuss the best location for your needs.

208 Cruz Alta Rd., Taos, NM 87571. ℂ **575/758-6200.** www.fs.fed.us/r3/carson. $7–$15 per night. No credit cards.

Taos Valley RV Park and Campground ★   Just 2½ miles south of the plaza, this lovely, well-maintained campground is surrounded by sage and offers views of the surrounding mountains. Each site has a picnic table and grill. The place has a small store, a laundry room, a playground, and tent shelters, as well as a dump station and very clean restrooms. Pets are welcome. Wireless Internet access is available throughout the park.

120 Este Rd., off NM 68 (7204 NDCBU), Taos, NM 87571. ℂ **800/999-7571** or 575/758-4469. Fax 575/758-4469. www.taosrv.com. 91 spaces. $22 without RV hookup; $30–$39 with RV hookup. AE, DISC, MC, V.

Taos Ski Valley

For information on the skiing and the facilities offered at Taos Ski Valley, see "Skiing," later in this chapter.

LODGES
Expensive

Powderhorn Suites and Condominiums ★ 🗝   A homelike feel and Euro-Southwestern ambience make this condo-inn one of the best buys in Taos Ski Valley, just a 2-minute walk from the lift. You'll find consistency and quality here, with clean medium-size rooms, mountain views, vaulted ceilings, well-planned bathrooms, and comfortable beds. The larger suites have stoves, balconies, and fireplaces. Adjoining rooms are good for families. As with almost all of the accommodations in Taos Ski Valley, this one has been condo-ized so each suite has a distinct owner; thus the service isn't what you would find at a full-service hotel, though it is still conscientious. There's no elevator, so if stairs are a problem for you, make sure to ask for a room on the ground floor.

5 Ernie Blake Rd. (P.O. Box 69), Taos Ski Valley, NM 87525. ℂ **800/776-2346** or 575/776-2341. Fax 575/776-2341. www.taospowderhorn.com. 16 units. Ski season $199–$245 double, $259–$290 suite,

$309–$370 condo; summer $89–$169 all room options. 2- to 6-person occupancy. MC, V. Valet parking. **Amenities:** 2 Jacuzzis. *In room:* TV, kitchenette (in some), Wi-Fi.

Moderate

Alpine Village Suites ★★ Alpine Village is a small village within Taos Ski Valley, a few steps from the lift. The complex also houses a ski shop and bar/restaurant. The owners began with seven rooms, still nice rentals, above their ski shop. Each has a sleeping loft for the agile who care to climb a ladder, as well as sunny windows. The newer section has elegantly decorated rooms, with attractive touches such as Mexican furniture and inventive tile work. Like most other accommodations at Taos Ski Valley, the rooms are not especially soundproof. Fortunately, most skiers go to bed early. In the newer building, rooms have fireplaces and private balconies. Request a south-facing room for a view of the slopes. The Jacuzzi sits below a lovely mural, and has a fireplace and a view of the slopes.

100 Thunderbird Rd. (P.O. Box 98), Taos Ski Valley, NM 87525. ✆ **800/576-2666** or 575/776-8540. Fax 575/776-8542. www.alpine-suites.com. 31 units. Ski season $150–$215 suite for 2, $216–$347 suite for 4, $216–$391 suite for up to 6; summer $90 suite for 2, $102–$132 suite for 4, $120–$270 suite for up to 6. Continental breakfast only in summer. AE, DISC, MC, V. Covered valet parking $15 per night. **Amenities:** Jacuzzi; massage; sauna. *In room:* TV, DVD and VCR (in some), kitchenette, Wi-Fi (in most).

CONDOMINIUMS
Expensive

Edelweiss Lodge & Spa ★★ Opened in 2005, this lodge at the base of the mountain took the place of a 1960s classic chalet. Now, it's a brand-new condo-hotel. The condominiums are upscale, each with a flagstone fireplace and full kitchen with marble countertops, stainless-steel appliances, and many with nice views of the slopes. All have luxury furnishings decorated in earth tones. For those looking for an upscale stay, this is your choice. Hotel rooms follow with the same luxury as the condos. Rooms are medium size with comfortable beds and medium-size bathrooms. Underground parking, a full spa, an excellent restaurant, and valet service for your skis add to the appeal.

106 Sutton Place, Taos Ski Valley, NM 87525. ✆ **800/458-8754** or 575/737-6900. Fax 575/737-6995. www.edelweisslodgeandspa.com. 31 units. Winter $220–$440 double, $275–$1,156 condo; summer $100 double, $160–$335 condo. AE, DISC, MC, V. Free parking. **Amenities:** Restaurant; bar; concierge; health club and full spa; Jacuzzi; sauna. *In room:* TV/DVD, CD player, hair dryer, kitchen, Wi-Fi.

Sierra del Sol Condominiums ★ I have wonderful memories of these condominiums, which are just a 2-minute walk from the lift; family friends used to invite me to stay with them when I was young. I'm happy to say that the units, built in the 1960s, with additions through the years, have been well maintained. Though they're privately owned, and therefore decorated at the whim of the owners, management does inspect them every year and make suggestions. They're smartly built and come in a few sizes: studio, one-bedroom, and two-bedroom. The one- and two-bedroom units have big living rooms with fireplaces and porches that look out on the ski runs. The bedrooms are spacious, and some have sleeping lofts. Two-bedroom units sleep up to six. Grills and picnic tables on the grounds sit near a mountain river.

13 Thunderbird Rd. (P.O. Box 84), Taos Ski Valley, NM 87525. ✆ **800/523-3954** or 575/776-2981. Fax 575/776-2347. www.sierrataos.com. 32 units. From $79 for studio in summer to $471 for 2-bedroom condo in high season. DISC, MC, V. Free parking. **Amenities:** Babysitting; 2 Jacuzzis; 2 saunas. *In room:* TV/DVD, hair dryer (upon request), kitchen, Wi-Fi.

Snakedance Condominiums and Spa ★★   The original structure that stood on this site was known as the Hondo Lodge. Before there was a Taos Ski Valley, Hondo Lodge served as a refuge for fishermen, hunters, and artists. A $3.5-million renovation has transformed the rooms of this once-time hotel into elegant condominiums. Skiers appreciate the inn's location, just steps from the lift, as well as amenities such as ski storage and boot dryers. The Snakedance Condominiums today are privately owned units, so each may differ some, though they are consistent in quality. All are bright, comfortable spaces with balconies with French doors, and kitchens with granite counters and a range, fridge, dishwasher, and microwave. All have gas fireplaces. The hotel also offers shuttle service to and from nearby shops and restaurants, and, at certain times, to Albuquerque and Santa Fe.

110 Sutton Place (P.O. Box 89), Taos Ski Valley, NM 87525. ℭ **800/322-9815** or 575/776-2277. Fax 575/776-1410. www.snakedancecondos.com. 33 units. Winter $272–$450 1-bedroom condo, $380–$700 2-bedroom condo for 4 people, $460–$800 2-bedroom loft condo for 6 people; summer $95 1-bedroom condo, $120 2-bedroom condo, $150 2-bedroom loft condo. Extra person $30 in winter, $10 in summer. Rates include continental breakfast. AE, DC, DISC, MC, V. Free parking at Taos Ski Valley parking lot. Closed mid-Apr to Memorial Day and mid-Oct to mid-Nov. **Amenities:** Restaurant; bar; free airport transfers; exercise room; Jacuzzi; sauna; spa. *In room:* TV/DVD, hair dryer, kitchen, Wi-Fi.

Moderate

Taos Mountain Lodge 🏂   These loft suites (which can each accommodate up to six) provide airy, comfortable lodging for a good price. Built in 1990, about a mile west of Taos Ski Valley on the road from Taos, the place has undergone some renovation over the years. Don't expect a lot of privacy in these condominiums, but they're good for a romping ski vacation. The beds are comfortable and the bathrooms are small but functional. Each unit has a small bedroom downstairs and a loft bedroom upstairs, as well as a foldout or futon couch in the living room. Regular rooms have kitchenettes, with minifridges and stoves, and deluxe rooms have full kitchens, with full refrigerators, stoves, and ovens.

Taos Ski Valley Rd. (P.O. Box 202), Taos Ski Valley, NM 87525. ℭ **866/320-8267** or 575/776-2229. Fax 575/776-3982. www.taosmountainlodge.net. 10 units. Ski season $120–$275 suite; May–Oct $85–$100 suite. AE, DISC, MC, V. *In room:* TV, hair dryer, kitchen or kitchenette.

WHERE TO DINE

Taos has some of the region's most inventive and fun restaurants. The creativity of the town flourishes in the flavors here. It's also a comfortable place to dine. Informality reigns; at a number of restaurants you can eat world-class food while wearing jeans or even ski pants. Nowhere is a jacket and tie mandatory. This informality doesn't extend to reservations, however; especially during the peak season, it's important to make reservations well in advance and keep them or else cancel. Also, be aware that Taos is not a late-night place; most restaurants finish serving at about 9pm.

Taos
EXPENSIVE

De La Tierra ★★★ NEW AMERICAN   Located in the ecoresort El Monte Sagrado (p. 205), this restaurant offers delectably inventive American cuisine in an old-world ambience, with a high ceiling, comfortable black silk chairs, and elegant contemporary art on the walls. Service is excellent, even down to the master sommelier overseeing the wine selections. The chef uses seasonal and local ingredients, including organic ones when he can. For starters, you might try the buffalo ravioli with green-chile Alfredo and cilantro pesto. For a main course, the Prairie Farms elk tenderloin with chestnut mashed potatoes and green-chile Brussels sprouts is delicious, as is the Kessler Canyon mountain trout with mint and green-pea potatoes and lemon caper sauce. Excellent food, including Sunday brunch, is served during the day at the Gardens, a more casual spot, with lots of exotic plants and a lovely patio. Meals are also served at the Anaconda Bar (p. 239).

In the El Monte Sagrado Hotel, 317 Kit Carson Rd. ℂ **800/828-8267** or 575/758-3502. www.elmonte-sagrado.com/dining/dining.asp. Reservations recommended. The Gardens main courses $7–$14 breakfast, $8–$16 lunch; De La Tierra $19–$39 dinner. AE, DC, DISC, MC, V. The Gardens daily 7am–3pm; De La Tierra daily 6–9:30pm.

Doc Martin's ★ NEW AMERICAN/NEW MEXICAN   Doc Martin's serves innovative food in a historic setting. The restaurant comprises Dr. Thomas Paul Martin's former home, office, and delivery room. In 1912, painters Bert Philips and Ernest Blumenschein hatched the concept of the Taos Society of Artists here.

The chef uses local and organic ingredients and wild game when available. The wine list has received numerous "Awards of Excellence" from *Wine Spectator* magazine. In the rich atmosphere of a thick-walled adobe home with a kiva fireplace, diners feast on breakfast fare such as a grilled organic buffalo patty and eggs, with wild mushroom gravy and home fries; or blue-corn and blueberry hotcakes. Lunch might include Doc's *chile rellenos*, or a turkey, avocado, bacon, and green-chile sandwich. For dinner, a good bet is the grilled buffalo steak with a red chile and roasted tomatillo sauce, served with beans, rice, and vegetables. If you have room, there's always a nice selection of desserts. The Adobe bar has live music with no cover charge.

In the Historic Taos Inn, 125 Paseo del Pueblo Norte. ℂ **575/758-1977.** www.taosinn.com. Reservations recommended. Main courses $5–$10 breakfast, $7–$15 lunch, $18–$30 dinner. AE, DISC, MC, V. Daily 5–9:30pm; Mon–Fri 7:30–11am and 11:30am–2:30pm; brunch Sat–Sun 7:30am–2:30pm.

El Meze ★★ 🍴 INTERNATIONAL/MEDITERRANEAN   Meaning "table" in Arabic, El Meze offers delicious Spanish/Mediterranean food with Moroccan influences. The setting is an 1847 hacienda with vigas, walls painted orange and green, a gold fireplace, and bright contemporary art on the walls. The classically trained chef puts much thought into his food and its preparation. Service is helpful and efficient. Dinner might begin with grilled prawns with lemon and Moroccan spices, or a butternut squash and chicken tortilla soup with avocado and feta. For an entree, I've enjoyed a tuna carpaccio with fresh grated horseradish, capers, lemon, and Spanish olive oil. Another excellent offering is the grilled bone-in rib-eye steak. For dessert, the chocolate truffle soufflé is as good as it sounds. A thoughtful beer and wine list accompanies the menu.

1017 Paseo del Pueblo Norte. ℂ **575/751-3337.** www.elmeze.com. AE, DISC, MC, V. Reservations recommended. Main courses $18–$32. AE, DISC, MC, V. Summer Mon–Sat 5:30–9:30pm; winter hours vary, call ahead.

Lambert's of Taos ★★★ NEW AMERICAN   Open since 1989 in the historic Randall Home near Los Pandos Road, this restaurant serves flavorful contemporary food in an elegant setting. Wood floors, lightly sponge-painted walls, and crisp tablecloths set the scene for imaginative food using seasonal and local ingredients whenever

Where to Dine in the Taos Area

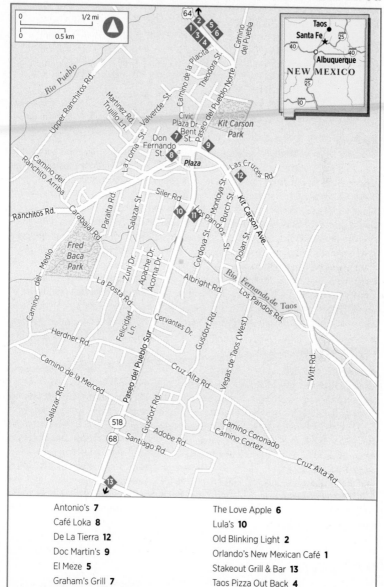

Antonio's **7**

Café Loka **8**

De La Tierra **12**

Doc Martin's **9**

El Meze **5**

Graham's Grill **7**

Guadalajara Grille **3**, **13**

Gutiz **3**

Lambert's of Taos **11**

The Love Apple **6**

Lula's **10**

Old Blinking Light **2**

Orlando's New Mexican Café **1**

Stakeout Grill & Bar **13**

Taos Pizza Out Back **4**

Trading Post Café **13**

Taos Cow **2**

possible. The meal begins with good crusty bread served with a head of roasted garlic and your choice of olive oil or butter. For an appetizer you might try the Maryland-style crab cakes with roasted garlic rémoulade. For an entree, the pepper-crusted lamb loin served with ravioli is a signature dish, but you might opt for one of the fresh fish specials, such as Scottish salmon with chard cream sauce, fingerling potatoes, and asparagus. For dessert, try the warm apple-and-almond crisp with white-chocolate ice cream or Zeke's chocolate truffle mousse. A full bar, with an interesting wine and beer list and espresso, is available. The restaurant also has a cozy lounge with its own menu—a real locals hangout.

309 Paseo del Pueblo Sur. ② **575/758-1009.** www.lambertsoftaos.com. Reservations recommended. Main courses $22–$38. AE, DC, DISC, MC, V. Daily 5–9pm or so.

Stakeout Grill & Bar ★★ CONTINENTAL/STEAK/SEAFOOD   This is one of northern New Mexico's most adventurous dining experiences. You drive about a mile up a dirt road toward the base of the Sangre de Cristo Mountains to reach the restaurant, and dine looking down on the Taos gorge while the sun sets over the Jemez Range. The warm, rustic decor of this sprawling hacienda with a broad patio (a great place to sit in summer) includes creaking hardwood floors—and a crackling fireplace in the winter. The fare, which focuses on steak and seafood, is fresh and thoughtfully prepared. Start with baked brie with sliced almonds and apples, or green-chile crab cakes with citrus aioli. Move on to a filet mignon served with béarnaise sauce, or sample one of the chef's excellent pasta specials. Recently, I had shrimp over linguine with goat cheese that was a bowl of pure joy. This is also the place to come if you have a craving for lobster. Try to time your reservation so you can see the sunset. A full bar, an extensive wine list, and cigars are available.

101 Stakeout Dr. (9 miles south of Taos, just off Hwy. 68). ② **575/758-2042.** www.stakeoutrestaurant. com. Reservations recommended. Main courses $20–$72. AE, DC, DISC, MC, V. Daily 5–9:30pm.

MODERATE

Antonio's ★★ 📷 MEXICAN/NEW MEXICAN   A summer afternoon on the patio of this new restaurant, with a fountain flowing and sun shining on flowers in garden beds, could just transport you to an idyllic Mexico. Add in a margarita and a plate of enchiladas or tacos, and you may never return. Just a block from the plaza, the food at this fun cafe is spirited, though the service could pay more attention. Start your meal with guacamole mixed at your table and move on to Rellenos en Nogada, a roasted poblano pepper stuffed with beef, pear, apple, raisins, onion, tomato, and spices, and smothered with walnut brandy cream sauce. Too rich for you? Try the beef, chicken, cheese, or spinach enchiladas with a red- or green-chile sauce. Finish with *tres leches*—cake in rich, whipped milk. A bar inside bustles at cocktail hour, as does the whole place during busy summer days. Under the same ownership, just a few blocks away at 135 Paseo del Pueblo Sur, **Rellenos Café** also serves the same delicious Mexican food but in a more modest setting (② **575/758-7001;** Mon–Sat 11am–3pm).

122-B Doña Luz. ② **575/751-4800.** www.antoniosoftaos.com. Reservations recommended on weekends. Main courses $8.50–$23. MC, V. Mon–Sat 11am–9pm.

Graham's Grille ★★ INTERNATIONAL/NEW AMERICAN   Opened in 2007, this restaurant offers comfort food with a Southwestern flair. It's set in a long, narrow space just off the plaza, a cozy urban atmosphere with hanging halogen lamps and a long *banco* along one wall. Meals start with delectable flour tortilla crisps. The must-have appetizer is the baked mac and cheese with green chile and bacon, but if that sounds too rich, the artichoke-and-fennel *fritti* will also please. Lunches offer soup, salad, and sandwich combinations, if you'd like. The town is buzzing about the salmon BLT, which is just what it sounds, salmon with good bacon, lettuce, and tomato. Burritos, tamale pie, and burgers—even veggie, buffalo, and lamb ones—come on house-made buns. For dinner, the cherry chipotle-grilled salmon is the most popular dish here. For dessert, the chocolate nachos are a real novelty, but my favorite is the mango coconut cake. A select beer and wine list accompanies the menu.

106 Paseo del Pueblo Norte. ⓒ **575/751-1350.** www.grahamstaos.com. Reservations recommended at dinner. Main courses $7–$13 lunch, $13–$32 dinner. AE, MC, V. Mon–Sat 11am–2:30pm and 5–9pm.

The Love Apple ★★★ 🍴 NEW AMERICAN/NEW MEXICAN   Set in the mid-1800s Placitas Chapel, this new restaurant serves inventive food in a warm and cozy atmosphere. The soulful setting includes candlelight, aged wood floors, thick adobe walls, and vigas adorning the ceiling. Service is attentive and intuitive. Diners feast on seasonal and often organic produce and meats in all the dishes. Good appetizer choices include a sautéed apple and roasted squash quesadilla; or a beet, pear, and mozzarella salad. The main course might bring a grilled lamb sausage with *posole* (hominy) or a ruby rainbow trout cooked in corn husks and served with a quinoa–piñon nut fritter. An eclectic list of wines accompanies the menu, with many value options. The seasons drive the dessert creations. My favorite thus far is hot apple pie a la mode. Be aware that this is a cash- or check-only establishment.

803 Paseo del Pueblo Norte, Taos, NM 87571. ⓒ **575/751-0050.** Reservations recommended. Main courses $13–$18. No credit cards. Tues–Sat 5:30–9:30pm.

Old Blinking Light ★ AMERICAN/MEXICAN   This restaurant on the Ski Valley Road provides tasty American food in a casual atmosphere. It's named for the blinking yellow light that was once the marker Taoseños used to give directions ("turn left at the blinking light," and so on), now replaced by a stoplight. Decorated with Spanish colonial furniture and an excellent art collection, this restaurant is a good place to stop after skiing or for a romping night of music. The service is friendly and efficient. To accompany the free chips and homemade salsa, order a margarita—preferably their standard, made with Sauza Gold Tequila—and sip it next to the patio bonfire, open evenings year-round. The menu ranges from salads and burgers to steaks, seafood, and Mexican food. I say head straight for the fajitas, especially the jumbo shrimp wrapped in bacon and stuffed with poblano peppers and jack cheese. Leave room for the Old Blinking Light Mud Pie, made with local Taos Cow Ice Cream. Live music plays on Monday and Friday nights.

US 150, mile marker 1. ⓒ **575/776-8787.** www.oldblinkinglight.com. Reservations recommended weekends and Mon nights. Main courses $9–$20. AE, MC, V. Restaurant daily 5–10pm. Bar opens at 4pm for happy hour. Wine shop daily noon–10pm.

Taos Pizza Out Back ★ ☺ ITALIAN/PIZZA   My kayaking buddies always go here after a day on the river. That will give you an idea of the level of informality (very), as well as the quality of the food and beer (great), and the size of the portions (large). It's a raucous old hippie-decorated adobe restaurant, with a friendly and eager waitstaff. What to order? I have one big word here: *PIZZA*. Sure the spicy Greek pasta is good, as is the Veggie Zone (a calzone filled with stir-fried veggies and

family-friendly RESTAURANTS

Lula's (p. 219) A relaxed atmosphere and lots of sandwich choices, as well as soups, are sure to please here.

Orlando's New Mexican Café (p. 219) The relaxed atmosphere and playfully colorful walls will please the kids almost as much as the tacos and quesadillas made especially for them.

Taos Cow (p. 219) Potpies and sandwiches will fill kids up before they dive into the all-natural ice cream at this cafe north of town.

Taos Pizza Out Back (p. 217) The pizza will please both parents and kids, and so will all the odd decorations, such as the chain with foot-long links hanging over the front counter.

two cheeses)—but, why? The pizzas are incredible. All come with a delicious thin crust that's folded over on the edges and sprinkled with sesame seeds. The sauce is unthinkably tasty, and the variations are broad. There's the Killer, with sun-dried tomatoes, Gorgonzola, green chile, and black olives; and my favorite, pizza Florentine (spinach, basil, sun-dried tomatoes, chicken breast, mushrooms, capers, and garlic). Don't leave without trying the house-made carrot cake. Check out the selection of wines and large selection of microbrews.

712 Paseo del Pueblo Norte (just north of Allsup's). ✆ **575/758-3112.** Reservations recommended weekends and holidays. Pizzas $13–$28; pastas and calzones $10–$13. MC, V. Daily 11am-10pm (winter Sun–Thurs until 9pm).

Trading Post Café ★★ 📖 NORTHERN ITALIAN/INTERNATIONAL   One of my tastiest writing assignments was when I did a profile of this restaurant for the *New York Times*. Chef/owner René Mettler served course after course prepared especially for me. But if you think this might color my opinion, just ask anyone in town where he or she most likes to eat. Don't expect quiet romance here: The place bustles. A bar encloses an open-exhibition kitchen. If you're dining alone or don't feel like waiting for a table, the bar is a fun place to sit. Diners can feel comfortable here, even if trying three appetizers and skipping the main course. The outstanding Caesar salad has an interesting twist—garlic chips. The *fettuccine alla carbonara* is tasty, as is the seafood pasta. Heartier appetites might like the New Zealand lamb chops with tomato-mint sauce. There's also a fresh fish of the day and usually some nice soups at very reasonable prices. A good list of beers and wines rounds out the experience. For dessert, try the tarts.

4179 Paseo del Pueblo Sur, Ranchos de Taos. ✆ **575/758-5089.** www.tradingpostcafe.com. Reservations accepted. Menu items $8–$30. AE, DC, DISC, MC, V. Tues–Sat 11:30am–9:30pm; Sun 5–9pm.

INEXPENSIVE

Guadalajara Grill ★ MEXICAN   This bustling restaurant set in a plain building on the south side serves authentic Mexican food in a casual setting. Glass-topped tables and wooden benches are highlighted by a mural of the plaza in the town of Teocuitatlán, the owner's original home. During warm months a wrap-around patio offers a great place to sip *cerveza*. The food is Mexican rather than New Mexican, a refreshing treat. I recommend the tacos, particularly pork or chicken, served in soft homemade corn tortillas, the meat artfully seasoned and grilled. The enchiladas and burritos are large and smothered in chile. *Platos* are served with rice and beans, and half orders are available for smaller appetites. The seafood dishes also offer real flavor—try the *mojo de ajo* (shrimp cooked with garlic), served with rice, beans, and guacamole. Beer and wine accompany the menu. Equally popular, and casual, is their north-side location, at 822 Paseo del Pueblo Norte (© **575/737-0816**).

1384 Paseo del Pueblo Sur. © **575/751-0063.** Main courses $5–$15. MC, V. Sun–Thurs 10:30am–9pm (winter until 8:30pm); Fri–Sat 10:30am–9:30pm (winter until 9pm).

Gutiz ★★ 🍴 FRENCH/SPANISH/NEW AMERICAN Between purple and apricot walls hung with bright contemporary art, this restaurant, recently under new ownership, serves unique and flavorful cuisine. The recipes combine flavors from Spain, France, Peru, and Bolivia and use organic greens and fresh meats and fish, and a broad variety of chile peppers. Service is friendly and efficient. Breakfast brings delicacies such as my favorite, the Taoseño—rice, potatoes, chile, cheese, and fresh herbs topped with scrambled eggs. The French toast is thick, made with home-baked bread. Lunch might begin with a niçoise salad made with fresh tuna, French beans, veggies, potatoes, and olives. The many varied sandwiches come on homemade bread. Alongside the great food, sip from a variety of coffees and chai tea.

812-B Paseo del Pueblo Norte. © **575/758-1226.** Main courses $7–$18. MC, V. Tues–Sun 8am–3pm.

Lula's ★★ ☺ DELI/CAFE A few blocks south of the plaza, this deli offers gourmet soups and sandwiches and diner-style meals between sun-colored walls or to go. The tables here, tall and glass, with stools, don't quite match the comfort level of the food, so diners tend to grab the few regular wooden ones. You order at a counter and the food is served at your table. The soups are gourmet, especially the vegetable stew, which has a rich broth and is served with a baguette. Paninis are a big draw here, the one with roasted eggplant, roasted red bell peppers, zucchini, spinach, provolone, and pesto a real favorite. The nightly blue-plate specials served after 4pm on weekdays and all day Saturday may include chicken alfresco—chicken in broth seasoned with garlic, tomato, and basil over linguini. A kids' menu pleases the tots. Don't leave without sampling a coconut macaroon with whipped ganache dipped in chocolate. Sample from the small select beer and wine list.

316 Paseo del Pueblo Sur. © **575/751-1280.** Main courses $7.50–$14. MC. V. Mon–Sat 11am–9pm (winter until 8pm).

Orlando's New Mexican Café ★ ☺ NEW MEXICAN Festivity reigns in this spicy little cafe on the north end of town. Serving some of northern New Mexico's best chile, this place has colorful tables set around a bustling open kitchen and airy patio dining during warmer months. Service is friendly but minimal. Try the Los Colores, their most popular dish, with three enchiladas (chicken, beef, and cheese) smothered in chile and served with beans and *posole*. The taco salad is another favorite. Portions are big here, and you can order a Mexican or microbrew beer, or a New Mexican or California wine.

114 Don Juan Valdez Lane (1¾ miles north of the plaza, off Paseo del Pueblo Norte). © **575/751-1450.** Reservations not accepted. Main courses under $12. MC, V. Daily 10:30am–3pm and 5–9pm.

North of town

Taos Cow ★ ☺ DELI/DESSERT Located about 10 minutes north of town in Arroyo Seco, Taos Cow offers fun breakfast and lunch fare in a relaxed atmosphere—and, of course, ice cream! Diners order and pick up at a counter. A unique item here is the potpies in chicken, buffalo, beef, or veggie, all with rich sauce and lots of vegetables. Village residents like to wake up to the breakfast tacos, made with fresh local eggs and lots of green chile. A different quiche special, such as a veggie with quinoa, tops the menu each day, and a variety of sandwiches are made with fresh ingredients ranging from black forest ham to portobello mushrooms. All that said, the real reason to come here is the hormone-free ice cream in a variety of flavors. My all-time favorite is the Cherry Ristra, with piñon nuts and chocolate chunks. Kids love their shakes. On chillier afternoons, there are espresso, cappuccino, and hot chocolate to warm you after a day on the slopes.

485 NM 150, Arroyo Seco. © **575/776-5640.** All menu items under $12. AE, DISC, MC, V. Daily 7am–7pm (winter until 6pm).

WHAT TO SEE & DO

With a history shaped by pre-Columbian civilization, Spanish colonialism, and the Wild West; outdoor activities that range from ballooning to world-class skiing; and a clustering of artists, writers, and musicians, Taos has something to offer almost everybody. Its pueblo is the most accessible in New Mexico, and its museums represent a world-class display of regional history and culture.

The Top Attractions

Millicent Rogers Museum of Northern New Mexico ★★   This museum will give you a glimpse of some of the finest Southwestern arts and crafts anywhere, but it's small enough to avoid being overwhelming. It was founded in 1953 by Millicent Rogers's family members after her death. Rogers was a wealthy Taos émigré who in 1947 began acquiring a magnificent collection of beautiful Native American arts and crafts. Included are Navajo and Pueblo jewelry, Navajo textiles, Pueblo pottery, Hopi and Zuni *katsina* dolls, paintings from the Rio Grande Pueblo people, and basketry from a wide variety of Southwestern tribes. The museum also presents exhibitions of Southwestern art, crafts, and design.

Since the 1970s, the scope of the museum's permanent collection has been expanded to include Anglo arts and crafts and Hispanic religious and secular arts and crafts, from Spanish and Mexican colonial to contemporary times. Included are *santos,* furniture, weavings, *colcha* embroideries, and decorative tinwork. Agricultural implements, domestic utensils, and tools dating from the 17th and 18th centuries are also displayed.

The museum gift shop has a fine collection of superior regional art. Classes, workshops, lectures, and field trips are held throughout the year.

Off US 64, 4 miles north of Taos Plaza, on Millicent Rogers Rd. © **575/758-2462.** www.millicentrogers. org. Admission $10 adults, $6 students, $8 seniors, $2 children 6–16, $18 family rate. Daily 10am–5pm. Closed Mon Nov–Mar, Easter, Thanksgiving, Christmas, New Year's Day.

San Francisco de Asis Church ★★   On NM 68, about 4 miles south of Taos, this famous church appears as a modern adobe sculpture with no doors or windows, an image that has often been photographed and painted, most notably by Ansel Adams and Georgia O'Keeffe. Visitors must walk through the garden on the east side to enter the two-story church and get a full perspective of its massive walls, authentic adobe plaster, and beauty.

Taos Attractions

Taos
Santa Fe
Albuquerque
NEW MEXICO

Taos
Municipal
Airport

Taos
Mesa

CARSON
NATIONAL FOREST

Airport ✈
Church ✝
Information ⓘ
Post Office ✉

Town Hall
Civic Center

Chamber of Commerce

State Hwy. 240

Visitor &
Information Center ⓘ

To Santa Fe

Arroyo Seco **14**
D. H. Lawrence Ranch **3**
Ernest L. Blumenschein Home
& Museum **8**
Governor Bent House Museum **10**
Harwood Museum of Art **7**
Martinez Hacienda **1**
Kit Carson Home and Museum **11**
Kit Carson Park and Cemetery **12**
Millicent Rogers Museum **4**
Rio Grande Gorge Bridge **2**
Rodeo **6**
San Francisco de Asis Church **5**
Taos Plaza **9**
Taos Art Museum **13**
Taos Pueblo **15**
Taos Ski Valley **16**

A Tip for Museumgoers

If you'd like to visit five museums that comprise the Museum Association of Taos—Blumenschein Home, Martinez Hacienda, Harwood Museum, Millicent Rogers Museum, and Taos Art Museum—you'll save money by purchasing a combination ticket for $25. The ticket allows one-time entry to each museum during a 1-year period and is fully transferable to other people. You may purchase the pass at any of the five museums. For more information, call ℂ 575/758-0505.

A video presentation is given in the church office every half-hour. Also, displayed on the wall is an unusual painting, *The Shadow of the Cross,* by Henri Ault (1896). Under ordinary light, it portrays a barefoot Christ at the Sea of Galilee; in darkness, however, the portrait becomes luminescent, and the perfect shadow of a cross forms over the left shoulder of Jesus' silhouette. The artist reportedly was as shocked as everyone else to see this. The reason for the illusion remains a mystery. A few crafts shops surround the square.

Ranchos de Taos Plaza. ℂ 575/758-2754. Admission $3 for video and mystery painting. Mon–Sat 9am–4pm. Visitors may attend Mass Mon–Wed and Fri 6:45am; Sat 6pm (Mass rotates from this church to the 3 mission chapels); Sun 7 (Spanish), 9, and 11:30am. Closed to the public 1st 2 weeks in June, when repairs are done; however, services still take place.

Taos Art Museum ★ 🏛 Set in the home of Russian artist Nicolai Fechin (*Feh-shin*), this collection displays works of the Taos Society of Artists, which give a sense of what Taos was like in the late 19th and early 20th centuries. The works are rich and varied, including panoramas and images of the Native American and Hispanic villagers. The setting in what was Fechin's home from 1927 until 1933 is truly unique. The historic building commemorates his career. Born in Russia in 1881, Fechin came to the United States in 1923, already acclaimed as a master of painting, drawing, sculpture, architecture, and woodwork. In Taos, he renovated the home and embellished it with hand-carved doors, windows, gates, posts, fireplaces, and other features of a Russian country home. Fechin died in 1955. If you don't care to pay the admission, you can see just Fechin's studio, which is attached to the gift shop, for free. Also, bear in mind that this museum is privately funded, so your dollars are a real help.

227 Paseo del Pueblo Norte. ℂ 575/758-2690. www.taosartmuseum.org. Admission $8 adults, $7 seniors, $5 students $4 children 6–12, free for 5 and under. Summer Tues–Sun 10am–5pm; call for winter hours.

Taos Historic Museums ★★ Two historical homes are operated as museums, affording visitors a glimpse of early Taos lifestyles. The Martinez Hacienda and Ernest Blumenschein home each has unique appeal.

The **Martinez Hacienda,** Lower Ranchitos Road, Hwy. 240 (ℂ 575/758-1000), is one of the only Spanish colonial haciendas in the United States that's open to the public year-round. This was the home of the merchant, trader, and *alcalde* (mayor) Don Antonio Severino Martinez, who bought it in 1804 and lived here until his death in 1827. His eldest son was Padre Antonio José Martinez, northern New Mexico's controversial spiritual leader from 1826 to 1867. Located on the west bank of the Rio Pueblo de Taos, about 2 miles southwest of the plaza, the museum is remarkably beautiful, with thick, raw adobe walls. The hacienda has no exterior windows—this was to protect against raids by Plains tribes.

Twenty-one rooms were built around two *placitas,* or interior courtyards. They give you a glimpse of the austerity of frontier lives, with only a few pieces of modest period furniture in each. You'll see bedrooms, stables, a kitchen, and a large fiesta room. Exhibits tell the story of the Martinez family and life in Spanish Taos between 1598 and 1821, when Mexico gained control.

Taos Historic Museums has developed the Martinez Hacienda into a living museum with weavers, blacksmiths, and woodcarvers. Demonstrations are scheduled daily, and during the **Taos Trade Fair** (held in late Sept) they run virtually nonstop. The Trade Fair commemorates the era when Native Americans, Spanish settlers, and mountain men met here to trade with each other.

The **Ernest L. Blumenschein Home & Museum,** 222 Ledoux St. (© 575/758-0505), 1½ blocks southwest of the plaza, re-creates the lifestyle of one of the founders of the Taos Society of Artists. An adobe home with garden walls and a courtyard, parts of which date from the 1790s, it became the home and studio of Blumenschein (1874–1960) and his family in 1919. Period furnishings include European antiques and handmade Taos furniture in Spanish colonial style.

Blumenschein was born and raised in Cincinnati. In 1898, after training in New York and Paris, he and fellow painter Bert Phillips were on assignment for *Harper's* and *McClure's* magazines of New York when a wheel of their wagon broke 30 miles north of Taos. Blumenschein drew the short straw and thus was obliged to bring the wheel by horseback to Taos for repair. He later recounted his initial reaction to the valley he entered: "No artist had ever recorded the New Mexico I was now seeing. No writer had ever written down the smell of this air or the feel of that morning sky. I was receiving . . . the first great unforgettable inspiration of my life. My destiny was being decided."

That spark later led to the foundation of Taos as an art colony. An extensive collection of works by early-20th-century Taos artists, including some by Blumenschein's wife, Mary, and daughter, Helen, are on display in several rooms of the home.

222 Ledoux St. © **575/758-0505** (information for both museums can be obtained at this number). www.taosmuseums.org. Admission for each museum $8 adults, $4 children 6-16, free for children 5 and under. Summer daily 9am–5pm; call for winter hours.

Taos Pueblo ★★★   This home to some 100 residents offers a peek into the traditional Pueblo culture. When you enter this UNESCO World Heritage Site, you'll see two large buildings, both with rooms piled on top of each other, forming structures that echo the shape of Taos Mountain (which sits to the northeast). Here, a portion of Taos residents lives without electricity and running water. The remaining 2,000 residents of Taos Pueblo live in conventional homes on the pueblo's 100,000 acres.

The main buildings' distinctive flowing lines of shaped mud, with a straw-and-mud exterior plaster, are typical of Pueblo architecture throughout the Southwest. It's architecture that blends in with the surrounding land. Bright blue doors are the same shade as the sky that frames the brown buildings.

The northernmost of New Mexico's 19 pueblos, Taos Pueblo has been home to the Tiwa-speaking people for more than a millennium. Many residents here still practice ancestral rituals. The center of their world is still nature; women use *hornos* to bake bread, and most still drink water that flows down from the sacred Blue Lake.

Meanwhile, arts and crafts and other tourism-related businesses support the economy, along with government services, ranching, and farming.

The village looks much the same today as it did when a regiment from Coronado's expedition first came upon it in 1540. Though the Tiwa were essentially a peaceful agrarian people, they are perhaps best remembered for spearheading the most successful revolt by Native Americans. Launched by Popé (Poh-*pay*) in 1680, the uprising drove the Spanish from Santa Fe until 1692 and from Taos until 1698.

As you explore the pueblo, you can visit the residents' studios, sample homemade bread, look into the **San Geronimo Chapel,** and wander past the fascinating ruins of the old church and cemetery. You're expected to ask permission from individuals before taking their photos; some will ask for a small payment. Do not trespass into kivas (ceremonial rooms) and other areas marked as restricted.

The **Feast of San Geronimo** (the patron saint of Taos Pueblo), on September 29 and 30, marks the end of the harvest season. The feast day is reminiscent of an ancient trade fair for the Taos Indians, when tribes from as far south as South America and as far north as the Arctic would come and trade for wares, hides, clothing, and harvested crops. The day is filled with footraces, pole climbing done by traditional Indian clowns, and artists and craftspeople dressed like early traders. Dance ceremonies are held the evening of September 29. Other annual events include a **turtle dance** on New Year's Day, **buffalo** or **deer dances** on Three Kings Day (Jan 6), and **corn dances** on Santa Cruz Day (May 3), San Antonio Day (June 13), San Juan Day (June 24), Santiago Day (July 25), and Santa Ana Day (July 26). The annual **Taos Pueblo Powwow** (www.taospueblopowwow.com), a dance competition and parade that brings together tribes from throughout North America, is held the second weekend of July on tribal lands off NM 522 (see "New Mexico Calendar of Events," in chapter 3). The pueblo Christmas celebration begins on Christmas Eve, with bonfires and a procession of the Blessed Mother. On Christmas Day, a variety of dances take place. These may include the **deer dance,** in which dancers act out a hunt, or the **Matachine dances,** which depicts the blending of the native and Spanish traditions.

During your visit to the pueblo you will have the opportunity to purchase traditional fried and oven-baked bread as well as a variety of arts and crafts. As with many of the other pueblos in New Mexico, Taos Pueblo has opened a casino. The smoke-free **Taos Mountain Casino** (© **888/946-8267;** www.taosmountaincasino.com) is on the main road to Taos Pueblo and features slot machines, blackjack, and poker.

Note: To learn more about the pueblo and its people, I recommend taking a 15-minute guided tour. Ask upon arrival when the next one will be given and where you should meet your guide.

Veterans Hwy. (P.O. Box 1846), Taos Pueblo. © **575/758-1028.** www.taospueblo.com. $10 adults, $5 students, children 10 and under free. Camera, video, and sketching fees subject to change on a yearly basis; be sure to ask about telephoto lenses and tripods, as the pueblo may not allow them; photography not permitted on feast days. Daily 8am–4:30pm in summer, 8am–4pm in winter, with a few exceptions. Guided tours available. Closed for 6 weeks every year late winter or early spring (call ahead). Because this is a living community, you can expect other periodic closures. From Paseo del Pueblo Norte, travel north 2 miles on Veterans Hwy.

More Attractions

D. H. Lawrence Ranch   A trip to this ranch north of Taos leads you into odd realms of devotion for the controversial early-20th-century author who lived and wrote in the area in the early 1920s. A short uphill walk from the ranch home (not open to visitors) is the D. H. Lawrence Memorial, a small stucco structure that is said to have Lawrence's ashes mixed in with the cement. The guest book is interesting: One couple wrote of trying for 24 years to get here from England.

Lawrence lived in Taos on and off between 1922 and 1925. The ranch was a gift to his wife, Frieda, from the art patron Mabel Dodge Luhan. Lawrence repaid Luhan the favor by giving her the manuscript of *Sons and Lovers*. When Lawrence died in southern France in 1930 of tuberculosis, his ashes were returned here for burial. The grave of Frieda, who died in 1956, is outside the memorial. The memorial is the only public building at the ranch, which is operated today by the University of New Mexico as an educational and recreational retreat.

NM 522, San Cristobal. © **575/776-2245.** Free admission. Daily 8am–6pm. To reach the site, head north from Taos about 15 miles on NM 522, then another 6 miles east into the forested Sangre de Cristo Range via a well-marked dirt road.

Governor Bent House Museum ☺ This residence of Charles Bent, New Mexico Territory's first American governor, offers an interesting peek into the region's at-times brutal history. Bent, a former trader who established Fort Bent, Colorado, was murdered during the 1847 Native American and Hispanic rebellion, while his wife and children escaped by digging through an adobe wall into the house next door. The hole is still visible. Period art and artifacts are on display at the museum, just a short block north of the plaza. Owned by the same family since the 1950s, the museum also has a charming gift shop with historic memorabilia.

117 Bent St. © **575/758-2376.** Admission $3 adults, $1 children 8–15, free for children 7 and under. MC, V. Daily 9:30am–5pm (winter from 10am). Closed Easter, Thanksgiving, Christmas, New Year's Day. Street parking.

Harwood Museum of Art of the University of New Mexico ★★ With its high ceilings and broad wood floors, this museum is a lovely place to wander among New Mexico–inspired images. A cultural and community center since 1923, the museum displays paintings, drawings, prints, sculpture, and photographs by Taos-area artists from 1800 to the present. Featured are paintings from the early days of the art colony by members of the Taos Society of Artists, including Oscar Berninghaus, Ernest Blumenschein, Herbert Dunton, Victor Higgins, Bert Phillips, and Walter Ufer. Also included are works by Emil Bisttram, Andrew Dasburg, Agnes Martin, Larry Bell, and Thomas Benrimo.

Upstairs are 19th-century pounded-tin pieces, *bultos* (carved statues) and *retablos* (religious paintings of saints that have traditionally been used for decoration and inspiration in the homes and churches of New Mexico). The permanent collection includes sculptures by Patrociño Barela, one of the leading Hispanic artists of 20th-century New Mexico. It's well worth seeing, especially his 3-foot-tall "Death Cart," a rendition of Doña Sebastiána, the bringer of death.

238 Ledoux St. © **575/758-9826.** www.harwoodmuseum.org. Admission $8 adults, $7 seniors, free for children 11 and under. Tues–Sat 10am–5pm; Sun noon–5pm (winter until 4pm).

Kit Carson Home and Museum If you want a glimpse into the modest lifestyle of Taos's frontiersmen, head to this three-room adobe home, a block east of the plaza. Built in 1825 and purchased in 1843 by Carson—the famous mountain man, Indian agent, and scout—it was a wedding gift for his young bride, Josefa Jaramillo.

It remained their home for 25 years, until both died (exactly a month apart) in 1868. Rooms have sparse displays such as buffalo hide and sheepskin bedding, a wooden chest, basic kitchen utensils, and a cooking fireplace. The treasure of the museum is interpreter Natívídad Mascarenas-Gallegos, a distant relative of Carson, who can tell you plenty about the family. The museum also includes a film on Carson produced by the History Channel. The price of a visit here is a bit steep for what you see, but if you decide to come, plan on spending about a half-hour. If you'd like to see more of Carson's possessions, visit the Martinez Hacienda (see above).

113 Kit Carson Rd. © **575/758-4945.** www.kitcarsonhomeandmuseum.com. Admission $5 adult, $4 seniors 65 years and older, $3 children 13–18, $2 children 6–12. Daily 9am–6pm.

Kit Carson Park and Cemetery   Major community events are held in the park in summer. The cemetery, established in 1847, contains the graves of Carson, his wife, Governor Charles Bent, the Don Antonio Martinez family, Mabel Dodge Luhan, and many other noted historical figures and artists. Their lives are described briefly on plaques.

211 Paseo del Pueblo Norte. © **575/758-8234.** Free admission. Daily 24 hr.

Rio Grande Gorge Bridge ★ ☺   This impressive bridge, west of the Taos airport, spans the Southwest's greatest river. At 650 feet above the canyon floor, it's one of America's highest bridges. If you can withstand the vertigo, it's interesting to come more than once, at different times of day, to observe how the changing light plays tricks with the colors of the cliff walls. A curious aside is that the wedding scene in the movie *Natural Born Killers* was filmed here.

US 64, 10 miles west of Taos. Free admission. Daily 24 hr.

Organized Tours

An excellent opportunity to explore the historic downtown area of Taos is offered by **Taos Historic Walking Tours** (© **575/758-4020**). Tours cost $12 and take 1½ to 2 hours, leaving from the Kit Carson Cemetery at 10am Monday to Saturday (June–Aug; closed holidays). Call to make an appointment.

If you'd really like a taste of Taos history and drama, call **Enchantment Dreams Walking Tours** ★ (© **575/776-2562;** storytel1@yahoo.com). Roberta Courtney Meyers, a theater artist, dramatist, and composer, will tour you through Taos's history while performing a number of characters, such as Georgia O'Keeffe and Kit Carson. Walking tours cost $25 per person.

SKIING ★★★

Downhill Skiing

Five alpine resorts are within an hour's drive of Taos; all offer complete facilities, including equipment rentals. Although exact opening and closing dates vary according to snow conditions, the season usually begins around Thanksgiving and continues into early April.

Ski clothing can be purchased, and ski equipment can be rented or bought, from several Taos outlets. Among them are **Cottam's Ski & Outdoor Shops,** with four locations (© **800/322-8267** or 575/758-2822; www.cottamsoutdoor.com), and **Taos Ski Valley Sportswear, Ski & Boot Co.,** in Taos Ski Valley (© **575/776-2291**).

Skiing with Kids

With its children's ski school, Taos Ski Valley has always been an excellent choice for skiing families, but with the 1994 addition of an 18,000-square-foot children's center (Kinderkäfig Center), skiing with your children in Taos is even better. Kinderkäfig offers many services, from equipment rental for children to babysitting services. Call ahead for more information.

Taos Ski Valley ★★★, P.O. Box 90, Taos Ski Valley, NM 87525 (✆ **575/776-2291;** www.skitaos.org), is the preeminent ski resort in the southern Rocky Mountains. It was founded in 1955 by a Swiss-German immigrant, Ernie Blake. According to local legend, Blake searched for 2 years in a small plane for the perfect location for a ski resort comparable to what he was accustomed to in the Alps. He found it at the abandoned mining site of Twining, high above Taos. Today, under the management of two younger generations of Blakes, the resort has become internationally renowned for its light, dry powder (as much as 300 in. annually), its superb ski school, and its personal, friendly service.

Taos Ski Valley can best be appreciated by the more experienced skier and snowboarder. It offers steep, high-alpine, high-adventure skiing. The mountain is more intricate than it might seem at first glance, and it holds many surprises and challenges—even for the expert. The *London Times* called the valley "without any argument the best ski resort in the world. Small, intimate, and endlessly challenging, Taos simply has no equal." The quality of the snow here (light and dry) is believed to be due to the dry Southwestern air and abundant sunshine. **Note:** In 2008, Taos Ski Valley began allowing snowboarders onto its slopes.

Between the 11,819-foot summit and the 9,207-foot base, there are 72 trails and bowls, more than half of them designated for expert and advanced skiers. Most of the remaining trails are suitable for advanced intermediates; there is little flat terrain for novices to gain experience and mileage. However, many beginning skiers find that after spending time in lessons they can enjoy the **Kachina Bowl,** which offers spectacular views as well as wide-open slopes.

The area has an uphill capacity of 15,000 skiers per hour on its five double chairs, one triple, four quads, and one surface tow. Full-day lift tickets, depending on the season, cost $45 to $69 for adults, $30 to $58 for ages 13 to 17, $20 to $41 for children 12 and under, $35 to $58 for seniors 65 to 79, and are free for seniors over 80 and for children 6 and under with an adult ticket purchase. Full rental packages are $29 for adults and $20 for children. Taos Ski Valley is open daily 9am to 4pm from Thanksgiving to around the second week of April. **Note:** Taos Ski Valley has one of the best ski schools in the country, specializing in teaching people how to negotiate steep and challenging runs.

Taos Ski Valley has many lodges and condominiums, with nearly 1,500 beds. (See "Taos Ski Valley," earlier, for details on accommodations.) All offer ski-week packages; three of them have restaurants. There are three restaurants on the mountain in addition to the many facilities of Village Center at the base. Call the **Taos Ski Valley** (✆ **800/776-1111** or 575/776-2233).

Not far from Taos Ski Valley is **Red River Ski & Snowboard Area,** P.O. Box 900, Red River, NM 87558 (✆ **800/331-7669** for reservations; 575/754-2223 for information; www.redriverskiarea.com). One of the bonuses of this ski area is that lodgers at Red River can walk out their doors and be on the slopes. Two other factors make this 40-year-old, family-oriented area special: First, most of its 58 trails are geared toward the intermediate skier, though beginners and experts also have some trails, and second, good snow is guaranteed early and late in the year by snowmaking equipment that can work on 87% of the runs, more than any other in New Mexico. However, be aware that this human-made snow tends to be icy, and the mountain is full of inexperienced skiers, so you really have to watch your back. Locals in the area refer to this as "Little Texas" because it's so popular with Texans and other Southerners. A very friendly atmosphere, with a touch of redneck attitude, prevails.

There's a 1,600-foot vertical drop here to a base elevation of 8,750 feet. Lifts include four double chairs, two triple chairs, and a surface tow, with a capacity of 7,920 skiers per hour. The cost of a ticket for all lifts is $59 for adults for a full day, $44 half-day; $48 for ages 13 to 19 for a full day, $35 half-day; and $39 for children 4 to 12 and seniors 60 through 69 for a full day, $32 half-day (free for seniors 70 and over). All rental packages start at $25 for adults, $17 for children. Lifts run daily 9am to 4pm approximately Thanksgiving through March. Ask about their lesson packages.

Also quite close to Taos (approx. 20 miles) is **Angel Fire Resort ★,** P.O. Drawer B, Angel Fire, NM 87710 (✆ **800/633-7463** or 575/377-6401; www.angelfire resort.com). If you (or your kids) don't feel up to skiing steeper Taos Mountain, Angel Fire is a good choice. The 73 trails are heavily oriented to beginner and intermediate skiers and snowboarders, with a few runs for more advanced skiers and snowboarders. The mountain has received over $7 million in improvements in past years. This is not an old village like you'll find at Taos and Red River. Instead, it's a Vail-style resort, built in 1960, with a variety of activities other than skiing (see "A Scenic Drive: The Enchanted Circle," later in this chapter). The snow-making capabilities here are excellent, and the ski school is good, though I hear it's so crowded that it's difficult to get in during spring break. Two high-speed quad lifts whisk you to the top quickly. There are also three double lifts and one surface lift. A large snowboard park contains a banked slalom course, rails, jumps, and other obstacles. Cross-country skiing, snowshoeing, and snow biking are also available. All-day lift tickets cost $59 for adults, $52 for ages 13 to 17, and $39 for children 7 to 12. Kids 6 and under and seniors 70 and over ski free. It's open daily 9am to 4pm from approximately mid-December to March 29 (depending on the weather).

The oldest ski area in the Taos region, founded in 1952, **Sipapu Ski and Summer Resort,** Hwy. 518, Rte. Box 29, Vadito, NM 87579 (✆ **505/587-2240;** www. sipapunm.com), is 25 miles southeast of Taos, on NM 518 in Tres Ritos Canyon. It prides itself on being a small local ski area, especially popular with schoolchildren. It has two triple chairs and two surface lifts, with a vertical drop of 1,025 feet to the 8,200-foot base elevation. There are 31 trails, half classified as intermediate, and two terrain park trails have been added. It's a nice little area, tucked way back in the mountains, with excellent lodging rates. Be aware that because the elevation is fairly low, runs can be icy. Lift tickets are $39 for adults for a full day, $29 for half-day; $34 for ages 13 through 20 full day, $26 for half-day; $29 for children 6 to 12 full day, $22 for half day; $29 for seniors 60 to 69 full day, $22 for half-day; free for seniors 70 and over and children 5 and under. A package including lift tickets, equipment rental, and a lesson costs $53 for adults and $42 for children. Also check out their lodging/skiing packages. Sipapu is open from about the end of November to March, and lifts run daily from 9am to 4pm.

Cross-Country Skiing

Numerous popular Nordic trails traverse **Carson National Forest.** If you call or write ahead, the ranger will send you a booklet titled *Where to Go in the Snow,* which gives cross-country skiers details about the maintained trails. One of the more popular trails is **Amole Canyon,** off NM 518 near the Sipapu Ski Area, where the Taos Nordic Ski Club maintains set tracks and signs along a 3-mile loop. It's closed to snowmobiles, a comfort to lovers of serenity.

Just east of Red River, with 16 miles of groomed trails (in addition to 6 miles of trails strictly for snowshoers) in 400 acres of forestlands atop Bobcat Pass, is the **Enchanted Forest Cross Country Ski Area ★** (© 575/754-6112; www.enchantedforestxc.com). Full-day trail passes, good from 9am to 4:30pm, are $15 for adults, $12 for teens 13 to 17 and seniors 62 to 69, $7 for children 7 to 12, and free for seniors 70 and over, as well as for children 6 and under. In addition to cross-country ski and snowshoe rentals, the ski area also rents pulk sleds—high-tech devices in which children are pulled by their skiing parents. The ski area offers a full ski shop and snack bar. Instruction in cross-country classic as well as freestyle skating is available. A new yurt (Mongolian-style hut) is also available for a ski-in accommodation. **Taos Mountain Outfitters,** 114 S. Plaza (© 575/758-9292; www.taosmountainoutfitters.com), offers telemark and cross-country sales and rentals.

MORE OUTDOOR ACTIVITIES

Taos County's 2,200 square miles embrace a great diversity of scenic beauty, from New Mexico's highest mountain, 13,161-foot **Wheeler Peak,** to the 650-foot-deep chasm of the **Rio Grande Gorge ★★. Carson National Forest,** which extends to the eastern city limits of Taos and cloaks a large part of the county, contains several major ski facilities as well as hundreds of miles of hiking trails through the **Sangre de Cristo Range.**

Recreation areas are mainly in the national forest, where pine and aspen provide refuge for abundant wildlife. Forty-eight areas are accessible by road, including 38 with campsites. There are also areas on the high desert mesa, carpeted by sagebrush, cactus, and, frequently, wildflowers. Two beautiful areas within a short drive of Taos are the **Valle Vidal Recreation Area,** north of Red River, and the **Wild Rivers Recreation Area** near Questa (see "A Scenic Drive: The Enchanted Circle," later in this chapter). For complete information, contact **Carson National Forest,** 208 Cruz Alta Rd. (© 575/758-6200; www.fs.fed.us/r3/carson), or the **Bureau of Land Management,** 226 Cruz Alta Rd. (© 575/758-8851; www.blm.gov/nm).

Ballooning

As in many other towns throughout New Mexico, hot-air ballooning is a top attraction. Recreational trips over the Taos Valley and Rio Grande Gorge are offered by **Paradise Hot Air Balloon Adventure** (© 575/751-6098; www.taosballooning.com). The company also offers ultralight rides.

ALONG A green shore

A sweet spot en route to Taos from Santa Fe, the **Orilla Verde** (Green Shore) **Recreation Area** offers just what its name implies: lovely green shores along the Rio Grande. It's an excellent place to camp or to simply have a picnic. If you're adventurous, the flat water in this section of the river makes for scenic canoeing, kayaking, rafting, and fishing. Hiking trails thread through the area as well. Along them, you may come across ancient cultural artifacts, but be sure to leave them as you find them.

While traveling to the area, you'll encounter two places of note. The village of **Pilar** ★ is a charming farming village, home to apple orchards, cornfields, and artists. The **Rio Grande Gorge Visitor Center** (at the intersection of NM

570 and NM 68; ℂ **575/751-4899**) provides information about the gorge and has very clean restrooms. It's open May to October daily 8:30am to 4:30pm (also Nov–Apr daily 10am–2pm if they can secure volunteer staff).

The day-use fee for Orilla Verde is $3 per day, camping is $7 per night, and RV camping is $15 per night. All campsites have picnic tables, grills, and restrooms. For information, contact the **Orilla Verde Visitor Station** (ℂ **575/751-4899**; www.blm.gov/nm), at the campground. To reach the recreation area, travel north from Santa Fe 50 miles or southwest from Taos 15 miles on NM 68; turn north on NM 570 and travel 1 mile.

Biking

Even if you're not an avid cyclist, it won't take long for you to realize that getting around Taos by bike is preferable to driving. You won't have the usual parking problems, and you won't have to sit in the line of traffic as it snakes through the center of town. If you feel like exploring the surrounding area, Carson National Forest rangers recommend several biking trails in the greater Taos area. Head to the **West Rim Trail** for a scenic and easy ride. To reach the trail, travel US 64 to the Taos Gorge Bridge, cross it, and find the trail head on your left, or head south on NM 68 for 17 miles to Pilar; turn west onto NM 570. Travel along the river for 6¼ miles, cross the bridge, and drive to the top of the ridge. Watch for the trail marker on your right. For a more technical and challenging ride, go to **Devisadero Loop.** From Taos, drive out of town on US 64 to your first pullout on the right, just as you enter the canyon at El Nogal Picnic Area. The **U.S. Forest Service** office, 208 Cruz Alta Rd. (ℂ **575/758-6200**), has excellent trail information. Also look for the *Taos Trails* map (created jointly by Carson National Forest, Native Sons Adventures, and Trails Illustrated) at area bookstores.

Bicycle rentals are available from the **Gearing Up Bicycle Shop,** 129 Paseo del Pueblo Sur (ℂ **575/751-0365;** www.gearingupbikes.com); daily rentals run $35 for a mountain bike with front suspension.

Fishing

In many of New Mexico's waters, fishing is possible year-round, though, due to conditions, many high lakes and streams are fishable only during the warmer months. Overall, the best fishing is in the spring and fall. Naturally, the Rio Grande is a favorite fishing spot, but there is also excellent fishing in the streams around Taos. Taoseños favor the Rio Hondo, Rio Pueblo (near Tres Ritos), Rio Fernando (in Taos Canyon), Pot Creek, and Rio Chiquito. Rainbow, cutthroat, German brown trout, and kokanee (a freshwater salmon) are commonly stocked and caught. Pike and catfish have been caught in the Rio Grande as well. Jiggs, spinners, or woolly worms are recommended as lure, or worms, corn, or salmon eggs as bait; many experienced anglers prefer fly-fishing.

Licenses are required, and are sold, along with tackle, at several Taos sporting-goods shops. For backcountry guides, try **Deep Creek Wilderness Outfitters and Guides,** P.O. Box 721, El Prado, NM 87529 (✆ **575/776-8423** or 575/776-5901), or **Taylor Streit Flyfishing Service,** 405 Camino de la Placita (✆ **575/751-1312;** www.streitflyfishing.com).

Fitness Facilities

The **Taos Spa and Tennis Club,** 111 Dona Ana Dr. (across from Sagebrush Inn; ✆ 575/758-1980; www.taosspa.com), is a fully equipped fitness center that rivals any you'd find in a big city. It has a variety of cardiovascular machines, bikes, and weight-training machines, as well as saunas, indoor and outdoor Jacuzzis, a steam room, and indoor and outdoor pools. Classes range from yoga to Pilates to water fitness. In addition, it has tennis and racquetball courts. Therapeutic massage, facials, and physical therapy are available daily by appointment. Children's programs include a tennis camp and swimming lessons, and babysitting programs are available in the morning and evening. The spa is open Monday to Thursday 5am to 9pm, Friday 5am to 8pm, and Saturday and Sunday 7am to 8pm. Monthly memberships are available for individuals and families, as are summer memberships. For visitors, there's a daily rate of $12.

The **Northside Health and Fitness Center,** at 1307 Paseo del Pueblo Norte (✆ 575/751-1242; www.taosnorthsidespa.com), is also a full-service facility, featuring top-of-the-line Cybex equipment, free weights, and cardiovascular equipment. Aerobics classes are scheduled daily (Jazzercise classes weekly), and there are indoor/outdoor pools and four tennis courts, as well as children's and seniors' programs. The center is open weekdays 5am to 9pm and weekends 8am to 8pm. The daily visitors' rate is $8. Also of note, with classes daily, is **Taos Pilates Studio,** 1103 Paseo del Pueblo Norte (✆ 575/758-7604; www.taospilates.net).

Golf

Since the summer of 1993, the 18-hole golf course at the **Taos Country Club,** 54 Golf Course Dr., Ranchos de Taos (✆ 575/758-7300; www.taoscountryclub.com), has been open to the public. Located off CR 110, just 6 miles south of the plaza, it's a first-rate championship golf course designed for all levels of play. It has open fairways and no hidden greens. The club also features a driving range, practice putting and chipping green, and instruction by PGA professionals. Greens fees are seasonal and start at $62; cart and club rentals are available. The country club has also added a clubhouse, featuring a restaurant and full bar. It's always advisable to call ahead for tee times 1 week in advance, but it's not unusual for people to show up unannounced and still manage to find a time to tee off.

The par-72, 18-hole course at the **Angel Fire Resort Golf Course** (✆ **800/633-7463** or 575/377-3055; www.angelfireresort.com/summer) is PGA endorsed. Surrounded by stands of ponderosa pine, spruce, and aspen, at 8,500 feet, it's one of the highest regulation golf courses in the world. It also has a driving range and putting green. Carts and clubs can be rented at the course, and the club pro provides instruction. Greens fees range from $47 to $99.

Hiking

There are hundreds of miles of hiking trails in Taos County's mountain and high-mesa country. The trails are especially well traveled in the summer and fall, although nights turn chilly and mountain weather may be fickle by September.

Free materials and advice on all **Carson National Forest** trails and recreation areas can be obtained from the **Forest Service Building,** 208 Cruz Alta Rd. (© **575/758-6200;** www.fs.fed.us/r3/carson), open Monday to Friday 8am to 4:30pm. Detailed USGS topographical maps of backcountry areas can be purchased from **Taos Mountain Outfitters,** 114 S. Plaza (© **575/758-9292;** www.taos mountainoutfitters.com).

One of the easiest hikes to access is the **West Rim Trail,** aptly named because it runs along the rim of the Rio Grande Gorge. Access this 9-mile-long trail by driving west from Taos on US 64, crossing the Rio Grande Gorge Bridge, and turning left into the picnic area. The 19,663-acre **Wheeler Peak Wilderness** is a wonderland of alpine tundra, encompassing New Mexico's highest peak (13,161 ft.). A favorite (though rigorous) hike to Wheeler Peak's summit (15 miles round-trip with a 3,700-ft. elevation gain) makes for a long but fun day. The trail head is at Taos Ski Valley. For year-round hiking, head to the **Wild Rivers Recreation Area ★** (© **575/770-1600**), near Questa (see "A Scenic Drive: The Enchanted Circle," later in this chapter).

Horseback Riding

The sage meadows and pine-covered mountains around Taos make it one of the West's most romantic places to ride. **Taos Indian Horse Ranch ★★**, on Pueblo land off Ski Valley Road, just before **Arroyo Seco** (© **575/758-3212;** www.taos indianhorseranch.com), offers a variety of guided rides. Open by appointment, the ranch provides horses for all types of riders (English, Western, Australian, and bareback) and ability levels. Call ahead to reserve and for prices, which will likely run about $100 for a 2-hour trail ride.

Horseback riding is also offered by **Rio Grande Stables,** P.O. Box 2122, El Prado (© **575/776-5913;** www.lajitasstables.com), with rides taking place during the summer months at Taos Ski Valley. Most riding outfitters offer lunch trips and overnight trips. Call for prices and further details.

Hunting

Hunters in **Carson National Forest** bag deer, turkey, grouse, band-tailed pigeons, and elk by special permit. Hunting seasons vary year to year, so it's important to inquire ahead with the New Mexico **Game and Fish Department** in Santa Fe (© **505/476-8000;** www.wildlife.state.nm.us).

Jogging

The paved paths and grass of Kit Carson Park (p. 226) provide a quiet place to stretch your legs.

Llama Trekking

For a taste of the unusual, you might want to try letting a llama carry your gear and food while you walk and explore, free of any heavy burdens. They're friendly, gentle animals that have keen senses of sight and smell. Often, other animals, such as elk, deer, and mountain sheep, are attracted to the scent of the llamas and will venture closer to hikers if the llamas are present.

Wild Earth Llama Adventures ★★ (ℭ **800/758-5262** or 575/586-0174; www.llamaadventures.com) offers a "Take a Llama to Llunch" day hike—a full day of hiking into the Sangre de Cristo Mountains, complete with a gourmet lunch for $99. Wild Earth also offers a variety of custom multiday wilderness adventures tailored to trekkers' needs and fitness levels for $165 per person per day. Children 11 and under receive discounts. Camping gear and food are provided. On the trips, experienced guides provide information about native plants and local wildlife, as well as natural and regional history of the area. The head guide has doubled as a chef in the off season, so the meals on these treks are quite tasty.

River Rafting

Half- or full-day white-water rafting trips down the Rio Grande and Rio Chama originate in Taos and can be booked through a variety of outfitters in the area. The wild **Taos Box** ★★★, a steep-sided canyon south of the Wild Rivers Recreation Area, offers a series of class IV rapids that rarely let up for some 17 miles. The water drops up to 90 feet per mile, providing one of the most exciting 1-day white-water tours in the West. May and June, when the water is rising, is a good time to go. Experience is not required, but you will be required to wear a life jacket (provided), and you should be willing to get wet.

Most of the companies listed run the **Taos Box** ($104–$115 per person) and **Pilar Racecourse** ($45–$56 per person for a half-day) on a daily basis.

I highly recommend **Los Rios River Runners** ★ in Taos, P.O. Box 2734 (ℭ **800/544-1181** or 575/776-8854; www.losriosriverrunners.com). Other safe bets are **Native Sons Adventures,** 1335 Paseo del Pueblo Sur (ℭ **800/753-7559** or 575/758-9342; www.nativesonsadventures.com), and **Far Flung Adventures,** P.O. Box 707, El Prado (ℭ **800/359-2627** or 575/758-2628; www.farflung.com).

Safety warning: Only experienced river runners should attempt these waters without a guide. Check with the **Bureau of Land Management** (ℭ **575/758-8851;** www.blm.gov/nm) to make sure that you're fully equipped to go white-water rafting. Have them check your gear to make sure that it's sturdy enough—this is serious rafting and kayaking!

Rock Climbing

Mountain Skills, P.O. Box 206, Arroyo Seco, NM 87514 (ℭ **575/776-2222;** www.climbingschoolusa.com), offers rock-climbing instruction for all skill levels, from beginners to more advanced climbers who would like to fine-tune their skills or just find out about the best area climbs.

Skateboarding

Try your board at **Taos Youth Family Center,** 407 Paseo del Cañon, 2 miles south of the plaza and about ¾ mile off Paseo del Pueblo Sur (ℭ **505/758-4160;**

GETTING PAMPERED: the spa scene

Taos doesn't have the spa scene that Tucson and Phoenix do, but you can get pampered with treatments ranging from body polishes to mud wraps to massages at **Estrella Massage & Day Spa,** 601 Callejon Rd. (© **575/751-7307;** www.estrellamassage.com). **Taos Spa and Tennis Club** (see "Fitness Facilities," above) also offers massages.

If you'd like to stay at a spa, **El Monte Sagrado,** 317 Kit Carson Rd. (© **800/828-8267** or 505/758-3502; www.elmontesagrado.com), and **Casa de las Chimeneas,** 405 Cordoba Rd. (© **877/758-4777** or 575/758-4777; www.visittaos.com), offer a variety of treatments to their guests (see earlier).

---

www.taosyouth.com). There is an in-line-skate and skateboarding park, open when there's no snow or ice. Admission is free.

Snowmobiling & ATV Riding

Native Sons Adventures, 1335 Paseo del Pueblo Sur (© **800/753-7559** or 575/758-9342; www.nativesonsadventures.com), runs fully guided tours in the Sangre de Cristo Mountains. Rates run $65 to $130. Advance reservations required.

Swimming

The indoors **Taos Swimming Pool,** Civic Plaza Drive at Camino de la Placita, opposite the Convention Center (© **575/758-4160;** www.taosyouth.com), admits swimmers 8 and over without adult supervision.

Tennis

Taos Spa and Tennis Club has four courts, and the **Northside Health and Fitness Center** has three tennis courts (see both under "Fitness Facilities," above). In addition, there are four free public courts in Taos—two at **Kit Carson Park,** on Paseo del Pueblo Norte, and two at **Fred Baca Memorial Park,** on Camino del Medio, south of Ranchitos Road.

SHOPPING

Given the town's historical associations with the arts, it isn't surprising that many visitors come to Taos to buy fine art. Some 50-odd galleries are within walking distance of the plaza, and a couple dozen more are just a short drive from downtown. Galleries and shops are generally open 7 days a week during summer and closed Sundays during winter. Hours vary but generally run from 10am to 5 or 6pm. Some artists show their work by appointment only.

The best-known artist in modern Taos is the late R. C. Gorman, a Navajo from Arizona who made his home in Taos for more than 2 decades. He was internationally acclaimed for his bright, somewhat surrealistic depictions of Navajo women. His **Navajo Gallery,** at 210 Ledoux St. (© **575/758-3250;** www.rcgormangallery. com), is a showcase for his widely varied work: acrylics, lithographs, silk screens, bronzes, tapestries, hand-cast ceramic vases, etched glass, and more.

My favorite spots to shop are the **Plaza and Bent Street** areas and the village of **Arroyo Seco** ★ on NM 150, about 5 miles north of Taos en route to Taos Ski Valley. At the village you'll find a lovely 1834 church, La Santísima Trinidad, along with a few cute little shops lining the winding lane through town. A few of my favorites there are **Arroyo Seco Mercantile** ★ (© 575/776-8806) at 488 NM 150, which is full of cowboy hats, antiques, and country home items; and **Jack Leustig Imaging** ★ (© 800/670-6651 or 575/776-3899; www.jliprints.com), which carries quality reproductions of fine artworks along with hundreds of art greeting cards.

Art

Act I Gallery   This gallery has a broad range of works in a variety of media. You'll find watercolors, *retablos,* furniture, paintings, Hispanic folk art, pottery, jewelry, and sculpture. 218 Paseo del Pueblo Norte. © **877/228-1278** or 575/758-7831. www.actonegallery.com.

Envision Gallery ★   Offering contemporary art with an elaborate sculpture garden, this is a fun place to browse for works on paper and of clay. Bold colors and innovative designs mark this work, with wind sculptures by Lyman Whitaker the real prize. 1405 Paseo del Pueblo Norte (in the Overland Sheepskin Complex), El Prado. © **505/751-1344.** www.envisiongallery.net.

Inger Jirby Gallery ★ 🎒   The word *expressionist* could have been created to define the work of internationally known artist Inger Jirby. Full of bold color and passionate brush strokes, Jirby's oils record the lives and landscapes of villages from the southwestern U.S. to Guatemala to Bali. This gallery, which meanders back through a 400-year-old adobe house, is a feast for the eyes and soul. 207 Ledoux St. © **575/758-7333.** www.jirby.com.

Lumina Contemporary Art ★★ 🎒   North of Taos (about 8 min.) outside the village of Arroyo Seco, this gallery, a new version of the notable gallery that was in Taos, offers a tranquil museum-quality experience. Set within a 3-acre Japanese garden, it has a water cascade and Buddhist teahouse accented with large stone sculptures. Inside, works offer a refreshing look at the world. Watch for Chacha's gold- and copper-leaf works on metal, and Annell Livingston's geometric paintings on handmade paper. It's open in summer Thursday to Monday 11am to 6:30pm; winter Friday to Monday 11am to 5pm. 11 NM 230, Arroyo Seco. © **877/5-558-6462** or 575/776-0123. www.luminagallery.com.

Michael McCormick Gallery ★ 🎒   Nationally renowned artists dynamically play with Southwestern themes in the works hanging at this gallery, steps from the plaza. Especially notable are the bright portraits by Miguel Martinez. If the gallery's namesake is in, strike up a conversation about art or poetry. 106C Paseo del Pueblo Norte. © **800/279-0879** or 575/758-1372. www.mccormickgallery.com.

Nichols Taos Fine Art Gallery   Here you will find traditional works in all media, including Western and cowboy art. 403 Paseo del Pueblo Norte. © **575/758-2475.**

Parks Gallery ★   Some of the region's finest contemporary art decks the walls of this gallery just off the plaza. Some of the top artists here include the late Melissa Zink, Jim Wagner, Susan Contreras, and Erin Currier. 127 Bent St. © **575/751-0343.** www.parksgallery.com.

Philip Bareiss Gallery The works of some 30 leading Taos artists, including sculptor and painter Ron Davis, and painter Norbert Voelke, are exhibited here, along with early Taos modernists. 15 NM 150. ℂ **800/458-2284** or 575/776-2284. www.taos artappraisal.com.

R. B. Ravens A trader for many years, including 25 years on the Ranchos Plaza, R. B. Ravens is skilled at finding incredible period artwork. Here, you'll find Navajo rugs and pottery, all in the setting of an old home with raw pine floors and hand-sculpted adobe walls. 4146 NM 68 (across from the St. Francis Church Plaza), Ranchos de Taos. ℂ **800/758-7322** or 575/758-7322. www.rbravens.com.

Robert L. Parsons Fine Art ★★ This gallery set in the 1859 Ferdinand Maxwell home carries works of the early Taos and Santa Fe artists, including Nicolai Fechin, Joseph Sharp, and O.E. Berninghaus. Fine Pueblo pottery and antique Navajo blankets dress the space as well. 131 Bent St. ℂ **575/751-0159.** www.parsonsart.com.

Books

Moby Dickens Bookshop ★ This is Taos's best bookstore, with comfortable places to sit and read. You'll find children's and adults' collections of Southwest, Native American, and out-of-print books. 124A Bent St. ℂ **888/442-9980** or 575/758-3050. www.mobydickens.com.

Children

Twirl ★ ☺ As well as a fun place to shop, this is an adventure. A play structure, hobbit home, and fountain keep kids occupied while those of all ages hunt for musical instruments, toys, and clothing. 225 Camino de la Placita. ℂ **575/751-1402.** www.twirl house.com.

Crafts

Taos Artisans Cooperative Gallery This 10-member cooperative gallery, owned and operated by local artists, sells local handmade jewelry, wearables, clay work, glass, leather work, and garden sculpture. You'll always find an artist in the shop. 107C Bent St. ℂ **575/758-1558.** www.taosartisansgallery.com.

Taos Blue This gallery has fine Native American and contemporary handcrafts. 101A Bent St. ℂ **575/758-3561.** www.taosblue.com.

Weaving Southwest Contemporary tapestries by New Mexico artists, as well as one-of-a-kind rugs, blankets, and pillows, are the woven specialties found here. 106-A Paseo del Pueblo Norte. ℂ **575/758-0433.** www.weavingsouthwest.com.

Fashions

Artemisia ★ Advertising "one-of-a-kind artwear and accessories," this shop delivers, with wearable art in bold colors, all hand-woven or hand-sewn, all for women. 115 Bent St. ℂ **575/737-9800.** www.artemisiataos.com.

Overland Sheepskin Company ★ You can't miss the romantically weathered barn sitting on a meadow north of town. Inside, you'll find anything you can imagine in leather: coats, gloves, hats, slippers. The coats here are exquisite, from oversize ranch styles to tailored blazers in a variety of leathers from sheepskin to buffalo hide. NM 522 (a few miles north of town). ℂ **575/758-8820.** www.overland.com.

Food

Cid's Food Market   This store has the best selection of natural and gourmet foods in Taos. It's a great place to stock your picnic basket with such items as roasted chicken and barbecued brisket, or with lighter fare such as sushi, Purple Onion–brand sandwiches, black-bean salad, and fresh hummus and tabbouleh. 623 Paseo del Pueblo Norte. ✆ **575/758-1148.** www.cidsfoodmarket.com.

Furniture

At Home in Taos ★ 🎁   If you're looking to brighten your abode, head to this brilliant shop just off the plaza. You'll find colorful, handmade place mats and bowls as well as bags made from recycled materials. 117 S. Plaza. ✆ **575/751-1486.**

Country Furnishings of Taos   Here you'll find unique hand-painted folk-art furniture. The pieces are as individual as the styles of the local folk artists who make them. There are also home accessories, unusual gifts, clothing, and jewelry. 534 Paseo del Pueblo Norte. ✆ **575/758-4633.**

Mineral & Fossil Gallery ★   This fine showroom offers an adventure into an ancient world of stunning geodes and fossils, both decorative and functional. Look for jewelry and fetishes here as well. 110 S. Plaza. ✆ **575/737-5001.**

Nambé ★   This company made a name for itself producing serving platters, picture frames, and candlesticks from a metal alloy. Over the years, Nambé has expanded into production of crystal and wood designs, all lovely for the home. 109 N. Plaza. ✆ **575/758-8221.** www.nambe.com.

Gifts & Souvenirs

Chimayo Trading del Norte   Specializing in Navajo weavings, pueblo pottery, and other types of pottery, this is a fun spot to peruse on the Ranchos de Taos Plaza. Look especially for the Casas Grandes pottery from Mexico. 1 Ranchos de Taos Plaza. ✆ **575/758-0504.**

El Rincón Trading Post 🎁   This shop has a real trading-post feel. It's a wonderful place to find turquoise jewelry, whether you're looking for contemporary or antique. In the back of the store is a museum full of Native American and Western artifacts. 114 Kit Carson Rd. ✆ **575/758-9188.**

Jewelry

Artwares Contemporary Jewelry   The gallery owners here call their contemporary jewelry "a departure from the traditional." True to this slogan, each piece here offers a new twist on traditional Southwestern and Native American design, by artists such as Roberto Coin, John Hardy, Diane Malouf, Judith Ripka, and Alex Sepkus. 129 N. Plaza. ✆ **800/527-8850** or 575/758-8850. www.artwaresjewelry.com.

Musical Instruments

Taos Drum Company ★   Taos Drums has one of the largest selections of Native American log and hand drums in the world. In addition to drums, the showroom displays Southwestern and wrought-iron furniture, cowboy art, more than 60 styles of rawhide lampshades, and an array of other items as well. To find Taos Drum Company, look for the tepees and drums off NM 68. Ask about the tour that

THE MAJOR concert & performance HALLS

Taos Convention Center, 121 Civic Plaza Dr. (© **575/758-5792**). This convention space has an exhibit center where presentations, lectures, and concerts are held.

Taos Community Auditorium, Kit Carson Memorial State Park (© **575/758-4677**). A comfortable, small-town space, this community auditorium makes a nice venue for films, concerts, and lectures.

demonstrates the drum-making process. 5 miles south of Taos Plaza (off NM 68). © **800/424-3786** or 575/758-3796. www.taosdrums.com.

Pottery

Stephen Kilborn Pottery   Visiting this shop in town is a treat, but for a real adventure, go 17 miles south of Taos toward Santa Fe to Stephen Kilborn's studio in Pilar, open daily 10am to 5pm June to October (shorter hours off season). There, you can watch how the pottery is made. 136A Paseo del Pueblo Norte. © **800/853-2519** or 575/758-5760. www.kilbornpottery.com.

TAOS AFTER DARK

For a small town, Taos has its share of top entertainment. The resort atmosphere and the arts community attract performers, and the city enjoys annual programs in music and literary arts. State troupes, such as the New Mexico Repertory Theater and New Mexico Symphony Orchestra, make regular visits.

Many events are scheduled by the **Taos Center for the Arts (TCA),** 133 Paseo del Pueblo Norte (© **575/758-2052;** www.tcataos.org), at the Taos Community Auditorium. The TCA imports local, regional, and national performers in theater, dance, and concerts (Robert Mirabal, among others, has performed here). Also, look for a weekly film series offered year-round.

You can obtain information on current events in the *Taos News,* published every Thursday. The **Taos County Chamber of Commerce** (© **800/732-8267** or 575/751-8800; www.taoschamber.com) is also a good resource. Taos Visitors Center (© **575/758-3873**) publishes semiannual listings of *Taos County Events,* as well as the annual *Taos Country Vacation Guide* that also lists events and happenings around town.

The Performing Arts

Music from Angel Fire   This acclaimed program of chamber music begins in mid-August, with weekend concerts, and continues up to Labor Day. Based in the small resort community of Angel Fire (located about 21 miles east of Taos, off US 64), it also presents numerous concerts in Taos, Las Vegas, and Raton. P.O. Box 502, Angel Fire. © **888/377-3300** or 575/377-3233. www.musicfromangelfire.org.

Taos School of Music ★ Founded in 1963, this music summer school located at the Hotel St. Bernard in Taos Ski Valley offers excellent concerts by notable artists. From mid-June to mid-August there is an intensive 8-week study and performance program for advanced students of violin, viola, cello, and piano. The 8-week **Chamber Music Festival,** an important adjunct of the school, offers 16 concerts and seminars for the public; performances are given by pianist Robert McDonald, the Borromeo, St. Lawrence, and Brentano String Quartets, and the Young Artists International orchestra. Performances are held at the Taos Community Auditorium and the Hotel St. Bernard. P.O. Box 1879. ℂ **575/776-2388.** www.taosschoolofmusic.com. Tickets for chamber music concerts $20 for adults, $10 for children 16 and under.

The Club & Music Scene

Adobe Bar ★ A favorite gathering place for locals and visitors, the Adobe Bar is known for its live music series (nights vary) devoted to the eclectic talents of Taos musicians. The schedule offers a little of everything—classical, jazz, folk, flamenco, and world music. The Adobe Bar features a wide selection of international beers, wines by the glass, light New Mexican dining, desserts, and an espresso menu. Their margarita consistently wins the "Best of Taos" competition in *Taos News.* It's open daily 11:30am to 10pm. In the Historic Taos Inn, 125 Paseo del Pueblo Norte. ℂ **575/758-2233.** www.taosinn.com.

Alley Cantina ★ 📷 This bar that touts its location as the oldest house in Taos has become the hot late-night spot. The focus is on interaction, as well as TV sports, but there's also a cozy outdoor patio. Patrons playing shuffleboard, pool, chess, and backgammon listen to live music 4 to 5 nights a week. Burgers, fish and chips, and other informal dishes are served until 11pm. 121 Teresina Lane. ℂ **575/758-2121.** www.alleycantina.com. Cover for live music only.

Anaconda Bar ★★ Set in the ecoresort El Monte Sagrado, this is Taos's most happening nightspot, with live entertainment—jazz, blues, Native American flute, or country—playing Thursday through Saturday. An anaconda sculpture snaking across the ceiling and an 11,000-gallon fish tank set the contemporary tone of the place, where a variety of the hotel's signature dishes are served. In the El Monte Sagrado hotel, 317 Kit Carson Rd. ℂ **575/758-3502.** www.elmontesagrado.com.

Caffe Tazza ★ This cozy three-room cafe, with a summer patio, attracts local community groups, artists, performers, and poets. Plays, films, comedy, and musical performances are given here on weekends (and some weeknights in summer). You can read one of the assorted periodicals available (including the *New York Times*) while sipping a cappuccino or *café Mexicano* (espresso with steamed milk and Mexican chocolate), made from organic coffee beans. The food—soups and sandwiches—is quite good. Pastries, which are imported from many bakeries around the region, are almost as big a draw here as the Taos Cow ice cream. Choose from 15 flavors. 122 Kit Carson Rd. ℂ **575/758-8706.**

Sagebrush Inn ★ This is a real hot spot for locals. The atmosphere is Old West, with a rustic wooden dance floor and plenty of rowdiness. Live country or rock music generally plays Thursdays to Saturdays from 8:30 to 11:30pm. Paseo del Pueblo Sur (P.O. Box 557). ℂ **575/758-2254.**

A SCENIC DRIVE: THE ENCHANTED CIRCLE

If you're in the mood to explore, take this 90-mile loop north of Taos, through the old Hispanic villages of Arroyo Hondo and Questa, into a pass that the Apaches, Kiowas, and Comanches once used to cross the mountains to trade with the Taos Indians. You'll come to the Wild West mining town of Red River, pass through the expansive Moreno Valley, and travel along the base of some of New Mexico's tallest peaks. Then you'll skim the shores of a high mountain lake at Eagle Nest, pass through the resort village of Angel Fire, and head back to Taos along the meandering Rio Fernando de Taos. Although one can drive the entire loop in 2 hours from Taos, most folks prefer to take a full day, and many take several days.

Arroyo Hondo

Traveling north from Taos via NM 522, it's a 9-mile drive to this village, the remains of an 1815 land grant along the Rio Hondo. Along the dirt roads that lead off NM 522, you may find a windowless *morada* or two, marked by plain crosses in front—places of worship for the still-active Penitentes, a religious order known for self-flagellation. This is also the turnoff point for trips to the Rio Grande Box, an awesome 1-day, 17-mile white-water run for which you can book trips in Santa Fe, Taos, Red River, and Angel Fire. (See the "Outdoor Activities" sections in chapter 7 and "More Outdoor Activities," earlier in this chapter, for booking agents in Santa Fe and Taos, respectively.)

Arroyo Hondo was also the site of the New Buffalo commune in the 1960s. Hippies flocked here, looking to escape the mores of modern society. Over the years, the commune members have dispersed throughout northern New Mexico, bringing an interesting creative element to the food, architecture, and philosophy of the state. En route north, the highway passes near **San Cristobal,** where a side road turns off to the **D. H. Lawrence Ranch** (see "More Attractions," earlier in this chapter) and **Lama,** site of an isolated spiritual retreat.

Questa

Next, NM 522 passes through Questa, most of whose residents are employed at a molybdenum mine about 5 miles east of town. Mining molybdenum (an ingredient in lightbulbs, television tubes, and missile systems) in the area has not been without controversy. The process has raked across hillsides along the Red River, and though the mine's owner treats the water it uses before returning it to the river, studies show that it has adversely affected the fish life. Still, the mine is a major employer in the area, and locals are grateful for the income it generates.

If you turn west off NM 522 onto NM 378 about 3 miles north of Questa, you'll travel 8 miles on a paved road to the Bureau of Land Management–administered **Wild Rivers Recreation Area ★★** (𝒞 575/586-1150; www.blm.gov/nm). Here, where the Red River enters the gorge, you'll find 22 miles of trails, some suited for biking and some for hiking, a few trails traveling 800 feet down into the gorge to the banks of the Rio Grande. Forty-eight miles of the Rio Grande, which extend south from the Colorado border, are protected under the national Wild and Scenic River Act of 1968. Information on geology and wildlife, as well as hikers' trail maps, can

Taos Area (Including Enchanted Circle)

To Alamosa

Antonito

Area of detail

Santa Fe ★ • Taos 25

Albuquerque

NEW MEXICO

25

40 40

10

To Colorado Springs

159

COLORADO

NEW MEXICO

Costilla

Valle Vidal

196

0   5 mi
0   5 km

8

TAOS | A Scenic Drive: The Enchanted Circle

Costilla Lake

522

Latir Lakes

Rio Grande

378

D.H. Lawrence Ranch **2**
Picuris Pueblo **3**
Orilla Verde Recreation Area **1**
Vietnam Veterans Memorial
   State Park **4**

285

Tres Piedras

To Farmington and Chama

64

Questa

Wild Rivers
Recreation Area

522

CARSON
NATIONAL
FOREST

2
San Cristobal

38

Red River

578

Red River Ski

Elizabethtown

150

Taos Ski Valley

To Raton

Eagle Nest

CRISTO

DE

Arroyo
Hondo

577

Valdez

Arroyo
Seco

Eagle Nest Lake

Taos Airport

Taos

4

Angel Fire

Ranchos
de Taos

64

Angel Fire
Ski Resort

567

Talpa

285

68

Fort Burgwin
Research Center

434

SANGRE

Ojo Caliente
Hot Springs

Rio Grande

1
Pilar

518

Embudo

75

Vadito

Dixon

3

Peñasco

518

Tres Ritos

68

Las Trampas

Trampas
Church

76

Sipapu
Ski Area

To Santa Fe
& Albuquerque

Truchas

Chimayo

CARSON
NATIONAL
FOREST

To Las Vegas, NM

Airport ✈
Church ♱
Ski Area 🎿
Enchanted
Circle

be obtained at the visitor center here. The stunning La Junta Trail (1.2 miles) is difficult, but travels into the canyon at the convergence of the Red River and Rio Grande. The Big Arsenic Springs Trail (1 mile) is moderate and offers a self-guided interpretive trail. Both are excellent ways to get down into the canyon.

The village of **Costilla,** near the Colorado border, is 20 miles north of Questa. This is the turnoff point for four-wheel-drive jaunts and hiking trips into **Valle Vidal,** a huge U.S. Forest Service–administered reserve with 42 miles of roads and many hiking trails. A day hike in this area can bring you sightings of hundreds of elk.

Red River

To continue on the Enchanted Circle loop, turn east at Questa onto NM 38 for a 12-mile climb to Red River, a rough-and-ready 1890s gold-mining town that has parlayed its Wild West ambience into a pleasant resort village that's especially popular with families from Texas and Oklahoma.

This community, at 8,750 feet, is a center for skiing, snowmobiling, fishing, hiking, off-road driving, horseback riding, mountain biking, river rafting, and other outdoor pursuits. Frontier-style celebrations, honky-tonk entertainment, and even staged shootouts on Main Street are held throughout the year.

Though it can be a charming and fun town, Red River's food and accommodations are mediocre at best. Its patrons are down-home folks, happy with a bed and a diner-style meal. If you decide to stay, try the **Lodge at Red River,** 400 E. Main St. (© **800/915-6343** or 575/754-6280; www.lodgeatredriver.com), in the center of town. It offers hotel rooms ranging in price from $84 to $225. Knotty pine throughout, the accommodations are clean and comfortable. Downstairs, **Texas Reds Steak House** ★ serves steaks, burgers, and chicken dishes in a country-diner atmosphere. It's open in summer and winter daily from 4:30 to 9pm. During the shoulder seasons in spring and fall, it's open on Friday and Saturday nights.

If you're passing through and want a tasty meal, **Mountain Treasures** ★, 121 E. Main St. (© **575/754-2700**), a gallery, bistro, and espresso bar, offers excellent sandwiches. Go straight for the muffulettas or "muffys," Italian sandwiches made popular in New Orleans. Salami, turkey, provolone, cheddar, and olive spread are set within homemade Sicilian round bread and heated until the outside is crusty, the inside gooey rich. For dessert try the Czech pastry *kolache* in a variety of fruits, including peach and cherry. Summer and winter ski season the cafe is open daily 6am to 8pm, and other times Monday to Saturday 7am to 2pm.

The **Red River Chamber of Commerce,** P.O. Box 870, Red River, NM 87558 (© **800/348-6444** or 575/754-2366; www.redrivernewmexico.com), lists more than 40 accommodations, including lodges and condominiums. Some are open winters or summers only.

Eagle Nest

About 16 miles southeast of Red River, on the other side of 9,850-foot Bobcat Pass, is the village of Eagle Nest, resting on the shore of Eagle Nest Lake in the Moreno Valley. Gold was mined in this area as early as 1866, starting in what is now the ghost town of **Elizabethtown** about 5 miles north; Eagle Nest itself (pop. 200) wasn't incorporated until 1976. The 4-square-mile **Eagle Nest Lake State Park** (© **888/667-2757** or 575/377-1594; www.emnrd.state.nm.us) stretches out below the village. Currently facilities include restrooms, a boat ramp, and visitor center. The lake is considered one of the top trout producers in the United States and attracts ice fishermen in winter as well as summer anglers. It's too cold for swimming, but sailboaters and windsurfers ply the waters.

One of New Mexico's more atmospheric country bars, the **Laguna Vista Saloon,** resides here, on US 64 at the center of Eagle Nest (© **800/821-2093** or 575/377-6522; www.lagunavistalodge.com).

If you're heading to Cimarron or Denver, proceed east on US 64 from Eagle Nest. But if you're circling back to Taos, continue southwest on NM 38 and US 64 to Agua Fría and Angel Fire.

Shortly before the Agua Fría junction, you'll see the **Vietnam Veterans Memorial State Park,** CR B-4, Angel Fire (© **575/377-6900;** www.angelfirememorial. com). It's a stunning structure with curved white walls soaring high against the backdrop of the Sangre de Cristo Range. Consisting of a chapel and an underground visitor center, it was built by Dr. Victor Westphall in memory of his son, David, a marine lieutenant killed in Vietnam in 1968. The 6,000-square-foot memorial houses exhibits, videos, and memorabilia. It also has a changing gallery of photographs of Vietnam veterans who lost their lives in the Southeast Asian war, but no photo is as poignant as this inscription written by young David Westphall, a promising poet:

> *Greed plowed cities desolate.*
> *Lusts ran snorting through the streets.*
> *Pride reared up to desecrate*
> *Shrines, and there were no retreats.*
> *So man learned to shed the tears*
> *With which he measures out his years.*

Angel Fire

If you like the clean efficiency of a resort complex, you may want to plan a night or two here—at any time of year. Angel Fire is approximately 150 miles north of Albuquerque and 21 miles east of Taos. Opened in the late 1960s, this resort offers a hotel, condominiums, and cabins. Winter is the biggest season. This medium-size beginner and intermediate mountain is an excellent place for families to roam about (see "Skiing," earlier in this chapter). Two high-speed quad lifts zip skiers to the top quickly, while allowing them a long ski down. The views of the Moreno Valley are awe inspiring. Fourteen miles of Nordic trail traverse the top of the mountain, and snow mobile tours are also available here.

During spring, summer, and fall, **Angel Fire Resort ★** offers golf, tennis, hiking, mountain biking (you can take your bike up on the quad lift), fly-fishing, river rafting, and horseback riding. There are other fun family activities, such as a video arcade, a miniature golf course, theater performances, and, throughout the year, a variety of festivals, including a hot-air balloon festival, Winterfest, and concerts of both classical and popular music.

The unofficial community center is the **Angel Fire Resort,** 10 Miller Lane (P.O. Box 130), Angel Fire, NM 87710 (© **800/633-7463** or 575/377-6401; www.angel fireresort.com), a 155-unit hotel with spacious, comfortable rooms, some with fireplaces and some with balconies. The resort is in the process of remodeling, so be sure to request one of its updated rooms. Rates range from $92 to $200.

If you'd like a good meal while in the area, stop in at the **Roasted Clove ★**, 48 N. Angel Fire Rd. (© **575/377-0636;** www.roastedclove.com), a fine-dining restaurant that serves contemporary American cuisine. Your best bet here is the filet-mignon tacos served with fresh guacamole, chile sauce, and lime crema. It's open during ski season and in summer Monday to Wednesday, Thursday, and Sunday from 5 to 8:30pm, and Friday to Saturday 5 to 9pm.

For more information on the Moreno Valley, including full accommodations listings, contact the **Angel Fire Chamber of Commerce,** P.O. Box 547, Angel Fire, NM 87710 (© **800/446-8117** or 575/377-6661; fax 575/377-3034; www.angel-firechamber.org).

A fascinating adventure you may want to try here is a 1-hour, 1-day, or overnight horseback trip with **Roadrunner Tours,** P.O. Box 274, Angel Fire, NM 87710 (© **575/377-6416;** www.rtours.com). One-and-a-half-hour rides run year-round for $70, but if you'd like a little more adventure, try an overnight. In winter, Roadrunner offers sleigh rides as well. Call for prices.

NORTHWESTERN NEW MEXICO

xotic adventure awaits you in New Mexico's "Indian Country." At **Acoma,** you may peek through a hole in the wall of an ancient cemetery on a mesa hundreds of feet above the ground. It's there so that the spirits of some children who were taken from the pueblo can return. In **Grants** (pop. 8,806), a former uranium-mining boomtown, travel deep into a mine. In **Gallup** (pop. 20,209), self-proclaimed "Indian capital of the world" and a mecca for silver jewelry shoppers, you can cruise along Route 66 and pick up some authentic "pawn." In **Farmington** (pop. 43,573), center of the fertile San Juan valley and gateway to the Four Corners region, you might sleep in a cave. And in **Chama** (pop. 1,199), ride on the Cumbres & Toltec Railroad—the longest and highest narrow-gauge steam railroad in the country.

Each is an adventure in its own right, but what really makes them special is the people you'll encounter along the way. The biggest presence here is the Native American culture, old and new. Each time I travel to this area, I'm pleasantly surprised by the number of Pueblos, Navajos, and Apaches who inhabit it. Truly, they are the majority, and they set the pace and tone of the place. The Zuni, Acoma, and Laguna pueblos are each within a short distance of I-40. Acoma's "Sky City" has been continually occupied for more than 9 centuries. A huge chunk of the northwest is taken up by a part of the Navajo Reservation, the largest in America; and the Jicarilla Apache Reservation stretches 65 miles south from the Colorado border. All share their arts and crafts as well as their distinctive cultures with visitors, but they ask that their personal privacy and religious traditions be respected.

The past lives here, too. The Pueblo people believe that their ancestors' spirits still inhabit the ruins. **Chaco Culture National Historical Park,** with 12 major ruins and hundreds of smaller ones, represents the development of ancient Puebloan civilization, which reached its peak in

Northwestern New Mexico

the 11th century. **Aztec Ruins National Monument** and the nearby **Salmon Ruins** are similarly spectacular Pueblo preservations.

Two other national monuments in northwestern New Mexico also speak of the region's history. **El Morro** is a sandstone monolith known as Inscription Rock, where travelers and explorers documented their journeys for centuries; **El Malpais** is a volcanic badland with spectacular cinder cones, ice caves, and lava tubes.

NORTHWESTERN NEW MEXICO'S GREAT OUTDOORS

Like the rest of New Mexico, the northwestern region offers much in the way of outdoor recreation. If you're an outdoor enthusiast, you could spend months here.

BIKING   Mountain biking is permitted in parts of **Cíbola National Forest** (© 505/346-2650; www.fs.fed.us/r3/cibola), which, in this region, is on both sides of I-40 in the Grants to Gallup area. The national forest has six districts; call the number above for a referral to the district you want to visit. Some of the best biking is in Farmington, which is where the "Durangatangs" come during the winter to train and ride (Durango is a mountain-biking mecca). **Cottonwood Cycles,** 4370 E. Main in Farmington (© 505/326-0429; www.cottonwoodcycles.com), will give directions to trails. Cottonwood also rents bikes. Be sure to check out the **Lions Wilderness Park,** where you'll find its renowned **Road Apple Trail** on the north end of town. Bikers are also welcome at the **Bureau of Land Management Conservation Area** just off NM 117 near **El Malpais National Monument** (see "Acoma & Laguna Pueblos & Grants," below). At Chaco Canyon, check out the Wijiji Ruin trail, nice and easy but through beautiful country leading to an Anasazi ruin.

BOATING   If you're towing a boat, good places to stop are **Bluewater Lake State Park** (© 505/876-2391), a reservoir between Gallup and Grants, and **Navajo Lake State Park** (© 505/632-2278), about 25 miles east of Bloomfield. Both of these state parks have boat ramps, and Navajo Lake has several marinas (from which visitors can rent boats), picnic areas, a visitor center, and groceries for those who plan to make a day of it. To find information on New Mexico state parks, go to www.nmparks.com. **Zuni Lakes,** six bodies of water operated by the Zuni tribe, also offers opportunities for boating, although you're not allowed to use gasoline motors and you must obtain a permit (© 505/782-5851) before setting out.

FISHING   **Bluewater Lake State Park** is one of the best places to fish in the area. In fact, some people believe it has the highest catch rate of all New Mexico lakes. Look to catch trout here. A world-renowned fishing destination, the **San Juan River** ★★, just below Navajo Dam, made *Field & Stream's* 2008 list of top fishing spots in the Rocky Mountain West.

The scenery is outstanding and excellent guides in the area can help you find the choicest spots. **Navajo Lake State Park** (see "Boating," above) features about 150 miles of shoreline where fishers go to catch trout, bass, catfish, and pike. Navajo Lake is one of the largest lakes in New Mexico, and the park is very heavily trafficked, so if crowds aren't your thing, look for another fishing hole. Just 4 miles south of Kirtland is **Morgan Lake,** a quiet spot for largemouth bass and catfish. If you need fishing gear or want to hire a guide while in the area, contact **Abe's Motel and Fly Shop,** 1791 US 173, Navajo Dam (📞 **505/632-2194**). In Farmington, contact **Dad's Boat Parts and Backyard Boutique,** 210 E. Piñon St. (📞 **505/326-1870**), or **Zia Sporting Goods,** 500 E. Main (📞 **505/327-6004**; www.ziasporting goods.net).

GOLF In 2002, *Golf Digest* rated **Piñon Hills Golf Course,** 2101 Sunrise Pkwy., in Farmington (📞 **505/326-6066**; www.fmtn.org), the "best municipal course" in the United States. Also in Farmington is the **Civitan Golf Course,** 2100 N. Dustin (📞 **505/599-1194**). In Kirtland (approx. 7 miles west of Farmington), your golf option is **Riverview Golf Course,** on US 64 (📞 **505/598-0140**). In Grants, tee off at the 18-hole Coyote del Malpais Golf Course, at the base of Mount Taylor (📞 **505/285-5544**; www.coyotedelmalpaisgolfcourse.com).

HIKING This part of the state has some great hiking trails. You'll get to see ancient archaeological ruins in places such as Aztec Ruins and Chaco Canyon. In **Cíbola National Forest** (📞 **505/346-2650**; www.fs.fed.us/r3/cibola), the hike to the summit of Mount Taylor is excellent. In cooler months, but not winter, try hiking around **El Malpais National Monument** (📞 **505/783-4774**; www.nps.gov/elma). Two good hikes to try in El Malpais are the Zuni-Acoma Trail (this one is extremely taxing, so if you're not in shape, don't expect to make the 15-mile round-trip hike) and the Big Lava Tubes Trail (1 mile round-trip). My favorite hike in the region is to the top of **El Morro National Monument ★★** (📞 **505/285-4641**; www.nps.gov/elmo), which takes you to some Anasazi ruins. For quiet hiking on fairly level ground, head to **Bluewater Lake State Park** (📞 **505/876-2391**), **Red Rock Park** (📞 **505/722-3839**), or **Angel Peak Recreation Area** (📞 **505/599-8900**).

Sporting goods stores where you can get hiking gear include **REI-Albuquerque,** 1550 Mercantile Ave. NE, in Albuquerque (📞 **505/247-1191**; www.rei.com); **Frontier Sports,** 300 NE Aztec Blvd., in Aztec (📞 **505/334-0009**); and **Zia Sporting Goods,** 500 E. Main, in Farmington (📞 **505/327-6004**; www.ziasportinggoods.net).

RAFTING & KAYAKING The Chama River Canyon Wilderness begins just below El Vado Dam and runs past the Monastery of Christ in the Desert, usually an overnight trip, though some last up to 3 nights. Half- and one-day trips are also available on the lower portion. The river snakes through one of the most spectacular canyons I've ever seen, at one point rising 1,500 feet above your head. Rapids are mostly class II (on a scale from I to VI), but there are some big waves. Water is released on most weekends throughout the summer, so you can count on enough to make the trip exciting. Full-day trips are $115 for adults, $104 for children 6 to 11. Contact **Far Flung Adventures,** P.O. Box 707, El Prado, NM 87529 (📞 **800/359-2627** or 505/758-2628; www.farflung.com).

SKIING Some of the best cross-country skiing in the state is in the Chama area. Lots of broad bowls make the area a favorite of backcountry skiers as well as day-touring skiers. If you're up for an overnight adventure, contact **Southwest Nordic Center** (📞 **575/758-4761**; www.southwestnordiccenter.com), a company that rents yurts (Russian-style huts). Skiers trek into them, carrying their clothing and food in backpacks. Guide service is provided, or you can go in on your own, following directions on a map. The yurts are rented by the night and range from $70 to

$125 per group. Call for reservations as much in advance as possible as they do book up. The season is from mid-November to April, depending on snow conditions.

Some like to ski the old logging roads of Mount Taylor, which go all the way to the summit in **Cíbola National Forest** near Grants. Contact the ranger station in Grants at ✆ 505/287-8833 for more information. If you need to rent ski equipment, try **Chama Ski Service** (✆ 575/756-2492), which also offers snow reports and trail information.

SWIMMING Good swimming is available at **Navajo Lake State Park** (✆ 505/632-2278). Before diving in at other lakes in state parks, make sure swimming is permitted.

ACOMA & LAGUNA PUEBLOS & GRANTS

Your best base for exploring the Acoma and Laguna pueblos, as well as the El Malpais and El Morro National Monuments (see "El Malpais & El Morro National Monuments," below), is the town of Grants, 1¼ hours west of Albuquerque on I-40 west.

Acoma Pueblo ★★★

This spectacular "Sky City," a walled adobe village perched high atop a sheer rock mesa 365 feet above the 6,600-foot valley floor, is believed to have been inhabited at least since the 11th century—the longest continuously occupied community in the United States. Native legend claims that it has been inhabited since before the time of Christ. Both the pueblo and **San Estevan del Rey Mission** are National Historic Landmarks. In 2006, the Sky City Cultural Center and Haak'u Museum opened below Acoma, showcasing pottery, textiles, baskets, and other art from the tribe.

The Keresan-speaking Acoma (*Ack*-oo-mah) Pueblo boasts 6,005 inhabitants, but only about 50 people reside year-round on the 70-acre mesa top. They make their living from tourists who come to see the village, the large church containing examples of Spanish colonial art, and to purchase the pueblo's thin-walled white pottery with polychrome designs. Many Acomas work in Grants, 15 miles west of the pueblo; in Albuquerque; or for one of Acoma's business enterprises, such as Sky City Casino. Others are cattle ranchers and farm individual family gardens.

ESSENTIALS

GETTING THERE To reach Acoma from Grants, drive east 15 miles on I-40 to McCartys, and then south 13 miles on paved tribal roads to the visitor center. From Albuquerque, drive west 55 miles to the Acoma–Sky City exit (102), and then 15 miles southwest.

VISITOR INFORMATION For additional information, contact the **Sky City Cultural Center and Pueblo of Acoma** (✆ 888/747-0181; www.acomaskycity.org).

ADMISSION FEES & HOURS Admission to the village is $20 for adults, $15 for seniors (60 and over) and military, $10 for children 6 to 17, and free for children 5 and under, with discounts for students and Native American visitors. The charge to take still photographs is $10; be aware that there are other restrictions on photography. The tours run daily in the summer 9am to 5pm; daily in the spring, fall, and winter 10am to 3pm. The 1-hour-and-20-minute tours begin every 45 minutes, depending on the demand. The pueblo is closed to visitors on Easter weekend (some years), June 24 and 29, July 10 to 13, the first or second weekend in October, and the first Saturday in December. It's best to call ahead to make sure that the tour is available when you're visiting.

SEEING THE HIGHLIGHTS

You absolutely cannot wander freely around Acoma Pueblo, but you can start your tour at the 40,000-square-foot museum, which gives a good look into this culture, and peruse their gallery, offering art and crafts for sale. You can even have a meal at the Yaak'a Café. Then board the **tour bus,** which climbs through a rock garden of 50-foot sandstone monoliths and past precipitously dangling outhouses to the mesa's summit. There's no running water or electricity in this medieval-looking village; a small reservoir collects rainwater for most purposes, but drinking water is transported up from below. Wood-hole ladders and mica windows are prevalent among the 300-odd adobe structures. As you tour the village, you'll have many opportunities to buy pottery and other pueblo treasures. Pottery is expensive here, but you're not going to find it any cheaper anywhere else, and you'll be guaranteed that it's authentic if you buy it directly from the craftsperson. Along the way, be sure to sample some Indian fry bread topped with honey.

DANCES & CEREMONIES

The annual San Esteban del Rey feast day is September 2, when the pueblo's patron saint is honored with an 8am Mass, a procession, an afternoon corn dance, and an arts-and-crafts fair, which includes homemade games of chance and food stalls. A Governor's Feast is held annually in February, and 4 days of Christmas festivals run from December 25 to 28.

WHERE TO STAY & DINE

The **Sky City Hotel & Casino,** off I-40 at exit 102 (© **888/759-2489;** www.sky city.com) offers good basic accommodations with prices ranging from $79 to $129 double. The hotel has a restaurant, snack bar, night club, casino, and RV park.

AN ATTRACTION NEAR LAGUNA

Seboyeta, the oldest Hispanic community in western New Mexico, is 3½ miles north of Paguate, outside Laguna Pueblo. Still in view are ruins of adobe fortress walls built in the 1830s to protect the village from Navajo attack. The Mission of Our Lady of Sorrows was built in the 1830s, as was the nearby Shrine of Los Portales, built in a cave north of town.

Grants

If you've ever wondered what a "boom-and-bust town" looks like, come to Grants and find out. Grants first boomed with the coming of the railroad in the late 19th century, when 4,000 workers descended on the tiny farm town. When the railroad was completed, the workers left, and the town was bust. Next, Grants saw high times in the 1940s, growing carrots and sending them to the East Coast, but when packaging became more advanced, Grants lost its foothold in the market and busted again. Then came the 1950s, when a Navajo sheep rancher named Paddy Martinez discovered some strange yellow rocks near Haystack Mountain, northwest of town. The United States needed uranium, and his find led to the biggest boom in the area. By the early 1980s, demand for uranium had dropped, and so went the big wages and big spenders that the ore's popularity had produced. However, recent demand may just revive that industry once again. Today, the city on a segment of Route 66 is a jumping-off point for outdoor adventures.

The city is the seat of expansive Cíbola County, which stretches from the Arizona border nearly to Albuquerque. For more information, contact the **Grants/Cíbola County Chamber of Commerce** at 100 N. Iron Ave. (P.O. Box 297), Grants, NM 87020 (© **800/748-2142** or 505/287-4802; www.grants.org). It's in the same building as the New Mexico Mining Museum.

AN ATTRACTION IN GRANTS

New Mexico Mining Museum ★ ☺   This enormously interesting little museum primes you for the underground adventure of traveling into a re-creation of a mine shaft by showing you, on ground level, some geology, such as a fossilized dinosaur leg bone and a piece of Malpais lava. The world's only underground uranium-mining museum also gives you a sense of the context within which uranium was mined, through photos of the uranium-mining pioneers. Thus, the stage is set for your walk into a mine-shaft-like doorway adorned with rusty metal hats. An elevator takes you down into a spooky, low-lit place with stone walls. You begin in the station where uranium was loaded and unloaded and travel through the earth to places defined on wall plaques. While exploring, you get a sense of the dark and dirty work that mining can be. Those with claustrophobia may have to content themselves with visiting the exhibits above ground.

100 N. Iron Ave., at Santa Fe Ave. © 800/748-2142 or 505/287-4802. www.grants.org. Admission $3 adults, $2 seniors 60 and over and children 7–18; free for children 6 and under. Mon–Sat 9am–4pm.

Northwest New Mexico Visitor Center ★   East of Grants, this center sits within an expansive Pueblo-style building with a broad atrium showing off views of the Malpais. It offers fliers and films on the region's parks, forests, and Indian country. A real treat here is a series of suggested driving tours displayed with large color photos and free cards describing the routes. One tour takes visitors along the volcanoes of the Malpais, another through the abandoned logging communities of the Zuni Mountains Historical Loop, and another to the stunning geologic formations of the Cabezon and Rio Puerco area. A fun shelf of Southwest book titles is worth perusing.

1900 Santa Fe Ave. © **505/876-2783.** Free admission. Daily 9am–6pm during daylight saving time; 8am–5pm during Mountain Standard Time.

WHERE TO STAY IN GRANTS

Grants hotels are all on or near Route 66, with major properties near I-40 interchanges, and smaller or older motels nearer downtown.

Best Western Inn & Suites   Built in 1976 with remodeling ongoing, this hotel provides spacious rooms and good amenities, though you have to like to walk. Rooms are built around a huge quadrangle with an indoor pool in a sunny, plant-filled courtyard at the center. Request a room at one of the four corner entrances to avoid trudging down the long hallways. Also, request a room that faces outside rather than in toward the courtyard, where noise from the pool carries. Though not as up-to-date

To see local and regional art, stop by the Cíbola Arts Council's **Double Six Gallery ★**, 1001 W. Santa Fe Ave. (**℅ 505/287-7311**), a community space featuring photos, sculpture, and paintings. As well, the gallery houses the **Cíbola Art and Artifacts Museum**, which mounts shows related to regional history and invites artists to display related works. Recent exhibitions include a homestead show and railroading show.

as the Holiday Inn Express (see below), more amenities are provided here. Rooms are bright, with comfortable beds, and decorated in floral prints with Aztec trim. Bathrooms are medium-size and clean.

1501 E. Santa Fe Ave. (I-40 exit 85), Grants, NM 87020. **℅ 800/528-1234** or 505/287-7901. Fax 505/285-5751. www.bestwestern.com. 126 units. $75–$89 double. Rates include full breakfast. AE, DC, DISC, MC, V. Pets welcome. **Amenities:** Exercise room; Jacuzzi; indoor pool; men's and women's saunas. *In room:* A/C, TV, fridge (some rooms), hair dryer, Wi-Fi.

Holiday Inn Express ★   This new hotel opened in 2010 and provides quiet, well-conceived lodgings just off the interstate. Rooms are medium size and comfortable, with a desk and some with views out across meadows. Suites have fold-out couches, a good option for families. Bathrooms have granite countertops. Service here is courteous and efficient.

1512 E. Santa Fe Ave., Grants, NM 87020. **℅ 800/465-4329** or 505/287-9252. Fax 505/285-6998. www.hiexpress.com. 76 units. $139 double; $149–$179 suite. Rates include hot breakfast. AE, DC, DISC, MC, V. Pets welcome. **Amenities:** Jacuzzi; indoor pool. *In room:* A/C, TV, fridge, hair dryer, microwave, Wi-Fi.

CAMPING

Grants has three decent campgrounds with both tent and RV facilities. All range in price from $12 to $17 for tent camping and $15 to $20 for full hookups. **Blue Spruce RV Park** (**℅ 505/287-2560**) has 25 sites and 16 full hookups and is open year-round. It has enough trees to block the wind, some grass, and the roads and parking spaces are gravel, so dust is minimized. Cable television hookups are available, as are laundry facilities and a recreation room. To reach the park, take I-40 to exit 81 and then go ¼ mile south on NM 53.

WHERE TO DINE IN GRANTS

In general, you won't find much to eat at pueblos or national monuments, so you're best off looking for a restaurant in Grants.

El Cafecito 🎣 ☺ AMERICAN/MEXICAN   This real locals' spot serves up tasty food in a relaxed atmosphere. At mealtime, the brightly lit space with Saltillo tile floors bustles with families eating huevos rancheros (eggs over tortillas, smothered in chile) for breakfast, and enchiladas, stuffed *sopaipillas,* and burgers for lunch and dinner. All meals are large and inexpensive. Kids enjoy their own menu selections.

820 E. Santa Fe Ave. **℅ 505/285-6229.** Main courses $4–$8 breakfast, $6–$12 lunch or dinner. AE, DISC, MC, V. Mon–Fri 7am–9pm; Sat 7am–8pm.

La Ventana NEW MEXICAN/STEAKS   Grants locals come here for a special lunch or dinner out. With one large room that seats about 50 people, the restaurant has a Southwestern decor, with a two-horse sculpture and some dancing *katsinas*. Ironically, the place is dark, with windows blinded, despite its name, which means "the window," referring to the natural arch south of town. If you can catch Grants on a nonwindy day, opt for the patio. Service is friendly but varies in its efficiency. Recommended dishes include chicken fajita salad and prime rib. You'll also find sandwiches such as turkey and guacamole served on seven-grain bread. You can order from a full bar.

110½ Geis St., Hillcrest Center. ✆ **505/287-9393.** Reservations recommended. Main courses $5–$12 lunch, $8–$20 dinner. AE, DC, DISC, MC, V. Mon–Sat 11am–11pm.

Wow Diner ★ ☺ DINER/NEW MEXICAN   This new cafe offers tasty food in a flashy stainless steel and tile building on the west side of town in Milan. Comfortable booths lining the walls and a soda fountain with stools create a classic Route 66 diner ambience. You might start your day with French toast stuffed with cream cheese and strawberries. For lunch you could try pork carnitas—pulled pork that you fold into corn tortillas—with Spanish rice and beans on the side. A good dinner offering is pan-fried trout, with beurre blanc and almond sauce and a potato, rice, or fries. Finish with a hot chocolate brownie with ice cream. The restaurant also serves some Asian dishes, steaks, and salads. Chase it all down with beer or wine. Kids have their own menu options. The diner is located across the street from the Petro Truck Stop.

1300 Motel Dr., Milan. ✆ **505/287-3801.** Main courses $6–$22. AE, DISC, MC, V. Tues–Sun 6am–midnight.

EL MALPAIS & EL MORRO NATIONAL MONUMENTS

Northwestern New Mexico has two national monuments that are must-sees for anyone touring this region: El Malpais and El Morro. The region is also home to the Cíbola National Forest, with its stately Mount Taylor, visible from miles away and an excellent place to hike and backcountry ski.

El Malpais: Exploring the Badlands ★

Designated a national monument in 1987, El Malpais (Spanish for "badlands") is an outstanding example of the volcanic landscapes in the United States. El Malpais contains 115,000 acres of cinder cones, vast lava flows, hundreds of lava tubes, ice caves, sandstone cliffs, natural bridges and arches, Anasazi ruins, ancient Native American trails, and Spanish and Anglo homesteads.

ESSENTIALS

GETTING THERE   You can take one of two approaches to El Malpais, via NM 117 or NM 53. NM 117 exits I-40 7 miles east of Grants; NM 53 exits I-40 on the west end of Grants (it's right on the edge of town).

VISITOR INFORMATION   Admission to El Malpais is free (unless you're visiting the privately owned Ice Caves), and it's open to visitors year-round. The **visitor center,** off NM 53 between mile markers 63 and 64, is open daily from 8:30am to 4:30pm. Here you can pick up maps of the park, leaflets on specific trails, and other details about exploring the monument. For more information, contact **El Malpais**

National Monument, NPS, P.O. Box 939, Grants, NM 87020 (© **505/783-4774;** www.nps.gov/elma).

SEEING THE HIGHLIGHTS

From **Sandstone Bluffs Overlook** (10 miles south of I-40 off NM 117), many craters are visible in the lava flow, which extends for miles along the eastern flank of the Continental Divide. The most recent flows are only 1,000 years old; Native American legends tell of rivers of "fire rock." Seventeen miles south of I-40 is **La Ventana Natural Arch,** the largest accessible natural arch in New Mexico.

From NM 53, which exits I-40 just west of Grants, visitors have access to the **Zuni-Acoma Trail,** an ancient Pueblo trade route that crosses four major lava flows in a 7½-mile (one-way) hike. A printed trail guide is available. **El Calderon,** a forested area 20 miles south of I-40, is a trail head for exploring a cinder cone, lava tubes, and a bat cave. (**Warning:** Hikers should not enter the bat cave or otherwise disturb the bats.)

The largest of all Malpais cinder cones, **Bandera Crater** is on private property 25 miles south of I-40. The National Park Service has laid plans to absorb this commercial operation, known as **Ice Caves Resort** (© **888/423-2283** or 505/783-4303; www.icecaves.com). For a fee ($10 for adults and $5 for children 5–12), visitors hike up the crater or walk to the edge of an ice cave. It's open daily from 8am to 6pm in summer, and from 8am to 4pm in winter.

Perhaps the most fascinating phenomenon of El Malpais is the lava tubes, formed when the outer surface of a lava flow cooled and solidified. When the lava river drained, tunnel-like caves were left. Ice caves within some of the tubes have delicate ice-crystal ceilings, ice stalactites, and floors like ice rinks.

HIKING & CAMPING

El Malpais has several hiking trails, including the above-mentioned Zuni-Acoma Trail. Most are marked with rock cairns; some are dirt trails. The best times to hike this area are during spring and fall, when it's not too hot. You're pretty much on your own when you explore this area, so prepare accordingly. Carry plenty of water with you; do not drink surface water. Carrying first-aid gear is always a good idea, as the lava rocks can be extremely sharp and inflict nasty cuts. Never go into a cave alone. The park service advises wearing hard hats, boots, protective clothing, and gloves, and carrying three sources of light when entering lava tubes. The weather can change suddenly, so be prepared; if lightning is around, move off the lava as quickly as possible.

Primitive camping is allowed in the park, but you must first obtain a free backcountry permit from the visitor center.

El Morro National Monument ★★

Travelers who like to look history straight in the eye are fascinated by "Inscription Rock," 43 miles west of Grants along NM 53. Looming up out of the sand and sagebrush is a bluff 200 feet high, holding some of the most captivating messages in North America. Its sandstone face displays a written record of the many who inhabited and traveled through this land, beginning with the ancestral Puebloans, who lived atop the formation around 1200. Carved with steel points are the signatures and comments of almost every explorer, conquistador, missionary, army officer, surveyor, and pioneer emigrant who passed this way between 1605, when Gov. Don Juan de Oñate carved the first inscription, and 1906, when it was preserved by the National Park Service. Oñate's inscription, dated April 16, 1605, was perhaps the first graffiti any European left in America.

A paved walkway makes it easy to walk to the writings, and a stone stairway leads up to other treasures. One entry reads: "Year of 1716 on the 26th of August passed by here Don Feliz Martinez, Governor and Captain General of this realm to the reduction and conquest of the Moqui." Confident of success as he was, Martinez actually got nowhere with any "conquest of the Moqui," or Hopi, peoples. After a 2-month battle, they chased him back to Santa Fe.

Another special group to pass by this way was the U.S. Camel Corps, trekking past on their way from Texas to California in 1857. The camels worked out fine in mountains and deserts, outlasting horses and mules 10 to 1, but the Civil War ended the experiment. When Peachy Breckinridge, fresh out of the Virginia Military Academy, came by with 25 camels, he noted the fact on the stone here.

El Morro was at one time as famous as the Blarney Stone of Ireland: Everybody had to stop by and make a mark. But when the Santa Fe Railroad was laid 25 miles to the north, El Morro was no longer on the main route to California, and from the 1870s, the tradition began to die out.

If you like to hike, be sure to take the full loop to the top of Inscription Rock. It's a spectacular trip that takes you along the rim of this mesa—offering 360-degree views—culminating in an up-close look at Ancestral Puebloan ruins, which occupy an area 200 by 300 feet. Inscription Rock's Zuni name, Atsinna, suggests that carving one's name here is a very old custom indeed: the word means "writing on rock."

ESSENTIALS

GETTING THERE   El Morro is 43 miles west of Grants on NM 53.

VISITOR INFORMATION   For information, contact **El Morro National Monument,** HC61, Box 43, Ramah, NM 87321-9603 (© **505/783-4226;** www.nps.gov/elmo). Admission to El Morro is $3 per person 16 and older. Self-guided trail booklets are available at the visitor center (turn off NM 53 at the El Morro sign and travel approximately ½ mile), open year-round from 9am to 5pm. Trails are also open year-round; check with the **visitor center** for hours. A **museum** at the visitor center features exhibits on the 700 years of human activity at El Morro. A 15-minute video gives a good introduction to the park. Also within the visitor center is a **bookstore** where you can pick up souvenirs and informational books. It takes approximately 2 hours to visit the museum and hike the trails. The park is closed on Christmas and New Year's Day.

CAMPING & LODGING

Though it isn't necessary to camp here in order to see most of the park, a nine-site campground at El Morro is open year-round, with a fee of $10 per night charged from approximately April to November. No supplies are available within the park, so if you're planning on spending a night or two, be sure to arrive well equipped.

One nearby private enterprise, **El Morro RV Park, Cabins & Cafe,** HC 61, Box 44, Ramah, NM 87321 (© **505/783-4612;** www.elmorro-nm.com), has cabins, RV and tent camping, and a cafe (see below). The cabins are well appointed, and the baths clean.

For a unique place to stay, check out **Cimarron Rose Bed & Breakfast ★★**, 30 miles southwest of Grants on NM 53 (© **800/856-5776;** www.cimarronrose. com). This ecofriendly inn offers three suites, a good place for families or a romantic getaway. The atmospheric country lodgings range in size from the Cimarron, with a 1930s mountain cabin feel, to the Zuni Mountain, with two cozy bedrooms and a living room with a wood-burning stove. All have full kitchens, with Mexican tile and generous food supplies in case you don't want to eat out. Prices range from $125 to $195 per night.

DINING

A fun stop while exploring this part of New Mexico is the **Ancient Way Café ★**, near mile marker 46 on NM 53 (© **505/783-4612**). Amid knotty pine walls, comfortable booths, and local art, this place serves imaginative food using such treats as free-range chicken and eggs, hormone-free beef, and seasonal vegetables. For breakfast you might have huevos rancheros along with house-made muffins. Lunch or dinner might bring a burger or salad or a grilled veggie wrap with Anasazi beans. On a recent visit I had their special: chicken and vegetable pesto over chile/tomato linguine, which was excellent. Follow it up with a piece of apple piñon-nut chile pie. Prices for main courses range from $10 to $20. It's open Monday to Friday 9am to 5pm (closed Wed). Dinner is served Friday and Saturday 5 to 8pm by reservation only.

Exploring the Area: Cibola National Forest

Cíbola National Forest is actually a combination of parcels of land throughout the state that total more than 1.6 million acres. Elevation varies from 5,000 to 11,301 feet, and the forest includes the Datil, Gallinas, Bear, Manzano, Sandia, San Mateo, and Zuni mountains.

Two major pieces of the forest flank I-40 on either side of Grants, near the pueblos and monuments described above. To the northeast of Grants, NM 547 leads some 20 miles into the San Mateo Mountains. The range's high point, and the highest point in the forest, 11,300-foot Mount Taylor, is home of the annual Mount Taylor Winter Quadrathlon in February. The route passes two campgrounds: Lobo Canyon and Coal Mine Canyon. Hiking and enjoying magnificent scenery and wildlife are popular in summer, cross-country skiing in winter.

JUST THE FACTS For more information about this section of Cíbola National Forest, contact the **Mount Taylor Ranger District,** 1800 Lobo Canyon Rd., Grants, NM 87020 (© **505/346-2650**). For general information about all six districts of the National Forest, contact **Cíbola National Forest,** 2113 Osuna Rd. NE, Suite A, Albuquerque, NM 87113-1001 (© **505/346-3900;** www.fs.fed.us/r3/cibola).

A modern road stop on I-40 heading west, 17 miles before Gallup, is the **Pilot Travel Center** (© **505/722-6655**). This is my idea of what a space station would be like. Not only can you get gas here, you also can also fill up at a Subway restaurant. There's also a restaurant with a salad bar and hot food bar. The center has plenty of pay phones, clean bathrooms, a post office, and a video arcade.

GALLUP: GATEWAY TO INDIAN COUNTRY ★

For me, **Gallup** has always been a mysterious place, home to many Native Americans, with dust left from its Wild West days, and with an unmistakable Route 66 architectural presence; it just doesn't seem to exist in this era. The best way to get a sense of the place is by walking around downtown, wandering through the trading posts and pawnshops and by the historic buildings. In doing so, you'll probably encounter many locals and get a real feel for this "Heart of Indian Country."

Gallup began as a town when the railroad from Arizona reached this spot in 1881. At that time, the town consisted of a stagecoach stop and a saloon, the Blue Goose. Within 2 years, coal mining had made the town boom, and some 22 saloons (including the Bucket of Blood) and an opera house filled the town, most of which was inhabited by immigrants from mining areas in eastern Europe, England, Wales, Germany, and Italy.

When the popularity of the railroads declined, Gallup turned briefly to the movie business as its boom ticket. The area's red-rock canyons and lonely desert were perfect for Westerns of the era, such as *Big Carnival,* with Kirk Douglas; *Four Faces West,* with Joel McCrea; and *The Bad Man,* starring Wallace Beery, Lionel Barrymore, and Ronald Reagan. These stars and many others stayed in a Route 66 hotel built by R. E. Griffith in 1937. Today, the El Rancho Hotel is one of Gallup's most notable landmarks and worth strolling through (see "Where to Stay in Gallup," and "Where to Dine in Gallup," below). Gallup now relies on trade and tourism, due to its central location within the Navajo Reservation and the Zuni lands, as well as its proximity to the ancient ruins at Chaco.

Gallup's most notable special event is the **Inter-Tribal Indian Ceremonial** held every August. Native Americans converge on the town for a parade, dances, and an all-Indian rodeo east of town, at Red Rock State Park. It's a busy time in Gallup, so make reservations far in advance. If you're not in town for the Ceremonial, try visiting on a Saturday, when many Native Americans come to town to trade. Best of all on this day is the **flea market,** north of town just off US 491. Here you can sample fry bread, Zuni bread, and Acoma bread, eat real mutton stew, and shop for anything from jewelry to underwear. After the flea market, most Gallup-area residents, native and nonnative alike, go to Earl's (see "Where to Dine in Gallup," below) to eat.

Essentials

GETTING THERE   From Albuquerque, take I-40 west (2½ hr.). From Farmington, take US 64 west to Shiprock, and then US 491 south (2½ hr.). From Flagstaff, Arizona, take I-40 east (3 hr.). Gallup is not served by any commercial airlines at this time.

VISITOR INFORMATION   The **Gallup–McKinley County Chamber of Commerce,** 103 W. US 66, Gallup, NM 87301 (© **800/380-4989** or 505/722-2228; www.thegallupchamber.com), is just south of the main I-40 interchange for downtown Gallup.

💬 FETISHES: gifts of power

According to Zuni lore, in the early years of human existence, the Sun sent down his two children to assist humans, who were under siege from earthly predators. The Sun's sons shot lightning bolts from their shields and destroyed the predators. For generations, Zunis, traveling across their lands in western New Mexico, have found stones shaped like particular animals. The Zunis believe the stones to be the remains of those long-lost predators, still containing their souls or last breaths.

In many shops in Santa Fe, you too can pick up a carved animal figure called a *fetish.* According to belief, the owner of the fetish is able to absorb the power of that creature. Many fetishes were long ago used for protection and might in the hunt. Today, a person might carry a bear for health and strength, or an eagle for keen perspective. A mole might be placed in a home's foundation for protection from elements underground, a frog buried with crops for fertility and rain, a ram carried in the purse for prosperity. For love, some locals recommend pairs of fetishes—often foxes or coyotes carved from a single piece of stone.

Many fetishes, arranged with bundles on top and attached with sinew, serve as an offering to the animal spirit that resides within the stone. Fetishes are still carved by many of the pueblos. A good fetish is not necessarily one that is meticulously carved. Some fetishes are barely carved at all, as the original shape of the stone already contains the form of the animal. When you have a sense of the quality and elegance available, decide which animal (and power) suits you best. Native Americans caution, however, that the fetish cannot be expected to impart an attribute you don't already possess. Instead, it will help elicit the power that already resides within you. A good source for fetishes is **Keshi,** 227 Don Gaspar Ave. (© **505/989-8728;** www.keshi.com). Expect to pay $25 to $50 or more for a good one.

What to See & Do

EXPLORING GALLUP

Gallup has 20 buildings that are either listed on or have been nominated to the National Register of Historic Places. Some hold trading posts worth visiting. A good place to start is at the **Santa Fe Railroad Depot,** which also houses the **Gallup Cultural Center ★**, at East 66 Avenue and Strong Street (© **505/863-4131**). Built in 1923 in modified Mission style, it has been renovated into a community transportation and cultural center, with a museum worth visiting, as well as a gift shop and diner. Note especially the exhibits on regional history and the Master's Exhibit of paintings, pottery, and basketry from area Native Americans (for more activities see "Sunset Dances," below). The center is open weekdays from 9am to 5pm, often with extended hours in the summer. Across the street, the **Drake Hotel** (later the Turquoise Club, but now vacant), built of blond brick in 1919, had the Prohibition-era reputation of being controlled by bootleggers, with wine running in the faucets in place of water.

The 1928 **White Cafe,** 100 W. 66 Ave., is an elaborate decorative brick structure that catered to the early auto tourist traffic. Now it's a jewelry store. Down the street, the **Eagle Café,** 220 W. 66 Ave. (© **505/722-3220**), open since 1920, serves diner food in an authentic atmosphere. A few doors down, **Richardson's Trading Company,** 222 W. 66 Ave. (© **505/722-4762;** www.richardsontrading.com), has been selling good Native American arts and crafts since 1913.

The **Rex Hotel,** 300 W. 66 Ave., constructed of locally quarried sandstone, was once known for its "ladies of the night." It's now the **Rex Museum** (© **505/863-1363**), a somewhat random display of items from the Gallup Historical Society Collection, but fun for history buffs. It's open daily but with unpredictable hours. Call before setting out.

Other architectural gems include the **Chief Theater,** 228 W. Coal Ave. This structure was built in 1920; in 1936, it was completely redesigned in Pueblo-Deco style, with zigzag relief and geometric form, by R. E. "Griff" Griffith (who also built the El Rancho Hotel), brother of Hollywood producer D. W. Griffith. Now this is **City Electric Shoe Shop** (© **505/863-5252;** www.cityelectricshoe.com), where Native Americans go to buy feathers, leather, and other goods to make ceremonial clothing. It's known to locals simply as City Electric, so called because it was the first shop in town to have an automated shoe-repair machine. It also has a good selection of moccasins and hats. Also visit the 1928 **El Morro Theater,** 207 W. Coal Ave., built in Spanish colonial revival style with Spanish baroque plaster carving and bright polychromatic painting; it's where locals come to see movies and dance performances.

GETTING OUTSIDE: A NEARBY PARK

Six miles east of downtown Gallup, **Red Rock Park,** NM 566 in Church Rock (© **505/722-3839,** or 505/722-3839 for campground; www.ci.gallup.nm.us/rrp/00182_redrock.html), has a natural amphitheater set against elegantly shaped red sandstone buttes. It includes an auditorium/convention center, a historical museum, a post office, a trading post, stables, and modern campgrounds.

The 8,000-seat arena is the site of numerous annual events, including the Inter-tribal Indian Ceremonial in mid-August. Red Rock Convention Center accommodates 600 for trade shows or concert performances.

A nature trail leads up into these stone monuments and makes for a nice break after hours on the road. See "Where to Stay in Gallup," below, for camping information. The park also has a playground, horseback riding trails, and a sports field.

The **Red Rock Museum** has displays on prehistoric Anasazi and modern Zuni, Hopi, and Navajo cultures, including an interesting collection of very intricate *katsinas*. A gallery features changing exhibits, often locally made crafts such as prayer and dancing fans, pottery, or weavings. It's open year-round Monday through Friday 8am to 4:30pm. There's a suggested donation of $2 for adults, $1 for seniors, and 50¢ for children.

Also at this site, in early December, is the **Red Rock Balloon Rally,** a high point on the sporting balloonist's calendar. For information, call the Gallup–McKinley County Chamber of Commerce (see "Visitor Information," above).

SHOPPING

Nowhere are the jewelry and crafts of Navajo, Zuni, and Hopi tribes less expensive than in Gallup. The most intriguing places to shop are the trading posts and pawnshops, which provide a surprising range of services for their largely Native American clientele and have little in common with the pawnshops of large U.S. cities.

Pawnbrokers here are essentially bankers, at least from the Navajo and Zuni viewpoint. Pawnshops provide safekeeping of valuable personal goods and make small-collateral loans. The trader will hold on to an item for months or even years before deeming it "dead" and putting it up for sale. Fewer than 5% of items ever go unredeemed, but over the years traders do accumulate a selection, so the shops are worth perusing.

Most shops are open Monday through Saturday from 9am to 5pm. For a look at everything from pawn jewelry to Pendleton robes and shawls to enamel and cast-iron kitchenware, visit **Ellis Tanner Trading Company** (© **505/863-4434;** www. etanner.com), Hwy. 602 Bypass, south from I-40 on NM 602 about 2 miles; it's at the corner of Nizhoni Boulevard. Also try **Perry Null-Tobe Turpen's Indian Trading Company,** 1710 S. Second St. (© **505/863-5249;** www.perrynulltrading. com), farther out on Second Street; it's a big free-standing brick building full of jewelry, rugs, *katsinas,* and pottery.

SUNSET DANCES ★

Every evening Memorial Day to Labor Day, dancers from a variety of area tribes sing, drum, and twirl in a stunning display of ritual from 7 to 8pm. The dances take place at the **Gallup Cultural Center** on East 66 Avenue and Strong Street (© **505/863-4131**). Admission to the center and dances is free.

Where to Stay in Gallup

Virtually every accommodation in Gallup is somewhere along Route 66, either near the I-40 interchanges or on the highway through downtown.

El Rancho Hotel ★ On the National Register of Historic Places, this hotel was built in 1937 by R. E. "Griff" Griffith, brother of movie mogul D. W. Griffith. It became the place for film companies to set up headquarters when filming here. Between the 1940s and 1960s, a who's who of Hollywood stayed here: Spencer Tracy, Katharine Hepburn, Burt Lancaster, Gene Autry, Lucille Ball, Jack Benny, Humphrey Bogart, James Cagney, Errol Flynn, Henry Fonda, the Marx Brothers—the list goes on and on.

Rooms differ and are named for the stars that stayed in them. Most are medium-size, with wagon-wheel headboards and dark, heavy pine furniture. The beds are comfortable. The bathrooms can be small, some with showers, others with tub/shower combos. All have lovely white hexagonal tiles. Many rooms have balconies. Two suites with kitchenettes are also available. My favorite rooms are on the ground floor, which is the quietest part of the hotel. Light sleepers should be aware that the train can be heard from rooms in the upper stories.

1000 E. 66 Ave., Gallup, NM 87301. © **800/543-6351** or 505/863-9311. Fax 505/722-5917. www. elranchohotel.com. 99 units. $82–$97 double; $138 suite. AE, DISC, MC, V. Pets welcome. **Amenities:** Restaurant (p. 262); lounge; outdoor pool (in summer); Wi-Fi (in lobby). *In room:* A/C, TV.

La Quinta ★ The challenge in Gallup is to find a quiet place to sleep. With busy train tracks running right through town, most accommodations stay noisy through the night. Sitting east of town, this is one of the quietest places I've found, but you'll have to reserve carefully. The trick here is to ask for a room on the side of the hotel that faces *away* from the tracks and you'll get a good night's sleep. Rooms are medium-size, with high ceilings and the calming green decor for which this chain is known. The rooms have comfortable beds and fairly spacious bathrooms. A hot breakfast adds to the appeal. On a recent visit I met a couple of professionals who work each month in Gallup and they said this is their choice of lodgings.

675 Scott Ave., Gallup, NM 87401. ⓒ **800/531-5900** or 505/327-4706. Fax 505/325-6583. www. laquinta.com. 106 units. $70–$100 double; $105–$125 suite. Rates include continental breakfast. AE, DISC, MC, V. **Amenities:** Outdoor pool. *In room:* A/C, TV, fridge upon request, hair dryer, Wi-Fi.

CAMPING

As in the rest of the state, the Gallup area offers plenty of places to pitch a tent or hook up your RV. **USA RV Park** (ⓒ **505/863-5021;** www.usarvpark.com) has 130 sites, 91 full hookups (cable TV costs extra), and cabins, as well as grocery and laundry facilities. Recreation facilities include arcade games, a seasonal heated swimming pool, and a playground. An outdoor dinner is served at an extra cost. Sites range from $21 for tents to $28 for full hookups. Cabins are $32. To reach the campground, take I-40 to the US 66/Business I-40 junction (exit 16); go 1 mile east on US 66/Business I-40.

Red Rock Park campground (ⓒ **505/722-3839**) has 106 sites—50 with no hookups and 56 with water and electricity. Tent sites are available. Sites range from $10 for tents to $20 for full hookups. The sites are right against the buttes, though in the spring they will surely be dusty because of little protection from the wind. Also accessible are a convenience store, picnic tables, and grills. For more information on Red Rock Park, see "Getting Outside: A Nearby Park," above.

Where to Dine in Gallup

Coal Street Pub ★ AMERICAN   In the center of downtown, this restaurant serves tasty food in a fun atmosphere full of Gallup memorabilia. Though the owners don't brew their own beer, they do a good job of creating a brewpub atmosphere. Hardwood floors and booths set the tone here along with ceiling fans and a curved bar at the back. Service is good. The big draw is the appetizers and sandwiches. You might start with fried zucchini strips or buffalo chicken wings. For a main course, half-pound burgers are popular, but the big winner is the Monte Cristo—ham, turkey, Swiss, and American cheese on bread, lightly battered and fried golden, served with raspberry preserves. At dinner, try the grilled chicken with a salad, sautéed veggies, and baked potato or fries. The pizzas are also good. For dessert, try the cheesecake. Beer and wine accompany the menu.

303 W. Coal Ave. ⓒ **505/722-0117.** www.coalstreetpub.com. Reservations accepted. Main courses $8–$17. AE, DISC, MC, V. Mon–Sat 11am–10pm.

The Coffee House ★ BAKED GOODS/SANDWICHES   This cafe in a historic building in the center of town offers a little big-city flair. Sparse decor with wood tables under an old copper ceiling is accented by local art shows. The espresso and cappuccino are delicious, as are the homemade cookies and muffins. For lunch or dinner, try the turkey and Swiss sandwich, the Waldorf chicken salad, or the chicken gyro. Wireless Internet is available.

203 W. Coal Ave. ⓒ **505/726-0291.** All menu items under $9. DISC, MC, V. Mon–Fri 7am–9:30pm; Sat 8am–3pm; closed Sun.

Earl's ★ ☺ AMERICAN/NEW MEXICAN   This is where the locals come to eat, particularly on weekends, en route to and from trading in Gallup. The place fills up with a variety of clientele, from college students to Navajo grandmothers. A Denny's-style diner, with comfortable booths and chairs, the restaurant allows Native Americans to sell their wares to you while you eat; however, you have the option of putting up a sign asking not to be disturbed. Often on weekends, vendors set up tables out front, so the whole place takes on a bustling bazaar atmosphere. And the food is good. I recommend the New Mexican dishes such as huevos rancheros, the enchilada plate, or the smothered grande burrito. Earl's offers a kids' menu and half-portion items for smaller appetites, as well as some salads and a "baked potato meal." Open since 1947, Earl's continues to please.

1400 E. 66 Ave. ② **505/863-4201.** Reservations accepted except Fri-Sat. Most menu items under $10. AE, MC, V. Mon-Sat 6am-9pm; Sun 7am-9pm.

El Rancho ★ 📷 ☺ AMERICAN/NEW MEXICAN   Set in the historic El Rancho Hotel (see above), this restaurant has fans all across the Southwest. They come to experience the Old West decor—with well-spaced, heavy wooden furniture and movie memorabilia on the walls—and the sense of the many movie stars who once ate here. The food is fine-diner-style, with dishes such as steak and eggs or hot cakes for breakfast, as well as regional delights such as *atole* (hot blue-corn cereal) or a breakfast taco. At lunch you can always count on a good burger here or select from a cast of sandwiches, such as the Doris Day (sirloin steak on French bread), or salads. At dinner, steaks are a big hit, as is the grilled salmon, both served with soup or salad, vegetable, and your choice of potato or rice. The New Mexican food is also good. Kids can select from the "little buckaroos" menu. A full bar is available.

In the El Rancho Hotel, 1000 E. 66 Ave. ② **800/543-6351** or 505/863-9311. www.historicelranchohotel.com. Reservations not accepted. Main courses $5-$12 breakfast, $8-$13 lunch, $9-$20 dinner. AE, DISC, MC, V. Daily 6:30am-10pm.

Jerry's Cafe 🍴 ☺ AMERICAN/NEW MEXICAN   This is where the locals go to eat New Mexican food. It's a narrow and cozy space with booths on both walls and dark-wood paneling. Usually it's packed with all manner of people, especially Native Americans, filling up on big plates of food smothered in chile sauces. You can't go wrong with any of the New Mexican dishes; I like the scrambled eggs with chile for breakfast. For lunch or dinner, try the flat enchiladas topped with an egg and served with a flour tortilla and *sopaipilla;* or the stuffed *sopaipilla,* with guacamole, beans, and beef, smothered in chile. Jerry's has a children's menu as well as burgers and basic sandwiches. Alcohol isn't served.

406 W. Coal Ave. ② **505/722-6775.** Reservations not accepted. Main courses $4-$7 breakfast, $8-$12 lunch and dinner. MC, V. Mon-Sat 8am-9pm.

ZUNI PUEBLO & THE NAVAJO RESERVATION

Zuni Pueblo

The largest of New Mexico's 19 pueblos, encompassing more than 600 square miles and home to over 12,000 people, Zuni still clings to its traditional language and culture, a great part of which includes art. It's estimated that 80% of its families are

Traditional Native American Bread Baking

While visiting the pueblos in New Mexico, you'll probably notice outdoor ovens (they look a bit like giant ant hills), known as *hornos,* which Native Americans have used to bake bread for hundreds of years. For Native Americans, making bread is a tradition that links them directly to their ancestors. Usually in the evening, the bread dough (made of white flour, lard, salt, yeast, and water) is made and kneaded, the loaves are shaped, and in the morning placed in the oven heated by a wood fire. They bake for about an hour. If you would like to try a traditional loaf, you can buy one at the Indian Pueblo Cultural Center in Albuquerque, at the Gallup Flea Market, and from vendors on the Zuni Reservation.

involved in creating art, most notably intricate stone inlay jewelry, carved stone animal fetishes, and *katsina* figures. Visitors to Zuni will encounter a place that's just beginning to welcome travelers, with a new roster of tours available. This is new to the pueblo, so be patient with the process. Tours include visits to the Middle Village, Zuni Mission, artists' studios, archaeological sites, as well as the experience of a Zuni meal. For details check with the Zuni Arts and Visitor Center (see below).

Zuni has a rich history. When the Spanish first arrived in the area, approximately 3,000 Zunis lived in six different villages, and they had occupied the region since at least the year 700. One of the main villages amid the high pink-and-gold sandstone formations of the area was **Hawikuh.** It was the first Southwestern village to encounter Europeans. In 1539, Fray Marcos de Niza, guided by Esteban the Moor (who had accompanied Cabeza de Baca in his earlier roaming of the area), came to New Mexico in search of the Seven Cities of Cíbola, which Baca had said were made of gold, silver, and precious stones. Esteban antagonized the inhabitants and was killed. De Niza was forced to retreat without really seeing the pueblo, although he described it in exaggerated terms on his return to Mexico, and the legend of the golden city was fueled.

The following year Coronado arrived at the village. Though the Zunis took up arms against him, he conquered the village easily, and the Zunis fled to **Towayalane** (Corn Mountain), a noble mile-long sandstone mesa near the present-day pueblo, as they would later do during the 1680 Pueblo Revolt.

At the time, the Zunis had a sophisticated civilization, with a relationship to the land and to each other that had sustained them for years. Today, the tribe continues efforts to preserve its cultural heritage. It has recovered valuable seed strains once used for dry farming, it's teaching the Zuni language in schools, and it's taking measures to preserve area wildlife that's critical to the Zuni faith.

The Zunis didn't fully accept the Christianity thrust upon them. Occasionally, they burned mission churches and killed priests. Though the Catholic mission, dedicated to Our Lady of Guadalupe, sits in the center of their village, clearly their primary religion is their own ancient one, and it's practiced most notably during the days of **Shalako,** an elaborate ceremony that takes place in late November or early December, reenacting the creation and migration of the Zuni people to Heptina, or the "Middle Place," which was destined to be their home.

ESSENTIALS

GETTING THERE   Zuni Pueblo is about 38 miles south of Gallup via NM 602 and NM 53.

VISITOR INFORMATION   For information, contact the **Zuni Arts and Visitor Center,** on 1239 NM 53 (© **505/782-7238;** www.zunitourism.com). This is the place to buy photography permits and inquire about pueblo tours and directions to sites. As at all Indian reservations, visitors are asked to respect tribal customs and individuals' privacy. No sketching or painting, photography or filming is allowed. Although the pueblo is never completely closed to outside visitors, certain areas may be off-limits during ceremonies, and no photography is allowed without a permit. At the website above you can download a brochure listing sites at the pueblo.

ADMISSION FEES & HOURS   Admission is free, and visitors are welcome daily from dawn to dusk.

SEEING THE HIGHLIGHTS

As you make your way around, you'll find a mix of buildings—modern ones, along with traditional adobes, and 100-year-old structures made from red carved sandstone. The **Old Zuni Mission** (Our Lady of Guadalupe Mission), on Old Mission Drive (© **505/782-7238**), was first built in 1629, then destroyed during the Pueblo Revolt, and rebuilt in 1699. It was renovated in 1966, but currently is in need of a major restoration. It's most famed for life-size murals of *katsinas* by Zuni Alex Seowtewa, which are now at the center of controversy over how to restore them. It's fronted by a picturesque cemetery. Contact the number above to see if a tour of the interior is available.

In addition, some Native American archaeological ruins on Zuni land date from the early 1200s, but you must obtain permission from the Visitor Center to see them. The **A:shiwi A:wan Museum and Heritage Center,** 1222 NM 53 (© **505/782-4403**), offers a glimpse into traditional Zuni culture. An exhibit under the auspices of the museum, "Echoes from the Past," set in a building in the heart of Zuni, presents artifacts from Hawikuh (on loan from the Smithsonian Institute). The main museum is open weekdays, year-round, from 9am to 5:30pm (same hours on Sat during the summer). Admission is free. Call first to be sure it is open and to ask for directions.

Today, Zuni tribal members are widely acclaimed for their jewelry, made from turquoise, shell, and jet, set in silver in intricate patterns called "needlepoint." The tribe also does fine beadwork, carving in shell and stone, and some pottery. Jewelry and other crafts are sold at **Turquoise Village,** on NM 53 (© **800/748-2405**). At this writing, it is open Monday to Saturday from 10:30am to 5pm. Another good option is the **Zuni Craftsman Co-op,** on NM 53 (© **888/926-1842** or 505/782-4521). At both shops, look especially for the hand-carved fetishes as well as the acclaimed needlepoint jewelry.

If you're planning your visit for late August, call ahead and find out if you're going to be around during the pueblo's annual fair and rodeo.

WHERE TO STAY IN ZUNI

Inn at Halona 🛏   Situated in the center of Zuni, this inn provides a peek into Zuni life. The inn itself fills two homes—one built in 1920, the other in 1940. I recommend the main house (built in 1920) as it's the brighter of the two and was remodeled in 1998. Both are filled with local art and decorated with handcrafted furniture. Most rooms are fairly small, and some rooms share bathrooms, so you'll want to reserve accordingly. All rooms have good linens and comfortably firm beds. My favorite, the Penthouse Room, is small but very sunny and quaint. Over a full and delicious breakfast served family-style in the dining room or out on the lovely patio, the innkeepers Roger Thomas and Elaine Dodson Thomas will delight you with stories of living at Zuni, where Elaine's Dutch family started the first trading post in 1903. Basic food is available in the trading post store.

23B Pia Mesa Rd. (P.O. Box 446), Zuni, NM 87327-0446. © **800/752-3278** or 505/782-4547. Fax 505/782-2155. www.halona.com. 8 units. $84 double. $10 for each extra person. Rates include full breakfast. MC, V. *In room:* No phone.

Navajo Indian Reservation

Navajos comprise the largest Native American tribe in the United States, with more than 298,215 members. Their reservation, known to them as the Navajo Nation, spreads across 26,000 square miles of Arizona, Utah, and New Mexico. The New Mexico portion, extending in a band 45 miles wide from just north of Gallup to the Colorado border, comprises only about 15% of the total area.

Until the 1920s, the Navajo Nation governed itself with a complex clan system. When oil was discovered on reservation land, the Navajos established a tribal government to handle the complexities of the 20th century. Today, the Navajo Tribal Council has 88 council delegates representing 110 regional chapters, some two dozen of which are in New Mexico. They meet at least four times a year as a full body in Window Rock, Arizona, capital of the Navajo Nation, near the New Mexico border, 24 miles northwest of Gallup.

Coal, oil, gas, and uranium earn much of the Navajo Nation's money, as does tourism, especially on the Arizona side of the border, which contains or abuts Grand Canyon National Park, Petrified Forest National Park, Canyon de Chelly National Monuments, Wupatki National Monuments, Navajo National Monument, and Monument Valley Navajo Tribal Park; and in Utah, Glen Canyon National Recreation Area, Rainbow Bridge National Monuments, Hovenweep National Monument, and Four Corners Monument.

The Navajos, like their linguistic cousins the Apaches, belong to the large family of Athapaskan Indians found across Alaska and northwestern Canada and in parts of the Northern California coast. They are believed to have migrated to the Southwest around the 14th century. In 1864, after nearly 2 decades of conflict with the U.S. Army, the entire tribe was rounded up and forced into internment at an agricultural colony near Fort Sumner, New Mexico—an event still recalled as "the Long March." Four years of near starvation later, the experiment was declared a failure, and the Navajos returned to their homeland.

During World War II, 320 Navajo young men served in the U.S. Marine Corps as communications specialists in the Pacific. The code they created, 437 terms based on the extremely complex Navajo language, was never cracked by the Japanese. Among those heroes was artist Carl Gorman, coordinator of the Navajo Medicine Man Organization and father of internationally famed painter R. C. Gorman. The 2002 movie *Windtalkers,* starring Nicholas Cage, was based on their story.

Although Navajos express themselves artistically in all media, they are best known for their work in silversmithing, sand painting, basketry, and weaving. Distinctive styles of hand-woven rugs from Two Grey Hills, Ganado, and Crystal are known worldwide.

ESSENTIALS

GETTING THERE   From Gallup, US 491 goes directly through the Navajo Indian Reservation up to Shiprock. From there you can head over to Farmington (see "Farmington & Environs," below) on US 64. *Warning:* US 491, previously labeled US 666, running between Gallup and Shiprock, has been called America's "most dangerous highway" by *USA Today*. In hopes of changing the fate of what many called the "Devil's Highway," the name was changed to a more benign set of numbers. Even with the new designation, you'll want to drive carefully!

VISITOR INFORMATION   For information before your trip, contact the **Navajo Tourism Department,** P.O. Box 663, Window Rock, AZ 86515 (Ⓒ **928/810-8501;** www.discovernavajo.com).

WHAT TO SEE & DO

Attractions in Window Rock, Arizona, include the Navajo Nation Council Chambers; the Navajo Nation Arts and Crafts Enterprise; the Navajo Museum, Library, and Visitors Center; and Window Rock Tribal Park, containing the natural red-rock arch after which the community is named.

Nearby attractions include **Hubbell Trading Post National Historic Site** (Ⓒ **928/755-3475;** www.nps.gov/hutr), on Arizona 264, ½ mile west of AZ 191, at Ganado, 30 miles west of Window Rock, and **Canyon de Chelly National Monument** (Ⓒ **928/674-5500;** www.nps.gov/cach), 39 miles north of Ganado on U.S. 191, at Chinle.

In early September, the annual 5-day **Navajo Nation Fair** (Ⓒ **928/871-6647;** www.navajonationfair.com) attracts more than 100,000 people to Window Rock for a huge rodeo, parade, carnival, Miss Navajo Nation contest, arts-and-crafts shows, intertribal powwow, concerts, country dancing, and agricultural exhibits. It's the country's largest Native American fair. A smaller but older and more traditional annual tribal fair is the early October **Northern Navajo Nation Fair** (Ⓒ **505/368-3727;** www.shiprocknavajofair.org), held 90 miles north of Gallup in the town of Shiprock.

WHERE TO STAY & DINE ON THE NAVAJO INDIAN RESERVATION

The place to stay on the reservation is the **Quality Inn Navajo Nation Capital,** 48 W. Hwy. 264 (P.O. Box 2340), Window Rock, AZ 86515 (Ⓒ **928/871-4108**).

Five Hunnerd, Six Hunnerd, Sold!

The **Crownpoint Rug Weavers Association** ★ holds 12 public auctions a year, normally on Friday evening, about 5 weeks apart. Travelers come from all over the world to sit in the stuffy Crownpoint Elementary School gymnasium (drive 20 miles north of I-40 on NM 371, turn west on Indian Rte. 9, and drive ½ mile) and bid on lovely rugs made throughout the Southwest. Prices are good, and the bidding can get exciting. Indian tacos and sodas are offered for sale outside. For more information, call Ⓒ **505/786-7386;** www.crownpointrugauction.com.

The modern guest rooms are comfortable and moderately priced (a double costs $72), and the restaurant offers Navajo specialties.

CHACO CULTURE NATIONAL HISTORICAL PARK ★★★

A combination of a stunning setting and well-preserved ruins makes the long drive to **Chaco Culture National Historic Park,** often referred to as Chaco Canyon, worth the trip. Whether you come from the north or south, you drive in on a dusty (and sometimes muddy) road that seems to add to the authenticity and adventure of this remote New Mexico experience.

When you finally arrive, you walk through stark desert country that seems perhaps ill suited as a center of culture. However, the ancestral Puebloan (Anasazi) people successfully farmed the lowlands and built great masonry towns, which connected with other towns over a wide-ranging network of roads crossing this desolate place.

What's most interesting here is how changes in architecture—beginning in the mid-800s, when the Ancestral Puebloans started building on a larger scale than they had previously—chart the area's cultural progress. The Ancestral Puebloans used the same masonry techniques that tribes had used in smaller villages in the region (walls one stone thick, with generous use of mud mortar), but they built stone villages of multiple stories with rooms several times larger than in the previous stage of their culture. Within a century, six large pueblos were underway. This pattern of a single large pueblo with oversize rooms, surrounded by conventional villages, caught on throughout the region. New communities built along these lines sprang up. Old villages built similarly large pueblos. Eventually there were more than 75 such towns, most of them closely tied to Chaco by an extensive system of roads. Aerial photos show hundreds of miles of roads connecting these towns with the Chaco pueblos, one of the longest running 42 miles straight north to Salmon Ruins and the Aztec Ruins. It is this road network that leads some scholars to believe that Chaco was the center of a unified society.

This progress led to Chaco becoming the economic center of the San Juan Basin by A.D. 1000. As many as 5,000 people may have lived in some 400 settlements in and around Chaco. As masonry techniques advanced through the years, walls rose more than four stories in height. Some of these are still visible today.

Chaco's decline after 1½ centuries of success coincided with a drought in the San Juan Basin between A.D. 1130 and 1180. Scientists still argue vehemently over why the site was abandoned and where the Chacoans went. Many believe that an influx of outsiders may have brought new rituals to the region, causing a schism among tribal members. Most agree, however, that the people drifted away to more hospitable places in the region and that their descendants are today's Pueblo people.

This is an isolated area, and there are **no services** available within or close to the park—no food, gas, auto repairs, firewood, lodging (besides the campground), or drinking water (other than at the visitor center) are available. Overnight camping is permitted year-round. If you're headed toward Santa Fe after a day at the park and looking for a place to spend the night, one nice option is the **Cañon del Rio Retreat & Spa,** 16445 NM 4, Jemez Springs, NM 87025 (© **505/829-4377;** www.canondelrio.com; p. 117).

Essentials

GETTING THERE To get to Chaco from Santa Fe, take I-25 south to Bernalillo and then US 550 northwest. Turn off US 550 at CR 7900 (3 miles southeast of Nageezi and about 50 miles west of Cuba at mile 112.5). Follow the signs from US 550 to the park boundary (21 miles). This route includes 8 miles of paved road (CR 7900) and 13 miles of dirt road (CR 7950). The trip takes about 3½ to 4 hours. Farmington is the nearest population center, a 1½-hour drive away. The park can also be reached from Grants via I-40 west to NM 371, which you follow north to Indian Route 9, east, and north again on NM 57 (IR 14), with the final 19 miles ungraded dirt. This route is rough to impassable and is not recommended for RVs.

Whichever way you come, call ahead to inquire about **road conditions** (© **505/827-5100;** www.nmroads.com) before leaving the paved highways. The dirt roads can get extremely muddy and dangerous after rain or snow, and afternoon thunderstorms are common in late summer. Roads often flood when it rains.

VISITOR INFORMATION Ranger-guided walks and campfire talks are available in the summer at the visitor center where you can get self-guided trail brochures and permits for the overnight campground (see "Camping," below). If you want information before you leave home, contact the Superintendent, Chaco Culture National Historical Park, 1808 County Rd. 7950, Nageezi, NM 87037 (© **505/786-7014;** www.nps.gov/chcu).

ADMISSION FEES & HOURS Admission is $8 per car; a campsite is $10 extra. The visitor center is open daily from 8am to 5pm. Trails are open from sunrise to sunset.

Seeing the Highlights

Exploring the ruins and hiking are the most popular activities here. A series of pueblo ruins stands within 5 or 6 miles of each other on the broad, flat, treeless canyon floor. Plan to spend at least 3 to 4 hours here driving to and exploring the different pueblos. A one-way road from the visitor center loops up one side of the canyon and down the other. Parking lots are scattered along the road near the various pueblos; from most, it's only a short walk to the ruins.

You may want to focus your energy on seeing **Pueblo Bonito,** the largest prehistoric Southwest Native American dwelling ever excavated. It contains giant kivas and 800 rooms covering more than 3 acres. Also, the **Pueblo Alto Trail** is a nice hike that takes you up on the canyon rim so that you can see the ruins from above—in the afternoon, especially when thunderheads are building, the views are spectacular. If you're a cyclist, stop at the visitor center to pick up a map outlining ridable trails.

Where to Stay & Dine

If you're driving from the northwest, your best bet is to stay in the Farmington/Aztec area (see below). If you're driving on US 550 from Albuquerque, the town of Cuba (pop. 600) boasts **El Bruno's Restaurante y Cantina** ★★, 6453 Main St. (US 550; © 575/289-9429). Within an adobe building with ceiling vigas and Mexican leather furniture, and with a lovely patio, this place serves tasty New Mexican food and steaks. It's open daily 11am to 10pm. Diners can order from a full bar. The lodging situation in this little town isn't quite so bright. Your only option is the **Frontier Motel,** on US 550 (© **505/289-3474**). Straddling both sides of the highway, it at least offers clean rooms to travelers. Be sure to get one on the south side of the highway, which is more upscale. Rooms have decent furnishings, fairly comfortable beds, and small bathrooms. Most have a fridge and microwave. Prices range from $45 to $60.

Camping

Gallo Campground, within the park, is quite popular with hikers. It's about 1 mile east of the visitor center; fees are $10 per night. The campground has 49 sites (group sites are also available), with fire grates (bring your own wood or charcoal), central toilets, and nonpotable water. Drinking water is available only at the visitor center. The campground cannot accommodate trailers over 30 feet.

As I said above, there's no place to stock up on supplies once you start the arduous drive to the canyon, so if you're camping, make sure you're well supplied, especially with water, before you head out.

FARMINGTON & ENVIRONS

Farmington has historic and outdoor finds that can keep you occupied for at least a day or two. It sits at the junction of the San Juan, Animas, and La Plata rivers. Adorned with arched globe willow trees, it's a lush place by New Mexico standards. A system of five parks along the San Juan River and its tributaries is its pride and joy. What's most notable for me, however, is the quaint downtown area, where century-old buildings still house thriving businesses and some trading posts with great prices. It's also an industrial center (coal, oil, natural gas, and hydroelectricity) and a shopping center for people within a 100-mile radius.

For visitors, Farmington is a takeoff point for explorations of the Navajo Reservation and Chaco Culture National Historical Park. For outdoors lovers, it's the spot to head to the Bisti/De-Na-Zin Wilderness; world-class fly-fishing on the San Juan River; lovely scenery at the Angel Peak Recreation Area; and even a trip up to Durango to enjoy some rafting, kayaking, skiing, and mountain biking. The nearby towns of Aztec and Bloomfield offer a variety of attractions as well.

Essentials

GETTING THERE   From Albuquerque, take US 550 (through Cuba) from the I-25 Bernalillo exit, and then head west on US 64 at Bloomfield (45 min.). From Gallup, take US 491 north to Shiprock, and then head east on US 64 (2¼ hr.). From Taos, follow US 64 all the way (4½ hr.). From Durango, Colorado, take US 500 south (1 hr.).

All commercial flights arrive at busy **Four Corners Regional Airport** on West Navajo Drive (© **505/599-1395;** www.fmtn.org). The principal carrier is **Great Lakes Airlines** (© **800/554-5111;** www.flygreatlakes.com).

Car-rental agencies at Four Corners Regional Airport include **Avis** (© **800/331-1212** or 505/327-9864), **Budget** (© **505/327-7304**), and **Hertz** (© **800/654-3131** or 505/327-6093).

VISITOR INFORMATION   The **Farmington Convention and Visitors Bureau,** 3041 E. Main St. (© **800/448-1240** or 505/326-7602; www.farmingtonnm.org), is the clearinghouse for tourist information for the Four Corners region. For more information, contact the **Farmington Chamber of Commerce,** 100 W. Broadway (✆ **505/325-0279;** www.gofarmington.com).

Seeing the Sights in the Area

IN FARMINGTON

E3 Children's Museum & Science Center ★ ☺   In downtown Farmington, kids can lose themselves in interactive fun at this expansive museum while they explore a range of exhibits on science, math, engineering, and art. Dinosaur puzzles the size of a car teach about ancient anatomy, a Bernoulli Ball explores how air moves over an object, and changing exhibits offer a chance to build a robot, learn about bats, or juggle. Plan to spend an hour to half-day here.

302 N. Orchard Ave. ✆ **505/599-1425.** www.farmingtonmuseum.org. Free admission. Tues–Sat 10am–5pm.

Farmington Museum at Gateway Park ★ ☺   Small-town museums can be completely precious, and this one and its neighbor in Aztec (see below) typify a tiny part of the world, but the truths they reveal span continents. Here you get to see the everyday struggle of a people to support themselves within a fairly inhospitable part of the world, spanning boom and bust years of agriculture, oil and gas production, and tourism. Located in the slick Gateway Visitor Center, exhibits vary, utilizing over 7,000 objects. You may walk through displays of a 1930s trading post with an old enameled scale, cloth bolts, and vintage saddles. Next, you can tour the Dinosaurs to Drill Bits exhibit, exploring the region's rich oil and gas history, including a 7-minute ride in the **Geovator,** which simulates a trip 7,285 feet into an oil well. Kids enjoy this! Excellent changing exhibits rotate through as well. A gift shop sells fun local art and some nice New Mexico–made crafts.

3041 E. Main St. ✆ **505/599-1174.** Fax 505/326-7572. www.farmingtonmuseum.org. Free admission. Mon–Sat 8am–5pm.

IN NEARBY AZTEC

VISITOR INFORMATION   The **Aztec Chamber of Commerce,** 110 N. Ash St. (✆ **505/334-9551;** www.aztecchamber.com), is a friendly place with a wealth of information about the area.

AZTEC MUSEUM AND PIONEER VILLAGE ☺   A real treat for kids, this museum and village transport visitors back over a century to a little frontier town. The museum has lots of memorabilia, but the outer **Pioneer Village** of replicas and real buildings, with all the trimmings, is what will hold interest. You'll walk through the actual 1912 Aztec jail—nowhere you'd want to live—into the sheriff's office. The blacksmith shop has an anvil and oddly shaped burro shoes. You'll see an authentic 1906 church and a schoolhouse. New additions include a farmhouse and historic drilling rigs. The second Saturday in September the museum celebrates Founders' Day, with living exhibits, food, and games.

125 N. Main Ave., Aztec. ✆ **505/334-9829.** www.aztecmuseum.org. Admission $3 adults, $1 children 12–17, free for children 11 and under. Summer Tues–Sat 10am–4pm; winter Thurs–Sat 10am–4pm.

IN NEARBY BLOOMFIELD

Salmon Ruins ★ ☺   What really marks the 150 rooms of these ruins 11 miles west of Farmington near Bloomfield is their setting on a hillside, surrounded by lush

Natural Fun

In the center of Farmington, a dirt road leads through Animas River bosque to the **Riverside Nature Center,** in Animas Park off Browning Parkway (© 505/599-1422; www.farmingtonmuseum.org). This jumping-off spot to the 3-mile long Riverwalk—a series of paved trails that contour and cross over the river—gives families up-close encounters with the wild. In the Center itself, a glassed-in viewing area allows kids to watch ducks and deer frolic. The Center also offers changing exhibits of nature-related art and photography and lots of hands-on learning exhibits. Meanwhile, special programs offered weekly take families on adventures: "Moonlight Stars and Stories" explores constellations and their accompanying myths, while "Making Tracks" helps participants identify animal tracks along the river. The Center is open Tuesday to Saturday 9am to 5pm and Sunday 1 to 4pm. Admission is free.

San Juan River bosque. You'll begin in the museum, where a number of informative displays range from one showing the variety of types of ancestral Puebloan vessels, from pitchers to canteens, to wild plants. Two strong architectural influences are visible here. First the Chacoan, who built the village around the 11th century, with walls of an intricate rubble-filled core with sandstone veneer. The more simple San Juan occupation masonry was added in the 12th century. A trail guide will lead you to each site.

Built in 1990, **Heritage Park,** on an adjoining plot of land, comprises a series of reconstructed ancient and historic dwellings representing the area's cultures, from a paleoarchaic sand-dune site to an Ancestral Puebloan pit house, from Apache wickiups and tepees to Navajo hogans, and an original pioneer homestead. Visitors are encouraged to enter the re-creations.

In the visitor center, you'll find a gift shop and a scholarly research library. Ask about their excellent guided tours to nearby ruins.

6131 US 64 (P.O. Box 125), Bloomfield, NM 87413. © **505/632-2013.** Fax 505/632-8633. www.salmonruins.com. Admission $3 adults, $1 children 6–16, $2 seniors, free for children 5 and under. Mon–Fri 8am–5pm; Sat–Sun 9am–5pm; Sun noon–5pm (winter only). Closed Thanksgiving, Christmas, and New Year's Day.

Aztec Ruins National Monument ★

These ruins offer an exciting and rare glimpse of a restored kiva, which visitors can enter and sit within, sensing the site's ancient history. The ruins of this 450-room Native American pueblo, left by the ancestral Puebloans 7 centuries ago, are 14 miles northeast of Farmington, in the town of Aztec on the Animas River. Early Anglo settlers, convinced that the ruins were of Aztec origin, misnamed the site. Despite the fact that this pueblo was built long before the Aztecs of central Mexico lived, the name persisted.

The influence of the Chaco culture is strong at Aztec, as evidenced in the pre-planned architecture, the open plaza, and the fine stone masonry in the old walls. But a later occupation shows as well. This second group of settlers remodeled the old pueblo and built others nearby, using techniques less elaborate and decorative than those of the Chacoans. Aztec Ruins is best known for its Great Kiva, the only completely reconstructed Anasazi great kiva in existence. Visiting Aztec Ruins National Monument will take you approximately 1 hour, even if you take the .25-mile self-guided trail and spend some time in the visitor center, which displays some outstanding examples of Anasazi ceramics and basketry. Add another half-hour if you plan to watch the video that imaginatively documents the history of native cultures in the area.

ESSENTIALS

GETTING THERE Aztec Ruins is approximately ½ mile north of US 550 on Ruins Road (CR 2900) on the north edge of the city of Aztec. Ruins Road is the first street immediately west of the Animas River Bridge on NM 516 in Aztec.

VISITOR INFORMATION For more information, contact **Aztec Ruins National Monument,** 84 CR 2900, Aztec, NM 87410-0640 (© **505/334-6174,** ext. 30; www.nps.gov/azru).

ADMISSION FEES & HOURS Admission is $5 for adults; children 16 and under are admitted free. The monument is open daily from 8am to 6pm Memorial Day through Labor Day and 8am to 5pm the rest of the year; it's closed Thanksgiving, Christmas, and New Year's Day.

CAMPING

Camping is not permitted at the monument. However, it is available at **Navajo Lake State Park** (© **505/632-2278**).

Nearby Parks & Recreation Areas

SHIPROCK PEAK

This distinctive landmark, on the Navajo Indian Reservation southwest of Shiprock, 29 miles west of Farmington via US 64, is known to the Navajo as *Tse bidá hi,* "Rock with wings." Composed of igneous rock flanked by long upright walls of solidified lava, it rises 1,700 feet off the desert floor to an elevation of 7,178 feet. There are scenic viewing points off US 491, 6 to 7 miles south of the town of Shiprock. You can get closer by taking the tribal road to the community of Red Rock, but you must have permission to get any nearer to this sacred Navajo rock. Climbing is not permitted.

The town named after the rock is a gateway to the Navajo reservation and the Four Corners region. There's a tribal visitor center here.

From Shiprock, you may want to make the 32-mile drive west on US 64 to Teec Nos Pos, Arizona, and then north on US 160, to the **Four Corners Monument** (© **928/871-6647;** www.navajonationparks.org). A concrete slab here sits astride the only point in the United States where four states meet: New Mexico, Colorado, Utah, and Arizona. Kids especially like the idea of standing at the center and occupying four states at once. There's no view here, but vendors sell crafts and food. Some people find a visit here not worth the trip or cost. The monument is open daily 7am to 8pm Memorial Day to Labor Day and 8am to 5pm the rest of the year. The cost is $3 per person for all ages.

NAVAJO LAKE STATE PARK

The **San Juan River, Pine River,** and **Sims Mesa recreation sites,** all with camping, fishing, and boating, make this the most popular watersports destination for residents of northwestern New Mexico. Trout, northern pike, largemouth bass, and catfish are caught in lake and river waters, and the surrounding hills attract hunters seeking deer and elk. A visitor center at Pine River Recreation Area has interpretive displays on natural history and on the construction and use of the dam.

Navajo Lake, with an area of 15,000 acres, extends from the confluence of the San Juan and Los Pinos rivers 25 miles north into Colorado. Navajo Dam, an earthen embankment, is ¾ mile long and 400 feet high. It provides Farmington-area cities, industries, and farms with their principal water supply. It's also the main storage reservoir for the Navajo Indian Irrigation Project, designed to irrigate 110,000 acres.

Anglers come from all over the world to fish the **San Juan River ★★** below the dam, a pastoral spot bordered by green hills, where golden light reflects off the water. Much of the water is designated "catch and release" and is teeming with rainbow, brown, and cutthroat trout. Experts will be heartily challenged by these fish that are attuned to the best tricks, while amateurs may want to hire a guide. With a guide I've pulled as many as 30 fish in a day from these waters; without a guide my experience was zip. For more information, see "Northwestern New Mexico's Great Outdoors," earlier in this chapter. The park is 40 miles east of Farmington on NM 511. For more information, call ✆ **505/632-2278.**

Not far from the park, **Wines of the San Juan,** 233 NM 511 at Turley (✆ **505/632-0879;** www.winesofthesanjuan.com), offers wine tastings and sells bottles of wines ranging from merlot to malvasia bianca. Call ahead to find out about the Sunday programs offered spring through fall, which might include flamenco guitar. The last weekend in September, the winery holds a festival featuring several bands and arts-and-crafts booths. The tasting room is open Monday to Saturday 10am to 6pm and Sunday noon to 6pm. Closed Tuesday.

ANGEL PEAK RECREATION AREA

The distinctive pinnacle of 6,991-foot Angel Peak can often be spotted from the hillsides around Farmington. The area offers a short nature trail and a variety of unusual, colorful geological formations and canyons to explore on foot. The Bureau of Land Management has developed a primitive campground with nine campsites and provided picnic tables in a few spots, but no drinking water is available here. The park is about 35 miles south of Farmington on US 550; the last 6 miles of access, after turning off US 550, are over a graded dirt road. For more information on the park, call ✆ **505/599-8900.**

Wet & Wild

If hiking through ruins and across desert sand has left you parched, head to the **Farmington Aquatic Center,** 1151 N. Sullivan (✆ **505/599-1167;** www.fmtn. org). Serious swimmers can do laps in an Olympic-size pool, while the kids play in their own large one, with slides and jungle-gym type games. It's open daily 1 to 4pm and Monday to Saturday 4:30 to 7:30pm in summer; Monday, Wednesday, and Friday 4:30 to 7:30pm and Wednesday 1 to 4pm in winter. Admission costs $5 for adults, $4.50 for teens 13 to 18, $3.25 for kids 3 to 12, and free for those 2 and under.

BISTI/DE-NA-ZIN WILDERNESS

Often referred to as Bisti Badlands (pronounced Bist-*eye*), this barren region may merit that name today, but it was once very different. Around 70 million years ago, large dinosaurs lived near what was then a coastal swamp, bordering a retreating inland sea. Today, their bones, and those of fish, turtles, lizards, and small mammals, are eroding slowly from the low shale hills.

Kirtland Shale, containing several bands of color, dominates the eastern part of the wilderness and caps the mushroom-shaped formations found there. Along with the spires and fanciful shapes of rock, hikers may find petrified wood sprinkled in small chips throughout the area, or even an occasional log. Removing petrified wood, fossils, or anything else from the wilderness is prohibited.

Hiking in the Bisti is fairly easy; from the small parking lot, follow an arroyo east 2 or 3 miles into the heart of the formations, which you'll see on your right (aim for the two red hills). The De-Na-Zin Wilderness to the east requires more climbing and navigational skills. It has no designated trails, bikes and motorized vehicles are prohibited, and it has no water or significant shade. The hour just after sunset or, especially, just before sunrise is a pleasant and quite magical time to see this starkly beautiful landscape. Primitive camping is allowed, but bring plenty of water and other supplies.

Bisti/De-Na-Zin Wilderness is just off NM 371, 37 miles south of Farmington. For more information, call the **Bureau of Land Management** at ✆ **505/599-8900.**

Where to Stay in Farmington & Aztec

Courtyard by Marriott ★ ☺ This hotel provides elegant rooms and all the amenities of a full-service inn, with the consistency you'd expect from Marriott. The expansive lobby looking out over Riverwalk Park is decorated in a Southwestern style. Just off it is a quiet lounge and a restaurant. The style carries into the rooms. They are spacious with comfortable beds and medium-size bathrooms with outer vanities. Southwestern landscape paintings adorn the walls. The suites are large and contain one bedroom and a living room with a foldout couch, wet bar, and microwave—a good choice for small families.

560 Scott Ave., Farmington, NM 87401. ✆ **800/228-9290** or 505/325-5111. Fax 505/325-5588. www. marriott.com. 125 units. $89–$119 double; $134–$144 suite. AE, DC, DISC, MC, V. **Amenities:** Restaurant; bar; exercise room; Jacuzzi; indoor pool w/sun deck; room service. *In room:* A/C, TV, hair dryer, Wi-Fi.

Soaring Eagle Lodge ★ ♟ This lodge offers basic and clean cabins on a poetic bend of the San Juan River. It's mostly a place for fishing enthusiasts, who come to ply these world-renowned waters, but those seeking to escape to the quiet of a lovely river will like it too. Each cabin has a kitchenette, partitioned-off bedroom space, and a front room with two easy chairs. Beds are comfortable and bathrooms very clean. A restaurant on-site serves tasty breakfasts and dinners. Be sure to reserve a cabin on the river edge where the views couldn't be finer. The lodge can set you up with a guide, and you may fish for free from shore on the lodge's private waters.

48 CR 4370, off NM 511, Navajo Dam, NM, 87419. ✆ **800/866-2719** or 505/632-3721. www.soaring eaglelodge.net. 11 units. $155 per person, double. Price includes a full breakfast and fishing privileges. MC, V. **Amenities:** Restaurant; guide service; Wi-Fi (in conference room). *In room:* A/C, TV, fridge, microwave.

Step Back Inn ★   This inn imparts a bit of Victorian charm to its fairly standard rooms. It's a friendly place offering iced tea and lemonade in their parlor throughout the day. Rooms are well planned and functional, with comfortable beds and medium-size bathrooms, as well as plenty of quiet. They also have pretty touches such as wallpaper, a recliner, and early American antique replica armoires, which hold the televisions. Each is named after a pioneer family of the area, some of whom are the ancestors of the hotel's owner, and each room includes a small booklet that tells their stories. Breakfast brings a warm, delicious cinnamon roll as large as a plate, served in a tearoom.

123 W. Aztec Blvd., Aztec, NM 87410. © **800/334-1255** or 505/334-1200. 39 units. $78 double. Rates include cinnamon roll, juice, and coffee. AE, MC, V. *In room:* A/C, TV, hair dryer, Wi-Fi.

BED & BREAKFASTS

Casa Blanca ★★★ 🎁☺   This B&B offers such nice rooms, it's a travel destination. In a quiet residential neighborhood just a few blocks from the shops and restaurants of Main Street, this inn, built in the 1940s, was once the home of a wealthy family that traded with the Navajos. In 2004, new owners expanded it, adding patios and fountains, creating a lovely oasis. The large rooms, decorated in an elegant Southwestern style, have original artwork and plenty of amenities. My favorite room is the Chaco, with red-brick floors, authentic Navajo rugs, and antique furnishings. Also of note is the Vista Grande, a large upstairs room with views in every direction. Travelers with disabilities are treated especially well here (there are two large suites especially for them), as are business travelers (there's high-speed and wireless Internet, a courtesy computer, and a meeting room). The full breakfast is always gourmet. Ask about their lovely two-bedroom, two-bathroom cottage, with a full kitchen—a great place for families, marked by the same elegance as the rest of the inn.

505 E. La Plata St., Farmington, NM 87401. © **800/550-6503** or 505/327-6503. Fax 505/326-5680. www.casablancanm.com. 8 units. $125–$255 double. Rates include full breakfast. AE, MC, V. *In room:* A/C, TV, fridge, hair dryer, microwave, Wi-Fi.

Kokopelli's Cave ★★   Retired geologist Bruce Black wanted to build a cave, so he gave some laid-off Grants miners $20,000 to bore as deeply as they could into the side of a cliff face. This apartment was the result. Built in a semicircle, both the entry hall and the bedroom have wide sliding glass doors leading to little balconies beyond which the cliff face drops hundreds of feet below. This really is a cliff dwelling, and you must hike a bit down to it, though good guardrails guide you. The apartment is laid out around a broad central pillar, and the ceilings and walls are thick, undulating stone. A grill is outside, as are chairs where you can relax in the mornings and evenings. Fruit, juice, coffee, and pastries make up a self-serve breakfast.

3204 Crestridge Dr., Farmington, NM 87401. © **505/326-2461.** Fax 505/325-9671. www.bbonline.com/nm/kokopelli. 1 unit. $260 double; $300 for 3–4 people. Closed Dec–Feb. AE, MC, V. **Amenities:** Jacuzzi. *In room:* TV/DVD, hair dryer, kitchen.

CAMPING

Mom and Pop RV Park (© **505/327-3200**) has 36 sites, 35 of them with full hookups, tent sites, a bathhouse, and a toy soldier shop. The sites are a bit desolate, around an asphalt central area, but a little grassy spot at the office has an incredible electric train set that Pop runs at certain times during the day. Mom and Pop RV Park is at 901 Illinois Ave., in Farmington (just off US 64).

Where to Dine in Farmington & Aztec

EXPENSIVE

The Bluffs ★★ 🍴 SANDWICHES/SEAFOOD/STEAKS   Ten minutes east of Farmington's town center, the Bluffs serves inventive food with attention to detail. A large room is sectioned off by wooden partitions crowned with elegantly glazed glass shaped like the bluffs prominent in the surrounding area. It's a comfortable atmosphere with roomy booths and stacked sandstone accents. Service is decent. The outdoor patio is a nice spot on not-so-hot days. For lunch, my pick is the turkey-bacon club, served on ciabatta bread. The Thai beef salad is also tasty. At dinner, try your favorite steak cut of Angus beef or one of many daily specials. Most recently, I had Scottish salmon with crispy spinach, and garlic mashed potatoes. Dinners come with salad and a choice of vegetable or potato. A full bar and carefully selected wine list accompanies the menu. For dessert, indulge in the chocolate mousse.

3450 E. Main St., Farmington. ✆ **505/325-8155.** Reservations recommended on weekend nights. Main courses $7–$12 lunch, $15–$33 dinner. AE, DISC, MC, V. Mon–Fri 11am–2pm; Mon–Sat 5–9pm; lounge daily 4–9 or 10pm.

MODERATE

Rubio's ★ NEW MEXICAN   Set in the center of Aztec, this restaurant and bar offers a festive dining experience. Amid brightly painted walls, with comfy booths, the restaurant portion provides a relaxing atmosphere for families. Meanwhile, the bar next door, with ceiling fans and a beach mural, gets livelier. Service is friendly and eager to please. Meals start with chips and salsa, followed by such tasty fare as breakfast burritos or French toast in the morning. Lunch and dinner might start with nachos or guacamole and move on to their "Sopaipilla el Grande," a favorite—*sopaipilla* topped with taco meat, cheese, guac, and sour cream. Grilled burgers, chicken, and steak also dress the menu here, as do a variety of combo plates. Kids have their own menu and adults a full bar. Live music, ranging from rock to country, plays on most Saturday nights.

116 S. Main St., Aztec. ✆ **505/334-0599.** Main courses $4–$8 breakfast, $5–$20 lunch and dinner. AE, DISC, MC, V. Mon–Thurs 11am–9pm; Fri–Sat 11am–10pm.

Three Rivers Eatery & Brewhouse ★ ☺ AMERICAN   This brewpub on an elegant corner in the center of downtown Farmington serves some of the region's best food and beer. After my first sip of their Arroyo Amber Ale, I was sold. The restaurant is set in a big two-story brick building that once housed the Farmington Drug Store and the Farmington *Times-Hustler* newspaper. Hardwood floors and vintage items, such as period bottles and posters found in the renovation, complete the experience. It's a comfortable place where the owner might just sit down in one of the comfy booths with you and chat about his passion, beer brewing. I recommend the burgers, which come in a variety of flavors, from grilled onion and Swiss to jack and green chile. You'll also find barbecue pork ribs, steaks, and seafood. A popular dish is the Cajun boil, with crawfish, andouille sausage, crab legs, and corn on the cob. Families enjoy the spacious booths in the back and a kid's menu.

If you're traveling with your brood, head next door to **Three Rivers Pizzeria,** 107 E. Main St. (✆ **505/325-0308**). Under the same ownership, this place offers kids many of their favorite toppings, while adults can savor a crust made with Papa Bear's Golden Honey Ale from the accompanying brewery.

Northwestern New Mexico's lush green fields and mild (mostly) climate are attracting more and more artists. A great place to sample some of the lively work is **Artifacts Gallery**, 302 E. Main St. (✆ **505/327-2907;** www. artifacts-gallery.com), in Farmington. Set in a Victorian-style lumber building is a collection of art studios whose artists are often on hand to discuss their work. Just down the street, step into **Andrea Kristina's Bookstore & Kafé**, 218 W. Main St. (✆ **505/327-3313**). This lively place, in a historic building with tables set amid bookshelves, has a great selection of books and offers live music, poetry, and films most Thursday through Saturday nights from 7 to 9pm. A range of coffee drinks and soups, salads, sandwiches, and pizza dress the menu. It's open Monday to Friday 7am to 9pm and Saturday 8am to 10pm. In nearby Aztec, stop in at **Feat of Clay**, 107 S. Main St. (✆ **505/334-4335**). A cooperative gallery, it holds the work of 14 local artists and has great prices. Look for "Molten Treasures," glass jewelry by Jinx Bolli. While in Aztec be sure to take some time to stroll through the town's newly renovated 19th-century **historic district**.

101 E. Main St., Farmington. ✆ **505/324-2187.** www.threeriversbrewery.com. Main courses $6–$25. AE, DISC, MC, V. Mon–Thurs 11am–10pm; Fri–Sat 11am–11pm; Sun 11am–9pm.

INEXPENSIVE

Main Street Bistro ★ BAKERY/CAFE   This imaginative little cafe in Aztec, with brightly colored floors and walls, offers tasty house-made breakfasts, sandwiches, soups, and salads. Order at the counter and the friendly waitstaff will bring your food to the table. Be aware that the place bustles during peak hours; so if you want quiet time, go midmorning or later in the afternoon. At breakfast, you might order the egg-centric—two eggs, hash browns, English muffin, and fruit. For lunch, you can't go wrong with the daily soup special, a salad, or sandwich (try the cordon bleu—ham and Swiss on ciabatta, grilled), or the frittata quiche, made fresh daily. Wash it all down with a full range of coffee drinks or their delicious raspberry iced tea.

122 N. Main St., Aztec. ✆ **505/334-0109.** All menu items under $9. DISC, MC, V. Mon–Fri 7am–4pm; Sat 7–noon.

Shopping in Farmington

Downtown Farmington shops are generally open from 10am to 6pm Monday through Saturday. Native American arts and crafts are best purchased at trading posts, either downtown on Main or Broadway streets, or west of Farmington on US 64 toward Shiprock. You may want to check out the following stores: One of the best in the city is **Fifth Generation Trading Company** ★, 232 W. Broadway (✆ **505/326-3211;** www.southwestshowrooms.com). Trading since 1875, the Tanner family offers jewelry, Navajo rugs, pottery, alabaster sculptures, old pawn, and *katsinas.* **Bob French Navajo Rugs,** on US 64, 18 miles west of Farmington (✆ **505/598-5621;** www.bobfrenchnavajorugs.com), sells silver and turquoise jewelry and a range of antique and new rugs. **Hogback Trading Company,** 3221 US 64, Waterflow, 17 miles west of Farmington (✆ **505/598-5154**), has large displays of Indian jewelry, rugs, and folk art. And **Navajo Trading Company,** 126 E. Main St. (© **505/325-1685**), is an actual pawnshop, with lots of exquisite old jewelry; you can peruse bracelets and necklaces while listening to clerks speaking Navajo.

Farmington After Dark

Sandstone Production's **Summer Outdoor Theater** ★ stages two fun shows each year. Presented in the Lions Wilderness Park Amphitheater (off College Blvd.) against a sandstone backdrop, the offerings are usually a dramatic piece and a musical. For information and advance ticket sales, contact © **505/599-1148;** www. fmtn.org/sandstone. Shows are Thursday through Saturday from mid-June through July, with dinner at 6:30pm and the performance at 8pm.

If you're looking for a pub, **Three Rivers Tap & Game Room,** 113 E. Main St. (© **505/325-6605;** www.threeriversbrewery.com), is a big hit with locals. This brewpub/game room has the feel of the bar from the television show *Cheers,* with wood floors, high ceilings, and lots of laughter and brew flowing. Pool tables, foosball, and shuffleboard fill patrons' time while they munch on popcorn and peanuts, and, some nights, listen to live music. Patrons can order food from the next-door brewpub/restaurant of the same name (see above).

THE JICARILLA APACHE RESERVATION

About 2,755 Apaches live on the Jicarilla Apache Indian Reservation along US 64 and NM 537. Its 768,000 acres stretch from the Colorado border south 65 miles to US 550 near Cuba, New Mexico.

The word *jicarilla* (pronounced hick-ah-*ree*-ah) means "little basket," so it's no surprise that tribal craftspeople are noted for their basket weaving and beadwork. See their work, both contemporary and of museum quality, at the **Jicarilla Apache Arts and Crafts Shop and Museum,** a green building along US 64 west of the central village on the reservation (© **575/759-1343;** www.jicarillaonline.com). In the back rooms here, I found women listening to 1950s rock while weaving baskets and stringing beads. Two isolated pueblo ruins, open to the public, are found on the reservation: **Cordova Canyon** ruins on tribal Road 13 and **Honolulu** ruins on Road 63.

Though the area is lovely, there's not much else to do unless you're interested in hunting and fishing. Tribe members guide fishers and trophy hunters, most of whom seek elk, mule deer, or bear, into the reservation's rugged wilderness backcountry. Highlights of the Jicarilla calendar are the **Little Beaver Celebration** (mid-July), which features a rodeo, a 5-mile run, a draft-horse pull, and a powwow. The **Stone Lake Fiesta** (Sept 14–15 annually) includes a rodeo, ceremonial dances, and a footrace.

Admission to Jicarilla Apache Reservation is free, and visitors are welcome year-round. For information on outdoor activities and for general information, contact the Tribal Office at P.O. Box 507 (© **575/759-3242**).

The **Best Western Jicarilla Inn and Casino** on US 64 (P.O. Box 233), Dulce, NM 87528 (© **800/742-1938** or 575/759-3663; www.bestwesternnewmexico. com), offers decent rooms and slot-machine play, though you'll find better accommodations in Chama (see below).

CHAMA & ITS SCENIC RAILROAD

Some of my best outdoor adventuring has taken place in the area surrounding this pioneer village of 1,250 people at the base of the 10,000-foot Cumbres Pass. With backpack on, I cross-country skied high into the mountains and stayed the night in a yurt (Mongolian hut), the next day waking to hundreds of acres of snowy fields to explore. Another time, I headed down **Rio Chama,** an official wild-and-scenic river, on rafts and in kayaks following the course that Navajos, Utes, and Comanches once traveled to raid the Pueblo Indians down river. The campsites along the way were pristine, with mule deer threading through the trees beyond our tents. In a more recent visit to the village, it was summertime, and I'd just come from Durango, which was packed with tourists, to hike, raft, and ride the train. Chama was still quiet, and I realized Chama is New Mexico's undiscovered Durango, without the masses.

Bordered by three wilderness areas, the Carson, Rio Grande, and Santa Fe national forests, the area is indeed prime for hunting, fishing, cross-country skiing, snowmobiling, snowshoeing, and hiking.

Another highlight here is America's longest and highest narrow-gauge coal-fired steam line, the **Cumbres & Toltec Scenic Railroad,** which winds through valleys and mountain meadows 64 miles between Chama and Antonito, Colorado. The village of Chama boomed when the railroad arrived in 1881. A rough-and-ready frontier town, the place still maintains that flavor, with lumber and ranching making up a big part of the economy.

Landmarks to watch for are the **Brazos Cliffs** and waterfall and **Heron and El Vado lakes.** Tierra Amarilla, the Rio Arriba County seat, is 14 miles south, and is at the center—along with Los Ojos and Los Brazos—of a wool-raising and weaving tradition where local craftspeople still weave masterpieces. Dulce, governmental seat of the Jicarilla Apache Indian Reservation, is 27 miles west.

Essentials

GETTING THERE   From Santa Fe, take US 84 north (2 hr.). From Taos, take US 64 west (2½ hr.). From Farmington, take US 64 east (2¼ hr.).

VISITOR INFORMATION   The **New Mexico Visitor Information Center,** P.O. Box 697, Chama, NM 87520 (© **575/756-2235**), is at 2372 US 17. It's open daily from 8am to 6pm in the summer, from 8am to 5pm in the winter. At the same address is the **Chama Valley Chamber of Commerce** (© **800/477-0149** or 575/756-2306; www.chamavalley.com).

All Aboard the Historic C&T Railroad

Cumbres & Toltec Scenic Railroad ★★ 📷   If you have a passion for the past and for incredible scenery, climb aboard America's longest and highest narrow-gauge steam railroad, the historic C&T. It operates on a 64-mile track between Chama and Antonito, Colorado. Built in 1880 as an extension of the Denver and Rio Grande line to serve the mining camps of the San Juan Mountains, it is perhaps the finest surviving example of what once was a vast network of remote Rocky Mountain railways.

Steam Power Shopping

After sitting on the steam train, you may want to stroll for a while, hitting a few of the shops in Chama. One of note is the **Local Color Gallery**, 567 Terrace Ave. (© 888/756-2604 or 575/756-2604) in the center of town. Here you'll find all kinds of locally made arts and crafts, from pottery to moody candles painted with petroglyph symbols to picturesque watercolors of the Chama area. Nearby, the Trackside Emporium, 611 Terrace Ave. (© 575/756-1848), offers train books and videos and model cars.

The C&T passes through forests of pine and aspen, past striking rock formations, and over the magnificent Toltec Gorge of the Rio de los Pinos. It crests at the 10,000-foot Cumbres Pass, the highest in the United States used by scheduled passenger trains.

Halfway through the route, at Osier, Colorado, the *New Mexico Express* from Chama meets the *Colorado Limited* from Antonito. They stop to exchange greetings, engines, and through passengers. A lunch of roast turkey, mashed potatoes, gravy, and other offerings is served in a big, barnlike dining hall in Osier. From there, through passengers continue on to Antonito and return by van, while round-trip passengers return to their starting point. Be aware that both trips are nearly full-day events. Those who find it uncomfortable to sit for long periods may instead want to opt for hiking or skiing in the area. Ask about their Parlor Car, a more luxurious alternative to coach seating.

A walking-tour brochure, describing 23 points of interest in the Chama railroad yards, can be picked up at the 1899 depot in Chama. These yards are a living, working museum, which fascinates history buffs. A registered National Historic Site, the C&T is owned by the states of Colorado and New Mexico. Special cars with lifts for people with disabilities are available with a 7-day advance reservation.

500 Terrace Ave., Chama, NM 87520. © **888/286-2737** or 575/756-2151. Fax 575/756-2694. www.cumbrestoltec.com. Lunch included with all fares. Round-trip to Osier: adults $75, children age 11 and under $38. Through trip to Antonito, return by van (or to Antonito by van, return by train): adults $91, children $50. Reservations highly recommended. Memorial Day to mid-Oct trains leave Chama daily at 10am; vans depart for Antonito at 8:30am.

Where to Stay in Chama

Most accommodations in this area are found on NM 17 or south of the US 64/84 junction, known as the "Y."

HOTELS/LODGES

Chama Station Inn ★ Set in downtown Chama, right across the street from the Cumbres & Toltec Scenic Railroad station, this inn offers clean, atmospheric rooms in a 1920s building. Wood floors, high ceilings, and quilts on the comfortable beds create a cozy atmosphere. Bathrooms are small, with only a shower, but functional. A portal on the two-story building allows a nice place to lounge next to an elaborate garden. Best of all, you can climb out of bed and walk to the train. Two of the rooms have kiva fireplaces. The only drawback here is that the inn is only open from late May to mid-October, when the train is running. Next door, a coffee shop offers breakfast. I'd give its name but it seems to change hands every year, so your guess is as good as mine.

423 Terrace Ave. Chama, NM 87520. © **888/726-8150** or 575/756-2315. www.chamastationinn.com. 9 units. $75–$85 double. AE, DISC, MC, V. Closed late May to mid-Oct. *In room:* TV, hair dryer.

River Bend Lodge   Set on a bend of the Chama River, this lodging offers the best cabins in town and clean motel rooms. Though they're prefab cabins, they're better than some of the more authentic and overly rustic ones at nearby lodgings. If you can reserve cabin no. 40, 50, or 60 at the back of the property, you'll have a sweet riverside stay. Some of these are split level, with a queen-size sleeping loft and a bedroom—not great for privacy, but good for a family that doesn't mind sharing space. Others are similar, but without the loft. Every cabin has a fold-out futon in the living room, an efficient little kitchen, and a small bathroom. The motel rooms are medium-size, with basic furnishing and a long portal to relax on in the afternoons.

2625 US 84/64, Chama, NM 87520. © **800/288-1371** or 575/756-2264. Fax 575/756-2664. www. chamariverbendlodge.com. 21 units. Motel rooms $68–$89 double; cabins $115–$135 double. Children 12 and under stay free in parent's room. AE, DC, DISC, MC, V. Pets accepted with $10 fee. **Amenities:** Jacuzzi; river for fishing and wading. *In room:* A/C, TV, fridge, hair dryer, Wi-Fi.

CAMPING

At **Rio Chama RV Campground** (© **575/756-2303**), you're within easy walking distance of the Cumbres & Toltec Scenic Railroad depot. This shady campground with 100 sites along the Rio Chama is ideal for RVers and tenters who plan to take train rides. The campground also offers great photo opportunities of the old steam trains leaving the depot. Hot showers, a dump station, and complete hookups are available. It's open from May to mid-October only. The campground is 2¼ miles north of the US 84/64 junction on NM 17.

  Twin Rivers Trailer Park (© **575/756-2218**) has 50 sites and 40 full hook-ups; phone hookups are offered. Tent sites are available, as are laundry facilities and ice and picnic tables. River swimming and fishing are popular activities; other sports facilities include basketball, volleyball, badminton, and horseshoes. Twin Rivers is open from April 15 to November 1 and is 100 yards west of the junction of NM 17 and US 84/64.

Where to Dine in Chama

High Country Restaurant and Saloon ★ STEAKS/SEAFOOD/NEW MEXI-CAN   This is definitely a country place, with functional furniture, orange vinyl chairs, brown carpet, and a big stone fireplace. But it's *the* place innkeepers recommend. The steaks are a big draw here. More sophisticated appetites may like the *trucha con piñon,* trout dusted in flour and cooked with pine nuts, garlic, and shallots. Meals are served with a salad and choice of potato. The New Mexican food is also good. Sunday brunch offers a buffet with biscuits and gravy as well as egg dishes, and pancakes. The attached saloon has a full bar and bustles with people eating peanuts and throwing the shells on the floor.

Main St. (⅒ mile north of the Y), Chama. © **575/756-2384.** Main courses $5–$20 lunch; $7–$20 dinner; Sun breakfast buffet $10. AE, DISC, MC, V. Mon–Sat 11am–10pm; Sun 8am–10pm. Closed Easter, Thanksgiving, Christmas.

What to See & Do on US 84 South

Distinctive yellow earth provided a name for the town of **Tierra Amarilla,** 14 miles south of Chama at the junction of US 84 and US 64. Throughout New Mexico, this name is synonymous with a continuing controversy over the land-grant rights of the descendants of the original Hispanic settlers. But the economy of this community of 1,000 is dyed in the wool—literally.

The organization Ganados del Valle (Livestock Growers of the Valley) is at work to save the longhaired Spanish churro sheep from extinction, to introduce other unusual wool breeds to the valley, and to perpetuate a 200-year-old tradition of shepherding, spinning, weaving, and dyeing. Many of the craftspeople work in conjunction with **Tierra Wools ★**, 91 Main St. Los Ojos, NM 87551 (✆ **575/588-7231**), which has a showroom and workshop in a century-old mercantile building just north of Tierra Amarilla. One-of-a-kind blankets and men's and women's apparel are among the products displayed and sold.

Just down the street, across from the Los Ojos General Store, is an interesting little art studio worth checking out. **Yellow Earth Studio** (✆ **575/588-7807**) the passion of Paul Trachtman, the resident artist, is a great place to see and purchase enchanting scenes of the Los Ojos area in the form of paintings and monotype, woodcut, and metal engraving prints. His work is part of the permanent collection of the New Mexico State Capitol. Paul will likely be working away in his studio in back, and if you're fortunate, he'll guide you through some of his techniques.

Two state parks are a short drive west from Tierra Amarilla. **El Vado Lake State Park,** 14 miles southwest on NM 112 (✆ **575/588-7247;** www.nmparks.com), offers boating and water-skiing, fishing, and camping in summer; cross-country skiing and ice fishing in winter. **Heron Lake State Park,** 11 miles west on US 64 and NM 95 (✆ **575/588-7470;** www.nmparks.com), has a no-wake speed limit for motor vessels, adding to its appeal for fishing, sailing, windsurfing, canoeing, and swimming. The park has an interpretive center, plus camping, picnic sites, hiking trails, and cross-country skiing in the winter. The 5.5-mile Rio Chama trail connects the two lakes.

East of Tierra Amarilla, the Rio Brazos cuts a canyon through the Tusas Mountains and around 11,403-foot Brazos Peak. Just north of Los Ojos, NM 512 heads east 7½ miles up the **Brazos Box Canyon.** High cliffs that rise straight from the valley floor give it a Yosemite-like appearance—which is even more apparent from an overlook on US 64, 18 miles east of Tierra Amarilla en route to Taos. **El Chorro,** an impressive waterfall at the mouth of the canyon, usually flows only from early May to mid-June. Several resort lodges are in the area.

About 37 miles south of Tierra Amarilla on US 84, and 3 miles north of Ghost Ranch, is **Echo Canyon Amphitheater** (✆ **575/684-2486**), a U.S. Forest Service campground and picnic area. The natural "theater," hollowed out of sandstone by thousands of years of erosion, is a natural work of art with layers of stone ranging from pearl-color to blood red. The walls send back eerie echoes and even clips of conversations. It's just a 10-minute walk from the parking area. The fee is $2 per car. Some 13 miles west of here, via the dirt Forest Service road 151 into the Chama River Canyon Wilderness, is the isolated **Monastery of Christ in the Desert** (www.christdesert.org), built in 1964 by Benedictine monks. The brothers produce crafts, sold at a small gift shop, and operate a guesthouse.

Along the same road (FS 151) is access to the Chama River, a good place to hike, mountain bike, kayak, and camp. The **Rim Vista Trail** will take you to the top of the rim, with vast views out across Abiquiu Lake and Ghost Ranch. Primitive campsites can be found all along the river.

A 3-mile drive from there is **Ghost Ranch,** a collection of adobe buildings that make up an adult study center maintained by the United Presbyterian Church. A number of hauntingly memorable hikes originate from this place, which gets its name from the *brujas,* or witches, said to inhabit the canyons. Most popular among the hikes is spectacular **Chimney Rock,** but even more notable in my opinion is **Kitchen Mesa.** Directions for the hikes can be obtained at the visitor center. World-renowned painter Georgia O'Keeffe spent time at Ghost Ranch painting these canyons and other land formations. Eventually she bought a portion of the ranch and lived in a humble adobe house there. The ranch now offers seminars on a variety of topics, ranging from art to literature to religion, that are open to all. For information, contact **Ghost Ranch,** 401 Old Taos Hwy., Santa Fe (© **877/804-4678** or 505/982-8539; www.ghostranch.org).

As a part of Ghost Ranch, the **Florence Hawley Ellis Museum of Anthropology** has interpretative exhibits of a Spanish ranch house and Native American anthropology, and the **Ruth Hall Paleontology Museum** (© **505/685-4333** both museums; www.ghostranch.org) displays fossils of the early dinosaur named coelophysis found on the ranch. A lightly built creature, it was very fast when chasing prey. It roamed the area 250 million years ago, making it the oldest dinosaur found in New Mexico.

Many dinosaur skeletons have been found in rocks along the base of cliffs near **Abiquiu Reservoir** (© **505/685-4371**), a popular boating and fishing spot formed by the Abiquiu Dam.

A good place to stay and dine in the area is the **Abiquiu Inn ★**, a small country inn, restaurant, art gallery, and gift shop, ½ mile north of the village of Abiquiu (© **505/685-4378;** www.abiquiuinn.com). The casitas are especially nice. Rates are $139 to $199.

Heading south from Abiquiu, watch for **Dar al Islam** (© **505/685-4515**), a spiritual center with a circular Middle Eastern–style mosque made of adobe; the small community of **Mendanales** is the home of renowned weaver Cordelia Coronado; and **Hernandez,** the village immortalized in Ansel Adams's famous 1941 photograph *Moonrise, Hernandez, New Mexico.* **Rancho de San Juan** (p. 199) is a wonderful nearby place to stay and dine.

If you're in the area and need gas, a snack, or goodies for a picnic, stop in at **Bode's,** on US 84 in Abiquiu (© **505/685-4422**). The general store for the area, this place has shovels and irrigation boots, and better yet, cold drinks, gourmet sandwiches, and other deli items—even Frito pies and a hearty green chile chicken stew.

9

NORTHWESTERN NEW MEXICO

Chama & Its Scenic Railroad

NORTHEASTERN NEW MEXICO

The long distances along the mountains from Las Vegas to Cimarron, or across the plains from Raton to Clayton, are worth the driving time. History is everywhere, from evidence of Coronado's passage during his 16th-century search of Cíbola, to the Santa Fe Trail ruts on the prairie made some 300 years later. In **Cimarron,** you'll see evidence of the holdings of cattle baron Lucien Maxwell, who controlled most of these prairies as his private empire in the latter half of the 19th century. During his era, this was truly the Wild West. Cimarron attracted nearly every gunslinger of the era, from Butch Cassidy to Clay Allison, Black Jack Ketchum to Jesse James. Bullet holes still decorate the ceiling of the St. James Hotel.

Established long before its Nevada namesake, **Las Vegas** was the largest city in New Mexico at the turn of the 20th century, with a fast-growing, cosmopolitan population. Doc Holliday, Bat Masterson, and Wyatt Earp walked its wild streets in the 1880s. A decade later, it was the headquarters of Teddy Roosevelt's Rough Riders, and early in the 20th century, it was a silent-film capital and the site of a world heavyweight boxing match. Today, with a population of approximately 15,000, it is the region's largest city and the proud home of 900 historic properties. **Raton** (pop. 6,500), on I-25 in the Sangre de Cristo foothills, is the gateway to New Mexico from the north. **Clayton** (pop. 2,200), **Tucumcari** (pop. 5,900), and **Santa Rosa** (pop. 2,700) are all transportation hubs and ranching centers.

Two national monuments are particular points of interest. **Fort Union,** 24 miles north of Las Vegas, was the largest military installation in the Southwest in the 1860s and 1870s. **Capulin Volcano,** 33 miles east of Raton, last erupted 60,000 years ago; visitors can now walk inside the crater. Also of note are the **Kiowa and Rita Blanca National Grasslands** preserves: 136,000 acres of pure prairie.

Northeastern New Mexico

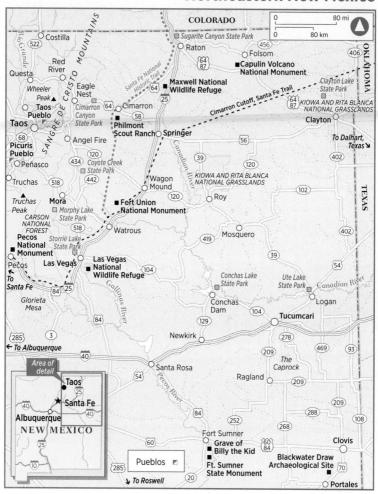

Drained by the Pecos and Canadian rivers, northeastern New Mexico is otherwise notable for the number of small lakes that afford opportunities for fishing, hunting, boating, camping, and even scuba diving. Eleven state parks and about a half-dozen designated wildlife areas are within the region. **Philmont Scout Ranch,** south of Cimarron, is known by Boy Scouts throughout the world.

NORTHEASTERN NEW MEXICO'S GREAT OUTDOORS

Northeastern New Mexico encompasses a variety of Southwestern landscapes. The undulating grasslands of the eastern portion of the region eventually give way to the cliffs, canyons, and forests of the mighty Sangre de Cristo Mountains, which offer some of the best hiking and camping in the state. The area is drained by the Pecos and Canadian rivers and has many small streams and lakes, including Ute Lake, the second-largest in the state, that afford opportunities for bait fishing, fly-fishing, boating, swimming, and sailing in this seemingly arid region. To find information on New Mexico state parks, go to www.nmparks.com.

BIRD-WATCHING Las Vegas National Wildlife Refuge (ⓒ 505/425-3581; www.fws.gov/southwest), 5 miles southeast of Las Vegas, is a great place for bird-watching. Species spotted year-round include prairie falcons and hawks; during late fall and early winter, migratory birds such as sandhill cranes, snow geese, Canada geese, and bald and golden eagles frequent the refuge. In all, more than 254 species can be sighted in the area. The **Maxwell National Wildlife Refuge** (ⓒ 575/375-2331), near Raton, also boasts a rich population of resident and migratory birds, including raptors and bald eagles.

BOATING You'll find opportunities for boating, windsurfing, and swimming throughout this region. Two of the most popular boating areas are **Storrie Lake State Park** (ⓒ 505/425-7278), 6 miles north of Las Vegas, and **Conchas Lake State Park** (ⓒ 575/868-2270), near Tucumcari. Storrie Lake is especially popular among **windsurfers,** who favor its consistent winds.

FISHING Isolated and primitive **Morphy Lake State Park** (ⓒ 575/387-2328), is a favorite destination for serious anglers. The lake is regularly stocked with rainbow trout. **Cimarron Canyon State Park** (ⓒ 575/377-6271), is also popular with fishers. Lake Alice in **Sugarite Canyon State Park** (ⓒ 575/445-5607), just north of Raton at the Colorado border, is a good spot for fly-fishing. For more information on the best fishing opportunities in the area, see chapters 7 and 8.

GOLF Duffers can get in a few holes in or near virtually every town covered in this section. I recommend the following courses: **Gene Torres Golf Course,** 1 Country Club Dr. in Las Vegas (ⓒ 505/425-7711; www.newmexicohighlandsugolf.com), was rebuilt and updated in 2007. **Raton Municipal Golf Course,** 510 Country Club Rd., Raton NM 87740 (ⓒ 575/445-8113; www.ratongolf.com); **Pendaries Village Mountain Resort,** in Rociada (ⓒ 505/425-3561; www.pendaries.net), 13 miles south of Mora and 27 miles northwest of Las Vegas; and **Tucumcari Municipal Golf Course,** Route 66 Boulevard, Tucumcari, NM 88401 (ⓒ 575/461-1849; www.cityoftucumcari.com/golf).

HIKING Northeastern New Mexico abounds in great places to hike, including the trails at Capulin Volcano; however, the best places are in the mountains to the north of Las Vegas and west of Santa Fe and Taos. The region's premier hike takes you to the top of **Hermit's Peak,** a lovely but strenuous 8-mile round-trip foray onto a stunning precipice. Take NM 65 about 15 miles northwest of Las Vegas to the El Porvenir Campground. It's probably best to acquire equipment and supplies in Albuquerque before you set out.

HORSEBACK RIDING   If you'd like to try your spurs at some real ranch riding, herding cattle, and spitting on the plains and such, contact the **Hartley Guest Ranch,** 50 Guest Ranch Lane, Roy (© **800/687-3833** or 575/673-2244). The ranch offers 3- and 5-night packages from April through September.

HOT SPRINGS   In this region, look for **Montezuma Hot Springs,** located on the campus of the Armand Hammer United World College of the American West, near Las Vegas (see "Exploring Las Vegas," below). Open daily from 8am to midnight.

SCUBA DIVING   There couldn't possibly be scuba diving in this dry, landlocked state, could there? Yes, there is, with the best at Santa Rosa, where you'll find the **Blue Hole,** an 81-foot-deep artesian well that's a favorite of divers from around the world. The best place to rent equipment is at the **Santa Rosa Dive Center** on Blue Hole Road, open only on weekends (© **575/472-3370**).

SWIMMING   In summer I always plan for a very cool dip at **Blue Hole** (see above). Swimming is also good (although chilly) at **Clayton, Conchas, Morphy, Storrie,** and **Ute lakes.** (You can find directions to and specifics about these lakes at various points in the rest of this chapter.) In addition, though it's an indoor rather than an outdoor experience, the **Abe Montoya Recreation Center's** (© **505/426-1739**) swimming pool, at 1751 N. Grand Ave., is an especially good place to take kids. It's Olympic-size and has a slide that will keep kids busy for hours. Call for more information.

LAS VEGAS & ENVIRONS ★★

Once known as the "gateway to New Mexico," **Las Vegas,** a pleasant town in the foothills of the Sangre de Cristo Mountains, was founded with a land grant from the Mexican government in 1835. A group of 29 Spanish colonists planted crops in the area and built a central plaza, which started out as a meeting place and a defense against Indian attack but soon became a main trading center on the Santa Fe Trail. Las Vegas boomed with the advent of the Atchison, Topeka, and Santa Fe Railway in 1879; almost overnight the town became the most important trading center and gathering place in the state and one of the largest towns in the Rocky Mountain West, rivaling Denver, Tucson, and El Paso in size.

Town settlers who arrived by train in the late 19th century shunned the indigenous adobe architecture, favoring instead building styles more typical of the Midwest or New England. They put up scores of fancy Queen Anne- and Victorian-style houses and hotels, and the town is noted to this day for its dazzling diversity of architectural styles. Some 900 buildings in Las Vegas are on the National Register of Historic Places.

Meanwhile, the town saw visits from many notable characters, including Billy the Kid, Wyatt Earp, and Doc Holliday (who practiced dentistry here). It continues to play its Old West part in movies: Scenes from *Wyatt Earp, The HiLo Country,* and *All the Pretty Horses* were shot here, as were Tom Mix's vintage westerns. Strolling the streets, you'll get a sense of those past times as you peruse Western-wear shops, bookstores, and old soda fountains that seem caught in a time warp, with their period architecture and friendly business owners.

Smiling Food

En route to Las Vegas from Santa Fe, along I-25, stop in at **La Risa Café** ★ (✆ 575/421-3883; www.thelarisacafe. com) on NM 3 in Ribera. In a cozy old house with brightly painted walls and on a fun patio, "the Smile" offers imaginative food made with fresh ingredients. For breakfast, their "Hangover stew" (green chile stew topped with eggs) is delicious. Lunch and dinner bring sandwiches, salads, and New Mexican dishes, as well as daily specials. Beer and wine accompany the menu. La Risa is open Thursday to Saturday 11am to 8pm and Sunday 8am to 6pm, with abbreviated hours in winter.

Essentials

GETTING THERE   From Santa Fe, take I-25 northeast 60 miles (1¼ hr.); from Raton, take I-25 south 105 miles (1¾ hr.); from Taos, follow NM 518 southeast 78 miles through Mora (2 hr.); from Tucumcari, follow NM 104 west 112 miles (2 hr.). **Las Vegas Municipal Airport** handles private flights and charters but has no regularly scheduled commercial service.

VISITOR INFORMATION   The **Las Vegas & San Miguel County Chamber of Commerce** is at 503 Sixth St. (P.O. Box 128), Las Vegas, NM 87701 (✆ **800/ 832-5947** or 505/425-8631; www.lasvegasnewmexico.com). It's open weekdays from 9am to 5pm.

Exploring Las Vegas
THE RAILROAD DISTRICT

When you first enter Las Vegas, you may want to take a brief driving tour through the railroad district and "east Las Vegas" to get a sense of how the railroad's arrival in the 1870s shaped that side of the city. Turn east on Douglas Avenue, which will take you to Railroad Avenue. In this district are turn-of-the-20th-century brick buildings housing such businesses as Moonlite Welding and Blue Dart Upholstery Shop. The center of the railroad district is the old Fred Harvey **Castañeda Hotel** at 510 Railroad. Built in 1898, it is one of the early Harvey Houses to be built in the Mission Revival style. It no longer operates as a hotel; however, you'll want to stop and take a peek into the lobby, which is still elegant, with a molded tin ceiling and arched windows.

THE HISTORIC DISTRICT

The chamber of commerce on Grand Avenue (see "Essentials," above) has a map of a self-guided tour of this area. What's most notable is the town's early Spanish history; adobe buildings dating from the first Spanish visits in the 16th century are still standing alongside the ornate structures of the late 1800s. In addition, you'll find a well-preserved collection of Territorial-style buildings. Most of the interesting structures can be found in the Plaza–Bridge Street area.

In particular, don't miss the **Plaza Hotel,** 230 Old Town Plaza, the finest hotel in the New Mexico Territory back in 1881. Its three-story facade, topped with a fancy broken pediment decoration, was the town's pride and joy, and it has been happily restored. (See "Where to Stay in Las Vegas," below.)

Another highlight is the **Dice Apartments,** 210 Old Town Plaza. Although the low adobe building is unimpressive, its history is distinguished—it is the sole building on the plaza that predates the U.S.-Mexican War of 1846. In that year, Gen. Stephen Kearny, commander of the Army of the West, stood on a one-story building on the north side of the plaza (probably this one) to address the town's population, claiming New Mexico for the United States.

For shopping, be sure to browse through **Rough Rider Antiques,** at 501 Railroad Ave. (ⓒ **505/454-8063**). You'll find Southwestern furniture, eclectic Western art, and quilts here. **War Dancer Designs & Gallery,** 125 Bridge St. (ⓒ **505/425-3877;** www.wardancerdesigns.com), carries Southwestern art and jewelry. Another good shopping stop is **Plaza Antiques,** 1805 Old Town Plaza (ⓒ **505/454-9447**), a fun place to browse for antique clothing and kitchen tables. A great place to browse for books on regional history is **Tome on the Range,** 158 Bridge St. (ⓒ **505/454-9944;** www.tomeontherange.com).

Housed in a 1940s-era Work Projects Administration (WPA) building, the **Las Vegas City Museum and Rough Riders Memorial Collection,** 727 Grand Ave. (ⓒ **505/426-3205;** www.lasvegasmuseum.org), is a fun spot to spend about an hour. The largest contingent of Rough Riders was recruited from New Mexico to fight in the 1898 Spanish-American War. This museum chronicles their contribution to U.S. history and also contains artifacts relating to the history of the city. Another exhibit documents the history of Las Vegas. Admission is free. The museum is open Tuesday to Sunday 10am to 4pm, and by appointment.

In the plaza area, the **Santa Fe Trail Interpretive Center,** 116 Bridge St. (ⓒ **505/425-8803;** www.santafetrailnm.org), offers a glimpse into efforts to restore the town's 918 historic buildings as well as information about the Santa Fe Trail. Set in the 1890s Winternitz Building, it's a fun stop, if you find it open. Hours vary greatly, as it is staffed by volunteers.

OTHER ATTRACTIONS NEAR TOWN

Las Vegas has two colleges. **New Mexico Highlands University** (ⓒ **877/850-9064;** www.nmhu.edu), a 4-year liberal arts school of almost 3,000 students, was

Weaving Magic

You can watch weavers at work at **Tapetes de Lana & The Traveler's Café** on the Las Vegas Plaza. Appropriately set in a late-1800s textile shop, this fun import shop, weavers' studio, and cafe offers a peek into the art as well as lovely works to buy. Hanging from antique stone walls are scarves, shawls, and Rio Grande–style rugs woven as part of a job-training program for people with low income, many of whom have mastered the art beautifully. Now the shop has a cafe selling organic free-trade coffee, baked goods, salads, sandwiches, and pizza. It's located at 1814 Plaza (ⓒ **505/426-8638;** www.worldtreasuresimports.com) and is open Monday through Saturday 7am to 6:30pm and Sunday 9am to 3pm. Prices for weavings are uncommonly reasonable. A sister store in nearby Mora, **Tapetes de Lana,** on NM 518 (ⓒ **575/387-2247;** www.tapetesdelana.com) carries rugs, scarves, and a good selection of yarns. It's open Monday to Friday 10am to 5pm.

established in 1893. The **Armand Hammer United World College,** 5 miles west of Las Vegas via NM 65 (© **505/454-4200;** www.uwc-usa.org), is an international school with students from more than 70 countries. It is housed in the former **Montezuma Hotel,** a luxury resort built by the Santa Fe Railroad in the 1880s and now a historic landmark. Three U.S. presidents, Germany's Kaiser Wilhelm II, and Japan's Meiji Emperor Mutsuhito stayed in the multistoried, turreted, 270-room "Montezuma Castle," as it came to be known. One-hour tours of the Castle are offered on select Saturdays at 1pm. Call © **505/454-4221** for a schedule.

Exploring the Area

Mora, a small village 31 miles north of Las Vegas via NM 518, is the main center between Las Vegas and Taos, and it's the seat of sparsely populated Mora County. The 15-mile-long Mora Valley is one of New Mexico's prettiest but most economically depressed regions, where families have for centuries lived by subsistence farming and are only recently having to adapt to other means of earning income. An interesting stop here is the **Tapetes de Lana** (see "Weaving Magic," above) shop in the middle of town.

Cleveland Roller Mill Museum ★ One vestige of a more prosperous past is this two-story adobe mill, which ground out wheat flour every day from 1901 to 1947. It was the last large merchant flour mill to be built in New Mexico and one of the last to stop running, and it is the only roller mill in the state to have its original milling works intact. Today, it has been converted into a museum with exhibits on local regional history and culture. The Millfest, on Labor Day weekend, features the mill in operation, dances, arts and crafts, music, and more. It's advisable to call ahead because the mill is closed from time to time. Plan to spend 1 to 2 hours exploring.

NM 518, about 2 miles west of Mora, Cleveland, NM 87715. © **575/387-2645.** www.clevelandrollermillmuseum.com. Free admission. Weekends only Memorial Day to Labor Day 10am–3pm.

La Cueva National Historic Site and Salman Ranch ★ 🎒 Each fall, I make a bit of a pilgrimage to this spot in a lush valley along the Mora River. Its history is rich, dating from the early 1800s, when a man named Vicente Romero began farming and raising sheep here. He completed an elegant two-story northern New Mexico home that still stands, as well as a mill that ground flour and supplied electricity for the area. Just north of these historic sites is the San Rafael Mission Church, with exquisite French Gothic windows. The trip through these sites is worth the time during any season, but in the fall, the raspberries ripen and turn this into a must-do trip to sample berries by the basket or crate, as well as in jams and over soft vanilla ice cream. Delicious.

NM 518, 6 miles east of Mora, Buena Vista, NM 87712. © **575/387-2900.** Free admission. Summer Mon–Sat 9am–5pm, Sun 10am–5pm; winter hours limited (call first).

Victory Alpaca Ranch ★ ☺ Few things surprise me in this strange part of the state, where images of Jesus are known to appear on stucco walls and ghosts are said to inhabit the old haciendas. But I must say that my head turned when I first saw alpacas grazing in a meadow here. I stopped immediately and stepped out of my car just in time for a tour. A guide took us out to a meadow where we fed the odd South American Andean creatures that greeted us with a harmonica-like hum. Very friendly, they ate from our hands while the babies roamed about, heads held high.

Also on-site is a store that sells a wide variety of yarns, hats, sweaters, and shawls made from alpaca wool.

1 mile north of Mora on NM 434, Mora, NM 87732. ✆ **505/387-2254.** www.victoryranch.com. Admission for feeding tour $3 adults, $2 children 11 and under. Daily 10am–4pm, with tours at 11am, 1pm, and 3pm. Closed Jan–Mar 14.

STATE PARKS & SCENIC HIGHLIGHTS

Storrie Lake State Park (✆ 505/425-7278; www.nmparks.com), 4 miles north via NM 518, open daily during daylight hours year-round, offers fishing, swimming, windsurfing, water-skiing, camping, a visitor center with historic exhibits, and a playground.

Villanueva State Park (✆ 575/421-2957; www.nmparks.com), 31 miles southwest via I-25 and NM 3 and open daily from 7am to 9pm (until 7pm in winter), offers excellent hiking, camping, and picnicking between red sandstone bluffs in the Pecos River Valley. Nearby are the Spanish colonial villages **Villanueva** and **San Miguel del Vado;** the latter is a national historic district built around an impressive 1805 church.

Fourteen miles north of Mora via NM 434 is an out-of-the-way beauty, **Coyote Creek State Park** (✆ 575/387-2328; www.nmparks.com), with fully developed and primitive campsites beside a stream. The fishing is good, and a few well-marked hiking trails head into the mountains.

If you prefer your nature a little less primitive, head for the **Pendaries Village Mountain Resort,** P.O. Box 820, Rociada, NM 87742 (✆ 505/425-3561; www.pendaries.net), located 13 miles south of Mora and 27 miles northwest of Las Vegas, on NM 105 off NM 94. This lovely foothills lodge boasts the region's finest 18-hole golf course and fishing. It also has overnight accommodations and a restaurant/lounge, open May to October.

FORT UNION NATIONAL MONUMENT ★

Established in 1851 to defend the Santa Fe Trail against attacks from Plains Indians, Fort Union was expanded in 1861 in anticipation of a Confederate invasion, which was subsequently thwarted at Glorieta Pass, 20 miles southeast of Santa Fe. Fort Union's location on the Santa Fe Trail made it a welcome way station for travelers, but when the railroad replaced the trail in 1879, the fort was on its way out. It was abandoned in 1891. Today, Fort Union, the largest military installation in the 19th-century Southwest, is in ruins. Though it offers little to see but adobe walls and chimneys, the very scope of the fort is impressive. Santa Fe Trail wagon ruts can still be seen nearby. Follow the 1.5-mile self-guided interpretive trail that wanders through the ruins and imagine yourself a weary 19th-century wagon traveler stopping for rest and supplies.

The national monument has a small visitor center and museum with exhibits and booklets on the fort's history. Visitors should allow 2 hours to tour the ruins.

JUST THE FACTS   To reach the site from Las Vegas, drive 18 miles north on I-25 to the Watrous exit, and then another 8 miles northwest on NM 161. Admission is $3 per person. Fort Union National Monument is open Memorial Day to Labor Day daily from 8am to 6pm; during the rest of the year, it is open daily from 8am to 4pm. It's closed Thanksgiving, Christmas, and New Year's Day.

A gift shop carries a wide selection of books on New Mexico history and women's history, and frontier military books. Camping is not available at the monument, but facilities are available in nearby Las Vegas.

For more information on the monument, contact Fort Union National Monument, P.O. Box 127, Watrous, NM 87753 (✆ **505/425-8025;** www.nps.gov/foun).

Where to Stay in Las Vegas

Most motels are on US 85 (Grand Ave.), the main north-south highway through downtown Las Vegas (an exception is the Plaza Hotel). All major chain hotels are represented in this town, so if that's your preference, call your favorite.

Plaza Hotel ★   This inn was built in Italianate bracketed style in 1882, in the days when Western towns, newly connected with the East by train, vied with one another in constructing fancy "railroad hotels." Considered the finest hotel in the New Mexico Territory when it was built, it underwent a $2-million renovation exactly 100 years later.

Don't expect to see the elegance of the Ritz. Instead, expect a more frontier style, with Old West antiques. However, the new **Ilfeld** section ★★ offers elegant accommodations, well worth requesting. Throughout the hotel, rooms vary in size, and have elegantly high ceilings, antique furnishings, comfortably firm beds, and armoires concealing some of the televisions. The rooms have windows facing either outward toward the plaza and surrounding streets or inward toward an atrium.

The hotel offers three meals daily and limited room service from its Landmark Grill (see below). Byron T's 19th-century saloon often features live music on Friday evenings.

230 Plaza, Las Vegas, NM 87701. ✆ **800/328-1882** or 505/425-3591. Fax 505/425-9659. www.plaza hotel-nm.com. 72 units. $109–$145 double; $129–$174 suite. Rates include cooked-to-order breakfast. AE, DC, DISC, MC, V. **Amenities:** Restaurant; bar; exercise room. *In room:* A/C, TV, hair dryer, Wi-Fi.

CAMPING

There's plenty of camping available in and around Las Vegas. I recommend the **Las Vegas KOA** (✆ **800/562-3423** or 505/454-0180; www.koa.com), which has 65 sites, 15 with full hookups, 26 with water and electricity. Laundry, grocery, ice, and recreational facilities (including a pool) are available, as is a large gift shop. Seasonal cookouts are offered. From I-25, go 1 block southeast on US 84, and then ½ mile southwest on Frontage Road (also called Sheridan Rd.).

Also in Las Vegas is **Vegas RV Park** (✆ **505/425-5640**), which offers 21 sites with full hookups and cable TV availability. It's located at 504 Harris Rd. in Las Vegas.

If you'd rather camp at a state park, try **Storrie Lake State Park** (✆ **505/425-7278;** www.nmparks.com), which offers 20 sites with electricity, 23 sites without it, and primitive camping in an open area close to the lake. Developed sites have water, picnic tables, and grills, and a visitor center is nearby.

Where to Dine in Las Vegas

The Landmark Grill ★★ 🍴 AMERICAN/NEW MEXICAN   This restaurant provides a tasty and atmospheric dining experience, with a view across the graceful Las Vegas plaza. Set in the historic 1882 Plaza Hotel, it has good food, especially the New Mexican and the grilled dishes. It is a sunny dining room, with tables well spaced, adorned by original 19th-century stenciling along the walls. Service is good. At breakfast you might have egg and pancake dishes, and on Sunday for brunch eggs Florentine (poached eggs, spinach, grilled tomato, and hollandaise sauce on an English muffin), served with hash browns. Lunch brings salads, sandwiches, burgers, pasta, and New Mexican food. I've enjoyed a grilled turkey with Swiss cheese and green chile on rye. At dinner, you might enjoy a filet with bleu cheese mushroom sauce, or grilled pecan-crusted trout with pecan butter, each served with salad, vegetable, and choice of starch. Beer and wine accompany the menu. Byron T's 19th-century saloon next door offers food daily from 2 to 5pm. A good wine list and full bar accompany the menu.

230 Plaza. (C) **800/328-1882** or 505/425-3591. www.plazahotel-nm.com. Reservations recommended on weekend nights. Main courses breakfast/brunch and lunch $5–$15, dinner $8–$26. AE, DC, DISC, MC, V. Daily 7am–2pm and 5–9pm.

ON THE SANTA FE TRAIL: CIMARRON & RATON

Cimarron ★

Few towns in the American West have as much lore or legend attached to them as Cimarron, 41 miles southwest of Raton via US 64. Nestled against the eastern slope of the Sangre de Cristo Mountains, the town (its name is Spanish for "wild" or "untamed") achieved its greatest fame as a "wild and woolly" outpost on the Santa Fe Trail between the 1850s and 1880s and a gathering place for area ranchers, traders, gamblers, gunslingers, and other characters.

ESSENTIALS

GETTING THERE   From Fort Union National Monument, head north on I-25, and then west on US 58 to Cimarron.

VISITOR INFORMATION   The **Cimarron Chamber of Commerce,** 104 N. Lincoln Ave. (P.O. Box 604), Cimarron, NM 87714 (C) **575/376-2417;** www. cimarronnm.com), has complete information on the region. It is open June to August daily 9am to 5pm, and November to April Monday through Saturday 10am to 3pm; the rest of the year Monday to Saturday 10am to 4pm.

EXPLORING THE WILD WEST TOWN

Frontier personalities such as Kit Carson and Wyatt Earp, Buffalo Bill Cody and Annie Oakley, Bat Masterson and Doc Holliday, Butch Cassidy and Jesse James, painter Frederic Remington and novelist Zane Grey all passed through and stayed in Cimarron—most of them at the **St. James Hotel** (p. 295). Even if you're not planning an overnight stay here, it's a fun place to visit for an hour or two.

Land baron Lucien Maxwell founded the town in 1848 as the base of operations for his 1.7-million-acre empire. In 1857, he built a mansion at his **Maxwell Ranch,** furnishing it opulently with heavy draperies, gold-framed paintings, and two grand pianos. The ranch isn't open for viewing today, but Maxwell's 1864 stone gristmill, built to supply flour to Fort Union, is. The **Aztec Mill** (C) **575/376-2417**), a grand, 1864 three-story stone museum that's well worth visiting, houses an interesting collection of early photos, as well as memorabilia including a saddle that belonged to Kit Carson. Head to the cellar to see the mill's workings. It's open Memorial Day to Labor Day Friday to Wednesday 10am to 5pm, Sunday noon to 5. Admission is by donation. Ask for a **Cimarron Historic Walking-Tour** map. Another map available here called "Ruts and Swales on the Santa Fe Trail," shows where travelers can find those historic marks on the prairie.

A block north of US 64, look for a few historic buildings housing shops. In particular check out the **Cimarron Art Gallery,** 337 E. 9th St. (✆ **800/253-1470** or 575/376-2614; www.cimarronartgallery.com), which has a 1937 soda fountain, and offers ice cream, flavored coffees, as well as jewelry, sculptures, and a huge selection of Boy Scout badges. Another good stop is **Blue Moon Eclectics,** 333 E. 9th St. (✆ **575/376-9040**), selling artful pottery, jewelry, books, and paintings. Down the street, stop in at **L. Martin Pavletich** studio, 428 E. 9th St. (✆ **575/376-2871;** www.lmartinpavletich.com), to see colorful landscape paintings of the region.

NEARBY ATTRACTIONS

Cimarron is the gateway to the **Philmont Scout Ranch** (✆ **575/376-2281;** www. scouting.org), a 137,500-acre property donated in pieces, beginning in 1938, to the Boy Scouts of America by Texas oilman Waite Phillips. Approximately 22,000 scouts from all over the world use the ranch for backcountry camping and leadership training each summer. Even if you have no interest in scouting, you'll want to visit the elegant Villa. It and two other museums on the ranch are open to the public.

GETTING OUTSIDE: CIMARRON CANYON STATE PARK

US 64 from Cimarron leads west 24 miles to Eagle Nest, passing en route the popular and often crowded **Cimarron Canyon State Park** (✆ **575/377-6271;** www. nmparks.com). A 32,000-acre designated state wildlife area, it sits at the foot of crenulated granite cliffs, 800 feet high in some areas, known as the Palisades. Rock climbing is allowed throughout the park except in the Palisades area. The river and the two park lakes attract anglers; for the best fishing, move away from the heavily populated campgrounds.

Just east of Cimarron, County Road 204 offers access to the Carson National Forest's **Valle Vidal** recreation area, a scenic and remote place to hike, backpack, and see hundreds of elk.

WHERE TO STAY & DINE IN CIMARRON

Casa del Gavilan ★ 🎖🛏 Built in 1910 on a broad hill overlooking Philmont and the mountains beyond, this sprawling adobe villa provides a quiet Southwestern ranch-style experience. The common areas have high ceilings with thick vigas (beams) and wooden floors. The rooms surround a central courtyard, a nice place to sit and relax in the cool evenings. The rooms are spacious, with comfortably firm beds and plenty of antiques. The bathrooms are medium-size and maintain an old-style charm. The two-bedroom suite, which is housed in what's called the Guest House, is good for families, though lower ceilings give it a slightly newer feel. There isn't a television on the premises, but a hiking trail just off the courtyard leads to amazing vistas. Breakfast is served in a big, sunny dining room; you'll find such specialties as baked French toast with ham-and-fruit salad and a baked apple pancake served with sausage.

6 miles south of Cimarron on NM 21 (P.O. Box 518), Cimarron, NM 87714. ✆ **800/428-4526** or 575/376-2246. Fax 575/376-2247. www.casadelgavilan.com. 5 units. $89–$149 per unit. Rates include full breakfast. Extra person $20, extra child between the ages of 5–10 $10. DISC, MC, V. *In room:* No phone.

Cold Beer

For a funky break between Raton and Cimarron, stop in at the **Colfax Tavern**. A bar since 1929, this lone building on the prairie is so popular that people call it Cold Beer, New Mexico, as though it were a town in itself. The owner says that Cold Beer is a "state of mind." Many ingredients go into creating that state, including a pool table, photos on the walls of locals imbibing, decent pizza and burgers, and a few tail-wagging mutts to welcome you. It's at the corner of US 64 and NM 505 (✆ **575/376-2229**).

St. James Hotel ★ This landmark hotel looks much the same today as it did in 1873, when it was built by Henri Lambert, previously a chef for Napoleon, Abraham Lincoln, and Ulysses S. Grant. In 2009, a new owner embarked on a major renovation. Rooms don't have televisions or phones—the better to evoke the days when famous guests such as Zane Grey were residents. Annie Oakley's bed is here, and a glass case holds a register with the signatures of Buffalo Bill Cody and Jesse James. One room just off the lobby stays open so that those not spending the night can have a peek. The most authentic and atmospheric rooms are next to this one.

The St. James was a place of some lawlessness: 26 men were said to have been killed within the 2-foot-thick adobe walls, and bullet holes can be seen in the pressed-tin ceiling of the bar. The ghosts of some are believed to inhabit the hotel.

Next door are 12 more rooms in a motel. These basic accommodations offer clean bathrooms, TVs, and telephones for those who prefer the 21st century.

The St. James serves good food three meals a day in an airy space, with hardwood floors and a grand fireplace. The offerings include a full breakfast buffet, sandwiches, burgers, salads, and New Mexican food at lunch, and grilled chicken, steaks, and fish at dinner. Prices range from $7 to $30. A patio with a fountain offers a nice place to relax, and live music in summer on Friday and Saturday nights. The Old West–style lounge, with a wooden bar from Santa Fe's St. Francis Hotel, draws locals and travelers. The restaurant is open daily 7am to 9pm, with the bar closing between 10:30pm and midnight.

617 S. Collison, Cimarron, NM 87714. ✆ **888/376-2664.** 575/376-2664. Fax 575/376-1009. www.exstjames.com. 22 units. Hotel $70–$140 double; motel $70–$100 double. AE, DISC, MC, V. **Amenities:** Restaurant; bar. *In room:* A/C, TV (in some rooms).

Raton

Raton was founded in 1879 at the site of Willow Springs, a watering stop on the Santa Fe Trail. Mountain man "Uncle Dick" Wooton, a closet entrepreneur, had blasted a pass through the Rocky Mountains just north of the spring and began charging tolls. When the railroad bought Wooton's road, Raton developed as the railroad, mining, and ranching center for this part of the New Mexico Territory. Today it has a well-preserved historic district and the finest shooting facility in the United States.

East of Raton is Capulin Mountain, home to Capulin Volcano National Monument. The volcanic crater of the majestic 8,182-foot peak, extinct for 60,000 years, is open to visitors. See below for more about Capulin Volcano National Monument.

ESSENTIALS

GETTING THERE   From Santa Fe, take I-25 north; from Taos, take US 64 east.

VISITOR INFORMATION   The tourist information center is at the **Raton Chamber and Economic Development Council,** 100 Clayton Rd., at the corner of 2nd Street (P.O. Box 1211), Raton, NM 87740 (✆ **800/638-6161** or 575/445-3689; www.raton.info). Memorial Day to Labor Day, the center is open daily from 8am to 6pm; hours are 8am to 5pm during the rest of the year.

STROLLING HISTORIC RATON

Five blocks of Raton's original town site are listed on the National Register of Historic Places, with some 70 significant buildings. It's best to explore the historic district by foot, allowing 1 to 2 hours. Start at the **Raton Museum ★**, 108 S. 2nd St. (✆ **575/445-8979**), which offers two floors full of displays on mining, railroad, and ranching history from the early days of the town, as well as lovely collections of Hispanic *santo* carvings and Native American basketry. The museum is open Tuesday through Saturday from 9am to 5pm. You can pick up a walking-tour map there. If you're not up for the full tour, at least take a stroll down 1st Street to see the **Mission Santa Fe Depot,** 1st St. and Cook Ave., a 1903 Spanish Mission Revival structure, where Amtrak still stops. Also of note is the **Wells Fargo Express Building,** 145 S. 1st St., erected in 1910, also in Spanish Mission Revival style. Now it houses the **Old Pass Gallery** (✆ **575/445-2052;** www.ratonarts.org), which features local, regional, and national art and crafts, including furnishings. Across the street is the **Abourezk Building,** 132 S. 1st St., which over time has been a drugstore, dry-good and grocery store, and is now home of the **Heirloom Shop** (✆ **575/445-8876**), a fun antiques shop. My mother likes to buy vintage handkerchiefs here.

A few blocks west on 2nd Street, be sure to take note of the **Shuler Theater,** 131 N. 2nd St. (✆ **575/445-4746**), which brings a variety of productions to Raton, including concerts of Music from Angel Fire. Across the street, shoppers will enjoy **Santa Fe Trail Traders,** 100 S. 2nd St. (✆ **575/445-2888**), which carries turquoise jewelry, Native American pottery, and weavings.

If you'd like a good latte or espresso, head to **Enchanted Grounds ★** 111 Park Ave. (✆ **575/445-2219**). The cafe also serves pastries, full breakfasts, salads, and sandwiches. All menu items cost less than $8. It is open Monday 7am to 2pm, Tuesday to Friday 7am to 4:30pm, and Saturday 7:30am to 4:30pm.

NEARBY ATTRACTIONS

The **NRA Whittington Center** (✆ **575/445-3615;** www.nrawc.org), off US 64 about 10 miles south of Raton, is considered the most complete nonmilitary shooting and training facility in the world. Operated by the National Rifle Association, it spans 50 square miles of rolling hills.

Hat Cemetery

While strolling Raton's main drag, step into **Solano's Boot & Western Wear,** 101 S. 2nd St. (✆ **575/445-2632**). As well as selling the latest in cowboy/cowgirl chic, the place has a "hat cemetery," with some 339 bent and sweaty favorites donated by northern New Mexico and southern Colorado ranchers.

In the little town of **Springer** (pop. 1,300), 39 miles south of Raton via I-25, the **Santa Fe Trail Museum,** in the center of town on Maxwell Avenue (𝒸 **575/483-2682;** www.santafetrailnm.org), is housed in the old three-story 1881 Colfax County Courthouse. It contains pioneer artifacts and memorabilia from travelers along the Santa Fe Trail and early residents of the area. Hours are Friday through Sunday 10:30am to 2:30pm. Admission is $4 for adults, $2 for seniors and students, and free for children 9 and under with an adult; free for all on Saturday. The **Colfax County Fair** takes place in Springer annually in mid-August, with a rodeo and 4-H fair. Call 𝒸 **575/445-8071** for more information.

If you want to stay or dine in Springer, stop in at the **Brown Hotel & Café,** 302 Maxwell Ave. (𝒸 **575/483-2269**). This old-time place has photos of area ranchers on the walls and sweet country-style rooms upstairs. The food is diner-style, with plenty of pancakes, burritos, and, of course, chicken-fried steak. The hotel owner bakes his own bread, so be sure to try a slice.

GETTING OUTSIDE

Sugarite Canyon State Park (𝒸 **575/445-5607;** www.nmparks.com), 10 miles northeast of Raton via NM 72 and NM 526, offers historic exhibits, camping, boating, and excellent fishing at two trout-stocked lakes. Lake Alice is the best place in the park for fly-fishing. Numerous hiking trails meander through the park, and a museum at the visitor center traces the canyon's mining history.

South of US 56 via NM 39 is the westernmost of the two parcels that comprise the **Kiowa and Rita Blanca National Grasslands** (𝒸 **575/374-9652**). The 263,954-acre area is a project to reclaim once-barren prairie land, the result of over-farming in the late 19th and early 20th centuries, and the Great Plains Dustbowl of the 1930s. Today the plains are grass-covered, and the area provides food, cover, and water for a wide variety of wildlife.

WHERE TO STAY IN RATON

Many major chains have hotels here, so you may want to contact your favorite.

Heart's Desire Bed & Breakfast ★ 🏠 Set in the Raton Historic District, this little crystal of history was built in 1885 to serve as a boardinghouse during Raton's railroad heyday. In 1997, Barbara Riley restored it, bringing splendor to the Victorian building. Guest rooms are medium-size, all decorated with Victorian touches, all with a shared bathroom. Each room has a sink and a comfortable bed. There's also a suite with a full kitchen and its own bathroom. Over a tasty breakfast such as eggs Benedict with fresh fruit, Barbara will regale you with tales of growing up on the plains.

301 S. 3rd St., Raton, NM 87740. 𝒸 **866/488-1028** or 575/445-1000. www.heartsdesireraton.com. 4 units. $75–$90 double with shared bathroom; $98–$130 suite. Rates include full breakfast. AE, DISC, MC, V. **Amenities:** Access to gym. *In room:* TV, Wi-Fi.

Holiday Inn Express ★★ ☺ This hotel on the south end of Raton offers comfortable rooms and excellent service. Six times running, it has earned the Torch-bearer award from Holiday Inn Express, which puts it in their top-20 properties in the Americas. Rooms come with a king or two queens, some with sleeper sofas as well. Each is medium size, with comfortable beds with good linens. Bathrooms are small with an outer vanity. This hotel also offers a variety of specialty suites—one for business travelers, which includes a large desk and two TVs; a "spa suite," which has a hot tub for two; and a "family suite," which offers a dining area and two separate bedrooms (one with bunk beds, so the space can sleep six or more).

101 Card Ave., Raton, NM 87740. ℭ **800/465-4329** or 575/445-1500. Fax 575/445-7650. www.hi express.com/ratonnm. 80 units. $109–$125 double; $150–$310 suite. Rates include full breakfast and evening snack. AE, DISC, MC, V. Pets $10 per night. **Amenities:** Free airport transfer; exercise room; Jacuzzi; indoor pool. *In room:* A/C, TV, hair dryer, Wi-Fi.

Camping

Quite a few campgrounds are in the Raton area, including the **Raton KOA,** in town at 1330 S. 2nd St. (ℭ **800/562-9033** or 575/445-3488; www.koa.com), with 54 sites, grocery and laundry facilities, and picnic tables and grills.

Summerland RV Park, at 1900 S. Cedar/I-25 and US 87 (ℭ **575/445-9536**), which is convenient to the interstate, has 44 sites (plus 16 monthly sites), laundry and grocery facilities, and picnic tables.

WHERE TO DINE IN RATON

Oasis Restaurant ★ ☺   At mealtime, area residents crowd this bright, open cafe on the south end of town, which serves quality diner-style food. With comfortable decor and tables and booths adequately spaced, the restaurant provides a good setting for locals to chat and gossip. "You gettin' old?" one man asked another. "Naw," his neighbor said. "I'm *already* old." All ages fill this place, though—they seem to enjoy the burgers (hand-patted) and fries (hand-cut). Soups are homemade, as are rolls, tortillas, and *sopaipillas.* Each day brings a special such as green-chile chicken casserole. Breakfasts are hearty, with lots of egg and pancake options.

1445 S. 2nd St. (from Clayton Hwy., turn south). ℭ **575/445-2221.** Main courses $4–$8 breakfast, $5–$16 lunch or dinner. AE, DISC, MC, V. Daily 6am–8pm (summer till 8:30pm).

Pappas' Sweet Shop Restaurant ★ SEAFOOD/STEAKS   Founded in 1923, this restaurant still draws praise from most locals. It's an interesting place, with counters full of chocolate candies and fudge up front. The big dining room has a comfortable tearoom feel, with soft chairs and low lighting. And though the food isn't sophisticated, it's tasty. Best known are the beef dishes; prime rib (on weekends) is a big seller here. I've enjoyed a filet that was well prepared. Meals come with homemade bread, a salad, vegetable, and your choice of a potato dish. A full-service lounge adjoins the restaurant, and there's also a gift shop.

1201 S. 2nd St. ℭ **575/445-9811.** Reservations suggested at dinner in summer. Main courses $6–$12 lunch, $10–$28 dinner. AE, DISC, MC, V. Mon–Sat 11:30am–2pm and 5–9pm.

CAPULIN VOLCANO NATIONAL MONUMENT ★★

Capulin Volcano National Monument offers visitors the rare opportunity to walk inside a volcanic crater. A 2-mile road spirals up from the visitor center more than 600 feet to the crater of the 8,182-foot peak, where two self-guided trails leave from the parking area: an energetic and popular 1-mile hike around the crater rim and a 100-foot descent into the crater to the ancient volcanic vent. One of the most interesting features here is the symmetry of the main cinder cone. The volcano was last active about 60,000 years ago, when it sent out the last of four lava flows. Scientists consider it extinct.

Because of the elevation, you should wear a light jacket in the summer and layers during the rest of the year. Be aware that the road up to the crater rim is frequently closed due to weather conditions. Plan on spending 1 to 3 hours at the volcano; a more in-depth exploration could take several days, but camping is not permitted.

A short nature trail behind the center introduces plant and animal life of the area and is great for kids and accessible to people with disabilities. The crater rim offers magnificent panoramic views of the surrounding landscape, the Sangre de Cristo Mountains, and, on clear days, portions of four contiguous states: Kansas, Texas, Colorado, and Oklahoma. During the summer, the volcano attracts swarms of lady-bird beetles (ladybugs).

Essentials

GETTING THERE   The monument is located 30 miles east of Raton via US 64/87 and north 3 miles on NM 325.

VISITOR INFORMATION   The visitor center, at the base of the western side of the volcano, is open daily Memorial Day to Labor Day from 8am to 5pm, the rest of the year daily from 8am to 4pm. An audiovisual program discusses volcanism, and park personnel will answer questions. Admission is $5 per car. For more information, contact **Capulin Volcano National Monument,** P.O. Box 40, Capulin, NM 88414 (© 575/278-2201; www.nps.gov/cavo).

Dining

Unfortunately, there is no quality food in the area. You might consider bringing food for a picnic at Capulin Volcano. Otherwise, the **Capulin Country Store,** US 64/87 and NM 325 (© 575/278-3900), offers ready-made sandwiches, microwave burritos, and chips. It is open daily 9am to 6pm. This is also a gift shop and liquor store.

Camping

Camping is not permitted inside the monument; however, camping facilities are available only 3 miles away, in Capulin (try the **Capulin RV Park,** at © 575/278-2921; www.capulinrvpark.com), as well as in the neighboring towns of Raton and Clayton. The RV park offers 25 sites with full hookups.

ALONG THE CLAYTON HIGHWAY

Folsom

Near here, cowboy George McJunkin discovered the 10,000-year-old remains of "Folsom Man." The find, excavated by the Denver Museum of Natural History in 1926, represented the first association of the artifacts of prehistoric people (spear points) with the fossil bones of extinct animals (a species of bison). The site is on private property and is closed to the public, but some artifacts (prehistoric as well as from the 19th c.) are displayed at the **Folsom Museum,** Main Street, Folsom (© 575/278-2122 in summer, or 575/278-3616 in winter; www.folsommuseum. org). The museum does not, however, contain any authentic Folsom points, only replicas. The museum has limited exhibits on prehistoric and historic Native

Americans of the area, as well as Folsom's settlement by whites. Hours are daily 10am to 5pm from Memorial Day to Labor Day, winter by appointment. The museum is open weekends only in May and September. Admission is $1.50 for adults, 50¢ for children 6 to 12, and free for children 5 and under. To get to Folsom, take NM 325 off the Clayton Highway (US 64/87, running 83 miles east-southeast from Raton to Clayton) for 7 miles.

Clayton

Clayton (pop. 2,500) is a ranching center 9 miles west of the Texas and Oklahoma panhandle borders. Rich prairie grasses, typical of nearby **Kiowa and Rita Blanca National Grasslands** (© 575/374-9652; www.fs.fed.us/r3/cibola), led to its founding in 1887 at the site of a longtime cowboy resting spot and watering hole. In the early 19th century, the Cimarron Cutoff of the Santa Fe Trail passed through here. This area was also the site of numerous bloody battles between Plains Indians and Anglo settlers and traders. Clayton is most known as the town where the notorious train robber Thomas "Black Jack" Ketchum was inadvertently decapitated while being hanged in 1901 (a doctor carefully reunited head and body before Ketchum was buried here).

ESSENTIALS

GETTING THERE   Clayton is located 9 miles west of the Texas and Oklahoma panhandles borders at the intersection of US 64/87 and US 56.

VISITOR INFORMATION   For information on area attractions, as well as more lodging and dining options, contact the **Clayton–Union County Chamber of Commerce,** 1103 S. 1st St. (P.O. Box 476), Clayton, NM 88415 (© **575/374-9253;** www.claytonnewmexico.org).

WHAT TO SEE & DO

Tracks from eight species of dinosaurs can be clearly seen on the **Dinosaur Track-way at Clayton Lake State Park ★**, 12 miles north of town off NM 370, near the distinctive Rabbit Ears Mountains (© **575/374-8808;** www.nmparks.com). The lake is crystalline blue and is strange to come upon after driving across these pale prairies. It offers fishing, swimming, boating, hiking, and camping. A half-mile trail on the southeast side of the lake leads across the dam to an exhibit describing the types of dinosaurs that roamed this area. From there, you can wander along a boardwalk to the amazingly intact dinosaur tracks. In 2006, the park gained an $85,000 observatory, where stargazers can take advantage of the region's especially dark skies to see to the edge of the universe.

WHERE TO STAY & DINE

A historic site of note in Clayton is the late 1800s **Eklund Hotel,** 15 Main St., which unfortunately closed recently. You can get a good night's rest at the **Day's Inn & Suites,** 1120 S. 1st St., Clayton, NM 88415 (© **800/329-7466** or 575/374-0133; www.daysinn.com). Dining options here include **Mary's Back Porch,** a little cafe at the back of a flower shop at 200 Main St. (© **575/374-8353**). Mary makes coffee drinks, soups, and sandwiches, specializing in smoked brisket. All menu items are under $10. The cafe is open Monday to Tuesday and Saturday 8am to 4pm, Wednesday to Friday 8am to 6pm. Another option, set in a brick, historic building is **Crossroads,** 2 Front St. (© **575/374-5282**). This cafe serves a variety of coffee drinks, pastries, and a few lunch/dinner offerings each day. You might find a grilled salmon salad or a chile bowl with cornbread, all excellent. All menu items are under $8. It is open Monday to Friday 6:30am to 2pm and 4 to 7pm; Saturday from 7 to 11am.

THE I-40 CORRIDOR

The 216 freeway miles on I-40 from Albuquerque to the Texas border cross feature-less prairie and very few towns. But the valleys of the Pecos River (site of Santa Rosa) and the Canadian River (Tucumcari is on its banks) have several attractions, including natural lakes. In recent years, both towns have revitalized their historic districts, creating little art centers, with a few galleries, shops, and restaurants. Start your tour of Santa Rosa along Historic Route 66, which is also a great place to peruse the Mother Road's neon signage. The historic district is just south of there. Tucumcari also has a great display of Route 66 neon and architecture along its main route, with the historic district a few blocks north. Both are well worth driving.

Essentials

GETTING THERE   Travel time from Albuquerque to Tucumcari via I-40 is 2 hours, 40 minutes; to Santa Rosa, 1 hour, 45 minutes. There's no regularly sched-uled commercial service into either Tucumcari or Santa Rosa. Private planes can land at **Tucumcari Municipal Airport** (© **575/461-3451**).

VISITOR INFORMATION   Contact the **Tucumcari–Quay County Chamber of Commerce,** 404 W. Rte. 66 Blvd. (P.O. Drawer E), Tucumcari, NM 88401 (© **575/461-1694;** www.tucumcarinm.com), or the **Santa Rosa City Informa-tion Center,** 244 S. Fourth St., Santa Rosa, NM 88435 (© **575/472-3404;** www.santarosanm.org).

Seeing the Sights

The **Mesalands Community College's Dinosaur Museum ★**, 222 E. Laughlin (© **575/461-3466;** www.mesalands.edu/museum/museum.htm), half a block east off 1st Street, is home to the largest collection of life-size bronze prehistoric skele-tons in the world. It's open from March to Labor Day, Tuesday through Saturday 10am to 6pm (noon–5pm the rest of the year). Admission is $6 for adults, $3.50 for children 5 to 11, free for children 4 and under, and $5 for seniors 65 and older.

A fun small-town stop is **Tucumcari Historical Museum,** 416 S. Adams (© **575/461-4201;** www.cityoftucumcari.com/museum), 1 block east of 1st Street. Renovated in 1999, the museum showcases Route 66 and other regional memora-bilia. It's open from 10am to 5pm Monday through Saturday in summer and from 9am to 4pm Monday through Friday in winter. Admission is $5 for adults, $4 for seniors and $1 for children 6 to 15; it's free for kids 5 and under. The moonlike **Mesa Redondo,** a round mesa rising 11 miles south of town via NM 209, was once train robber "Black Jack" Ketchum's hideout—he was eventually captured and exe-cuted in Clayton in 1901.

To the northwest, 34 miles distant from Tucumcari over NM 104, is **Conchas Lake State Park** (© **575/868-2270;** www.nmparks.com), with a reservoir 25 miles long. Though the water is a beautiful aqua, it sits within a desert environment, with lots of sand and little shade. A marina on the northern side provides facilities for boating, fishing, and water-skiing, while nearby you'll find a store, cafe, RV park with hookups, and trailers available to rent. If you'd like to spend a few days here, contact the **Adobe Belle ★**, P.O. Box 131, Conchas Dam, NM 88416 (🕿 **575/868-3351**), an inn just above the lake's shore that offers adobe cabins. The decor is a little dated, but the cabins provide plenty of space.

Ute Lake State Park (🕿 **575/487-2284;** www.nmparks.com) is 22 miles northeast of Tucumcari on US 54, near the town of Logan. It has a full-service marina, docking facilities, picnic tables, campsites, and rental boats.

Quay County around Tucumcari is noted for its blue-quail hunting, said to be the best anywhere in the United States.

Santa Rosa calls itself "the city of natural lakes." Those bodies of water include **Blue Hole ★** (turn south off Rte. 66 onto Lake Dr. then left onto Blue Hole Rd.; 🕿 **575/472-3763**), a crystal-clear, 81-foot-deep artesian well just east of downtown. Fed by a subterranean river that flows 3,000 gallons per minute at a constant 61°F (16°C), it's a favorite of scuba divers and is deep enough to merit open-water certification. Divers must either be certified or be with a certified instructor. Equipment can be rented at the nearby **Santa Rosa Dive Center** (🕿 **575/472-3370**), open on weekends only. Swimming and snorkeling are also fun here, with a bathhouse on-site. This is a great place to cool off on a hot summer day. **Park Lake** (🕿 **575/472-3763**), in the middle of town, serves as the town's municipal pool. It's a natural lake so the water is fresh, and visitors can rent paddleboats and canoes. The kids can swim with the geese while you cool off under the elm trees. The lake offers free swimming, picnicking, and fishing, as well as a softball field and playground. **Santa Rosa Lake State Park,** P.O. Box 384, Santa Rosa, NM 88435 (🕿 **575/472-3110;** www.nmparks.com), on a dammed portion of the Pecos River, has camping, hiking, boating, and excellent fishing. Ten miles south of town via NM 91, the village of **Puerto de Luna** is a 19th-century county seat with a mid-1800s courthouse and church, Nuestra Señora del Refugio. Francisco Vásquez de Coronado was believed to have camped here as he traveled en route to Kansas. For insight into village life here, read Rudolfo Anaya's *Bless Me, Ultima,* a tale of growing up on the *llano* (plains) of the area.

Where to Stay

Major chain hotels are at I-40 interchanges in both Tucumcari and Santa Rosa. Smaller ma-and-pa motels can be found along the main streets through town that were once segments of legendary Route 66—still bearing that historic name.

IN TUCUMCARI

Hampton Inn ★   With the consistency of its brand name, this hotel provides a bit of an oasis in this part of the state. It's located near I-40, but has some very quiet rooms. Each is medium size with earth-tone decor and comfortable beds with luxury bedding. Some have microwaves and fridges. The bathrooms are standard size with floor tiles. The west side rooms offer the most quiet and a bit of a view out across meadows and ponds.

3409 E. Rte. 66. (at I-40 exit 335), Tucumcari, NM 88401. 🕿 **800/426-7866** or 575/461-1111. Fax 575/461-0000. www.hamptoninn.com. 58 units. $99–$115. Rates include hot breakfast. AE, DC, DISC, MC, V. **Amenities:** Exercise room; Jacuzzi; indoor pool; sauna. *In room:* A/C, TV, hair dryer, Wi-Fi.

route 66 REVISITED: REDISCOVERING NEW MEXICO'S STRETCH OF THE MOTHER ROAD

As the old Bobby Troupe hit suggests: Get your kicks on Route 66. The highway that once stretched from Chicago to California was hailed as the road to freedom. During the Great Depression, it was the way west for farmers escaping Dust Bowl poverty out on the plains. If you found yourself in a rut in the late 1940s and '50s, all you had to do was hop in the car and head west on Route 66.

Of course, the road existed long before it gained such widespread fascination. Built in the late 1920s and paved in 1937, it was the lifeblood of communities in eight states. Nowadays, however, US 66 is as elusive as the fantasies that once carried hundreds of thousands west in search of a better life. Replaced by other roads, covered up by interstates (mostly I-40), and just plain out of use, Route 66 still exists in New Mexico, but you'll have to do a little searching and take some extra time to find it.

Motorists driving west from Texas can take a spin (make that a slow spin) on a 20-mile gravel stretch of the original highway running from Glenrio (Texas) to San Jon. From San Jon to Tucumcari, you can enjoy nearly 24 continuous paved miles of vintage 66. In Tucumcari,

the historic route sliced through the center of town along what is now Route 66 Boulevard. Santa Rosa's Historic Route 66 is that city's 4-mile claim to the Mother Road. In Albuquerque, US 66 follows Central Avenue for 18 miles, from the 1936 State Fairgrounds (now Expo New Mexico), past original 1930s motels and the historic Nob Hill district, on west through downtown.

One of the best spots to pretend you are a 1950s road warrior crossing the desert—whizzing past rattlesnakes, tepees, and tumbleweeds—is along NM 124, which winds 25 miles from Mesita to Acoma in northwestern New Mexico. You can next pick up old Route 66 in Grants, along the 6-mile Santa Fe Avenue. In Gallup, a 9-mile segment of US 66 is lined with restaurants and hotels reminiscent of the city's days as a Western film capital from 1929 to 1964. Just outside Gallup, the historic route continues west to the Arizona border as NM 118.

For more information about Route 66, contact the **Grants/Cíbola County Chamber of Commerce** (✆ **800/748-2142;** www.grants.org) or the **New Mexico Department of Tourism** (✆ **505/827-7400;** www.newmexico.org).

Camping near Tucumcari

There are three good campgrounds around Tucumcari. **Tucumcari KOA** (✆ **800/562-1871** or 575/461-1841; www.koa.com) has 111 sites, laundry and grocery facilities, RV supplies, picnic tables, and grills. It also offers a recreation hall with video games, a heated swimming pool, a hot tub, a basketball hoop, a playground, horseshoes, and shuffleboard, along with lots of elm trees for shade. To get there from I-40, get off the interstate at exit 335, and then go ¼ mile east on South Frontage Road.

Mt. Road RV Park (✆ **575/461-9628**) has 60 sites with full hookups, tent sites, laundry facilities, and picnic tables. From I-40, take exit 333 to Mountain Road; the park is on the US 54 bypass.

The campground in **Conchas Lake State Park** (✆ **575/868-2270;** www.emnrd.state.nm.us/prd/conchas.htm) has 104 sites, 40 full hookups, lake swimming, boating, and fishing.

IN SANTA ROSA

La Quinta ★ Perched on a hill above Santa Rosa, this newer whitewashed chain hotel offers clean and functional rooms. All are medium-size, decorated in tasteful earth tones. Each has an extremely small bathroom with an outer sink/vanity. Beds are comfy and are accompanied by a table and chairs. The place is inventively landscaped with a rock grotto patio where the Jacuzzi sits.

1701 Will Rogers Dr., Santa Rosa, NM 88435. ℂ **800/753-3757** or 575/472-4800. Fax 575/472-4809. www.laquinta.com. 60 units. $90–$114 double. Rates include continental breakfast. AE, DC, DISC, MC, V. **Amenities:** Exercise room; outdoor Jacuzzi; indoor pool. *In room:* A/C, TV, hair dryer, Wi-Fi.

Camping near Santa Rosa

The **Santa Rosa Campground** (ℂ **575/472-3126**) offers 94 sites, 33 full hookups, laundry and grocery facilities, Wi-Fi, fire rings, grills, a heated swimming pool, and a playground for the kids. Situated in a piñon and juniper forest near town, the campground has a few small elm trees on the grounds. Coming from the east on I-40, take exit 277 and go 1 mile west on the Business Loop; coming from the west on I-40, take exit 275 and go ¼ mile east on the Business Loop.

Also in the area is **Santa Rosa Lake State Park** (ℂ **575/472-3110**; www.emnrd.state.nm.us/prd/santarosa.htm), with year-round camping featuring 75 sites (about a third with electric hookups) as well as grills, boating, fishing, and hiking trails. Swimming in the lake is permitted but not encouraged because of the lake's uneven bottom and lack of beaches; children would be safer swimming in Park Lake in Santa Rosa.

Two Good Places to Eat in the Area

Del's Family Restaurant AMERICAN/NEW MEXICAN The big cow atop Del's neon sign is not only a Route 66 landmark; it also points to the fine steaks inside. The restaurant has big windows along most every wall, letting in plenty of daylight or neon light at night. It's a casual, diner-style eatery with lots of plants. At lunch, sample sandwiches and salads. The roast beef is a big seller here at dinnertime, served with a scoop of mashed potatoes and a trip to the salad bar. You can also order a grilled chicken breast. The New Mexican food is good but not great. Del's is not licensed for alcoholic beverages.

1202 E. Rte. 66, Tucumcari. ℂ **575/461-1740.** Main courses $5–$10 lunch, $8–$16 dinner. MC, V. Mon-Sat 11am–9pm.

Joseph's Restaurant & Cantina ★ AMERICAN/NEW MEXICAN You may want to plan your drive so that you can eat a meal at "Joe's." In business since 1956, it's a real Route 66 diner, with linoleum tables, comfortable booths, and plenty of memorabilia, from license plates to vintage RC Cola posters. The locals all eat here: You'll see Hispanic grandmothers, skinny cowboys in straw hats, and dusty farmhands just in from the fields. The varied menu offers excellent fare. Breakfast brings eggs and bacon or omelets. At lunch, I've enjoyed a salad topped with tender grilled chicken. The New Mexican dishes are large and chile-smothered, and the burgers juicy, with a variety of toppings, from the Rio Pecos topped with green chile to the Acapulco, with guacamole. Steaks are a big seller, also at a good price. For dessert, try a piece of pie or a shake. Also on the premises are a bakery, a full-service bar, and a gift shop.

865 Historic Rte. 66, Santa Rosa. ℂ **575/472-3361.** Main courses $4–$8 breakfast, $6–$9 lunch, $7–$15 dinner. AE, DISC, MC, V. Daily 7am–10pm (winter till 9pm).

SOUTHWESTERN NEW MEXICO

This region, defined by the border with Mexico and cloaked by the 3.3-million-acre **Gila National Forest,** offers ruggedness and remoteness, and always an echo of history. It's the region that wealthy Zacatecan mine owner Juan de Oñate passed through in 1598 to take possession of the territory for the Spanish king.

It was and still is a good place to hide out. Billy the Kid lived here; so did Geronimo. You'll stumble upon relics of their past at many junctures. You'll see thousands of snow geese taking flight at the **Bosque del Apache National Wildlife Refuge.** You can even contemplate the vastness of space at the **Very Large Array (VLA),** the world's most powerful radio telescope.

The most settled part of the area is down the center of the state, where the Rio Grande marks a distinct riparian line. Throughout history, this river has nourished the Native American, Hispanic, and Anglo settlers who have built their homes beside its banks. The river land was especially fertile around modern Las Cruces; the settlement of La Mesilla was southern New Mexico's major center for 3 centuries.

West of the river, the Black Range and Mogollon Mountains rise in the area now cloaked by Gila National Forest. This was the homeland of the Mogollon Indians 1,000 years ago. **Gila Cliff Dwellings National Monument** preserves one of their great legacies. This was also the homeland of the fiercely independent Chiricahua Apaches in the 19th century. Considered the last North American Indians to succumb to the whites, they counted Cochise and Geronimo among their leaders.

Mining and outdoor recreation, centered in historic **Silver City** (pop. 10,000), are the economic stanchions of the region. But dozens of mining towns have boomed and busted in the past 140 years, as a smattering of ghost towns throughout the region attest. Mining continues in the region but with little certainty. Some towns such as Silver City and Hillsboro now survive because artists have opened galleries on the Old West streets.

Las Cruces, at the foot of the Organ Mountains, is New Mexico's second largest city, with 95,000 people. It's a busy agricultural and education center. North up the valley are **Truth or Consequences** (pop. 6,800), a spa town named for the 1950s radio and TV game show, and **Socorro** (pop. 9,000), a historic city with Spanish roots. West, on the I-10

Southwestern New Mexico

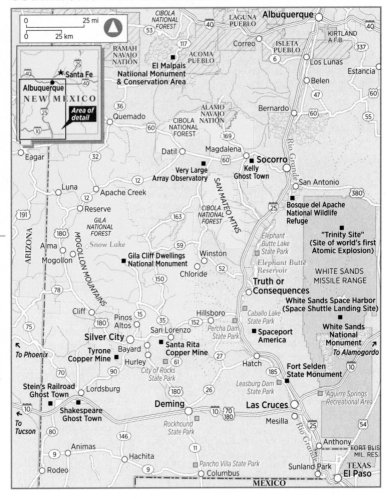

corridor to Arizona, are the ranching centers of **Deming** (pop. 15,500) and **Lordsburg** (pop. 2,800).

SOUTHWESTERN NEW MEXICO'S GREAT OUTDOORS

Rugged, remote, forested, and fascinating all describe southwestern New Mexico, where few tourists venture—lucky for you if you're looking for backcountry

Hummingbird Safari at Lake Roberts

At the **Annual Hummingbirds of New Mexico Festival** (© 575/536-3206; www.hbnm.org) in the village of Lake Roberts, the third week in July, bird lovers can watch as little cuffs are placed on hummingbird ankles, a remarkable process called "banding" to help identify them and learn about their lives. The weekend includes talks, guided walks, arts-and-crafts booths, and baked goods for sale.

adventure. The general website for all the **New Mexico State Parks** listed below is **www.nmparks.com**.

BIKING   Bikes are not allowed in the Gila Wilderness, but they are permitted on trails in other parts of **Gila National Forest** (© 575/388-8201; www.fs.usda.gov/gila). Refer to "Other Adventures in Gila National Forest," later in this chapter, for some specific ride suggestions and contact **Gila Hike and Bike** (© 575/388-3222) in Silver City for rentals and guidebooks to riding in the Gila National Forest.

BIRD-WATCHING   Bosque del Apache National Wildlife Refuge (© 575/835-1828) is a refuge for migratory waterfowl such as snow geese and cranes. (See "Seeing the Sights Near Socorro," below.) **North Monticello Point** (© 575/517-7720), on Elephant Butte Lake, is a great place to see pelicans, bald eagles, and a variety of waterfowl, while **Water Canyon** (© 575/854-2281), 14 miles west of Socorro in the **Cíbola National Forest,** is home to golden eagles. The **Sevilleta National Wildlife Refuge** (© 575/864-4021; www.fws.gov/southwest), north of Socorro between La Joya and Chamizal, is a long-term ecological research site under the direction of the National Science Foundation. Its visitor center has exhibits about the refuge. The **Mesilla Valley Bosque State Park,** southwest of Mesilla in Las Cruces (© 575/523-4398), has a visitor center with displays that describe the bosque restoration here and offers Saturday guided birding tours. Call for a schedule. The refuge offers free tours during its open house, the second Saturday in October. In recent years, the **Gila National Forest** (© 575/388-8201; www.fs.usda.gov/gila) has become quite popular with birders. In the Gila, my favorite birding spot is **Lake Roberts,** where hummingbirds abound.

BOATING   In the Gila National Forest, both **Lake Roberts** (© 575/536-2250), about 40 miles north of Silver City on NM 15, and **Snow Lake** (© 575/533-6231), north on US 180 from Silver City and then east on NM 159, allow boating. Lake Roberts features motorboat rentals, whereas Snow Lake only permits canoes, rowboats, and other boats without gas motors.

Elephant Butte Lake State Park (© 575/744-5923) boasts the largest body of water in New Mexico. The lake is 43 miles long and popular with boating enthusiasts. Three ramps provide boating access to the lake, and there are launching areas for smaller vessels.

FISHING   Caballo Lake State Park (© 575/743-3942), about 18 miles south of Truth or Consequences, offers smallmouth and largemouth bass, stripers, bluegill, crappie, catfish, and walleye fishing in its 11,500-acre lake. **Elephant Butte Lake State Park** (© 575/744-5923), also near Truth or Consequences, is another great fishing location. Look to catch white bass, black bass, catfish, walleye, crappie, and stripers here. **Lake Roberts** (© 575/536-2250), about 40 miles north of Silver City in the Gila National Forest, is prime rainbow trout fishing waters. A fishing license and habitat stamp are both required. You'll find fly-fishing in the **Gila River** year-round, but the best seasons are spring and fall. Mainly rainbow trout swim these waters, with catfish on the lower Gila. For more information, contact the **New Mexico Game and Fish Department** (© 505/476-8000; www.wildlife.state.nm.us).

GOLF   In Socorro, the 18-hole **New Mexico Tech Golf Course** (© 575/835-5335; www.nmt.edu) offers tree-lined fairways and water on more than half of its holes. The **Truth or Consequences Golf Course** (© 575/894-2603) offers 9 fairly traditional holes in a desert setting. But the new **Sierra del Rio Golf Course** at Turtleback Mountain Resort (© 575/744-4653; www.sierradelrio.com), opened in 2007, offers 18 holes that area golfers are talking about. Another contemporary course is in Las Cruces, at the 18-hole **Sonoma Ranch Golf Course** (© 575/521-1818; www.sonomaranchgolf.com), which opened in 2000. Las Cruces also has the **New Mexico State University Golf Course** (© 575/646-3219; www.nmsugolf.com), built with collegiate golf in mind. With wide-spanning views and undulating terrain, this Cal Olsen–designed course has much to offer. Deming has the 18-hole **Rio Mimbres Country Club** (© 575/546-9481), while Silver City golfers go to the 18-hole **Silver City Golf Course** (© 575/538-5041; www.silvercity.org/golf), home to the annual Billy Casper Golf Tournament.

HIKING   It goes without saying that there's great hiking available in the **Gila National Forest** (© 575/388-8201; www.nps.gov/gicl), which has approximately 1,500 miles of trails, ranging in length and difficulty. Your best bet for hiking in the area is to purchase a guidebook devoted entirely to hiking the Gila National Forest, but popular areas include the Crest Trail, the West Fork Trail, and the Aldo Leopold Wilderness. One favorite day hike in the forest is the Catwalk, a moderately strenuous hike along a series of steel bridges and walkways suspended over Whitewater Canyon. See "Other Adventures in Gila National Forest," later in this chapter, for more hiking suggestions. Whenever and wherever you go hiking, be sure to carry plenty of water.

HORSEBACK RIDING   If you want to go horseback riding, the **Double E Guest Ranch** (© 575/535-2048; www.doubleranch.com) offers authentic ranch riding in the southwestern New Mexico desert and forest lands. Because the ranch is also a working cattle ranch, it has an authentic feel, and a guest capacity of only 12 adds to the experience. About a half-hour from Silver City, the ranch sits on a shady bend of Bear Creek, which draws plenty of wildlife. The accommodations are in old ranch buildings, which range from cozy to expansive. These are not luxury rooms—they're real ranch lodgings. The ranch does not have a separate children's program but does accept kids.

HOT SPRINGS   This is hot springs country. For locations in Truth or Consequences, call © 800/831-9487 or 575/894-3536, or see "Truth or Consequences," later in this chapter for my choices of bathhouses. **Lightfeather Hot Spring** is a spring near the Gila Cliff Dwellings National Monument visitor center.

SWIMMING   Swimming is permitted at **Elephant Butte Lake State Park** (© 575/744-5923) and **Caballo Lake State Park** (© 575/743-3942), but not at some others. Be sure to ask first.

SOCORRO & THE VLA

Socorro, a quiet, pleasant town of about 9,000, is an unusual mix of the 19th, 20th, and 21st centuries. Established as a mining settlement and ranching center, its downtown area is dominated by numerous mid-1800s buildings and the 17th-century San Miguel Mission. **The New Mexico Institute of Mining and Technology** (New Mexico Tech) is a major research center. Socorro is also the gateway to a vast and varied two-county region that includes the **Bosque del Apache National Wildlife Refuge,** the **Very Large Array National Radio Astronomy Observatory (VLA),** and three national forests.

Essentials

GETTING THERE From Albuquerque, take I-25 south (1¼ hr.). From Las Cruces, take I-25 north (2¾ hr.).

VISITOR INFORMATION The **Socorro County Chamber of Commerce,** which is also the visitor information headquarters, is at 101 Plaza (P.O. Box 743), Socorro, NM 87801 (© **575/835-0424;** www.socorro-nm.com).

Exploring Socorro

The best introduction to Socorro is a walking tour of the historic district. A brochure with a map and guidebook, available at the chamber of commerce on the **plaza,** where the tour begins, points out several historic buildings, many on the National Register of Historic Places.

You'll definitely want to check out the old **Val Verde Hotel.** The horseshoe-shaped Val Verde, a National Historic Landmark, was built in 1919 in California Mission style. It's been converted to apartments. Another interesting spot is the **Fullingim-Isenhour-Leard Gallery,** 113-C W. Abeyta St., just off the plaza (© **575/835-4487;** www.figalleries.com). In a historic building, four artists share their bronze-work, paintings, and etchings. If you're craving a cappuccino or latte while in Socorro, head to the **Manzanares Street Coffee House ★**, 110 Manzanares St. (© **575/838-0809**). As well as coffee drinks, the shop offers good sandwiches on focaccia, salads, and house-made gelato and pastries. It's also a wireless Internet zone.

Cruising the Royal Road

As you skim across the open desert on Interstate 25, take heart in knowing that you're following an ancient route: El Camino Real, or the Royal Road that ran from Mexico to San Juan Pueblo north of Santa Fe. It's older than recorded history, traveled first by indigenous people. Later the Spaniards, beginning with Juan de Oñate in 1598, made their way north on it, seeking adventure and prosperity. They brought herds of horses and cattle, flocks of sheep and goats, and, most transformative, Catholicism. In subsequent centuries it continued to be the main road for travelers and traders carrying goods and ideas. Eventually it connected up with the Santa Fe Trail, which was the east-west route from Missouri. To find out more about this route, visit the **El Camino Real International Heritage Center.** See below for details.

Other Attractions

El Camino Real International Heritage Center ★ This museum, opened in 2005, tells the story of El Camino Real, the 1,500-mile international trade route from Mexico to San Juan Pueblo, near Santa Fe. The impressive $5-million, 20,000-square-foot structure, set in the middle of the desert, is an award-winning building perched like a ship above Sheep Canyon between Socorro and Truth or Consequences. In fact, the center is designed with ship elements, including a bowsprit on the helm. "The journey across this area reminded travelers of crossing the sea, with its tufts of grass, mirages, and overwhelming silence," says Monument Ranger Dave Wunker. The real fun starts in the exhibit hall, where visitors get to travel the trail themselves, beginning at Zacatecas Plaza in Mexico, one of many stops along the road. Artifacts from the Camino days—a *caja fuerte* (strong box) and an Apache water jug—help tell the story.

CR 1598, 30 miles south of Socorro. From I-25 take exit 115 and follow the signs. ℂ **575/854-3600.** www.nmmonuments.org. Admission $5 adults; free for children 16 and under. Wed–Sun 8:30am–5pm.

Mineral Museum Run by the New Mexico Bureau of Geology and Mineral Resources, this museum has the largest geological collection in the state. Its more than 15,000 specimens include mineral samples from all over the world, fossils, mining artifacts, and photographs.

Campus Rd., New Mexico Tech campus. ℂ **575/835-5420.** www.geoinfo.nmt.edu/museum. Free admission. Mon–Fri 8am–5pm; Sat–Sun 10am–3pm.

Old San Miguel Mission ★★ Built between 1615 and 1626 and abandoned during the Pueblo Revolt of 1680, this graceful church was subsequently restored, and a new wing was built in 1853. It boasts thick adobe walls, large carved vigas (rafters), and supporting corbel arches. English-language Masses are Saturday at 5 and 7pm and Sunday at 8am, 10am, and 12:30pm.

403 El Camino Real NW, 2 blocks north of the plaza. ℂ **575/835-2891.** www.sdc.org/~smiguel. Free admission. Mon–Fri 8am–7:30pm (winter till 6:30pm).

Seeing the Sights Near Socorro

SOUTH OF SOCORRO The village of San Antonio, the boyhood home of Conrad Hilton, is 10 miles from Socorro via I-25. During the financial panic of 1907, his merchant father, Augustus Hilton, converted part of his store into a rooming house. This gave Conrad his first exposure to the hospitality industry, and he went on to worldwide fame as a hotelier. Only ruins of the store/boardinghouse remain.

WEST OF SOCORRO US 60, running west to Arizona, is the avenue to several points of interest. Magdalena, 27 miles from Socorro, is a mining and ranching town that preserves an 1880s Old West spirit. In mid-November, this little town holds its Fall Festival, which includes a variety of studio tours, artist demonstrations, and a silent auction. If you want to stay in Magdalena, I recommend the **Western Bed and Breakfast & RV Park,** 404 First St. (ℂ 575/854-2417; www.thewestern motel.com), a rustic motel with pine walls decorating most rooms. The **Magdalena Café & Steakhouse** ★, 109 S. Main St. (ℂ 575/854-2696), set in a historic building, serves burgers, enchiladas, and steaks. It's open Monday to Friday 7am to 1:30pm, Thursday and Friday 5 to 7pm, and Saturday 7am to 12:30pm.

The Pie Way

The long stretch of highway on US 60 between Socorro and Quemado offers few islands in its vast sea of grass. One of them is Pie Town. In the 1920s, a Texan named Clyde Norman settled here, started baking and selling pies, and his talent won the town a name. It has even been written up in *Smithsonian Magazine*. Set along the Continental Divide, today the **Pie-O-Neer** cafe, on US 60 (📞 575/772-2711; www.pie-o-neer.com) offers up a treat worth clocking the miles for. The cafe bakes a variety of pies daily—the specialty is apple. Simple meals, such as burgers and green-chile stew, are offered as well. The town's **Pie Festival** takes place in mid-September.

Three miles south, the ghost town of **Kelly** produced more than $40 million worth of lead, zinc, copper, silver, and gold in the late 19th and early 20th centuries.

Fifty-four miles west of Socorro via US 60 is the **Very Large Array National Radio Astronomy Observatory (VLA)** ★★ (the Socorro office is at 1003 Lopezville Rd. NW; 📞 575/835-7000; www.nrao.edu). Here, 27 dish-shaped antennas, each 82 feet in diameter, are spread across the plains of San Agustin, forming a single gigantic radio telescope. Many recognize the site from the 1997 movie *Contact*, starring Jodie Foster. Photographs taken with this apparatus are similar to those taken with the largest optical telescopes, except that radio telescopes are sensitive to low-frequency radio waves. All types of celestial objects are photographed, including the sun and its planets, stars, quasars, galaxies, and even the faint remains of the "big bang" that scientists believe occurred some 10 billion years ago. On the outdoor, self-guided walking tour, you'll have a chance to get a closer look at the massive antennas. Admission is free, and visitors are welcomed daily from 8:30am to sunset. Free guided tours are offered every half hour from 11am to 4pm.

Where to Stay in the Socorro Area

Most accommodations are along California Street, the main highway through town, or the adjacent I-25 frontage road. Most lodgings provide free parking.

Casa Blanca ★   The ideal situation in this part of the world is to be just a few minutes away from the Bosque del Apache. That way, you only have to get out of bed a half-hour or so before sunup in order to get to the wildlife refuge and see the morning flight (see "Bosque del Apache National Wildlife Refuge," below). Casa Blanca is the place to stay for this reason. It's a cozy Victorian farmhouse and home to proprietor Phoebe Wood, a former schoolteacher. The place has a genuine homelike quality—comfortable and well maintained. The best room is the Heron with a queen-size bed and private bathroom with a whirlpool tub. An early morning snack and coffee are offered for those leaving early to the Bosque, and upon your return, a full breakfast is available. Fruit, cereals, eggs, and home-baked muffins are served in a homey kitchen. Smoking is not permitted.

13 Montoya St. (P.O. Box 31), San Antonio, NM 87832. 📞 **575/835-3027.** www.casablancabedand breakfast.com. 3 units. $80–$100 double. Rates include generous breakfast. MC, V. Closed June–Sept. Children and pets welcome.

Holiday Inn Express ★ ☺ Opened in 2007, this hotel right within town with good access to I-25 offers the region's best lodgings. Rooms come in kings, two queens, and suites. All are medium size, with a lounge chair and/or desk and/or two chairs and a table. The rooms, decorated in earth tones, have comfortable beds and nice linens. The suites have fold-out couches, a good option for those traveling with children. Bathrooms are medium-size, with granite countertops. Service here is courteous and efficient. A hot breakfast is served in the sunny breakfast room or on the patio.

1040 California St. NE, Socorro, NM 87801. ℂ **800/465-4329** or 575/838-4600. Fax 575/838-4700. www.hiexpress.com/socorronm. 77 units. $105 double; $135 suite. Rates include breakfast. AE, DISC, MC, V. **Amenities:** Exercise room; indoor Jacuzzi; indoor pool. *In room:* A/C, TV, fridge, hair dryer, microwave, Wi-Fi.

CAMPING

Casey's Socorro RV Park (ℂ **800/674-2234** or 575/835-2234) offers mountain and valley views and plenty of shade, as well as 100 sites and 30 full hookups. Tent sites are available, as are picnic tables, grills, and ice. A playground and swimming pool are open year-round. To reach Casey's, take I-25 to exit 147, go 1 block west on Business I-25 and then 1 block south on West Frontage Road.

Where to Dine in the Socorro Area

El Sombrero ★ NEW MEXICAN This is a real locals' place. My Socorran friends call it "the Hat" and always request the garden room, where tables surround a fountain. This is some of the best New Mexican food around. I especially enjoy the chicken enchiladas, with tortillas made in-house. They come rolled, with beans, rice, and a *sopaipilla*. Most popular on the menu are the fajitas, beef or chicken, served with rice, beans, tortillas, and guacamole. The restaurant is known for its trademark sauces, especially the poblano chile and mole sauces, which are served over enchiladas or meats such as chicken. For dessert, try the *churro*, a cinnamon sugared stick, with vanilla ice cream. Beer and wine are available.

210 Mesquite NE, Socorro. ℂ **575/835-3945.** www.frankandlupes.com. Main courses $6–$12. AE, DC, DISC, MC, V. Daily 11am–9pm.

Manny's Buckhorn Tavern ★★ AMERICAN For years, the cafe across the street from this place in San Antonio (10 miles south of town), the Owl Bar, held the state's title for the best green chile cheeseburger. More recently this spry contender has come to dominate the ring. With the title has come a slew of press, including *GQ* magazine naming its burgers on their national top-20 burger list. *Travel + Leisure* and the *New York Times* have also written about this charming place that's full of local color. It has hardwood floors, beer neons, and memorabilia on the walls—a crucifix, antelope antlers—set above cozy booths. Order their specialty, a Buckhorn Burger, made with hand-patted 80% lean beef topped with green chile and cheese. On the side, choose fries or onion rings, both good and crispy. If you're not a burger fan, try the tacos or tamales. Wash your meal down with a beer or margarita from the full bar.

Building 68, NM 380, San Antonio (10 miles south of Socorro). ℂ **575/835-4423.** www.buckhorn burgers.com. All menu items under $8. MC, V. Mon–Fri 11am–8pm; Sat 11am–3pm.

Socorro Springs Brewing Company ★★ AMERICAN/PIZZA This little pocket of sophistication is a nice addition to small-town Socorro. On most any day, the place is full of happy diners sampling the brew and eating tasty wood-oven and grilled cuisine. It's a casual place with a refined brewpub atmosphere, with wooden tables and colorful walls. The service is congenial though not quick. You may choose from salads and sandwiches, calzones and pizzas, and more upscale dishes. A good pizza choice is the Bandido, with pepperoni, Italian sausage, prosciutto, and jalapeños, or the El Cerdo with red-chile marinated pork, capicola ham, cheddar-jack cheese, olives, and cilantro. Most recently, I enjoyed the baked penne carbonara—penne pasta with a cheddar/bacon sauce baked in the wood-fired oven. The beer is nice, with a bit of a smoky taste.

1012 W. California St., Socorro. ✆ **575/838-0650.** www.socorrosprings.com. Reservations accepted. Main courses $8–$24. AE, DISC, MC, V. Daily 10:30am–10pm.

BOSQUE DEL APACHE NATIONAL WILDLIFE REFUGE

by Ian Wilker

The barren lands to either side of I-25 south of Albuquerque seem hardly fit for rattlesnakes, much less one of the Southwest's greatest concentrations of wildlife. The plants that do find purchase in the parched washes and small canyons along the road—forbiddingly named hardies such as creosote bush, tarbush, and white thorn—serve notice that you are indeed within the northernmost finger of the great Chihuahuan Desert, which covers southern New Mexico and southwestern Texas, and runs deep into Mexico.

However, to the east of the interstate is the green-margined Rio Grande. In the midst of such a blasted landscape, the river stands out as an inviting beacon to wildlife, and nowhere does it shine more brightly than at Bosque del Apache's 7,000 acres of carefully managed riparian habitat, which includes marshlands, meadows, agricultural fields, arrow-weed thickets on the riverbanks, and big old-growth cottonwoods lining what were once the oxbows of the river. The refuge supports a riot of wildlife, including all the characteristic mammals and reptiles of the Southwest (mule deer, jackrabbits, and coyotes are common) and about 377 species of birds.

A visit here during the peak winter season—from November to March—is one of the most consistently thrilling wildlife spectacles you can see anywhere in the lower 48 states, especially if you're an avid bird-watcher. Bosque del Apache is, you might say, the LAX of the Central Flyway, one of four paths that migratory birds follow every year between their summer breeding grounds in the tundral north and wintering grounds in the southern United States, Mexico, even as far away as South America—and many of these birds either stop over here to recharge their batteries or settle down for the winter.

It's not enough to say that hundreds of species of birds are on hand. The wonder is in the sheer numbers of them. In early December the refuge may harbor as many as 45,000 snow geese, 57,000 ducks of many different species, and 18,000 sandhill cranes—huge, ungainly birds that nonetheless have a special majesty in flight, pinkish in the sun at dawn or dusk. Plenty of raptors are also about—numerous red-tailed hawks and northern harriers (sometimes called marsh hawks), Cooper's hawks and kestrels, and even bald and golden eagles—as well as Bosque del Apache's many year-round avian residents: pheasants and quail, wild turkeys, and much mythologized roadrunners (*El Paisano,* in Mexican folklore). Everyone will be mesmerized by the huge societies of sandhills, ducks, and geese, going about their daily business of feeding, gabbling, quarreling, honking, and otherwise making an immense racket.

The refuge has a 12-mile auto tour loop, which you should drive very slowly; the south half of the loop travels past numerous water impoundments, where the majority of the ducks and geese hang out, and the north half has the meadows and farmland, where you'll see the roadrunners and other land birds, and where the cranes and geese feed from midmorning through the afternoon.

A few special experiences bear further explanation. Dawn is definitely the best time to be here—songbirds are far more active in the first hours of the day, and the cranes and geese take flight en masse. This last is not to be missed. Dusk, when the birds return to the water, is also a good time. At either dawn or dusk, find your way to one of the observation decks and wait for what birders call the "fly out" (off the water to the fields) or "fly in" (from the fields to the water).

Don't despair if you can't be at the Bosque del Apache during the prime winter months, for it's a special place any time of year. By April, the geese and ducks have flown north, and the refuge drains the water impoundments to allow the marsh plants to regenerate; the resulting mud flats are an ideal feeding ground for the migrating shorebirds that arrive in April and May.

If you'd like to stretch your legs a bit, check out the **Chupadera Peak Trail,** which follows a 2.5-mile loop or a 10-mile loop to a high point overlooking the refuge. Ask for directions at the visitor center.

JUST THE FACTS   The Bosque del Apache National Wildlife Refuge is about a 1½-hour drive from Albuquerque. Follow I-25 for 9 miles south of Socorro, and then take the San Antonio exit. At the main intersection of San Antonio, turn south onto NM 1. In 3 miles, you'll be on refuge lands, and another 4 miles will bring you to the excellent visitor center, which has a small museum with interpretive displays and a large shelf of field guides, natural histories, and other books of interest for visitors to New Mexico. The visitor center is open from 7:30am to 4pm weekdays, and from 8am to 4:30pm weekends. The refuge itself is open year-round daily from 1 hour before sunrise to 1 hour after sunset. Admission is $3 per vehicle. For more information, contact **Bosque del Apache National Wildlife Refuge,** P.O. Box 1246, Socorro, NM 87801 (© **575/835-1828;** www.fws.gov/southwest/refuges/newmex/bosque).

TRUTH OR CONSEQUENCES

Originally known as Hot Springs, after the therapeutic mineral springs bubbling up near the river, the town took the name Truth or Consequences—usually shortened to "T or C"—in 1950. That was the year that Ralph Edwards, producer of the popular radio and television program *Truth or Consequences,* began his weekly broadcast with these words: "I wish that some town in the United States liked and respected our show so much that it would like to change its name to Truth or Consequences."

The reward to any city willing to do so was to become the site of the 10th-anniversary broadcast of the program, which would put it on the national map in a big way. The locals voted for the name change, which has survived three protest elections over the years.

Although the TV program was canceled decades ago, Ralph Edwards continued to return for the annual **Truth or Consequences Fiesta,** the first weekend of May. He died in 2005. Another popular annual festival is **Geronimo Days,** the second weekend of October. Despite its festive roots, T or C seems to have an identity crisis—perhaps a consequence of giving up its name for the fame and fortune of television. The city displays a forlorn quality, possibly due to the struggling economy. However, in recent years, a few of the bathhouses have undergone renovation, and a number of galleries and restaurants have opened up, bringing new life to the town.

Essentials

GETTING THERE   From Albuquerque, take I-25 south (2½ hr.). From Las Cruces, take I-25 north (1¼ hr.). Though no commercial flight service exists, those who fly themselves may contact the **Truth or Consequences Municipal Airport,** Old North Hwy. 85 (☏ **575/894-6199**).

VISITOR INFORMATION   A **visitor information center** is at 211 Main St. next to the Geronimo Springs Museum (☏ **575/894-6600**) in downtown Truth or Consequences. Also there is the **Truth or Consequences & Sierra County Chamber of Commerce,** 207 S. Foch St., Truth or Consequences, NM 87901 (☏ **575/894-3536**; www.truthorconsequenceschamberofcommerce.com).

CITY LAYOUT   This year-round resort town and retirement community is spread along the Rio Grande between the Elephant Butte and Caballo reservoirs, two of the three largest bodies of water in the state. Business Loop 25 branches off from I-25 to wind through the city, splitting into Main Street (one-way west) and South Broadway (one-way east) in the downtown area. Third Avenue connects T or C with the Elephant Butte resort community, 5 miles east.

 ### Next Stop—Space

Fasten your seat belt and settle back for an orbit or two of Earth—that's what space-minded folks, such as New Mexico Governor Bill Richardson and British tycoon Richard Branson, foresee as a reality soon. Space tourists would take off from the proposed $225-million Spaceport America near Truth or Consequences. In its embryonic stages now, the spaceport will include one or more runways, hangars, a control building, and launch pads. The first test flights took place in 2007, while the completion date for the spaceport is 2011.

When it's complete, Branson plans to headquarter Virgin Galactic here. Currently Virgin is selling tickets for $200,000 apiece for a 2½-hour flight, including 5 minutes of weightlessness. The first of these flights will likely fly out of the Mojave Airport in California, where SpaceShipOne became the first privately manned rocket to reach space in 2004. For updates, log onto www.virgingalactic.com or www.edd.state.nm.us.

Taking the Waters at the Historic Hot Springs

The town's "original" attraction is its hot springs. The entire downtown area is located over a table of odorless hot mineral water, 98° to 115°F (37°–46°C), that bubbles to the surface through wells or pools. The first bathhouse was built in the 1880s; most of the half-dozen historic spas operating today date from the 1930s. Generally open from morning to early evening, these spas welcome visitors for soaks and massages. Baths of 20 minutes or longer start at $7 per person.

The chamber of commerce has information on all the local spas (see "Essentials," above). Among them is **Sierra Grande Lodge & Spa ★★**, 501 McAdoo St. (© **575/894-6976;** www.sierragrandelodge.com), where Geronimo himself is rumored to have taken a break. (See "Where to Stay in & Around Truth or Consequences," below.) As well as luxurious soaking tubs, this inn offers a full line of spa treatments, including some innovative massages.

I highly recommend the **Hay-Yo-Kay Hot Springs ★**, 300 Austin St. (© **575/894-2228;** www.hay-yo-kay.com). It has natural-flow pools (versus tubs filled with spring water). The tub rooms are private and gracefully tiled. Hay-Yo-Kay is open Wednesday through Sunday 11am to 7pm. Massages and reflexology are also available. Newly renovated, the **Riverbend Springs Resort & Spa ★** 100 Austin St. (© **575/894-7625;** www.riverbendhotsprings.com) offers clean tubs that overlook the Rio Grande River. The pools are open daily from 8am to 10pm.

A Museum in T or C

Geronimo Springs Museum Outside this museum is Geronimo's Spring, where the great Apache shaman is said to have taken his warriors to bathe their battle wounds. Turtleback Mountain, looming over the Rio Grande east of the city, is believed to have been sacred to Native Americans.

Exhibits include prehistoric Mogollon and Mimbres pottery (A.D. 950–1250); the Spanish Heritage Room, with artifacts of the first families of Sierra County; and artists' work, including historical murals and sculptured bronzes. An authentic miner's cabin has been moved here from the nearby mountains. The Ralph Edwards Wing contains the history and highlights of the annual fiestas and celebrates the city's name change, including television footage from the shows filmed in T or C.

211 Main St. © **575/894-6600.** Admission $5 adults, $2.50 students; family rates available. DISC, MC, V. Mon–Sat 9am–5pm; Sun noon–5pm.

Getting Outside

Elephant Butte Lake State Park encompasses New Mexico's largest body of water, with 36,500 lake surface acres. It's one of the most popular state parks in New Mexico, attracting watersports enthusiasts and fishers from throughout the south and central regions of the state. Fishing for white bass, black bass, catfish, walleye, crappie, and stripers goes on year-round. Trout are stocked in the Rio Grande below Elephant Butte Dam. The park has sandy beaches for tanning and swimming (though don't expect the white sands of the Cayman Islands here). You can also find boating, sailing, water-skiing, windsurfing, jet-skiing, scuba diving, nature trails, and camping. Beware of going to the lake on summer weekends—Fourth of July and Labor Day weekend in particular—when the crowds are overwhelming. However, in the other seasons and during the week in summer, it's a quiet place.

Bird-watchers also enjoy the park, spotting hundreds of species, including bald eagles, great blue herons, and more than 20 species of duck during migrations in spring and fall. The lake was named for a huge rock formation that makes an island; before the inundation that created the lake, it clearly looked like an elephant. Today, it's partially submerged.

The park is about 5 miles north of Truth or Consequences via I-25. For more information, contact ℂ **575/744-5923;** www.nmparks.com.

About 18 miles south of Truth or Consequences via I-25 is another recreation area, **Caballo Lake State Park** (ℂ **575/743-3942;** www.nmparks.com), which, like Elephant Butte, has year-round watersports, fishing, swimming, and campsites. The lofty ridge of the Caballo Mountains just to the east of the lake makes a handsome backdrop. Park facilities include a full-service marina with a shop for boaters and full hookups for recreational vehicles.

Reached from the same exit off I-25 is yet another recreation area, **Percha Dam State Park** (ℂ **575/743-3942;** www.nmparks.com), a lovely shaded spot under great cottonwood trees, part of the ancient bosque, or woods, the Spanish found bordering the Rio Grande when they first arrived in this area in the 1530s. The dam here diverts river water for irrigation. The park offers campsites, restrooms and showers, hiking trails, and access to fishing.

Exploring the Ghost Towns in the Area

NORTH OF TRUTH OR CONSEQUENCES About 40 miles from Truth or Consequences are the precarious remains of Winston and Chloride, two so-called ghost towns—abandoned mining centers that nevertheless do have a few residents. Exploring these towns makes for a nice side trip off I-25. You may want to include a visit to the Very Large Array and the old mining town of Magdalena in the trip (see "Socorro & the VLA," earlier in this chapter). However, be aware that if you do, much of the journey from Winston to the VLA is on graded dirt road.

Winston, 37 miles northwest of Truth or Consequences on NM 52, was abandoned in the early 1900s when silver prices dropped and local mining became unprofitable. Some of the original structures from that era are still standing. A similar fate befell **Chloride,** 5 miles west of Winston on a side road off NM 52, where famed silver mines had such names as Nana, Wall Street, and Unknown. Chloride also figured in many battles in the turn-of-the-20th-century war between cattle-ranching and sheep-ranching interests. In the very center of town is the "hanging tree," where the town used to tie drunks to "dry" in the sun.

SOUTH OF TRUTH OR CONSEQUENCES Thirty-two miles from Truth or Consequences, via I-25 south to NM 152, then west, is **Hillsboro ★**, another ghost town that's fast losing its ghosts to a small invasion of artists and craftspeople, antiques shops, and galleries. This town boomed after an 1877 gold strike nearby, and during its heyday it produced $6 million in silver and gold. It was the county seat from 1884 to 1938. You may want to plan your drive to include breakfast or lunch at **Hillsboro General Store & Country Café ★**, on NM 152 in the center of town (ℂ **575/895-5306**). Serving excellent burgers and burritos in a historic general store ambience, this spot also has some of the best pie in the region; it's called bumbleberry and combines many berries in a flaky crust. Open Sunday to Wednesday and Friday from 8am to 6:30pm.

The **Black Range Historical Museum** (📞 575/895-5233 or 575/895-5685) contains exhibits and artifacts from Hillsboro's mining boom. In the former Ocean Grove Hotel, a turn-of-the-20th-century brothel operated by Sadie Orchard, the museum collection includes some of the madam's effects. This volunteer-staffed museum is supposed to be open daily 10am to 4pm, but it isn't always. It's closed most major holidays. Suggested donation is $2 for adults, $1 for children, and $5 for a family.

The **Enchanted Villa** bed-and-breakfast inn, a quarter mile west of Hillsboro on NM 152 (no street address), P.O. Box 456, Hillsboro, NM 88042 (📞 575/895-5686), is a 1941 adobe structure that offers decent accommodations. The rates, $84 for a double and $55 for a single, include full hot breakfasts.

Nine miles west of Hillsboro on NM 152, just after you've entered the Gila National Forest, is **Kingston,** born with a rich silver strike in 1880 and reputed to have been among the wildest mining towns in the region, with 7,000 people, 22 saloons, a notorious red-light district (conveniently located on Virtue Ave.), and an opera house. Kingston was also once the home of Albert Fall, a U.S. secretary of state who gained notoriety for his role in the Teapot Dome Scandal.

Your headquarters in Kingston should be the **Black Range Lodge Bed & Breakfast,** 119 Main St., Kingston, NM 88042 (📞 575/895-5652; www.black rangelodge.com), a rustic stone lodge that dates from the 1880s, and over the years has housed miners and soldiers. The lodge has seven rooms—all with private bathrooms and some with private balconies—a large game room with a pool table and video games, and family suites, as well as a guesthouse. Rates are $95 for a double, with multiple-night discounts; the guesthouse is $149 per night, which includes a full breakfast. Well-behaved pets are welcome for a $5 per day fee.

Among historic buildings in Kingston are the **brick assay office,** the **Victorio Hotel,** and the **Percha Bank,** now a museum open by appointment—ask at Black Range Lodge. Also ask for a Kingston Walking Tour map. The town bell in front of the Volunteer Fire Department was once used to warn residents of Native American attacks.

Where to Stay in & Around Truth or Consequences

Blackstone Hot Springs ★★ Set in a 1930s motor court, this resort offers a fun and funky theme-room stay. The real draw here is the mineral baths in the rooms, which allow guests to bathe all they want. As befits this town named for a television show, the rooms are as well, with such themes as the Twilight Zone, Golden Girls, and my favorite, The Jetsons, with a space-age couch and posters of the TV show on the walls. All rooms are set around a quiet courtyard and offer fine bedding and kitchenettes. The real star of this show is the Wet Room, reserved on the hour ($25), which has a large soaking tub and a geothermal steam room with a waterfall. Whether you're a guest or not, you should try this out because breathing in the notable T or C minerals can induce an otherworldly experience.

410 Austin St. Truth or Consequences, NM 87901. 📞 **575/894-0894.** www.blackstonehotsprings.com. 7 units. $75–$125 double. AE, DISC, MC, V. **Amenities:** Soaking tub; steam room. *In room:* A/C, TV, hair dryer, kitchenette, mineral bath, Wi-Fi.

Elephant Butte Inn ★ For a comfortable stay and a unique experience, try this hotel above Elephant Butte Lake that offers panoramic views as well as a relaxing resortlike feel. It caters to boaters, fishers, and other relaxation lovers. Rooms are standard size, furnished with king- or queen-size beds. Bathrooms are small but functional, with an outer sink vanity. I recommend the lakeside view, where a big grassy lawn stretches down to tennis courts. These rooms are a bit more upscale, with unique decor in each, and equipped with plasma TVs, fridges, and microwaves. For golfers, packages are available that include greens fees at the Sierra del Rio Golf Course at Turtleback Mountain Resort (p. 308). The Ivory Spa here offers a full range of treatments, including reasonably priced spa packages. A courtesy computer with Internet is available in the lobby.

401 NM 195 (P.O. Box 996), Elephant Butte, NM 87935. © **575/744-5431.** Fax 575/744-5044. www. elephantbutteinn.com. 45 units. $80–$129 double. Golf and spa packages available. AE, DC, DISC, MC, V. Pets welcome ($15–$20 per visit). **Amenities:** Restaurant; lounge w/outdoor patio; outdoor pool; room service; spa; tennis courts. *In room:* A/C, TV, fridge/microwave (some rooms), hair dryer, Wi-Fi.

Sierra Grande Lodge & Spa ★★ Prepare yourself for a sensual oasis at this historic resort. The biggest draw is the springs. Here you stay in luxury while partaking of warm, healing waters rich in minerals. The medium-size rooms in this renovated 1920s lodge, which is listed on the National Register of Historic Places, have handcrafted furnishings, hardwood floors, high ceilings, and many have balconies. All have comfortable beds with good linens. Bathrooms are small but functional. Some come with in-room Jacuzzis. Best of all here are a variety of spa treatments including massages, wraps, facials, and most notably Ashiatsu, in which the masseuse massages with her feet.

501 McAdoo St., Truth or Consequences, NM 87901. © **575/894-6976.** www.sierragrandelodge.com. 18 units. $99–$169 double; $249–$279 suite. Rates includes gourmet continental breakfast and 30-min. mineral bath for each day of stay. AE, DISC, MC, V. **Amenities:** Concierge; spa. *In room:* A/C, TV, DVD player upon request, hair dryer, Wi-Fi.

CAMPING

Elephant Butte Lake State Park (© 575/744-5923; www.nmparks.com) welcomes backpackers and RVs alike, with 200 developed campsites, 150 RV hookups, picnic tables, and access points for swimming, hiking, boating, and fishing. Kids love the playground.

Not far from Elephant Butte Lake is **Monticello Point RV Park** (© 575/894-6468), which offers tent sites and 69 sites with full hookups. Laundry and grocery facilities are also on the premises, as are restrooms with showers. To reach Monticello Point, take I-25 to exit 89, and proceed 5½ miles east on the paved road—follow the signs.

Lakeside RV Park and Lodging (© 575/744-5996), also near Elephant Butte, has 70 sites, two overflow sites (all 64 are full hookups), as well as a recreation room with cable and laundry facilities. The RV park is 4 miles southeast of the I-25 and NM 195 junction (exit 83) on NM 195. To reach the RV park when you're headed north on I-25, take exit 79, go half a mile east on the paved road, 1½ miles north on NM 181, then 1½ miles east on NM 171, and finally a quarter mile south on NM 195.

Camping is also available at **Caballo Lake State Park** and **Percha Dam State Park.** For information on either park, call © **575/743-3942** or visit www.nmparks. com.

Where to Dine in & Around Truth or Consequences

Café Bella Luca ★★ TUSCAN/ITALIAN   Set in a historic building, renovated to have a clean, contemporary look, with high ceilings, stained concrete floors, and warm earth tones, this restaurant serves some of the best food in the region. Chef Byron Harrel makes all the sauces and breads here, and the seafood is flown in fresh. Lunch or dinner might start with crispy fried calamari or a crab cake. At lunch, one of the many sandwiches is a good bet. I've enjoyed the turkey pancetta on focaccia with house-made fries or a salad. The menu also offers pizzas and calzones. The pasta Alfredo with grilled shrimp is also nice. At dinner, the seafood *puttanesca* has a nice bite, and the ravioli, which varies with the season, is always excellent. An extensive wine and beer list with organic options accompanies the menu, as do a variety of house-made desserts. This is a Wi-Fi hotspot.

303 Jones St. ⓒ **575/894-9866.** www.cafebellaluca.com. Reservations recommended on weekends. Main courses $7–$12 lunch, $10–$30 dinner. AE, DISC, MC, V. Wed–Mon 11am–4pm; Wed–Thurs and Sun–Mon 5–9pm; Fri–Sat 5–10pm.

Happy Belly Deli ★ AMERICAN   This prime spot for breakfast and lunch offers homestyle cooking in a friendly, cozy cafe decked with original art. A *bonhomie* atmosphere pervades, with diners talking table-to-table. A full range of egg and pancake dishes fill the breakfast roster. At lunch, try one of the chef's inspired soup creations, such as the Thai chicken rice, which change daily. The green-chile Philly is a popular sandwich here, and independent eaters can build their own.

313 Broadway. ⓒ **575/894-3354.** All menu items under $8. MC, V. Mon–Fri 7am–3pm; Sat 8am–3pm; Sun 8am–noon.

Los Arcos Steak & Lobster ★ AMERICAN   A favorite of my late father's, this spacious hacienda-style restaurant fronted by a lovely desert garden is intimate and friendly in atmosphere, as if you're at an old friend's home. Its steaks are regionally

---

Wandering in T or C

Truth or Consequences has become a bit of an art hot spot recently, with many artists moving here to enjoy the temperate climate and low cost of living. As a result, many galleries have opened up. Unfortunately, they seem to close just as quickly. So rather than give you a list that will surely change by press time, I recommend you check out **www.torcart.com**, the website for the **Downtown Gallery District Association**. The site provides a map of its members' locations and dates for their monthly art hop, when they hold receptions into the evening.

While you're out wandering, if you need a little energy, head to **Little Sprout** ★, 400 N. Broadway (ⓒ 575/894-4114) to get a health fix. This cafe serves coffee, a broad range of freshly squeezed juices and smoothies, as well as sandwiches and baked goods. A favorite is the roast chicken panini, with mozzarella, roasted red peppers, basil leaves; and pesto on a ciabatta bun. The cafe is open Monday to Saturday 8am to 6pm, and Sunday 8am to 4:30pm.

famous; my choice is always the filet mignon, served with salad and your choice of potato or rice. The fish dishes are also good, with offerings that include king crab and lobster. The restaurant also has a fine dessert list and cordial selection. During warmer months, diners enjoy the outdoor patio. The bar here hops at happy hour.

1400 Date St. ✆ **575/894-6200.** Main courses $11–$40. AE, DISC, MC, V. Sun–Thurs 5–9:30pm; Fri–Sat 5–10:30pm.

Pacific Grill ★ SEAFOOD With salmon-colored walls and palm tree art, this restaurant serves decent fish prepared inventively. It's a good family spot or a fun place for a night out with friends. Service is friendly but it can be overworked. Though the fish is brought to the restaurant frozen, the preparations make it seem fresh. I've enjoyed the lemon-pepper salmon and the island-style sweet-and-sour chicken.

304 S. Pershing St. (behind the State National Bank). ✆ **575/894-7687.** Main courses $6–$21. AE, DISC, MC, V. Tues–Sun 11am–2pm and 5–8pm.

LAS CRUCES

Picture a valley full of weathered wooden crosses marking graves of settlers brutally murdered by Apaches, behind them mountains with peaks so jagged they resemble organ pipes. Such was the scene that caused people to begin calling this city Las Cruces, meaning "the crosses." Even today, the place has a mysterious presence, its rich history haunting it still. Reminders of characters such as Billy the Kid, who was sentenced to death in this area, and Pancho Villa, who spent time here, are present throughout the region.

Established in 1849 on El Camino Real, the "royal highway" between Santa Fe and Mexico City, Las Cruces became a supply center for miners prospecting the Organ Mountains and soldiers stationed at nearby Fort Selden. Today, it's New Mexico's second-largest urban area, with 95,000 people. It's noted as an agricultural center, especially for its cotton, pecans, and chiles; as a regional transportation hub; and as the gateway to the White Sands Missile Range and other defense installations.

Las Cruces manages to survive within a desert landscape that gets only 8 inches of moisture a year, pulling enough moisture from the Rio Grande, which runs through, to irrigate a broad swath of valley.

Essentials

GETTING THERE From Albuquerque, take I-25 south (4 hr.). From El Paso, take I-10 north (¾ hr.). From Tucson, take I-25 east (5 hr.).

Las Cruces International Airport (✆ **575/541-2471;** www.las-cruces.org/facilities/airport), 8 miles west of the city, offers no commercial flights at this time. **El Paso International Airport** (**ELP;** ✆ **915/780-4749;** www.elpasointernational airport.com), 47 miles south, has daily flights to and from Albuquerque, Phoenix, Dallas, and Houston, among other cities. The **Las Cruces Shuttle Service,** P.O. Box 3172, Las Cruces, NM 88003 (✆ **800/288-1784** or 575/525-1784; www.lascrucesshuttle.com), provides service between the El Paso airport and Las Cruces. It leaves Las Cruces 12 times daily between 5am and 9:30pm for a charge of $40 one-way or $70 round-trip per person, with large discounts for additional passengers traveling together. A $10 charge is added for pickup or drop-off at places other than

Las Cruces

ACCOMMODATIONS ■
Hotel Encanto de Las Cruces **13**
La Quinta **5**
The Lundeen Inn of the Arts **3**

DINING ◆
Double Eagle **8**
Chope's Bar & Cafe **9**
Farley's **12**
La Posta de Mesilla **8**
Lemongrass **10**
Lorenzo's Restaurante Italiano de Old Mesilla **6**
Old Mesilla Pastry Café: The Shed **4**
Sunset Grill & Wine Bar **11**
Tiffany's Pizza & Greek American Cuisine **15**

ATTRACTIONS ●
Branigan Cultural Center **2**
Las Cruces Museum of Art **2**
Las Cruces Museum of Natural History **14**
Las Cruces Railroad Museum **1**
Mesilla **7**
New Mexico Farm & Ranch Heritage Museum **16**
San Albino Church **7**

its regular stops at major hotels. Connections can also be made three times a day from Las Cruces to Deming and Silver City.

VISITOR INFORMATION The **Las Cruces Convention and Visitors Bureau** is at 211 N. Water St., Las Cruces, NM 88001 (🕿 **877/266-8252** or 575/541-2444; www.lascrucescvb.org). The **Greater Las Cruces Chamber of Commerce,** 760 W. Picacho Ave., can be reached at 🕿 **575/524-1968** or www. lascruces.org.

danse MACABRE

The **Dance of the Matachines,** a ritualistic dance performed at northern New Mexico pueblos and in many Hispanic communities, reveals the cultural miscegenation, identities, and conflicts that characterize northern New Mexico. It's a dark and vivid ritual in which a little girl, Malinche, is wedded to the church. The dance, depicting the taming of the native spirit, is difficult even for historians to decipher.

Brought to the New World by the Spaniards, the dance has its roots in the painful period during which the Moors were driven out of Spain. However, some symbols seem obvious: At one point, men bearing whips tame "El Toro," a small boy dressed as a bull who has been charging about rebelliously. The whip-men symbolically castrate him and then stroll through the crowd, pretending to display the dismembered body parts, as if to warn villagers of the consequences of disobedience. At another point, a hunched woman-figure births a small troll-like doll, perhaps representative of the union between Indian and Hispanic cultures.

The Dance of the Matachines ends when two *abuelo* (grandparent) figures dance across the dirt, holding up the just-born baby, while the Matachines, adorned with bishoplike headdresses, follow them away in a recessional march. The Matachines' dance, often performed in the early mornings, is so dark and mystical that every time I see it, my passion for this area deepens. The image of that baby always stays with me, and in a way represents New Mexico itself: a place born of disparate beliefs that have melded with the sand, sage, and sun, and produced incredible richness.

What to See & Do in Las Cruces

On a hot day, when the church bells are ringing and you're wandering the brick streets of **Mesilla ★★**, you may for a moment feel you have slipped back into the late 16th century. This village on Las Cruces's southwestern flank was established in the late 1500s by Mexican colonists. It became the crossroads of El Camino Real and the Butterfield Overland Mail route. The Gadsden Purchase, which annexed Mesilla to the United States and fixed the current international boundaries of New Mexico and Arizona, was signed here in 1854.

Mesilla's most notorious resident, William Bonney, otherwise known as Billy the Kid, was sentenced to death at the county courthouse here. He was sent back to Lincoln, New Mexico, to be hanged, but escaped before the sentence was carried out. Legendary hero Pat Garrett eventually tracked down and killed the Kid at Fort Sumner; later, Garrett was mysteriously murdered in an arroyo just outside Las Cruces. He is buried in the local Masonic cemetery.

Thick-walled adobe buildings, which once protected residents against Apache attacks, now house art galleries, restaurants, museums, and gift shops. Throughout Mesilla, colorful red chile *ristras* decorate homes and businesses. On Fridays 11am to 4pm and Sundays noon to 4pm year-round locals sell crafts and seasonal produce.

TOURING MESILLA

For a fun and easy jaunt that will familiarize you with the history and architecture of this interesting village, purchase the booklet *A Walking Tour of Mesilla, NM*, sold at shops around the plaza and at the **J. Paul Taylor Visitor Center** in the Mesilla Town Hall, 2231 Avenida de Mesilla (𝐶 **575/524-3262,** ext. 117), where you'll find period photos and plenty of brochures on the area, as well as clean public restrooms. A good source for Mesilla events is **www.oldmesilla.org**.

Some places of note include the **San Albino Church** (see "Other Attractions," below), from which you can get a view of the plaza and even peek down the side streets, where some of the old adobe houses have been restored and painted bold pinks and greens. On the southwest corner of the plaza is the **oldest documented brick building in New Mexico,** built by Augustin Maurin in 1860. It has a sad history of its proprietors being murdered by robbers.

If you'd like a treat, head to **Stahmann's on the Plaza,** 2030 Calle de Parian (𝐶 **575/527-0667;** www.stahmanns.com). A retail outlet for the notable Stahmann Farms, Stahmann's sells cookies, pecan candy, and just plain, but delicious, pecans. Find other nutty treats at **Heart of the Desert Pistachios & Wines,** 2355 Calle de Guadalupe (𝐶 **575/647-2115**). I especially enjoy their pistachio white chocolate chunk ice cream. Chocolate lovers will find chocolate-dipped frozen strawberries and homemade ice cream at the **Chocolate Lady,** 2379 Calle de Guadalupe (𝐶 **575/526-2744**).

If you prefer a guided historic walking tour, contact **Preciliana Sandoval,** 2488 Calle Principal, P.O. Box 981, Mesilla, NM 88046 (behind El Patio Bar; 𝐶 **575/ 647-2639**). This bold artist/historian, a fifth-generation Mesilla Valley native, will regale you with stories of ghosts and historic battles in the area. Tours cost $10 per person and take about an hour, and group discounts are available.

PLACES OF NOTE IN HISTORIC LAS CRUCES

Though it has a much less romantic atmosphere than Mesilla, downtown Las Cruces has a few historical buildings, which make visiting it worthwhile. If you'd like to do a walking tour of the area, pick up a map at the **Las Cruces Convention and Visitors Bureau** at 211 N. Water St.

Central to the area is **Downtown Mall** (𝐶 **575/541-2155**), an open-air arcade that hosts the **Las Cruces Farmers' & Crafts Market ★**, which specializes in locally handcrafted items and seasonal local produce, on Wednesday and Saturday from 8am to noon. Established in 1888, **New Mexico State University,** University Avenue and Locust Street (𝐶 **575/646-0111;** www.nmsu.edu), has an enrollment of 24,000 students and is especially noted for its schools of engineering and agriculture. It has a museum and two galleries.

OTHER ATTRACTIONS

Branigan Cultural Center If you'd like to learn about Las Cruces history, this museum will inform you of the region's prehistory to its settlement as a city, with an excellent array of period photos, and military, ranching, railroad, and rocket memorabilia. Another gallery houses changing shows of local and regional art and traveling exhibitions. The center also presents performing arts, educational programs, and special events. It's set in an elegant historic 1935 Branigan Library and still has its original desk, skylight, and mural.

500 N. Water St. 𝐶 **575/541-2155.** http://museums.las-cruces.org. Free admission. Tues–Sat 9am– 4:30pm.

Las Cruces Museum of Art   This museum houses galleries, art studios, and classrooms, with frequently changing exhibitions of contemporary art in a variety of media. It offers art classes year-round. Two recent exhibitions included traveling shows by Salvador Dalí and Auguste Rodin.

490 N. Water St. ℂ **575/541-2137.** http://museums.las-cruces.org. Free admission. Tues–Sat 9am–4:30pm.

Las Cruces Museum of Natural History ☺   This small city-funded museum offers a variety of exhibits that emphasize science and natural history. The museum features live animals of the Chihuahuan Desert and hands-on science activities. The Paleozoic Trackway offers a peek at some of the oldest fossil footprints in the world—280 million years. Exhibits, such as "Insects and Bugs" and "Every Body Eats," change every few months.

Mesilla Valley Mall, 700 S. Telshor Blvd. ℂ **575/522-3120.** http://museums.las-cruces.org. Free admission. Mon–Thurs and Sat 10am–5pm; Fri 10am–8pm; Sun 1–5pm.

Las Cruces Railroad Museum   Located in the historic Santa Fe Depot, which is on the National Registry of Historic Buildings, this museum offers exhibits of Las Cruces railroad history from the train's arrival in 1881 to the present. Exhibits include period photos, antique equipment and tools, and model trains. Driving through residential neighborhoods en route to the museum you'll get a feel for the many styles of architecture that the train's arrival sparked, including Queen Anne, Mission Revival, and Gothic Revival. My favorite part of the display is a photo of Theodore Roosevelt on a train during his 1912 visit to Las Cruces.

Corner of Mesilla St. and Las Cruces Ave. ℂ **575/647-4480.** http://museums.las-cruces.org. Free admission. Thurs–Sat 9am–4:30pm.

New Mexico Farm and Ranch Heritage Museum ★★   This 47-acre interactive museum brings to life the 3,000-year history of farming, ranching, and rural living in New Mexico. It's housed within a huge structure that's designed to look like a hacienda-style barn, with a U-shaped courtyard in back and exhibits surrounding it on expansive grounds. Visitors can watch a cow being milked, stroll along corrals filled with livestock, enjoy several gardens, and drop by the blacksmith shop. Tape recordings enliven the ranching exhibit, with messages by the region's first settlers and enduring ranchers, along with the tools and machinery of their trade. Annual events at the museum are the Blessing of the Fields in May and Cowboy Days the second weekend in March.

4100 Dripping Springs Rd. (follow University Ave. east beyond the edge of town). ℂ **575/522-4100.** www.nmfarmandranchmuseum.org. Admission $5 adults, $3 seniors 60 and over, $2 children 5–17; free for children 4 and under. Mon–Sat 9am–5pm; Sun noon–5pm.

San Albino Church ★★   The present structure was built in 1906 on the foundation of the original church, constructed in 1851. It was named for St. Albin, a medieval English bishop of North Africa, on whose day an important irrigation ditch from the Rio Grande was completed. The church bells date from the early 1870s; the pews were made in Taos of Philippine mahogany.

North side of Old Mesilla Plaza. ℂ **575/526-9349.** www.sanalbino.org. Free admission; donations appreciated. Usually Mon–Sat 1–3pm (call ahead). English-language Mass Sat 5:30pm and Sun 11am; Spanish Mass Sun 8am, weekdays 7am.

SPECTATOR SPORTS

New Mexico State University football, basketball, baseball, softball, and volleyball teams play intercollegiate schedules in the Big West Conference, against schools from California, Nevada, and Utah. The Aggies play their home games on the NMSU campus, south of University Avenue on Locust Street. Football is played in the Aggie Memorial Stadium, and basketball games are held in the Pan American Center arena. For information about the games, call the **Pan Am Ticket Office** (© 575/646-1420; www.nmstatesports.com).

New Mexico's longest horse-racing season takes place 45 miles south of Las Cruces at **Sunland Park Racetrack and Casino** (© 575/874-5200; www.sunland-park.com). Live races run Friday, Saturday, Sunday, and Tuesday, from December to April. The casino, which features 700 slot machines, is open Sunday through Thursday from 9:30am to 1am, Friday and Saturday until 2am.

SHOPPING

Shoppers should be aware that in Las Cruces, Monday is a notoriously quiet day. Some stores close for the day, so it's best to call ahead before traveling to a specific store.

For art, visit **Lundeen's Inn of the Arts ★**, 618 S. Alameda Blvd. (© 575/526-3326; www.innofthearts.com), displaying the works of about 30 Southwest painters, sculptors, and potters; **Rising Sky Artworks,** 415 E. Foster (© 877/525-8454; www.risingskypottery.com), which features works in clay by local and Western artists; **Mesilla Valley Fine Arts,** 2770A Calle de Guadalupe (© 575/522-2933; www.mesillavalleyfinearts.com), which offers works by 30 Southwestern artists—a great place to pick up a New Mexico landscape painting; and **Preston Contemporary Art Center ★★**, 1755 Avenida de Mesilla (© 575/523-8713; www.preston contemporaryart.com), which exhibits midcareer and emerging international artists in an airy contemporary space. For clothing, check out **La Mariposa,** 2470 Calle de Guadalupe (© 575/647-2636), for brightly colored whimsical women's wear and jewelry at a reasonable price.

On the plaza, the **Nambe Showroom** (© 575/527-4623; www.nambe.com) displays handcrafted tableware by Nambe Mills in Santa Fe. It's a great place to shop for gifts.

For books, try **Mesilla Book Center,** in an 1856 mercantile building on the west side of Old Mesilla Plaza (© 575/526-6220).

For native crafts and jewelry, check out **Silver Assets ★**, 1948 Calle de Santiago (© 575/523-8747; www.silverassetsonline.com), 1½ blocks east of San Albino Church in Mesilla. Set back from the plaza itself, look for **Galeri Azul,** Mesilla Plaza (© 575/523-8783), offering whimsical T-shirts and sun hats, and kitschy jewelry.

Mesilla Valley Mall is a full-service shopping center at 700 S. Telshor Blvd., just off the I-25 interchange with Lohman Avenue (© 575/522-1001; www.mesilla valleymall.com), with well over 100 stores. The mall is open Monday through Saturday from 10am to 9pm and Sunday from noon to 6pm.

Southern New Mexico is a big wine-producing region. A few options for wine tastings include **Blue Teal Vineyards,** 2461 Calle de Guadalupe, south of Old Mesilla Plaza (© 877/669-4637 or 575/524-0390; www.blueteal.com). It's open Monday through Thursday 11am to 6pm, Friday and Saturday 11am to 8pm, and

Sunday noon to 6pm. The tasting room at **La Viña Winery** (✆ **575/882-7632**; www.lavinawinery.com), south of Las Cruces off NM 28, is open Thursday to Tuesday from noon to 5pm, and by appointment. New to Mesilla is **Vintage Wines**, 2461 Calle de Principal (✆ **575/523-9463**; www.vintagewinesandcigars.com), with a wine bar, cozy patio, and cigar offerings. It is open Wednesday and Thursday noon to 8pm, Friday and Saturday noon to 10pm, and Sunday noon to 5pm.

Las Cruces After Dark

National recording artists frequently perform at NMSU's **Pan Am Center** (✆ **575/646-1420**; www.panam.nmsu.edu). The **NMSU Music Department** (✆ **575/646-2421**) offers free jazz, classical, and pop concerts from August to May, and the **Las Cruces Symphony Orchestra** (✆ **575/646-3709**; www.lascruces symphony.com) often performs here as well.

Hershel Zohn Theater (✆ **575/646-4515**), at NMSU, presents plays of the professional/student **American Southwest Theatre Company** from September to May, featuring dramas, comedies, musicals, and original works. Visit **http://theatre. nmsu.edu/astc** for information. The **No Strings Theatre Company** at the Black Box Theatre, 430 N. Downtown Mall (✆ **575/523-1223**; www.no-strings.org), presents an eclectic selection of plays in a relaxed atmosphere, including some excellent local works.

The **Las Cruces Community Theatre** (✆ **575/523-1200**; www.lcctnm.org) mounts six productions a year at its own facility on the downtown mall.

The **Mesilla Valley Film Society** (✆ **575/524-8287**; www.mesillavalleyfilm. org) runs a good selection of contemporary and vintage art films at the Fountain Theatre, 2469 Calle de Guadalupe, a half-block south of the plaza in Mesilla, nightly at 7:30pm and sometimes 9:45pm, and Sunday at 2:30pm and sometimes 5pm.

If you'd like a cocktail in a fun atmosphere, check out **Azul Nightclub ★** in the Hotel Encanto, 705 S. Telshor Blvd. (✆ **866/383-0443** or 575/522-4300; www. hhandr.com). In a contemporary setting reminiscent of a Spanish nightclub, the city's youngish business set has drinks and hors d'oeuvres.

Rambling Downtown

The first Friday of each month all the galleries on the Downtown Mall stay open until 7pm for the **Downtown Ramble.** Most serve refreshments and have artists on-hand to visit with patrons. While wandering in the area stop in the **Rio Grande Theatre,** 211 N. Downtown Mall (✆ **575/523-6403**; www.daarts. org). Built in 1926 as a movie palace, it has been restored to an elegant performing arts center. With Art Deco touches inside and out, including a restored neon sign and elaborate tile work, it's worth seeing in its own right.

But plenty happens in the theater, including some major productions. Past shows include Eliza Gilkyson in concert and a rendition of *Prairie Home Companion.* The theater sits along Main Street in downtown, also restored, offering a great place to stroll, though at this writing few shops had as yet opened up. One gallery worth checking out is **M. Phillip's,** 300 N. Downtown Mall (✆ **575/525-1367**; www.mphillips gallery.com), which carries Russian and European fine art.

Exploring the Area

NORTH OF LAS CRUCES   The town of **Hatch,** 39 miles north via I-25 or 34 miles north via NM 185, calls itself the "chile capital of the world." It's the center of a 22,000-acre agricultural belt that grows and processes more chile than anywhere else in the world. The annual Hatch Chile Festival over Labor Day weekend celebrates the harvest. For information, call the **Hatch Chamber of Commerce** (© **575/267-5050**) or check out www.villageofhatch.org.

Fort Selden State Monument is 15 miles north of Las Cruces between I-25 (exit 19) and NM 185. Founded in 1865, Fort Selden housed the famous Black Cavalry, the "Buffalo Soldiers" who protected settlers from marauding natives. It was subsequently the boyhood home of Gen. Douglas MacArthur, whose father, Arthur, was in charge of troops patrolling the U.S.-Mexico border in the 1880s. The fort closed permanently in 1891. Today, elegantly eroded ruins remain. Displays in the visitor center tell Fort Selden's story, including photos of young Douglas and his family. The monument is open Wednesday to Monday from 8:30am to 5pm; admission is $3 for adults and free for children age 16 and under. For more information, call © **575/526-8911** or visit www.nmmonuments.org. Adjacent to the state monument, **Leasburg Dam State Park** (© **575/524-4068;** www.nmparks.com) offers picnicking, camping, canoeing, and fishing.

SOUTH OF LAS CRUCES   **Stahmann Farms,** 10 miles south of La Mesilla on NM 28, is one of the world's largest single producers of pecans. Several million pounds are harvested, mostly during November, from orchards in the bed of an ancient lake. **Stahmann's Country Store** ★ (© **800/654-6887;** www.stahmanns. com) sells pecans, pecan candy, ice cream, and other specialty foods, and it has a small cafe. It's open Monday through Saturday from 10am to 6pm, Sunday from 11am to 6pm. If you'd like to stay south of Las Cruces, book a night or two at **Casa de Sueños** ★, 405 Mountain Vista Rd., La Union, NM 88021 (© **575/874-9166;** www.casaofdreams.com). Set high on a plain overlooking the Rio Grande River Valley, with the Franklin Mountains in the distance, it offers atmospheric Southwest-style rooms about a half-hour south of Las Cruces, with good access to El Paso.

War Eagles Air Museum ★ (© **575/589-2000;** www.war-eagles-air-museum. com), at the Santa Teresa Airport, about 35 miles south of Las Cruces via I-10 (call or check the website for directions), has an extensive collection of historic aircraft

---

  Weaving Dreams

One day after enchiladas at Chope's Café in La Mesa, I wandered down a dirt road nearby and found a little adobe garden house, the studio of weaver Rosie Chavarria-Jones. "I use whatever I have around and let the yarn solar dye," she says. That might include marigolds, prickly pear cactus, purple cabbage, or pomegranates. Once the wool is dyed, she spins it and weaves it into scarves and shawls, which she sells from her shop. Her "A Mano Weaving Workshop" is at 216 E. Bellman in La Mesa (© 575/233-4363; amano4@ peoplepc.com). Call to be sure she's in.

from World War II and the Korean War, plus automobiles and a tank. The museum is open Tuesday through Sunday from 10am to 4pm; admission is $5 for adults, $4 for senior citizens age 65 and over; free for children age 11 and under.

EAST OF LAS CRUCES The **Organ Mountains,** so-called because they resemble the pipes of a church organ, draw inevitable comparisons to Wyoming's Grand Tetons. Organ Peak, at 9,119 feet, is the highest point in Doña Ana County.

The **Aguirre Springs Recreation Area ★★** (*©* 575/525-4300; www.blm.gov. nm), off US 70 on the western slope of the Organ Mountains, is one of the most spectacular places I've ever camped. Operated by the Bureau of Land Management, the camping and picnic sites sit at the base of the jagged Organ Mountains. Visitors to the area can hike, camp, picnic, or ride horseback (no horse rentals on-site). If you'd like to hike, don't miss the **Baylor Pass** trail, which crosses along the base of the Organ peaks, up through a pass, and over to the Las Cruces side. Though the hike is 6 miles one-way, just over 2 miles will get you to the pass, where there's a meadow with amazing views.

Where to Stay in & Around Las Cruces

Hotel Encanto de Las Cruces ★★ Spanish Colonial elegance defines this seven-story hotel on the east side of town, about a 15-minute drive from Mesilla, with an incredible view of the city and the Organ Mountains. The hotel was built in 1986, and implemented a major remodel in 2006, including new bedding and furnishings, all with a lovely Old World Mexican/Colonial motif. The lobby has a tiered fountain, colorful tile, and museum-quality furnishings. Rooms are spacious and outfitted with handcrafted furniture and comfortable beds with good linens. Photography by the noted artist Miguel Gandert dresses the walls. Baths are medium-size with granite countertops. Some rooms flank the pool and have little patios. The service here is excellent. The Café España serves breakfast, lunch, and dinner in an elegant Spanish Colonial ambience, and the Azul Nightclub offers drinks with a contemporary Southwest flair.

705 S. Telshor Blvd., Las Cruces, NM 88011. *©* **866/383-0443** or 575/522-4300. Fax 575/521-4707. www.hhandr.com. 203 units. $109–$159 double; $179–$199 suite. AE, DC, DISC, MC, V. Pets welcome ($25/day). **Amenities:** Restaurant; lounge; exercise room; Jacuzzi; heated outdoor pool (open in summer); room service. *In room:* A/C, TV, hair dryer, Wi-Fi.

La Quinta Five minutes from Old Mesilla, this chain hotel provides relatively quiet and comfortable rooms with plenty of amenities. The clean and well-designed rooms range from medium to large, all with desks and medium-size bathrooms. An outdoor pool sits within a comfortable courtyard, an important addition in this warm climate. Guests eat their continental breakfast in a bright garden room off the lobby. When you reserve here ask for one of the "annex" rooms, which are the largest and newest. Also, be aware that trains pass near this area at night. A few casual dining restaurants have opened across the street.

790 Av. de Mesilla, Las Cruces, NM 88005. *©* **800/531-5900** or 575/524-0331. Fax 575/525-8360. www.laquinta.com. $55–$97 double. Rates include continental breakfast. AE, DISC, MC, V. Pets welcome. **Amenities:** Small fitness room; outdoor pool. *In room:* A/C, TV, hair dryer, Wi-Fi.

A BED & BREAKFAST

The Lundeen Inn of the Arts ★ This boutique inn is a late-1890s adobe home, with whitewashed walls, narrow alleys, and arched doorways. It offers a range of rooms, each named for an artist. My favorites are in the main part of the house, set around a two-story garden room, with elegant antiques and arched windows. Most rooms are medium-size with comfortably firm beds dressed in good linens. Bathrooms are generally small and simple but clean. The inn is also an art gallery, displaying the works of about 30 Southwestern painters, sculptors, and potters. Breakfast includes fresh fruit and such specialties as pumpkin pancakes and huevos rancheros.

618 S. Alameda Blvd., Las Cruces, NM 88005. © **888/526-3326** or 575/526-3326. Fax 575/647-1334. www.innofthearts.com. 7 units. $85–$99 double; $85–$120 suite. Rates include full breakfast. AE, DC, DISC, MC, V. Pets welcome. **Amenities:** Concierge. In room: A/C, TV, hair dryer, Wi-Fi.

CAMPING

Quite a few campgrounds are within or near Las Cruces. All the ones listed here include full hookups for RVs, tent areas, and recreation areas. **KOA Las Cruces** (© **575/526-6555;** www.koa.com) also offers cabins and laundry and grocery facilities. From the junction of I-10 and US 70 (exit 135), go 1½ miles east on US 70, and then half a block south on Weinrich Road.

Another option is **Dalmont's RV Park** (© **575/523-2992**). If you're coming from the west, when you reach the junction of I-25 and I-10, go 2½ miles northwest on I-10 to the Main Street exit, and then go 2 blocks west on Valley Drive. If you're coming from the east, at the junction of I-10 and Main Street, go ¼ mile north on Main Street and then 1 block west on Valley Drive. To reach **Siesta RV Park** (© **575/523-6816;** www.siestarvpark.com), at the junction of I-10 and NM 28, take exit 140 and go half a mile south on NM 28. **Leasburg Dam State Park** (© **575/524-4068;** www.nmparks.com) is a smaller park that also offers RV and tent camping, but it has no laundry or grocery facilities. A general country store is about 1 mile down the road, and hiking and fishing are available.

Where to Dine in & Around Las Cruces

EXPENSIVE

Double Eagle ★★ CONTINENTAL   When I was a kid, whenever we went to Las Cruces, we always made a special trip to this elegant restaurant imbued with Old West style. I'm pleased to say that it's still a quality place to dine. This 150-year-old Territorial-style hacienda that was once the governor's mansion is on the National Register of Historic Places. Built around a central courtyard, it has numerous rooms, one of which is said to be frequented by a woman's ghost. The menu is varied and includes pasta, chicken, fish, and steak dishes, with the beef aged in-house. My favorite is the filet mignon. All entrees come with salad, vegetable, and choice of potato or pasta. There's a full bar, from which you might want to order a mango margarita, and for dessert you can end it all with the Death by Chocolate Cake. **Peppers Café,** set in the courtyard, serves inventive New Mexican fare at lunch. Try their signature dish, stuffed seafood chile rellenos.

2355 Calle de Guadalupe, on the east side of Mesilla Plaza. © **575/523-6700.** www.double-eagle-mesilla.com. Reservations recommended. Main courses $8–$15 lunch (at Peppers), $14–$36 dinner. AE, DC, DISC, MC, V. Mon–Sat 11am–10pm; Sun 11am–9pm.

MODERATE

Lemongrass ★★ 🍴 THAI   This addition to the Las Cruces dining scene offers delicious flavors in a comfortably elegant atmosphere. It's set in an open room accented with Thai tapestries on the walls. Service is congenial, though be prepared to wait a bit for the food. Chef Kimberly Ming uses very fresh ingredients and brings her own touch to traditional Thai dishes such as pad Thai—rice noodles with egg, bean sprouts, tofu, tamarind sauce, and shrimp or chicken. I've also enjoyed a delicious *pad pong kari*—broccoli, bell pepper, straw mushrooms, and chicken or shrimp in a yellow curry and coconut milk sauce. Unique to this Thai restaurant, the chef is open to dialing the spice way down so even tender palates can enjoy eating here. Enjoy beer and wine with your meal.

2540 El Paseo Rd. ℂ **575/523-8778.** Reservations recommended on weekends in summer. Main courses $7–$15 lunch, $16–$20 dinner. AE, DISC, DC, MC, V. Daily 11am–2pm and 5–9pm.

Mix Pacific Rim Cuisine ★★ ASIAN/SUSHI   With moody lighting and lots of fine details, this intimate restaurant serves artful Pacific Rim cuisine. Chinese paper lamps seem to float on the ceiling, while the wood tables are topped with inlaid Asian knickknacks, and a sushi bar lines one wall. Service is good. You might start with one of their fun drinks such as a Pacific Pleasure—silver *sake* with mango, orange, and apple juice. Next, move on to some Polynesian spring rolls with mango salsa. A number of salads dress the menu, as do a full range of sushi offerings. For lunch, the *bento* combinations are a good buy; such entrees as grilled salmon come with soup, salad, and steamed or fried rice. Dinner offerings are more upscale. You might try the steak wrap—fresh asparagus wrapped with grilled New York steak, or the spicy *miso* sea bass. Both come with soup, salad, *wasabi*-mashed potatoes and stir-fried vegetables. A fun choice for dessert is the banana spring rolls with ice cream. Beer and wine accompany the menu. Next door, the same restaurateur serves quality fast Asian food at Mix Express.

1001 University Ave. D4. ℂ **575/532-2042.** www.mixpacificrim.com. Reservations accepted. Main courses lunch $7–$10, dinner $13–$20. AE, DISC, MC, V. Mon–Fri 11am–2pm and 5–9pm; Sat noon–2pm and 5–9pm.

Sunset Grill & Wine Bar ★★ 🍴 NEW AMERICAN/STEAKS   With moody lighting and lots of fine details, this restaurant serves up good food and even better views. Located at Sonoma Ranch, an upscale golf community, the restaurant looks out over their golf course and serves three meals daily. The interior has a corner fireplace, stacked flagstone accents, and broad windows. The menu changes seasonally and always features some New Mexican entrees. Breakfast brings many selections of egg and pancake type dishes. Lunch offers soups, salads, and sandwiches, including an Asiago-and-steak sandwich with ranch dressing. Dinner focuses primarily on steak and seafood. Most recently, I enjoyed grilled halibut with white wine butter sauce, with mashed potatoes and grilled asparagus. The entrees include a choice of soup or salad, which makes the meals here a real value. A thoughtful wine list accompanies the menu. Live music plays nights Wednesday to Friday.

1274 Golf Club Rd. ℂ **575/521-1826.** www.sonomaranch.com. Reservations recommended for weekend dinners. Main courses $8–$14 breakfast and lunch, $21–$38 dinner. AE, DISC, MC, V. Daily 7am–10pm.

INEXPENSIVE

Chope's Bar & Cafe ★ ☺ NEW MEXICAN   This is one of those legendary spots, a requisite weekly pilgrimage for many. Drive 15 minutes south of Old Mesilla through pecan orchards to its door, and you'll encounter a real locals' scene. The dining rooms are plain. Set in an old house, they have tile floors, faux wood paneling, and closely set tables, usually full of families, businesspeople, and college students. You'll feast on *chile rellenos,* enchiladas, and burritos. Whatever you order, make sure it's smothered with red or green chile, if you can handle the heat. If not, opt for tacos or a hamburger. Kids like the place because it's casual and they have their own menu. Service is friendly but very overworked. With your meal, order up margaritas or a Mexican beer, or, if you really wish to partake, head next door to the cantina, a dark and raucous place reminiscent of a border-town bar.

NM 28 (in the center of town in La Mesa; no street address). ☎ **575/233-3420** or 575/233-9976. Main courses $5-$10. MC, V. Tues-Sat 11:30am-1:30pm and 5:30-8:30pm; cantina Tues-Sat 11:30am-9:30pm.

Farley's ☺ BURGERS/SANDWICHES   This big barnlike redbrick place offers pub food in a festive ambience. Part of a chain throughout southern New Mexico, it has entertainment along with food. While awaiting their meals kids and adults enjoy foosball, air hockey, and video games in the game room. The main part of the restaurant is a bar with tall tables for mixing with the scene or booths for more privacy. The third room is quieter and more family-oriented. Food here is rib-sticking, with such offerings as chicken Alfredo, pork ribs, fajitas, soups, salads, and burgers.

3499 Foothills Rd. ☎ **575/522-0466.** Main courses $7-$13. AE, DISC, MC, V. Daily 11am-11pm.

La Posta de Mesilla ☺ NEW MEXICAN/STEAKS   If you're on the Mesilla Plaza and want to eat New Mexican food for not much money, walk in here. The restaurant occupies a mid-18th-century adobe building that is the only surviving stagecoach station of the Butterfield Overland Mail route from Tipton, Missouri, to San Francisco. Kit Carson, Pancho Villa, General Douglas MacArthur, and Billy the Kid were all here at one time. The entrance leads through a jungle of tall plants beneath a Plexiglas roof, past a tank of piranhas and a noisy aviary of macaws and Amazon parrots, to nine dining rooms with bright, festive decor. (Kids love this and their own menu selections.) The tables are basic, with vinyl and metal chairs. Try the enchiladas, which come with a nice chile sauce. The tostadas (tortilla cups filled with beans and topped with chile and cheese) are a house specialty. There's a full-service bar.

2410 Calle de San Albino (southeast corner of Old Mesilla Plaza). ☎ **575/524-3524.** www.laposta-de-mesilla.com. Reservations recommended. Main courses $7-$16. AE, DC, DISC, MC, V. Daily 11am-9pm (Fri-Sat till 9:30pm).

Lorenzo's Restaurante Italiano de Old Messilla ★★ SICILIAN   In a spirited building with lots of brick and with murals depicting rural scenes on the walls, the restaurant offers the feel of a Sicilian village cafe, a good indication of the quality of the food here. Rather than fancy Italian food like you find in many cities, this restaurant serves traditional Sicilian meals, with lots of red sauces and homemade pasta. It's big with locals, and it fills up fast. The atmosphere is jovial and the service is good. You can't go wrong with standards such as spaghetti marinara or lasagna, or for something more adventurous, try the linguini and clams. Meals are served with a salad of freshly tossed greens and bread so good you'll have a tough time stopping yourself from eating it all. Wash it down with a carafe of Chianti or your favorite beer.

1750 Calle de Mercado #4 (Onate Plaza, a block from Old Mesilla Plaza). ☎ **575/525-3174.** Reservations recommended. Main courses $8-$19. AE, DISC, MC, V. Sun-Tues 11am-8:30pm; Wed-Thurs 11am-9pm; Fri-Sat 11am-9:30pm.

Old Mesilla Pastry Café: The Shed ★★ NEW MEXICAN   This small cafe with a colorful contemporary ambience serves terrific food. Tile floors and plum and orange art make for a friendly place to savor breakfast or lunch. The service is attentive. A good bet here is the breakfast enchiladas—corn tortillas with turkey sausage, onion, and cheese smothered in a red or green sauce with potatoes. The oatmeal pancakes are also delicious. At lunch, the wood-fired pizza is a good choice for those seeking an alternative to chile dishes. Pick up a loaf of their green chile cheddar bread to take with you.

810 S. Valley Dr. ℂ **575/525-2636.** All menu items under $10. AE, DISC, MC, V. Daily 7:30am–2pm.

Tiffany's Pizza & Greek American Cuisine ★★ ☺ GREEK/PIZZA   Between sky-blue walls decorated with photos of Greece, this cafe serves flavorful pizza, sandwiches, and entrees to the tune of festive music. It's a casual place with faux wood tables and tile floors and a TV with the sound off, but the food is authentic. One favorite is the Tiffany's Pizza, which comes with sausage, pepperoni, pastrami, bell peppers, onion, and mushrooms, a good dish to take back to your hotel room after a long day. Or you could have a lamb gyro sandwich. My favorite here is the moussaka or the baked chicken; the latter comes with potatoes, vegetables, and salad at a great price. In fact, the portions are so large here, a couple could easily split a meal. Kids have their own menu, and the relaxed attitude will make them comfortable. Though no alcohol is served, there is Greek coffee, and baklava or Greek wedding cookies for dessert.

Telshor Tower Plaza G-1 (2 buildings behind the Hotel Encanto). ℂ **575/532-5002.** Main courses $8–$15; pizza $15–$19. AE, DISC, MC, V. Tues–Thurs 9am–8pm; Fri 9am–9pm; Sat 11am–9pm.

DEMING & LORDSBURG

New Mexico's least populated corner is this one, which includes the "boot heel" of the Gadsden Purchase, poking 40 miles down toward Mexico (a great place for backpacking). These two railroad towns, an hour apart on I-10, see a lot of traffic; but whereas **Deming** (pop. 15,500) is thriving as a ranching and retirement center, **Lordsburg's** population has declined to approximately 2,800. This is a popular area for rockhounds, aficionados of ghost towns, and history buffs: **Columbus,** 32 miles south of Deming, was attacked by the Mexican bandit-revolutionary Pancho Villa in 1916. The U.S. military retaliated by sending 10,000 troops into Mexico to find him, to no avail.

Essentials

GETTING THERE   From Las Cruces, take I-10 west (1 hr. to Deming, 2 hr. to Lordsburg). From Tucson, take I-10 east (3 hr. to Lordsburg, 4 hr. to Deming).

Great Lakes Airlines (ℂ **575/388-4115;** www.flygreatlakes.com) flies daily to **Grant County Airport** (ℂ **575/388-4554**), 15 miles south of Silver City near Hurley. The **Las Cruces Shuttle Service,** P.O. Box 3172, Las Cruces, NM 88003 (ℂ **800/288-1784** or 575/525-1784; www.lascrucesshuttle.com), runs several times daily between Deming and the El Paso airport by way of Las Cruces.

VISITOR INFORMATION   The **Deming–Luna County Chamber of Commerce** is at 800 E. Pine St., Deming (ℂ **800/848-4955** or 575/546-2674; www. demingchamber.com). The **Greater Hidalgo Area Chamber of Commerce** is at 117 E. 2nd St., Lordsburg, NM 88045 (ℂ **575/542-9864**).

FRENCH & ITALIAN vintages

As one of New Mexico's best wine growing regions, this area offers two quality vineyards, each with a tasting room well worth visiting. **St. Clair Winery & Visitor Center ★★**, 1325 DeBaca Rd. SE (© **866/336-7357** or 575/546-1179; www.stclairvineyards.com), the largest wine producer in the state, is run by Florent Lescombe, a sixth-generation French wine grower. It is open Monday to Saturday 9am to 6pm and Sunday noon to 6pm. **Luna Rossa Winery ★★**, 3710 West Pine St. (© **575/544-1160;** www.lunarossawinery.com), features vintages designed by Paolo and Sylvia D'Andrea from northeastern Italy. Paolo comes from a heritage of four generations of wine growers. The tasting room is open Monday to Saturday 10am to 6pm and Sunday noon to 6pm.

What to See & Do Near Deming

Deming Luna Mimbres Museum ★ Deming was the meeting place of the second east-west railroad to connect the Pacific and Atlantic coasts, and that heritage is recalled in this museum, run by the Luna County Historical Society. It has a stellar geode collection; a room featuring the John and Mary Alice King Collection of Mimbres pottery; and a doll room with more than 800 dolls. A 5,000-square-foot adjacent space displays transportation-related exhibits, including a replica of a railroad depot, a Harvey House, and vintage fire trucks. Across the street is the Custom House, a turn-of-the-20th-century adobe home that has been turned into a walk-through exhibit.

301 S. Silver Ave., Deming. © **575/546-2382.** Fax 575/544-0121. Free admission; donations encouraged. Mon–Sat 9am–4pm; Sun 1:30–4pm.

GETTING OUTSIDE

At **Rockhound State Park ★**, 14 miles southeast of Deming via NM 11, visitors are encouraged to pick up and take home with them as much as 15 pounds of minerals—jasper, agate, quartz crystal, flow-banded rhyolite, and others. At the base of the Little Florida Mountains, the park is a lovely, arid, cactus-covered land with paths leading down into dry gullies and canyons. (You may have to walk a bit, as the more accessible minerals have been largely picked out.)

The campground ($10 for nonelectric hookup; $18 with sewage and electric hookup), which has shelters, restrooms, and showers, offers a distant view of mountain ranges all the way to the Mexican border. The park also has one marked hiking trail and a playground. Admission is $5 per vehicle, and the park is open year-round from dawn to dusk. For more information, contact © **575/546-6182;** www.nmparks.com.

Some 35 miles south of Deming is the tiny border town of **Columbus,** which looks across at Mexico. The **Pancho Villa State Park ★** here marks the last foreign invasion of American soil. A temporary fort, where a tiny garrison was housed in tents, was attacked in 1916 by 600 Mexican revolutionaries, who cut through the boundary fence at Columbus. Eighteen Americans were killed, 12 wounded; an estimated 200 Mexicans died. The Mexicans immediately retreated across their border. An American punitive expedition, headed by Gen. John J. Pershing, was launched into Mexico but got nowhere. Villa restricted his banditry to Mexico after that, until his assassination in 1923.

The state park includes ruins of the old fort and a visitor center and 7,000-square-foot museum offering exhibits and a film. The park also has a strikingly beautiful desert botanical garden (worth the trip alone), plus campsites, restrooms, showers, an RV dump station, and a playground. There's a $5-per-vehicle entrance fee; the park is staffed daily from 8am to 5pm. For more information, contact ✆ 575/531-2711; www.nmparks.com.

Across the street from the state park is the old Southern Pacific Railroad Depot, which has been restored by the Columbus Historical Society and now houses the **Columbus Historical Museum** (✆ 575/531-2620), which contains railroad memorabilia and exhibits on local history. Call for hours, which vary.

If you'd like to stay in Columbus, call **Martha's Place Bed & Breakfast,** Main and Lima streets (✆ 575/531-2467; www.marthasplacebb.com). It's a two-story stucco Pueblo-style adobe painted cream and green, with Victorian touches inside. The medium-size rooms have comfortable beds and French doors leading to a balcony. Prices are $75 double. Rates include breakfast. Pets are welcome.

Three miles south across the border in Mexico is **Las Palomas, Chihuahua** (pop. 1,500). The port of entry is open 24 hours. A few desirable restaurants and tourist-oriented businesses are in Las Palomas. Mostly, though, it's a drug-trafficking town. **Beware of barhopping in Palomas at night,** as it can be dangerous.

What to See & Do Near Lordsburg

Visitors to Lordsburg can go **rockhounding** in this area rich in minerals of many kinds. Desert roses can be found near Summit, and agate is known to exist in many abandoned mines locally. Mine dumps, southwest of Hachita, contain lead, zinc, and gold; the Animas Mountains have manganese. Volcanic glass can be picked up in Coronado National Forest, and you can pan for gold in Gold Gulch.

Rodeo, 30 miles southwest via I-10 and NM 80, is the home of the **Chiricahua Gallery** (✆ 575/557-2225; www.rodeonewmexico.com), open Monday through Saturday from 10am to 4pm. Regional artists have joined in a nonprofit, cooperative venture to exhibit works and offer classes in a variety of media. Many choose to live on the high-desert slopes of the Chiricahua Range. Look especially for the inspirational bird-filled landscapes of Jean Bohlender. The gallery is on NM 80 en route to Douglas, Arizona.

Shakespeare Ghost Town ☺ A national historic site, Shakespeare was once the home of 3,000 miners, promoters, and dealers of various kinds. Under the name Ralston, it enjoyed a silver boom in 1870. This was followed by a notorious diamond fraud in 1872, in which a mine was salted with diamonds in order to raise prices on mining stock; many notables were sucked in, particularly William Ralston, founder of the Bank of California. It enjoyed a mining revival in 1879 under its new name, Shakespeare. Since 1935, it's been privately owned by the Hill family, which has kept it uncommercialized, with no souvenir hype or gift shops. Six original buildings and two reconstructed buildings survive in various stages of repair. Two-hour guided tours are offered on a limited basis, and reenactments and living history are staged on the fourth weekends of April, June, August, and October, if performers are available. Phone to confirm the performances.

2½ miles south of Lordsburg (no street address), P.O. Box 253, Lordsburg, NM 88045. ☏ **575/542-9034.** www.shakespeareghostown.com. Admission $4 adults, $3 children 6–12; for shootouts and special events $5 adults, $4 children. Open only 10am–2pm on the 2nd Sun and preceding Sat of each month. Special events by appointment. To reach Shakespeare, drive 1½ miles south from I-10 on Main St. Just before the town cemetery, turn right, proceed ½ mile, and turn right again. Follow the dirt road another ½ mile into Shakespeare.

Where to Stay in Deming & Lordsburg

IN DEMING

Holiday Inn ★   Just off I-10, the Holiday Inn brings a bit of style to dusty Deming. Though from the outside the 1974 two-story white brick structure appears basic, the rooms—with renovations in 2009—tell another story. Each is medium-size with light pine furniture and decorated in Aztec prints, with bold expressionist paintings on the walls. Bathrooms are small but each has a vanity with granite counters. Some of the suites come with Jacuzzis. The large pool is surrounded by lush grass; request a poolside room and you'll have a bit of a resort feel. The hotel's restaurant is open for breakfast, lunch, and dinner, serving New Mexican and American food.

Off I-10, exit 85 (P.O. Box 1138), Deming, NM 88031. ☏ **800/465-4329** or 575/546-2661. Fax 575/546-6308. www.ichotels.com. 116 units. $67–$85 double. AE, DC, DISC, MC, V. Pets welcome. **Amenities:** Restaurant; exercise room; Jacuzzi; outdoor heated pool (summer); room service. *In room:* A/C, TV, fridge, hair dryer, Wi-Fi.

La Quinta Inn ★   True to its origins, this new whitewashed hotel provides consistent and comfortable rooms at a decent price. Each is medium size with high ceilings, red-wood furniture, and earth-tone decor. The beds are comfortable and the bathrooms spacious enough and with granite countertops. This is a good option if you'd like a newer-style hotel than the Holiday Inn next door.

4300 E. Pine St., Deming, NM 88030. ☏ **800/753-3757** or 575/546-0600. Fax 575/544-8207. www.laquinta.com. 58 units. $79–$105 double. Rates include continental breakfast. AE, DC, DISC, MC, V. **Amenities:** Exercise room; outdoor heated pool (summer). *In room:* A/C, TV, fridge, hair dryer, microwave, Wi-Fi.

IN LORDSBURG

Comfort Inn Lordsburg ★ ☺   This new three-story hotel remains true to its brand, providing clean and comfortable rooms at a reasonable price. All rooms are spacious with earth-tone decor, contemporary mahogany-style furnishings, and a desk. The king rooms have a sleeper sofa, a good option for families. This is definitely your best option in town.

400 W. Wabash St., Lordsburg, NM 88045. ☏ **877/526-3938** or 575/542-3355. Fax 575/542-3360. www.comfortinn.com. 64 units. $84–$99 double. Rates include full hot breakfast. AE, DC, DISC, MC, V. Pets ($10 fee). **Amenities:** Jacuzzi; indoor pool; sauna. *In room:* A/C, TV, hair dryer, Wi-Fi.

CAMPING IN & AROUND DEMING & LORDSBURG

City of Rocks State Park, in Deming (☏ **575/536-2800;** www.nmparks.com), has 55 campsites, 10 with electric hookups; tent sites are available, and picnic tables and a hiking trail are nearby. **Dreamcatcher RV Park** (☏ **575/544-4004**), also in Deming (take exit 85, Motel Dr., off I-10 and go 1 block south on Business I-10), has 92 sites, all with full hookups. It also offers free access to a nearby swimming pool and on-site laundry facilities. **Little Vineyard RV Park** (☏ **575/546-3560**) in Deming (from I-10 take exit 85 and go 1 mile southwest on Business I-10 toward Deming) is larger than those already mentioned. It has 150 with full hookups, limited groceries, an indoor pool and hot tub, cable TV hookups, Wi-Fi, and a small RV parts store. The campground at **Rockhound State Park** (© **575/546-6182; www.nmparks.com**) is picturesque and great for rockhounds who can't get enough of their hobby. RV sites with hookups and tent sites are both available, as are shelters, restrooms, and showers.

If you'd rather camp near Lordsburg, try **Lordsburg KOA** (© **800/562-5772** or 575/542-8003; www.koa.com). It's in a desert setting but with shade trees, and tenting is permitted. Grocery and laundry facilities are available, in addition to a recreation area, a swimming pool, a playground, and horseshoes. To reach the campground, take I-10 to exit 22 and then go 1 block south; next, turn right at the Chevron station and follow the signs to the campground.

Where to Dine in Deming & Lordsburg

IN DEMING

Palma's Italian Grill ★ ☺ ITALIAN   Set in an old bank building still equipped with its late 1800s vault, this restaurant serves traditional Italian dishes in a festive atmosphere. With checkered tablecloths and high ceilings, the place is airy and the service friendly. A big seller here is the spaghetti and meatballs with sausage, as is the lasagna, both served with a salad and fresh-baked bread. The steaks are also good, served with soup or salad, and baked potato or pasta. Lighter dishes such as a Caesar salad with grilled chicken, shrimp, or salmon, are available as well. A kids' menu, including some American offerings, makes them feel at home. Finish with a piece of homemade pie, a cannoli, or spumoni ice cream. A beer and wine list accompanies the menu.

110 S. Silver Ave., Deming. © **575/544-3100.** Main courses $7–$24. DISC, MC, V. Tues–Sat 11am–9pm; Sun 11am–3pm.

Si Señor ★ NEW MEXICAN   Locals crowd this downtown cafe to eat platters full of tasty New Mexican food. The interior has functional furniture and a lovely tile floor. At breakfast, try the huevos rancheros. The big seller here for lunch and dinner is the deluxe combination, with a *chile relleno,* a tamale, a cheese enchilada, a taco, refried beans, Spanish rice, and red or green chile. The menu also sports salads, hamburgers, and chicken and fish dishes. All come with chips and salsa, and wine and beer are served.

200 E. Pine, Deming. © **575/546-3938.** Main courses $6–$10 breakfast, $5–$12 lunch and dinner. DISC, MC, V. Mon–Sat 9am–8pm; Sun 1–10pm.

IN LORDSBURG

Kranberry's Family Restaurant AMERICAN/MEXICAN   A friendly, casual Denny's-style family restaurant decorated with Southwestern art, Kranberry's offers American favorites, including eggs and pancakes for breakfast; and burgers, chicken, beef, and salads, as well as Mexican selections for lunch and dinner. Baked goods are made on the premises daily. My favorite is the corn bread, served with the soup special.

1405 S. Main St., Lordsburg. © **575/542-9400.** Main courses $4–$7 breakfast, $6–$17 lunch and dinner. AE, DC, DISC, MC, V. Daily 6am–9:30pm.

SILVER CITY ★★

Silver City (pop. 10,000) is an old mining town, in the foothills of the Pinos Altos Range of the Mogollon Mountains, and gateway to the Gila Wilderness and the Gila Cliff Dwellings. It is also a cultural center that offers imaginative galleries and inventive dining.

Early Native Americans mined turquoise from these hills, and by 1804, Spanish settlers were digging for copper. In 1870, a group of prospectors discovered silver, and the rush was on. In 10 short months, the newly christened Silver City grew from a single cabin to more than 80 buildings. Early visitors included Billy the Kid, Judge Roy Bean, and William Randolph Hearst.

This comparatively isolated community kept pace with every modern convenience: telephones in 1883, electric lights in 1884 (only 2 years after New York City installed its lighting), and a water system in 1887. The town should have gone bust with the crash of silver prices in 1893. But unlike many Western towns, Silver City did not become a picturesque memory. It capitalized on its high, dry climate to become today's county seat and trade center. Copper mining and processing is still the major industry. But Silver City also can boast a famous son: The late Harrison (Jack) Schmitt, the first civilian geologist to visit the moon, and later a U.S. senator, was born and raised in nearby Santa Rita.

Essentials

GETTING THERE From Albuquerque, take I-25 south, 15 miles past Truth or Consequences; then west on NM 152 and US 180 (5 hr.). From Las Cruces, take I-10 west to Deming, and then north on US 180 (2 hr.).

Great Lakes Airlines (✆ 575/388-4115) flies daily to **Grant County Airport** (✆ 575/388-4554), 15 miles south of Silver City near Hurley. **Silver Stage Lines** (✆ 800/522-0162) offers daily shuttle service to and from the El Paso airport, and charter service to and from Tucson. The **Las Cruces Shuttle Service** (✆ 800/288-1784 or 575/525-1784; www.lascrucesshuttle.com) runs several times daily between Silver City and the El Paso airport, by way of Las Cruces.

VISITOR INFORMATION The **Murray Ryan Visitor Center,** at 201 N. Hudson St., Silver City, NM 88061 (✆ 800/548-9378 or 575/538-3785; www.silver city.org), also houses the Silver City Grant County Chamber of Commerce and is a good source of information. The chamber produces extremely useful tourist publications. Also of note at this site is a replica 1870s log cabin donated to the city by movie producer Ron Howard. It was built for the filming of the 2005 movie *The Missing.* A plaque on it says that Billy the Kid likely lived in one similar to it when he was a young resident of this town.

What to See & Do in Silver City

Silver City's downtown **Historic District ★**, the first such district to receive National Register recognition, is a must for visitors. The downtown core is marked by the extensive use of brick in construction: Brick clay was discovered in the area soon after the town's founding in 1870, and an 1880 ordinance prohibited frame construction within the town limits. Mansard-roofed Victorian houses, Queen Anne and Italianate residences, and commercial buildings show off the cast-iron architecture of the period. Some are still undergoing restoration.

An 1895 flood washed out Main Street and turned it into a gaping chasm, which was eventually bridged over; finally, the **Big Ditch,** as it's called, was made into a green park in the center of town. Facing downtown, in the 500 block of North Hudson Street, was a famous red-light district from the turn-of-the-20th-century until the late 1960s.

Billy the Kid lived in Silver City as a youth. You can see his cabin site a block north of the Broadway Bridge, on the east side of the Big Ditch. The Kid (William Bonney) waited tables at the Star Hotel, at Hudson Street and Broadway. He was jailed (at 304 N. Hudson St.) in 1875 at the age of 15, after being convicted of stealing from a Chinese laundry, but he escaped—a first for the Kid. The grave of Bonney's mother, Catherine McCarty, is in Silver City Cemetery, east of town on Memory Lane, off US 180. She died of tuberculosis about a year after the family moved here in 1873.

Silver City Walking Tours ★ (🕐 575/534-4841; www.silvercitywalks.com) offers a "leisurely stroll" through town highlighting tales of Billy the Kid, Geronimo and other historic characters. Tours are by appointment and cost $15.

Silver City Museum ★   This very well-presented museum of city and regional history contains collections relating to southwestern New Mexico history, mining, Native American pottery, and early photographs. Exhibits include a southwestern New Mexico history timeline, a parlor displaying Victorian decorative arts, and a chronicle of commerce in early Silver City. A local history research library is available to visitors also. The main gallery features changing exhibits. The museum is lodged in the 1881 H. B. Ailman House, a former city hall and fire station, remarkable for its cupola and Victorian mansard roof. Ailman came to Silver City penniless in 1871, made a fortune in mining, and went on to start the Meredith and Ailman Bank. Guided historic district walking tours are offered on Memorial Day and Labor Day. There's also a museum store. Take a fun trip up into the cupola for a nice view of the city.

312 W. Broadway. 🕐 **575/538-5921.** Fax 575/388-1096. www.silvercitymuseum.org. Suggested donation $3 per person. Tues-Fri 9am-4:30pm; Sat-Sun 10am-4pm. Closed Mon except Memorial Day and Labor Day.

Western New Mexico University Museum (WNMU)   Spread across 80 acres on the west side of Silver City, WNMU celebrated its centennial in 1993. The university boasts a 2,800-student enrollment and 24 major buildings. Among them is historic 1916 Fleming Hall, which houses this interesting museum. The WNMU museum has the largest permanent exhibit of prehistoric Mimbres pottery in the world. Also displayed are Casas Grandes Indian pottery, stone tools, ancient jewelry, historic photographs, and mining artifacts. Displays change regularly, so there's always something new to see, such as vanishing Americana, riparian fossils, Nigerian folk art, or a collection of 18th- to 20th-century timepieces. There is a gift shop here.

1000 W. College, Fleming Hall, WNMU. 🕐 **575/538-6386.** www.wnmu.edu/univ/museum.htm. Free admission. Mon-Fri 9am-4:30pm; Sat-Sun 10am-4pm.

Silver City After Dark

Silver City Brewing Co. ★ 101 E. College (🕐 575/534-2739; www.swnmbeer. com), the town's brewpub, offers tasty beer and a menu including pizza, pasta, sandwiches, and salads. Best of all here, during warm months, live music plays on the

---

Way Beyond Silver

Silver City has become an artists' mecca, as creative people retreat to the small town for the peace it offers. You can spend a fun day wandering the streets. Some of my favorite shops and galleries include **Silver City Trading Company's Antique Mall,** 205 W. Broadway (© 575/388-8989), which is packed with a range of items, from fun junk to Western antiques. **Copper Quail Gallery,** 211-A N. Texas St. (© 575/388-2646), offers wonderful regional art. **Blue Dome Gallery,** 307 N. Texas St. (© 575/534-8671; www.bluedomegallery.com), carries inventive contemporary art and crafts, while **Seedboat Gallery,** 214 W.

Yankee St. (© 575/534-1136; www.seedboatgallery.com), offers more earthy fare. Look for photos by Robert Medina Cook. A fun stop for coffee and a look at period photos of Silver City's "Big Ditch" is **Yankie Creek Coffee House,** 112 W. Yankie (© 575/534-9025), open Monday to Saturday 7am to 6pm, and Sunday 7am to 4pm. If you're craving a cold treat, head to **Alotta Gelato,** 619 N. Bullard St. © 575/534-4995; www.alottagelato.com), serving a broad range of gelato flavors, including Romeo and Juliet, their primo chocolate chip. Open Sunday to Thursday noon to 9pm, Friday and Saturday noon to 10pm.

---

patio on weekends. It's open daily 11am to 8pm. **Isaac's Bar & Grill ★** offers live entertainment on Saturday nights and fun activities on other nights as well, including a Trivia Night on Wednesdays. See "Where to Dine in & Around Silver City," below.

Exploring the Area

NORTH OF SILVER CITY   The virtual ghost town of **Pinos Altos ★**, straddling the Continental Divide, is 6 miles north of Silver City on NM 15. Dubbed "Tall Pines" when it was founded in the gold- and silver-rush era, Apache attacks and mine failures took their toll.

The adobe **Methodist-Episcopal Church** was built with William Randolph Hearst's money in 1898 and now houses the Grant County Art Guild. The town also has the **Log Cabin Curio Shop and Museum,** set in an 1866 cabin (© 575/388-1882), and the **Buckhorn Saloon and Opera House** (p. 343). **Pinos Altos Horse Drawn Carriage Rides** (© 575/534-9605) will tour you around the town on a carriage pulled by draft horses Bonnie and Clyde from Wednesdays to Sundays 11am to 4:30pm. Call for reservations.

If you'd like to stay in the village, contact **Bear Creek Motel & Cabins,** on NM 15 (© 575/388-4501; www.bearcreekcabins.com). Set among ponderosa pines, it's a nice, cool place to spend time. The cabins are a little dark, but quite cozy, most with a porch where guests grill their own food. Prices range from $119 to $159.

SOUTH OF SILVER CITY   City of Rocks State Park ★ (© 575/536-2800; www.nmparks.com), 25 miles from Silver City via US 180 and NM 61, is an area of fantastically shaped volcanic rock formations, formed in ancient times from thick blankets of ash that hardened into tuff. This soft stone, eroded by wind and rain, was shaped into monolithic blocks reminiscent of Stonehenge. For some, the park resembles a medieval village; for others, it's a collection of misshapen, albeit benign, giants. Complete with a desert garden, the park offers excellent camping and picnic sites. It's also a renowned spot for bouldering, a type of rock climbing in which participants don't use ropes. Day use is allowed from 7am to 9pm for $5 per vehicle; a campsite costs $8 to $18 (pay at self-service pay station). The visitor center is typically open daily from 9:30am to 4:30pm, but its hours may vary, depending on volunteer staffing.

WEST OF SILVER CITY   US 180, heading northwest from Silver City, is the gateway to Catron County and most of the Gila National Forest, including the villages of Glenwood, Reserve, and Quemado. For details on this area, see "Other Adventures in Gila National Forest," later.

Where to Stay in & Around Silver City

Silver City now offers a full range of chain hotels, many with reasonable prices, so if you have a favorite, call their 800 number to see if it's represented. Most lodgings in town provide free parking.

Holiday Inn Express ★ ☺   East of downtown, this hotel offers clean and quiet rooms with standards you expect from the brand name. Rooms are medium-size, decorated with earth tones, and have high ceilings, large windows letting in lots of sunlight, and a desk and chair. Beds are comfortable. The medium-size bathrooms are very clean. Be sure *not* to book room no. 121, which has noisy pipes playing tunes through the night.

1103 Superior St., Silver City, NM 88061. ℂ **800/465-4329** or 575/538-2525. Fax 575/538-2525. 60 units. $114 double; $140 suite. AE, DC, DISC, MC, V. Pets allowed in some rooms. **Amenities:** Exercise room; Jacuzzi. *In room:* A/C, TV, hair dryer, Wi-Fi.

Thar's Copper in Them Thar Hills

Southern New Mexico has carried on its mining legacy into the present, with two fully operating mines. 12 miles south of Silver City on NM 90 is the Freeport-McMoRan Tyrone Inc. **Open Pit Copper Mine** (ℂ 575/538-5331). Some 60 million tons of rock are taken out every year. Former mine owner Phelps Dodge consolidated its Tyrone holdings in 1909 and hired famous architect Bertram Goodhue to design a "Mediterranean-style" company town. Tyrone, later referred to as the Million Dollar Ghost Town, was constructed between 1914 and 1918. A drop in copper prices caused it to be abandoned virtually overnight. After a pre–World War II incarnation as a luxurious dude ranch, Tyrone lay dormant for years until the late 1960s, when the town made way for the present-day open pit mine and mill.

The oldest active mine in the Southwest, and among the largest in America, is the Freeport-McMoRan **Chino Mines Co. Open Pit Copper Mine** (commonly called the Santa Rita Copper Mine; ℂ 575/537-3381) at Santa Rita, 15 miles east of Silver City via US 180 and NM 152. The multicolored open pit is a mile wide and 1,000 feet deep, and can be viewed from an observation point. Even if you scorn such catastrophic gashes in the earth, it's worth stopping to look out over the mine. Unfortunately, no tours are available at this writing.

The Palace Hotel If you like the feel of an Old West downtown hotel in the center of the historic district, this is your spot. First established in 1882 as a bank, then opened as a hotel in 1900, it closed for many years but was reopened in 1990 as a small European-style hotel. Each of the rooms on the second floor is shaped and decorated differently. All are eclectic, some with antiques. The beds are medium firm, and the standard-size bathrooms are very clean with old fixtures, some with new toilets. Suites have a microwave and fridge. The rooms closest to the upstairs sitting room and breakfast area are the nicest. If you're not accustomed to city noise, you'll want to avoid this place, as traffic noise can be loud into the night.

106 W. Broadway (P.O. Box 5093), Silver City, NM 88061. ☏ **575/388-1811.** www.zianet.com/palace hotel. 19 units. $48–$63 double; $79 suite. Rates include continental breakfast. AE, DC, DISC, MC, V. **Amenities:** Lounge; Wi-Fi (in some parts of hotel). *In room:* No phone.

SMALLER INNS

Inn on Broadway ★★ This bed-and-breakfast set on a quiet street in the historic district offers an atmospheric stay in an 1883 Victorian home. The inn has marble fireplaces, hardwood floors, and is decorated with antiques. Each guestroom has its own style, such as the Garden Suite, with bright flower-trimmed walls, lots of light, and a sitting room with a sleeper sofa. A full breakfast is served in the sunny southwest-facing dining room. The innkeepers here go out of their way to provide guests with an enjoyable stay.

411 W. Broadway, Silver City, NM 88061. ☏ **575/388-5485.** www.innonbroadwayweb.com. 4 units. $95–$155 double. AE, DISC, MC, V. Rates include full breakfast. *In room:* A/C, TV, hair dryer.

> ### Relax in History
>
> Set in a Queen Anne–style home dating from 1906, the **Ciénega Spa & Salon,** 101 N. Cooper St. (☏ 575/534-1600; www.cienegaspasalon.com), offers a full range of treatments between bisque- and azure-colored walls. The place also serves as an art gallery, representing many local artists as well as pottery from the villagers of Mata Ortiz, Mexico.

Casitas de Gila ★★ If you're looking for a remote and peaceful stay in the quintessential southern New Mexico terrain, this inn is for you. Set on a little bluff above Bear Creek, about a half-hour from Silver City, these five casitas offer the epitome of Southwestern style. The adobe-style dwellings are decorated with Spanish-style furniture and Mexican rugs. The medium-size guestrooms come well equipped with comfortable beds, bath supplies, and bathrobes. Each also has a kiva fireplace and a small porch with a *chiminea* (Mexican ceramic fireplace) and a grill. On hand is a hot tub with a view of the creek, canyon, and sky. The area is great for birding and hiking, and horseback riding can be arranged. Also on the property are 226 acres with hiking trails, an art gallery, and a courtyard.

50 Casita Flats Rd. (P.O. Box 325), Gila, NM 88038. ☏ **877/923-4827** or 575/535-4455. Fax 575/535-4456. www.casitasdegila.com. 5 casitas. $130–$210 double. Rates include continental breakfast. AE, DISC, MC, V. **Amenities:** Concierge; Jacuzzi. *In room:* Kitchen, Wi-Fi.

CAMPING

Silver City KOA (☏ **800/562-7623** or 575/388-3351; www.silvercitykoa.com) has 82 sites and 42 full hookups, and it offers groceries, laundry facilities, a pool, basketball and volleyball courts, a playground, and pet park. The campground is

5 miles east of the NM 90/US 180 junction, 11824 US 180. **Silver City RV Park** (© **575/538-2239;** www.silvercityrv.com) has 48 sites (45 with full hookups), showers, laundry facilities, and picnic tables. It's downtown on Bennett Street, behind Food Basket supermarket. Camping is also available at the Gila Cliff Dwellings (see "Gila Cliff Dwellings National Monument," below).

Where to Dine in & Around Silver City

Buckhorn Saloon and Opera House ★★ BURGERS/SEAFOOD/STEAKS
Seven miles north of Silver City in Pinos Altos, the Buckhorn offers fine dining in 1860s decor. It's completely authentic, with vigas on the ceiling and thick adobe walls, and a recent renovation has brought a more contemporary touch. The restaurant is noted for its Western-style steaks, seafood, and excellent wine list. If you've got a big appetite, try the New York strip or the center-cut pork chop. Entrees come with bread, a salad or soup, and choice of potatoes or onion rings. The high-personality saloon offers an Old West feel with a grand fireplace and a wooden bar, where the mannequin Indian Joe always presides. Many come to this saloon to have excellent burgers and hear live music on selected nights. In the attached opera house, live music also plays some nights, so check the website for a schedule.

32 Main St., Pinos Altos. © **575/538-9911.** www.buckhornsaloonandoperahouse.com. Reservations recommended. Main courses $10–$30. AE, DISC, MC, V. Mon–Sat 5–10pm; saloon Mon–Sat 3–11pm.

The Curious Kumquat ★★ NEW AMERICAN It's challenging enough for chefs in locales such as Santa Fe and Albuquerque—where small farms are fairly common—to supply their restaurants with local, seasonal ingredients. But doing so in a remote place like this takes real courage. Chef Rob Connoley manages the feat boldly. At lunch you'll select from a variety of salads and sandwiches as well as a daily special. A favorite is the Robwich—Black Forest ham, Swiss cheese, applewood-smoked bacon, greens, and tomatoes on grilled sourdough. At dinner, the candied pork belly blue corn taco has a blue corn cone filled with pork that's accented with sugar-salt and smoked paprika and cooked for 24 hours, served with crispy kale and tomato chutney. You'll feast on such delicacies in the simple setting of a novelty food store set in a restored 1876 home, with modern furnishings set on hardwood floors. During summer, the shaded patio provides a nice retreat. A well-conceived wine list accompanies the menu.

111 E. College Ave. © **575/534-0337.** www.curiouskumquat.com. Main courses $4.50–$7 lunch, $15–$30 dinner. AE, DISC, MC, V. Mon–Sat 11am–2pm; Thurs–Sat 5:30–10pm.

Diane's Bakery & Cafe ★★ NEW AMERICAN This is a wonderful find in such a small town. Diane Barrett, who was once a pastry chef at La Traviata and Eldorado in Santa Fe, has brought refined city food to this small town. At lunch, the atmosphere is bustling, usually with a slight wait for a table. At dinner, the tone is romantic and low key, with more nouveau specialties. The service is friendly and adequate. You can't go wrong with any of the baked goods here. At brunch, try the hatch Benedict, a version of eggs Benedict made with home-baked chile cheddar toast. At lunch I suggest the spanakopita, a baked spinach pastry, served with a salad; the quiche of the day is also delicious. At dinner, you may want to order the pork loin, with mashed potatoes and house-made apple sauce, or the seafood Thai coconut curry. Diane's also serves great steaks. There's a small but creative wine and beer menu. Don't leave without sampling one of the desserts, such as the four-layer chocolate cake. Next door, Diane's Parlor serves wine and light fare, with more extended hours.

510 N. Bullard St., Silver City. © **575/538-8722.** www.dianesrestaurant.com. Reservations recommended for dinner. Main courses $6–$9 breakfast and lunch, $15–$25 dinner. MC, V. Tues–Sat 11am–2pm and 5:30–9pm; brunch Sat–Sun 9am–2pm.

Isaac's Bar & Grill ★ PUB FOOD/AMERICAN   With the charm of an 1881 historic building, once housing Isaac N. Cohen's mercantile business, this restaurant and bar serves good sandwiches, burgers, salads, and grilled meat and fish dishes. The main room is a pub, with tall tables and lots of locals talking among them. The second room is large with tables spread about. Both rooms have hardwood floors, aged brick walls, and high ceilings. The service here can be somewhat evasive, though friendly. Brunch is served Saturday and Sunday, with standards such as eggs Benedict and French toast. A big seller here at lunch and dinner is the buffalo burger, with a choice of salad, soup, or the restaurant's special duck fat french fries. Lighter appetites might like the Greek salad, with veggies, kalamata olives, and feta, served with pita bread. Local live music, ranging from rock to Western to folk to blues, plays on Saturday nights.

200 N. Bullard. © **575/388-4090.** www.isaacsbarandgrill.com. Main courses $8–$19. MC, V. Mon–Tues 11am–midnight; Wed–Sat 11am–1:30am; Sun noon–midnight.

Jalisco's ★ ☺ NEW MEXICAN   Set within an enchanting brick building in the historic district, this festive, nonsmoking restaurant serves big portions of good food. Three dining rooms fill the old structure, which has been Latinized with arched doorways and bold Mexican street-scene calendars on the walls. The combination plates are large and popular, as are the enchiladas. There are also burgers and a children's menu. Whatever you do, be sure to order a *sopaipilla* for dessert. They're delicious and huge. Beer and wine are served.

103 S. Bullard St., Silver City. © **575/388-2060.** Main courses $6–$12. DISC, MC, V. Mon–Sat 11am–8:30pm.

Shevek & Company Restaurant ★★ 📖 INTERNATIONAL   You can travel to many places at this sweet restaurant in the center of town. Chef Shevek Barnhart has spent much of his life absorbing culinary magic from relatives and friends with backgrounds ranging from Italian to Moroccan. The ambience is clean bistro in the main room, a little more formal in a connecting dining room, and more casual on the patio. At lunch, the kosher pastrami Reuben is piled with goodies. Dinner brings such delights as Tunisian barbecue chicken over couscous. Shevek & Co. boasts the largest selection of wines and microbrews in the region.

602 N. Bullard St. © **575/534-9168.** www.silver-eats.com. Reservations recommended on weekends. Main courses $3–$12 brunch, $5–$18 lunch, $10–$24 dinner. DISC, MC, V. Sun–Tues and Thurs 5–9pm; Fri–Sat 5–9:30pm. Closes 1/2-hour earlier in winter.

Vicki's Eatery ★ SALADS/SANDWICHES   Set in a historic building, with hardwood floors and high ceilings, this cafe serves comfort food using fresh ingredients. The place specializes in soups, salads, and sandwiches ranging from healthful to decadent. For breakfast, you might have chorizo or smoked sausage and eggs. At lunch, the Reuben sandwich is thick and served on robust pumpernickel, with German potato salad on the side. Quesadillas are also popular. Heart-healthy selections are available as well. Their carrot cake is stellar.

315 Texas St. (at Market St.). ℂ **575/388-5430.** Main courses $5–$11. AE, DC, DISC, MC, V. Mon–Sat 7am–3pm; Sun 8am–2pm.

GILA CLIFF DWELLINGS NATIONAL MONUMENT ★★

It takes 1½ to 2 hours to reach the **Gila Cliff Dwellings** from Silver City, but it's definitely worth the trip. First-time visitors are inevitably awed by the remains of an ancient civilization set in the mouths of caves, abandoned for 7 centuries. You reach the dwellings on a 1-mile moderate hike along which you catch glimpses of the ruins. This walk is an elaborate journey into the past. It winds its way into a narrow canyon, from which you first spot the poetic ruins perched in six caves 180 feet up on the canyon wall, stone shiny and hard as porcelain. Then the ascent begins up innumerable steps and rocks until you're standing face-to-face with these ancient relics, which offer a glimpse into the lives of Native Americans who lived here from the late 1270s through the early 1300s. Tree-ring dating indicates their residence didn't last longer than 30 to 40 years.

What's remarkable about the journey through the cliff dwellings is the depth of some of the caves. At one point, you'll climb a ladder and pass from one cave into the next, viewing the intricate little rooms (42 total) and walls that once made up a community dwelling. Probably not more than 10 to 15 families (about 40–50 people) lived in the cliff dwellings at any one time. The inhabitants were excellent weavers and skilled potters.

The cliff dwellings were discovered by Anglo settlers in the early 1870s, near where the three forks of the Gila River rise. Once you leave the last cave, you'll head down again traversing some steep steps to the canyon floor. Pets are not allowed within the monument, but they can be taken on trails within the Gila Wilderness. Be sure to pick up a trail guide at the visitor center.

Essentials

GETTING THERE   From Silver City, take NM 15 north 44 miles to the Gila Cliff Dwellings. Travel time from Silver City is approximately 2 hours. You won't find any gas stations between Silver City and Gila Cliff Dwellings, so plan accordingly. Also know that at the monument, vehicles are permitted on paved roads only.

VISITOR INFORMATION   For more information, contact **Gila Cliff Dwellings National Monument,** HC 68, Box 100, Silver City, NM 88061 (ℂ **575/536-9461;** www.nps.gov/gicl).

ADMISSION FEES & HOURS   Admission to the monument is $3 per person, $10 per family with children age 12 and under admitted free. The visitor center, where you can pick up detailed brochures, is open daily from 8am to 5pm Memorial Day to Labor Day and from 8am to 4:30pm the rest of the year. The cliff dwellings are open daily from 8am to 6pm in the summer and from 9am to 4pm the rest of the year.

Seeing the Highlights

Today, the dwellings allow a rare glimpse inside the homes and lives of prehistoric Native Americans. About 75% of what is seen is original, although the walls have been capped and the foundations strengthened to prevent further deterioration. It took a great deal of effort to build these homes: The stones were held in place by mortar, and all the clay and water for the mortar had to be carried by hand up from the stream, as the Mogollon did not have any pack animals. The vigas for the roof were cut and shaped with stone axes or fire.

The people who lived here were farmers, as shown by the remains of beans, squash, and corn in their homes. The fields were along the valley of the west fork of the Gila River and on the mesa across the canyon. No signs of irrigation have been found.

Near the visitor center, about a mile away, the remains of an earlier pit house (A.D. 100–400), built below ground level, and later pit houses (up to A.D. 1000), above ground structures of adobe or wattle, have been found.

Camping

Camping and picnicking are encouraged in the national monument, with four developed campgrounds. Camping is free and some sites are RV accessible, though there are no hookups. Overnight lodging can be found in Silver City and in the nearby town of Gila Hot Springs, which also has a grocery store, horse rentals, and guided pack trips. For information, contact the visitor center (℡ **575/536-9461**).

OTHER ADVENTURES IN GILA NATIONAL FOREST

Gila National Forest, which offers some of the most spectacular mountain scenery in the Southwest, comprises 3.3 million acres in four counties. Nearly one-fourth of that acreage (790,000 acres) comprises the **Gila, Aldo Leopold,** and **Blue Range wildernesses.** Its highest peak is Whitewater Baldy, at 10,892 feet. Within the forest, six out of seven life zones can be found, so the range of plant and wildlife is broad. You may see mule deer, elk, antelope, black bear, mountain lion, and bighorn sheep. Nearly 400 miles of streams and a few small lakes sustain healthy populations of trout as well as bass, bluegill, and catfish. Anglers can head to Lake Roberts, Snow Lake, and Quemado Lake.

JUST THE FACTS   For more information on the national forest, contact the **U.S. Forest Service,** Forest Supervisor's Office, 3005 E. Camino del Bosque, Silver City, NM 88061 (℡ **575/388-8201;** www.fs.fed.us).

The national forest has 29 campgrounds, all with toilets and six with drinking water. Car and backpack camping are also permitted throughout the forest.

Hiking & Other Activities

Within the forest are 1,490 miles of trails for hiking and horseback riding, and in winter, cross-country skiing. Outside the wilderness areas, trail bikes and off-road vehicles are also permitted. Hiking trails in the Gila Wilderness, especially the

A Shocking Experience

If you'd like to have an electrifying moment or two, plan a visit to the **Lightning Field,** near Quemado (✆ **505/898-3335;** www.lightningfield.org). An enormous sculpture by American artist Walter De Maria, it consists of 400 stainless-steel poles arranged in a rectangular grid. Its purpose? To attract those most picturesque and deadly bolts. Visitors are welcome May through October but must reserve months in advance.

41-mile Middle Fork Trail, with its east end near Gila Cliff Dwellings, are among the most popular in the state and can sometimes be crowded. If you are more interested in communing with nature than with fellow hikers, however, you will find plenty of trails to suit you, both in and out of the officially designated wilderness areas.

Most of the trails are maintained and easy to follow. Trails along river bottoms, however, have many stream crossings (so be prepared for hiking with wet feet) and may be washed out by summer flash floods. It's best to inquire about trail conditions before you set out. More than 50 trail heads provide roadside parking.

Some of the best hikes in the area are the Frisco Box, Pueblo Creek, Whitewater Baldy, the Catwalk and Beyond, the Middle Fork/Little Bear Loop, and the Black Range Crest Trail. The Gila National Forest contains several wilderness areas that are off-limits to **mountain bikes,** including the Gila, Aldo Leopold, and the Blue Range Primitive Area. However, cyclists can access quite a few trails. Some to look for are the Cleveland Mine trail, Silver City Loop, Continental Divide, Signal Peak, Pinos Altos Loop, Fort Bayard Historical Trails, and Forest Trail 100.

The Catwalk National Recreation Trail ★ (✆ **575/539-2481**), 68 miles north of Silver City on US 180, then 5 miles east of Glenwood via NM 174, is a great break after a long drive. Kids are especially thrilled with this hike. It follows the route of a pipeline built in 1897 to carry water to the now-defunct town of Graham and its electric generator. About ¼ mile above the parking area is the beginning of a striking 250-foot metal causeway clinging to the sides of the boulder-choked Whitewater Canyon, which in spots is 20 feet wide and 250 feet deep. Along the way, you'll find water pouring through caves and waterfalls spitting off the cliff side. Farther up the canyon, a suspension bridge spans the chasm. Picnic facilities are near the parking area. There's a $3 fee per car.

Other Highlights

The scenic ghost town of **Mogollon** is 3½ miles north of Glenwood on US 180, and then 9 miles east on NM 159, a narrow mountain road that takes a good 25 minutes to negotiate. The village bears witness to silver and gold mining booms beginning in the late 19th century, and to the disastrous effects of floods and fire in later years. Remains of its last operating mine, the Little Fanny (which ceased operation in the 1950s), are still visible, along with dozens of other old buildings, miners' shacks, and mining paraphernalia. An art gallery and museum are found along Mogollon's main street. The movie *My Name Is Nobody,* starring Henry Fonda, was filmed here.

ELFEGO BACA—local folk hero

As you make your way on NM 12 into Reserve, a village of some 350 residents with a few charming Old West storefronts, you'll note its quietness—such a contrast from what Elfego Baca must have encountered in 1884. Back then the 19-year-old boy had heard about atrocities taking place here: A man named El Burro had been castrated by some cowboys from Texas. Meanwhile, farmer Epitacio Martinez had tried to stop the misdeed and was taken outside and used as target practice. He survived, but barely, and was left to nurse four bullet wounds.

Along the main street, Milligan's Store and Whiskey Bar was full of cowboys shooting up the ceiling. Such behavior gave Elfego his first chance to exercise his self-appointed deputy status. Brandishing a badge he'd found, he arrested a man named Charley McCarthy. In the next few days, Elfego stood up to the bullies. Soon word of his bravado spread, and backup troops came from area ranches.

"He must have had supreme confidence," says Henry Martinez, owner of the gas station/store Henry's Corner at the center town. Henry has a private stake in this history: his great-great grandfather was the farmer who took four bullets in an attempt to help El Burro.

This history set Henry on a mission to honor Elfego's life. "It's fascinating that one man took such a stand and changed history in the Reserve area," he says. Elfego's visit ended in a standoff as he hid out in a jacal—a dilapidated mud hut— while some 80 cowboys shot 4,000 holes in the place. Through the ordeal, two were killed. Elfego, a known sharp shooter, survived by ducking into the jacal's partly dug-out floor and by the grace of a statue of Our Lady of Santa Ana—which came out unscathed, as did Elfego, after fighting for 33 hours.

To honor the event, Henry, with the help of other community members, acquired funds from the state of New Mexico and hired artist James N. Muir to create a statue. "The accuracy and realism" are what sold Henry on Muir's work. "Elfego is stepping out of the jacal fully in charge, without a scratch," he says. The statue stands in the center of town, on the spot that Henry says is "within yards" of the original jacal.

Cochise, Geronimo, and other Apache war chiefs held forth in these mountains in the late 19th century. **Reserve** (pop. 389), 100 miles northwest of Silver City, has a few homes, a store, and a bar. A good stop in town is **Henry's Corner,** 109 Main St. (© **866/291-2732;** www.elfegobacaathenryscorner.com), where you'll find gas, ice cream, and books, including ones on Elfego Baca, and my own *King of the Road*.

SOUTHEASTERN NEW MEXICO

Whether you're an adult or a child, the wonder of nature in this part of the world will inspire you. Here you'll find Carlsbad Caverns National Park and White Sands National Monument, whose immensity and intricate beauty speak in unique ways to each individual.

Running east of the Rio Grande (the I-25 corridor) and south of I-40, southeastern New Mexico has other sites as well. Along with the natural wonders, this is the home of the fierce Mescalero Apaches and the world's richest quarter-horse race. Billy the Kid lived and died in southeastern New Mexico in the 19th century, and the world's first atomic bomb was exploded here in the 20th. From west to east, barren desert gives way to high, forested peaks, snow-covered in winter; to the fertile valley of the Pecos River; and to plains beloved by ranchers along the Texas border.

The main population center in this section of the state is **Roswell** (pop. 46,000), famous as the purported landing place of an unidentified flying object (UFO). **Ruidoso** (pop. 10,000), in the mountains between Alamogordo and Roswell, is a booming resort town. **Carlsbad** (pop. 25,500), 76 miles south of Roswell, and **Alamogordo** (pop. 36,000), 117 miles west of Roswell, are of more immediate interest to tourists. Other sizable towns are **Clovis** (pop. 33,000) and **Hobbs** (pop. 28,500), both on the Texas border, and **Artesia** (pop. 11,000), between Roswell and Carlsbad, has a pretty restored historic district.

SOUTHEASTERN NEW MEXICO'S GREAT OUTDOORS

This region of the state offers a wealth of outdoor opportunities. To research any of the state parks listed in this section, go to www.nmparks.com.

BIKING Several forest roads and single-track trails in this region are favorites with mountain bikers. In the Ruidoso area, near Cloudcroft, the

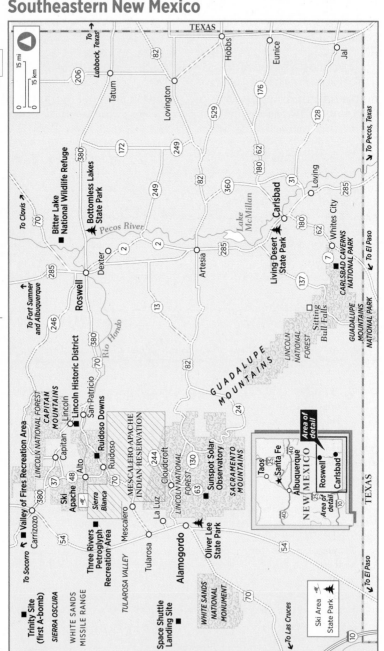

Rim Trail, a 17-mile intermediate trail that offers views of the White Sands, is considered one of the top-10 trails in the nation. To reach the trail, take NM 130 from Cloudcroft to NM 6563, turn right, and look for the Rim Trail signs. The Cloudcroft area offers three other good trails: La Luz Canyon, Silver Springs Loop, and Pumphouse Canyon. For directions, contact the Cloudcroft Ranger Station (☎ 575/682-2551). The paved road up to **Carlsbad Caverns National Park** is scenic, and the auto traffic drives slowly, but it's very hot in the summer.

BIRD-WATCHING **Bitter Lake National Wildlife Refuge** (☎ 575/622-6755; www.fws.gov/southwest), northeast of Roswell, is particularly good for watching migratory waterfowl, and **Bluff Springs** (☎ 575/682-2551), south of Cloudcroft, is popular with turkeys and hummingbirds. If you find turkey vultures particularly fascinating, **Rattlesnake Springs** (☎ 575/785-2232; www.nature.org), south of Carlsbad, is the place to go.

BOATING Boating, water-skiing, jet-skiing, and sailing are permitted at **Carlsbad Municipal Park,** which runs through town for just over a mile along the west bank of Lake Carlsbad. The lake also has a beach that's open to swimmers. **Brantley Lake State Park** (☎ 575/457-2384), 15 miles north of Carlsbad, is popular with windsurfers who favor its consistent desert winds.

FISHING **Bonito Lake** and **Rio Ruidoso** are popular destinations for trout fishing. The scenic **Oasis State Park** (☎ 575/356-5331) just north of Portales, also offers fishing.

GOLF This region has plenty of golfing opportunities. In Ruidoso, **Cree Meadows Country Club,** Country Club Drive off Sudderth Drive (☎ 575/257-2733; www.playcreemeadows.com), is an 18-hole public course. Also public in the Ruidoso area are the 18-hole courses at the **Inn of the Mountain Gods Resort & Casino,** 287 Carrizo Canyon Rd. (☎ 800/545-9011 or 575/464-4100; www.innofthemountaingods.com); and the **Links at Sierra Blanca,** 105 Sierra Blanca Dr. (☎ 575/258-5330; www.thelodgeatsierrablanca.com). In Cloudcroft, the 9-hole **Lodge at Cloudcroft Golf Course** (☎ 800/395-6343 or 575/682-2566; www.thelodgeresort.com) boasts an elevation of 9,200 feet; it's one of the highest courses in the world and one of the oldest in the United States. Alamogordo's **Desert Lakes Golf Course** (☎ 575/437-0290; www.desertlakesgolf.com) has views of Sierra Blanca and the Sacramento Mountains.

HIKING More than 225 miles of trails weave a web through the Smokey Bear Ranger District of the **Lincoln National Forest.** From Ruidoso, a favorite destination of hikers is the White Mountain Wilderness, with nine trails, and the Capitan Mountains Wilderness, with 11 trails. **Smokey Bear Ranger District office,** 901 Mechem Dr., Ruidoso (☎ 575/257-4095; www.fs.fed.us/r3/lincoln), has excellent and inexpensive maps of each wilderness area. Monjeau Lookout is a popular destination off Ski Run Road (NM 532). **Carlsbad Caverns National Park** has an extensive trail system as well (outside the caves, of course).

HORSEBACK RIDING Horseback riding is popular in Ruidoso. Try the **Inn of the Mountain Gods Resort & Casino** (☎ 800/545-9011 or 575/464-4100; www.innofthemountaingods.com) or **Cowboys Riding Stables** (☎ 575/378-8217; www.cowboysridingstables.com).

SKIING Southern New Mexico's premier ski resort is **Ski Apache** (© 575/257-9001 for snow reports, 575/336-4356 for information; www.skiapache.com), only 20 miles northwest of Ruidoso in the Mescalero Apache Indian Reservation. Situated on an 11,500-foot ridge of the 12,000-foot Sierra Blanca, the resort boasts a gondola, two quad chairs, five triple chairs, one double chair, a day lodge, a sport shop, a rental shop, a ski school, a first-aid center, four snack bars, and a lounge. Ski Apache has 55 trails and slopes (20% beginner, 35% intermediate, and 45% advanced), with a vertical drop of 1,900 feet and a total skier capacity of 16,500 an hour. Though its location seems remote, a lot of skiers fill this mountain during weekends and holidays. Because the mountain is owned and run by the Apaches, you can experience another culture while skiing. All-day lift tickets cost $51 for adults, $45 for seniors, $43 for teens 13 to 17, and $25 for children 12 and under. The mountain is open Thanksgiving to Easter daily from 8:45am to 4pm. Lift-and-lodging packages can be booked through the **Inn of the Mountain Gods Resort & Casino** (© 800/545-9011 or 575/464-4100; www.innofthemountaingods.com).

ALAMOGORDO

Famous for its leading role in America's space research and military technology industries, **Alamogordo** (pop. 36,000) achieved worldwide fame on July 16, 1945, when the first atomic bomb was exploded at nearby Trinity Site. Today, it is home of the New Mexico Museum of Space History, White Sands National Monument, and Holloman Air Force Base. Twenty miles east and twice as high, the resort village of **Cloudcroft** (elevation 8,650 ft.) attracts vacationers to the forested heights of the Sacramento Mountains.

Essentials

GETTING THERE From Albuquerque, take I-25 south 87 miles to San Antonio; turn east on US 380, go 66 miles to Carrizozo; then turn south on US 54 for 58 miles (4 hr.). From Las Cruces, take US 70 northeast (1½ hr.). *Note:* US 70 may be closed for up to 2 hr. during tests on White Sands Missile Range. From El Paso, take US 54 north (1½ hr.).

The nearest major airport is **El Paso International.** The local airport, **Alamogordo–White Sands Regional Airport** (© 575/439-4110) does not offer commercial service.

VISITOR INFORMATION The **Alamogordo Chamber of Commerce** and visitor center is at 1301 N. White Sands Blvd., Alamogordo, NM 88311 (© 800/826-0294 or 575/437-6120; www.alamogordo.com).

CITY LAYOUT Alamogordo is on the eastern edge of the Tularosa Valley, at the foot of the Sacramento Mountains. US 54 (White Sands Blvd.) is the main street, extending several miles north and south. The downtown district is a few blocks east of White Sands Boulevard, off 10th Street.

What to See & Do in Alamogordo

In addition to the attractions in Alamogordo itself, also enjoyable is the small, historic village of **La Luz,** just 3 miles north of Alamogordo. It has attracted a number

The Nut House

While traveling this area, you'll likely see signs pointing into thick groves of pecan trees directing you to the **Nut House**, 32 Ivy Lane, in La Luz (© 575/437-6889). When you step inside, you'll be greeted by the scent of pecan pie with a hint of chocolate. The airy space with a long, aged-wood bar is packed with local art, much of it made by the artists of the legendary La Luz art colony from the 1960s and some of their children. As well as perusing art, you can sip a latte and eat homemade soups and sandwiches on a lovely patio within the pecan trees. Don't leave without sampling a piece of apple, peach, or chocolate pie, all laced with pecans. It's open Tuesday to Friday 9am to 5:30pm, Saturday and Sunday 10am to 4pm.

of resident artists and craftspeople who live, work, and display some of their products for sale. Worth seeing are the cactus-filled park and the small Our Lady of Light Church.

New Mexico Museum of Space History ★★   The New Mexico Museum of Space History comes in two parts: the International Space Hall of Fame and the Clyde W. Tombaugh IMAX Dome Theater. Both are on the lower slopes of the Sacramento Mountains (with stunning views of the Tularosa Basin), 2 miles east of US 54, and just above New Mexico State University's Alamogordo branch campus.

The Space Hall of Fame occupies the "Golden Cube," a five-story building with walls of golden glass. Visitors are encouraged to start on the top floor and work their way down. En route, they recall the accomplishments of the first astronauts and cosmonauts, including America's Mercury, Gemini, and Apollo programs, and the early Soviet orbital flights. Spacecraft and a lunar exploration module are exhibited. The museum also presents an exhibit on the first successful private flight in space—winner of the Ansari X-Prize. Most fun is a simulator in which visitors get to land the Space Shuttle.

At Tombaugh Theater, IMAX projection and Spitz 512 Planetarium Systems create earthly and cosmic experiences on a 2,700-square-foot dome screen.

Located at the top of NM 2001. © 877/333-6589 outside New Mexico, or 575/437-2840. Fax 575/434-2245. www.nmspacemuseum.org. Admission to International Space Hall of Fame $6 adults, $5 seniors 60 and older and military, $4 children age 4–12, free for children 3 and under. IMAX Theater $6 adults, $5.50 seniors and military, $4.50 children age 4–12, free for children 3 and under; additional charge for double feature. Ask about their combination ticket. Daily 9am–5pm.

Toy Train Depot ☺   The brainchild of John Koval (whom you're likely to meet at the door), this is an interesting attraction for train fanatics and laypeople. Koval started the nonprofit museum, housed in a genuine 1898 railroad depot, as a means to celebrate the railroad's important presence in the area. The museum meanders back through three rooms, each filled with tracks laid along colorful miniature cityscapes and countryside—1,200 feet of track altogether. The highlight is a re-creation of the Alamogordo, Carrizozo, and Cloudcroft train system. Rides through the grounds on 12-inch and 16-inch gauge trains are offered. There's also a railroad hobby shop.

1991 N. White Sands Blvd. ☏ **888/207-3564** or 575/437-2855. www.toytraindepot.homestead.com. Admission $4. Train rides $4. Wed–Sun 12:30–4:30pm.

SOMETHING UNUSUAL

Eagle Ranch Pistachio Groves   This is a tasty and fun step into the nutty world of pistachio farming. New Mexico's first and largest pistachio groves, Eagle Ranch offers free 45-minute tours weekdays at 10am and 1:30pm in summer and at 1:30pm in winter. The tour offers a brief history of the pistachio groves and a tour of the shipping and receiving facility, salting and roasting department, and out through the groves. A visitor center with an art gallery displays the work of local artists, and at the gift shop, you can buy pistachio nuts, custom baskets, and a variety of other items, including wines. Try the pistachio-white-chocolate-chunk ice cream!

7288 US 54/70 (5 miles north of Alamogordo). ☏ **800/432-0999** or 575/434-0035. www.heartof thedesert.com. Free admission. Gift shop and gallery Mon–Sat 8am–6pm; Sun 9am–6pm.

TRINITY SITE

The world's first atomic bomb was exploded in this desert never-never land on July 16, 1945. It is strictly off-limits to civilians—except twice a year, on the first Saturday of April and October. A small lava monument commemorates the explosion, which left a crater a quarter mile across and 8 feet deep, and transformed the desert sand into a jade green glaze called "Trinitite" that remains today. The McDonald House, where the bomb's plutonium core was assembled 2 miles from ground zero, has been restored to its 1945 condition. The site is on the west slope of Sierra Oscura, 90 air miles northwest of Alamogordo. For more information, call the public affairs office of **White Sands Missile Range** (☏ **575/678-1134;** www.wsmr. army.mil).

Getting Outside

Fifteen miles southeast of Alamogordo via US 54 and Dog Canyon Road, you'll find **Oliver Lee Memorial State Park.** Nestled at the mouth of Dog Canyon, a stunning break in the steep escarpment of the Sacramento Mountains, the site has drawn human visitors for thousands of years. Springs and seeps support a variety of rare and endangered plant species, as well as a rich animal life. Hiking trails into the foothills are well marked; the park also offers a visitor center with excellent exhibits on local history, and picnic and camping grounds, with showers, electricity, and a dump station.

Dog Canyon was one of the last strongholds of the Mescalero Apache, and it was the site of battles between Native Americans and the U.S. Cavalry in the 19th century. Around the turn of the 20th century, rancher Oliver Lee built a home near here and raised cattle. Guided tours from the visitor center to Lee's restored house give a taste of early ranch life in southern New Mexico.

The park is open 24 hours a day; admission is $5 per car. The visitor center is open daily from 9am to 4pm. Guided tours are offered Saturday and Sunday at 3pm, weather permitting. For more information, call ☏ **575/437-8284.**

Exploring the Surrounding Area

Cloudcroft ★ is a picturesque mountain village of 765 people high in the Sacramento Mountains, surrounded by Lincoln National Forest. Though only about 20 miles east of Alamogordo via US 82, it is twice as high, overlooking the Tularosa Valley from a dizzying elevation of almost 9,000 feet. It was founded in 1899 when railroad surveyors reached the mountain summit and built a lodge for Southern Pacific Railroad workers. Today, the Lodge is Cloudcroft's biggest attraction and biggest employer (see "Nearby Places to Stay & Dine," below). Other accommodations are also available in town, as are lots of recreational opportunities and community festivals. For information, contact the **Cloudcroft Chamber of Commerce,** P.O. Box 1290, Cloudcroft, NM 88317 (✆ **866/874-4447** or 575/682-2733; www. cloudcroft.net). It's in a log cabin in the center of town, on the south side of US 82.

The **Sacramento Mountains Historical Museum and Pioneer Village,** US 82 east of downtown Cloudcroft (✆ **575/682-2932**), recalls the community's early days, with several pioneer buildings, historic photos, and exhibits of turn-of-the-20th-century railroad memorabilia, clothing, and other artifacts. Call for hours. Nearby, **Lincoln National Forest** (✆ **575/682-2551**) maintains the unique **La Pasada Encantada Nature Trail,** a short footpath from Sleepygrass Campground, off NM 130 south of town, with signs in Braille inviting walkers to touch the various plants, leaves, and trees. Also look for the several-mile moderate trail to the historic **Mexican Canyon Railroad Trestle.** The trail head is in a U.S. Forest Service picnic area, west of the junction of US 82 and NM 130, where you'll also find a short walk to an observation point offering spectacular views across White Sands Missile Range and the Tularosa Basin. The picnic area also has tables, grills, drinking water, and restrooms.

National Solar Observatory–Sacramento Peak (✆ **575/434-7000;** www. nso.edu), 18 miles south of Cloudcroft via NM 6563, a National Scenic Byway, attracts astronomers from around the world to study the sun and its effects on our planet. Actually, three observatories are here, with two open to the public for self-guided tours (allow at least 1 hr.), open daily from 8am to 5pm, with more limited hours in winter—so call. The visitor center is open daily March through January from 9am to 5pm, and the rest of the year on Saturday and Sunday from 9am to 5pm. It has exhibits about the observatory and astronomy, as well as some geared toward children, and a gift shop.

If you'd like a tasty meal in this mountain town, head to where the locals eat, **Big Daddy's Diner,** 1705 NM 82 (✆ **575/682-1224;** www.bigdaddysdinercloudcroft. com). In a cozy, diner-style atmosphere, the restaurant serves egg and pancake breakfasts; salads, burgers, and sandwiches at lunch; and chicken, seafood, and steak at dinner, with barbecue on weekends. It's generally open three meals daily, with abbreviated hours during the winter.

If you like outdoor gear and items such as scented candles and tie-dyed clothes, stop at **High Altitude,** 310 Burro Ave. (✆ **575/682-1229**).

Where to Stay in Alamogordo

All accommodations in Alamogordo are along White Sands Boulevard, the north-south highway through town, and parking is free.

Best Western Desert Aire 🍴 ☺ This motel, remodeled in 2007, provides a comfortable and quiet night's rest, which is likely why it fills up most every night during Alamogordo's busier months. The medium-size rooms have contemporary furnishings and comfortable new beds. The bathrooms are small, with an outer sink vanity. Also available are kitchenettes, which contain stoves, ovens, and microwaves. The suites are inexpensive and have 3-foot-deep Jacuzzi tubs. The central point of this motel is the pool, a great place to cool off on hot days, though it can fill up with kids.

1021 S. White Sands Blvd., Alamogordo, NM 88310. ✆ **800/565-1988** or 575/437-2110. Fax 575/437-1898. www.bestwestern.com. 99 units. $68–$107 double; $75–$120 suite. Rates include continental breakfast. AE, DISC, MC, V. Pets welcome ($50 deposit). **Amenities:** Exercise room; Jacuzzi; outdoor pool; sauna. *In room:* A/C, TV, fridge, hair dryer, microwave, Wi-Fi.

Holiday Inn Express ★ This newer hotel on the south end of town provides what you'd expect from this chain—clean, comfortable rooms with a bit of flair. The hotel is steps above the Best Western, though it doesn't offer even near the competitive price. Rooms are medium size, with high ceilings and come in standards and suites. All are spacious, decorated in natural hues, with comfortable beds, while the bathrooms are medium size with granite countertops. A full, hot breakfast comes with the room.

100 Kerry Ave. ✆ **800/465-4329** or 575/434-9773. Fax 575/434-3279. www.hiexpress.com. 80 units. $114 double; $130–$150 suite. Rates include full breakfast. AE, DC, DISC, MC, V. **Amenities:** Exercise room; indoor pool. *In room:* A/C, TV, fridge, hair dryer, Wi-Fi.

CAMPING

I recommend camping at **White Sands National Monument** (see "Camping," under "White Sands National Monument," below), though be aware that it is a backcountry experience.

If you'd rather have amenities, try **Alamogordo Roadrunner** (✆ **877/437-3003** or 575/437-3003; www.roadrunnercampground.com). It has laundry and grocery facilities as well as a recreation area, swimming pool, playground, shuffleboard, Wi-Fi at some sites, and planned group activities in winter. The campground is on 24th Street in Alamogordo, just east of the US 54/70/82 junction. If you're looking for something in between, **Oliver Lee State Park,** 15 miles southeast of Alamogordo via US 54 and Dog Canyon Road (✆ **575/437-8284;** www.nmparks. com), is a good choice, with 44 sites, 10 full hookups, picnic tables, grills, tent sites, a playground, and hiking trails.

Where to Dine in Alamogordo

CJ's Si Señor ★ ☺ NEW MEXICAN Set along the town's main drag, this cozy spot remains packed during mealtime for good reason: the food is excellent. Saltillo tile floors and arched doorways lend a festive feel to the casual place. Order anything smothered in chile sauce. Tender palates can order a special mild green chile. Lunch and dinner start with complimentary chips and salsa. The combination plate, with a cheese enchilada, beef taco, flauta, Spanish rice, and refried beans is a delicious choice, as is the chicken enchilada plate. Kids have their own menu here.

1480 N. White Sands Blvd. ✆ **575/437-7879.** Main courses $4.25–$13. AE, DISC, MC, V. Mon–Sat 11am–8pm.

Memories Restaurant ★ 🎁 AMERICAN Set in a 1907 Victorian home in a residential neighborhood right on the edge of historic downtown, this restaurant serves good food in an old-world setting. Functional tables sit on carpeted floors within what was once the living room and den, or sun porch, creating a casual, comfortable atmosphere. Diners come to sample salads and croissant sandwiches for lunch and grilled steaks and seafood for dinner. At lunch, I recommend the crab salad served over avocado, or the turkey and avocado croissant sandwich. For dinner, a big seller is the prime rib, which comes with bread, a side dish, and vegetable. The grilled shrimp is also good. For dessert, try the chocolate cream pie. Beer and wine are available.

1223 New York Ave. (corner of 13th St.). ℂ **575/437-0077.** Reservations recommended. Main courses $6-$13 lunch, $11-$27 dinner. AE, DISC, MC, V. Mon-Sat 11am-9pm.

Nature's Pantry ★ 🍴 DELI/HEALTH FOOD If many days on the road have left your stomach weary, step into this downtown oasis of healthiness. Linda Jungling offers all manner of vitamins and tonics, but she also has a few tables and a juice bar, where locals come to eat baked goods, sandwiches, and salads. At lunchtime, try the chicken salad sandwich with avocado and sprouts served on whole grain bread, or any number of salads, all made with fresh vegetables.

2909 N. White Sands Blvd. ℂ **575/437-3037.** AE, DISC, MC, V. All menu items under $11. Mon-Sat 8am-7pm.

NEARBY PLACES TO STAY & DINE

Casa de Sueños ★ ☺ NEW MEXICAN For tasty New Mexican fare, with a good dose of the whimsy of Mexico, check out this fun restaurant about 15 miles north of Alamogordo, outside Tularosa. Decorated with Mexican folk paintings and a country home mural, it exudes a fiesta atmosphere. Outside, the broad patio is lit with little Christmas lights and has chile peppers printed on the tablecloths. For breakfast, try the huevos rancheros. A lunch buffet provides a good sampling of enchiladas and beans. To start your meal, try the guacamole, made with red onions. For an entree, order anything with the green chile sauce, made with fresh chiles and well seasoned. Vegetarian and children's selections round out the menu. You can order from a variety of beers and wines.

35 St. Francis Dr., Tularosa, NM. ℂ **575/585-3494.** Reservations recommended on weekends. Main courses $5-$8 breakfast, $7-$15 lunch and dinner. AE, DISC, MC, V. Mon-Thurs 11am-8pm; Fri-Sat 11am-8:30pm; Sun 10:30am-8pm.

The Lodge at Cloudcroft ★★ This lodge is an antique jewel of another era. From the grand fireplace in the lobby to the homey Victorian decor in the guest rooms, it exudes gentility and class. Its 9-hole golf course, one of the nation's highest, challenges golfers across rolling hills between 8,600 and 9,200 feet elevation. Most rooms in the Lodge have views and all are filled with antiques, from sideboards and lamps to mirrors and steam radiators. The standard rooms are small so you may want to reserve one of their suites, which have a bedroom and a sitting room with a fold-out couch. Some suites have Jacuzzi tubs. In 1991, more rooms were added in the form of the Pavilion and the Retreat, which were built adjacent to the Lodge. These are most often rented out in blocks and are less desirable than those in the main hotel. The hotel's new Spirit of the Mountain Spa offers a variety of massage treatments.

Rebecca's (ℂ **575/682-2566**), the lodge's restaurant, is named for the resident ghost, believed to have been a chambermaid in the 1930s who was killed by her lumberjack lover. Three meals, plus a midday snack menu, are served daily. Service is friendly and very efficient, and the atmosphere is elegant, with bright sunshine during the day and romantic lighting at night. I especially enjoy breakfast here, where I order eggs Benedict or anything that comes with their biscuits. Lunch brings sandwiches and salads. At dinner try the rack of lamb. The champagne Sunday brunch is a must here, offering a prime rib serving station and an array of side selections.

601 Corona Place (P.O. Box 497), Cloudcroft, NM 88317. © **800/395-6343** or 575/682-2566. Fax 575/682-2715. www.thelodgeresort.com. 59 units. $115–$165 double; $175–$335 suite. AE, DC, DISC, MC, V. Free parking. **Amenities:** Restaurant; lounge; babysitting; concierge; golf course; exercise room; Jacuzzi; outdoor heated pool; sauna; spa; access to nearby tennis courts. *In room:* A/C, TV, hair dryer upon request, Wi-Fi.

WHITE SANDS NATIONAL MONUMENT ★★★

Arguably the most memorable natural area in this part of the southwestern U.S., **White Sands National Monument** preserves the best part of the world's largest gypsum dune field, an area of 275 square miles of pure white gypsum sand reaching out over the floor of the Tularosa Basin in wavelike dunes. Plants and animals have evolved in special ways to adapt to the bright white environment here. Some creatures have a bleached coloration to match the whiteness all around them, and some plants have developed means for surviving against the smothering pressures of the blowing sands.

The surrounding mountains—the Sacramentos to the east, with their forested slopes, and the serene San Andres to the west—are composed of sandstone, limestone, sedimentary rocks, and pockets of gypsum. Over millions of years, rains and melting snows dissolved the gypsum and carried it down into Lake Lucero. Here the hot sun and dry winds evaporate the water, leaving the pure white gypsum to crystallize. Then the persistent winds blow these crystals, in the form of minuscule bits of sand, in a northeastern direction, adding them to growing dunes. As each dune grows and moves farther from the lake, new ones form, rank after rank, in what seems an endless procession.

The dunes are especially enchanting at sunrise and under the light of a full moon, but you'll have to camp here to experience this extraordinary sight (see "Camping," below). If you're not camping, you'll probably want to spend only a couple of hours here. Refreshments and snacks can be purchased at the visitor center, along with books, maps, posters, and other souvenirs; however, no dining or grocery facilities are available here.

Essentials

GETTING THERE   The visitor center is 15 miles southwest of Alamogordo on US 70/82. (**Note:** Due to missile testing on the adjacent White Sands Missile Range, this road is sometimes closed for up to 2 hr. at a time.) The nearest major airport is **El Paso International,** 90 miles away (see "Getting to New Mexico," in chapter 3).

VISITOR INFORMATION   For more information, contact **White Sands National Monument,** P.O. Box 1086, Holloman AFB, NM 88330-1086 (© **575/679-2599;** www.nps.gov/whsa). When driving near or in the monument, tune your radio to 1610 AM for information on what's happening.

Safety Tips

The National Park Service emphasizes that (1) tunneling in this sand can be dangerous because it collapses easily and could suffocate a person; (2) sand-surfing down the dune slopes, although permitted, can also be hazardous, so it should be undertaken with care, and never near an auto road; and (3) hikers can get lost in a sudden sandstorm if they stray from marked trails or areas.

ADMISSION FEES & HOURS   Admission is $3 (free for children 15 and under). Memorial Day to Labor Day, the visitor center is open daily from 8am to 7pm, and Dunes Drive is open daily from 7am to sunset. Ranger talks and sunset strolls are given nightly at 7 and 8:30pm during summer. During the rest of the year, the visitor center is open daily from 9am to 5pm, and Dunes Drive is open daily from 7am to sunset.

Seeing the Highlights

The 16-mile **Dunes Drive** loops through the "heart of sands" from the visitor center. Information available at the center tells you what to look for on your drive. Sometimes the winds blow the dunes over the road, which must then be rerouted. All the dunes are in fact moving slowly to the northeast, pushed by prevailing southwest winds, some at the rate of as much as 20 feet per year.

In the center of the monument, the road itself is made of hard-packed gypsum. (**Note:** It can be especially slick after an afternoon thunderstorm, so drive cautiously!) Visitors are invited to get out of their cars at established parking areas and explore a bit; some like to climb a dune for a better view of the endless sea of sand. If you'd rather experience the park by hiking than on the long drive, try the Big Dune Trail, a good trail right near the entrance. It takes you on a 45-minute loop along the edges of the dunes and then into their whiteness, ending atop a 60-foot-tall one. In summer, ranger-guided nature walks and evening programs take place in the dunes.

Camping

I recommend camping here, especially to see the dunes at sunrise or under a full moon. The park closes at dusk, and you'll have to leave if you're not camping. It doesn't reopen until after dawn, so you'll have no way to see the sunrise unless you camp. White Sands has no facilities, however, so this is strictly a backcountry adventure. Only tent camping is allowed, and you'll hike ¾ mile to the campsite where you can pitch a tent. On a full moon, the campsites go quickly; you may want to arrive early in the morning. At other times, availability shouldn't be a problem. You must register at the visitor center, get clearance, and pay a small fee of $3 per person. Call ☏ **575/679-2599** for information.

If backcountry camping isn't your speed, try one of the other campgrounds in nearby Alamogordo and Las Cruces (see the "Where to Stay" sections under "Alamogordo," earlier in this chapter, and "Las Cruces," in chapter 11).

RUIDOSO ★ & ENVIRONS

Ruidoso (most New Mexicans pronounce it "Ree-uh-*do*-so") is situated at 6,900 feet in the timbered Sacramento Mountains, the southernmost finger of the Rockies. It is a mountain resort town most famous for the nearby Ruidoso Downs racetrack, where the world's richest quarter-horse race is run for a $2-million purse. Outdoors lovers, hikers, horseback riders, fishers, and hunters are drawn to the surrounding Lincoln National Forest. Southern New Mexico's most important ski resort, Ski Apache, is just out of town. The nearby **Mescalero Apache Indian Reservation** includes the Inn of the Mountain Gods Resort & Casino. Not far away, the historic village of **Lincoln** recalls the Wild West days of Billy the Kid. Be aware that during the busiest of months, Ruidoso seems to live up to its Spanish name—which translates as "noisy," although the name originally referred to the sound of the river running through town.

Essentials

GETTING THERE   From Albuquerque, take I-25 south 87 miles to San Antonio; turn east on US 380 and travel 74 miles; then head south on NM 37/48 (4 hr.). From Alamogordo, take US 70 northeast via Tularosa (1 hr.). From Roswell, take US 70 west (1½ hr.). No commercial service is available to **Sierra Blanca Regional Airport** (𝄐 575/336-8111), 17 miles north, near Alto.

VISITOR INFORMATION   The **Ruidoso Valley Chamber of Commerce** and visitor center is at 720 Sudderth Dr. (𝄐 877/784-3676 or 575/257-7395; www.ruidosonow.com).

Exploring Ruidoso

GALLERY HOPPING

Many noted artists—among them Peter Hurd, Henriette Wyeth, and Gordon Snidow—made their homes in Ruidoso and the surrounding Lincoln County. Dozens of other art-world hopefuls have followed them here, resulting in a proliferation of galleries in town. Most are open Monday to Saturday from 10am to 5pm, except where noted. Among my favorites are **De Carol Designs,** 2616 Sudderth Dr. (𝄐 575/257-5024); **McGary Studios,** a bronze foundry at 2002 Sudderth Dr. (𝄐 575/257-1000; www.davemcgary.com); and **Hurd–La Rinconada** (𝄐 575/653-4331; www.wyethartists.com), in San Patricio, 20 miles east of Ruidoso on US 70 (see "A Scenic Drive Around the Lincoln Loop," later in this chapter), open Monday through Saturday from 9am to 5pm. Check out the contemporary masters and historic works of art at **Ann Buell Fine Art ★**, 2825 Sudderth Dr. (𝄐 575/257-9102; www.annbuellfineart.com).

SHOPPING

Ruidoso's best shopping is at 2801 Sudderth Dr., where a cluster of shops fulfill many desires. Slip on sassy sandals and other contemporary shoes at **Steppin' Out** (𝄐 575/257-5924). Next door, tots and teens can find upscale duds at **Klassy Kids** (𝄐 575/257-3857). Meanwhile, wine lovers may want to sample New Mexico varieties and artisanal cheeses at **End of the Vine** (𝄐 575/630-9463; www.endofthevine.com). And finally, foodies will like the kitchen selection at **House of Kelham** (𝄐 575/257-2492). Head north on Mechem to **Casa Décor,**

1214 Mechem Dr. (📞 **575/258-2912;** www.casadecorruidoso.com) to find reasonably priced rustic furnishings as well as a good selection of Mexican tile and artful crosses.

PAMPER YOURSELF

If you want a sweet break from your travels, book a massage or other treatment at the Healing Room at the **Lodge at Sierra Blanca,** 107 Sierra Blanca Dr. 📞 **866/211-7727** or 575/937-2304. Treatments range from Swedish massage to hot-stone therapy to body wraps to salt glows and facials.

RUIDOSO DOWNS

In a stunning setting surrounded by green grass and pine trees, the famous **Ruidoso Downs racetrack** and **Billy the Kid Casino** (📞 **575/378-4431;** www.ruidowns racing.com), 2 miles east of Ruidoso on US 70, is home to the world's richest quarter-horse race, the $2 million **All American Futurity,** run each year on Labor Day. Many other days of quarter-horse and thoroughbred racing lead up to the big one, beginning in May and running to Labor Day. Post time is 1pm Thursday through Sunday. Grandstand admission is free; call about reserved seating prices.

The on-site casino has all the neon and noise gamblers love. Though you'll find only slots at this casino (for more variety, head to Inn of the Mountain Gods Resort & Casino, p. 365), bonuses here include simulcast racing on big-screen TVs in the bar and a well-priced buffet with tables overlooking the track. It's open Saturday through Thursday from 11am to 11pm, and Friday from noon to midnight.

AN INTERESTING MUSEUM

The Hubbard Museum of the American West ★   This museum contains a collection of thousands of horse-related items, including saddles from all over the world, a Russian sleigh, a horse-drawn "fire engine," and an 1860 stagecoach. Several great American artists, including Frederic Remington and Charles M. Russell, are represented in the museum's permanent collection. A gift shop has some interesting books and curios.

841 W. US 70, Ruidoso Downs, NM 88346. 📞 **575/378-4142.** Fax 575/378-4166. www.hubbard museum.org. Admission $6 adults, $5 seniors and military, $2 children 6–16, free for children 5 and under. Daily 9am–5pm. Closed Thanksgiving and Christmas.

SPENCER THEATER FOR THE PERFORMING ARTS ★★

The dream of Alto, New Mexico, residents Dr. A. N. and Jackie Spencer, the 514-seat Spencer Theater, on Sierra Blanca Airport Hwy. 220, 4½ miles east of NM 48 (📞 **888/818-7872** or 575/336-4800; www.spencertheater.com), is a model

---

 Family Fun

Families enjoy the excitement at **Fun-trackers Family Fun Center,** 101 Carrizo Canyon Rd. (📞 **575/257-3275;** www. funtrackers-ruidoso.net), which offers go-kart courses, bumper boats, bull riding, and miniature golf. *Beware:* It can be crammed with people midsummer. It's open Memorial Day to Labor Day from Sunday to Thursday 10am to 9pm and Friday and Saturday 10am to 10pm; from September to May it's open weekends only, with limited hours.

performance space that cost more than $22 million to construct. Opened in 1997, the theater has drawn such talents as Ottmar Liebert and Chuck Mangione and presented Broadway shows. Free tours are offered at 10am Tuesday and Thursday. Performances take place both weekends and weekdays. The theater runs two seasons year-round, and tickets cost from $10 to $98.

Mescalero Apache Indian Reservation

Immediately south and west of Ruidoso, the Mescalero Apache Indian Reservation covers over 460,000 acres (719 sq. miles) and is home to about 4,000 members of the Mescalero, Chiricahua, and Lipan bands of Apaches. Established by order of President Ulysses S. Grant in 1873, it sustains a profitable cattle-ranching industry and the Apache-run logging firm of Mescalero Forest Products.

SEEING THE HIGHLIGHTS

Even if you're not staying or dining here, be sure to visit the **Inn of the Mountain Gods Resort & Casino,** a luxury resort owned and operated by the tribe (p. 365); it's the crowning achievement of Wendell Chino, former president of the Mescalero Apache tribe.

Also on the reservation, on US 70 about 17 miles southwest of Ruidoso, is the **Mescalero Cultural Center** (© 575/671-4494; www.mescaleroapache.com), open weekdays from 8am to 4:30pm. Photos, artifacts, clothing, crafts, and other exhibits demonstrate the history and culture of the tribe.

St. Joseph's Apache Mission ★ (© 575/464-4473; www.stjosephmission. org), just off US 70 in Mescalero, on a hill overlooking the reservation, is a grand, stone Romanesque-style structure that stands 103 feet tall and has walls 4 feet thick. Built between 1920 and 1939, the mission church also contains an icon of the Apache Christ, with Christ depicted as a Mescalero holy man, as well as other Apache religious art. Local arts and crafts and religious items are for sale at the parish office. The church is open daily during daylight hours.

A locals' secret worth discovering is the **Old Road Restaurant,** 692 Old Road in Mescalero (© 575/464-4674). In a historic adobe home, with tile and wood floors and chile-ristra accents, this restaurant has served delicious New Mexican food for more than 30 years. Try the combination plate. Checks and cash only. It's open Tuesday to Sunday 9am to 9pm.

RUIDOSO AT NIGHT

If you'd like a rollicking night out, check out **Mountain Annie's Dinner Theater ★,** 2710 Sudderth Dr. (© 575/257-7982; www.mountainannies.com). Set in a 7,000 square-foot building with chandeliers and red velvet drapes, the dinner theater features a variety of types of performances, but most are music variety shows, with tunes ranging from rock to country. The cost for a beef brisket or chicken dinner is $33 adults and $12 for children. Doors open at 6:30pm; dinner is served at 7pm, and the show begins at 8pm. Children can either watch the show or hang out in the supervised playhouse, free of charge. In an Old West vein, the **Flying J Ranch,** on NM 48, 1 mile north of Alto (© 888/458-3595 or 575/336-4330; www.flying jranch.com), offers fun family entertainment and chuck-wagon fare. This ranch is like a Western village, complete with staged gunfights and pony rides for the kids. Gates open at 5:30pm; the gunfight commences at 6:50pm; a hearty chuck-wagon dinner of barbecue beef or chicken is served promptly at 7pm. Then, at 7:50pm, the Flying J Wranglers present a fast-paced stage show with Western music and a world-champion yodeler. Reservations are highly recommended. It costs $24 for ages 13 and up, $14 for ages 4 to 12, and is free for ages 3 and under. It's open May to Labor Day Monday to Saturday, and Labor Day to mid-October Saturday only.

DANCES & CEREMONIES

Throughout the year, the Mescalero Cultural Center hosts powwows of colorful dancing and traditional drumming, open to the public and with unrestricted photography. The most accessible to visitors are dances and a rodeo on July 4.

For more information about the reservation, write to the Tribal Office at P.O. Box 227, Mescalero, NM 88340 or call ☎ 575/671-4494.

LINCOLN HISTORIC DISTRICT ★★

One of the last historic yet uncommercialized 19th-century towns remaining in the American West, the tiny community of Lincoln lies 37 miles northeast of Ruidoso on US 380, in the valley of the Rio Bonito. Only some 50 people live here today, but it was once the seat of the largest county in the United States, and the focal point of the notorious Lincoln County War of 1878–79. Though the town contains a number of museums today, a single ticket will get you entry into all of them.

The bloody Lincoln County War was fought between various ranching and merchant factions over the issue of beef contracts for nearby Fort Stanton. A sharpshooting teenager named William Bonney—soon to be known as "Billy the Kid"—took sides in this issue with "the good guys," escaping from the burning McSween House after his employer and colleague were shot and killed. Three years later, after shooting down a sheriff, he was captured in Lincoln and sentenced to be hanged. But he shot his way out of his cell in what is now the **Lincoln County Courthouse Museum,** which still has a hole made by a bullet from the Kid's gun. Of special note here is a letter handwritten by Billy defending himself to Governor Lew Wallace.

Many of the original structures from that era have been preserved and restored by the Museum of New Mexico, Partners in Preservation of Lincoln State Monument, and the Lincoln County Historical Society.

JUST THE FACTS   At the **Visitor Center,** on NM 380 on the east side of town (☎ 575/653-4025; www.nmmonuments.org), exhibits explain the role in Lincoln's history of Apaches, Hispanics, Anglo cowboys, and the black Buffalo Soldiers, and detail the Lincoln County War. A 12-minute film on Lincoln history is presented in an old-fashioned theater. Start your visit here and learn more from docents at the various museums. Also of note in the town is the round **Torreon** fortress, which served as protection from Apache raids; the **Montaño Store,** once a saloon and boarding house; **Dr. Wood's House,** filled with pre-1920s furnishings, books, and instruments; and the **Tunstall Store Museum,** with late-19th- and early-20th-century clothes, hardware, and butter churns.

An annual **folk pageant,** *The Last Escape of Billy the Kid,* has been presented outdoors since 1949 as a highly romanticized version of the Lincoln County War. It's staged Friday and Saturday night and Sunday afternoon during the first full weekend in August as part of the **Old Lincoln Days** celebration. The festival also includes living-history demonstrations of traditional crafts, musical programs, and food booths throughout the village.

The historic district is open year-round daily from 8:30am to 4:30pm. Admission is $5 for adults (which includes entry to six buildings during summer and four in winter); free for children 16 and under.

For lodging recommendations in Lincoln, see "Where to Stay in & Around Ruidoso," below. The village has three dining options. Set in an 1883 building, the **Dolan House,** 826 Calle la Placita (✆ 575/653-4670; dolansoutpost@yahoo.com), serves home-style soups and sandwiches Friday to Tuesday 9am to 3:30pm and Friday 5 to 8pm. Try their pecan pie. Just down the road, the **Wortley Hotel & Dining Room,** on US 380 in the center of Lincoln (✆ 575/653-4300; www.wortleyhotel.com), offers another historic property dining experience. The restaurant serves hearty egg and pancake breakfasts and lunches that include burgers, salads, and New Mexican food. The restaurant is open during summer Wednesday to Sunday 8am to 3pm, with abbreviated hours in spring and fall. Closed in winter. One mile west of Lincoln on US 380, the **Laughing Sheep Farm Restaurant** (✆ 575/653-4041) serves their own farm-grown produce and meats in a sunny room with rural surroundings. It's open during the warmer months, Wednesday to Sunday from 11am to 3pm and, with reservations only, Friday and Saturday from 5 to 8pm.

If you would like to shop in Lincoln, stop in at **Ran La Roca Glass,** 3112 US 380 (✆ 575/653-4219; ranlaroca@pvtn.net). The artists, often working in back, make enameled-glass jewelry, sculptures, and vessels. Down the street, **La Placita,** on US 380 (✆ 575/653-4047; www.lincolnnewmexico.com), sells rugs, blankets, and wall hangings made by owner Ralph Dunlap.

Where to Stay in & Around Ruidoso

If you're looking for a budget stay in Ruidoso, the **Motel 6** (✆ 800/466-8356; www.motel6.com), on the outskirts of town has reliably clean rooms. In recent years Ruidoso has landed many other major chains including Ramada, La Quinta, Comfort Inn, and Days Inn.

IN TOWN

Best Western at Pine Springs   Nestled within ponderosa pines well above Ruidoso Downs, this inn offers the consistency of a Best Western, with a few extras. Rooms are fairly spacious, set either motel-style so you can park nearby, or in a grassy courtyard, which I recommend, all only minutes from town and a stone's throw from the racetrack and casino. Rooms are decorated in soft colors and have comfortable beds and medium-size, clean bathrooms. Though they could use some updating, as could the cracked sidewalks, the setting and price still recommend this place. The inn's two best points: It's located away from the town of Ruidoso, which during busy months is unbearably noisy, and it has a lovely outdoor pool with a view of the mountains.

1420 US 70, Ruidoso Downs, NM 88346. ✆ **800/237-3607** or 575/378-8100. Fax 575/378-8215. www.bestwestern.com. 100 units. $81–$139 double. Rates include continental breakfast. AE, DC, DISC, MC, V. Pets (no charge). **Amenities:** Exercise room; Jacuzzi; outdoor pool (summer only). *In room:* A/C, TV, fridge, hair dryer, microwave, Wi-Fi (in downstairs rooms).

Escape Resort ★★★ 🛏   For years Ruidoso has needed a really upscale lodging, one with elegance and functionality. Now it has one. This cluster of five casitas, set within town a little off the main road and surrounded by pine trees, offers accommodations of a level one would find in Santa Fe. They come in one- and two-bedroom sizes and have large rooms with high ceilings, marble counters, fine linens, contemporary furnishings in muted earth tones, gas fireplaces fashioned from stacked sandstone, and private patios. The bathrooms have a Jacuzzi tub and steam-shower. All have fully equipped kitchens with stainless-steel appliances. Calling this a "resort" is a bit of a stretch, since it has few amenities, but all else here is stellar.

1016 Mechem Rd., Ruidoso, NM 88345. © **888/762-8551** or 575/258-1234. www.theescaperesort.com. 5 units. $229 1-bedroom casita; $279 2-bedroom casita. Rates include complimentary wine. AE, DISC, MC, V. **Amenities:** Access to nearby golf course; outdoor pool (summer only). *In room:* A/C, TV, hair dryer, kitchen, Wi-Fi.

Hotel Ruidoso ★★ ☺
This new hotel, set in the center of town within walking distance of shopping and entertainment, but a little back from the main street and surrounded by pines, offers clean, contemporary rooms with a bit of flair. Currently, it's one of the town's best values. It's a big, blocky looking three-story building, but it has well-appointed accommodations. Rooms are medium size and come in standards or minisuites. All have comfortable beds and are decorated in earth tones, with medium-size bathrooms with granite sinks and tile work in the bathrooms. Minisuites have a fold-out couch, a good option for small families. Service is good. The breakfast room is a comfortably airy place to spend the morning.

110 Chase St. © **866/734-5197** or 575/257-2007. Fax 575/257-2008. www.hotelruidoso.net. 55 units. $79–$99 weekdays; $119–$169 weekends. Rates include full breakfast. AE, DISC, MC, V. **Amenities:** Exercise room; Jacuzzi; indoor pool. *In room:* A/C, TV, fridge, hair dryer, microwave, Wi-Fi.

Inn of the Mountain Gods Resort & Casino ★★
What's most impressive about this resort is its location, set on a grassy slope above a mountain lake on the Mescalero Apache Indian Reservation, 3½ miles southwest of Ruidoso. It's built in the style of a Lake Tahoe casino, with glossy gaming rooms, a variety of restaurants, and a golf course. Though the architecture has a cool modernity, the rooms are comfortable with luxurious touches. You're greeted outside by an impressive Crown Dancer fountain, and inside by banks of windows looking out on the lake. The rooms come in a few sizes, though standard ones are fairly spacious, all with quality bedding, comfortable beds, and medium-size bathrooms. I recommend paying a little more for a lakeside view. Wendell's, with a mountain and lake view, features steak and seafood, with extensive wine offerings. The resort also has a sports bar, a nightclub with live music Friday and Saturday nights, and a casino with more than 1,000 slot machines and 34 table games.

287 Carrizo Canyon Rd., Mescalero, NM 88340. © **800/545-9011** or 575/464-7777. www.innofthe mountaingods.com. 273 units. $129–$209 forest-view double, $169–$289 lake-view double; $269–$349 suite. Golf and ski packages available. AE, DC, DISC, MC, V. **Amenities:** 3 restaurants; 2 bars; concierge; golf course; Jacuzzi; indoor pool; room service. *In room:* A/C, TV, hair dryer, Wi-Fi.

The Lodge at Sierra Blanca ★★
Surrounded by a golf course and plenty of quiet, this hotel offers clean, reliable rooms in a picturesque setting. However, if you find convention traffic daunting, you'll want to ask what's scheduled at the next-door convention center before reserving. When I visited, the hotel was quiet and serene. The lobby centers around an Anasazi-style stacked sandstone fireplace, creating an elegance that carries into the rooms. The rooms are medium size, decorated in a contemporary Southwestern style, with comfortable beds and medium-size baths. The suites, which are large, have sofa beds, fireplaces, and balconies. Many of the rooms have two-person Jacuzzi tubs. The hotel offers golf packages.

107 Sierra Blanca Dr., Ruidoso, NM 88345. ✆ **866/211-7727** or 575/258-5500. Fax 575/258-2419. www.
thelodgeatsierrablanca.com. 120 units. $149–$189 double; $169–$199 suite. Rates include full breakfast. AE,
DISC, MC, V. Take Mechem Dr. 5 min. north of Sudderth. Pets allowed ($50 fee). **Amenities:** Golf course;
exercise room; Jacuzzi; indoor pool. *In room:* A/C, TV, fridge (in most), hair dryer, microwave, Wi-Fi.

Ruidoso Lodge Cabins ★   This 1950s cabin complex ranks as one of the quaint-
est accommodations in the Ruidoso area. Set on the banks of the Ruidoso River, these
cabins have knotty-pine walls and small rooms decorated with quilts and some
antiques. All cabins are very clean, with full kitchens, small bathrooms, and porches
with gas grills. My favorite, newly remodeled, is #6, right on the river and with a fireplace and Jacuzzi tub. Newer units adjacent to these, the **Riverside Cottages** ★★,
where kids aren't welcome, are more upscale, decorated in a country inn style, with
vaulted ceilings and in-room Jacuzzis. Though the road passing close to the cabins can
prove noisy, it quiets down at night. During the day, the river is a nice spot to fish (for
trout) or simply watch the minnows swim by. The lodge restricts outside visitors in
order to keep the grounds quiet for all guests. If you're looking for complete quiet, ask
about their new **Hidden Canyon** ★★, three cabins on 50 acres of forested land.

300 Main Rd., Ruidoso, NM 88345. ✆ **800/950-2510** or 575/257-2510. www.ruidosolodge.com. 23
cabins. Sept–June $99–$189 double; July–Aug and major holidays $139–$209 double. Ask about midweek specials. DISC, MC, V. Children not permitted in Riverside Cottages or Hidden Canyon. *In room:*
TV, hair dryer, kitchenette, Wi-Fi.

IN LINCOLN: A FEW HISTORIC LODGINGS

Ellis Store and Co. Country Inn ★   With part of this house dating from 1850,
this is believed to be the oldest existing residence in Lincoln County, and as a B&B,
it gives visitors a real taste of 19th-century living but with most of today's luxuries.
The house has plenty of history. Billy the Kid spent several weeks here, although
somewhat unwillingly, according to court records that show payment of $64 for 2
weeks' food and lodging for the Kid and a companion held under house arrest.

Three rooms in the main house are a step back into the 1800s, with wood-burning
fireplaces or stoves providing heat, antique furnishings, and handmade quilts. The
separate Mill House, built of adobe and hand-hewn lumber in the 1880s, isn't quite
as cozy as the main house, but it definitely offers an Old West feel.

US 380 (mile marker 98, P.O. Box 15), Lincoln, NM 88338. ✆ **800/653-6460** or 575/653-4609. 8 units,
4 with private bathroom. $89–$119 double. Rates include gourmet breakfast. AE, DISC, MC, V. **Amenities:** Restaurant by reservation only. *In room:* No phone.

Wortley Hotel ★   Built in 1872, this restored hotel offers frontier-style rooms and
excellent service. A key locale in the Lincoln County War, this hotel exudes history.
A broad front porch is a great place to lounge in the afternoons. The rooms are basic
but comfortable and sweetly decorated, with hardwood floors, fireplaces, antique
furniture, queen beds, and small bathrooms with showers. A common room has a
television. The dining room, with oak tables, a fireplace, and sun-porch, is a nice
place to lounge over one of the tasty meals served here. Open spring through fall.

US 380, Lincoln, NM 88338. ✆ **575/653-4300.** www.wortleyhotel.com. 5 rooms. $95 double. Rates include
full breakfast. DISC, MC, V. Pets welcome ($10 fee). **Amenities:** Restaurant. *In room:* No phone, Wi-Fi.

IN SAN PATRICIO

Sentinel Ranch Guest Homes ★★ ☺   About 20 miles east of Ruidoso on the
2,500-acre Sentinel Ranch, these attractive casitas are part of the Hurd–La Rinconada

One of the region's most cherished relics has been restored. **Tinnie Silver Dollar Steakhouse and Saloon,** on US 70, 43 miles west of Roswell and 28 miles east of Ruidoso (✆ 575/653-4425; www.tinniesilverdollar.com), offers excellent food and fine accommodations. The elegant 1870s Victorian structure provides a perfect backdrop for frontier-style dining. A meal here might start with coconut shrimp and move on to a filet mignon with green-chile au gratin potatoes or roasted chicken with mashed potatoes and light gravy. Tinnie also serves Sunday champagne brunch 10am to 3pm, including such traditional favorites as eggs Benedict and prime rib. The steakhouse is open Monday to Thursday from 5 to 9pm, and Friday and Saturday from 5 to 10pm, with the saloon opening at 4pm. While eating, enjoy the view of the gardens and fountain from the veranda and the original Peter Hurd paintings that hang in each room of the restaurant.

The same location has a deli (Mon–Sat 10am–9pm and Sun 10am–8pm) offering packaged liquor sales, a gift shop, and two suites for overnight guests. The suites range in price from $89 to $175, depending on the season.

Gallery, which displays the work of well-known artists Peter and Michael Hurd, Henriette Wyeth Hurd, N. C. Wyeth, and Andrew Wyeth.

Units available are two historic one-bedroom casitas, built in the early part of the 20th century, and three new and much larger units. Of the casitas, Orchard House is my favorite; it sits on the edge of an apple orchard and is furnished in weathered Southwestern antiques. Both of the larger units are elegant, especially La Helenita, a pitched-roofed adobe house that's large enough for two families. All also have fireplaces and comfortable living areas and are decorated with antiques, primitives, and art by the Hurd-Wyeth family. These casitas serve as good bases for families that enjoy having a kitchen.

NM 70 (mile marker 281), San Patricio, NM 88348. ✆ **800/658-6912** or 575/653-4331. Fax 575/653-4218. www.wyethartists.com. 5 units. $140–$410 per casita. AE, DISC, MC, V. Pets welcome (some limitations; $20/day). **Amenities:** Access to e-mail and fax at gallery. *In room:* A/C, TV/VCR, kitchen.

CAMPING

Lincoln National Forest has more than a dozen campgrounds in the region; four of them are within the immediate area. The **Smokey Bear Ranger Station,** 901 Mechem Dr., Ruidoso (✆ **575/257-4095**), is open Memorial Day to Labor Day Monday through Saturday from 7:30am to 4:30pm, and the same hours Monday through Friday the rest of the year.

Where to Dine in & Around Ruidoso

IN TOWN
Expensive

Willmon's Prime Grille ★★ STEAK/SEAFOOD This restaurant at the center of town offers a relaxing retreat from the bustle of the main drag. In a cozy atmosphere of earth tones accented with comfy *bancos* along the walls, Willmon's serves elegant contemporary American cuisine. Service is good. For a starter, you might try the jumbo lump crab cakes served with Key lime mustard sauce. For an entree I recommend any of the steaks, served with a variety of topping options including a porcini mushroom or au poivre sauce. All entrees come with one side, which for the price in this part of the state is a little skimpy. Choices include baked potato, mac 'n Gruyère cheese, and asparagus. Willmon's wine list won the Wine Spectator Award in 2009.

2523 Sudderth Dr. ✆ **575/257-2954.** www.ruidosofinedining.com. Reservations recommended. Main courses $18–$45. AE, DC, DISC, MC, V. Mon–Sat 5:30–9pm; Sun 5:30–8pm.

Moderate

Cattle Baron ★ SEAFOOD/STEAK   This is the place to go if you really have an appetite. It's a casually elegant restaurant, part of a chain with six locations around the Southwest, that may not serve the best steaks and seafood you've tasted, but still provides good-quality food. It's a casual restaurant decorated in an opulent Western style with lots of burgundy upholstery and brass. Often the place is busy and festive, so it's not ideal for a romantic getaway. Service is efficient and friendly. For lunch, try the turkey-and-avocado sandwich or the teriyaki kabob. For dinner, I usually order the filet mignon or the scampi. An extensive salad bar dominates the main dining room, and a comfortable lounge sits near the entryway.

657 Sudderth Dr. ✆ **575/257-9355.** www.cattlebaron.com. Reservations recommended for 6 or more. Main courses $7.50–$10 lunch, $9–$40 dinner. AE, DC, DISC, MC, V. Mon–Thurs 11am–9:30pm; Fri–Sat 11am–10pm; Sun 11am–9pm.

Texas Club Grill & Bar ★ SEAFOOD/STEAK   Hidden away and somewhat hush-hush, this steakhouse isn't really a club, but because it advertises only by word of mouth, it has an exclusive quality, accented by plenty of Texas twang in the air and longhorns hanging on the walls. The place's secrets are a hometown friendliness and steaks hand-rubbed with signature seasonings. The dining room, which over-looks a small lake, has comfy booths and sturdy chairs. It's a lively place with a broad menu, including many cuts of beef and other dishes, such as chicken, shrimp, pasta, and salads. My favorite dish is the filet, and my mom's is the jumbo charbroiled shrimp, both served with hot rolls and a choice of potato, pasta, or vegetable. Service is efficient. Also on-site is a lounge with a dance floor, where a DJ spins music every night the place is open, and live music often plays on weekends.

212 Metz Dr. ✆ **575/258-3325.** Reservations recommended. Main courses $12–$35. AE, DC, DISC, MC, V. Wed–Thurs and Sun 5–9pm; Fri–Sat 5–10pm. From Mechem Dr., turn east on Cree Meadows Dr.

Inexpensive

Casa Blanca ★ ☺ NEW MEXICAN   This is a real locals' favorite for the margaritas and fun New Mexican food. You can count on a good meal here, made with fresh ingredients. The decor is casual—four rooms in a sprawling house on a hill within town, each with brick or tile floors and colorful art on the walls. The garden room and patio are my choices. All of them can get a little noisy from the many kids who like the menu selections here. Your efficient and friendly server will start you out with complimentary chips and salsa. The best bet here is the chicken enchiladas with sour cream, or the beef or chicken fajitas. Recently I enjoyed a tasty habañero-blackened chicken. Salads and burgers are also available. For dessert? Try the chocolate flan cake.

501 Mechem Dr. ✆ **575/257-2495.** Main courses $7–$17. AE, MC, V. Mon–Thurs 7am–9pm; Fri–Sat 7am–10pm; Sun 7am–8pm. Closed Thanksgiving and Christmas.

Cornerstone Bakery and Café ★ BAKERY/CAFE   In this cafe on the east side of town, amid yellow walls covered with nature scenes, diners eat hearty breakfasts while sipping espresso and cappuccino. During breakfast, this place can get crowded, serving omelets and eggs Benedict to locals and travelers. Lunch is equally bustling, with offerings such as quiche, an almond-chicken salad croissant, or one of their daily specials. This might include a pulled pork sandwich on green chile cheddar bun. All the breads and pastries are baked fresh daily including a delicious chocolate cream pie.

359 Sudderth Dr. (3 miles east of downtown). ✆ **575/257-1842.** www.cornerstonebakerycafe.com. Most menu items under $10. AE, DISC, MC, V. Daily 7:30am–2pm (3pm in summer).

Hummingbird Tearoom ★ ☺ AMERICAN   If you're looking for a light lunch, head to this little room pinched into a corner of a small strip mall in the center of town. Though you won't find anything extravagant on the menu, everything is well prepared and tasty. I've had a tuna salad sandwich made with sweet pickles the way my mother makes them. You can also order their daily frittata, made with cheese and various types of vegetables. A kid's menu features such favorites as a PB&J and macaroni and cheese. During warm months, their patio offers a nice refuge.

2306 Sudderth Dr., Village Plaza. ✆ **575/257-5100.** Main courses $5–$9. AE, DISC, MC, V. Mon–Sat 11am–3pm.

Sacred Grounds Coffee ★★ CAFE   In a contemporary space with stainless steel tables and big windows, this cafe serves excellent organic and fair-trade coffees including lattes, espressos, and also chai tea. The often-present owner makes pastries, quiches, soups, and sandwiches. With free Wi-Fi, it's a good place to hang out.

2825 Sudderth Dr., Ste. B. ✆ **575/257-2273.** All menu items under $8. MC, V. Mon–Sat 6:30am–6pm; Sun 8am–2pm.

Village Buttery ★★ LIGHT FARE   You'll likely be greeted by an enthusiastic, "Hi, darlin'," when you step into this little place on the east end of town, an indication of homestyle food served here. Run by a covey of kind women, it is a cozy place decorated with tile-topped tables and local art. A broad roadside patio is popular in the warmer months. The Buttery serves a variety of soups, salads, sandwiches, and quiches, along with house-baked pies. Most recently, I enjoyed a chicken salad sandwich with rotini pasta (broccoli, celery, feta cheese, and olives with a broccoli-and-raspberry walnut vinaigrette). Their tomato-basil soup is also good. For something different, try a piece of their signature buttermilk pie.

2107 Sudderth Dr. ✆ **575/257-9251.** www.thevillagebuttery.com. All menu items under $10. DISC, MC, V. Mon–Sat 10:30am–2:30pm.

A SCENIC DRIVE AROUND THE LINCOLN LOOP

An enjoyable way to see many of the sights of the area while staying in Ruidoso is on a 1- or 2-day 162-mile loop tour. Heading east from Ruidoso on US 70, about 18 miles past Ruidoso Downs, is the small community of **San Patricio,** where you'll find (watch for signs) the **Hurd–La Rinconada Gallery** (✆ 575/653-4331; www.wyethartists.com). Late artist Peter Hurd, a Roswell native, flunked out of West Point

No Scum Allowed

In the "ghost town" of White Oaks, the **No Scum Allowed Saloon** (© 575/648-5583; www.noscumallowedsaloon.com) sits in an atmospheric 1880s brick building, with signed dollar bills plastered to the ceiling and vintage license plates nailed all over the walls. While there, ask the owner, Tony Marsh, how he got the place. You're in for many laughs. On NM 349 near Carrizozo, it's well worth a stop to have refreshments and see the art town of White Oaks. Open most weekends.

---

before studying with artist N. C. Wyeth and marrying Wyeth's daughter, Henriette, eventually returning with her to New Mexico. This gallery shows and sells works by Peter Hurd, Henriette Wyeth, their son Michael Hurd, Andrew Wyeth, and N. C. Wyeth. Many of the works capture the ambience of the landscape in the San Patricio area. In addition to original works, signed reproductions are available. The gallery is open Monday through Saturday from 9am to 5pm and Sunday from 10am to 4pm. Several rooms and guesthouses are also available by the night or for longer periods (see p. 366).

From San Patricio, continue east on US 70 for 4 miles to the community of Hondo, at the confluence of the Rio Hondo and Rio Bonito, and turn west onto US 380. From here, it's about 10 miles to **Lincoln,** a fascinating little town that is also a National Historic Landmark (see "Lincoln Historic District," earlier in this chapter). From Lincoln, continue west on US 380 about a dozen miles to **Capitan** and **Smokey Bear Historical Park,** 118 Smokey Bear Blvd. (© 575/354-2748; www.smokeybearpark.com), open daily from 9am to 5pm. Smokey, the national symbol of forest fire prevention, was found near here as an orphaned cub by firefighters in the early 1950s. Admission to this park is $2 for adults, $1 for children age 7 to 12, and free for children 6 and under. The park has exhibits on Smokey's rescue and life at the National Zoo in Washington, D.C.; fire prevention; and forest health. Visitors can also stop at Smokey's grave and explore a nature path that represents six vegetation zones of the area. If you'd like to stay in Capitan, check out **Capitan Cabins,** 321 3rd St. (© 575/354-6010; www.capitancabins.com), which has well-appointed cabins on one of the town's back streets.

Heading west from Capitan about 20 miles takes you to **Carrizozo,** the Lincoln County seat since 1912. One of the best green-chile cheeseburgers in the Southwest can be found at the **Outpost** (© 575/648-9994), 415 Central Ave. They're served in a basket, with fries if you'd like. Inside this dark, cool bar/restaurant, you'll find cowboys and farmers chowing under the gaze of bison and deer heads. If you'd like a light lunch or latte, stop in at **La Brewja Café,** 113 Central Ave. (© 575/648-3090), a fun joint with free Wi-Fi and a guest computer. Look for breakfast burritos, soups, salads, sandwiches, and quiches. The cafe doesn't take itself too seriously, as they advertise their "hours of create chaos" to be Monday to Friday 7am to 4pm.

From there, take 2nd Street east to 12th Street, where five lively galleries have opened up in the historic district. Especially look for **Gallery 408,** 408 12th St. (© 575/648-2598; www.gallery408.com). Also of note is the **Carrizozo Heritage Museum,** 103 12th St. (© 575/648-2102; www.carrizozochamber.org—click on businesses, then museums). It features displays on the history of this small railroad town and Lincoln County, and is open Friday and Saturday 10am to 2pm.

Continue west on US 380 for 4 miles to **Valley of Fires Recreation Area** (© 575/648-2241), where you'll find what is considered one of the youngest and best-preserved lava fields in the United States. Among the black lava formations is a .8-mile self-guided nature trail, which is well worth the walk. Part of it is wheelchair accessible. You'll discover a strange new landscape that at first glance appears inhospitable but really is rich with plant life and wildlife. Be sure to walk far enough to see the 400-year-old juniper wringing itself from the black stone. A small visitor center and bookstore is in the park campground. Admission is $3 per person or $5 per car for day use, and camping costs $7 to $18. The park is open year-round.

To continue the loop tour, return 4 miles to Carrizozo, turn south onto US 54, and go about 28 miles to the turnoff to **Three Rivers Petroglyph National Recreation Area** (© 575/525-4300), about 5 miles east on a paved road. Some 20,000 individual rock-art images are here, carved by Mogollon peoples who lived in the area centuries ago. A trail about .8 mile long links many of the most interesting petroglyphs; and the view surrounding the area, with mountains to the east and White Sands to the southwest, is outstanding. The park also includes the partially excavated ruins of an ancient Native American village, including a multiroom adobe building, pit house, and masonry house that have been partially reconstructed. Administered by the U.S. Bureau of Land Management, the park has facilities for picnicking and camping. The day-use fee is $2 per vehicle. Overnight camping is $10. The U.S. Forest Service also has a campground in the area, about 5 miles east via a gravel road.

From the recreation area, return 5 miles to US 54 and continue south about 15 miles to **Tularosa Vineyards** (© 575/585-2260; www.tularosavineyards.com), which offers tastings daily from noon until 5pm. Tours by appointment. Using all New Mexico grapes, the winery is especially known for its award-winning reds. Wines can be purchased by the bottle, with prices ranging from $10 to $25. (**Note:** A fun pastime while traveling in this area is to read *Tularosa* by Michael McGarrity. Set in the Tularosa Basin, it's a thrilling mystery about the White Sands Missile Range and Spanish gold.)

Continuing south from the winery, drive about 2 miles to Tularosa and turn east onto US 70, which you take for about 16 miles to the village of **Mescalero** on the Mescalero Apache Indian Reservation. From US 70, take the exit for the Bureau of Indian Affairs and follow the signs to the imposing **St. Joseph's Apache Mission** (see "Mescalero Apache Indian Reservation," earlier in this chapter). After you return to US 70, it's about 19 miles back to Ruidoso.

ROSWELL

Best known as a destination for UFO enthusiasts and conspiracy theorists, Roswell has become a household name thanks to old Mulder and Scully. And even if you're not glued to your set for reruns of *The X-Files,* you may remember Roswell as the setting for major scenes from the 1996 blockbuster *Independence Day.* Government cover-ups, alien autopsies, and cigarette-smoking feds . . . come along as we venture into the UFO capital of the world.

THE INCIDENT AT roswell

In July 1947, something "happened" in Roswell. What was it? Debate still rages. On July 8, 1947, a local rancher named MacBrazel found unusual debris scattered across his property. The U.S. military released a statement saying the debris was wreckage from a spaceship crash. Four hours later, however, the military retracted the statement, claiming what fell from the sky was "only a weather balloon." Most of the community didn't believe the story, although some did suspect that the military was somehow involved—Robert Goddard had been working on rockets in this area since the 1930s, and the Roswell Air Base was nearby. Eyewitnesses to the account, however, maintain the debris "was not of this world."

Theorists believe that the crash actually involved two spacecraft. One disintegrated, hence the debris across the MacBrazel ranch, and the other crash-landed, hence the four alien bodies that were also claimed to have been discovered.

UFO believers have remained dissatisfied with the U.S. Air Force's weather balloon story and have insisted on an explanation for the "alien bodies." The most recent comment from the Air Force came in 1997, 2 weeks before the 50th anniversary of the "crash." The Air Force said that the most likely explanation for the unverified alien reports was that people were simply remembering and misplacing in time a number of life-size dummies dropped from the sky during a series of experiments in the 1950s.

The main place to go in Roswell to learn more about the incident is the **International UFO Museum and Research Center** (© **575/625-9495;** www.roswellufomuseum.com), in the old Plains Theater on Main Street. Staffers will be more than happy to discuss the crash and the alleged military cover-up. As well as displaying an hour-by-hour timeline of the "incident," the museum has photographs of bizarre and elaborate crop circles, and a variety of films about paranormal experiences. A gift shop sells all manner of little green men and related books. The museum is open daily from 9am to 5pm; admission is $5 for adults, $2 for those 5 to 15, and free for kids 4 and under.

Roswell hosts a **UFO Festival** every year during the first week in July. Some of the events include guest speakers, celebrity appearances, an Alien Village, and parade. For details on the event, call © **888/767-3378** or visit www. roswellufofestival.com.

—Su Hudson

Essentials

GETTING THERE   From Albuquerque, take I-40 east 59 miles to Clines Corners; turn south on US 285, and travel 140 miles to Roswell (4 hr.). From Las Cruces, take US 70 east (4 hr.). From Carlsbad, take US 285 north (1½ hr.).

Roswell Airport, at Roswell Industrial Air Center on South Main Street (© **575/347-5703**), is served commercially by **American Eagle Airlines** (© **800/ 433-7300;** www.aa.com), directly from Dallas, Texas, twice daily.

VISITOR INFORMATION   The **Roswell Chamber of Commerce** is at 131 W. 2nd St. (P.O. Box 70), Roswell, NM 88202 (© **575/623-5695;** www.roswellnm.org). The Roswell Convention and Visitors Center is at 912 N. Main (© **575/624-6860**).

Seeing the Sights

Historical Society for Southeast New Mexico   The handsome mansion that houses this historical collection is as much a part of the museum as the collection itself. A three-story, yellow-brick structure, it was built between 1910 and 1912 by rancher J. P. White. Its gently sweeping rooflines and large porches reflect the prairie style of architecture made popular by Frank Lloyd Wright. The White family lived here until 1972; today, this home, on the National Register of Historic Places, is a monument to early-20th-century lifestyles. First- and second-floor rooms, including the parlor, bedrooms, dining room, and kitchen, have been restored and furnished with early-20th-century antiques. The second floor has a gallery of changing historic exhibits, from fashions to children's toys. The third floor, once White's private library, now houses the Pecos Valley Collection and the center's archives. A gift shop sells books and other gift items.

200 N. Lea Ave. (at W. 2nd St.), Roswell, NM 88201. ✆ **575/622-8333.** Fax 575/623-8746. www.hssnm. net. Admission by donation. Daily 1–4pm.

Roswell Museum and Art Center ★   This highly acclaimed small museum is a good place to stop in order to get a sense of this area before heading out to explore. The art center contains an excellent collection of works by Peter Hurd and his wife, Henriette Wyeth, many of which depict the gentry-ranching lifestyle in this area. You'll also find works by Georgia O'Keeffe, Ernest Blumenschein, Joseph Sharp, and others famed from the early-20th-century Taos and Santa Fe art colonies. The museum has an early historical section, but its pride and joy is the **Robert Goddard Collection,** which presents actual engines, rocket assemblies, and specialized parts developed by Goddard in the 1930s, when he lived and worked in Roswell. Goddard's workshop has been re-created for the exhibit.

100 W. 11th St., Roswell, NM 88201. ✆ **575/624-6744.** Fax 575/624-6765. www.roswellmuseum.org. Free admission. Mon–Sat 9am–5pm; Sun and holidays 1–5pm. Closed Thanksgiving, Christmas Eve, Christmas Day, and New Year's Day.

Spring River Park and Zoo ☺   This lovely park, covering 36 acres on either side of a stream a mile east of the New Mexico Military Institute, incorporates a miniature train, an antique carousel, a large prairie-dog town, a children's fishing pond, a picnic area, and playgrounds. The zoo features 150 native and exotic animals, as well as some Texas longhorns.

1306 E. College Blvd. (at Atkinson Ave.), Roswell, NM 88203. ✆ **575/624-6760.** Fax 575/624-6941. Free admission. Summer daily 10am–8pm; winter daily 10am–5:30pm. Gift shop Wed–Sun 1–5pm (summer only).

Getting Outside

Fifteen miles northeast of Roswell, on the Pecos River, at the **Bitter Lake National Wildlife Refuge ★**, a great variety of waterfowl—including cormorants, herons, and pelicans—find a winter home. The refuge, reached via US 380 and NM 265 from Roswell, comprises 24,000 acres of river bottomland, marsh, stands of salt cedar, and open range. All told, more than 300 species of birds have been sighted here. You can get information at the headquarters building at the entrance, or contact ✆ **575/622-6755;** www.fws.gov/southwest. Fall and early winter are the best times to visit.

Bottomless Lakes State Park is a chain of seven lakes surrounded by rock bluffs 16 miles east of Roswell via NM 409, off US 380. It got its name from early cowboys, who tried to fathom the lakes' depth by plumbing them with lariats. No matter how many ropes they tied together and lowered into the limpid water, they never touched bottom. In truth, though, none of the lakes are deeper than 100 feet. The park offers fishing for rainbow trout, swimming and windsurfing, campsites for trailers or tents, shelters, showers, a dump station, and a concession area with vending machines and paddleboat rentals. The lake is open daily 24 hours; admission is $5 per vehicle. The visitor center is open daily 9am to 6pm Memorial Day to Labor Day, the rest of the year daily 8am to 5pm. For more information, contact ✆ **575/624-6058;** www.nmparks.com.

Originally built to raise bass and catfish, the **Dexter National Fish Hatchery,** 1½ miles east of Dexter on NM 190, about 16 miles southeast of Roswell via NM 2, is now a center for the study and raising of 15 threatened and endangered fish species, such as the razorback sucker, Colorado squawfish, and Chihuahuan chub. Year-round, visitors can take self-guided tours among the hatchery's ponds; from late March to October, the visitor center is open, with exhibits and an aquarium containing endangered fish. The hatchery (✆ **575/734-5910;** www.fws.gov/southwest) is open weekdays from 6:30am to 4pm, and admission is free.

Where to Stay in Roswell

In recent years most major motel chains have opened in Roswell, including Hampton Inn, Holiday Inn Express, Motel 6, and Comfort Suites.

Fairfield Inn & Suites by Marriott ★ This inn at the center of town offers bright rooms with plenty of amenities. The lobby and breakfast area have a living room feel, and the whole place offers the convenience and good prices one can expect from a Fairfield. Elements such as marble and tile in the bathrooms and a nice pool further enhance the place. The suites offer an interesting angled two-room configuration, with a big TV and a CD player, and the standard rooms are medium size, each with a desk. All rooms have comfortable beds.

1201 N. Main St., Roswell, NM 88201. ✆ **800/228-2800** or 575/624-1300. www.marriott.com. 67 units. $139–$169 double. Rates include full hot breakfast. AE, DC, DISC, MC, V. **Amenities:** Exercise room; Jacuzzi; outdoor pool; Wi-Fi (in lobby). *In room:* A/C, TV, CD player, hair dryer, microwave.

CAMPING

Town and Country RV Park (✆ **800/499-4364** or 575/624-1833; www.townand countryrvpark.com), south of Roswell, is your best bet for camping, with some grass and cottonwood and elm trees for shade. The campground has 75 sites, most with full hookups. Prices range from $30 to $35. Tent campers can set up here as well. Bathrooms are clean and convenient, as is the large pool. The campground is at 331 W. Brasher Rd. Head south on Main Street for 3 miles; turn west on West Brasher Road.

Where to Dine in Roswell

Cattle Baron ★ SEAFOOD/STEAK This popular restaurant is always busy during mealtimes. You can usually get a table, however, and they are nicely spaced so that the noise level is minimal. It's an informal place with a wealthy ranch feel—lots of burgundy and brass. Service is fast and friendly. Many come here just to feast at the salad bar, which is one of the best I've seen and includes many potato and pasta dishes, as well as a choice of two soups. Everything is made fresh here—the bread baked in-house, the beef even hand cut by the manager. You can't go wrong with the steaks, such as the tender filet mignon wrapped in bacon. You can also get dishes such as shrimp scampi at a price that will make you glad for Roswell's provincialism. The lounge is a comfortable place to come for evening drinks, and there's a full bar here.

1113 N. Main St. © **575/622-2465.** www.cattlebaron.com. Reservations recommended. Main courses $7.50-$10 lunch, $9-$40 dinner. AE, DISC, MC, V. Mon-Thurs 11am-9:30pm; Fri-Sat 11am-10pm; Sun 11am-9pm.

Farley's ☺AMERICAN   This raucous place can really draw crowds. Folks come for the barnlike atmosphere, where they can throw peanut shells on the floor and scream at TVs. Lots of booths inside and a patio outside please kids and their parents, as does the menu variety. Soups and salads, pizza, sandwiches, and burgers are the big sellers. Entrees such as chicken Alfredo and baby back ribs will fill you up if you want a real meal. ***Note:*** On weekend nights and holidays, you'll have to wait for a table. A full bar is available.

1315 N. Main St. © **575/627-1100.** Main courses $8-$20. AE, DC, DISC, MC, V. Daily 11am-midnight or so, depending on the crowd.

Tia Juana's Mexican Grille & Cantina ★★ ☺NEW MEXICAN   On the north end of town, this spot serves tasty New Mexican fare in a festive Mexican cantina ambience. Red chile lights and photos of Oaxaca accent the large dining area, which is made intimate with booths and tables nicely spaced. Service is friendly and on the mark. The food is prepared with fresh ingredients and good chile—the restaurant even makes its own tortillas daily. You can't go wrong with the enchiladas, served rolled or stacked, or the tacos, served soft or crisp. Kids have plenty of menu options, as well as crayons to draw with, and adults can enjoy a full bar.

3601 N. Main St. © **575/627-6113.** www.tiajuanas.net. Main courses $8-$20. AE, DC, DISC, MC, V. Mon-Thurs 11am-9:30pm; Fri-Sat 11am-10pm; Sun 11am-9pm.

ALSO WORTH A LOOK: FORT SUMNER & ENVIRONS

The little town of **Fort Sumner,** home to 1,250 people, 84 miles north of Roswell via US 285 and NM 20, is important in New Mexico history because it's the site of Fort Sumner State Monument and the burial place of the notorious Billy the Kid. Stop by if you're in the vicinity and have some time to spare.

Fort Sumner State Monument ★ (© 575/355-2573; www.nmmonuments. org) recalls a tragic U.S. Army experiment (1864–68) to create a self-sustaining agricultural colony for captive Navajos and Mescalero Apaches. Many still recall the "Long March," during which some Navajos walked a distance of more than 400 miles. By fall 1864, some 9,000 people were held captive here, site of the Bosque Redondo Reservation. Disaster followed: disease, blighted crops, alkaline water, Comanche raids, and the Navajos' devastating alienation from their homelands. Some 3,000 Native Americans died here. Part of the fort where the military lived and worked has been reconstructed at the site. A short walking tour takes you to various signposts that explain what was once on the land, illustrated with sad photographs of the dismal conditions. The visitor center (open daily 8:30am–5pm) gives you a good background before you head out to the site. The monument is 7 miles southeast of the modern town, via US 60/84 and NM 272. Admission is $5 for adults, free for children age 17 and under.

Nearby, the **Old Fort Sumner Museum** (© 575/355-2942) displays artifacts, pictures, and documents. It's a private enterprise that may not quite be worth the $3.50 admission.

Behind the museum (you don't have to go through the museum) is the **Grave of Billy the Kid,** its 6-foot tombstone engraved to "William H. Bonney, alias 'Billy the Kid,' died July 16, 1881," and to two previously slain comrades with whom he was buried. Also in the graveyard is the tomb of Lucien Maxwell, the land czar from the Cimarron area, who purchased Fort Sumner after the military abandoned it.

If you're curious about the notorious Kid, you can learn more at the **Billy the Kid Museum** (© 575/355-2380; www.billythekidmuseumfortsumner.com), 1 mile east of downtown Fort Sumner on US 60/84. In operation for over half a century, it contains more than 60,000 relics of the Old West, including some that recall the life of young Bonney himself, such as his rifle. Admission is $5 for adults, $4 for seniors 62 and older, $3 for ages 7 to 15, free ages 6 and under.

The **Old Fort Days** celebration, the second week of June, is Fort Sumner's big annual event. It includes the World's Richest Tombstone Race (inspired by the actual theft of Billy's tombstone, since recovered), 2 nights of rodeo, a country music show, a barbecue, and a parade.

Sumner Lake State Park (© 575/355-2541; www.nmparks.com), 16 miles northwest of Fort Sumner via US 84 and NM 203, is a 1,000-acre property with a campground (with electric and water hookups). Boating, fishing, swimming, and water-skiing are popular recreations.

For more information on the town, contact the **Fort Sumner Chamber of Commerce,** P.O. Box 28, Fort Sumner, NM 88119 (© 575/355-7705; www. ftsumnerchamber.com).

Clovis/Portales

Clovis, 110 miles northeast of Roswell via US 70, is a major market center on the Texas border. Founded in 1906 as a railway town, it is now the focus of an active ranching and farming region. The **Lyceum Theatre,** 409 Main St. (© 575/763-6085), is a significant restoration of a former vaudeville theater; it's now the city's center for performing arts. A major rodeo on the national circuit is held the first weekend in June. "Clovis Man," who hunted mammoths in this region about 10,000 B.C., was first discovered at a site near the city. For more information, contact the **Clovis/Curry County Chamber of Commerce** (© 575/763-3435; www.clovis nm.org).

Nineteen miles south of Clovis is **Portales,** a town of 11,000 people that is the home of the main campus of **Eastern New Mexico University.** On campus are the **Roosevelt County Historical Museum** (© 575/562-2592; www.enmu. edu—look for "quick links") of regional ranching history and the **Natural History Museum** (© 575/562-2753), with wildlife exhibits, including a bee colony. Anthropology and paleontology exhibits are at the **Blackwater Draw Archaeological**

Site and Museum ★ (✆ 575/562-2202), 7 miles northeast of Portales on US 70 toward Clovis. The museum isn't much, but the archaeological site draws bone buffs from around the world. Especially notable is the Interpretive Center, where visitors can watch an excavation in progress. The site is on NM 467, 5 miles north of US 70. For more information, contact the **Roosevelt County Chamber of Commerce** at ✆ 575/356-8541; or www.portales.com.

For lodging in the Clovis/Portales area, try the **La Quinta Inn,** 4521 N. Prince, Clovis, NM 88101 (✆ 800/753-3757 or 575/763-8777; www.lq.com). A good dining bet in the area is **Juanito's,** 1608 Mabry Dr., Clovis (✆ 575/762-7822).

In Portales, stay at the **Super 8 Motel,** 1805 W. 2nd St. (✆ 800/800-8000 or 575/356-8518; www.super8.com). The **Cattle Baron,** 1600 S. Avenue D (✆ 575/356-5587; www.cattlebaron.com), has good steaks and a nice salad bar.

CARLSBAD & ENVIRONS

Carlsbad, named for a spa in Bohemia, offers almost 3 miles of beaches and paths along the tree-shaded Pecos River. Founded in the late 1800s, its back streets have many elegant homes, and its town square encircles a Pueblo-style courthouse designed by New Mexico architect John Gaw Meem. Besides getting a good tourist business from Carlsbad Caverns, the town survives on farming, with irrigated crops of cotton, hay, and pecans.

Carlsbad Caverns National Park (see below) offers an unforgettable nature experience, drawing some 500,000 visitors each year.

Essentials

GETTING THERE From Albuquerque, take I-40 east 59 miles to Clines Corners; turn south on US 285, and travel 216 miles to Carlsbad via Roswell (6 hr.). From El Paso, take US 62/180 east (3 hr.).

New Mexico Airlines (✆ 888/564-6119; www.pacificwings.com/nma) provides commercial service, with daily flights between Albuquerque and **Cavern City Air Terminal** (✆ 575/887-3060), 4 miles south of the city via National Parks Highway (US 62/180). You can rent a car from **Enterprise,** 609 N. Canal St. (✆ 575/887-3039); with an advance reservation they will pick you up at the airport.

VISITOR INFORMATION The **Carlsbad Chamber of Commerce** and the **Carlsbad Convention and Visitors Bureau,** both at 302 S. Canal St. (US 285), P.O. Box 910, Carlsbad, NM 88220 (✆ 800/221-1224 or 575/887-6516; www.carlsbadchamber.com), are open Monday from 9am to 5pm and Tuesday through Friday from 8am to 5pm.

Seeing the Sights

Carlsbad's pride and joy is the broad Pecos River, with a 3½-mile **river walk** along the tree-shaded banks, beginning near the north end of Riverside Drive. This is a lovely place for a picnic, and if you'd like to cool off, a municipal beach at the north end has changing rooms and showers. Annual **Christmas on the Pecos** ★★ pontoon boat rides take place each evening from Thanksgiving to New Year's Eve (except Christmas Eve), past a stunning display of Christmas lights on riverside homes and businesses. Advance reservations, available from the chamber of commerce, are required.

The **Carlsbad Museum and Art Center,** 418 W. Fox St., 1 block west of Canal Street (📞 **575/887-0276**), contains Apache relics, pioneer artifacts, and an impressive art collection. The museum's store has a small but fine selection of jewelry and books at reasonable prices. The museum is open Monday through Saturday from 10am to 5pm; admission is free, although donations are welcome. If you're looking to shop, check out the **Artist Gallery,** 120 S. Canyon St. (📞 **575/887-1210**), selling local and regional art. Look especially for Helen Gwinn's mixed-media pieces.

Getting Outside

Recreational facilities in the Carlsbad area include some two dozen parks, several golf courses, numerous tennis courts and swimming pools, a municipal beach, and a shooting and archery range. Contact the **City of Carlsbad Recreation Department** (📞 **575/887-1191;** www.cityofcarlsbadnm.com).

Living Desert Zoo & Gardens State Park ★ ☺   Situated within 1,200 acres of authentic Chihuahuan Desert, this park contains more than 50 species of desert mammals, birds, and reptiles, and almost 500 varieties of plants. Even for someone like me, who cringes at the thought of zoos, this is a pleasant 1.3-mile walk. You pass through displays with plaques pointing out vegetation such as mountain mahogany, and geologic formations such as gypsum sinkholes. In addition to a nocturnal exhibit, you're likely to see lizards and other wild creatures, as well as captive ones.

Rehabilitation programs provide for the park's animals, which have been sick or injured and are no longer able to survive in the wild. You'll see golden eagles and great horned owls among the birds of prey in the aviary, and large animals such as deer and elk in outdoor pastures. One of the main highlights is the endangered gray wolf exhibit. The view from the park, high atop the Ocotillo Hills on the northwest side of Carlsbad, is superb.

1504 Miehls Dr. (P.O. Box 100), Carlsbad, NM 88221-0100. 📞 **575/887-5516.** www.emnrd.state.nm.us/prd/livingdesert.htm. Admission $5 adults, $3 children 7-12, free for children 6 and under. Memorial Day weekend to Labor Day daily 8am–5pm, last park entry by 3:30pm; rest of year daily 9am–5pm, last park entry by 3:30pm. Gift shop closes 45 min. before zoo. Closed Christmas. Take Miehls Dr. off US 285 west of town and proceed just over a mile.

Where to Stay in & Around Carlsbad

Most lodgings are in the center of Carlsbad. Only the Best Western Cavern Inn is near the National Park, and I do not recommend it, as it needs more care than it is getting.

Best Western Stevens Inn ★   This is a comfortable and welcoming place after the rigor of traveling in this part of the state, where there are miles between stops. The grounds are carefully landscaped, and the inn offers numerous types of rooms built in different eras. Some need to be upgraded, so be sure to request a remodeled one or, better yet, request one of the newest rooms at the south end of the property, which are large and have large bathrooms; each has a fridge and microwave, and some have full kitchens. The rooms in the 400 and 600 numbered buildings are also updated. All the rooms are medium size, decorated in a Southwestern style, and have firm beds. Bathrooms are small but have outer double-sink vanities. The Flume (p. 385) is one of the better restaurants in town.

1829 S. Canal St., Carlsbad, NM 88220. © **800/730-2851,** 800/528-1234, or 575/887-2851. Fax 575/887-6338. www.bestwestern.com. 221 units. $109 double; $129 suite. Rates include breakfast buffet. AE, DISC, MC, V. Small pets allowed ($25 deposit). **Amenities:** Restaurant; bar; free airport transfer; exercise room; playground; large outdoor pool; executive level rooms; room service. *In room:* A/C, TV, fridge, hair dryer, kitchen (in some), microwave, Wi-Fi.

Holiday Inn Express ★★ ☺   One of Carlsbad's newest lodgings, this hotel, opened in 2007, provides well-planned, comfortable rooms on the north side of town. Rooms are medium-size, with comfortable beds dressed in earthy colors, and a desk, and with lots of amenities. The medium-size bathrooms have granite countertops and tile tubs. As well, the hotel has king and queen suites, which include two TVs and a fold-out couch, a good option for families. Service here is courteous and professional.

2210 W. Pierce St., Carlsbad, NM 88220. © **800/465-4329** or 575/234-1252. Fax 575/234-1253. www. hiexpress.com. 80 units. $99–$105 double; $133–$143 suite. Rates include full hot breakfast. AE, DISC, MC, V. **Amenities:** Exercise room; Jacuzzi; indoor pool. *In room:* A/C, TV, fridge, hair dryer, microwave, Wi-Fi.

Trinity Hotel Suites ★★ 🏠   In an 1892 bank building that's a National Historic Landmark, this new hotel provides a luxurious old-world stay. The lobby, attached restaurant (see "Where to Dine," below), wine bar, and small gift shop selling locally sourced products have high ceilings and hardwood floors, an elegance that carries into the guestrooms. They are spacious, with black, carved wood furniture, quality bedding, and large luxurious bathrooms, including some with Jacuzzi tubs. Service is very conscientious. The town's best restaurant also resides here, where guests enjoy a delicious full breakfast included in the price of the room. The wine bar is a happening place, where guests can sample locally made wines including ones from the hotel owners' vineyard.

201 S. Canal, Carlsbad, NM 88220. © **575/234-9891.** www.thetrinityhotel.com. 9 units. $169–$269 double. Rates include full gourmet breakfast. AE, DISC, MC, V. **Amenities:** Restaurant; lounge; concierge. *In room:* A/C, TV, hair dryer, MP3 docking station, Wi-Fi.

CAMPING

Brantley Lake State Park (© **575/457-2384;** www.nmparks.com) in Carlsbad has RV hookups as well as tent campsites. Picnic tables, grills, and recreational facilities are available. Boating and lake fishing are popular here. **Carlsbad RV Park and Campground,** on the south end of town at 4301 National Parks Hwy. (© **888/878-7275** or 575/885-6333; www.carlsbadrvpark.com), is a large, full-service campground with a swimming pool and playground. In Artesia, try **Artesia RV Park** (© **575/746-6184;** www.artesiarvpark.net), a more moderately sized campground, on Hermosa Drive just south of the junction of US 82/285. Laundry facilities and a game room are available.

Where to Dine in & Around Carlsbad

Blue House ★ 🏠 BAKERY/CAFE   In a quest to find good coffee in even the smallest of New Mexico towns, I now rate Carlsbad high. On a quiet residential street just north of historic downtown is this gem, set in a Queen Anne–style blue house with morning-glory vines adorning the front fence. Inside, subtle colors warm the walls, contrasting with brightly painted chairs and small round tables. The fare is simple, fresh, and imaginative, with espresso, lattes, and Italian sodas the biggest draws, along with special sandwiches and soups daily. Excellent baked goods top the breakfast menu, including homemade cinnamon rolls. For lunch, try any of the fresh organic salads such as the grilled chicken or Oriental. For something sweeter, order the cream cheese–raspberry coffee cake.

609 N. Canyon Rd. ℂ 575/628-0555. All menu items under $8. DISC, MC, V. Mon–Fri 6am–2pm; Sat 6am–noon (lunch served Tues–Fri 11am–1pm). Take Canal St. to Church St. east, and then go south on Canyon Rd.

Danny's Place ★ ☺ BARBECUE   In a country atmosphere with tile floors, pine chairs, and colorful plates adorning the walls, this restaurant serves excellent barbecue cooked over wood flames. More than 35 years ago, Danny Gaulden started marinating beef, pork, and chicken in his own sauce and he still does. At the back of the kitchen, a flaming cauldron cooks it to perfection. This place bustles while the competent waitstaff meets the pace. Your best bet here is the brisket, which accounts for 75% of their meals served. It comes with your choice of sides including coleslaw and potato salad, as does the rib dinner. Half-portion orders are offered. The restaurant also serves burgers, New Mexican dishes, and barbecue sandwiches, while a kids' menu offers burgers, chicken, and burritos.

902 South Canal St. ℂ 575/885-8739. www.dannysbbq.com. Main courses $4–$14. AE, DISC, MC, V. Wed–Mon 11am–9pm.

Trinity Hotel Suites, Fine Foods & Wine ★★ 🍴 ITALIAN   Set in an 1892 bank building complete with hardwood floors, high ceilings, crystal chandeliers, and a safe that now houses a cigar humidor, this lively restaurant serves an excellent selection of Italian dishes prepared with local ingredients, when possible. The service is courteous and efficient. At breakfast, order a latte or espresso with a variety of egg and pancake dishes, while lunch brings soups, salads, and sandwiches, including an Italian meatball one, with mozzarella and marinara sauce. Dinner is when this place really shines, with a variety of pasta, meat and fish, and vegetarian dishes. My favorite is the chicken marsala, with the classic mushroom wine sauce, and served over pasta. The lobster ravioli in a vodka sauce is also delicious. Definitely save room for the tiramisu. A short but well-considered wine and beer list accompanies the menu, with many by-the-glass options.

201 S. Canal, Carlsbad, NM 88220. ℂ 575/234-9891. www.thetrinityhotel.com. Reservations recommended for dinner. Main courses $5–$12 breakfast, $7–$10 lunch, $10–$15 dinner. AE, DISC, MC, V. Daily 7am–2pm; Mon–Sat 5–8:30pm or later if busy.

Carlsbad After Dark

Carlsbad has a bit of a night scene. You have two options. The **Blue Cactus,** 1829 S. Canal St. (ℂ **575/887-2851**), offers a variety of DJ music Monday through Saturday nights, as well as big-screen TVs. The **Post Time Saloon,** 313 W. Fox St. (ℂ **575/628-1977**), is a huge place with pool tables, three bars, and a dance floor. The club offers a range of DJ mixes, including country, Tejano, and karaoke.

Exploring the Environs

A SIDE TRIP TO TEXAS: GUADALUPE MOUNTAINS NATIONAL PARK ★★

Some 250 million years ago, the Guadalupe Mountains were an immense reef poking up through a tropical ocean. Marine organisms fossilized this 400-mile-long

Capitan Reef as limestone; later, as the sea evaporated, a blanket of sediments and mineral salts buried the reef. Then, just 10 to 12 million years ago, a mountain-building uplift exposed a part of the fossil reef. This has given modern scientists a unique opportunity to explore earth's geologic history, and outdoor lovers a playground for wilderness experience.

The steep southern end of the range makes up **Guadalupe Mountains National Park** and includes Guadalupe Peak, at 8,749 feet the highest in Texas, while the northern part lies within Lincoln National Forest and Carlsbad Caverns National Park. Deer, elk, mountain lion, and bear are found in the forests, which contrast strikingly with the desert around them.

JUST THE FACTS To reach the park, take US 62/180, 55 miles southwest of Carlsbad. Admission to the park is $5, and the visitor center is open daily June through August from 8am to 6pm; September through May from 8am to 4:30pm. For more information, contact **Park Ranger,** HC-60, Box 400, Salt Flat, TX 79847 (© **915/981-3251;** www.nps.gov/gumo). The park has more than 80 miles of trails; most are steep, rugged, and rocky. No lodging, restaurants, stores, or gas exist within 35 miles of the park. Leashed pets are permitted only in the campground parking area.

SEEING THE HIGHLIGHTS The visitor center offers a variety of exhibits and slide programs that tell the story of the Guadalupe Mountains, as well as ranger-guided walks and lectures. Information, maps, and backcountry permits can also be obtained at **McKittrick Canyon Visitor Center** (10 miles northeast via US 62/180 and a side road; © **915/828-3381**) and the **Dog Canyon Ranger Station** (reached through Carlsbad via NM 137 and CR 414, about 70 miles; © **575/981-2418**).

One of the most spectacular hikes in Texas is to the top of **Guadalupe Peak,** an 8.5-mile round-trip trek accessed from the Pine Springs Campground. **McKittrick Canyon,** protected by its high sheer walls, with a green swath of trees growing along the banks of its spring-fed stream, is a beautiful location. It is a great spot for hiking, bird-watching, and viewing other wildlife, and it's an especially lovely sight during fall foliage season, from late October to mid-November.

CAMPING Pine Springs and Dog Canyon both have developed camping areas, with restrooms and water, but no hookups or showers. Fires, including charcoal, are not permitted.

ARTESIA

A downtown rejuvenation project has brought a sparkle to **Artesia,** a town of nearly 11,000 people, 36 miles north of Carlsbad on US 285. If you'd like to tour the town, pick up a **Walking Tour** map from local businesses or the Artesia Chamber of Commerce (see below), or download it at www.artesiamainstreet.com, to see 17 historic or notable sites. The **Artesia Historical Museum and Art Center,** housed in a Victorian home at 505 W. Richardson Ave. (© **575/748-2390;** www.artesia museum.com), is worth visiting just to see the Queen Anne–style home with the outside covered with round river stones. Open Tuesday through Friday from 9am to 5pm (closed noon–1pm), and Saturday from 1 to 5pm, the museum exhibits Native American and pioneer artifacts, traveling exhibits, and art shows. Admission is free.

If you want to stop over in Artesia, consider the **Best Western Pecos Inn,** 2209 W. Main St. (US 82), Artesia, NM 88211 (© **575/748-3324;** www.bestwestern.

com). For a historic option, try the **Heritage Inn** ★, 209 W. Main St., Artesia, NM 88210 (*C* **575/748-2552;** www.artesiaheritageinn.com). In the center of town, the 1906 hotel offers cozy rooms decorated with antiques, many with hardwood floors. A good place to eat is the **Wellhead** ★, 332 W. Main St. (*C* **575/746-0640;** www. thewellhead.com), a brewpub designed around the theme of oil wells. It's open Sunday through Thursday from 11am to 11pm and Friday and Saturday from 11am to midnight. Reservations are recommended on weekends and holidays. Main courses range from $8 to $32, and most major credit cards are accepted. Further information can be obtained from the **Artesia Chamber of Commerce,** P.O. Box 99, Artesia, NM 88211 (*C* **575/746-2744;** www.artesiachamber.com).

HOBBS

Located 69 miles east of Carlsbad on US 62/180, on the edge of the Llano Estacado tableland, Hobbs is at the center of New Mexico's richest oil field. Many oil companies base their headquarters here.

The **Lea County Cowboy Hall of Fame and Western Heritage Center** near New Mexico Junior College, on the Lovington Highway (*C* **575/392-6730;** www. museumshobbsnm.org), honors the area's ranchers (both men and women) and rodeo performers and is open Tuesday through Saturday from 10am to 5pm (closed college holidays).

Twenty-two miles northwest of Hobbs via NM 18, at the junction with US 82, is the town of **Lovington** (pop. 9,500), another ranching and oil center. The **Lea County Historical Museum,** 103 S. Love St. (*C* **575/396-4805;** www.leacounty museum.org), presents memorabilia of the region's unique history in a World War I–era hotel (ca. 1918).

If you plan to stay in Hobbs, try the **Holiday Inn Express,** 3610 N. Lovington Hwy. (*C* **800/377-8660** or 575/392-8777; www.hiexpress.com). **Harry McAdams Park,** 4 miles north of Hobbs on NM 18 (*C* **575/397-9291**), has campsites and a visitor center set on acres of lovely grass. You can get a good square meal at the **Cattle Baron,** 1930 N. Grimes St. (*C* **575/393-2800;** www.cattlebaron. com). Gamblers and horse-racing fans enjoy the **Black Gold Casino at Zia Park,** 3901 W. Millen Dr. (*C* **888/942-7275** or 575/492-7000; www.blackgoldcasino. net), with more than 700 slot machines. Live horse racing takes place September to December. For more information on the area, contact the **Hobbs Chamber of Commerce,** 400 N. Marland Blvd. (*C* **800/658-6291** or 575/397-3202; www. hobbschamber.org), or the **Lovington Chamber of Commerce,** 201 S. Main St. (*C* **575/396-5311;** www.lovingtonchamber.org).

CARLSBAD CAVERNS NATIONAL PARK ★★★

One of the largest and most spectacular cave systems in the world, **Carlsbad Caverns** comprise some 100 known caves that snake through the porous limestone reef of the Guadalupe Mountains. Fantastic and grotesque formations fascinate visitors, who find every shape imaginable (and unimaginable) naturally sculpted in the underground world—from frozen waterfalls to strands of pearls, from soda straws to miniature castles, from draperies to ice-cream cones.

Although Native Americans had known of the caverns for centuries, they were not discovered by Anglos until about a century ago, when settlers were attracted by sunset flights of bats from the cave. Jim White, a guano miner, began to explore the main cave in the early 1900s and to share its wonders with tourists. By 1923, the caverns had become a national monument, upgraded to national park status in 1930.

Essentials

GETTING THERE Take US 62/180 from either Carlsbad (see "Essentials," under "Carlsbad & Environs," earlier in this chapter), which is 23 miles to the northeast, or El Paso, Texas, which is 150 miles to the west. The scenic entrance road to the park is 7 miles long and originates at the park gate at White's City.

VISITOR INFORMATION For more information about the park, contact **Carlsbad Caverns National Park,** 3225 National Parks Hwy., Carlsbad, NM 88220 (*C* **877/444-6777;** www.recreation.gov for tour reservations, 575/785-2232 for information about guided tours, or 575/785-3012 for bat flight information; www.nps.gov/cave).

ADMISSION FEES & HOURS General admission to the park is $6 for adults, free for children age 15 and under. Admission is good for 3 days and includes entry to the two self-guided walking tours. Guided tours range in price from $8 to $20, depending on the type of tour, and reservations are required. The visitor center and park are open daily approximately from Memorial Day to Labor Day from 8am to 7pm; however, the last entry into the cave via the Natural Entrance is 3:30pm and via the elevator is 5pm. The rest of the year the visitor center and park are open from 8am to 5pm; the last entry into the cave via the Natural Entrance is 2pm and via the elevator is 3:30pm. The park is closed Christmas.

Touring the Caves

Two caves, **Carlsbad Cavern** and **Slaughter Canyon Cave,** are open to the public. The National Park Service has provided facilities, including elevators, to make it easy for everyone to visit the cavern, and a kennel for pets is available. Visitors in wheelchairs are common. Baby strollers are not allowed in the caves, and children 15 and under must be accompanied by an adult.

In addition to the tours described below, inquire at the visitor center information desk about other ranger-guided tours, including climbing and crawling "wild" cave tours. Be sure to call days in advance because some tours are offered only 1 day per week. Spelunkers who seek access to the park's undeveloped caves require special permission from the park superintendent.

CARLSBAD CAVERN TOURS

You can tour Carlsbad Cavern in one of three ways, depending on your time, interest, and level of ability. The first, and least difficult, option is to take the elevator from the visitor center down 750 feet to the start of the self-guided tour of the Big Room. More difficult and time consuming, but vastly more rewarding, is the 1-mile self-guided tour along the Natural Entrance route, which follows the traditional explorer's route, entering the cavern through the large historic natural entrance. The paved walkway through the natural entrance winds into the depths of the cavern and leads through a series of underground rooms; this tour takes about an hour. Parts of

> ## Carlsbad Cavern Tour Tips
>
> Wear flat shoes with rubber soles and heels because of the slippery paths. A light sweater or jacket feels good in the constant temperature of 56°F (13°C), especially when it's 100°F (38°C) outside in the sun. The cavern is well lit, but you may want to bring along a flashlight as well. Rangers are stationed in the cave to answer questions.

it are steep. At its lowest point, the trail reaches 750 feet below the surface, ending finally at an underground rest area.

Visitors who take either the elevator or the Natural Entrance route begin the self-guided tour of the spectacular Big Room near the rest area. The floor of this room covers 14 acres; the tour, over a relatively level path, is 1¼ miles long and takes about an hour.

The third option is the 1½-hour ranger-guided Kings Palace tour, which also departs from the underground rest area. This tour descends 830 feet beneath the surface of the desert to the deepest portion of the cavern open to the public. Reservations are required, and an additional fee is charged.

OTHER GUIDED TOURS

Be sure to ask about the Slaughter Canyon Cave, Left Hand Tunnel, Lower Cave, Hall of the White Giant, and Spider Cave tours. These vary in degree of difficulty and adventure, from Left Hand, which is an easy half-mile lantern tour, to Spider Cave, where you can expect tight crawlways and canyonlike passages, to Hall of the White Giant, a strenuous tour in which you're required to crawl long distances, squeeze through tight crevices, and climb up slippery flow-stone-lined passages. Call in advance for times of each tour. All these tours depart from the visitor center.

Bat Flights

Every sunset from Memorial Day to mid-October, a crowd gathers at the natural entrance of the cave to watch 400,000 bats take flight for a night of insect feasting. (The bats winter in Mexico.) All day long, the Mexican free-tailed bats sleep in the cavern; at night, they strike out on an insect hunt. A ranger program is offered around sunset (verify the time at the visitor center) at the outdoor Bat Flight Amphitheater. A dawn bat fly-in is also impressive. Midsummer, the park sponsors a **Bat Flight Breakfast** from 5 to 7am, during which visitors watch the bats return to the cavern. Participants purchase their own breakfasts at the Carlsbad Caverns Trading Restaurant. For information call © **575/785-3012** for bat flights; 575/785-2232, ext. 0 for bat flight breakfast; or check www.nps.gov/cave.

Other Park Activities

The new Carlsbad Caverns Visitor Center has virtual tours of the caves, a variety of films, and an expansive book and gift shop, as well as a restaurant. Aside from the caves, the park offers a 10-mile one-way scenic-loop drive through the Chihuahuan Desert to view Rattlesnake and Upper Walnut canyons. Picnickers can head for

Rattlesnake Springs Picnic Area, on CR 418 near Slaughter Canyon Cave, a water source for hundreds of years for Native Americans, and a primo birding spot. Backcountry hikers must register at the visitor center before going out on any of the trails in the park's 46,766 acres. Watch the Caverns website for dates for **Star Party** events given during the summer. The park is an excellent place to view the night sky.

Dining

The new Carlsbad Caverns Visitor Center has a **cafeteria-style restaurant** serving tasty food salads, sandwiches, and hot dishes. It's open daily in summer from 8am to 7pm, with hot food served until 6:15pm; in winter daily from 8am to 5pm, with hot food until 4:15pm. A **cafe** at the base of the caverns serves light food and other refreshments.

The Flume ★ AMERICAN   Named for the irrigation ditch that brings water to the region's farmers, the Flume serves reliable beef, pork, and chicken dishes in a comfortable atmosphere. This is where Carlsbad locals come for their special nights out. The decor in the two-room dining area, separated by arches, has a bit of a 1970s feel, but includes comfortable chairs. Service is good. Breakfast brings standard egg and pancake offerings. For lunch you might try one of their sandwiches such as the smoked turkey with Swiss cheese and avocado. The salads and burgers are also tasty. At dinner, I've enjoyed a nice grilled chicken here, and my mother liked her fettuccine Alfredo with shrimp. Others seem to order the rib-eye or prime rib, which is served on Friday and Saturday nights. Entrees come with a trip to the salad bar, a vegetable, and choice of a starch. Diners can order from a full bar. A senior menu is available.

1829 S. Canal St., ✆ **575/887-2851.** www.bestwestern.com. Breakfast and lunch $5–$12; dinner $13–$23. AE, DISC, MC, V. Daily 6am–10pm.

FAST FACTS

FAST FACTS: NEW MEXICO

Area Codes   The telephone area code for northwestern New Mexico, including Albuquerque and Santa Fe, is **505.** For the rest of the state, including Taos, the code is **575.**

Business Hours   **Offices** and **stores** are generally open Monday to Friday 9am to 5pm, with many stores also open Friday night, Saturday, and Sunday. Most **banks** are open Monday to Thursday 9am to 5pm and Friday 9am to 6pm. Some may also be open Saturday morning. Most branches have ATMs available 24 hours. Call establishments for specific hours.

Cellphones (Mobile Phones)   See "Staying Connected," in chapter 3.

Drinking Laws   The legal age for purchase and consumption of alcoholic beverages is 21; proof of age is required and often requested at bars, nightclubs, and restaurants, so it's always a good idea to bring ID when you go out.

Bars may remain open until 2am Monday to Saturday and until midnight on Sunday. Wine, beer, and spirits are sold at licensed supermarkets and liquor stores, but there are no package sales on election days until after 7pm, and on Sundays before noon. It is illegal to transport liquor through most Native American reservations.

Do not carry open containers of alcohol in your car or any public area that isn't zoned for alcohol consumption. The police can fine you on the spot. Don't even think about driving while intoxicated.

Driving Rules   See "Getting There & Around," in chapter 3.

Electricity   Like Canada, the United States uses 110 to 120 volts AC (60 cycles), compared to 220 to 240 volts AC (50 cycles) in most of Europe, Australia, and New Zealand. Downward converters that change 220–240 volts to 110–120 volts are difficult to find in the United States, so bring one with you.

Embassies & Consulates   All embassies are in the nation's capital, Washington, D.C. Some consulates are in major U.S. cities, and most nations have a mission to the United Nations in New York City. If your country isn't listed below, call for directory information in Washington, D.C. (✆ **202/555-1212**), or check **www.embassy.org/embassies**.

The embassy of **Australia** is at 1601 Massachusetts Ave. NW, Washington, DC 20036 (✆ **202/797-3000;** www.australia.visahq.com). Consulates are in New York, Honolulu, Houston, Los Angeles, and San Francisco.

The embassy of **Canada** is at 501 Pennsylvania Ave. NW, Washington, DC 20001 (✆ **202/682-1740;** www.canadainternational.gc.ca/washington). Other Canadian consulates are in Buffalo (New York), Detroit, Los Angeles, New York, and Seattle.

The embassy of **Ireland** is at 2234 Massachusetts Ave. NW, Washington, DC 20008 (✆ **202/462-3939;** www.embassyofireland.org). Irish consulates are in Boston, Chicago, New York, San Francisco, and other cities. See website for complete listing.

The embassy of **New Zealand** is at 37 Observatory Circle NW, Washington, DC 20008 (© **202/328-4800;** www.nzembassy.com). New Zealand consulates are in Los Angeles, Salt Lake City, San Francisco, and Seattle.

The embassy of the **United Kingdom** is at 3100 Massachusetts Ave. NW, Washington, DC 20008 (© **202/588-6500;** www.ukinusa.fco.gov.uk). Other British consulates are in Atlanta, Boston, Chicago, Cleveland, Houston, Los Angeles, New York, San Francisco, and Seattle.

Emergencies In case of emergency, dial © **911.** For more specific information, see "Fast Facts" in chapters 6, 7, and 8.

Gasoline (Petrol) At press time, the cost of gasoline in the U.S. (also known as gas, but never petrol) is abnormally high. In New Mexico, prices run a little above the national average. Taxes are already included in the printed price. One U.S. gallon equals 3.8 liters or .85 imperial gallons.

Holidays Banks, government offices, post offices, and many stores, restaurants, and museums are closed on the following legal national holidays: January 1 (New Year's Day), the third Monday in January (Martin Luther King, Jr., Day), the third Monday in February (Presidents' Day), the last Monday in May (Memorial Day), July 4 (Independence Day), the first Monday in September (Labor Day), the second Monday in October (Columbus Day), November 11 (Veterans' Day/Armistice Day), the fourth Thursday in November (Thanksgiving Day), and December 25 (Christmas). The Tuesday after the first Monday in November is Election Day, a federal government holiday in presidential-election years (held every 4 years, and next in 2012). For more information on holidays see "Calendar of Events," in chapter 3.

Insurance In these uncertain times, travel insurance is always a good idea, but if you find that option costly, here is something to consider: In this region the weather and political climate are fairly reliable, so your trip won't likely be interrupted by those conditions. For information on traveler's insurance, trip cancellation insurance, and medical insurance while traveling, please visit www.frommers.com/tips.

Internet Access See "Staying Connected," in chapter 3.

Legal Aid If you are "pulled over" for a minor infraction (such as speeding), never attempt to pay the fine directly to a police officer; this could be construed as attempted bribery, a much more serious crime. Pay fines by mail, or directly into the hands of the clerk of the court. If accused of a more serious offense, say and do nothing before consulting a lawyer. Here the burden is on the state to prove a person's guilt beyond a reasonable doubt, and everyone has the right to remain silent, whether he or she is suspected of a crime or actually arrested. Once arrested, a person can make one telephone call to a party of his or her choice. The international visitor should call his or her embassy or consulate.

Mail At press time, domestic postage rates were 28¢ for a postcard and 44¢ for a letter. For international mail, a first-class letter of up to 1 ounce costs 98¢ (75¢ to Canada and 79¢ to Mexico); a first-class postcard costs the same as a letter. For more information go to **www.usps.com**.

If you aren't sure what your address will be in the United States, mail can be sent to you, in your name, c/o General Delivery at the main post office of the city or region where you expect to be. (Call © **800/275-8777** for information on the nearest post office.) The addressee must pick up mail in person and must produce proof of identity (driver's license, passport, and so on). Most post offices will hold mail for up to 1 month, and are open Monday to Friday from 8am to 6pm, and Saturday from 9am to 3pm.

Always include zip codes when mailing items in the U.S. If you don't know your zip code, visit **www.usps.com/zip4**.

Newspapers & Magazines   See "Staying Connected," in chapter 3.

Passports   See "Embassies & Consulates," above, for whom to contact if you lose your passport while traveling in the U.S. For other information, contact the following agencies:

For Residents of Australia   Contact the **Australian Passport Information Service** at ✆ **131-232,** or visit www.passports.gov.au.

For Residents of Canada   Contact the central **Passport Office,** Department of Foreign Affairs and International Trade, Ottawa, ON K1A 0G3 (✆ **800/567-6868;** www.ppt.gc.ca).

For Residents of Ireland   Contact the **Passport Office,** Setanta Centre, Molesworth Street, Dublin 2 (✆ **01/671-1633;** www.foreignaffairs.gov.ie).

For Residents of New Zealand   Contact the **Passports Office,** Department of Internal Affairs, 47 Boulcott St., Wellington, 6011 (✆ **0800/225-050** in New Zealand, or 04/474-8100; www.passports.govt.nz).

For Residents of the United Kingdom   Visit your nearest passport office, major post office, or travel agency, or contact the **Identity and Passport Service (IPS),** 89 Eccleston Sq., London, SW1V 1PN (✆ **0300/222-0000;** www.ips.gov.uk).

For Residents of the United States   To find your regional passport office, check the U.S. State Department website (www.travel.state.gov/passport) or call the **National Passport Information Center** (✆ **877/487-2778**) for automated information.

Police   In case of emergencies, dial ✆ **911.** For local police stations, see "Fast Facts" in chapters 6, 7, and 8.

Smoking   New Mexico recently outlawed smoking at indoor public places, including restaurants and nightclubs. Some hotels offer rooms that allow smoking, though the number of these is dwindling.

Taxes   Please see "Fast Facts" in chapters 6, 7, and 8 for specifics about city taxes. The United States has no value-added tax (VAT) or other indirect tax at the national level. Every state, county, and city may levy its own local tax on all purchases, including hotel and restaurant checks and airline tickets. These taxes will not appear on price tags.

Telephones   See "Staying Connected," in chapter 3.

Time   New Mexico is on **Mountain Standard Time,** 1 hour ahead of the West Coast and 2 hours behind the East Coast. When it's 10am in Santa Fe, it's noon in New York, 11am in Chicago, and 9am in San Francisco.

Daylight saving time (summer time) is in effect from 1am on the second Sunday in March to 1am on the first Sunday in November, except in Arizona, Hawaii, the U.S. Virgin Islands, and Puerto Rico. Daylight saving time moves the clock 1 hour ahead of standard time.

Tipping   In hotels, tip **bellhops** at least $1 per bag ($2–$3 if you have a lot of luggage) and tip the **chamber staff** $1 to $2 per day (more if you've left a big mess for him or her to clean up). Tip the **doorman** or **concierge** only if he or she has provided you with some specific service (for example, calling a cab for you or obtaining difficult-to-get theater tickets). Tip the **valet-parking attendant** $1 every time you get your car.

In restaurants, bars, and nightclubs, tip **service staff** and **bartenders** 15% to 20% of the check, tip **checkroom attendants** $1 per garment, and tip **valet-parking attendants** $1 per vehicle.

As for other service personnel, tip **cab drivers** 15% of the fare; tip **skycaps** at airports at least $1 per bag ($2–$3 if you have a lot of luggage); and tip **hairdressers** and **barbers** 15% to 20%.

Toilets   You won't find public toilets or restrooms on the streets in most U.S. cities, but they can be found in hotel lobbies, bars, restaurants, museums, department stores, railway and bus stations, and service stations. Large hotels and fast-food restaurants are often the best bet for clean facilities. Restaurants and bars in resorts or heavily visited areas may reserve their restrooms for patrons.

Visas   For information about U.S. visas, go to **www.travel.state.gov** and click on "Visas." Or go to one of the following websites:

Australian citizens can obtain up-to-date visa information from the **U.S. Embassy Canberra,** Moonah Place, Yarralumla, ACT 2600 (© **02/6214-5600**), or by checking the U.S. Diplomatic Mission's website at **http://canberra.usembassy.gov**.

British subjects can obtain up-to-date visa information by calling the **U.S. Embassy Visa Information Line** (© **0891/200-290**) or by visiting the "Visas" section of the American Embassy London's website at **www.usembassy.org.uk**.

Irish citizens can obtain up-to-date visa information through the **U.S. Embassy Dublin,** 42 Elgin Rd., Ballsbridge, Dublin 4 (© **353/1-668-8777**; http://dublin.usembassy.gov).

Citizens of **New Zealand** can obtain up-to-date visa information by contacting the **U.S. Embassy New Zealand,** 29 Fitzherbert Terrace, Thorndon, Wellington (© **644/ 472-2068;** http://newzealand.usembassy.gov).

Visitor Information   Numerous agencies can assist you with planning your trip. The Visitors Information Center for the **New Mexico Department of Tourism** is located at 491 Old Santa Fe Trail, Santa Fe, NM 87501 (© **800/733-6396** or 505/827-7400). You can also find general New Mexico information on the Department of Tourism's website at **www.newmexico.org**. Santa Fe, Taos, and Albuquerque each have their own information service for visitors (see the "Orientation" sections in chapters 6, 7, and 8, respectively).

A valuable resource for information on outdoor recreation is the **Public Lands Information Center,** on the south side of town at 301 Dinosaur Trail, Santa Fe, NM 87508 (© **877/276-9404** or 505/954-2002; www.publiclands.org). Here, adventurers can find out what's available on lands administered by the National Forest Service, the Bureau of Land Management, the Fish and Wildlife Service, the National Park Service, the New Mexico Department of Game and Fish (which sells hunting and fishing licenses), and the New Mexico State Parks Division. The New Mexico Department of Tourism will send you a free state map if you call **800/733-6396** or 505/827-7400. Or, check out **www.mapquest.com**.

Water   All municipal water in the region is potable.

Wi-Fi   See "Staying Connected," in chapter 3.

AIRLINE WEBSITES

MAJOR AIRLINES

American Airlines & American Eagle
www.aa.com

Continental Airlines
www.continental.com

Delta Air Lines
www.delta.com

United Airlines
www.united.com

US Airways
www.usairways.com

BUDGET AIRLINES

Frontier Airlines
www.frontierairlines.com

Southwest Airlines
www.southwest.com

Airline Websites

FAST FACTS

Index